The Princeton Review

Cracking the
AP*
CALCULUS
AB & BC
Exams
2008 Edition

David S. Kahn

PrincetonReview.com

Random House, Inc. New York

The Princeton Review, Inc.
2315 Broadway
New York, NY   10024
E-mail: editorialsupport@review.com

ISBN: 978-0-375-76641-1
ISSN: 1092-4086

Editor: Briana Gordon
Production Editor: M. Tighe Wall
Production Coordinator: Stephen White

Printed in the United States of America.

10 9 8 7 6 5 4 3 2

2008 Edition

John Katzman, Chairman, Founder
Michael J. Perik, CEO
Mark Chernis, President, Test Preparation, COO
Andy Lutz, VP, Product Development
Robert Franek, VP, Publishing

Editorial
Melody Marcus, Editorial Director
Briana Gordon, Senior Editor
Rebecca Lessem, Editor

Production Services
Stephen White, Executive Director, Production Services

Production Editorial
M. Tighe Wall, Senior Production Editor
Meave Shelton, Production Editor
Heather Brady, Production Editor

Print Production
Suzanne Barker, Director, Print Production
Kim Howie, Production Coordinator
Ryan Tozzi, Production Staff
Effie Hadjiioannou, Production Staff

Research & Development
Kris Gamache, AVP, Retail Products
Tricia McCloskey, Executive Director, Graduate Programs
Christine Parker, Executive Director, HS Programs
Joy Grieco, Executive Director, School-Based Products
Vanessa Coggshall, Senior Director
Judene Wright, Senior Director, MCAT Programs

Marketing
Keri Hoyt, VP of Sales and Marketing
Liz Wands, Executive Director, Field Sales
Jeffrey Meanza, Director of Graduate Programs, Field Sales
Christy Jehn, Director of Secondary School Programs, Field Sales
Erin Elizabeth Stockdill, Manager of High School Programs, Field Sales
Caren Hector, Creative Director
Irina Bromme, Senior Graphic Designer
Shannon Summer, Graphic Designer

Random House Publishing Team
Tom Russell, Publisher
Nicole Benhabib, Publishing Manager
Ellen L. Reed, Production Manager
Alison Skrabek, Associate Managing Editor

ABOUT THE AUTHOR

David S. Kahn studied applied mathematics and physics at the University of Wisconsin and has taught courses in calculus, precalculus, algebra, trigonometry, and geometry at the college and high school levels. He has worked as an educational consultant for many years and tutored more students in mathematics than he can count! He has worked for The Princeton Review since 1989, and, in addition to AP calculus, he has taught math and verbal courses for the SAT, SAT II, LSAT, GMAT, and the GRE, trained other teachers, and written several other math books as well.

ACKNOWLEDGMENTS

First of all, I would like to thank Arnold Feingold and Peter B. Kahn for once again doing every problem, reading every word, and otherwise lending their invaluable assistance. I also want to thank Ellen Mendlow for being a terrific editor on past editions and Anthony Keene for his first-rate reading, analysis, and contributions. Thanks to Frank, without whose advice I never would have taken this path. Thanks to Jeffrey, Miriam, and Vicki for moral support. Thanks Mom.

Finally, I would like to thank the people who really made all of this effort worthwhile — my students. I hope that I haven't omitted anyone, but if I have, the fault is entirely mine.

Aaron and Sasha, Aaron, Abby B., Abby F., Abby H., Abbye, Aidan, Alex and Claire, Alex A., Alex F., Alex G., Alex H., Alex S., Alex and Gabe, Alexa, Alexandra and Natalie, Alexes, Alexis and Brittany, Ali and Jon, Alicia, Allie and Lauren, Allison and Andrew, Allison R., Ally, Aly and Lauren, Alyssa and Courtney, Amanda and Pamela B., Amanda C., Amanda H., Amanda M., Amanda R., Amparo, Andrea T., Andrea V., Andrew B., Andrew D., Andrew S., Andy R., Andy and Allison, Ann, Anna D., Anna and Jon, Anna and Max, Anna L., Anna M., Annie, Anu, April, Ariane, Ariel, Arielle and Gabrielle, Arthur and Annie, Arya, Asheley and Freddy, Ashley A., Ashley K., Ashley and Sarah, Ashley and Lauren, Avra, Becky B., Becky H., Ben S., Ben and Andrew Y., Benji, Beth and Sarah, Bethany and Lesley, Betsy and Jon, Blythe, Brett, Brette and Josh, Brian, Brian N., Brooke, Devon, and Megan, Butch, Caitlin, Caitlin and Anna S., Camilla and Eloise, Caroline H., Caroline S., Caroline and Peter W., Chad, Charlie, Charlotte, Chloe, Chrissie, Christine, Christine W., Claire H., Claudia, Corey, Corinne, Courtney and Keith, Courtney S., Craig, Daisy, Dana J., Dani and Adam, Daniel, Daniel and Jen, Daniella, Danielle and Andreas, Danielle and Nikki D., Danielle G., Danny K., Dara and Stacey, Dara M., Darcy, David R., Deborah and Matthew, Deniz and Destine, Devon and Jenna, Dora, Eairinn, Elana, Elexa and Nicky, Elisa, Eliza, Elizabeth, Elizabeth F., Emily A., Emily B., Emily and Allison, Emily C., Emily G., Emily K., Emily L., Emily M., Emily S., Emily T., Emma and Sophie, Erica H., Erica R., Erica S., Eric and Lauren, Erika, Erin, Eugenie, Eva, Evan, Eve H., Eve M., Frank, Gabby, Geoffrey, George and Julian, George M., Gloria, Graham and Will, Hallie, Harrison, Harry and Sidney, Hazel, Heather D., Heather F., Heather and Gillian, Hernando and Vicki, Hilary and Lindsay, Hilary F., Holli, Holly G., Holly K., Honor, Ingrid, Isabel, Jackie and Vicky, Jacob, Jackson, Jackie, Jackie S., Jaclyn and Adam,

Ian, Jason P., Jason and Andrew, Jay, Jay and Gideon, Jed D., Jed F., Jenna, Jen, Jennifer B., Jennifer W ., Jenny K., Jenny and Missy, Jeremy C., Jeremy K., Jess, Jess P., Jesse, Jessica, Jessica and Eric H., Jessica L., Jessica T., Jessie, Jessie C., Jessie and Perry N., Jill, Jillian, Daniel and Olivia, Jillian S., Joanna, Joanna C., Joanna G., Joanna and Julia M., Joanna W., Jocelyn, Jody and Kim, Johanna, John, John and Dan, Jonah and Zoe, Jonathan P., Jordan C., Jordan and Blair F., Jordan G., Jordana, Jordyn, Josh and Jesse, Judie and Rob, Julia and Caroline, Julia, Julia G., Julia and Charlotte P., Julie H., Julie and Dana, Julie P., Juliet, Kara B., Kara O., Kasia and Amy, Kat R., Kate D., Kate F., Kate G., Kate L., Kate P., Kate S., Kate W., Kathryn and Leslie, Katie, Katie M., Katrina, Kimberly, Kitty and Alex, Krista, Erika, and Caroline, Kristen, Laura F., Laura G., Laura S., Laura T., Laura Z., Lauren and Eric, Lauren R., Lauren T., Lauren and Allie, Leah, Lee R., Leigh and Ruthie, Leigh, Lila, Lilaj, Lili C., Lily and Ben, Lily Hayes, Lisbeth and Charlotte, Lindsay F., Lindsay K., Lindsay L., Lindsay N., Lindsay R., Lindsay and Jessie S., Lindsey and Kari, Lisa, Liz D., Liz H., Liz M., Lizzie A., Lizzi B., Lizzy, Lizzy T., Louis, Lucinda, Lucy, Lucy D., Maddie, Madeline, Magnolia, Mara and Steffie, Marcia, Margaret S., Mariel L., Mariel S., Marielle K., Marielle S., Marietta, Marissa, Marnie and Sam, Mary M., Matt, Matthew B., Matt F., Matt G., Matt V., Matt W., Matthew G., Maxx and Ben, Maya and Rohit, Meesh, Melissa, Meredith, Meredith and Gordie B., Meredith and Katie, Meredith S-K., Michael M., Michael and Danny, Michael R., Michaela, Miles, Milton, Miranda, Moira, Molly and Annie, Morgan, Morgan C., Morgan H., Nadia and Alexis, Naomi, Natalie, Nathania, Nico, Nicole B., Nicole N., Nicole S., Nikki, Nina R., Nina V., Nora, Nushien, Oliver, Omar, Oren, Pam, Paige, Peter, Philip and Peter, Phoebe, Priscilla, Quinn and Chris, Rachel A., Rachel B., Rachel and Adam., Rachel H., Rachel I., Rachel and Jake, Rachel K., Rachel L., Rachel and Mitchell M., Rachel S., Rachel and Eli, Rachel and Steven, Ramit, Randi, Rayna, Rebecca B., Rebecca G., Rebecca and Gaby, Rebecca R., Rebecca W., Richard, Tina, and Alice, Richie D., Ricky, Rose, Sally, Sam C., Sam L., Sam R., Sam S., Sam W ., Samuel C., Samar, Sara H., Sara L., Sara R., Sarah, Patty, and Kat, Sarah and Beth, Sarah A., Sarah and Michelle K., Sarah L., Sarah M-D., Sarah and Michael, Sarah S., Sascha, Samara, Saya, Skye, Simone, Sofia, Sonja, Sonja and Talya, Sophie and Tess, Sophie D., Sophie S., Sophie W., Stacey, Stacy, Stephanie, Stephen C., Sydney, Tammy and Hayley, Tara and Max, Taylor, Tenley and Galen, Terrence, Tess, Tom, Tracy, Tripp H., Tripp W., Vana, Vanessa and John, Victoria, Victoria H., Vivek, Vladimir, Waleed, Will A., Will, Teddy and Ellie, Wyatt and Ryan, Wyna, Zach, Zoë, and Zoey.

CONTENTS

Introduction

If you're reading this book, you're probably about to take the Advanced Placement (AP) Calculus Exam. Calculus is a very difficult subject and one that a lot of students have trouble with. If it's any consolation, you should remember that, generally, only *strong* math students take AP calculus. If you weren't a math whiz, you wouldn't have made it this far! So be proud of yourself, and realize that you're not alone. Most people find calculus very hard.

One of the reasons why calculus is so difficult arises from a lack of understanding about the nature of the subject. You probably think that calculus is the end of a sequence of courses in mathematics that you arrive at after passing through algebra, geometry, trigonometry, etc. Wrong! It's the beginning of a whole new branch of mathematics. You must learn a whole new set of tools and a whole new approach to problem solving. Calculus is going to teach you a new way of thinking and of looking at mathematics and at nature. Maybe it will even stick.

What do we mean by a whole new approach to problem solving? Well, before calculus, most of the problems that you had to do were one-step problems. You were asked a question, and you had one thing that you had to figure out. For example: *If you raise the price of an item that originally cost $50 to $80, by what percent did you raise the price*? This isn't terribly hard. You set up an equation, and you solve it. In fact, only in geometry do you have to do multi-stage thinking involving proofs, not problem solving. This means that up until now, your thinking has tended to be oriented towards the method that ought to be used to solve the problem, and how to execute the method.

In calculus, you are going to be solving multi-step problems. For example: *If two cars start at the same point and travel in directions 120 degrees apart, and if the first car is traveling at 60 miles per hour and the second car is traveling at 75 miles per hour, how fast is the distance between the two cars growing after three hours?* This problem requires you to figure out how far the cars have gone after three hours, set up an equation relating the speed of each car to the rate of change of the distance between them, and solve it. It's going to require some trigonometry, some algebra, some geometry, and some calculus. Much harder, isn't it?

The good news about AP calculus is that, because it is an introductory course, you probably won't delve too deeply into any of the topics, but you will concentrate on learning a lot of techniques. There's a lot of memorization involved in calculus, and you'll be expected to look at a problem and immediately know which type of problem it is and which technique to use to solve it. This book will help you do that. It's broken down into many small units, each of which concentrates on a particular type of problem and the technique(s) you'll need to solve it.

The other good news is that this is not college calculus, which could be taught any number of different ways. This is AP calculus. This means that the curriculum and the test are standardized. You'll be expected to learn certain things, and you will *not* be expected to learn others. Furthermore, the exam tends to ask the same kinds of questions year after year. So once you learn how to do those types of problems, you'll be in good shape for the test.

The final bit of good news is that the curve on the test is *very* generous. If you can get 70 percent of the questions right, you'll get a very good score. You should understand, of course, that it's hard to get a lot of the questions right! If 70 percent is a very good score, then a lot of people will be getting under 50 percent right. But after you finish this book, you won't be one of them!

WHAT'S THE DIFFERENCE?

AP calculus is divided into two types: AB and BC. The former is supposed to be the equivalent of a semester of college calculus; the latter, a year. In truth, AB calculus covers closer to three quarters of a year of college calculus. In fact, the main difference between the two is that BC calculus tests some more theoretical aspects of calculus and it covers a few additional topics. In addition, BC calculus is harder than AB calculus. The AB exam usually tests straightforward problems in each topic. They're not too tricky and they don't vary very much. The BC exam asks harder questions. But neither exam is tricky in the sense that the SAT is tricky. Nor do they test esoteric aspects of calculus. Rather, both tests tend to focus on testing whether you've learned the basics of differential and integral calculus. The tests are difficult because of the breadth of topics that they cover, not the depth. You will probably find that many of the problems in this book seem easier than the problems you've had in school. This is because your teacher is giving you problems that are harder than those on the AP.

ABOUT THE TEST

Now, some words about the test itself. The AP exam comes in three parts. First, there is a section of multiple-choice questions covering a variety of calculus topics. You're not permitted to use your calculator for this first section of the test. Second, there is a section of multiple-choice questions similar to the first, except that you are permitted to use a calculator for these questions. These two sections comprise a total of 45 questions.

Third, there's a section of six questions, each of which requires you to write out the solutions and the steps by which you solved it. You are permitted to use a calculator for the first three problems but not for the second three. Partial credit is given for various steps in the solution of each problem. You'll usually be required to sketch a graph in one of the questions. The Educational Testing Service (ETS) does you a big favor here: You may use a graphing calculator. In fact, ETS recommends it! And they allow you to use programs as well. But here's the truth about calculus: Most of the time, you don't need the calculator anyway. Remember: These are the people who bring you the SAT. Any gift from them should be regarded skeptically!

SOME FRIENDLY ADVICE

The key to doing well on the exam is to memorize a variety of techniques for solving calculus problems, and to recognize when to use them. There's so much to learn in AP calculus that it's difficult to remember everything. Instead, you should be able to derive or figure out how to do certain things based on your mastery of a few essential techniques. In addition, you'll be expected to remember a lot of the math that you did before calculus—particularly trigonometry. **If you're not strong in this area, take some time to review the appendix on prerequisite mathematics located at the back of this book.**

Furthermore, if you can't derive certain formulae, you should memorize them! A lot of students don't bother to memorize the trigonometry special angles and formulae because they can do them on their calculators. This is a big mistake. You'll be expected to be very good with these in calculus, and if you can't recall them easily, you'll be slowed down and the problems will seem much harder. Make sure that you're also comfortable with analytic geometry. If you rely on your calculator to graph for you, you'll get a lot of questions wrong because you won't recognize the curves when you see them.

This advice is going to seem backward compared to what your teachers are telling you. In school you're often yelled at for memorizing things. Teachers tell you to *understand* the concepts, not just memorize the answers. Well, things are different here. The understanding will come later, after you're comfortable with the mechanics. In the meantime, you should learn techniques, practice them, and, through repetition, you will ingrain them in your memory.

Each chapter is divided into three types of problems: examples, solved problems, and practice problems. The first type is contained in the explanatory portion of the unit. The examples are designed to further your understanding of the subject and to show you how to get the problems right. Each step of the solution to the example is worked out, except for some simple algebraic and arithmetic steps that should come easily to you at this point.

The second type is solved problems. The solutions are worked out in approximately the same detail as the examples. Before you start work on each of these, cover the solution with an index card or something, then check the solution afterward. And you should read through the solution, not just assume that you knew what you were doing because your answer was correct.

The third type of problem is practice problems. Only the answers to them are given. We hope you'll find that each chapter offers you enough practice problems for you to be comfortable with the material. The topics that are emphasized on the exam have more problems; those that are de-emphasized have fewer. In other words, if a chapter has only a few practice problems, it's not an important topic on the AP exam and you shouldn't worry too much about it.

The recipe for success follows these guidelines:

- **Do all of the problems!** As with many other things in life, if you want to do well in calculus, you must practice! You should work carefully through the examples and solved problems, so that you really understand the method involved for getting the right answer. Often it won't be the calculus that you get wrong, it will be the algebra.

- **Know your algebra!** One of the main reasons that students have trouble with calculus is that their algebra is weak. You must be good at factoring, reducing, simplifying, expanding, inverting, and so on. Otherwise, you won't be able to perform the proper steps that reduce the problem to following a simple technique. Many of the answer choices on the AP exam differ only by a constant or two, so you have to be strong at algebra to get those correct.

- **Do the practice tests!** After you've finished going through all of the chapters, there are practice tests for you to do. Each has step-by-step solutions to the problems. You should carefully go through the solutions to all of the problems you get wrong, and you might want to review the units on the ones that you got correct as well. (You might just have been lucky!) Each of the answers will tell you the chapter you should review if you got the question wrong.

- **Don't always trust your teachers or your textbooks!** Some of the material that your teachers will show you is not on the AP exam. Furthermore, many classes use a college textbook for the AP calculus course. These tend to cover far more than you'll ever need for the exam. Although you need to know this extra material for class, don't worry about it for the exam. Just stick to what this book covers.

- **If the test is in three weeks, what do I do?!** Some of you will be buying this book right before the AP exam. In that case, you should proceed directly to the practice exams. Once you know where your weaknesses lie, you can go back to the relevant chapters and improve your skills.

WHAT IS ON THE AP EXAM?

Topics in italics are BC Topics. This list is drawn from the topical outline for AP calculus furnished by The College Board. You might find that your teacher covers some additional topics, or omits some, in your course. Some of the topics are very broad, so we cannot guarantee that this book covers these topics exhaustively.

I. Functions, Graphs, and Limits
A. Analysis of Graphs

- You should be able to analyze a graph based on "the interplay between geometric and analytic information." The preceding phrase comes directly from The College Board. Don't let it scare you. What the College Board really means is that you should have covered graphing in precalculus, and you should know (a) how to graph, and (b) how to read a graph. **This is a precalculus topic and we won't cover it in this book.**

B. Limits

- You should be able to calculate limits algebraically, or to estimate them from a graph or from a table of data.

- You do **not** need to find limits using the Delta-Epsilon definition of a limit.

C. Asymptotes

- You should understand asymptotes graphically and be able to compare the growth rates of different types of functions (namely polynomial functions, logarithmic functions, and exponential functions). **This is a topic that should have been covered in precalculus, and we won't cover it in this book.**

- You should understand asymptotes in terms of limits involving infinity.

D. Continuity

- You should be able to test the continuity of a function in terms of limits and you should understand continuous functions graphically.

- You should understand the intermediate value theorem and the extreme value theorem.

E. *Parametric, Polar, and Vector Functions*

- *You should be able to analyze plane curves given in any of these three forms. Usually, you will be asked to convert from one of these three forms back to Rectangular Form (also known as Cartesian Form).*

II. Differential Calculus

A. The Definition of the Derivative

- You should be able to find a derivative by finding the limit of the difference quotient.

- You should also know the relationship between differentiability and continuity. That is, if a function is differentiable at a point, it's continuous there. But if a function is continuous at a point, it's not necessarily differentiable there.

B. Derivative at a Point

- You should know the Power Rule, the Product Rule, the Quotient Rule, and the Chain Rule.

- You should be able to find the slope of a curve at a point, and the tangent and normal lines to a curve at a point.

- You should also be able to use local linear approximation and differentials to estimate the tangent line to a curve at a point.

- You should be able to find the instantaneous rate of change of a function using the derivative or the limit of the average rate of change of a function.

- You should be able to approximate the rate of change of a function from a graph or from a table of values.

- You should be able to find Higher-Order Derivatives and to use Implicit Differentiation. These may look like a lot of topics, but they all cover the same few ideas, namely: Can you find a derivative exactly? Can you find a derivative approximately? And, do you know what the slope of a tangent line means?

C. Derivative of a Function

- You should be able to relate the graph of a function to the graph of its derivative, and vice-versa. This is tricky.

- You should know the relationship between the sign of a derivative and whether the function is increasing or decreasing (positive derivative means increasing; negative means decreasing).

- You should know how to find relative and absolute maxima and minima.

- You should know the mean value theorem for derivatives and Rolle's theorem.

D. Second Derivative

- You should be able to relate the graph of a function to the graph of its derivative and its second derivative, and vice-versa. This is tricky.

- You should know the relationship between concavity and the sign of the second derivative (positive means concave up; negative means concave down).

- You should know how to find points of inflection.

E. Applications of Derivatives

- You should be able to sketch a curve using first and second derivatives and be able to analyze the critical points.

- You should be able to solve Optimization problems (Max/Min problems), and Related Rates problems.

- You should be able to find the derivative of the inverse of a function.

- You should be able to solve Rectilinear Motion problems.

F. *More Applications of Derivatives*

- *You should be able to analyze planar curves in parametric, polar, and vector form, including velocity and acceleration vectors.*

- *You should be able to interpret differential equations via slope fields. Don't be intimidated. These look harder than they are.*

- *You should be able to use Euler's Method to find numerical solutions of differential equations.*

- *You should know L'Hôpital's Rule.*

G. Computation of Derivatives

- You should be able to find the derivatives of Trig functions, Logarithmic functions, Exponential functions, and Inverse Trig functions.

- *BC students should be able to find the derivatives of parametric, polar, and vector functions.*

III. Integral Calculus
A. Riemann Sums

- You should be able to find the area under a curve using left, right, and midpoint evaluations and the Trapezoidal Rule.

- You should know the fundamental theorem of calculus:

$$\int_a^b f'(x)dx = f(b) - f(a)$$

B. Applications of Integrals

- You should be able to find the area of a region, the volume of a solid of known cross-section, the volume of a solid of revolution, and the average value of a function.

- You should be able to solve acceleration, velocity, and position problems.

- *BC students should also be able to find the length of a curve (including a curve in parametric form) and the area of a region bounded by polar curves.*

C. Fundamental Theorem of Calculus

- You should know the first and second fundamental theorems of calculus and be able to use them to find the derivative of an integral, and in analytical and graphical analysis of functions.

D. Techniques of Antidifferentiation

- You should be able to integrate using the power rule and *U*-Substitution. *BC students should be able to do Integration by Parts and simple Partial Fractions.*

- *You should also be able to evaluate Improper Integrals as limits of definite integrals.*

E. Applications of Antidifferentiation

- You should be able to find specific antiderivatives using initial conditions.

- You should be able to solve separable differential equations and logistic differential equations.

IV. Polynomial Approximations and Series

A. *The Concept of a Series*

- *You should know that a series is a sequence of partial sums and that convergence is defined as the limit of the sequence of partial sums.*

B. *Series of Concepts*

- *You should understand and be able to solve problems involving Geometric Series, the Harmonic Series, Alternating Series, and P-Series.*

- *You should know the Integral Test, the Ratio Test, and the Comparison Test, and how to use them to determine whether a series converges or diverges.*

C. *Taylor Series*

- *You should know Taylor Polynomial Approximation; the general Taylor Series centered at $x = a$; and the Maclaurin Series for e^x, $\sin x$, $\cos x$, and $\dfrac{1}{1-x}$.*

- *You should know how to differentiate and antidifferentiate Taylor Series and how to form new series from known series.*

- *You should know functions defined by power series and radius of convergence.*

- *You should know the Lagrange error bound for Taylor Series.*

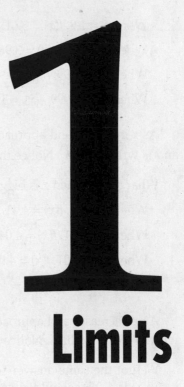

Limits

WHAT IS A LIMIT?

In order to understand calculus, you need to know what a "limit" is. A limit is the value a function (which usually is written "$f(x)$" on the AP exam) approaches as the variable within that function (usually "x") gets nearer and nearer to a particular value. In other words, when x is very close to a certain number, what is $f(x)$ very close to? As far as the AB test is concerned, that's all you have to know about evaluating limits. There's a more technical method that you BC students have to learn, but we won't discuss it until we have to—at the end of this chapter.

Let's look at an example of a limit: What is the limit of the function $f(x) = x^2$ as x approaches 2?

In limit notation, the expression "the limit as x approaches 2" is written like this: $\lim_{x \to 2}$. In order to

evaluate the limit, let's check out some values of $\lim_{x \to 2}$ as x increases and gets closer to 2 (without ever

exactly getting there).

When $x = 1.9$, $f(x) = 3.61$.

When $x = 1.99$, $f(x) = 3.9601$.

When $x = 1.999$, $f(x) = 3.996001$.

When $x = 1.9999$, $f(x) = 3.99960001$.

As x increases and approaches 2, $f(x)$ gets closer and closer to 4. This is called the **left-hand limit** and is written: $\lim\limits_{x \to 2^-}$. Notice the little minus sign!

What about when x is bigger than 2?

When $x = 2.1$, $f(x) = 4.41$.

When $x = 2.01$, $f(x) = 4.0401$.

When $x = 2.001$, $f(x) = 4.004001$.

When $x = 2.0001$, $f(x) = 4.00040001$.

As x decreases and approaches 2, $f(x)$ still approaches 4. This is called the **right-hand limit** and is written like this: $\lim\limits_{x \to 2^+}$. Notice the little plus sign!

We got the same answer when evaluating both the left- and right-hand limits, because when x is 2, $f(x)$ is 4. You should always check both sides of the independent variable because, as you'll see shortly, sometimes you don't get the same answer. Therefore, we write that $\lim\limits_{x \to 2} x^2 = 4$.

We didn't really need to look at all of these decimal values to know what was going to happen when x got really close to 2. But it's important to go through the exercise because, typically, the answers get a lot more complicated. Let's do a few examples.

Example 1: Find $\lim\limits_{x \to 5} x^2$.

The approach is simple: plug in 5 for x, and you get 25.

Example 2: Find $\lim\limits_{x \to 3} x^3$.

Here the answer is 27.

There are some simple algebraic rules of limits that you should know. These are:

$$\lim_{x \to a} kf(x) = k \lim_{x \to a} f(x)$$

Example: $\lim\limits_{x \to 5} 3x^2 = 3 \lim\limits_{x \to 5} x^2 = 75$

$$\lim_{x \to a} \left[f(x) + g(x) \right] = \lim_{x \to a} f(x) + \lim_{x \to u} g(x)$$

Example: $\lim_{x \to 5} \left[x^2 + x^3 \right] = \lim_{x \to 5} x^2 + \lim_{x \to 5} x^3 = 150$

$$\lim_{x \to a} \left[f(x) \cdot g(x) \right] = \lim_{x \to a} f(x) \cdot \lim_{x \to a} g(x)$$

Example: $\lim_{x \to 5} \left[\left(x^2 + 1 \right) \sqrt{x-1} \right] = \lim_{x \to 5} \left(x^2 + 1 \right) \lim_{x \to 5} \sqrt{x-1} = 52$

Example 3: Find $\lim_{x \to 0} \left(x^2 + 5x \right)$.

Plug in 0, and you get 0.

So far, so good. All you do to find the limit of a simple polynomial is plug in the number that the variable is approaching and see what the answer is. Naturally, the process can get messier—especially if x approaches zero.

Example 4: Find $\lim_{x \to 0} \dfrac{1}{x^2}$.

If you plug in some very small values for x, you'll see that this function approaches ∞. And it doesn't matter whether x is positive or negative, you still get ∞. Look at the graph of $y = \dfrac{1}{x^2}$:

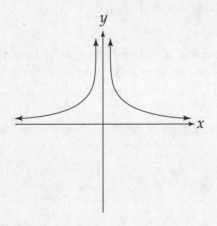

On either side of $x = 0$ (the y-axis), the curve approaches ∞.

Example 5: Find $\lim\limits_{x \to 0} \dfrac{1}{x}$.

Here you have a problem. If you plug in some very small positive values for x (0.1, 0.01, 0.001, etc.), you approach ∞. In other words, $\lim\limits_{x \to 0^+} \dfrac{1}{x} = \infty$. But, if you plug in some very small negative values for x (–0.1, –0.01, –0.001, etc.) you approach $-\infty$. That is, $\lim\limits_{x \to 0^-} \dfrac{1}{x} = -\infty$. Because the right-hand limit is not equal to the left-hand limit, this limit does not exist.

Look at the graph of $\dfrac{1}{x}$:

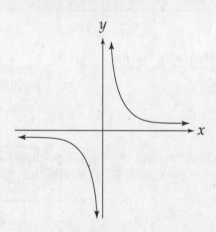

You can see that on the left side of $x = 0$, the curve approaches $-\infty$, and on the right side of $x = 0$, the curve approaches ∞. There are some very important points that we need to emphasize from the last two examples.

(1) If the left-hand limit of a function is not equal to the right-hand limit of the function, then the limit does not exist.

(2) A limit equal to infinity is not the same as a limit that does not exist, but sometimes you will see the expression "no limit," which serves both purposes.

(3) If k is a positive constant, then $\lim\limits_{x \to 0^+} \dfrac{k}{x} = \infty$, $\lim\limits_{x \to 0^-} \dfrac{k}{x} = -\infty$, and $\lim\limits_{x \to 0} \dfrac{k}{x}$ does not exist.

(4) If k is a positive constant, then $\lim\limits_{x \to 0^+} \dfrac{k}{x^2} = \infty$, $\lim\limits_{x \to 0^-} \dfrac{k}{x^2} = \infty$, and $\lim\limits_{x \to 0} \dfrac{k}{x^2} = \infty$.

Why does the limit exist in Example 4 but not for Example 5? Because when we have $\dfrac{k}{x^2}$, the function is always positive no matter what the sign of x is and thus the function has the same limit from the left and the right. But when we have $\dfrac{k}{x}$, the function's sign depends on the sign of x, and you get a different limit from each side.

Let's look at a few examples in which the variable approaches infinity.

Example 6: Find $\lim\limits_{x \to \infty} \dfrac{1}{x}$.

As x gets bigger and bigger, the value of the function gets smaller and smaller. Therefore, $\lim\limits_{x \to \infty} \dfrac{1}{x} = 0$.

Example 7: Find $\lim\limits_{x \to -\infty} \dfrac{1}{x}$.

It's the same situation as the one in Example 6; as x decreases (approaches negative infinity), the value of the function increases (approaches zero). We write this:

$$\lim_{x \to -\infty} \frac{1}{x} = 0$$

We don't have the same problem here that we did when x approached zero because "positive zero" is the same thing as "negative zero," whereas positive infinity is different from negative infinity.

Here's another rule:

If k and n are constants, $|x| > 1$, and $n > 0$, then $\lim\limits_{x \to \infty} \dfrac{k}{x^n} = 0$, and $\lim\limits_{x \to -\infty} \dfrac{k}{x^n} = 0$.

Example 8: Find $\lim\limits_{x \to \infty} \dfrac{3x + 5}{7x - 2}$.

When you have variables in both the top and the bottom, you can't just plug ∞ into the expression. You'll get $\dfrac{\infty}{\infty}$. We solve this by using the following technique:

When an expression consists of a polynomial divided by another polynomial, divide each term of the numerator and the denominator by the highest power of x that appears in the expression.

The highest power of x in this case is x^1, so we divide every term in the expression (both top and bottom) by x, like so:

$$\lim_{x \to \infty} \frac{3x + 5}{7x - 2} = \lim_{x \to \infty} \frac{\dfrac{3x}{x} + \dfrac{5}{x}}{\dfrac{7x}{x} - \dfrac{2}{x}} = \lim_{x \to \infty} \frac{3 + \dfrac{5}{x}}{7 - \dfrac{2}{x}}$$

Now when we take the limit, the two terms containing x approach zero. We're left with $\dfrac{3}{7}$.

Example 9: Find $\lim\limits_{x\to\infty}\dfrac{8x^2-4x+1}{16x^2+7x-2}$

Divide each term by x^2. You get:

$$\lim_{x\to\infty}\frac{8-\dfrac{4}{x}+\dfrac{1}{x^2}}{16+\dfrac{7}{x}-\dfrac{2}{x^2}}=\frac{8}{16}=\frac{1}{2}$$

Example 10: Find $\lim\limits_{x\to\infty}\dfrac{-3x^{10}-70x^5+x^3}{33x^{10}+200x^8-1000x^4}$.

Here, divide each term by x^{10}:

$$\lim_{x\to\infty}\frac{-3x^{10}-70x^5+x^3}{33x^{10}+200x^8-1000x^4}=\lim_{x\to\infty}\frac{-3-\dfrac{70}{x^5}+\dfrac{1}{x^7}}{33+\dfrac{200}{x^2}-\dfrac{1000}{x^6}}=-\frac{3}{33}=-\frac{1}{11}$$

Focus your attention on the highest power of x. The other powers don't matter, because they're all going to disappear. Now we have three new rules for evaluating the limit of a rational expression as x approaches infinity:

> (1) If the highest power of x in a rational expression is in the numerator, then the limit as x approaches infinity is infinity.

Example: $\lim\limits_{x\to\infty}\dfrac{5x^7-3x}{16x^6-3x^2}=\infty$

> (2) If the highest power of x in a rational expression is in the denominator, then the limit as x approaches infinity is zero.

Example: $\lim\limits_{x\to\infty}\dfrac{5x^6-3x}{16x^7-3x^2}=0$

> (3) If the highest power of x in a rational expression is the same in both the numerator and denominator, then the limit as x approaches infinity is the coefficient of the highest term in the numerator divided by the coefficient of the highest term in the denominator.

Example: $\lim\limits_{x\to\infty}\dfrac{5x^7-3x}{16x^7-3x^2}=\dfrac{5}{16}$

LIMITS OF TRIGONOMETRIC FUNCTIONS

At some point during the exam, you'll have to find the limit of certain trig expressions, usually as x approaches either zero or infinity. There are four standard limits that you should memorize—with those, you can evaluate all of the trigonometric limits that appear on the test. As you'll see throughout this book, calculus requires that you remember all of your trig from previous years.

Rule No. 1: $\lim\limits_{x \to 0} \dfrac{\sin x}{x} = 1$ (x is in radians, *not* degrees)

This may seem strange, but if you look at the graphs of $f(x) = \sin x$ and $f(x) = x$, they have approximately the same slope near the origin (as x gets closer to zero). Since x and the sine of x are about the same as x approaches zero, their quotient will be very close to one. Furthermore, because $\lim\limits_{x \to 0} \cos x = 1$ (review cosine values if you don't get this!), we know that $\lim\limits_{x \to 0} \tan x = \lim\limits_{x \to 0} \dfrac{\sin x}{\cos x} = 0$.

Now we will find a second rule. Let's evaluate the limit $\lim\limits_{x \to 0} \dfrac{\cos x - 1}{x}$. First, multiply the top and bottom by $\cos x + 1$. We get: $\lim\limits_{x \to 0} \dfrac{\cos x - 1}{x} \dfrac{\cos x + 1}{\cos x + 1}$. Now simplify the limit to: $\lim\limits_{x \to 0} \dfrac{\cos^2 x - 1}{x(\cos x + 1)}$. Next, we can use the trigonometric identity $\sin^2 x = 1 - \cos^2 x$ and rewrite the limit as: $\lim\limits_{x \to 0} \dfrac{-\sin^2 x}{x(\cos x + 1)}$.

Now, break this into two limits: $\lim\limits_{x \to 0} \dfrac{-\sin x}{x} \dfrac{\sin x}{(\cos x + 1)}$. The first limit is –1 (see Rule No. 1) and the second is 0 (why?), so the limit is 0.

Rule No. 2: $\lim\limits_{x \to 0} \dfrac{\cos x - 1}{x} = 0$

Example 11: Find $\lim\limits_{x \to 0} \dfrac{\sin 3x}{x}$.

Use a simple trick: Multiply the top and bottom of the expression by 3. This gives us: $\lim\limits_{x \to 0} \dfrac{3 \sin 3x}{3x}$. Next, substitute a letter for $3x$; for example, a. Now, we get the following:

$$\lim\limits_{a \to 0} \dfrac{3 \sin a}{a} = 3 \lim\limits_{a \to 0} \dfrac{\sin a}{a} = 3(1) = 3$$

Example 12: Find $\lim\limits_{x \to 0} \dfrac{\sin 5x}{\sin 4x}$.

Now we get a bit more sophisticated. First, divide both the numerator and the denominator by x, like so:

$$\lim_{x \to 0} \frac{\dfrac{\sin 5x}{x}}{\dfrac{\sin 4x}{x}}$$

Next, multiply the top and bottom of the numerator by 5, and the top and bottom of the denominator by 4, which gives us:

$$\lim_{x \to 0} \frac{\dfrac{5\sin 5x}{5x}}{\dfrac{4\sin 4x}{4x}}$$

From the work we did in Example 11, we can see that this limit is $\dfrac{5}{4}$. Guess what! You have two more rules!

Rule No. 3: $\lim\limits_{x \to 0} \dfrac{\sin ax}{x} = a$

Rule No. 4: $\lim\limits_{x \to 0} \dfrac{\sin ax}{\sin bx} = \dfrac{a}{b}$

Example 13: Find $\lim\limits_{x \to 0} \dfrac{x^2}{1 - \cos^2 x}$.

Using trigonometric identities, you can replace $(1 - \cos^2 x)$ with $\sin^2 x$:

$$\lim_{x \to 0} \frac{x^2}{1 - \cos^2 x} = \lim_{x \to 0} \frac{x^2}{\sin^2 x} = \lim_{x \to 0} \left(\frac{x}{\sin x} \cdot \frac{x}{\sin x} \right) = 1 \cdot 1 = 1$$

Here are other examples for you to try, with answers right beneath them. Give 'em a try, and check your work.

PROBLEM 1. Find $\lim\limits_{x \to 3} \dfrac{x-3}{x+2}$.

Answer: If you plug in 3 for x, you get $\lim\limits_{x \to 3} \dfrac{3-3}{3+2} = \dfrac{0}{5} = 0$.

PROBLEM 2. Find $\lim\limits_{x \to 3} \dfrac{x+2}{x-3}$.

Answer: The left-hand limit is: $\lim\limits_{x \to 3^-} \dfrac{x+2}{x-3} = -\infty$

The right-hand limit is: $\lim\limits_{x \to 3^+} \dfrac{x+2}{x-3} = \infty$

These two limits are not the same. Therefore, the limit does not exist.

PROBLEM 3. Find $\lim\limits_{x \to 3} \dfrac{x+2}{\left(x-3\right)^2}$.

Answer: The left-hand limit is: $\lim\limits_{x \to 3^-} \dfrac{x+2}{\left(x-3\right)^2} = \infty$

The right-hand limit is: $\lim\limits_{x \to 3^+} \dfrac{x+2}{\left(x-3\right)^2} = \infty$

These two limits are the same, so the limit is ∞.

PROBLEM 4. Find $\lim\limits_{x \to -4} \dfrac{x^2+6x+8}{x+4}$.

Answer: If you plug –4 into the top and bottom, you get $\dfrac{0}{0}$. You have to factor the top into

$(x+2)(x+4)$ to get this: $\lim\limits_{x \to -4} \dfrac{(x+2)(x+4)}{(x+4)}$

Now it's time to cancel like terms: $\lim\limits_{x \to -4} \dfrac{(x+2)(x+4)}{(x+4)} = \lim\limits_{x \to -4}(x+2) = -2$

PROBLEM 5. Find $\lim\limits_{x \to \infty} \dfrac{15x^2-11x}{22x^2+4x}$.

Answer: Divide each term by x^2: $\lim\limits_{x \to \infty} \dfrac{15x^2-11x}{22x^2+4x} = \lim\limits_{x \to \infty} \dfrac{15-\dfrac{11}{x}}{22+\dfrac{4}{x}} = \dfrac{15}{22}$

PROBLEM 6. Find $\lim\limits_{x \to 0} \dfrac{4x}{\tan x}$.

Answer: Replace $\tan x$ with $\dfrac{\sin x}{\cos x}$, which changes the expression into:

$$\lim_{x\to 0}\frac{4x}{\tan x}=\lim_{x\to 0}\frac{4x}{\dfrac{\sin x}{\cos x}}=\lim_{x\to 0}\frac{4x\cos x}{\sin x}$$

Since $\lim_{x\to 0}\dfrac{x}{\sin x}=1$ and $\lim_{x\to 0}\cos x=1$, the answer is 4.

Note: Pay careful attention to this next solved problem. It will be very important when you work on problems in Chapter 4.

PROBLEM 7. Find $\lim_{h\to 0}\dfrac{(5+h)^2-25}{h}$.

Answer: First, expand and simplify the numerator like this:

$$\lim_{h\to 0}\frac{(5+h)^2-25}{h}=\lim_{h\to 0}\frac{25+10h+h^2-25}{h}=\lim_{h\to 0}\frac{10h+h^2}{h}.$$

Next, factor h out of the numerator and the denominator like this:

$$\lim_{h\to 0}\frac{10h+h^2}{h}=\lim_{h\to 0}\frac{h(10+h)}{h}=\lim_{h\to 0}(10+h).$$

Taking the limit you get: $\lim_{h\to 0}(10+h)=10$.

PRACTICE PROBLEM SET 1

Try these 30 problems to test your skill with limits. The answers are in Chapter 21.

1. $\lim_{x\to 8}\left(x^2-5x-11\right)=$

2. $\lim_{x\to 5}\left(\dfrac{x+3}{x^2-15}\right)=$

3. $\lim_{x\to 0}\pi^2=$

4. $\lim_{x\to 3}\left(\dfrac{x^2-2x-3}{x-3}\right)=$

5. $\lim_{x\to\infty}\left(\dfrac{10x^2+25x+1}{x^4-8}\right)=$

6. $\lim_{x\to\infty}\left(\dfrac{x^4-8}{10x^2+25x+1}\right)=$

7. $\lim\limits_{x \to \infty} \left(\dfrac{x^4 - 8}{10x^4 + 25x + 1} \right) =$

8. $\lim\limits_{x \to \infty} \left(\dfrac{\sqrt{5x^4 + 2x}}{x^2} \right) =$

9. $\lim\limits_{x \to 6^+} \left(\dfrac{x + 2}{x^2 - 4x - 12} \right) =$

10. $\lim\limits_{x \to 6^-} \left(\dfrac{x + 2}{x^2 - 4x - 12} \right) =$

11. $\lim\limits_{x \to 6} \left(\dfrac{x + 2}{x^2 - 4x - 12} \right) =$

12. $\lim\limits_{x \to 0^+} \left(\dfrac{x}{|x|} \right) =$

13. $\lim\limits_{x \to 0^-} \left(\dfrac{x}{|x|} \right) =$

14. $\lim\limits_{x \to 7^+} \left(\dfrac{x}{x^2 - 49} \right) =$

15. $\lim\limits_{x \to 7} \left(\dfrac{x}{x^2 - 49} \right) =$

16. $\lim\limits_{x \to 7} \dfrac{x}{(x - 7)^2} =$

17. Let $f(x) = \begin{cases} x^2 - 5, x \le 3 \\ x + 2, x > 3 \end{cases}$

   Find: (a) $\lim\limits_{x \to 3^-} f(x)$; (b) $\lim\limits_{x \to 3^+} f(x)$; and (c) $\lim\limits_{x \to 3} f(x)$

18. Let $f(x) = \begin{cases} x^2 - 5, x \le 3 \\ x + 1, x > 3 \end{cases}$

   Find: (a) $\lim\limits_{x \to 3^-} f(x)$; (b) $\lim\limits_{x \to 3^+} f(x)$; and (c) $\lim\limits_{x \to 3} f(x)$

19. Find $\lim\limits_{x \to \frac{\pi}{4}} 3 \cos x$.

20. Find $\lim\limits_{x \to 0} 3 \dfrac{x}{\cos x}$.

21. Find $\lim\limits_{x \to 0} 3 \dfrac{x}{\sin x}$.

22. Find $\lim\limits_{x \to 0} \dfrac{\sin 3x}{\sin 8x}$.

23. Find $\lim\limits_{x \to 0} \dfrac{\tan 7x}{\sin 5x}$.

24. Find $\lim\limits_{x \to \infty} \sin x$.

25. Find $\lim\limits_{x \to \infty} \sin \dfrac{1}{x}$.

26. Find $\lim\limits_{x \to 0} \dfrac{x^2 \sin x}{1 - \cos^2 x}$.

27. Find $\lim\limits_{x \to 0} \dfrac{\sin^2 7x}{\sin^2 11x}$.

28. Find $\lim\limits_{h \to 0} \dfrac{(3+h)^2 - 9}{h}$.

29. Find $\lim\limits_{h \to 0} \dfrac{\sin(x+h) - \sin x}{h}$.

30. Find $\lim\limits_{h \to 0} \dfrac{\dfrac{1}{x+h} - \dfrac{1}{x}}{h}$.

2

Continuity

Every AP exam has a few questions on continuity, so it's important to understand the basic idea of what it means for a function to be continuous. The concept is very simple: If the graph of the function doesn't have any breaks or holes in it within a certain interval, the function is continuous over that interval.

Simple polynomials are continuous everywhere; it's the other ones—trigonometric, rational, piecewise—that might have continuity problems. Most of the test questions concern these last types of functions. In order to learn how to test whether a function is continuous, you'll need some more mathematical terminology.

THE DEFINITION OF CONTINUITY

In order for a function $f(x)$ to be continuous at a point $x = c$, it must fulfill *all three* of the following conditions:

Condition 1: $f(c)$ exists.

Condition 2: $\lim\limits_{x \to c} f(x)$ exists.

Condition 3: $\lim\limits_{x \to c} f(x) = f(c)$

Let's look at a simple example of a continuous function. (Incidentally, you'll find that these functions are continuous almost everywhere, and the only possible difficulty will occur at a few specific values of x.)

Example 1: Is the function $f(x) = \begin{cases} x+1, \ x < 2 \\ 2x-1, \ x \geq 2 \end{cases}$ continuous at the point $x = 2$?

Condition 1: Does $f(2)$ exist?
Yes. It's equal to $2(2) - 1 = 3$.

Condition 2: Does $\lim\limits_{x \to 2} f(x)$ exist?

You need to look at the limit from both sides of 2. The left-hand limit is: $\lim\limits_{x \to 2^-} f(x) = 2 + 1 = 3$. The right-hand limit is: $\lim\limits_{x \to 2^-} f(x) = 2(2) - 1 = 3$.

Because the two limits are the same, the limit exists.

Condition 3: Does $\begin{cases} x+1, \ x < 2 \\ 2x \ - \ 1, \ x > 2 \end{cases} f(x) = f(2)$?

The two equal each other, so yes; the function is continuous at $x = 2$.

A simple and important way to check whether a function is continuous is to sketch the function. If you can't sketch the function without lifting your pencil from the paper at some point, then the function is not continuous.

Now let's look at some examples of functions that are not continuous.

Example 2: Is the function $f(x) = \begin{cases} x+1, \ x < 2 \\ 2x \ - \ 1, \ x > 2 \end{cases}$ continuous at $x = 2$?

Condition 1: Does $f(2)$ exist?
Nope. The function of x is defined if x is greater than or less than 2, but not if x is equal to 2. Therefore, the function is not continuous at $x = 2$. Notice that we don't have to bother with the other two conditions. Once you find a problem, the function is automatically not continuous, and you can stop.

Example 3: Is the function $f(x) = \begin{cases} x+1, & x < 2 \\ 2x+1, & x \geq 2 \end{cases}$ continuous at $x = 2$?

Condition 1: Does $f(x)$ exist?
Yes. It is equal to $2(2) + 1 = 5$.

Condition 2: Does $\lim\limits_{x \to 2} f(x)$ exist?

The left-hand limit is: $\lim\limits_{x \to 2^-} f(x) = 2 + 1 = 3$.

The right-hand limit is: $\lim\limits_{x \to 2^+} f(x) = 2(2) + 1 = 5$.

The two limits don't match, so the limit doesn't exist and the function is not continuous at $x = 2$.

Example 4: Is the function $f(x) = \begin{cases} x+1, & x < 2 \\ x^2, & x = 2 \\ 2x-1, & x > 2 \end{cases}$ continuous at $x = 2$?

Condition 1: Does $f(2)$ exist?
Yes. It's equal to $2^2 = 4$.

Condition 2: Does $\lim\limits_{x \to 2} f(x)$ exist?

The left-hand limit is: $\lim\limits_{x \to 2^-} f(x) = 2 + 1 = 3$.

The right-hand limit is: $\lim\limits_{x \to 2^+} f(x) = 2(2) - 1 = 3$.

Because the two limits are the same, the limit exists.

Condition 3: Does $\lim\limits_{x \to 2} f(x) = f(2)$?

The $\lim\limits_{x \to 2} f(x) = 3$, but $f(2) = 4$. Because these aren't equal, the answer is "no" and the function is not continuous at $x = 2$.

TYPES OF DISCONTINUITIES

There are four types of discontinuities you have to know: jump, point, essential, and removable.

A **jump** discontinuity occurs when the curve "breaks" at a particular place and starts somewhere else. In other words, $\lim\limits_{x \to a^-} f(x) \neq \lim\limits_{x \to a^+} f(x)$.

A sample looks like this:

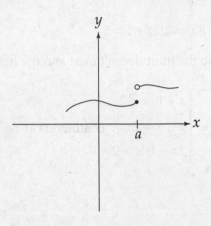

A **point** discontinuity occurs when the curve has a "hole" in it from a missing point because the function has a value at that point that's "off the curve." In other words, $\lim\limits_{x \to a} f(x) \neq f(a)$.

Here's what a point discontinuity looks like:

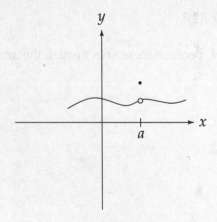

An **essential** discontinuity occurs when the curve has a vertical asymptote.

Like so:

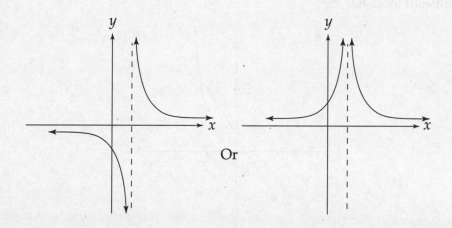

Or

A **removable** discontinuity occurs when you have a rational expression with common factors in the numerator and denominator. Because these factors can be canceled, the discontinuity is "removable."

Here's an example:

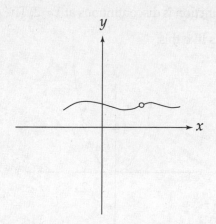

This curve looks very similar to a point discontinuity, but notice that with a removable discontinuity, $f(x)$ is not defined at the point, whereas with a point discontinuity, $f(x)$ is defined there.

Now that you know what these four types of discontinuities look like, let's see what types of functions are not everywhere continuous.

Example 5: Consider the function:

$$f(x) = \begin{cases} x+3, & x \le 2 \\ x^2, & x > 2 \end{cases}$$

The left-hand limit is 5 as x approaches 2, and the right-hand limit is 4 as x approaches 2. Because the curve has different values on each side of 2, the curve is discontinuous at $x = 2$. We say that the curve "jumps" at $x = 2$ from the left-hand curve to the right-hand curve because the left and right-hand limits differ. It looks like this:

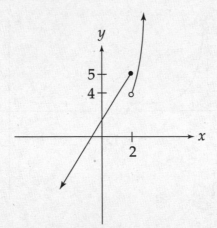

This is an example of a jump discontinuity.

Example 6: Consider the function:

$$f(x) = \begin{cases} x^2, & x \neq 2 \\ 5, & x = 2 \end{cases}$$

Because $\lim\limits_{x \to 2} f(x) \neq f(2)$; the function is discontinuous at $x = 2$. The curve is continuous everywhere except at the point $x = 2$. It looks like this:

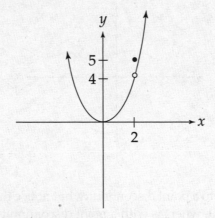

This is an example of a point discontinuity.

Example 7: Consider the function: $f(x) = \dfrac{5}{x - 2}$

The function is discontinuous because it's possible for the denominator to equal zero (at $x = 2$). This means that $f(2)$ doesn't exist, and the function has an asymptote at $x = 2$. In addition,

$$\lim_{x \to 2^-} f(x) = -\infty \text{ and } \lim_{x \to 2^+} f(x) = \infty$$

The graph looks like this:

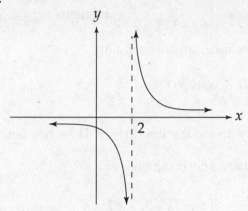

This is an example of an essential discontinuity.

Example 8: Consider the function:

$$f(x) = \frac{x^2 - 8x + 15}{x^2 - 6x + 5}$$

If you factor the top and bottom, you can see where the discontinuities are:

$$f(x) = \frac{x^2 - 8x + 15}{x^2 - 6x + 5} = \frac{(x-3)(x-5)}{(x-1)(x-5)}$$

The function has a zero in the denominator when $x = 1$ or $x = 5$, so the function is discontinuous at those two points. But, you can cancel the term $(x - 5)$ from both the numerator and the denominator, leaving you with:

$$f(x) = \frac{x-3}{x-1}$$

Now the reduced function *is* continuous at $x = 5$. Thus the original function has a removable discontinuity at $x = 5$. Furthermore, if you now plug $x = 5$ into the reduced function, you get:

$$f(5) = \frac{2}{4} = \frac{1}{2}$$

The discontinuity is at $x = 5$, and there's a hole at $\left(5, \frac{1}{2}\right)$. In other words, if the original function were continuous at $x = 5$, it would have the value $\frac{1}{2}$. Notice that this is the same as: $\lim\limits_{x\to5} f(x)$.

These are the types of discontinuities that you can expect to encounter on the AP examination. Here are some sample problems and their solutions. Cover the answers as you work, then check your results.

PROBLEM 1. Is the function $f(x) = \begin{cases} 2x^3 - 1, & x < 2 \\ 6x - 3, & x \geq 2 \end{cases}$ continuous at $x = 2$?

Answer: Test the conditions necessary for continuity.

Condition 1: $f(2) = 9$, so we're okay so far.

Condition 2: The $\lim\limits_{x \to 2^-} f(x) = 15$ and the $\lim\limits_{x \to 2^+} f(x) = 9$. These two limits don't agree, so the $\lim\limits_{x \to 2} f(x)$ doesn't exist and the function is not continuous at $x = 2$.

PROBLEM 2. Is the function $f(x) = \begin{cases} x^2 + 3x + 5, & x < 1 \\ 6x + 3, & x \geq 1 \end{cases}$ continuous at $x = 1$?

Answer: Condition 1: $f(1) = 9$.

Condition 2: The $\lim\limits_{x \to 1^-} f(x) = 9$ and the $\lim\limits_{x \to 1^+} f(x) = 9$.

Therefore, the $\lim\limits_{x \to 1} f(x)$ exists and is equal to 9.

Condition 3: $\lim\limits_{x \to 1} f(x) = f(1) = 9$.

The function satisfies all three conditions, so it is continuous at $x = 1$.

PROBLEM 3. For what value of a is the function $f(x) = \begin{cases} ax + 5, & x < 4 \\ x^2 - x, & x \geq 4 \end{cases}$ continuous at $x = 4$?

Answer: Because $f(4) = 12$, the function passes the first condition.

For Condition 2 to be satisfied, the $\lim\limits_{x \to 4^-} f(x) = 4a + 5$ must equal the $\lim\limits_{x \to 4^+} f(x) = 12$. So, set $4a + 5 = 12$. If $a = \dfrac{7}{4}$, the limit will exist at $x = 4$ and the other two conditions will also be fulfilled.

Therefore, the value $a = \dfrac{7}{4}$ makes the function continuous at $x = 4$.

PROBLEM 4. Where does the function $f(x) = \dfrac{2x^2 - 7x - 15}{x^2 - x - 20}$ have: (a) an essential discontinuity; and (b) a removable discontinuity?

Answer: If you factor the top and bottom of this fraction, you get:

$$f(x) = \frac{2x^2 - 7x - 15}{x^2 - x - 20} = \frac{(2x+3)(x-5)}{(x+4)(x-5)}$$

Thus, the function has an essential discontinuity at $x = -4$. If we then cancel the term $(x - 5)$, and substitute $x = 5$ into the reduced expression, we get $f(5) = \frac{13}{9}$. Therefore, the function has a removable discontinuity at $\left(5, \frac{13}{9}\right)$.

Note: Don't confuse coordinate parentheses with interval notation. In interval notation, square brackets include endpoints and parentheses do not. For example, the interval $2 \leq x \leq 4$ is written [2, 4] and the interval $2 < x < 4$ is written (2, 4).

PRACTICE PROBLEM SET 2
Now try these problems. The answers are in Chapter 21.

1. Is the function $f(x) = \begin{cases} x+7, & x<2 \\ 9, & x=2 \\ 3x+3, & x>2 \end{cases}$ continuous at $x = 2$?

2. Is the function $f(x) = \begin{cases} 4x^2 - 2x, & x<3 \\ 10x-1, & x=3 \\ 30, & x>3 \end{cases}$ continuous at $x = 3$?

3. Is the function $f(x) = \begin{cases} 5x+7, & x<3 \\ 7x+1, & x>3 \end{cases}$ continuous at $x = 3$?

4. Is the function $f(x) = \sec x$ continuous everywhere?

5. Is the function $f(x) = \sec x$ continuous on the interval $\left[-\frac{\pi}{2}, \frac{\pi}{2}\right]$?

6. Is the function $f(x) = \sec x$ continuous on the interval $\left(-\frac{\pi}{2}, \frac{\pi}{2}\right)$?

7. For what value(s) of k is the function $f(x) = \begin{cases} 3x^2 - 11x - 4, & x \leq 4 \\ kx^2 - 2x - 1, & x>4 \end{cases}$ continuous at $x = 4$?

8. For what value(s) of k is the function $f(x) = \begin{cases} -6x-12, & x < -3 \\ k^2 - 5k, & x = -3 \\ 6, & x > -3 \end{cases}$ continuous at $x = -3$?

9. At what point is the removable discontinuity for the function $f(x) = \dfrac{x^2 + 5x - 24}{x^2 - x - 6}$?

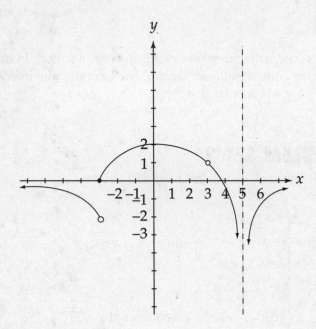

10. Given the graph of $f(x)$ above, find:

    (a) $\displaystyle\lim_{x \to -\infty} f(x)$

    (b) $\displaystyle\lim_{x \to \infty} f(x)$

    (c) $\displaystyle\lim_{x \to 3^-} f(x)$

    (d) $\displaystyle\lim_{x \to 3^+} f(x)$

    (e) $f(3)$

    (f) Any discontinuities.

3

The Definition of the Derivative

The main tool that you'll use in differential calculus is called the **derivative**. All of the problems that you'll encounter in differential calculus make use of the derivative, so your goal should be to become an expert at finding, or "taking," derivatives by the end of Chapter 4. However, before you learn a simple way to take a derivative, your teacher will probably make you learn how derivatives are calculated by teaching you something called the "Definition of the Derivative."

DERIVING THE FORMULA

The best way to understand the definition of the derivative is to start by looking at the simplest continuous function: a line. As you should recall, you can determine the slope of a line by taking two points on that line and plugging them into the slope formula:

$$m = \frac{y_2 - y_1}{x_2 - x_1} \qquad\qquad m \text{ stands for slope.}$$

For example, suppose a line goes through the points (3, 7) and (8, 22). First, you subtract the y-coordinates $(22 - 7) = 15$. Next, subtract the corresponding x-coordinates $(8 - 3) = 5$. Finally, divide the first number by the second: $\frac{15}{5} = 3$. The result is the slope of the line: $m = 3$.

Notice that you can use the coordinates in reverse order and still get the same result. It doesn't matter in which order you do the subtraction as long as you're consistent (and you remember to put the y-coordinates in the numerator and the x-coordinates in the denominator).

Let's look at the graph of that line. The slope measures the steepness of the line, which looks like this:

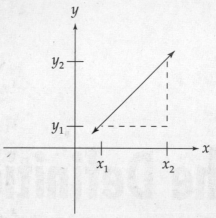

You probably remember your teachers referring to the slope as the "rise" over the "run." The rise is the difference between the y-coordinates, and the run is the difference between the x-coordinates. The slope is the ratio of the two.

Now for a few changes in notation. Instead of calling the x-coordinates x_1 and x_2, we're going to call them x_1 and $x_1 + h$, where h is the difference between the two x-coordinates. (Sometimes, instead of h, some books use Δx.) Second, instead of using y_1 and y_2, we use $f(x_1)$ and $f(x_1 + h)$. So now the graph looks like this:

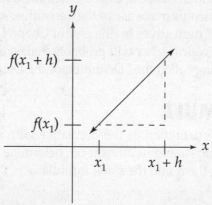

The picture is exactly the same—only the notation has changed.

THE SLOPE OF A CURVE

Suppose that instead of finding the slope of a line, we wanted to find the slope of a curve. Here, the slope formula no longer works because the distance from one point to the other is curved, not straight. But we could find the approximate slope if we took the slope of the line between the two points. This is called the **secant line**.

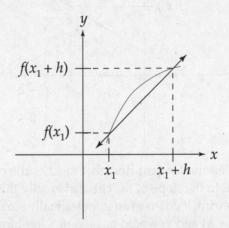

The equation for the slope of the secant line is:

$$\frac{f(x_1 + h) - f(x_1)}{h}$$

Remember this formula! This is called the **Difference Quotient**.

THE SECANT AND THE TANGENT

As you can see, the farther apart the two points are, the less the slope of the line corresponds to the slope of the curve.

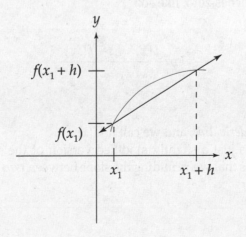

Conversely, the closer the two points are, the more accurate the approximation is.

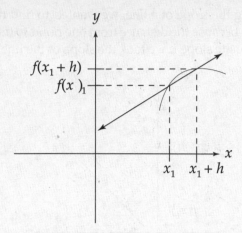

In fact, there is one line, called the **tangent line**, that touches the curve at exactly one point. The slope of the tangent line is equal to the slope of the curve at exactly this point. The object of using the above formula, therefore, is to shrink h down to an infinitesimally small amount. If we could do that, then the difference between $(x_1 + h)$ and x_1 would be a point. Graphically, it looks like this:

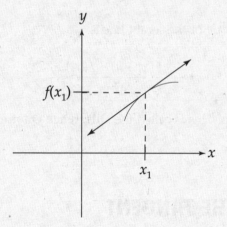

How do we perform this shrinking act? By using the limits we discussed in Chapter 1. We set up a limit during which h approaches zero, like so:

$$\lim_{h \to 0} \frac{f(x_1 + h) - f(x_1)}{h}$$

This is the *definition of the derivative*, and we call it $f'(x)$.

Notice that the equation is just a slightly modified version of the slope formula, with different notation. The only difference is that we're finding the slope between two points that are almost exactly next to each other.

Example 1: Find the slope of the curve $f(x) = y = x^2$ at the point (2, 4).

This means that $x_1 = 2$ and $f(2) = 2^2 = 4$. If we can figure out $f(x_1 + h)$, then we can find the slope. Well, how did we find the value of $f(x)$? We plugged x_1 into the equation $f(x) = x^2$. To find $f(x_1 + h)$ we plug $x_1 + h$ into the equation, which now looks like this:

$$f(x_1 + h) = (2 + h)^2 = 4 + 4h + h^2$$

Now plug this into the slope formula:

$$\lim_{h \to 0} \frac{f(x_1 + h) - f(x_1)}{h} = \lim_{h \to 0} \frac{4 + 4h + h^2 - 4}{h} = \lim_{h \to 0} \frac{4h + h^2}{h}$$

Next, simplify by factoring h out of the top:

$$\lim_{h \to 0} \frac{4h + h^2}{h} = \lim_{h \to 0} \frac{h(4 + h)}{h} = \lim_{h \to 0}(4 + h)$$

Taking the limit as h approaches 0, we get 4. Therefore, the slope of the curve $y = x^2$ at the point (2, 4) is 4. Now we've found the slope of a curve at a certain point, and the notation looks like this: $f'(2) = 4$. Remember this notation!

Example 2: Find the derivative of the equation in Example 1 at the point (5, 25). This means that $x_1 = 5$ and $f(x) = 25$. This time,

$$(x_1 + h)^2 = (5 + h)^2 = 25 + 10h + h^2$$

Now plug this into the formula for the derivative:

$$\lim_{h \to 0} \frac{f(x_1 + h) - f(x_1)}{h} = \lim_{h \to 0} \frac{25 + 10h + h^2 - 25}{h} = \lim_{h \to 0} \frac{10h + h^2}{h}$$

Once again, simplify by factoring h out of the top:

$$\lim_{h \to 0} \frac{10h + h^2}{h} = \lim_{h \to 0} \frac{h(10 + h)}{h} = \lim_{h \to 0}(10 + h)$$

Taking the limit as h goes to 0, you get 10. Therefore, the slope of the curve $y = x^2$ at the point (5, 25) is 10, or: $f'(5) = 10$.

Using this pattern, let's forget about the arithmetic for a second and derive a formula.

Example 3: Find the slope of the equation $f(x) = x^2$ at the point $\left(x_1, x_1^2\right)$.

Follow the steps in the last two problems, but instead of using a number, use x_1. This means that $f(x_1) = x_1^2$ and $(x_1 + h)^2 = x_1^2 + 2x_1h + h^2$. Then the derivative is:

$$\lim_{h \to 0} \frac{x_1^2 + 2x_1h + h^2 - x_1^2}{h} = \lim_{h \to 0} \frac{2x_1h + h^2}{h}$$

Factor h out of the top:

$$\lim_{h\to 0}\frac{h(2x_1 + h)}{h} = \lim_{h\to 0}(2x_1 + h)$$

Now take the limit as h goes to 0: you get $2x_1$. Therefore, $f'(x_1) = 2x_1$.

This example gives us a general formula for the derivative of this curve. Now we can pick any point, plug it into the formula, and determine the slope at that point. For example, the derivative at the point $x = 7$ is 14. At the point $x = \dfrac{7}{3}$, the derivative is $x = \dfrac{7}{3}$.

DIFFERENTIABILITY

One of the important requirements for the differentiability of a function is that the function be continuous. But, even if a function is continuous at a point, the function is not necessarily differentiable there. Check out the graph below:

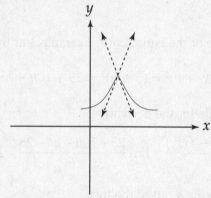

If a function has a "sharp corner," you can draw more than one tangent line at that point, and because the slopes of their tangent lines are not equal, the function is not differentiable there.

Another possible problem occurs when the tangent line is vertical, (which can also occur at a cusp) because a vertical line has an infinite slope. For example, if the derivative of a function is $\dfrac{1}{x+1}$, it doesn't have a derivative at $x = -1$.

Try these problems on your own, then check your work against the answers immediately beneath each problem.

PROBLEM 1. Find the derivative of $f(x) = 3x^2$ at (4, 48).

Answer: $f(4 + h) = 3(4 + h)^2 = 48 + 24h + 3h^2$. Use the definition of the derivative:

$$f'(4) = \lim_{h\to 0}\frac{48 + 24h + 3h^2 - 48}{h}$$

Simplify:

$$\lim_{h \to 0} \frac{24h + 3h^2}{h} = \lim_{h \to 0}(24 + 3h) = 24$$

The slope of the curve at the point (4, 48) is 24.

PROBLEM 2. Find the derivative of $f(x) = 3x^2$.

Answer: $f(x + h) = 3(x + h)^2 = 3x^2 + 6xh + 3h^2$. Use the definition of the derivative:

$$f'(x) = \lim_{h \to 0} \frac{3x^2 + 6xh + 3h^2 - 3x^2}{h}$$

Simplify:

$$\lim_{h \to 0} \frac{6xh + 3h^2}{h} = \lim_{h \to 0}(6x + 3h) = 6x$$

The derivative is $6x$.

PROBLEM 3. Find the derivative of $f(x) = x^3$.

Answer: $f(x + h) = (x + h)^3 = x^3 + 3x^2h + 3xh^2 + h^3$. First, use the definition of the derivative:

$$f'(x) = \lim_{h \to 0} \frac{x^3 + 3x^2h + 3xh^2 + h^3 - x^3}{h}$$

And simplify:

$$\lim_{h \to 0} \frac{3x^2h + 3xh^2 + h^3}{h} = \lim_{h \to 0}\left(3x^2 + 3xh + h^2\right) = 3x^2$$

The derivative is $3x^2$.
This next one will test your algebraic skills. Don't say we didn't warn you!

PROBLEM 4. Find the derivative of $f(x) = \sqrt{x}$.

Answer: $f(x + h) = \sqrt{x + h}$.
Use the definition of the derivative:

$$f'(x) = \lim_{h \to 0} \frac{\sqrt{x + h} - \sqrt{x}}{h}$$

Notice that this one doesn't cancel as conveniently as the other problems did. In order to simplify this expression, we have to multiply both the top and the bottom of the expression by $\sqrt{x + h} + \sqrt{x}$ (the conjugate of the numerator).

$$f'(x) = \lim_{h \to 0} \frac{\sqrt{x+h} - \sqrt{x}}{h} \left(\frac{\sqrt{x+h} + \sqrt{x}}{\sqrt{x+h} + \sqrt{x}} \right) = \lim_{h \to 0} \frac{x+h-x}{h \left(\sqrt{x+h} + \sqrt{x} \right)} = \lim_{h \to 0} \frac{h}{h \left(\sqrt{x+h} + \sqrt{x} \right)}$$

Simplify:

$$\lim_{h \to 0} \frac{1}{\left(\sqrt{x+h} + \sqrt{x} \right)} = \frac{1}{2\sqrt{x}}$$

The derivative is $\dfrac{1}{2\sqrt{x}}$.

PROBLEM 5. Find the derivative of $f(x) = \sin x$.

Answer: $f(x + h) = \sin(x + h) = \sin x \cos h + \cos x \sin h$.

Note: Don't confuse the sine of h with hyperbolic sine, which is abbreviated "sinh." The same is true for "cosh." The AP exam doesn't cover hyperbolic functions anyway, so you don't need to worry about them. Also, if you didn't remember the formula for the sine of the sum of two angles, review it!

Using the definition, you get this:

$$f'(x) = \lim_{h \to 0} \frac{\sin x \cos h + \cos x \sin h - \sin x}{h}$$

First, rearrange the numerator:

$$f'(x) = \lim_{h \to 0} \frac{\sin x (\cos h - 1) + \cos x \sin h}{h}$$

Next, split the expression into two fractions:

$$\lim_{h \to 0} \frac{\sin x (\cos h - 1)}{h} + \lim_{h \to 0} \frac{\cos x \sin h}{h}$$

As you learned in Chapter 2, $\lim\limits_{h \to 0} \dfrac{\cos h - 1}{h} = 0$ and $\lim\limits_{h \to 0} \dfrac{\sin h}{h} = 1$. Therefore, we have:

$$\lim_{h \to 0} \sin x (0) + \lim_{h \to 0} \cos x (1) = \cos x$$

The derivative of $\sin x$ is $\cos x$.

PRACTICE PROBLEM SET 3

Now find the derivative of the following expressions. The answers are in Chapter 21.

1. $f(x) = 5x$ at $x = 3$

2. $f(x) = 4x$ at $x = -8$

3. $f(x) = 2x^2$ at $x = 5$

4. $f(x) = 5x^2$ at $x = -1$

5. $f(x) = 8x^2$

6. $f(x) = -10x^2$

7. $f(x) = 20x^2$ at $x = a$

8. $f(x) = 2x^3$ at $x = -3$

9. $f(x) = -3x^3$

10. $f(x) = x^4$

11. $f(x) = x^5$

12. $f(x) = 2\sqrt{x}$ at $x = 9$

13. $f(x) = 5\sqrt{2x}$ at $x = 8$

14. $f(x) = \sin x$ at $x = \dfrac{\pi}{3}$

15. $f(x) = \cos x$

16. $f(x) = x^2 + x$

17. $f(x) = x^3 + 3x + 2$

18. $f(x) = \dfrac{1}{x}$

19. $f(x) = ax^2 + bx + c$

20. $f(x) = \dfrac{1}{x^2}$

4

Basic Differentiation

In calculus, you'll be asked to do two things: differentiate and integrate. In this section, you're going to learn differentiation. Integration will come later, in the second half of this book. Before we get about the business of learning how to take derivatives, however, here's a brief note about notation. Read this!

NOTATION

There are several different notations for derivatives in calculus. We'll use two different types interchangeably throughout this book, so get used to them now.

We'll refer to functions three different ways: $f(x)$, u or v, and y. For example, we might write: $f(x) = x^3$, $g(x) = x^4$, $h(x) = x^5$. Or we might use: $y = \sqrt{x}$. We'll also use notation like: $u = \sin x$ and $v = \cos x$. Usually, we pick the notation that causes the least confusion.

The derivatives of the functions will use notation that depends on the function. In other words:

Function	First Derivative	Second Derivative
$f(x)$	$f'(x)$	$f''(x)$
$g(x)$	$g'(x)$	$g''(x)$
y	y' or $\dfrac{dy}{dx}$	y'' or $\dfrac{d^2y}{dx^2}$

In addition, if we refer to a derivative of a function in general (for example, $ax^2 + bx + c$), we might enclose the expression in parentheses and use either of the following notations:

$$\left(ax^2 + bx + c\right)', \text{ or } \frac{d}{dx}\left(ax^2 + bx + c\right)$$

Sometimes math books refer to a derivative using either D_x or f_x. We're not going to use either of them.

THE POWER RULE

In the last chapter, you learned how to find a derivative using the definition of the derivative, a process that is very time-consuming and sometimes involves a lot of complex algebra. Fortunately, there's a shortcut to taking derivatives, so you'll never have to use the definition again—except when it's a question on an exam!

The basic technique for taking a derivative is called the **Power Rule**.

> Rule No. 1: If $y = x^n$, then $\dfrac{dy}{dx} = nx^{n-1}$

That's it. Wasn't that simple? Of course, this and all of the following rules can be derived easily from the definition of the derivative. Look at these next few examples of the Power Rule in action:

Example 1: If $y = x^5$, then $\dfrac{dy}{dx} = 5x^4$.

Example 2: If $y = x^{20}$, then $\dfrac{dy}{dx} = 20x^{19}$.

Notice that when the power of the function is negative, the power of the derivative is more negative.

Example 3: If $f(x) = x^{-5}$, then $f'(x) = -5x^{-6}$.

When the power is a fraction, you should be careful to get the subtraction right (you'll see the powers $\frac{1}{2}, \frac{1}{3}, \frac{3}{2}, -\frac{1}{2},$ and $-\frac{1}{3}$ often, so be comfortable with subtracting 1 from them).

Example 4: If $u = x^{\frac{1}{2}}$, then $\frac{du}{dx} = \frac{1}{2}x^{-\frac{1}{2}}$.

When the power is 1, the derivative is just a constant.

Example 5: If $y = x^1$, then $\frac{dy}{dx} = 1x^0 = 1$. (Because x^0 is 1!)

When the power is 0, the derivative is 0.

Example 6: If $y = x^0$, then $\frac{dy}{dx} = 0$.

This leads to the next three rules:

Rule No. 2: If $y = x$, then $\frac{dy}{dx} = 1$.

Rule No. 3: If $y = kx$, then $\frac{dy}{dx} = k$ (where k is a constant)

Rule No. 4: If $y = k$, then $\frac{dy}{dx} = 0$ (where k is a constant)

Note: For future reference, $a, b, c, n,$ and k always stand for constants.

Example 7: If $y = 8x^4$, then $\frac{dy}{dx} = 32x^3$.

Example 8: If $y = 5x^{100}$, then $y' = 500x^{99}$.

Example 9: If $y = -3x^{-5}$, then $\frac{dy}{dx} = 15x^{-6}$.

Example 10: If $f(x) = 7x^{\frac{1}{2}}$, then $f'(x) = \dfrac{7}{2}x^{-\frac{1}{2}}$.

Example 11: If $y = x\sqrt{15}$, then $\dfrac{dy}{dx} = \sqrt{15}$.

Example 12: If $y = 12$, then $\dfrac{dy}{dx} = 0$.

If you have any questions about any of these 12 examples (especially the last two), review the rules. Now for one last rule.

THE ADDITION RULE

If $y = ax^n + bx^m$, where a and b are constants, then $\dfrac{dy}{dx} = a\left(nx^{n-1}\right) + b\left(mx^{m-1}\right)$

This works for subtraction, too.

Example 13: If $y = 3x^4 + 8x^{10}$, then $\dfrac{dy}{dx} = 12x^3 + 80x^9$.

Example 14: If $y = 7x^{-4} + 5x^{-\frac{1}{2}}$, then $\dfrac{dy}{dx} = -28x^{-5} - \dfrac{5}{2}x^{-\frac{3}{2}}$.

Example 15: If $y = 5x^4(2 - x^3)$, then $\dfrac{dy}{dx} = 40x^3 - 35x^6$.

Example 16: If $y = (3x^2 + 5)(x - 1)$, then $y = 3x^3 - 3x^2 + 5x - 5$ and $\dfrac{dy}{dx} = 9x^2 - 6x + 5$.

Example 17: If $y = ax^3 + bx^2 + cx + d$, then $\dfrac{dy}{dx} = 3ax^2 + 2bx + c$.

After you've worked through all 17 of these examples, you should be able to take the derivative of any polynomial with ease.

As you may have noticed from the examples above, in calculus, you are often asked to convert from fractions and radicals to negative powers and fractional powers. In addition, don't freak out if your answer doesn't match any of the answer choices. Since answers to problems are often presented in simplified form, your answer may not be simplified enough.

There are two basic expressions that you'll often be asked to differentiate. You can make your life easier by memorizing the following derivatives:

$$\text{If } y = \frac{k}{x} \text{, then } \frac{dy}{dx} = -\frac{k}{x^2}$$

$$\text{If } y = k\sqrt{x} \text{, then } \frac{dy}{dx} = \frac{k}{2\sqrt{x}}$$

HIGHER ORDER DERIVATIVES

This may sound like a big deal, but it isn't. This term only refers to taking the derivative of a function more than once. You don't have to stop at the first derivative of a function; you can keep taking derivatives. The derivative of a first derivative is called the second derivative. The derivative of the second derivative is called the third derivative, and so on.

Generally, you'll only have to take first and second derivatives.

Function	First Derivative	Second Derivative
x^6	$6x^5$	$30x^4$
$8\sqrt{x}$	$\dfrac{4}{\sqrt{x}}$	$-2x^{-\frac{3}{2}}$

Notice how we simplified the derivatives in the latter example? You should be able to do this mentally.

Here are some sample problems involving the rules we discussed above. As you work, cover the answers with an index card, and then check your work after you're done. By the time you finish them, you should know the rules by heart.

PROBLEM 1. If $y = 50x^5 + \dfrac{3}{x} - 7x^{-\frac{5}{3}}$, then $\dfrac{dy}{dx} =$

Answer: $\dfrac{dy}{dx} = 50\left(5x^4\right) + \left(-\dfrac{3}{x^2}\right) - 7\left(-\dfrac{5}{3}\right)x^{-\frac{8}{3}} = 250x^4 - \dfrac{3}{x^2} + \dfrac{35}{3}x^{-\frac{8}{3}}$

PROBLEM 2. If $y = 9x^4 + 6x^2 - 7x + 11$, then $\dfrac{dy}{dx} =$

Answer: $\dfrac{dy}{dx} = 9\left(4x^3\right) + 6\left(2x\right) - 7\left(1\right) + 0 = 36x^3 + 12x - 7$

PROBLEM 3. If $f(x) = 6x^{\frac{3}{2}} - 12\sqrt{x} - \dfrac{8}{\sqrt{x}} + 24x^{-\frac{3}{2}}$, then $f'(x) =$

Answer: $f'(x) = 6\left(\dfrac{3}{2}x^{\frac{1}{2}}\right) - \left(\dfrac{12}{2\sqrt{x}}\right) - 8\left(-\dfrac{1}{2}x^{-\frac{3}{2}}\right) + 24\left(-\dfrac{3}{2}x^{-\frac{5}{2}}\right) = 9\sqrt{x} - \dfrac{6}{\sqrt{x}} + 4x^{-\frac{3}{2}} - 36x^{-\frac{5}{2}}$

How'd you do? Did you notice the changes in notation? How about the fractional powers, radical signs, and x's in denominators? You should be able to switch back and forth between notations, between fractional powers and radical signs, and between negative powers in a numerator and positive powers in a denominator.

PRACTICE PROBLEM SET 4

Find the derivative of each expression and simplify. The answers are in Chapter 21.

1. $(4x^2 + 1)^2$

2. $(x^5 + 3x)^2$

3. $11x^7$

4. $8x^{10}$

5. $18x^3 + 12x + 11$

6. $\dfrac{1}{2}(x^{12} + 17)$

7. $-\dfrac{1}{3}(x^9 + 2x^3 - 9)$

8. π^5

9. $\dfrac{1}{a}\left(\dfrac{1}{b}x^2 - \dfrac{2}{a}x - \dfrac{d}{x}\right)$

10. $-8x^{-8} + 12\sqrt{x}$

11. $6x^7 - 4\sqrt{x}$

12. $x^{-5} + \dfrac{1}{x^8}$

13. $\sqrt{x} + \dfrac{1}{x^3}$

14. $(6x^2 + 3)(12x - 4)$

15. $(3 - x - 2x^3)(6 + x^4)$

16. $e^{10} + \pi^3 - 7$

17. $\left(\dfrac{1}{x} + \dfrac{1}{x^2}\right)\left(\dfrac{4}{x^3} - \dfrac{6}{x^4}\right)$

18. $\sqrt{x} + \dfrac{1}{\sqrt{3}}$

19. $(x^2 + 8x - 4)(2x^2 + x^4)$

20. 0

21. $(x + 1)^3$

22. $\sqrt{x} + \sqrt[3]{x} + \sqrt[3]{x^2}$

23. $x(2x + 7)(x - 2)$

24. $\sqrt{x}\left(\sqrt[3]{x} + \sqrt[5]{x}\right)$

25. $ax^5 + bx^4 + cx^3 + dx^2 + ex + f$

THE PRODUCT RULE

Now that you know how to find derivatives of simple polynomials, it's time to get more complicated. What if you had to find the derivative of this?

$$f(x) = (x^3 + 5x^2 - 4x + 1)(x^5 - 7x^4 + x)$$

You could multiply out the expression and take the derivative of each term, like this:

$$f(x) = x^8 - 2x^7 - 39x^6 + 29x^5 - 6x^4 + 5x^3 - 4x^2 + x$$

And the derivative is:

$$f'(x) = 8x^7 - 14x^6 - 234x^5 + 145x^4 - 24x^3 + 15x^2 - 8x + 1$$

Needless to say, this process is messy. Naturally, there's an easier way. When a function involves two terms multiplied by each other, we use the **Product Rule**.

The Product Rule: If $f(x) = uv$, then $f'(x) = u\dfrac{dv}{dx} + v\dfrac{du}{dx}$

To find the derivative of two things multiplied by each other, you multiply the first function by the derivative of the second, and add that to the second function multiplied by the derivative of the first. With the product rule, the order of these two operations doesn't matter. It *does* matter with other rules, though, so it helps to use the same order each time, just to be sure.

Let's use the Product Rule to find the derivative of our example.

$$f'(x) = (x^3 + 5x^2 - 4x + 1)(5x^4 - 28x^3 + 1) + (x^5 - 7x^4 + x)(3x^2 + 10x - 4)$$

If we were to simplify this, we'd get the same answer as before. But, here's the best part: We're not going to simplify it. One of the great things about the AP exam is that when it's difficult to simplify an expression, you almost never have to. Nonetheless, you'll often need to simplify expressions when you're taking second derivatives, or when you use the derivative in some other equation. Practice simplifying whenever possible.

Example 1: $f(x) = (9x^2 + 4x)(x^3 - 5x^2)$

$$f'(x) = (9x^2 + 4x)(3x^2 - 10x) + (x^3 - 5x^2)(18x + 4)$$

Example 2: $y = \left(\sqrt{x} + 4\sqrt[3]{x}\right)\left(x^5 - 11x^8\right)$

$$y' = \left(\sqrt{x} + 4\sqrt[3]{x}\right)\left(5x^4 - 88x^7\right) + \left(x^5 - 11x^8\right)\left(\frac{1}{2\sqrt{x}} + \frac{4}{3\sqrt[3]{x^2}}\right)$$

Example 3: $y = \left(\dfrac{1}{x} + \dfrac{1}{x^2} - \dfrac{1}{x^3}\right)\left(\dfrac{1}{x} - \dfrac{1}{x^3} + \dfrac{1}{x^5}\right)$

$$y' = \left(\frac{1}{x} + \frac{1}{x^2} - \frac{1}{x^3}\right)\left(-\frac{1}{x^2} + \frac{3}{x^4} - \frac{5}{x^6}\right) + \left(\frac{1}{x} - \frac{1}{x^3} + \frac{1}{x^5}\right)\left(-\frac{1}{x^2} - \frac{2}{x^3} + \frac{3}{x^4}\right)$$

THE QUOTIENT RULE

What happens when you have to take the derivative of a function that is the quotient of two other functions? You guessed it: use the **Quotient Rule**.

The Quotient Rule: If $f(x) = \dfrac{u}{v}$, then $f'(x) = \dfrac{v\dfrac{du}{dx} - u\dfrac{dv}{dx}}{v^2}$

In this rule, as opposed to the Product Rule, the order in which you take the derivatives is very important, because you're subtracting instead of adding. It's always the bottom function times the derivative of the top minus the top function times the derivative of the bottom. Then divide the whole thing by the bottom function squared. A good way to remember this is to say the following:

$$\frac{"LoDeHi - HiDeLo"}{(Lo)^2}$$

You could also write:

$$f(x) = \frac{u}{v} \text{ as } f(x) = u\frac{1}{v}$$

Then you could derive the Quotient Rule using the Product Rule:

$$f'(x) = u\left(-\frac{1}{v^2}\frac{dv}{dx}\right) + \frac{du}{dx}\frac{1}{v} = \frac{v\dfrac{du}{dx} - u\dfrac{dv}{dx}}{v^2}$$

Here are some more examples:

Example 4: $f(x) = \dfrac{\left(x^5 - 3x^4\right)}{\left(x^2 + 7x\right)}$

$$f'(x) = \frac{\left(x^2 + 7x\right)\left(5x^4 - 12x^3\right) - \left(x^5 - 3x^4\right)\left(2x + 7\right)}{\left(x^2 + 7x\right)^2}$$

Example 5: $y = \dfrac{\left(x^{-3} - x^{-8}\right)}{\left(x^{-2} + x^{-6}\right)}$

$$\frac{dy}{dx} = \frac{\left(x^{-2} + x^{-6}\right)\left(-3x^{-4} + 8x^{-9}\right) - \left(x^{-3} - x^{-8}\right)\left(-2x^{-3} - 6x^{-7}\right)}{\left(x^{-2} + x^{-6}\right)^2}$$

We're not going to simplify these, although the Quotient Rule often produces expressions that simplify more readily than those involving the Product Rule. Sometimes it's helpful to simplify, but avoid it otherwise. When you have to find a second derivative, however, you do have to simplify the quotient. If this is the case, the AP exam usually will give you a simple expression to deal with, such as in the example below.

Example 6: $y = \dfrac{3x+5}{5x-3}$

$$\frac{dy}{dx} = \frac{(5x-3)(3)-(3x+5)(5)}{(5x-3)^2} = \frac{(15x-9)-(15x+25)}{(5x-3)^2} = \frac{-34}{(5x-3)^2}$$

In order to take the derivative of $\dfrac{dy}{dx}$, you have to use the Chain Rule.

THE CHAIN RULE

The most important rule in this chapter (and sometimes the most difficult one) is called the **Chain Rule**. It's used when you're given composite functions—that is, a function inside of another function. You'll always see one of these on the exam, so it's important to know the Chain Rule cold.

A composite function is usually written as: $f(g(x))$.

For example: If $f(x) = \dfrac{1}{x}$ and $g(x) = \sqrt{3x}$, then $f(g(x)) = \dfrac{1}{\sqrt{3x}}$

We could also find: $g(f(x)) = \sqrt{\dfrac{3}{x}}$

When finding the derivative of a composite function, we take the derivative of the "outside" function, with the inside function g considered as the variable, leaving the "inside" function alone. Then, we multiply this by the derivative of the "inside" function, with respect to its variable x.

Another way to write the Chain Rule is like this:

The Chain Rule: If $y=f\left(g(x)\right)$, then $y' = \left(\dfrac{df\left(g(x)\right)}{dg}\right)\left(\dfrac{dg}{dx}\right)$

This rule is tricky, so here are several examples. The last couple incorporate the Product Rule and the Quotient Rule as well.

Example 7: If $y = (5x^3 + 3x)^5$, then $\dfrac{dy}{dx} = 5(5x^3 + 3x)^4(15x^2 + 3)$

We just dealt with the derivative of something to the fifth power, like this:

$$y = (g)^5 \qquad \frac{dy}{dg} = 5(g)^4, \text{ where } g = 5x^3 + 3x$$

Then we multiplied by the derivative of g: $(15x^2 + 3)$.

Always do it this way. The process has several successive steps, like peeling away the layers of an onion until you reach the center.

Example 8: If $y = \sqrt{x^3 - 4x}$, then $\dfrac{dy}{dx} = \dfrac{1}{2}\left(x^3 - 4x\right)^{-\frac{1}{2}}\left(3x^2 - 4\right)$

Again, we took the derivative of the outside function, leaving the inside alone. Then we multiplied by the derivative of the inside.

Example 9: If $y = \sqrt{\left(x^5 - 8x^3\right)\left(x^2 + 6x\right)}$, then

$$\frac{dy}{dx} = \frac{1}{2}\left[\left(x^5 - 8x^3\right)\left(x^2 + 6x\right)\right]^{-\frac{1}{2}}\left[\left(x^5 - 8x^3\right)\left(2x + 6\right) + \left(x^2 + 6x\right)\left(5x^4 - 24x^2\right)\right]$$

Messy, isn't it? That's because we used the Chain Rule and the Product Rule. Now for one with the Chain Rule and the Quotient Rule.

Example 10: If $y = \left(\dfrac{2x + 8}{x^2 - 10x}\right)^5$, then

$$\frac{dy}{dx} = 5\left[\frac{2x + 8}{x^2 - 10x}\right]^4\left[\frac{\left(x^2 - 10x\right)(2) - (2x + 8)(2x - 10)}{\left(x^2 - 10x\right)^2}\right]$$

As you can see, these grow quite complex, so we only simplify these as a last resort. If you must simplify, the AP exam will only have a very simple Chain Rule problem, like the following example:

Example 11: If $y = \sqrt{5x^3 + x}$ then $\dfrac{dy}{dx} = \dfrac{1}{2}\left(5x^3 + x\right)^{-\frac{1}{2}}\left(15x^2 + 1\right)$

Now we use the Product Rule and the Chain Rule to find the second derivative:

$$\frac{d^2y}{dx^2} = \frac{1}{2}\left(5x^3 + x\right)^{-\frac{1}{2}}\left(30x\right) + \left(15x^2 + 1\right)\left[-\frac{1}{4}\left(5x^3 + x\right)^{-\frac{3}{2}}\left(15x^2 + 1\right)\right]$$

You can also simplify this further, if necessary.

There's another representation of the Chain Rule that you need to learn.

$$\text{If } y = y(v) \text{ and } v = v(x), \text{ then } \frac{dy}{dx} = \frac{dy}{dv}\frac{dv}{dx}$$

Example 12: $y = 8v^2 - 6v$ and $v = 5x^3 - 11x$, then

$$\frac{dy}{dx} = (16v - 6)(15x^2 - 11)$$

Then substitute for v:

$$\frac{dy}{dx} = \left(16\left(5x^3 - 11x\right) - 6\right)\left(15x^2 - 11\right) = \left(80x^3 - 176x - 6\right)\left(15x^2 - 11\right)$$

Here are some solved problems. Cover the answers first, then check your work.

PROBLEM 1. Find $\dfrac{dy}{dx}$ if $y = \left(5x^4 + 3x^7\right)\left(x^{10} - 8x\right)$.

Answer: $\dfrac{dy}{dx} = \left(5x^4 + 3x^7\right)\left(10x^9 - 8\right) + \left(x^{10} - 8x\right)\left(20x^3 + 21x^6\right)$

PROBLEM 2. Find $\dfrac{dy}{dx}$ if $y = \left(x^3 + 3x^2 + 3x + 1\right)\left(x^2 + 2x + 1\right)$.

Answer: $\dfrac{dy}{dx} = \left(x^3 + 3x^2 + 3x + 1\right)(2x + 2) + \left(x^2 + 2x + 1\right)\left(3x^2 + 6x + 3\right)$

PROBLEM 3. Find $\dfrac{dy}{dx}$ if $y = \left(\sqrt{x} + \dfrac{1}{x}\right)\left(\sqrt[3]{x^2} - \dfrac{1}{x^3}\right)$.

Answer: $\dfrac{dy}{dx} = \left(\sqrt{x} + \dfrac{1}{x}\right)\left(\dfrac{2}{3}x^{-\frac{1}{3}} + \dfrac{3}{x^4}\right) + \left(\sqrt[3]{x^2} - \dfrac{1}{x^3}\right)\left(\dfrac{1}{2\sqrt{x}} - \dfrac{1}{x^2}\right)$

PROBLEM 4. Find $\dfrac{dy}{dx}$ if $y = \left(x^3 + 1\right)\left(x^2 + 5x - \dfrac{1}{x^5}\right)$.

Answer: $\dfrac{dy}{dx} = \left(x^3 + 1\right)\left(2x + 5 + \dfrac{5}{x^6}\right) + \left(x^2 + 5x - \dfrac{1}{x^5}\right)\left(3x^2\right)$

PROBLEM 5. Find $\dfrac{dy}{dx}$ if $y = \dfrac{2x-4}{x^2-6}$.

Answer: $\dfrac{dy}{dx} = \dfrac{\left(x^2-6\right)(2)-(2x-4)(2x)}{\left(x^2-6\right)^2} = \dfrac{-2x^2+8x-12}{\left(x^2-6\right)^2}$

PROBLEM 6. Find $\dfrac{dy}{dx}$ if $y = \dfrac{x^2+1}{x^2+x+4}$.

Answer: $\dfrac{dy}{dx} = \dfrac{\left(x^2+x+4\right)(2x)-\left(x^2+1\right)(2x+1)}{\left(x^2+x+4\right)^2} = \dfrac{x^2+6x-1}{\left(x^2+x+4\right)^2}$

PROBLEM 7. Find $\dfrac{dy}{dx}$ if $y = \dfrac{x+5}{x-5}$.

Answer: $\dfrac{dy}{dx} = \dfrac{(x-5)(1)-(x+5)(1)}{(x-5)^2} = \dfrac{-10}{(x-5)^2}$

PROBLEM 8. Find $\dfrac{dy}{dx}$ at $x = 1$ if $y = \dfrac{(x+3)\left(x^3-9\right)}{\left(x^2+4\right)(x-8)}$.

Answer: You might be tempted to use the Product Rule to find the derivatives of the top and bottom, but this problem is much easier if you expand the numerator and denominator first:

$$y = \frac{x^4+3x^3-9x-27}{x^3-8x^2+4x-32}$$

$$\frac{dy}{dx} = \frac{\left(x^3-8x^2+4x-32\right)\left(4x^3+9x^2-9\right)-\left(x^4+3x^3-9x-27\right)\left(3x^2-16x+4\right)}{\left(x^3-8x^2+4x-32\right)^2}$$

You'd have to be deranged to attempt to simplify this expression. Luckily, you don't have to. Just plug in $x = 1$ and simplify.

$$\left.\frac{dy}{dx}\right|_{x=1} = \frac{(-35)(4)-(-32)(-9)}{\left[(-35)\right]^2} = -\frac{428}{1225}$$

PROBLEM 9. Find $\dfrac{dy}{dx}$ if $y = (x^4 + x)^2$.

Answer: $\dfrac{dy}{dx} = 2(x^4 + x)(4x^3 + 1)$

PROBLEM 10. Find $\dfrac{dy}{dx}$ if $y = \left(\dfrac{x+3}{x-3}\right)^3$.

Answer: $\dfrac{dy}{dx} = 3\left(\dfrac{x+3}{x-3}\right)^2 \left(\dfrac{(x-3)(1)-(x+3)(1)}{(x-3)^2}\right) = -18\left(\dfrac{(x+3)^2}{(x-3)^4}\right)$

PROBLEM 11. Find $\dfrac{dy}{dx}$ if $y = \left(\dfrac{x}{4} + \dfrac{4}{x}\right)^4$.

Answer: $\dfrac{dy}{dx} = 4\left(\dfrac{x}{4} + \dfrac{4}{x}\right)^3 \left(\dfrac{1}{4} - \dfrac{4}{x^2}\right)$

PROBLEM 12. Find $\dfrac{dy}{dx}$ at $x = 1$ if $y = \left[(x^3 + x)(x^4 - x^2)\right]^2$.

Answer: $\dfrac{dy}{dx} = 2\left[(x^3 + x)(x^4 - x^2)\right]\left[(x^3 + x)(4x^3 - 2x) + (x^4 - x^2)(3x^2 + 1)\right]$

Once again, plug in right away. Never simplify until after you've substituted.

At $x = 1$, $\dfrac{dy}{dx} = 0$.

PRACTICE PROBLEM SET 5

Simplify when possible. The answers are in Chapter 21.

1. Find $f'(x)$ if $f(x) = \left(\dfrac{4x^3 - 3x^2}{5x^7 + 1}\right)$.

2. Find $f'(x)$ if $f(x) = \left(x^2 - 4x + 3\right)\left(x + 1\right)$.

3. Find $f'(x)$ if $f(x) = \left(x + 1\right)^{10}$.

4. Find $f'(x)$ if $f(x) = 8\sqrt{\left(x^4 - 4x^2\right)}$.

5. Find $f'(x)$ if $f(x) = \left(\dfrac{x}{x^2 + 1}\right)^3$.

6. Find $f'(x)$ if $f(x) = \sqrt[4]{\left(\dfrac{2x - 5}{5x + 2}\right)}$.

7. Find $f'(x)$ if $f(x) = \dfrac{4x^8 - \sqrt{x}}{8x^4}$.

8. Find $f'(x)$ if $f(x) = \left(x + \dfrac{1}{x}\right)\left(x^2 - \dfrac{1}{x^2}\right)$.

9. Find $f'(x)$ if $f(x) = \left(\dfrac{x}{x + 1}\right)^4$.

10. Find $f'(x)$ if $f(x) = \left(x^2 + x\right)^{100}$.

11. Find $f'(x)$ if $f(x) = \sqrt{\dfrac{x^2 + 1}{x^2 - 1}}$.

12. Find $f'(x)$ at $x = 2$ if $f(x) = \dfrac{(x + 4)(x - 8)}{(x + 6)(x - 6)}$.

13. Find $f'(x)$ at $x = 1$ if $f(x) = \dfrac{x^6 + 4x^3 + 6}{\left(x^4 - 2\right)^2}$.

14. Find $f'(x)$ at $x = 1$ if $f(x) = \left[\dfrac{x - \sqrt{x}}{x + \sqrt{x}}\right]^2$.

15. Find $f'(x)$ if $f(x) = \dfrac{x^2 - 3}{(x-3)}$.

16. Find $f'(x)$ at $x = 1$ if $f(x) = (x^4 - x^2)(2x^3 + x)$.

17. Find $f'(x)$ at $x = 2$ if $f(x) = \dfrac{x^2 + 2x}{x^4 - x^3}$.

18. Find $f'(x)$ if $f(x) = \sqrt{x^4 + x^2}$.

19. Find $f'(x)$ at $x = 1$ if $f(x) = \dfrac{x}{\left(1 + x^2\right)^2}$.

20. Find $\dfrac{dy}{dx}$ if $y = u^2 - 1$ and $u = \dfrac{1}{x-1}$.

21. Find $\dfrac{dy}{dx}$ at $x = 1$ if $y = \dfrac{t^2 + 2}{t^2 - 2}$ and $t = x^3$.

22. Find $\dfrac{dy}{dt}$ if $y = (x^6 - 6x^5)(5x^2 + x)$ and $x = \sqrt{t}$.

23. Find $\dfrac{du}{dv}$ at $v = 2$ if $u = \sqrt{x^3 + x^2}$ and $x = \dfrac{1}{v}$.

24. Find $\dfrac{dy}{dx}$ at $x = 1$ if $y = \dfrac{1 + u}{1 + u^2}$ and $u = x^2 - 1$.

25. Find $\dfrac{du}{dv}$ if $u = y^3$ and $y = \dfrac{x}{x + 8}$ and $x = v^2$.

DERIVATIVES OF TRIG FUNCTIONS

There are a lot of trigonometry problems in calculus and on the AP Calculus Exam. If you're not sure of your trig, you should definitely go to the Appendix and review the unit on Prerequisite Math. You'll need to remember your trig formulas, the values of the special angles, and the trig ratios, among other stuff.

In addition, angles are *always* referred to in radians. You can forget all about using degrees.

You should know the derivatives of all six trig functions. The good news is that the derivatives are pretty easy, and all you have to do is memorize them. Because the AP exam might ask you about this, though, let's use the definition of the derivative to figure out the derivative of sin x.

If $f(x) = \sin x$, then $f(x + h) = \sin(x + h)$.

Substitute this into the definition of the derivative:

$$\lim_{h \to 0} \frac{f(x+h)-f(x)}{h} = \lim_{h \to 0} \frac{\sin(x+h)-\sin x}{h}$$

Remember that $\sin(x + h) = \sin x \cos h + \cos x \sin h$! Now simplify it:

$$\lim_{h \to 0} \frac{\sin x \cos h + \cos x \sin h - \sin x}{h}$$

Next, rewrite this as:

$$\lim_{h \to 0} \frac{\sin x (\cos h - 1) + \cos x \sin h}{h} = \lim_{h \to 0} \frac{\sin x (\cos h - 1)}{h} + \lim_{h \to 0} \frac{\cos x \sin h}{h}$$

Next, use some of the trigonometric limits that you memorized back in Chapter 1. Specifically:

$$\lim_{h \to 0} \frac{(\cos h - 1)}{h} = 0 \text{ and } \lim_{h \to 0} \frac{\sin h}{h} = 1$$

This gives you:

$$\lim_{h \to 0} \frac{\sin x (\cos h - 1)}{h} + \lim_{h \to 0} \frac{\cos x \sin h}{h} = \sin x (0) + \cos x (1) = \cos x$$

$$\frac{d}{dx} \sin x = \cos x$$

Example 1: Find the derivative of $\sin\left(\frac{\pi}{2} - x\right)$.

$$\frac{d}{dx} \sin\left(\frac{\pi}{2} - x\right) = \cos\left(\frac{\pi}{2} - x\right)(-1) = -\cos\left(\frac{\pi}{2} - x\right)$$

Use some of the rules of trigonometry you remember from last year. Because

$$\sin\left(\frac{\pi}{2} - x\right) = \cos x \text{ and } \cos\left(\frac{\pi}{2} - x\right) = \sin x ,$$

you can substitute into the above expression and get: $\frac{d}{dx} \cos x = -\sin x$.

Now, let's derive the derivatives of the other four trigonometric functions.

Example 2: Find the derivative of $\dfrac{\sin x}{\cos x}$.

Use the Quotient Rule:

$$\frac{d}{dx}\frac{\sin x}{\cos x} = \frac{(\cos x)(\cos x)-(\sin x)(-\sin x)}{(\cos x)^2} = \frac{\cos^2 x + \sin^2 x}{\cos^2 x} = \frac{1}{\cos^2 x} = \sec^2 x$$

Because $\dfrac{\sin x}{\cos x} = \tan x$, you should get: $\dfrac{d}{dx}\tan x = \sec^2 x$.

Example 3: Find the derivative of $\dfrac{\cos x}{\sin x}$.

Use the Quotient Rule:

$$\frac{d}{dx}\frac{\cos x}{\sin x} = \frac{(\sin x)(-\sin x)-(\cos x)(\cos x)}{(\sin x)^2} = \frac{-(\cos^2 x + \sin^2 x)}{\sin^2 x} = -\frac{1}{\sin^2 x} = -\csc^2 x$$

Because $\dfrac{\cos x}{\sin x} = \cot x$, you get: $\dfrac{d}{dx}\cot x = -\csc^2 x$.

Example 4: Find the derivative of $\dfrac{1}{\cos x}$.

Use the Reciprocal Rule.

$$\frac{d}{dx}\frac{1}{\cos x} = \frac{-1}{(\cos x)^2}(-\sin x) = \frac{\sin x}{\cos^2 x} = \frac{1}{\cos x}\frac{\sin x}{\cos x} = \sec x \tan x$$

Because $\dfrac{1}{\cos x} = \sec x$, you get: $\dfrac{d}{dx}\sec x = \sec x \tan x$.

Example 5: Find the derivative of $\dfrac{1}{\sin x}$.

You get the idea by now.

$$\frac{d}{dx}\frac{1}{\sin x} = \frac{-1}{(\sin x)^2}(\cos x) = \frac{-\cos x}{\sin^2 x} = \frac{-1}{\sin x}\frac{\cos x}{\sin x} = -\csc x \cot x$$

Because $\dfrac{1}{\sin x} = \csc x$, you get: $\dfrac{d}{dx}\csc x = -\csc x \cot x$.

There you go. We have now found the derivatives of all six of the trigonometric functions. (A chart of them appears at the end of the book.) Now memorize them. You'll thank us later.

Let's do some more examples:

Example 6: Find the derivative of sin(5x).

$$\frac{d}{dx}\sin(5x) = \cos(5x)(5) = 5\cos(5x)$$

Example 7: Find the derivative of sec(x^2).

$$\frac{d}{dx}\sec(x^2) = \sec(x^2)\tan(x^2)(2x)$$

Example 8: Find the derivative of csc($x^3 - 5x$).

$$\frac{d}{dx}\csc(x^3 - 5x) = -\csc(x^3 - 5x)\cot(x^3 - 5x)(3x^2 - 5).$$

These derivatives are almost like formulas. You just follow the pattern and use the Chain Rule when appropriate.

Here are some solved problems. Do each problem, covering the answer first, then checking your answer.

PROBLEM 1. Find $f'(x)$ if $f(x) = \sin(2x^3)$.

Answer: Follow the rule: $f'(x) = \cos(2x^3)6x^2$

PROBLEM 2. Find $f'(x)$ if $f(x) = \cos\left(\sqrt{3x}\right)$.

Answer: $f'(x) = -\sin\left(\sqrt{3x}\right)\left[\frac{1}{2}(3x)^{-\frac{1}{2}}(3)\right] = \dfrac{-3\sin\left(\sqrt{3x}\right)}{2\sqrt{3x}}$

PROBLEM 3. Find $f'(x)$ if $f(x) = \tan\left(\dfrac{x}{x+1}\right)$.

Answer: $f'(x) = \sec^2\left(\dfrac{x}{x+1}\right)\left[\dfrac{(x+1)-x}{(x+1)^2}\right] = \left(\dfrac{1}{(x+1)^2}\right)\sec^2\left(\dfrac{x}{x+1}\right)$

PROBLEM 4. Find $f'(x)$ if $f(x) = \csc(x^3 + x + 1)$.

Answer: Follow the rule: $f'(x) = -\csc(x^3 + x + 1)\cot(x^3 + x + 1)(3x^2 + 1)$

PRACTICE PROBLEM SET 6

Now try these problems. The answers are in Chapter 21.

1. Find $\dfrac{dy}{dx}$ if $y = \sin^2 x$.

2. Find $\dfrac{dy}{dx}$ if $y = \cos x^2$.

3. Find $\dfrac{dy}{dx}$ if $y = (\tan x)(\sec x)$.

4. Find $\dfrac{dy}{dx}$ if $y = \cot 4x$.

5. Find $\dfrac{dy}{dx}$ if $y = \sqrt{\sin 3x}$.

6. Find $\dfrac{dy}{dx}$ if $y = \dfrac{1 + \sin x}{1 - \sin x}$.

7. Find $\dfrac{dy}{dx}$ if $y = \csc^2 x^2$.

8. Find $\dfrac{dy}{dx}$ if $y = 2 \sin 3x \cos 4x$.

9. Find $\dfrac{d^4 y}{dx^4}$ if $y = \sin 2x$.

10. Find $\dfrac{dy}{dx}$ if $y = \sin t - \cos t$ and $t = 1 + \cos^2 x$.

11. Find $\dfrac{dy}{dx}$ if $y = \left(\dfrac{\tan x}{1 - \tan x}\right)^2$.

12. Find $\dfrac{dr}{d\theta}$ if $r = \sec\theta \tan 2\theta$.

13. Find $\dfrac{dr}{d\theta}$ if $r = \cos(1 + \sin\theta)$.

14. Find $\dfrac{dr}{d\theta}$ if $r = \dfrac{\sec\theta}{1 + \tan\theta}$.

15. Find $\dfrac{dy}{dx}$ if $y = \left(1 + \cot\left(\dfrac{2}{x}\right)\right)^{-2}$.

16. Find $\dfrac{dy}{dx}$ if $y = \sin\left(\cos\left(\sqrt{x}\right)\right)$.

5

Implicit Differentiation

HOW TO DO IT

By now, it should be easy for you to take the derivative of an equation such as $y = 3x^5 - 7x$. If you're given an equation such as $y^2 = 3x^5 - 7x$, you can still figure out the derivative by taking the square root of both sides, which gives you y in terms of x. This is known as finding the derivative **explicitly**. It's messy, but possible.

If you have to find the derivative of $y^2 + y = 3x^5 - 7x$, you don't have an easy way to get y in terms of x, so you can't differentiate this equation using any of the techniques you've learned so far. That's because each of those previous techniques needs to be used on an equation in which y is in terms of x. When you can't isolate y in terms of x (or if isolating y makes taking the derivative a nightmare), it's time to take the derivative **implicitly**.

Implicit differentiation is one of the simpler techniques you need to learn to do in calculus, but for some reason it gives many students trouble. Suppose you have the equation $y^2 = 3x^5 - 7x$. This means that the value of y is a function of the value of x. When we take the derivative, $\dfrac{dy}{dx}$, we're looking at the rate at which y changes as x changes. Thus, given $y = x^2 + x$, when we write:

$$\frac{dy}{dx} = 2x + 1$$

we're saying that "the rate" at which y changes, with respect to how x changes, is $2x + 1$.

Now, suppose you want to find $\dfrac{dx}{dy}$. As you might imagine:

$$\frac{dx}{dy} = \frac{1}{dy \, / \, dx}$$

So here, $\dfrac{dx}{dy} = \dfrac{1}{2x+1}$. But notice that this derivative is in terms of x, not y, and you need to find the derivative with respect to y. This derivative is an **implicit** one. When you can't isolate the variables of an equation, you often end up with a derivative that is in terms of both variables.

Another way to think of this is that there is a hidden term in the derivative, $\dfrac{dx}{dx}$, and when we take the derivative, what we really get is:

$$\frac{dy}{dx} = 2x\left(\frac{dx}{dx}\right) + 1\left(\frac{dx}{dx}\right)$$

A fraction that has the same term in its numerator and denominator is equal to 1, so we write:

$$\frac{dy}{dx} = 2x(1) + 1(1) = 2x + 1$$

Every time we take a derivative of a term with x in it, we multiply by the term $\dfrac{dx}{dx}$, but because this is 1, we ignore it. Suppose however, that we wanted to find out how y changes with respect to t (for time). Then we would have:

$$\frac{dy}{dt} = 2x\left(\frac{dx}{dt}\right) + 1\left(\frac{dx}{dt}\right)$$

If we wanted to find out how y changes with respect to r, we would have:

$$\frac{dy}{dr} = 2x\left(\frac{dx}{dr}\right) + 1\left(\frac{dx}{dr}\right)$$

and if we wanted to find out how y changes with respect to y, we would have:

$$\frac{dy}{dy} = 2x\left(\frac{dx}{dy}\right) + 1\left(\frac{dx}{dy}\right) \text{ or } 1 = 2x\frac{dx}{dy} + \frac{dx}{dy}$$

This is how we really do differentiation. Remember:

$$\frac{dx}{dy} = \frac{1}{\dfrac{dy}{dx}}$$

When you have an equation of x in terms of y, and you want to find the derivative with respect to y, simply differentiate. But if the equation is of y in terms of x, find $\dfrac{dy}{dx}$ and take its reciprocal to find $\dfrac{dx}{dy}$. You should use implicit differentiation any time you can't write a function explicitly in terms of the variable that we want to take the derivative with respect to. Go back to our original example:

$$y^2 + y = 3x^5 - 7x$$

To take the derivative according to the information in the last paragraph, you get:

$$2y\left(\frac{dy}{dx}\right) + 1\left(\frac{dy}{dx}\right) = 15x^4\left(\frac{dx}{dx}\right) - 7\left(\frac{dx}{dx}\right)$$

Notice how each variable is multiplied by its appropriate $\dfrac{d}{dx}$. Now, remembering that $\dfrac{dx}{dx} = 1$, rewrite the expression this way: $2y\left(\dfrac{dy}{dx}\right) + 1\left(\dfrac{dy}{dx}\right) = 15x^4 - 7$

Next, factor $\dfrac{dy}{dx}$ out of the left-hand side: $\dfrac{dy}{dx}(2y + 1) = 15x^4 - 7$

Isolating $\dfrac{dy}{dx}$ gives you: $\dfrac{dy}{dx} = \dfrac{15x^4 - 7}{(2y + 1)}$

This is the derivative you're looking for. Notice how the derivative is defined in terms of y **and** x. Up until now, $\dfrac{dy}{dx}$ has been strictly in terms of x. This is why the differentiation is "implicit."

Confused? Let's do a few examples and you will get the hang of it.

Example 1: Find $\dfrac{dy}{dx}$ if $y^3 - 4y^2 = x^5 + 3x^4$.

Using implicit differentiation, you get:

$$3y^2\left(\frac{dy}{dx}\right) - 8y\left(\frac{dy}{dx}\right) = 5x^4\left(\frac{dx}{dx}\right) + 12x^3\left(\frac{dx}{dx}\right)$$

Remember that $\dfrac{dx}{dx} = 1$: $\dfrac{dy}{dx}(3y^2 - 8y) = 5x^4 + 12x^3$

After you factor out $\dfrac{dy}{dx}$, divide both sides by $3y^2 - 8y$:

$$\frac{dy}{dx} = \frac{5x^4 + 12x^3}{(3y^2 - 8y)}$$

Note: Now that you understand that the derivative of an x term with respect to x will always be multiplied by $\dfrac{dx}{dx}$, and that $\dfrac{dx}{dx} = 1$, we won't write $\dfrac{dx}{dx}$ anymore. You should understand that the term is implied.

Example 2: Find $\dfrac{dy}{dx}$ if $\sin y^2 - \cos x^2 = \cos y^2 + \sin x^2$.

Use implicit differentiation:

$$\cos y^2 \left(2y \frac{dy}{dx} \right) + \sin x^2 \left(2x \right) = -\sin y^2 \left(2y \frac{dy}{dx} \right) + \cos x^2 \left(2x \right)$$

Then simplify:

$$2y \cos y^2 \left(\frac{dy}{dx} \right) + 2x \sin x^2 = -2y \sin y^2 \left(\frac{dy}{dx} \right) + 2x \cos x^2$$

Next, put all of the terms containing $\dfrac{dy}{dx}$ on the left and all of the other terms on the right:

$$2y \cos y^2 \left(\frac{dy}{dx} \right) + 2y \sin y^2 \left(\frac{dy}{dx} \right) = -2x \sin x^2 + 2x \cos x^2$$

Next, factor out $\dfrac{dy}{dx}$:

$$\frac{dy}{dx} \left(2y \cos y^2 + 2y \sin y^2 \right) = -2x \sin x^2 + 2x \cos x^2$$

And isolate $\dfrac{dy}{dx}$:

$$\frac{dy}{dx} = \frac{-2x \sin x^2 + 2x \cos x^2}{\left(2y \cos y^2 + 2y \sin y^2 \right)}$$

This can be simplified further to:

$$\frac{dy}{dx} = \frac{-x \left(\sin x^2 - \cos x^2 \right)}{y \left(\cos y^2 + \sin y^2 \right)}$$

Example 3: Find $\dfrac{dy}{dx}$ if $3x^2 + 5xy^2 - 4y^3 = 8$.

Implicit differentiation should result in: $6x + \left[5x\left(2y\dfrac{dy}{dx}\right) + (5)y^2 \right] - 12y^2\left(\dfrac{dy}{dx}\right) = 0$

(Did you notice the use of the Product Rule to find the derivative of $5xy^2$? The AP exam loves to make you do this. All of the same differentiation rules that you've learned up until now still apply. We're just adding another technique.) You can simplify this to:

$$6x + 10xy\dfrac{dy}{dx} + 5y^2 - 12y^2\dfrac{dy}{dx} = 0$$

Next, put all of the terms containing $\dfrac{dy}{dx}$ on the left and all of the other terms on the right:

$$10xy\dfrac{dy}{dx} - 12y^2\dfrac{dy}{dx} = -6x - 5y^2$$

Next, factor out $\dfrac{dy}{dx}$:

$$\left(10xy - 12y^2\right)\dfrac{dy}{dx} = -6x - 5y^2$$

Then, isolate $\dfrac{dy}{dx}$:

$$\dfrac{dy}{dx} = \dfrac{-6x - 5y^2}{\left(10xy - 12y^2\right)}$$

Example 4: Find the derivative of $3x^2 - 4y^2 + y = 9$ at $(2, 1)$.

You need to use implicit differentiation to find $\dfrac{dy}{dx}$:

$$6x - 8y\left(\dfrac{dy}{dx}\right) + \left(\dfrac{dy}{dx}\right) = 0$$

Now, instead of rearranging to isolate $\dfrac{dy}{dx}$, plug in $(2, 1)$ immediately and solve for the derivative:

$$6(2) - 8\left(\dfrac{dy}{dx}\right) + \left(\dfrac{dy}{dx}\right) = 0$$

Simplify: $12 - 7\left(\dfrac{dy}{dx}\right) = 0$, so $\dfrac{dy}{dx} = \dfrac{12}{7}$

Getting the hang of implicit differentiation yet? We hope so, because these next examples are slightly harder.

Example 5: Find $\dfrac{dy}{dx}$ if $\dfrac{y^2 + x^3}{y^3 - x^2} = x$.

First, cross-multiply. Do this whenever you have a quotient because the Product Rule is a lot less messy than the Quotient Rule for implicit differentiation.

We get:

$$y^2 + x^3 = x(y^3 - x^2)$$

Distribute:

$$y^2 + x^3 = xy^3 - x^3$$

Take the derivative:

$$2y\frac{dy}{dx} + 3x^2 = x\left(3y^2\frac{dy}{dx}\right) + y^3 - 3x^2$$

Simplify:

$$2y\frac{dy}{dx} + 3x^2 = 3xy^2\frac{dy}{dx} + y^3 - 3x^2$$

Put all of the terms containing $\dfrac{dy}{dx}$ on the left and all of the other terms on the right:

$$2y\frac{dy}{dx} - 3xy^2\frac{dy}{dx} = y^3 - 6x^2$$

Factor out $\dfrac{dy}{dx}$:

$$\frac{dy}{dx}\left(2y - 3xy^2\right) = y^3 - 6x^2$$

Now you can isolate $\dfrac{dy}{dx}$:

$$\frac{dy}{dx} = \frac{y^3 - 6x^2}{2y - 3xy^2}$$

Example 6: Find the derivative of $\dfrac{2x - 5y^2}{4y^3 - x^2} = -x$ at $(1, 1)$.

First, cross-multiply:

$$2x - 5y^2 = -x\left(4y^3 - x^2\right)$$

Distribute:

$$2x - 5y^2 = -4xy^3 + x^3$$

Take the derivative:

$$2 - 10y\frac{dy}{dx} = -4x\left(3y^2\frac{dy}{dx}\right) - 4y^3 + 3x^2$$

Do not simplify now. Rather, plug in $(1, 1)$ right away. This will save you from the algebra:

$$2 - 10(1)\frac{dy}{dx} = -4(1)\left(3(1)^2\frac{dy}{dx}\right) - 4(1)^3 + 3(1)^2$$

Now solve for $\dfrac{dy}{dx}$:

$$2 - 10\frac{dy}{dx} = -12\frac{dy}{dx} - 1$$

$$2\frac{dy}{dx} = -3$$

$$\frac{dy}{dx} = \frac{-3}{2}$$

SECOND DERIVATIVES

Sometimes, you'll be asked to find a second derivative implicitly.

Example 7: Find $\dfrac{d^2y}{dx^2}$ if $y^2 + 2y = 4x^2 + 2x$.

Differentiating implicitly, you get:

$$2y\frac{dy}{dx} + 2\frac{dy}{dx} = 8x + 2$$

Next, simplify and solve for $\dfrac{dy}{dx}$:

$$\frac{dy}{dx} = \frac{4x+1}{y+1}$$

Now it's time to take the derivative again:

$$\frac{d^2y}{dx^2} = \frac{4(y+1)-(4x+1)\left(\dfrac{dy}{dx}\right)}{(y+1)^2}$$

Finally, substitute for $\dfrac{dy}{dx}$:

$$\frac{4(y+1)-(4x+1)\left(\dfrac{4x+1}{y+1}\right)}{(y+1)^2} = \frac{4(y+1)^2-(4x+1)^2}{(y+1)^3}$$

Try these solved problems without looking at the answers. Then check your work.

PROBLEM 1. Find $\dfrac{dy}{dx}$ if $x^2+y^2=6xy$.

Answer: Differentiate with respect to x:

$$2x+2y\frac{dy}{dx} = 6x\frac{dy}{dx}+6y$$

Group all of the $\dfrac{dy}{dx}$ terms on the left and the other terms on the right:

$$2y\frac{dy}{dx}-6x\frac{dy}{dx} = 6y-2x$$

Now factor out $\dfrac{dy}{dx}$:

$$\frac{dy}{dx}(2y-6x) = 6y-2x$$

Therefore, the first derivative is the following:

$$\frac{dy}{dx} = \frac{6y - 2x}{2y - 6x} = \frac{3y - x}{y - 3x}$$

PROBLEM 2. Find $\frac{dy}{dx}$ if $x - \cos y = xy$

Answer: Differentiate with respect to x:

$$1 + \sin y \frac{dy}{dx} = x \frac{dy}{dx} + y$$

Grouping the terms, you get:

$$\sin y \frac{dy}{dx} - x \frac{dy}{dx} = y - 1$$

Now factor out $\frac{dy}{dx}$:

$$\frac{dy}{dx}(\sin y - x) = y - 1$$

The derivative is:

$$\frac{dy}{dx} = \frac{y - 1}{\sin y - x}$$

PROBLEM 3. Find $\frac{dy}{dx}$ if $x^2y^2 = 25$ at $(1,-5)$.

Answer: Once again, differentiate with respect to x:

$$x^2\left(2y\frac{dy}{dx}\right) + 2xy^2 = 0$$

Now, plug in $x = 1$ and $y = -5$, and solve for $\frac{dy}{dx}$:

$$-10\frac{dy}{dx} + 50 = 0 \qquad \frac{dy}{dx} = 5$$

PROBLEM 4. Find the derivative of each variable with respect to t of $x^2 + y^2 = z^2$

Answer: $2x\dfrac{dx}{dt} + 2y\dfrac{dy}{dt} = 2z\dfrac{dz}{dt}$

PROBLEM 5. Find the derivative of each variable with respect to t of $V = \dfrac{1}{3}\pi r^2 h$.

Answer: $\dfrac{dV}{dt} = \dfrac{1}{3}\pi\left(r^2\dfrac{dh}{dt} + 2r\dfrac{dr}{dt}h\right)$

PROBLEM 6. Find $\dfrac{d^2y}{dx^2}$ if $y^2 = x^2 - 2x$.

Answer: First, take the derivative with respect to x:

$$2y\dfrac{dy}{dx} = 2x - 2$$

Then solve for $\dfrac{dy}{dx}$:

$$\dfrac{dy}{dx} = \dfrac{2x-2}{2y} = \dfrac{x-1}{y}$$

The second derivative with respect to x becomes:

$$\dfrac{d^2y}{dx^2} = \dfrac{y(1) - (x-1)\dfrac{dy}{dx}}{y^2}$$

Now substitute for $\dfrac{dy}{dx}$ and simplify:

$$\dfrac{d^2y}{dx^2} = \dfrac{y - (x-1)\left(\dfrac{x-1}{y}\right)}{y^2} = \dfrac{y^2 - (x-1)^2}{y^3}$$

PRACTICE PROBLEM SET 7

Use implicit differentiation to find the following derivatives. The answers are in Chapter 21.

1. Find $\dfrac{dy}{dx}$ if $x^3 - y^3 = y$.

2. Find $\dfrac{dy}{dx}$ if $x^2 - 16xy + y^2 = 1$.

3. Find $\dfrac{dy}{dx}$ at (2, 1) if $\dfrac{x+y}{x-y} = 3$.

4. Find $\dfrac{dy}{dx}$ if $\cos y - \sin x = \sin y - \cos x$.

5. Find $\dfrac{dy}{dx}$ if $16x^2 - 16xy + y^2 = 1$ at (1, 1).

6. Find $\dfrac{dy}{dx}$ if $x^{\frac{1}{2}} + y^{\frac{1}{2}} = 2y^2$ at (1, 1).

7. Find $\dfrac{dy}{dx}$ if $x\sin y + y\sin x = \dfrac{\pi}{2\sqrt{2}}$ at $\left(\dfrac{\pi}{4}, \dfrac{\pi}{4}\right)$.

8. Find $\dfrac{d^2y}{dx^2}$ if $x^2 + 4y^2 = 1$.

9. Find $\dfrac{d^2y}{dx^2}$ if $\sin x + 1 = \cos y$.

10. Find $\dfrac{d^2y}{dx^2}$ if $x^2 - 4x = 2y - 2$.

6

Basic Applications of the Derivative

EQUATIONS OF TANGENT LINES AND NORMAL LINES

Finding the equation of a line tangent to a certain curve at a certain point is a standard calculus problem. This is because, among other things, the derivative is the slope of a tangent line to a curve at a particular point. Thus, we can find the equation of the tangent line to a curve if we have the equation of the curve and the point at which we want to find the tangent line. Then all we have to do is take the derivative of the equation, plug in the *x*-coordinate of the point to find the slope, then use the point and the slope to find the equation of the line. Let's take this one step at a time.

Suppose we have a point (x_1, y_1) and a slope m. Then the equation of the line through that point with that slope is:

$$(y - y_1) = m(x - x_1)$$

You should remember this formula from algebra. If not, memorize it!

Next, suppose that we have an equation $y = f(x)$, where (x_1, y_1) satisfies that equation. Then $f'(x_1) = m$, and we can plug all of our values into the equation for a line and get the equation of the tangent line. This is much easier to explain with a simple example.

Example 1: Find the equation of the tangent line to the curve $y = 5x^2$ at the point $(3, 45)$.

First of all, notice that the point satisfies the equation: when $x = 3$, $y = 45$. Now take the derivative of the equation:

$$\frac{dy}{dx} = 10x$$

Now, if you plug in $x = 3$, you'll get the slope of the curve at that point. By the way, the notation for plugging in a point is $\big|_{x=}$. Learn to recognize it!

$$\frac{dy}{dx}\bigg|_{x=3} = 10(3) = 30$$

Thus, we have the slope and the point, and the equation is:

$$(y - 45) = 30(x - 3)$$

It's customary to simplify the equation if it's not too onerous:

$$y = 30x - 45$$

Example 2: Find the equation of the tangent line to $y = x^3 + x^2$ at $(3, 36)$.

The derivative looks like this:

$$\frac{dy}{dx} = 3x^2 + 2x$$

So, the slope is:

$$\frac{dy}{dx}\bigg|_{x=3} = 3(3)^2 + 2(3) = 33$$

The equation looks like:

$$(y - 36) = 33(x - 3), \text{ or } y = 33x - 63$$

Naturally, there are a couple of things that can be done to make the problems harder. First of all, you can be given only the x-coordinate. Second, the equation can be more difficult to differentiate.

In order to find the y-coordinate, all you have to do is plug the x value into the equation for the curve and solve for y. Remember this: You'll see it again!

Example 3: Find the equation of the tangent line to $y = \dfrac{2x+5}{x^2-3}$ at $x = 1$.

First, find the y-coordinate:

$$y\,(1) = \frac{2(1)+5}{1^2-3} = -\frac{7}{2}$$

Second, take the derivative:

$$\frac{dy}{dx} = \frac{(x^2-3)(2)-(2x+5)(2x)}{(x^2-3)^2}$$

You're probably dreading having to simplify this derivative. Don't waste your time! Plug in $x = 1$ right away.

$$\left.\frac{dy}{dx}\right|_{x=1} = \frac{\left(1^2-3\right)(2)-\left(2(1)+5\right)\left(2(1)\right)}{\left(1^2-3\right)^2} = \frac{-4-14}{4} = -\frac{9}{2}$$

Now, we have a slope and a point, so the equation is:

$$y + \frac{7}{2} = -\frac{9}{2}(x-1), \text{ or } 2y = -9x+2$$

Sometimes, instead of finding the equation of a tangent line, you will be asked to find the equation of a normal line. A **normal** line is simply the line perpendicular to the tangent line at the same point. You follow the same steps as with the tangent line, but you use the slope that will give you a perpendicular line. Remember what that is? It's the negative reciprocal of the slope of the tangent line.

Example 4: Find the equation of the line normal to $y = x^5 - x^4 + 1$ at $x = 2$.

First, find the y-coordinate:

$$y\,(2) = 2^5 - 2^4 + 1 = 17$$

Second, take the derivative:

$$\frac{dy}{dx} = 5x^4 - 4x^3$$

Third, find the slope at $x = 2$:

$$\frac{dy}{dx}\bigg|_{x=2} = 5(2)^4 - 4(2)^3 = 48$$

Fourth, take the negative reciprocal of 48, which is $-\frac{1}{48}$.
Finally, the equation becomes:

$$y - 17 = -\frac{1}{48}(x - 2)$$

Try these solved problems. Do each problem, covering the answer first, then checking your answer.

PROBLEM 1. Find the equation of the tangent line to the graph of $y = 4 - 3x - x^2$ at the point (2, –6).

Answer: First, take the derivative of the equation:

$$\frac{dy}{dx} = -3 - 2x$$

Now, plug in $x = 2$ to get the slope of the tangent line:

$$\frac{dy}{dx} = -3 - 2(2) = -7$$

Third, plug the slope and the point into the equation for the line:

$$y - (-6) = -7\,(x - 2)$$

This simplifies to $y = -7x + 8$.

PROBLEM 2. Find the equation of the normal line to the graph of $y = 6 - x - x^2$ at $x = -1$.

Answer: Once again, take that derivative:

$$\frac{dy}{dx} = -1 - 2x$$

And then plug in $x = -1$ to get the slope of the tangent:

$$\frac{dy}{dx} = -1 - 2(-1) = 1$$

Plug $x = -1$ into the original equation to get the y-coordinate:

$$y = 6 + 1 - 1 = 6$$

Use the negative reciprocal of the slope in the second step to get the slope of the normal line:

$$m = -1$$

Finally, plug the slope and the point into the equation for the line:

$$y - 6 = -1 (x + 1)$$

This simplifies to $y = -x + 5$.

Problem 3. Find the equations of the tangent and normal lines to the graph of $y = \dfrac{10x}{x^2 + 1}$ at the point (2, 4).

Answer: This problem will put your algebra to the test. You have to use the Quotient Rule to take the derivative of this mess:

$$\frac{dy}{dx} = \frac{(x^2 + 1)(10) - (10x)(2x)}{(x^2 + 1)^2}$$

Second, plug in $x = 2$ to get the slope of the tangent:

$$\frac{dy}{dx} = \frac{(5)(10) - (20)(4)}{5^2} = -\frac{30}{25} = -\frac{6}{5}$$

Now, plug the slope and the point into the equation for the tangent line:

$$y - 4 = -\frac{6}{5}(x - 2)$$

That simplifies to $6x + 5y = 32$. The equation of the normal line must then be:

$$y - 4 = \frac{5}{6}(x - 2)$$

That, in turn, simplifies to $-5x + 6y = 14$.

Problem 4. Find the equation of the tangent line to the graph of $y = \sqrt{x^2 + 5}$ at the point (–2, 3).

Answer: First, take the derivative of the equation:

$$\frac{dy}{dx} = \frac{1}{2}\left(x^2 + 5\right)^{-\frac{1}{2}}(2x)$$

Now, we plug in $x = -2$ to get the slope of the tangent line:

$$\frac{dy}{dx} = \frac{1}{2}(9)^{-\frac{1}{2}}(-4) = -\frac{2}{3}$$

Third, we plug the slope and the point into the equation for the line:

$$y - 3 = -\frac{2}{3}(x + 2)$$

That can be simplified to $2x + 3y = 5$.

PROBLEM 5. The curve $y = ax^2 + bx + c$ passes through the point $(2, 4)$ and is tangent to the line $y = x + 1$ at $(0, 1)$. Find a, b, and c.

Answer: The curve passes through $(2, 4)$, so if you plug in $x = 2$, you'll get $y = 4$. Therefore,

$$4 = 4a + 2b + c$$

Second, the curve also passes through the point $(0, 1)$, so $c = 1$.

Because the curve is tangent to the line $y = x + 1$ at $(0, 1)$, they must both have the same slope at that point. The slope of the line is 1. The slope of the curve is the first derivative:

$$\frac{dy}{dx} = b$$

At $(0, 1)$ $\frac{dy}{dx} = b$. Therefore, $b = 1$.

Now that you know b and c, plug them back into the equation from the first step and solve for a:

$$4 = 4a + 2 + 1, \text{ and } a = \frac{1}{4}$$

PROBLEM 6. Find the points on the curve $y = 2x^3 - 3x^2 - 12x + 20$ where the tangent is parallel to the x-axis.

Answer: The x-axis is a horizontal line, so it has slope zero. Therefore, you want to know where the derivative of this curve is zero. Take the derivative:

$$\frac{dy}{dx} = 6x^2 - 6x - 12$$

And set it equal to zero and solve for x. Get accustomed to doing this: It's one of the most common questions in differential calculus.

$$\frac{dy}{dx} = 6x^2 - 6x - 12 = 0$$

$$6(x^2 - x - 2) = 0$$

$$6(x - 2)(x + 1) = 0$$

$$x = 2 \text{ or } x = -1$$

Third, find the *y*-coordinates of these two points.

$$y = 2(8) - 3(4) - 12(2) + 20 = 0$$

$$y = 2(-1) - 3(1) - 12(-1) + 20 = 27$$

Therefore, the points are (2, 0) and (-1, 27).

PRACTICE PROBLEM SET 8

Now try these problems. The answers are in Chapter 21.

1. Find the equation of the tangent to the graph of $y = 3x^2 - x$ at $x = 1$.

2. Find the equation of the tangent to the graph of $y = x^3 - 3x$ at $x = 3$.

3. Find the equation of the normal to the graph of $y = \sqrt{8x}$ at $x = 2$.

4. Find the equation of the tangent to the graph of $y = \dfrac{1}{\sqrt{x^2 + 7}}$ at $x = 3$.

5. Find the equation of the normal to the graph of $y = \dfrac{x+3}{x-3}$ at $x = 4$.

6. Find the equation of the tangent to the graph of $y = 4 - 3x - x^2$ at (0, 4).

7. Find the equation of the tangent to the graph of $y = 2x^3 - 3x^2 - 12x + 20$ at $x = 2$.

8. Find the equation of the tangent to the graph of $y = \dfrac{x^2 + 4}{x - 6}$ at $x = 5$.

9. Find the equation of the tangent to the graph of $y = \sqrt{x^3 - 15}$ at (4, 7).

10. Find the equation of the tangent to the graph of $y = (x^2 + 4x + 4)^2$ at $x = -2$.

11. Find the values of x where the tangent to the graph of $y = 2x^3 - 8x$ has a slope equal to the slope of $y = x$.

12. Find the equation of the normal to the graph of $y = \dfrac{3x + 5}{x - 1}$ at $x = 3$.

13. Find the values of x where the normal to the graph of $(x - 9)^2$ is parallel to the *y*-axis.

14. Find the coordinates where the tangent to the graph of $y = 8 - 3x - x^2$ is parallel to the *x*-axis.

15. Find the values of a, b, and c where the curves $y = x^2 + ax + b$ and $y = cx + x^2$ have a common tangent line at (-1, 0).

THE MEAN VALUE THEOREM FOR DERIVATIVES

If $y = f(x)$ is continuous on the interval $[a, b]$, and is differentiable everywhere on the interval (a, b), then there is at least one number c between a and b such that:

$$\frac{f(b) - f(a)}{b - a} = f'(c)$$

In other words, there's some point in the interval where the slope of the tangent line equals the slope of the secant line that connects the endpoints of the interval. (The function has to be continuous at the endpoints of the interval, but it doesn't have to be differentiable at the endpoints. Is this important? Maybe to mathematicians, but probably not to you!) You can see this graphically in the figure below:

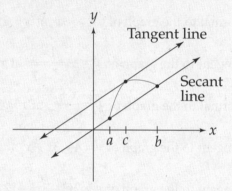

Example 1: Suppose you have the function $f(x) = x^2$, and you're looking at the interval $[1, 3]$. The mean value theorem for derivatives (this is often abbreviated MVTD) states that there is some number c such that:

$$f'(c) = \frac{3^2 - 1^2}{3 - 1} = 4$$

Because $f'(x) = 2x$, plug in c for x and solve: $2c = 4$ so $c = 2$. Notice that 2 is in the interval. This is what the MVTD predicted! If you don't get a value for c within the interval, something went wrong; either the function is not continuous and differentiable in the required interval, or you made a mistake.

Example 2: Consider the function $f(x) = x^3 - 12x$ on the interval $[-2, 2]$. The MVTD states that there is a c such that:

$$f'(c) = \frac{\left(2^3 - 24\right) - \left((-2)^3 + 24\right)}{2 - (-2)} = -8$$

Then $f'(c) = 3c^2 - 12 = -8$ and $c = \pm\dfrac{2}{\sqrt{3}}$ (which is approximately 1.155).

Notice that here there are two values of c that satisfy the MVTD. That's allowed. In fact, there can be infinitely many values, depending on the function.

Example 3: Consider the function $f(x) = \dfrac{1}{x}$ on the interval $[-2, 2]$.

Follow the MVTD:

$$f'(c) = \frac{\dfrac{1}{2} - \left(-\dfrac{1}{2}\right)}{2 - (-2)} = \frac{1}{4}$$

Then:

$$f'(c) = \frac{-1}{c^2} = \frac{1}{4}$$

There is no value of c that will satisfy this equation! We expected this. Why? Because $f(x)$ is not continuous at $x = 0$, which is in the interval. Suppose the interval had been $[1, 3]$, eliminating the discontinuity. The result would have been:

$$f'(c) = \frac{\dfrac{1}{3} - (1)}{3 - 1} = -\frac{1}{3} \ \text{ and } \ f'(c) = \frac{-1}{c^2} = -\frac{1}{3}; \ c = \pm\sqrt{3}$$

$c = -\sqrt{3}$ is not in the interval, but $c = \sqrt{3}$ is. The answer is $c = \sqrt{3}$.

Example 4: Consider the function $f(x) = x^2 - x - 12$ on the interval $[-3, 4]$.

Follow the MVTD:

$$f'(c) = \frac{0 - 0}{7} = 0 \ \text{ and } f'(c) = 2c - 1 = 0 \text{, so } c = \frac{1}{2}$$

In this last example, you discovered where the derivative of the equation equaled zero. This is going to be the single most common problem you'll solve in differential calculus. So now, we've got an important tip for you:

> When you don't know what to do, take the derivative of the equation and set it equal to zero!!!

Remember this advice for the rest of AP calculus.

Rolle's Theorem

Now let's learn Rolle's theorem, which is a special case of the MVTD.

> If $y = f(x)$ is continuous on the interval $[a, b]$, and is differentiable everywhere on the interval (a, b), and if $f(a) = f(b) = 0$, then there is at least one number c between a and b such that $f'(c) = 0$.

Graphically, this means that a continuous, differentiable curve has a horizontal tangent between any two points where it crosses the x-axis.

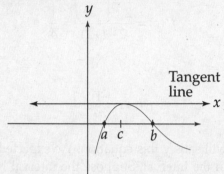

Example 4 was an example of Rolle's theorem, but let's do another.

Example 5: Consider the function $f(x) = \dfrac{x^2}{2} - 6x$ on the interval $[0, 12]$.

First, show that:

$$f(0) = \frac{0}{2} - 6(0) = 0 \text{ and } f(12) = \frac{144}{2} - 6(12) = 0$$

Then find:

$$f'(x) = x - 6, \text{ so } f'(c) = c - 6$$

If you set this equal to zero (remember what we told you!), you get $c = 6$. This value of c falls in the interval, so the theorem holds for this example.

As with the MVTD, you'll run into problems with the theorem when the function is not continuous and differentiable over the interval. This is where you need to look out for a trap set by ETS. Otherwise, just follow what we did here and you won't have any trouble with either Rolle's theorem or the MVTD. Try these example problems, and cover the responses until you check your work.

Problem 1. Find the values of c that satisfy the MVTD for $f(x) = x^2 + 2x - 1$ on the interval $[0, 1]$.

Answer: First, find $f(0)$ and $f(1)$:

$$f(0) = 0^2 + 2(0) - 1 = -1 \text{ and } f(1) = 1^2 + 2(1) - 1 = 2$$

Then,

$$\frac{2 - (-1)}{1 - 0} = \frac{3}{1} = 3 = f'(c)$$

Next, find $f'(x)$:

$$f'(x) = 2x + 2$$

Thus, $f'(c) = 2c + 2 = 3$, and $c = \dfrac{1}{2}$.

PROBLEM 2. Find the values of c that satisfy the MVTD for $f(x) = x^3 + 1$ on the interval $[1, 2]$.

Answer: Find $f(1) = 1^3 + 1 = 2$ and $f(2) = 2^3 + 1 = 9$. Then:

$$\frac{9-2}{2-1} = 7 = f'(c)$$

Next, $f'(x) = 3x^2$, so $f'(c) = 3c^2 = 7$ and $c = \pm\sqrt{\dfrac{7}{3}}$.

Notice that there are two answers for c, but only one of them is in the interval. The answer is $c = \sqrt{\dfrac{7}{3}}$.

PROBLEM 3. Find the values of c that satisfy the MVTD for $f(x) = x + \dfrac{1}{x}$ on the interval $[-4, 4]$.

Answer: First, because the function is not continuous on the interval, there may not be a solution for c. Let's show that this is true. Find $f(-4) = -4 - \dfrac{1}{4} = -\dfrac{17}{4}$ and $f(4) = 4 + \dfrac{1}{4} = \dfrac{17}{4}$. Then,

$$\frac{\dfrac{17}{4} - \left(-\dfrac{17}{4}\right)}{4 - (-4)} = \frac{17}{16} = f'(c)$$

Next, $f'(x) = 1 - \dfrac{1}{x^2}$. Therefore, $f'(c) = 1 - \dfrac{1}{c^2} = \dfrac{17}{16}$

There's no solution to this equation.

PROBLEM 4. Find the values of c that satisfy Rolle's theorem for $f(x) = x^4 - x$ on the interval $[0, 1]$.

Answer: Show that $f(0) = 0^4 - 0 = 0$ and that $f(1) = 1^4 - 1 = 0$.

Next, find $f'(x) = 4x^3 - 1$. By setting $f'(c) = 4c^3 - 1 = 0$ and solving, you'll see that $c = \sqrt[3]{\dfrac{1}{4}}$, which is in the interval.

PRACTICE PROBLEM SET 9

Now try these problems. The answers are in Chapter 21.

1. Find the values of c that satisfy the MVTD for $f(x) = 3x^2 + 5x - 2$ on the interval $[-1, 1]$.

2. Find the values of c that satisfy the MVTD for $f(x) = x^3 + 24x - 16$ on the interval $[0, 4]$.

3. Find the values of c that satisfy the MVTD for $f(x) = x^3 + 12x^2 + 7x$ on the interval $[-4, 4]$.

4. Find the values of c that satisfy the MVTD for $f(x) = \dfrac{6}{x} - 3$ on the interval $[1, 2]$.

5. Find the values of c that satisfy the MVTD for $f(x) = \dfrac{6}{x} - 3$ on the interval $[-1, 2]$.

6. Find the values of c that satisfy Rolle's theorem for $f(x) = x^2 - 8x + 12$ on the interval $[2, 6]$.

7. Find the values of c that satisfy Rolle's theorem for $f(x) = x^3 - x$ on the interval $[-1, 1]$.

8. Find the values of c that satisfy Rolle's theorem for $f(x) = x(1 - x)$ on the interval $[0, 1]$.

9. Find the values of c that satisfy Rolle's theorem for $f(x) = 1 - \dfrac{1}{x^2}$ on the interval $[-1, 1]$.

10. Find the values of c that satisfy Rolle's theorem for $f(x) = x^{\frac{2}{3}} - x^{\frac{1}{3}}$ on the interval $[0, 1]$.

7

Maxima and Minima

Here's another chapter of material involving more ways to apply the derivative to several other types of problems. This stuff focuses mainly on using the derivative to aid in graphing a function, etc.

APPLIED MAXIMA AND MINIMA PROBLEMS

One of the most common applications of the derivative is to find a maximum or minimum value of a function. These values can be called extreme values, optimal values, or critical points. Each of these problems involves the same, very simple principle:

> A maximum or a minimum of a function occurs at a point where the derivative of a function is zero, or where the derivative fails to exist.

At a point where the first derivative equals zero, the curve has a horizontal tangent line, at which point it could be reaching either a "peak" (maximum) or a "valley" (minimum).

There are a few exceptions to every rule. This rule is no different.

> If the derivative of a function is zero at a certain point, it is usually a maximum or minimum—but not always.
>
> There are two different kinds of maxima and minima: relative and absolute. A **relative** or **local** maximum or minimum means that the curve has a horizontal tangent line at that point, but it is not the highest or lowest value that the function attains. In the figure below, the two indicated points are relative maxima/minima.

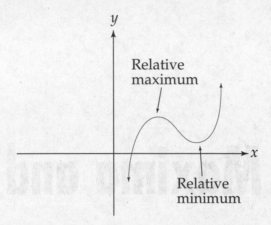

> An **absolute** maximum or minimum is either a point where the curve has a horizontal tangent line or a point at an end of the domain of the function where the function attains its highest or lowest value. In the figure below, the two indicated points are absolute maxima/minima. A relative maximum can also be an absolute maximum.

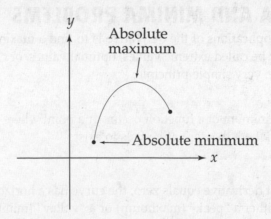

A typical word problem will ask you to find a maximum or a minimum value of a function, as it pertains to a certain situation. Sometimes you're given the equation; other times, you have to figure it out for yourself. Once you have the equation, you find its derivative and set it equal to zero. The values you get are called critical values. That is, if $f'(c) = 0$ or $f'(c)$ does not exist, then c is a critical value. Then, test these values to determine whether each value is a maximum or a minimum. The simplest way to do this is with the second derivative test.

> If a function has a critical value at x = c, then that value is a relative maximum if f''(c) < 0 and it is a relative minimum if f''(c) > 0.

If the second derivative is also zero at $x = c$, then the point is neither a maximum or a minimum but a point of inflection. More about that later.

It's time to do some examples.

Example 1: Find the minimum value on the curve $y = ax^2$, if $a > 0$.

Take the derivative and set it equal to zero:

$$\frac{dy}{dx} = 2ax = 0$$

The first derivative is equal to zero at $x = 0$. By plugging 0 back into the original equation, we can solve for the y-coordinate of the minimum (the y-coordinate is also 0, so the point is at the origin).

In order to determine if this is a maximum or a minimum, take the second derivative:

$$\frac{d^2y}{dx^2} = 2a$$

Because a is positive, the second derivative is positive and the critical point we obtained from the first derivative is a minimum point. Had a been negative, the second derivative would have been negative and a maximum would have occurred at the critical point.

Example 2: A manufacturing company has determined that the total cost of producing an item can be determined from the equation $C = 8x^2 - 176x + 1800$, where x is the number of units that the company makes. How many units should the company manufacture in order to minimize the cost?

Once again, take the derivative of the cost equation and set it equal to zero:

$$\frac{dC}{dx} = 16x - 176 = 0$$

$$x = 11$$

This tells us that 11 is a critical point of the equation. Now we need to figure out if this is a maximum or a minimum using the second derivative:

$$\frac{d^2C}{dx^2} = 16$$

Since 16 is always positive, any critical value is going to be a minimum. Therefore, the company should manufacture 11 units in order to minimize its cost.

Example 3: A rocket is fired into the air, and its height in meters at any given time t can be calculated using the formula $h(t) = 1600 + 196t - 4.9t^2$. Find the maximum height of the rocket and the time at which it occurs.

Take the derivative and set it equal to zero:

$$\frac{dh}{dt} = 196 - 9.8t$$

$$t = 20$$

Now we know that 20 is a critical point of the equation. Now use the second derivative test:

$$\frac{d^2h}{dt^2} = -9.8$$

This is always negative, so any critical value is a maximum. To determine the maximum height of the rocket, plug $t = 20$ into the equation:

$$h(20) = 1600 + 196(20) - 4.9(20^2) = 3560 \text{ meters}$$

The technique is always the same: (a) take the derivative of the equation; (b) set it equal to zero; and (c) use the second derivative test. The hardest part of these word problems is when you have to set up the equation yourself. The following is a classic AP problem:

Example 4: Max wants to make a box with no lid from a rectangular sheet of cardboard that is 18 inches by 24 inches. The box is to be made by cutting a square of side x from each corner of the sheet and folding up the sides (see figure below). Find the value of x that maximizes the volume of the box.

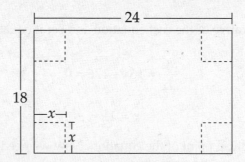

After we cut out the squares of side x and fold up the sides, the dimensions of the box will be:

width: $18 - 2x$
length: $24 - 2x$
depth: x

Using the formula for the volume of a rectangular prism, we can get an equation for the volume in terms of x:

$$V = x(18 - 2x)(24 - 2x)$$

Multiply the terms together (and be careful with your algebra):

$$V = x(18 - 2x)(24 - 2x) = 4x^3 - 84x^2 + 432x$$

Now take the derivative:

$$\frac{dV}{dx} = 12x^2 - 168x + 432$$

Set the derivative equal to zero, and solve for x:

$$12x^2 - 168x + 432 = 0$$

$$x^2 - 14x + 36 = 0$$

$$x = \frac{14 \pm \sqrt{196 - 144}}{2} = 7 \pm \sqrt{13} \approx 3.4, 10.6$$

Common sense tells us that you can't cut out two square pieces that measure 10.6 inches to a side (the sheet's only 18 inches wide!), so the maximizing value has to be 3.4 inches. Here's the second derivative test, just to be sure:

$$\frac{d^2V}{dx^2} = 24x - 168$$

At $x = 3.4$,

$$\int \tan^6 x \sec^2 x \, dx = \int u^6 du$$

So, the volume of the box will be maximized when $x = 3.4$.

Therefore, the dimensions of the box that maximize the volume are approximately:
11.2 in. × 17.2 in. × 3.4 in.

Sometimes, particularly when the domain of a function is restricted, you have to test the endpoints of the interval as well. This is because the highest or lowest value of a function may be at an endpoint of that interval; the critical value you obtained from the derivative might be just a local maximum or minimum. For the purposes of the AP exam, however, endpoints are considered separate from critical values.

Example 5: Find the absolute maximum and minimum values of $y = x^3 - x$ on the interval $[-3,3]$.

So far, the song remains the same. Take the derivative and set it equal to zero:

$$\frac{dy}{dx} = 3x^2 - 1 = 0$$

Solve for x:

$$x = \pm \frac{1}{\sqrt{3}}$$

Test the critical points:

$$\frac{d^2y}{dx^2} = 6x$$

At $x = \frac{1}{\sqrt{3}}$, we have a minimum. At $x = -\frac{1}{\sqrt{3}}$, we have a maximum.

$$\text{At } x = -\frac{1}{\sqrt{3}}, y = -\frac{1}{3\sqrt{3}} + \frac{1}{\sqrt{3}} = \frac{2}{3\sqrt{3}} \approx .385$$

$$\text{At } x = \frac{1}{\sqrt{3}}, y = \frac{1}{3\sqrt{3}} - \frac{1}{\sqrt{3}} = -\frac{2}{3\sqrt{3}} \approx -.385$$

Now it's time to check the endpoints of the interval:

$$\text{At } x = -3 \text{ , } y = -24$$
$$\text{At } x = 3 \text{ , } y = 24$$

We can see that the function actually has a *lower* value at $x = -3$ than at its "minimum" when $x = \frac{1}{\sqrt{3}}$. Similarly, the function has a *higher* value at $x = 3$ than at its "maximum" of $x = -\frac{1}{\sqrt{3}}$. This means that the function has a "local minimum" at $x = \frac{1}{\sqrt{3}}$, and an "absolute minimum" when $x = -3$.

And, the function has a "local maximum" at $x = -\frac{1}{\sqrt{3}}$, and an "absolute maximum" at $x = 3$.

Example 6: A rectangle is to be inscribed in a semicircle with radius 4, with one side on the semicircle's diameter. What is the largest area this rectangle can have?

Let's look at this on the coordinate axes. The equation for a circle of radius 4, centered at the origin, is $x^2 + y^2 = 16$; a semicircle has the equation $y = \sqrt{16 - x^2}$. Our rectangle can then be expressed as a function of x, where the height is $\sqrt{16 - x^2}$ and the base is $2x$. See the figure below:

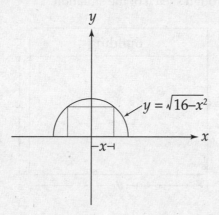

The area of the rectangle is: $A = 2x\sqrt{16 - x^2}$. Let's take the derivative of the area:

$$\frac{dA}{dx} = 2\sqrt{16 - x^2} - \frac{2x^2}{\sqrt{16 - x^2}}$$

The derivative is not defined at $x = \pm 4$. Setting the derivative equal to zero we get:

$$2\sqrt{16 - x^2} - \frac{2x^2}{\sqrt{16 - x^2}} = 0$$

$$2\sqrt{16 - x^2} = \frac{2x^2}{\sqrt{16 - x^2}}$$

$$2\left(16 - x^2\right) = 2x^2$$

$$32 - 2x^2 = 2x^2$$

$$32 = 4x^2$$

$$x = \pm\sqrt{8}$$

Note that the domain of this function is $-4 \leq x \leq 4$, so these numbers serve as endpoints of the interval. Let's compare the critical values and the endpoints:

When $x = -4$, $y = 0$ and the area is 0.

When $x = 4$, $y = 0$ and the area is 0.

When $x = \sqrt{8}$, $y = \sqrt{8}$ and the area is 16.

Thus, the maximum area occurs when $x = \sqrt{8}$ and the area equals 16.

Try some of these solved problems on your own. As always, cover the answers as you work.

PROBLEM 1. A rectangular field, bounded on one side by a building, is to be fenced in on the other three sides. If 3,000 feet of fence is to be used, find the dimensions of the largest field that can be fenced in.

Answer: First, let's make a rough sketch of the situation.

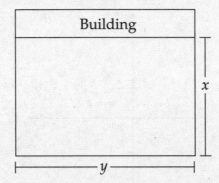

If we call the length of the field y and the width of the field x, the formula for the area of the field becomes:

$$A = xy$$

The perimeter of the fencing is equal to the sum of two widths and the length:

$$2x + y = 3000$$

Now, solve this second equation for y:

$$y = 3000 - 2x$$

When you plug this expression into the formula for the area, you get a formula for A in terms of x:

$$A = x(3000 - 2x) = 3000x - 2x^2$$

Next, take the derivative, set it equal to zero, and solve for x:

$$\frac{dA}{dx} = 3000 - 4x = 0$$

$$x = 750$$

Let's check to make sure it's a maximum. Find the second derivative:

$$\frac{d^2A}{dx^2} = -4$$

Since we have a negative result, $x = 750$ is a maximum. Finally, if we plug in $x = 750$ and solve for y, we find that $y = 1500$. The largest field will measure 750 feet by 1,500 feet.

PROBLEM 2. A poster is to contain 100 square inches of picture surrounded by a 4-inch margin at the top and bottom and a 2-inch margin on each side. Find the overall dimensions that will minimize the total area of the poster.

Answer: First, make a sketch.

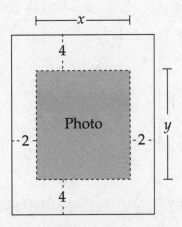

Let the area of the picture be $xy = 100$. The total area of the poster is $A = (x + 4)(y + 8)$. Then, expand the equation:

$$A = xy + 4y + 8x + 32$$

Substitute $xy = 100$ and $y = \dfrac{100}{x}$ into the area equation, and we get:

$$A = 132 + \frac{400}{x} + 8x$$

Now take the derivative and set it equal to zero:

$$\frac{dA}{dx} = 8 - \frac{400}{x^2} = 0$$

Solving for x, we find that $x = \sqrt{50}$. Now solve for y by plugging $x = \sqrt{50}$ into the area equation: $y = 2\sqrt{50}$. Then check that these dimensions give us a minimum:

$$\frac{d^2A}{dx^2} = \frac{800}{x^3}$$

This is positive when x is positive, so the minimum area occurs when $x = \sqrt{50}$. Thus, the overall dimensions of the poster are $4 + \sqrt{50}$ inches by $8 + 2\sqrt{50}$ inches.

PROBLEM 3. An open-top box with a square bottom and rectangular sides is to have a volume of 256 cubic inches. Find the dimensions that require the minimum amount of material.

Answer: First, make a sketch of the situation:

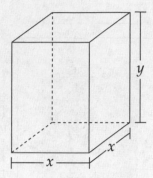

The amount of material necessary to make the box is equal to the surface area:

$$S = x^2 + 4xy$$

The formula for the volume of the box is $x^2y = 256$.

If we solve the latter equation for y, $y = \dfrac{256}{x^2}$, and plug it into the former equation, we get:

$$S = x^2 + 4x\frac{256}{x^2} = x^2 + \frac{1,024}{x}$$

Now take the derivative and set it equal to zero:

$$\frac{dS}{dx} = 2x - \frac{1,024}{x^2} = 0$$

If we solve this for x, we get $x^3 = 512$ and $x = 8$. Solving for y, we get $y = 4$. Check that these dimensions give us a minimum:

$$\frac{d^2A}{dx^2} = 2 + \frac{2,048}{x^3}$$

This is positive when x is positive, so the minimum surface area occurs when $x = 8$. The dimensions of the box should be 8 inches by 8 inches by 4 inches.

PROBLEM 4. Find the point on the curve $y = \sqrt{x}$ that is a minimum distance from the point (4, 0).

Answer: First, make that sketch.

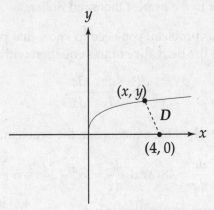

Using the distance formula:

$$D^2 = (x - 4)^2 + (y - 0)^2 = x^2 - 8x + 16 + y^2$$

Because $y = \sqrt{x}$:

$$D^2 = x^2 - 8x + 16 + x = x^2 - 7x + 16$$

Next, let $L = D^2$. We can do this because the minimum value of D^2 will occur at the same value of x as the minimum value of D. Therefore, it's simpler to minimize D^2 rather than D (because we won't have to take a square root!):

$$L = x^2 - 7x + 16$$

Now take the derivative and set it equal to zero:

$$\frac{dL}{dx} = 2x - 7 = 0$$

$$x = \frac{7}{2}$$

Solving for y, we get $y = \sqrt{\dfrac{7}{2}}$.

Finally, because $\dfrac{d^2L}{dx^2} = 2$, the point $\left(\dfrac{7}{2}, \sqrt{\dfrac{7}{2}} \right)$ is the minimum distance from the point (4, 0).

PROBLEM 5. Suppose that the revenue of a company can be represented with the function $r(x) = 48x$, and the company's cost function is $c(x) = x^3 - 12x^2 + 60x$, where x represents thousands of units and revenue and cost are represented in thousands of dollars. What production level maximizes profit, and what is the maximum profit to the nearest thousand dollars?

Answer: In order to solve this problem, you need to know that profit equals revenue minus cost. Since $P = r - c$, you should take the derivative of this equation with respect to x:

$$\frac{dP}{dx} = \frac{dr}{dx} - \frac{dc}{dx}.$$

Now, take the derivative of each of the equations in the problem:

$$\frac{dr}{dx} = 48 \text{ and } \frac{dc}{dx} = 3x^2 - 24x + 60$$

Plug these values into the previous equation to get:

$$\frac{dP}{dx} = 48 - 3x^2 + 24x - 60 = -3x^2 + 24x - 12$$

Now set $\dfrac{dP}{dx}$ equal to zero and solve for x:

$$-3x^2 + 24x - 12 = 0$$

$$x^2 - 8x + 4 = 0$$

$$x = \frac{8 \pm \sqrt{48}}{2} \approx 7.46, \ 0.54$$

At $x = 0.54$, revenue is 25.92 and cost is 29.06. At $x = 7.46$, revenue is 358.08 and cost is 194.94. The first value of x gives us a negative profit and the second value of x gives us a positive one, so the maximum profit must occur at $x \approx 7.46$ (thousand) units. The maximum profit, therefore, must be approximately $358.08 - 194.94 = 163.14$, or \$163,000 (to the nearest thousand dollars).

PRACTICE PROBLEM SET 10

Now try these problems on your own. The answers are in Chapter 21.

1. A rectangle has its base on the x-axis and its two upper corners on the parabola $y = 12 - x^2$. What is the largest possible area of the rectangle?

2. An open rectangular box is to be made from a 9×12 inch piece of tin by cutting squares of side x inches from the corners and folding up the sides. What should x be to maximize the volume of the box?

3. A 384-square-meter plot of land is to be enclosed by a fence and divided into two equal parts by another fence parallel to one pair of sides. What dimensions of the outer rectangle will minimize the amount of fence used?

4. What is the radius of a cylindrical soda can with volume of 512 cubic inches that will use the minimum material?

5. A swimmer is at a point 500 m from the closest point on a straight shoreline. She needs to reach a cottage located 1800 m down shore from the closest point. If she swims at 4 m/s and she walks at 6 m/s, how far from the cottage should she come ashore so as to arrive at the cottage in the shortest time?

6. Find the closest point on the curve $x^2 + y^2 = 1$ to the point (2, 0).

7. A window consists of an open rectangle topped by a semicircle and is to have a perimeter of 288 inches. Find the radius of the semicircle that will maximize the area of the window.

8. The range of a projectile is $R = \dfrac{v_0^2 \sin 2\theta}{g}$, where v_0 is its initial velocity, g is the acceleration due to gravity and is a constant, and θ is its firing angle. Find the angle that maximizes the projectile's range.

9. A computer company determines that its profit equation (in millions of dollars) is given by $P = x^3 - 48x^2 + 720x - 1000$, where x is the number of thousands of units of software sold and $0 \le x \le 40$. Optimize the manufacturer's profit.

CURVE SKETCHING

Another topic on which students spend a lot of time in calculus is curve sketching. In the old days, whole courses (called "Analytic Geometry") were devoted to the subject, and students had to master a wide variety of techniques to learn how to sketch a curve accurately.

Fortunately (or unfortunately, depending on your point of view), students no longer need to be as good at analytic geometry. There are two reasons for this: (1) the AP exam only tests a few types of curves; and (2) you can use a graphing calculator. Because of the calculator, you can get an idea of the shape of the curve, and all you need to do is find important points to label the graph. We use calculus to find some of these points.

When it's time to sketch a curve, we'll show you a four-part analysis that'll give you all the information you need.

TEST THE FUNCTION

Find where $f(x) = 0$. This tells you the function's x-intercepts (or roots). By setting $x = 0$, we can determine the y-intercepts. Then, find any horizontal and/or vertical asymptotes.

TEST THE FIRST DERIVATIVE

Find where $f'(x) = 0$. This tells you the critical points. We can determine whether the curve is rising or falling, as well as where the maxima and minima are. It's also possible to determine if the curve has any points where it's nondifferentiable.

TEST THE SECOND DERIVATIVE

Find where $f''(x) = 0$. This shows you where any points of inflection are. (These are points where the graph of a function changes concavity.) Then we can determine where the graph curves upward and where it curves downward.

TEST END BEHAVIOR

Look at what the general shape of the graph will be, based on the values of y for very large values of $\pm x$. Using this analysis, we can always come up with a sketch of a curve.

And now, the rules:

(1) When $f'(x) > 0$, the curve is rising; when $f'(x) < 0$, the curve is falling; when $f'(x) = 0$, the curve is at a critical point.

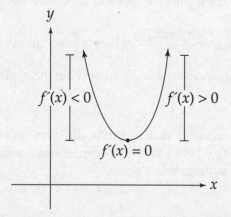

(2) When $f''(x) > 0$, the curve is "concave up"; when $f''(x) < 0$, the curve is "concave down"; when $f''(x) = 0$, the curve is at a point of inflection.

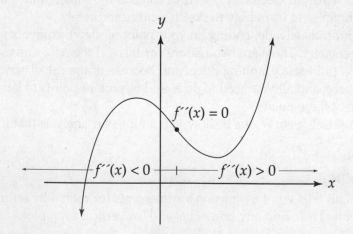

(3) The y-coordinates of each critical point are found by plugging the x-value into the original equation.

As always, this stuff will sink in better if we try a few examples.

Example 1: Sketch the equation $y = x^3 - 12x$.

Step 1: Find the x-intercepts:

$$x^3 - 12x = 0$$

$$x(x^2 - 12) = 0$$

$$x\left(x - \sqrt{12}\right)\left(x + \sqrt{12}\right) = 0$$

$$x = 0, \pm\sqrt{12}$$

The curve has x-intercepts at $\left(\sqrt{12},\ 0\right), \left(-\sqrt{12},\ 0\right),$ and $(0, 0)$.

Next, find the y-intercepts:

$$y = (0)^3 - 12(0) = 0$$

The curve has a y-intercept at $(0, 0)$.

There are no asymptotes, because there's no place where the curve is undefined (you won't have asymptotes for curves that are polynomials).

Step 2: Take the derivative of the function to find the critical points:

$$\frac{dy}{dx} = 3x^2 - 12$$

Set the derivative equal to zero and solve for x:

$$3x^2 - 12 = 0$$
$$3(x^2 - 4) = 0$$
$$3(x - 2)(x + 2) = 0$$
$$\text{so } x = 2, -2$$

Next, plug $x = 2, -2$ into the original equation to find the y-coordinates of the critical points:

$$y = (2)^3 - 12(2) = -16$$
$$y = (-2)^3 - 12(-2) = 16$$

Thus, we have critical points at $(2, -16)$ and $(-2, 16)$.

Step 3: Now, take the second derivative to find any points of inflection:

$$\frac{d^2y}{dx^2} = 6x$$

This equals zero at $x = 0$. We already know that when $x = 0$, $y = 0$, so the curve has a point of inflection at $(0, 0)$.

Now, plug the critical values into the second derivative to determine whether each is a maximum or a minimum. $f''(2) = 6(2) = 12$. This is positive, so the curve has a minimum at $(2, -16)$ and the curve is concave up at that point. $f''(-2) = 6(-2) = -12$. This value is negative, so the curve has a maximum at $(-2, 16)$ and the curve is concave down there."

Armed with this information, we can now plot the graph:

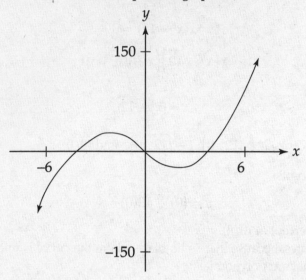

Example 2: Sketch the graph of $y = x^4 + 2x^3 - 2x^2 + 1$.

Step 1: First let's find the x-intercepts:

$$x^4 + 2x^3 - 2x^2 + 1 = 0$$

If the equation doesn't factor easily, it's best not to bother to find the function's roots. Convenient, huh? The good news is that if the roots aren't easy to find, ETS won't ask you to find them, or you can find them with your calculator.

Next, let's find the y-intercepts:

$$y = (0)^4 + 2(0)^3 - 2(0)^2 + 1$$

The curve has a y-intercept at $(0, 1)$.

There are no vertical asymptotes because there is no place where the curve is undefined.

Step 2: Now we take the derivative to find the critical points:

$$\frac{dy}{dx} = 4x^3 + 6x^2 - 4x$$

Set the derivative equal to zero:

$$4x^3 + 6x^2 - 4x = 0$$
$$2x(2x^2 + 3x - 2) = 0$$
$$2x(2x - 1)(x + 2) = 0$$

$$x = 0, \frac{1}{2}, -2$$

Next, plug these three values into the original equation to find the y-coordinates of the critical points. We already know that when $x = 0$, $y = 1$.

$$\text{When } x = \frac{1}{2}, \; y = \left(\frac{1}{2}\right)^4 + 2\left(\frac{1}{2}\right)^3 - 2\left(\frac{1}{2}\right)^2 + 1 = \frac{13}{16}$$

$$\text{When } x = -2, \; y = (-2)^4 + 2(-2)^3 - 2(-2)^2 + 1 = -7$$

Thus, we have critical points at $(0, 1)$, $\left(\frac{1}{2}, \frac{13}{16}\right)$, and $(-2, -7)$.

Step 3: Take the second derivative to find any points of inflection:

$$\frac{d^2y}{dx^2} = 12x^2 + 12x - 4$$

Set this equal to zero:

$$12x^2 + 12x - 4 = 0$$
$$3x^2 + 3x - 1 = 0$$

$$x = \frac{-3 \pm \sqrt{21}}{6} \approx .26, -1.26$$

Therefore, the curve has points of inflection at $x = \frac{-3 \pm \sqrt{21}}{6}$.

Now, solve for the y-coordinates:

$$(.26, .90) \text{ and } (-1.26, -3.66)$$

We can now plug the critical values into the second derivative to determine whether each is a maximum or a minimum:

$$12(0)^2 + 12(0) - 4 = -4$$

This is negative, so the curve has a maximum at $(0, 1)$; the curve is concave down there:

$$12\left(\frac{1}{2}\right)^2 + 12\left(\frac{1}{2}\right) - 4 = 5$$

This is positive, so the curve has a minimum at $\left(\frac{1}{2}, \frac{13}{16}\right)$; the curve is concave up there:

$$12(-2)^2 + 12(-2) - 4 = 20$$

This is positive, so the curve has a minimum at $(-2, -7)$ and the curve is also concave up there. We can now plot the graph:

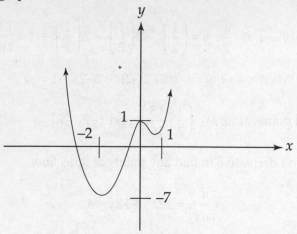

FINDING A CUSP

If the derivative of a function approaches ∞ from one side of a point and $-\infty$ from the other, and if the function is continuous at that point, then the curve has a "cusp" at that point. In order to find a cusp, you need to look at points where the first derivative is undefined, as well as where it's zero.

Example 3: Sketch the graph of $y = 2 - x^{\frac{2}{3}}$.

Step 1: Find the x-intercepts:

$$2 - x^{\frac{2}{3}} = 0$$

$$x^{\frac{2}{3}} = 2 \qquad x = \pm 2^{\frac{3}{2}} = \pm 2\sqrt{2}$$

The x-intercepts are at $\left(\pm 2\sqrt{2},\ 0\right)$.

Next, find the y-intercepts:

$$y = 2 - (0)^{\frac{2}{3}} = 2$$

The curve has a y-intercept at $(0, 2)$.
There are no asymptotes because there is no place where the curve is undefined.

Step 2: Now take the derivative to find the critical points:

$$\frac{dy}{dx} = -\frac{2}{3} x^{-\frac{1}{3}}$$

What's next? You guessed it! Set the derivative equal to zero:

$$-\frac{2}{3}x^{\frac{1}{3}} = 0$$

There are no values of x for which the equation is zero. But here's the new stuff to deal with: At $x = 0$, the derivative is undefined. If we look at the limit as x approaches 0 from both sides, we can determine whether the graph has a cusp.

$$\lim_{x \to 0^+} -\frac{2}{3}x^{-\frac{1}{3}} = -\infty \quad \text{and} \quad \lim_{x \to 0^-} -\frac{2}{3}x^{-\frac{1}{3}} = \infty$$

Therefore, the curve has a cusp at (0, 2).

There aren't any other critical points. But, we can see that when $x < 0$, the derivative is positive (which means that the curve is rising to the left of zero); and when $x > 0$ the derivative is negative (which means that the curve is falling to the right of zero).

Step 3: Now, we take the second derivative to find any points of inflection.

$$\frac{d^2y}{dx^2} = \frac{2}{9}x^{-\frac{4}{3}}$$

Again, there's no x value where this is zero. In fact, the second derivative is positive at all values of x except 0. Therefore, the graph is concave up everywhere.

Now it's time to graph this:

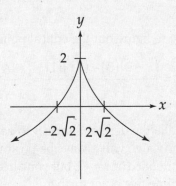

There's one other type of graph you should know about: a rational function. In order to graph a rational function, you need to know how to find that function's asymptotes.

How To Find Asymptotes

A line $y = c$ is a horizontal asymptote of the graph of $y = f(x)$ if:

$$\lim_{x \to \infty} f(x) = c \text{ or if } \lim_{x \to -\infty} f(x) = c$$

A line $x = k$ is a vertical asymptote of the graph of $y = f(x)$ if:

$$\lim_{x \to k^+} f(x) = \pm\infty \text{ or if } \lim_{x \to k^-} f(x) = \pm\infty$$

Example 4: Sketch the graph of $y = \dfrac{3x}{x+2}$.

Step 1: Find the x-intercepts. A fraction can be equal to zero only when its numerator is equal to zero (provided that the denominator is not also zero there). All we have to do is set $3x = 0$, and you get $x = 0$. Thus, the graph has an x-intercept at $(0, 0)$. Note: This is also the y-intercept.

Next, look for asymptotes. The denominator is undefined at $x = -2$, and if we take the left- and right-hand limits of the function:

$$\lim_{x \to -2^+} \frac{3x}{x+2} = -\infty \text{ and } \lim_{x \to -2^-} \frac{3x}{x+2} = \infty$$

The curve has a vertical asymptote at $x = -2$.

If we take $\lim_{x \to \infty} \dfrac{3x}{x+2} = 3$ and $\lim_{x \to -\infty} \dfrac{3x}{x+2} = 3$, the curve has a horizontal asymptote at $y = 3$.

Step 2: Now take the derivative to figure out the critical points:

$$\frac{dy}{dx} = \frac{(x+2)(3) - (3x)(1)}{(x+2)^2} = \frac{6}{(x+2)^2}$$

There are no values of x that make the derivative equal to zero. Because the numerator is 6 and the denominator is squared, the derivative will always be positive (the curve is always rising). You should note that the derivative is undefined at $x = -2$, but you already know that there's an asymptote at $x = -2$, so you don't need to examine this point further.

Step 3: Now it's time for the second derivative:

$$\frac{d^2y}{dx^2} = \frac{-12}{(x+2)^3}$$

This is never equal to zero. The expression is positive when $x < -2$, so the graph is concave up when $x < -2$. The second derivative is negative when $x > -2$, so it's concave down when $x > -2$.

Now plot the graph:

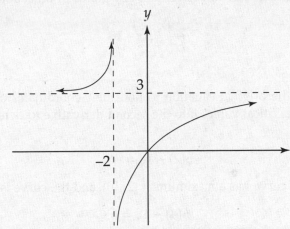

Now it's time to practice some problems. Do each problem, covering the answer first, then check your answer.

PROBLEM 1. Sketch the graph of $y = x^3 - 9x^2 + 24x - 10$. Plot all extrema, points of inflection, and asymptotes.

Answer: Follow the three steps.

First, see if the x-intercepts are easy to find. This is a cubic equation that isn't easily factored. So skip this step.

Next, find the y-intercepts by setting $x = 0$.

$$y = (0)^3 - 9(0)^2 + 24(0) - 10 = -10$$

The curve has a y-intercept at $(0, -10)$.

There are no asymptotes, because the curve is a simple polynomial.

Next, find the critical points using the first derivative:

$$\frac{dy}{dx} = 3x^2 - 18x + 24$$

Set the derivative equal to zero and solve for x:

$$3x^2 - 18x + 24 = 0$$
$$3(x^2 - 6x + 8) = 0$$
$$3(x - 4)(x - 2) = 0$$
$$x = 2, 4$$

Plug $x = 2$ and $x = 4$ into the original equation to find the y-coordinates of the critical points:

When $x = 2$, $y = 10$

When $x = 4$, $y = 6$

Thus, we have critical points at $(2, 10)$ and $(4, 6)$.

In our third step, the second derivative indicates any points of inflection:

$$\frac{d^2y}{dx^2} = 6x - 18$$

This equals zero at $x = 3$.

Next, plug $x = 3$ into the original equation to find the y-coordinates of the point of inflection, which is at (3, 8). Plug the critical values into the second derivative to determine whether each is a maximum or a minimum:

$$6(2) - 18 = -6$$

This is negative, so the curve has a maximum at (2, 10), and the curve is concave down there.

$$6(4) - 18 = 6$$

This is positive, so the curve has a minimum at (4, 6), and the curve is concave up there.
It's graph-plotting time:

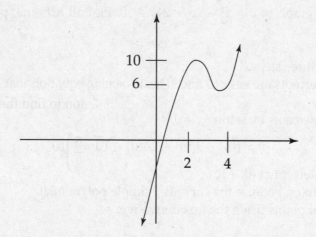

PROBLEM 2. Sketch the graph of $y = 8x^2 - 16x^4$. Plot all extrema, points of inflection, and asymptotes.

Answer: Factor the polynomial:

$$8x^2(1 - 2x^2) = 0$$

Solving for x, we get $x = 0$ (a double root), $x = \dfrac{1}{\sqrt{2}}$, and $x = -\dfrac{1}{\sqrt{2}}$.

Find the y-intercepts: when $x = 0$, $y = 0$.
There are no asymptotes, because the curve is a simple polynomial.
Find the critical points using the first derivative:

$$\frac{dy}{dx} = 16x - 64x^3$$

Set the derivative equal to zero and solve for x. You get $x = 0$, $x = \dfrac{1}{2}$, and $x = -\dfrac{1}{2}$.

Next, plug $x = 0$, $x = \dfrac{1}{2}$, and $x = -\dfrac{1}{2}$ into the original equation to find the y-coordinates of the critical points:

$$\text{When } x = 0, y = 0$$

$$\text{When } x = \frac{1}{2}, y = 1$$

$$\text{When } x = -\frac{1}{2}, y = 1$$

Thus, there are critical points at $(0, 0)$, $\left(\dfrac{1}{2}, 1\right)$, and $\left(-\dfrac{1}{2}, 1\right)$.

Take the second derivative to find any points of inflection:

$$\frac{d^2y}{dx^2} = 16 - 192x^2$$

This equals zero at $x = \dfrac{1}{\sqrt{12}}$ and $x = -\dfrac{1}{\sqrt{12}}$.

Next, plug $x = \dfrac{1}{\sqrt{12}}$ and $x = -\dfrac{1}{\sqrt{12}}$ into the original equation to find the y-coordinates of the points of inflection, which are at $\left(\dfrac{1}{\sqrt{12}}, \dfrac{5}{9}\right)$ and $\left(-\dfrac{1}{\sqrt{12}}, \dfrac{5}{9}\right)$.

Now determine whether the points are maxima or minima.

At $x = 0$, we have a minimum; the curve is concave up there.

At $x = \dfrac{1}{2}$, it's a maximum, and the curve is concave down.

At $x = -\dfrac{1}{2}$, it's also a maximum (still concave down).

Now plot:

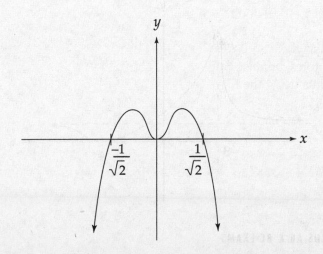

PROBLEM 3. Sketch the graph of $y = \left(\dfrac{x-4}{x+3}\right)^2$. Plot all extrema, points of inflection, and asymptotes.

Answer: This should seem rather routine by now.

Find the x-intercepts by setting the numerator equal to zero; $x = 4$. The graph has an x-intercept at $(4, 0)$. (It's a double root.)

Next, find the y-intercept by plugging in $x = 0$:

$$y = \frac{16}{9}$$

The denominator is undefined at $x = -3$, so there's a vertical asymptote at that point. Look at the limits:

$$\lim_{x \to \infty} \left(\frac{x-4}{x+3}\right)^2 = 1 \text{ and } \lim_{x \to -\infty} \left(\frac{x-4}{x+3}\right)^2 = 1$$

The curve has a horizontal asymptote at $y = 1$.

It's time for the first derivative:

$$\frac{dy}{dx} = 2\left(\frac{x-4}{x+3}\right)\frac{(x+3)(1)-(x-4)(1)}{(x+3)^2} = \frac{14x-56}{(x+3)^3}$$

The derivative is zero when $x = 4$, and the derivative is undefined at $x = -3$. (There's an asymptote there, so we can ignore the point. If the curve were *defined* at $x = -3$, then it would be a critical point, as you'll see in the next example.)

Now for the second derivative:

$$\frac{d^2y}{dx^2} = \frac{(x+3)^3(14)-(14x-56)3(x+3)^2}{(x+3)^6} = \frac{-28x+210}{(x+3)^4}$$

This is zero when $x = \dfrac{15}{2}$. The second derivative is positive (and the graph is concave up) when $x < \dfrac{15}{2}$, and it's negative (and the graph is concave down) when $x > \dfrac{15}{2}$.

We can now plug $x = 4$ into the second derivative. It's positive there, so $(4, 0)$ is a minimum. Your graph should look like this:

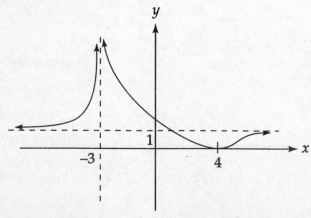

PROBLEM 4. Sketch the graph of $y - (x-4)^{\frac{2}{3}}$. Plot all extrema, points of inflection, and asymptotes.

Answer: By inspection, the x-intercept is at $x = 4$.

Next, find the y-intercepts. When $x = 0$, $y = \sqrt[3]{16} \approx 2.52$.
No asymptotes exist because there's no place where the curve is undefined.

The first derivative is:

$$\frac{dy}{dx} = \frac{2}{3}(x-4)^{-\frac{1}{3}}$$

Set it equal to zero:

$$\frac{2}{3}(x-4)^{-\frac{1}{3}} = 0$$

This can never equal zero. But, at $x = 4$ the derivative is undefined, so this is a critical point. If you look at the limit as x approaches 4 from both sides, you can see if there's a cusp:

$$\lim_{x \to 4^+} \frac{2}{3}(x-4)^{-\frac{1}{3}} = \infty \text{ and } \lim_{x \to 4^-} \frac{2}{3}(x-4)^{-\frac{1}{3}} = -\infty$$

The curve has a cusp at (4, 0).

There were no other critical points. But, we can see that when $x > 4$, the derivative is positive and the curve is rising; when $x < 4$ the derivative is negative, and the curve is falling.

The second derivative is:

$$\frac{d^2y}{dx^2} = -\frac{2}{9}(x-4)^{-\frac{4}{3}}$$

No value of x can set this equal to zero. In fact, the second derivative is negative at all values of x except 4. Therefore, the graph is concave down everywhere.

Your graph should look like this:

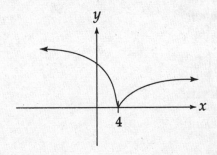

PRACTICE PROBLEM SET 11

It's time for you to try some of these on your own. Sketch each of the graphs below and check the answers in Chapter 21.

1. $y = x^3 - 9x - 6$

2. $y = -x^3 - 6x^2 - 9x - 4$

3. $y = (x^2 - 4)(9 - x^2)$

4. $y = (x^2 - 4)(9 - x^2)$

5. $y = \dfrac{x^4}{4} - 2x^2$

6. $y = \dfrac{x - 3}{x + 8}$

7. $y = \dfrac{x^2 - 4}{x - 3}$

8. $y = 3 + x^{\frac{2}{3}}$

9. $y = x^{\frac{2}{3}}\left(3 - 2x^{\frac{1}{3}}\right)$

10. $y = \dfrac{3x^2}{x^2 - 4}$

8
Motion

This chapter deals with two different types of word problems that involve motion: related rates and the relationship between velocity and acceleration of a particle. The subject matter might seem arcane, but once you get the hang of them, you'll see that these aren't so hard, either. Besides, the AP exam only tests a few basic problem types.

RELATED RATES

The idea behind these problems is very simple. In a typical problem, you'll be given an equation relating two or more variables. These variables will change with respect to time, and you'll use derivatives to determine how the rates of change are related. (Hence the name: related rates.) Sounds easy, doesn't it?

Example 1: A circular pool of water is expanding at the rate of $16\pi \dfrac{\text{in}^2}{\text{sec}}$. At what rate is the radius expanding when the radius is 4 inches?

Note: The pool is expanding in square inches per second. We've been given the rate that the area is changing, and we need to find the rate of change of the radius. What equation relates the area of a circle to its radius? $A = \pi r^2$.

Step 1: Set up the equation and take the derivative of this equation with respect to t (time), and you'll get this:

$$\frac{dA}{dt} = 2\pi r \frac{dr}{dt}$$

In this equation, $\dfrac{dA}{dt}$ represents the rate at which the area is changing, and $\dfrac{dr}{dt}$ is the rate at which the radius is changing. The simplest way to explain this is that whenever you have a variable in an equation (r, for example), the derivative with respect to time $\left(\dfrac{dr}{dt}\right)$ represents the rate at which that variable is increasing or decreasing.

Step 2: Now we can plug in the values for the rate of change of the area and for the radius. (Never plug in the values until after you have taken the derivative or you will get nonsense!)

$$16\pi = 2\pi(4)\frac{dr}{dt}$$

Solving for $\dfrac{dr}{dt}$, we get:

$$16\pi = 8\pi \frac{dr}{dt} \text{ and } \frac{dr}{dt} = 2$$

The radius is changing at a rate of $2\dfrac{\text{in}}{\text{sec}}$. It's important to note that this is the rate only when the radius is 4 inches. As the circle gets bigger and bigger, the radius will expand at a slower and slower rate.

Example 2: A 25-foot long ladder is leaning against a wall and sliding toward the floor. If the foot of the ladder is sliding away from the base of the wall at a rate of $15\dfrac{\text{feet}}{\text{sec}}$, how fast is the top of the ladder sliding down the wall when the top of the ladder is 7 feet from the ground?

Here's another classic related rates problem. As always, a picture is worth 1,000 words.

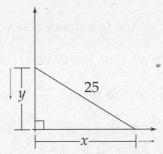

You can see that the ladder forms a right triangle with the wall. Let x stand for the distance from the foot of the ladder to the base of the wall, and let y represent the distance from the top of the ladder to the ground. What's our favorite theorem that deals with right triangles? The Pythagorean theorem tells us here that $x^2 + y^2 = 25^2$. Now we have an equation that relates the variables to each other.

Now take the derivative of the equation with respect to t:

$$2x\frac{dx}{dt} + 2y\frac{dy}{dt} = 0$$

Just plug in what you know and solve. Since we're looking for the rate at which the vertical distance is changing, we're going to solve for $\frac{dy}{dt}$.

Let's see what we know. We're given the rate at which the ladder is sliding away from the wall: $\frac{dx}{dt} = 15$. The distance from the ladder to the top of the wall is 7 feet ($y = 7$). To find x, use the Pythagorean theorem. If we plug in $y = 7$ to the equation $x^2 + y^2 = 25^2$, $x = 24$. Now plug all this information into the derivative equation:

$$2(24)(15) + 2(7)\frac{dy}{dt} = 0$$

$$\frac{dy}{dt} = \frac{-360}{7}\frac{\text{feet}}{\text{sec}}$$

Example 3: A spherical balloon is expanding at a rate of $60\pi\dfrac{\text{in}^3}{\text{sec}}$. How fast is the surface area of the balloon expanding when the radius of the balloon is 4 in?

Step 1: You're given the rate at which the volume's expanding, and you know the equation that relates volume to radius. But you have to relate radius to surface area as well, because you have to find the surface area's rate of change. This means that you'll need the equations for volume and surface area of a sphere:

$$V = \frac{4}{3}\pi r^3$$

$$A = 4\pi r^2$$

You're trying to find $\dfrac{dA}{dt}$, but A is given in terms of r, so you have to get $\dfrac{dr}{dt}$ first. Because we know the volume, if we work with the equation that gives us volume in terms of radius, we can find $\dfrac{dr}{dt}$. From there, work with the other equation to find $\dfrac{dA}{dt}$. If we take the derivative of the equation with respect to t we get: $\dfrac{dV}{dt} = 4\pi r^2 \dfrac{dr}{dt}$. Plugging in for $\dfrac{dV}{dt}$ and for r, we get: $60\pi = 4\pi(4)^2 \dfrac{dr}{dt}$. Solving for $\dfrac{dr}{dt}$ we get:

$$\frac{dr}{dt} = \frac{15}{16}\frac{\text{in}}{\text{sec}}$$

Step 2: Now, we take the derivative of the other equation with respect to t:

$$\frac{dA}{dt} = 8\pi r \frac{dr}{dt}$$

We can plug in for r and $\dfrac{dr}{dt}$ from the previous step and we get:

$$\frac{dA}{dt} = 8\pi(4)\frac{15}{16} = \frac{480\pi}{16}\frac{\text{in}^2}{\text{sec}} = 30\pi \frac{\text{in}^2}{\text{sec}}$$

One final example.

Example 4: An underground conical tank, standing on its vertex, is being filled with water at the rate of $18\pi \dfrac{\text{ft}^3}{\text{min}}$. If the tank has a height of 30 feet and a radius of 15 feet , how fast is the water level rising when the water is 12 feet deep?

This "cone" problem is also typical. The key point to getting these right is knowing that the ratio of the height of a right circular cone to its radius is constant. By telling us that the height of the cone is 30 and the radius is 15, we know that at any level, the height of the water will be twice its radius, or $h = 2r$.

The volume of a cone is $V = \dfrac{1}{3}\pi r^2 h$. (You'll learn to derive this formula through integration in Chapter 15.)

You must find the rate at which the water is rising (the height is changing), or $\dfrac{dh}{dt}$. Therefore, you want to eliminate the radius from the volume. By substituting $\dfrac{h}{2} = r$ into the equation for volume, we get:

$$V = \frac{1}{3}\pi\left(\frac{h}{2}\right)^2 h = \frac{\pi h^3}{12}$$

Differentiate both sides with respect to t:

$$\frac{dV}{dt} = \frac{\pi}{12} 3h^2 \frac{dh}{dt}$$

Now we can plug in and solve for $\frac{dh}{dt}$:

$$18\pi = \frac{\pi}{12} 3(12)^2 \frac{dh}{dt}$$

$$\frac{dh}{dt} = \frac{1}{2} \frac{\text{feet}}{\text{min}}$$

In order to solve related rates problems, you have to be good at determining relationships between variables. Once you figure that out, the rest is a piece of cake. Many of these problems involve geometric relationships, so review the formulas for the volumes and areas of cones, spheres, boxes, etc. Once you get the hang of setting up the problems, you'll see that these problems follow the same predictable patterns. Look through these sample problems.

PROBLEM 1. A circle is increasing in area at the rate of $16\pi \frac{\text{in}^2}{\text{s}}$. How fast is the radius increasing when the radius is 2 in?

Answer: Use the expression that relates the area of a circle to its radius: $A = \pi r^2$
Next, take the derivative of the expression with respect to t:

$$\frac{dA}{dt} = 2\pi r \frac{dr}{dt}$$

Now, Plug In $\frac{dA}{dt} = 16\pi$ and $r = 2$

$$16\pi = 2\pi(2)\frac{dr}{dt}$$

When you solve for $\frac{dr}{dt}$, you'll get $\frac{dr}{dt} = 4 \frac{\text{in}}{\text{sec}}$.

PROBLEM 2. A rocket is rising vertically at a rate of 5,400 miles per hour. An observer on the ground is standing 20 miles from the rocket's launch point. How fast (in radians per second) is the angle of elevation between the ground and the observer's line of sight of the rocket increasing when the rocket is at an elevation of 40 miles? (Notice that velocity is given in miles per hour and the answer asks for radians per second. In situations like this one, you have to be sure to convert the units properly, or you'll get nailed.)

Answer: First, draw a picture:

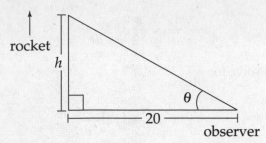

Now find the equation that relates the angle of elevation to the rocket's altitude:

$$\tan\theta = \frac{h}{20}$$

If we take the derivative of both sides of this expression with respect to t, we get:

$$\sec^2\theta\,\frac{d\theta}{dt} = \frac{1}{20}\frac{dh}{dt}$$

We know that $\dfrac{dh}{dt} = 5400$ miles per hour, but the problem asks for time in seconds, so we need to convert this number. There are 3,600 seconds in an hour, so $\dfrac{dh}{dt} = \dfrac{3}{2}$ miles per second. Next, we know that $\tan\theta = \dfrac{h}{20}$, so when $h = 40$, $\tan\theta = 2$. Because $1 + \tan^2\theta = \sec^2\theta$, we get $\sec^2\theta = 5$.

Plug in this information:

$$5\frac{d\theta}{dt} = \frac{1}{20}\left(\frac{3}{2}\right) \text{ and } \frac{d\theta}{dt} = \frac{3}{200} \text{ radians per second}$$

PRACTICE PROBLEM SET 12

Now try these problems on your own. The answers are in Chapter 21.

1. Oil spilled from a tanker spreads in a circle whose circumference increases at a rate of 40 ft/sec. How fast is the area of the spill increasing when the circumference of the circle is 100π ft?

2. A spherical balloon is inflating at a rate of 27π in³/sec. How fast is the radius of the balloon increasing when the radius is 3 in?

3. Cars A and B leave a town at the same time. Car A heads due south at a rate of 80 km/hr and car B heads due west at a rate of 60 km/hr. How fast is the distance between the cars increasing after three hours?

4. A cylindrical tank with a radius of 6 meters is filling with fluid at a rate of 108π m³/sec. How fast is the height increasing?

5. The sides of an equilateral triangle are increasing at the rate of 27 in/sec. How fast is the triangle's area increasing when the sides of the triangle are each 18 inches long?

6. An inverted conical container has a diameter of 42 in and a depth of 15 in. If water is flowing out of the vertex of the container at a rate of 35π in³/sec, how fast is the depth of the water dropping when the height is 5 inches?

7. A boat is being pulled toward a dock by a rope attached to its bow through a pulley on the dock 7 feet above the bow. If the rope is hauled in at a rate of 4 ft/sec, how fast is the boat approaching the dock when 25 feet of rope is out?

8. A 6-foot-tall woman is walking at the rate of 4 ft/sec away from a street lamp that is 24 feet tall. How fast is the length of her shadow changing?

9. The voltage, V, in an electrical circuit is related to the current, I, and the resistance, R, by the equation $V = IR$. The current is decreasing at –4 amps/sec as the resistance increases at 20 ohms/sec. How fast is the voltage changing when the voltage is 100 volts and the current is 20 amps?

10. The minute hand of a clock is 6 inches long. Starting from noon, how fast is the area of the sector swept out by the minute hand increasing in in²/min at any instant?

POSITION, VELOCITY, AND ACCELERATION

Almost every AP exam has a question on position, velocity, or acceleration. It's one of the traditional areas of physics where calculus comes in handy. Some of these problems require the use of integral calculus, which we won't talk about until the second half of this book. So, this unit is divided in half; you'll see the other half later.

If you have a function that gives you the position of an object (usually called a "particle") at a specified time, then the derivative of that function with respect to time is the velocity of the object, and the second derivative is the acceleration. These are usually represented by the following:

Position: $x(t)$ or sometimes $s(t)$

Velocity: $v(t)$, which is $x'(t)$

Acceleration: $a(t)$, which is $x''(t)$ or $v'(t)$

By the way, speed is the absolute value of velocity.

Example 1: If the position of a particle at a time t is given by the equation $x(t) = t^3 - 11t^2 + 24t$, find the velocity and the acceleration of the particle at time $t = 5$.

First, take the derivative of $x(t)$:

$$x'(t) = 3t^2 - 22t + 24 = v(t)$$

Second, plug in $t = 5$ to find the velocity at that time:

$$v(5) = 3(5^2) - 22(5) + 24 = -11$$

Third, take the derivative of $v(t)$ to find $a(t)$:

$$v'(t) = 6t - 22 = a(t)$$

Finally, plug in $t = 5$ to find the acceleration at that time:

$$a(5) = 6(5) - 22 = 8$$

See the negative velocity? The sign of the velocity is important, because it indicates the direction of the particle. Make sure that you know the following:

When the velocity is negative, the particle is moving to the left.

When the velocity is positive, the particle is moving to the right.

When the velocity and acceleration of the particle have the same signs, the particle's speed is increasing.

When the velocity and acceleration of the particle have opposite signs, the particle's speed is decreasing (or slowing down).

When the velocity is zero and the acceleration is not zero, the particle is momentarily stopped and changing direction.

These equations are usually functions of time (t). Typically, t is greater than zero, but it doesn't have to be.

Example 2: If the position of a particle is given by $x(t) = t^3 - 12t^2 + 36t + 18$, where $t > 0$, find the point at which the particle changes direction.

The derivative is:

$$x'(t) = v(t) = 3t^2 - 24t + 36$$

Set it equal to zero and solve for t:

$$x'(t) = 3t^2 - 24t + 36 = 0$$
$$t^2 - 8t + 12 = 0$$
$$(t - 2)(t - 6) = 0$$
$$t = 2 \text{ or } t = 6$$

You need to check that the acceleration is not 0. $x''(t) = 6t - 24$. This equals 0 at $t = 4$. Therefore, the particle is changing direction at $t = 2$ and $t = 6$.

Example 3: Given the same position function as in Example 2, find the interval of time during which the particle is slowing down.

When $0 < t < 2$ and $t > 6$, the particle's velocity is positive; when $2 < t < 6$, the particle's velocity is negative. You can verify this by graphing the function and seeing when it's above or below the x-axis. Or, try some points in the regions between the roots and outside the roots. Now, we need to determine the same information about the acceleration:

$$a(t) = v'(t) = 6t - 24$$

So the acceleration will be negative when $t < 4$, and positive when $t > 4$.
So we have:

Time	Velocity	Acceleration
$0 < t < 2$	Positive	Negative
$2 < t < 4$	Negative	Negative
$4 < t < 6$	Negative	Positive
$t > 6$	Positive	Positive

Whenever the velocity and acceleration have opposite signs, the particle is slowing down. Here the particle is slowing down during the first two seconds ($0 < t < 2$) and between the fourth and sixth seconds ($4 < t < 6$).

Another typical question you'll be asked is to find the distance a particle has traveled from one time to another. This is the distance that the particle has covered without regard to the sign, not just the displacement. In other words, if the particle had an odometer on it, what would it read? Usually, all you have to do is plug the two times into the position function and find the difference.

Example 4: How far does a particle travel between the eighth and tenth seconds if its position function is $x(t) = t^2 - 6t$?

Find $x(10) - x(8) = (100 - 60) - (64 - 48) = 24$.

Be careful about one very important thing: **If the velocity changes sign during the problem's time interval**, you'll get the wrong answer if you simply follow the method in the paragraph above. For example, suppose we had the same position function as above but we wanted to find the distance that the particle travels from $t = 2$ to $t = 4$:

$$x(4) - x(2) = (-8) - (-8) = 0$$

This is wrong. The particle travels from –8 back to –8, but it hasn't stood still. To fix this problem, divide the time interval into the time when the velocity is negative and the time when the velocity is positive, and add the absolute values of each distance. Here, the velocity is $v(t) = 2t - 6$. The velocity is negative when $t < 3$ and positive when $t > 3$. So we find the absolute value of the distance traveled from $t = 2$ to $t = 3$ and add to that the absolute value of the distance traveled from $t = 3$ to $t = 4$.

Because $x(t) = t^2 - 6t$:

$$|x(3) - x(2)| + |x(4) - x(3)| = |-9 + 8| + |-8 + 9| = 2$$

This is the distance that the particle traveled.

Example 5: Given the position function $x(t) = t^4 - 8t^2$, find the distance that the particle travels from $t = 0$ to $t = 4$.

First, find the first derivative $(v(t) = 4t^3 - 16t)$ and set it equal to zero:

$$4t^3 - 16t = 0 \quad 4t(t^2 - 4) = 0 \quad t = 0, 2, -2$$

So we need to divide the time interval into $t = 0$ to $t = 2$ and $t = 2$ to $t = 4$:

$$|x(2) - x(0)| + |x(4) - x(2)| = 16 + 144 = 160$$

Here are some solved problems. Do each problem, covering the answer first, then checking your answer.

Problem 1. Find the velocity and acceleration of a particle whose position function is $x(t) = 2t^3 - 21t^2 + 60t + 3$, for $t > 0$.

Answer: Find the first two derivatives:

$$v(t) = 6t^2 - 42t + 60$$

$$a(t) = 12t - 42$$

Problem 2. Given the position function in problem 1, find when the particle's speed is increasing.

Answer: First, set $v(t) = 0$:

$$6t^2 - 42t + 60 = 0$$
$$t^2 - 7t + 10 = 0$$
$$(t - 2)(t - 5) = 0$$
$$t = 2, t = 5$$

You should be able to determine that the velocity is positive from $0 < t < 2$, negative from $2 < t < 5$, and positive again from $t > 5$.

Now, set $a(t) = 0$:

$$12t - 42 = 0$$

$$t = \frac{7}{2}$$

You should be able to determine that the acceleration is negative from $0 < t < \frac{7}{2}$ and positive from $t > \frac{7}{2}$.

The intervals where the velocity and the acceleration have the same sign are $2 < t < \frac{7}{2}$ and $t > 5$.

PROBLEM 3. Given that the position of a particle is found by $x(t) = t^3 - 6t^2 + 1$; $t > 0$, find the distance that the particle travels from $t = 2$ to $t = 5$.

Answer: First, find $v(t)$.

$$v(t) = 3t^2 - 12t$$

Second, set $v(t) = 0$ and find the critical values:

$$3t^2 - 12t = 0 \quad 3t(t - 4) = 0 \quad t = \{0, 4\}$$

Since the particle changes direction after four seconds, you have to figure out two time intervals separately (from $t = 2$ to $t = 4$ and from $t = 4$ to $t = 5$) and add the absolute values of the distances:

$$\left|x(4) - x(2)\right| + \left|x(5) - x(4)\right| = \left|(-31) - (-15)\right| + \left|(-24) - (-31)\right| = 23$$

PROBLEM 4. If $x(t) = t^3 - 6t^2 + 9t + 1$; $t > 0$, find when the particle is changing direction.

Answer: First, find $v(t)$:

$$v(t) = 3t^2 - 12t + 9$$

Second, set $v(t) = 0$:

$$3t^2 - 12t + 9 = 0$$

$$t^2 - 4t + 3 = 0$$

$$t = 1,3$$

Third, find $a(t)$:

$$a(t) = 6t - 12$$

Check to see if the acceleration is zero at either $t = 1$ or $t = 3$: $a(1) = -6$, $a(3) = 6$. Because the acceleration is not zero at these times, and the velocity is zero, the particle changes direction at $t = 1$ and $t = 3$.

PRACTICE PROBLEM SET 13

Now try these problems. The answers are in Chapter 21.

1. Find the velocity and acceleration of a particle whose position function is $x(t) = t^3 - 9t^2 + 24t$, $t > 0$.

2. Find the velocity and acceleration of a particle whose position function is $x(t) = \sin(2t) + \cos(t)$.

3. If the position function of a particle is $x(t) = \dfrac{t}{t^2 + 9}$, $t > 0$, find when the particle is changing direction.

4. If the position function of a particle is $x(t) = \sin\left(\dfrac{t}{2}\right)$, $0 < t < 4\pi$, find when the particle is changing direction.

5. If the position function of a particle is $x(t) = 3t^2 + 2t + 4$, $t > 0$, find the distance that the particle travels from $t = 2$ to $t = 5$.

6. If the position function of a particle is $x(t) = t^2 + 8t$, $t > 0$, find the distance that the particle travels from $t = 0$ to $t = 4$.

7. If the position function of a particle is $x(t) = 2\sin^2 t + 2\cos^2 t$, $t > 0$, find the velocity and acceleration of the particle.

8. If the position function of a particle is $x(t) = t^3 + 8t^2 - 2t + 4$, $t > 0$, find when the particle is changing direction.

9. If the position function of a particle is $x(t) = 2t^3 - 6t^2 + 12t - 18$, $t > 0$, find when the particle is changing direction.

10. If the position function of a particle is $x(t) = \sin^2 2t$, $t > 0$, find the distance that the particle travels from $t = 0$ to $t = 2$.

9

Exponential and Logarithmic Functions, Part One

As with trigonometric functions, you'll be expected to remember all of the logarithmic and exponential functions you've studied in the past. If you're not sure about any of this stuff, review the unit on Prerequisite Mathematics. Also, this is only part one of our treatment of exponents and logs. Much of what you need to know about these functions requires knowledge of integrals (the second half of the book), so we'll discuss them again later.

THE DERIVATIVE OF ln *x*

When you studied logs in the past, you probably concentrated on common logs (that is, those with a base of 10), and avoided natural logarithms (base *e*) as much as possible. Well, we have bad news for you: Most of what you'll see from now on involves natural logs. In fact, common logs almost never show up in calculus. But that's okay. All you have to do is memorize a bunch of rules, and you'll be fine.

Rule No. 1: If $y = \ln x$, then $\dfrac{dy}{dx} = \dfrac{1}{x}$

This rule has a corollary that incorporates the Chain Rule and is actually a more useful rule to memorize:

Rule No. 2: If $y = \ln u$, then $\dfrac{dy}{dx} = \dfrac{1}{u}\dfrac{du}{dx}$

Remember: *u* is a function of *x*, and $\dfrac{du}{dx}$ is its derivative.

You'll see how simple this rule is after we try a few examples.

Example 1: Find the derivative of $f(x) = \ln(x^3)$.

$$f'(x) = \frac{3x^2}{x^3} = \frac{3}{x}$$

You could have done this another way. If you recall your rules of logarithms:

$$\ln(x^3) = 3\ln x$$

Therefore, $f'(x) = 3\left(\dfrac{1}{x}\right) = \dfrac{3}{x}$.

Example 2: Find the derivative of $f(x) = \ln(5x - 3x^6)$.

$$f'(x) = \frac{\left(5 - 18x^5\right)}{\left(5x - 3x^6\right)}$$

Example 3: Find the derivative of $f(x) = \ln(\cos x)$.

$$f'(x) = \frac{-\sin x}{\cos x} = -\tan x$$

Finding the derivative of a natural logarithm is just a matter of following a simple formula.

THE DERIVATIVE OF e^x

As you'll see in Rule No. 3, the derivative of e^x is probably the easiest thing that you'll ever have to do in calculus.

> Rule No. 3: If $y = e^x$, then $\dfrac{dy}{dx} = e^x$

That's not a typo. The derivative is the same thing as the original function!
Incorporating the Chain Rule, we get a good formula for finding the derivative:

> Rule No. 4: If $y = e^u$, then $\dfrac{dy}{dx} = e^u \dfrac{du}{dx}$

And you were worried that all of this logarithm and exponential stuff was going to be hard!

Example 4: Find the derivative of $f(x) = e^{3x}$.

$$f(x) = e^{3x}(3) = 3e^{3x}$$

Example 5: Find the derivative of $f(x) = e^{x^3}$.

$$f'(x) = e^{x^3}\left(3x^2\right) = 3x^2 e^{x^3}$$

Example 6: Find the derivative of $f(x) = e^{\tan x}$.

$$f(x) = \left(\sec^2 x\right) e^{\tan x}$$

Example 7: Find the second derivative of $f(x) = e^{x^2}$.

$$f'(x) = 2xe^{x^2}$$
$$f''(x) = 2e^{x^2} + 4x^2 e^{x^2}$$

Once again, it's just a matter of following a formula.

THE DERIVATIVE OF $\log_a x$

This derivative is actually a little trickier than the derivative of a natural log. First, if you remember your logarithm rules about change of base, we can rewrite $\log_a x$ this way:

$$\log_a x = \frac{\ln x}{\ln a}$$

Review the unit on Prerequisite Mathematics if this leaves you scratching your head. Anyway, because ln a is a constant, we can take the derivative and we get:

$$\frac{1}{\ln a}\frac{1}{x}$$

This leads us to our next rule:

Rule No. 5: If $y = \log_a x$, then $\dfrac{dy}{dx} = \dfrac{1}{x \ln a}$

Once again, incorporating the Chain Rule gives us a more useful formula:

Rule No. 6: If $y = \log_a u$, then $\dfrac{dy}{dx} = \dfrac{1}{u \ln a}\dfrac{du}{dx}$

Example 8: Find the derivative of $f(x) = \log_{10} x$.

$$f'(x) = \frac{1}{x \ln 10}$$

Note: We refer to the $\log_{10} x$ as $\log x$.

Example 9: Find the derivative of $f(x) = \log_8 (x^2 + x)$.

$$f'(x) = \frac{2x+1}{(x^2 + x)\ln 8}$$

Example 10: Find the derivative of $f(x) = \log_e x$.

$$f'(x) = \frac{1}{x \ln e} = \frac{1}{x}$$

You can expect this result from Rules 1 and 2 involving natural logs.

THE DERIVATIVE OF a^x

You should recall from your precalculus days that we can rewrite a^x as $e^{x \ln a}$. Keep in mind that ln a is just a constant, which gives us the next rule:

Rule No. 7: If $y = a^x$, then $\dfrac{dy}{dx} = \left(e^{x\ln a}\right)\ln a = a^x \left(\ln a\right)$

Given the pattern of this chapter, you can guess what's coming: another rule that incorporates the Chain Rule.

Rule No. 8: If $y = a^u$, then $\dfrac{dy}{dx} = a^u \left(\ln a\right)\dfrac{du}{dx}$

And now, some examples:

Example 11: Find the derivative of $f(x) = 3^x$.

$$f'(x) = 3^x \ln 3$$

Example 12: Find the derivative of $f(x) = 8^{4x^5}$.

$$f'(x) = 8^{4x^5}\left(20x^4\right)\ln 8$$

Example 13: Find the derivative of $f(x) = \pi^{\sin x}$.

$$f'(x) = \pi^{\sin x}\left(\cos x\right)\ln \pi$$

Finally, here's every nasty teacher's favorite exponential derivative:

Example 14: Find the derivative of $f(x) = x^x$.

First, rewrite this as: $f(x) = e^{x \ln x}$. Then take the derivative:

$$f'(x) = e^{x \ln x}\left(\ln x + \frac{x}{x}\right) = e^{x\ln x}\left(\ln x + 1\right) = x^x\left(\ln x + 1\right)$$

Would you have thought of that? Remember this trick. It might come in handy!
Okay. Ready for some practice? Here are some more solved problems. Cover the solutions and get cracking.

Problem 1. Find the derivative of $y = 3\ln(5x^2 + 4x)$.

Answer: Use Rule No. 2:

$$\frac{dy}{dx} = 3\frac{10x + 4}{5x^2 + 4x} = \frac{30x + 12}{5x^2 + 4x}$$

PROBLEM 2. Find the derivative of $f(x) = \ln\left(\sin\left(x^5\right)\right)$.

Answer:

$$f'(x) = \frac{5x^4 \cos\left(x^5\right)}{\sin\left(x^5\right)} = 5x^4 \cot\left(x^5\right)$$

PROBLEM 3. Find the derivative of $f(x) = e^{3x^7 - 4x^2}$.

Answer: Use Rule No. 4:

$$f'(x) = \left(21x^6 - 8x\right)e^{3x^7 - 4x^2}$$

PROBLEM 4. Here's a doozy: find the derivative of $y = e^{\frac{\cos\ 3x}{\sin\ 2x}}$.

Answer:

$$\frac{dy}{dx} = e^{\frac{\cos 3x}{\sin 2x}}\left[\frac{\sin 2x(-3\sin 3x) - \cos 3x(2\cos 2x)}{(\sin 2x)^2}\right] = e^{\frac{\cos 3x}{\sin 2x}}\left[\frac{-3\sin 2x \sin 3x - 2\cos 3x \cos 2x}{\sin^2 2x}\right]$$

PROBLEM 5. Find the derivative of $f(x) = \log_4(\tan x)$.

Answer: Use Rule No. 6:

$$f'(x) = \frac{1}{\ln 4}\frac{\sec^2 x}{\tan x}$$

PROBLEM 6. Find the derivative of $y = \log_8 \sqrt{\dfrac{x^3}{1+x^2}}$.

Answer: First use the rules of logarithms to rewrite the equation:

$$y = \frac{1}{2}\left[3\log_8 x - \log_8\left(1 + x^2\right)\right]$$

Now it's much easier to find the derivative:

$$\frac{dy}{dx} = \frac{1}{2}\left[3\frac{1}{x\ln 8}\right] - \frac{1}{2}\left[\frac{2x}{\ln 8\left(1 + x^2\right)}\right] = \frac{1}{2\ln 8}\left[\frac{3}{x} - \frac{2x}{\left(1 + x^2\right)}\right]$$

PROBLEM 7. Find the derivative of $y = 5^{\sqrt{x}}$

Answer: Use Rule No. 8:

$$\frac{dy}{dx} = 5^{\sqrt{x}} \frac{1}{2\sqrt{x}} \ln 5 = \frac{5^{\sqrt{x}} \ln 5}{2\sqrt{x}}$$

PROBLEM 8. Find the derivative of $y = \dfrac{e^{x^3}}{5^{\cos x}}$.

Answer: Here, you need to use the Quotient Rule and Rules Nos. 4 and 8:

$$\frac{dy}{dx} = \frac{5^{\cos x}\left(3x^2 e^{x^3}\right) - e^{x^3}\left(5^{\cos x} \ln 5 (-\sin x)\right)}{\left(5^{\cos x}\right)^2} = 5^{\cos x} e^{x^3} \frac{\left(3x^2\right) + \left(\sin x \ln 5\right)}{5^{2\cos x}} = e^{x^3} \frac{3x^2 + \sin x \ln 5}{5^{\cos x}}$$

PROBLEM 9. Find the derivative of $y = \sqrt[4]{\log_5 e^{x^3}}$.

Answer: First use the rules of logarithms to rewrite the equation:

$$y = \sqrt[4]{\log_5 e^{x^3}} = \sqrt[4]{\frac{\ln e^{x^3}}{\ln 5}} = \sqrt[4]{\frac{x^3}{\ln 5}} = \frac{x^{\frac{3}{4}}}{(\ln 5)^{\frac{1}{4}}}$$

Now, the derivative's easy:

$$\frac{dy}{dx} = \frac{\dfrac{3}{4}}{(x \ln 5)^{\frac{1}{4}}} = \frac{3}{4(x \ln 5)^{\frac{1}{4}}}$$

PRACTICE PROBLEM SET 14

Now find the derivative of each of the following functions. The answers are in Chapter 21.

1. $f(x) = \ln(x^4 + 8)$

2. $f(x) = \ln(3x\sqrt{3+x})$

3. $f(x) = \ln(\cot x - \csc x)$

4. $f(x) = x \ln \cos 3x - x^3$

5. $f(x) = \ln\left(\dfrac{5x^2}{\sqrt{5+x^2}}\right)$

6. $f(x) = e^{x\cos x}$

7. $f(x) = e^{-3x} \sin 5x$

8. $f(x) = \dfrac{e^{\tan 4x}}{4x}$

9. $f(x) = e^{\pi x} - \ln e^{\pi x}$

10. $f(x) = \log_{12}(x^3)$

11. $f(x) = \log_6(3x \tan x)$

12. $f(x) = \dfrac{\log_4 x}{e^{4x}}$

13. $f(x) = \log \sqrt{10^{3x}}$

14. $f(x) = \ln x \log x$

15. $f(x) = e^{3x} - 3^{ex}$

16. $f(x) = 10^{\sin x}$

17. $f(x) = 5^{\tan x}$

18. $f(x) = \ln(10^x)$

19. $f(x) = x^5 5^x$

10
Other Topics in Differential Calculus

This chapter is devoted to other topics involving differential calculus that don't fit into a specific category.

THE DERIVATIVE OF AN INVERSE FUNCTION

ETS occasionally asks a question about finding the derivative of an inverse function. To do this, you only need to learn this simple formula.

Suppose we have a function $x = f(y)$ that is defined and differentiable at $y = a$ where $x = c$. Suppose we also know that the $f^{-1}(x)$ exists at $x = c$. Thus, $f(a) = c$ and $f^{-1}(c) = a$. Then, because $\dfrac{dy}{dx} = \dfrac{1}{\dfrac{dx}{dy}}$,

$$\frac{d}{dx} f^{-1}(x) \bigg|_{x=c} = \frac{1}{\left[\dfrac{d}{dy} f(y) \right]_{y=a}}$$

The short translation of this is: We can find the derivative of a function's inverse at a particular point by taking the reciprocal of the derivative at that point's corresponding y-value. These examples should help clear up any confusion.

Example 1: If $f(x) = x^2$, find a derivative of $f^{-1}(x)$ at $x = 9$.

First, notice that $f(3) = 9$. One of the most confusing parts of finding the derivative of an inverse function is that when you're asked to find the derivative at a value of x, they're *really* asking you for the derivative of the inverse of the function at the value that *corresponds* to $f(x) = 9$. This is because x-values of the inverse correspond to $f(x)$ values of the original function.

The rule is very simple: When you're asked to find the derivative of $f^{-1}(x)$ at $x = c$, you take the reciprocal of the derivative of $f(x)$ at $x = a$, where $f(a) = c$.

We know that $\dfrac{d}{dx} f(x) = 2x$. This means that we're going to plug $x = 3$ into the formula (because $f(3) = 9$). This gives us:

$$\frac{1}{2x}\Big|_{x=3} = \frac{1}{6}$$

We can verify this by finding the inverse of the function first and then taking the derivative. The inverse of the function $f(x) = x^2$ is the function $f^{-1}(x) = \sqrt{x}$. Now we find the derivative and evaluate it at $f(3) = 9$:

$$\frac{d}{dx}\sqrt{x} = \frac{1}{2\sqrt{x}}\Big|_{x=9} = \frac{1}{6}$$

Remember the rule: Find the value, a, of $f(x)$ that gives you the value of x that the problem asks for. Then plug that value, a, into the reciprocal of the derivative of the *inverse* function.

Example 2: Find a derivative of the inverse of $y = x^3 - 1$ when $y = 7$.

First, we need to find the x-value that corresponds to $y = 7$. A little algebra tells us that this is $x = 2$. Then:

$$\frac{dy}{dx} = 3x^2 \text{ and } \frac{1}{\dfrac{dy}{dx}} = \frac{1}{3x^2}$$

Therefore, the derivative of the inverse is:

$$\frac{1}{3x^2}\Big|_{x=2} = \frac{1}{12}$$

Verify it: The inverse of the function $y = x^3 - 1$ is the function $y = \sqrt[3]{x+1}$. The derivative of this latter function is:

$$\frac{1}{3\sqrt[3]{(x+1)^2}}\Big|_{x=7} = \frac{1}{12}$$

Let's do one more.

Example 3: Find a derivative of the inverse of $y = x^2 + 4$ when $y = 29$.

At $y = 29$, $x = 5$, the derivative of the function is:

$$\frac{dy}{dx} = 2x$$

So, a derivative of the inverse is:

$$\frac{1}{2x}\bigg|_{x=5} = \frac{1}{10}$$

Note that $x = -5$ also gives us $y = 29$, so $\dfrac{-1}{10}$ is also a derivative. It's not that hard, once you get the hang of it. This is all you'll be required to know involving derivatives of inverses. Naturally, there are ways to create harder problems, but the AP exam stays away from them and sticks to simpler stuff.

Here are some solved problems. Do each problem, cover the answer first, and then check your answer.

PROBLEM 1. Find a derivative of the inverse of $y = f(x) = 2x^3 + 5x + 1$ at $y = 8$.

Answer: First, we take the derivative of $f(x)$:

$$f'(x) = 6x^2 + 5$$

A possible value of x is $x = 1$.

Then, we use the formula to find the derivative of the inverse:

$$\frac{1}{f'(1)} = \frac{1}{11}$$

PROBLEM 2. Find a derivative of the inverse of $y = f(x) = 3x^3 - x + 7$ at $y = 9$.

Answer: First, take the derivative of $f(x)$:

$$f'(x) = 9x^2 - 1$$

A possible value of x is $x = 1$.

Then, use the formula to find the derivative of the inverse:

$$\frac{1}{f'(1)} = \frac{1}{8}$$

PROBLEM 3. Find a derivative of the inverse of $y = \dfrac{8}{x^3}$ at $y = 1$.

Answer: Take the derivative of $f(x)$:

$$f'(x) = -\frac{24}{x^4}$$

Find the value of x where $y = 1$:

$$1 = \frac{8}{x^3}$$
$$x = 2$$

Use the formula:

$$\frac{1}{\left.\dfrac{dy}{dx}\right|_{x=2}} = \frac{1}{\left.\left(-\dfrac{24}{x^4}\right)\right|_{x=2}} = -\frac{2}{3}$$

Here's one more.

PROBLEM 4. Find a derivative of the inverse of $y = 2x - x^3$ at $y = 1$.

Answer: The derivative of the function is:

$$\frac{dy}{dx} = 2 - 3x^2$$

Next, find the value of x where $y = 1$. By inspection, $y = 1$ when $x = 1$. Then, we use the formula to find the derivative of the inverse:

$$\frac{1}{\left.\dfrac{dy}{dx}\right|_{x=1}} = \frac{1}{\left.(2 - 3x^2)\right|_{x=1}} = -1$$

PRACTICE PROBLEM SET 15

Find a derivative of the inverse of each of the following functions. The answers are in Chapter 21.

1. $y = x + \dfrac{1}{x}$ at $y = \dfrac{17}{4}$; where $x > 1$

2. $y = 3x - 5x^3$ at $y = 2$

3. $y = e^x$ at $y = e$

4. $f(x) = x^7 - 2x^5 + 2x^3$ at $f(x) = 1$

5. $y = x + x^3$ at $y = -2$

6. $y = 4x - x^3$ at $y = 3$

7. $y = \ln x$ at $y = 0$

8. $y = x^{\frac{1}{3}} + x^{\frac{1}{5}}$ at $y = 2$

DERIVATIVES OF PARAMETRIC FUNCTIONS

Although these can seem very difficult, the questions about parametric equations on the AP exam tend to be very straightforward. As we keep pointing out, don't be intimidated by the difficult topics; ETS tends to keep the questions simple. By contrast, ETS's questions on simpler topics tend to be trickier.

WHAT IS A PARAMETRIC FUNCTION?

Let's use an analogy. Suppose you're driving a car and you want to determine a function that describes your position on the road. There are two ways that you could arrive at your position. You could figure it out based on how far you've traveled, or you could determine it based on how long you've been traveling. If you let y represent your position and x the distance, you could find your position by $y = f(x)$.

If, on the other hand, you wanted to use the time that you've traveled, you can use two functions: $x = g(t)$, to determine the distance you've traveled, and $y = h(t)$, to determine your position. These latter equations are called "parametric equations." They enable you to define x and y in terms of another variable (usually t), rather than in terms of each other. Parametric equations also follow all of the standard derivative rules.

> To find $\dfrac{dy}{dx}$ using parametric equations, use this rule:
>
> $$\frac{dy / dt}{dx / dt} = \frac{dy}{dx}$$

For example, suppose that $x = t^2$ and $y = t^4$. Then:

$$\frac{dx}{dt} = 2t \text{ and } \frac{dy}{dt} = 4t^3$$

$$\frac{dy}{dx} = \frac{4t^3}{2t} = 2t^2$$

Now, because $x = t^2$, $\dfrac{dy}{dx} = 2x$.

We can verify this by first solving for y in terms of x and then differentiating. The result is:

$$y = x^2 \text{ and } \frac{dy}{dx} = 2x$$

You might also be asked to turn an equation in parametric form into an equation in Cartesian form. The simplest thing to do is to solve the equation for t and substitute that equation into the other one. Sometimes the relationship is not so obvious, as in this example.

Example 1: What curve is represented by $x = \cos t$ and $y = \sin t$, where $0 \le t \le 2\pi$?

We know from trigonometry that $\sin^2 t + \cos^2 t = 1$, so we can substitute y for $\sin t$ and x for $\cos t$. If we square both and add them, we get $x^2 + y^2 = 1$. This is the equation of a circle, centered at the origin, with radius 1.

You can test this by picking values of t and finding the coordinates by using the two equations. For example:

$$\text{At } t = \frac{\pi}{2}, \quad x = 0 \text{ and } y = 1; \text{ or}$$

$$\text{At } t = \frac{\pi}{6}, \quad x = \frac{\sqrt{3}}{2} \text{ and } y = \frac{1}{2}$$

Example 2: What curve is represented by $x = t$ and $y = t^2$?

If you substitute x for t, you'll find that $y = x^2$. Thus, this curve is a parabola with vertex at the origin.

Example 3: What curve is represented by $x = a \cos t$ and $y = b \sin t$, where $0 \le t \le 2\pi$?

First, rewrite the two equations:

$$\frac{x}{a} = \cos t \text{ and } \frac{y}{b} = \sin t$$

Now, because we know that $\sin^2 t + \cos^2 t = 1$, we know that:

$$\left(\frac{x}{a}\right)^2 + \left(\frac{y}{b}\right)^2 = 1$$

If $a \ne b$, this figure is an ellipse, centered at the origin, with axes of length $2a$ and $2b$. If $a = b$, it's a circle, centered at the origin, with radius a.

Now you know how to convert an equation from parametric form to Cartesian form. You'll also need to know how to work with the parametric equations, even if you can't figure out how to convert them into Cartesian form (sometimes you don't have to). These frequently will be equations of motion.

Example 4: A particle's position in the xy-plane at any time t is given by $x = 2t^2 + 3$ and $y = t^4$. Find: (a) the x-component of the particle's velocity at time $t = 5$; (b) $\dfrac{dy}{dx}$; and (c) the times at which the x- and y-components of the velocity are the same.

(a) All you do is take the derivative with respect to t:

$$\frac{dx}{dt} = 4t$$

At time $t = 5$, this is 20.

(b) You know $\dfrac{dx}{dt}$ from part (a), so now compute $\dfrac{dy}{dt}$. This is $4t^3$. Using the rule, $\dfrac{dy}{dx} = \dfrac{dy/dt}{dx/dt}$:

$$\frac{4t^3}{4t} = t^2$$

To express the answer in terms of x instead of the parameter, solve for t^2 in terms of x:

$$\frac{x-3}{2} = t^2$$

Then substitute:

$$\frac{dy}{dx} = \frac{x-3}{2}$$

(c) The components of the velocity are the same when $4t^3 = 4t$.

$$4t^3 - 4t = 0$$
$$4t\left(t^2 - 1\right) = 0$$
$$t = 0, \pm 1$$

Now you know all you need to about the basics of parametrized curves. There will be other types of problems involving parametric equations, but you'll see them later in the book.

Try these sample problems, working with an index card, as usual.

PROBLEM 1. Find the Cartesian equation represented by the parametric equations $x = 4 \cos t$ and $y = 4 \sin t,\ 0 \le t \le 2\pi$.

Answer: From Example 1, you know that $\sin^2 t + \cos^2 t = 1$. If you take each equation and rearrange the terms:

$$\frac{x}{4} = \cos t \quad \text{and} \quad \frac{y}{4} = \sin t$$

Next, substitute into $\sin^2 t + \cos^2 t = 1$:

$$\frac{x^2}{16} + \frac{y^2}{16} = 1, \text{ or}$$

$$x^2 + y^2 = 16$$

This is a circle, centered at the origin, with radius 4.

PROBLEM 2. Find the Cartesian equation represented by the parametric equations $x = \sqrt{t}$ and $y = t, \ t \geq 0$.

Answer: Here, you need to notice that if you square the equation for x, you get $x^2 = t$. Therefore, $y = x^2$. This is half of a parabola with a vertex at the origin.

PROBLEM 3. Find an equation of the line tangent to the curve $x = 2 \cos t$ and $y = 3 \sin t$ at $t = \frac{\pi}{4}$.

Answer: You can, of course, eliminate t, as before, obtaining:

$$\left(\frac{x}{2}\right)^2 + \left(\frac{y}{3}\right)^2 = 1$$

Proceed as in Example 4 in Chapter 5, but it's easier to retain the parameter t here and reach the answer. First, find the slope of the tangent line $\frac{dy}{dx}$ using the formula $\frac{dy}{dx} = \frac{dy/dt}{dx/dt}$:

$$\frac{dy}{dt} = 3 \cos t \ \text{ and } \ \frac{dx}{dt} = -2 \sin t \ .$$

Therefore, $\dfrac{dy}{dx} = \dfrac{3 \cos t}{-2 \sin t}$.

If we evaluate this at $t = \dfrac{\pi}{4}$:

$$\frac{dy}{dx} = \frac{3\left(\dfrac{1}{\sqrt{2}}\right)}{-2\left(\dfrac{1}{\sqrt{2}}\right)} = -\frac{3}{2}$$

At $t = \dfrac{\pi}{4}$, $x = \dfrac{2}{\sqrt{2}}$ and $y = \dfrac{3}{\sqrt{2}}$. Now you can find the equation of the tangent line:

$$\left(y - \frac{3}{\sqrt{2}}\right) = -\frac{3}{2}\left(x - \frac{2}{\sqrt{2}}\right)$$

This can be rewritten as $3x + 2y - 6\sqrt{2} = 0$.

PROBLEM 4. A particle's position at time t is determined by the equations $x = 3 + 2t^2$ and $y = 4t^4$, $t \geq 0$. Find the x- and y-components of the particle's velocity and the times when these components are equal.

Answer: First, figure out the x- and y-components of the velocity:

$$\frac{dx}{dt} = 4t \text{ and } \frac{dy}{dt} = 16t^3$$

These are equal when $16t^3 = 4t$. Solving for t:

$$t = 0, \pm \frac{1}{2}$$

Throw out the negative value of t, the answer is $t = 0, \dfrac{1}{2}$.

PRACTICE PROBLEM SET 16

Now try these problems. The answers are in Chapter 21.

1. Find the Cartesian equation of the curve represented by $x = \sec^2 t - 1$ and $y = \tan t$, $-\dfrac{\pi}{2} < t < \dfrac{\pi}{2}$.

2. Find the Cartesian equation of the curve represented by $x = t$ and $y = \sqrt{1 - t^2}$, $-1 < t < 1$.

3. Find the Cartesian equation of the curve represented by $x = 4t + 3$ and $y = 16t^2 - 9$, $-\infty < t < \infty$.

4. Find the equation of the tangent line to $x = t^2 + 4$ and $y = 8t$ at $t = 6$.

5. Find the equation of the tangent line to $x = \sec t$ and $y = \tan t$ at $t = \dfrac{\pi}{4}$.

6. The motion of a particle is given by $x = -2t^2$ and $y = t^3 - 3t + 9$, $t \geq 0$. Find the coordinates of the particle when its instantaneous direction of motion is horizontal.

7. The motion of a particle is given by $x = \ln t$ and $y = t^2 - 4t$. Find the coordinates of the particle when its instantaneous direction of motion is horizontal.

8. The motion of a particle is given by $x = 2 \sin t - 1$ and $y = \sin t - \dfrac{t}{2}$, $0 \leq t < 2\pi$. Find the times when the horizontal and vertical components of the particle's velocity are the same.

L'HÔPITAL'S RULE

L'Hôpital's Rule is a way to find the limit of certain kinds of expressions that are indeterminate forms. If the limit of an expression results in $\frac{0}{0}$ or $\frac{\infty}{\infty}$, the limit is called "indeterminate" and you can use L'Hôpital's Rule to evaluate these expressions:

> If $f(c) = g(c) = 0$, and if $f'(c)$ and $g'(c)$ exist, and if $g'(c) \neq 0$, then:
>
> $$\lim_{x \to c} \frac{f(x)}{g(x)} = \frac{f'(c)}{g'(c)}.$$

Similarly,

> If $f(c) = g(c) = \infty$, and if $f'(c)$. and $g'(c)$ exist, and if $g'(c) \neq 0$, then:
>
> $$\lim_{x \to c} \frac{f(x)}{g(x)} = \frac{f'(c)}{g'(c)}$$

In other words, if the limit of the function gives us an undefined expression, like $\frac{0}{0}$ or $\frac{\infty}{\infty}$, L'Hôpital's Rule says we can take the derivative of the top and the derivative of the bottom and see if we get a determinate expression. If not, we can repeat the process.

Example 1: Find $\lim_{x \to 0} \frac{\sin x}{x}$.

First, notice that plugging in 0 results in $\frac{0}{0}$, which is indeterminate. Take the derivative of the top and of the bottom:

$$\lim_{x \to 0} \frac{\cos x}{1}$$

The limit equals 1.

Example 2: Find $\lim_{x \to 0} \frac{2x - \sin x}{x}$.

If you plug in 0, you get $\frac{0-0}{0}$, which is indeterminate. Now, take the derivative of the top and of the bottom.

$$\lim_{x \to 0} \frac{2 - \cos x}{1}$$

This limit also equals 1.

Example 3: Find $\lim\limits_{x \to 0} \dfrac{\sqrt{4+x} - 2}{2x}$.

Again, plugging in 0 is no help; you get $\dfrac{0}{0}$. Take the derivative of the top and bottom:

$$\lim_{x \to 0} \frac{\dfrac{1}{2\sqrt{4+x}}}{2} = \frac{1}{8}$$

Example 4: Find $\lim\limits_{x \to 0} \dfrac{\sqrt{4+x} - 2 - \dfrac{x}{4}}{2x^2}$.

Take the derivative of the top and bottom:

$$\lim_{x \to 0} \frac{\dfrac{1}{2\sqrt{4+x}} - \dfrac{1}{4}}{4x}$$

Now if you take the limit, we still get $\dfrac{0}{0}$. So do it again.

$$\lim_{x \to 0} \frac{-\dfrac{1}{4}\left(4+x\right)^{-\frac{3}{2}}}{4} = -\frac{1}{128}$$

Now let's try a couple of $\dfrac{\infty}{\infty}$ forms.

Example 5: Find $\lim\limits_{x \to \infty} \dfrac{5x - 8}{3x + 1}$.

Now, the limit is $\dfrac{\infty}{\infty}$. The derivative of the top and bottom is:

$$\lim_{x \to \infty} \frac{5}{3} = \frac{5}{3}$$

Don't you wish that you had learned this back when you first did limits?

Example 6: Find $\lim\limits_{x \to \frac{\pi}{2}} \dfrac{\sec x}{1 + \sec x}$.

The derivative of the top and bottom is:

$$\lim_{x \to \frac{\pi}{2}} \frac{\sec x \tan x}{\sec x \tan x} = 1$$

Example 7: Find $\lim\limits_{x \to 0^+} x \cot x$.

Taking this limit results in $(0)(\infty)$, which is also indeterminate. (But you can't use the rule yet!) If

you rewrite this expression as $\lim\limits_{x \to 0^+} \dfrac{x}{\tan x}$, it's of the form $\dfrac{0}{0}$ and we can use L'Hôpital's Rule:

$$\lim_{x \to 0^+} \frac{1}{\sec^2 x} = 1$$

That's all that you need to know about L'Hôpital's Rule. Just check to see if the limit results in an indeterminate form. If it does, use the rule until you get a determinate form.

Here are some more examples.

PROBLEM 1. Find $\lim\limits_{x \to 0} \dfrac{\sin 8x}{x}$.

Answer: First, notice that plugging in 0 gives us an indeterminate result: $\dfrac{0}{0}$. Now, take the derivative of the top and of the bottom:

$$\lim_{x \to 0} \frac{8 \cos 8x}{1} = 8$$

PROBLEM 2. Find $\lim\limits_{\theta \to 0} \dfrac{\tan \theta}{\theta}$.

Answer: You still get $\dfrac{0}{0}$ if you plug in 0. Take the derivative of the top and of the bottom:

$$\lim_{x \to 0} \frac{\sec^2 \theta}{1} = 1$$

PROBLEM 3. Find $\lim\limits_{x \to \infty} x e^{-2x}$.

Answer: First, rewrite this expression as $\dfrac{x}{e^{2x}}$. Notice that when x nears infinity, the expression becomes $\dfrac{\infty}{\infty}$, which is indeterminate.

Take the derivative of the top and bottom:

$$\lim_{x \to \infty} \frac{1}{2e^{2x}} = 0$$

PROBLEM 4. Find $\lim\limits_{x \to \infty} \dfrac{5x^3 - 4x^2 + 1}{7x^3 + 2x - 6}$.

Answer: We learned this in Chapter 1, remember? Now we'll use L'Hôpital's Rule. At first glance, the limit is indeterminate: $\dfrac{\infty}{\infty}$. Let's take some derivatives:

$$\frac{15x^2 - 8x}{21x^2 + 2}$$

This is still indeterminate, so it's time to take the derivative of the top and bottom again:

$$\frac{30x - 8}{42x}$$

It's still indeterminate! If you try it one more time, you'll get a fraction with no variables: $\dfrac{30}{42}$, which can be simplified to $\dfrac{5}{7}$ (as we expected).

PROBLEM 5. Find $\lim\limits_{x \to \frac{\pi}{2}} \dfrac{x - \dfrac{\pi}{2}}{\cos x}$.

Answer: Plugging in $\dfrac{\pi}{2}$ gives you the indeterminate response of $\dfrac{0}{0}$. The derivative is:

$$-\frac{1}{\sin x}$$

When we take the limit of this expression, we get –1.

PRACTICE PROBLEM SET 17

Now find these limits using L'Hôpital's Rule. The answers are in Chapter 21.

1. Find $\lim\limits_{x \to 0} \dfrac{\sin 3x}{\sin 4x}$.

2. Find $\lim\limits_{x \to \pi} \dfrac{x - \pi}{\sin x}$.

3. Find $\lim\limits_{x \to 0} \dfrac{x - \sin x}{x^3}$.

4. Find $\lim\limits_{x \to 0} \dfrac{e^{3x} - e^{5x}}{x}$.

5. Find $\lim\limits_{x \to 0} \dfrac{\tan x - x}{\sin x - x}$.

6. Find $\lim\limits_{x \to \infty} \dfrac{x^5}{e^{5x}}$.

7. Find $\lim\limits_{x \to \infty} \dfrac{x^5 + 4x^3 - 8}{7x^5 - 3x^2 - 1}$.

8. Find $\lim\limits_{x \to 0^+} \dfrac{\ln(\sin x)}{\ln(\tan x)}$.

9. Find $\lim\limits_{x \to 0^+} \dfrac{\cot 2x}{\cot x}$.

10. Find $\lim\limits_{x \to 0^+} \dfrac{x}{\ln(x + 1)}$.

DIFFERENTIALS

Sometimes this is called "linearization." A differential is a very small quantity that corresponds to a change in a number. We use the symbol Δx to denote a differential. What are differentials used for? The AP exam mostly wants you to use them to approximate the value of a function or to find the error of an approximation.

Recall the formula for the definition of the derivative:

$$f'(x) = \lim\limits_{h \to 0} \dfrac{f(x + h) - f(x)}{h}$$

Replace h with Δx, which also stands for a very small increment of x, and get rid of the limit:

$$f'(x) \approx \frac{f(x+\Delta x) - f(x)}{\Delta x}$$

Notice that this is no longer equal to the derivative, but an approximation of it. If Δx is kept small, the approximation remains fairly accurate. Next, rearrange the equation as follows:

$$f(x+\Delta x) \approx f(x) + f'(x)\Delta x$$

This is our formula for differentials. It says that "the value of a function, at x plus a little bit, equals the value of the function at x, plus the product of the derivative of the function at x with the little bit."

Example 1: Use differentials to approximate $\sqrt{9.01}$.

You can start by letting $x = 9$, $\Delta x = +.01$, $f(x) = \sqrt{x}$. Next we need to find $f'(x)$:

$$f'(x) = \frac{1}{2\sqrt{x}}$$

Now plug in to the formula:

$$f(x+\Delta x) \approx f(x) + f'(x)\Delta x$$

$$\sqrt{x+\Delta x} \approx \sqrt{x} + \frac{1}{2\sqrt{x}}\Delta x$$

Now if we plug in $x = 9$ and $\Delta x = +.01$:

$$\sqrt{9.01} \approx \sqrt{9} + \frac{1}{2\sqrt{9}}(.01) \approx 3.001666666$$

If you enter $\sqrt{9.01}$ into your calculator, you get: 3.001666204. As you can see, our answer is a pretty good approximation. It's not so good, however, when Δx is too big. How big is too big? Good question.

Example 2: Use differentials to approximate $\sqrt{9.5}$.

Let $x = 9$, $\Delta x = +.5$, $f(x) = \sqrt{x}$ and plug in to what you found in Example 1:

$$\sqrt{9.5} \approx \sqrt{9} + \frac{1}{2\sqrt{9}}(.5) \approx 3.083333333$$

However, $\sqrt{9.5}$ equals 3.082207001 on a calculator. This is only good to two decimal places.

As the ratio of $\dfrac{\Delta x}{x}$ grows larger, the approximation gets less accurate and we start to get away from the actual value.

There's another approximation formula that you'll need to know for the AP exam. This formula is used to estimate the error in a measurement, or to find the effect on a formula when a small change in measurement is made. The formula is:

$$dy = f'(x)dx$$

This notation may look a little confusing. It says that the change in a measurement dy, due to a differential dx, is found by multiplying the derivative of the equation for y by the differential. Let's do an example.

Example 3: The radius of a circle is increased from 3 to 3.04. Estimate the change in area.

Let $A = \pi r^2$. Then our formula says that $dA = A'dr$, where A' is the derivative of the area with respect to r, and $dr = .04$ (the change). First, find the derivative of the area: $A' = 2\pi r$. Now plug in to the formula:

$$dA = 2\pi r dr = 2\pi(3)(.04) = .754$$

The actual change in the area is from 9π to 9.2416π, which is approximately .759. As you can see, this approximation formula is pretty accurate.

Here are some sample problems involving this differential formula. Try them out, then check your work against the answers directly beneath.

PROBLEM 1. Use differentials to approximate $(3.98)^4$.

Answer: Let $f(x) = x^4$, $x = 4$, and $\Delta x = -.02$. Next, find $f'(x)$, which is: $f'(x) = 4x^3$.
Now plug in to the formula:

$$f(x + \Delta x) \approx f(x) + f'(x)\Delta x$$
$$\sqrt{x + \Delta x} \approx x^4 + 4x^3\Delta x$$

If you plug in $x = 4$ and $\Delta x = -.02$, you get:

$$(3.98)^4 \approx 4^4 + 4(4)^3(-.02) \approx 250.88$$

Check $(3.98)^4$ by using your calculator; you should get 250.9182722. Not a bad approximation.

You're probably asking yourself, why can't I just use my calculator every time? Because most math teachers are dedicated to teaching you several complicated ways to calculate things without your calculator.

PROBLEM 2. Use differentials to approximate $\sin 46°$.

Answer: This is a tricky question. The formula doesn't work if you use degrees. Here's why: Let $f(x) = \sin x$, $x = 45°$, and $\Delta x = 1°$. The derivative is $f'(x) = \cos x$.

If you plug this information into the formula, you get: $\sin 46° \approx \sin 45° + \cos 45°(1°) = \sqrt{2}$. You should recognize that this is nonsense for two reasons: (1) the sine of any angle is between –1 and 1; and (2) the answer should be close to $\sin 45° = \dfrac{1}{\sqrt{2}}$.

What went wrong? You have to use radians! As we mentioned before, angles in calculus problems are measured in radians, not degrees.

Let $f(x) = \sin x$, $x = \dfrac{\pi}{4}$, and $\Delta x = \dfrac{\pi}{180}$. Now plug in to the formula:

$$\sin\left(\frac{46\pi}{180}\right) \approx \sin\frac{\pi}{4} + \left(\cos\frac{\pi}{4}\right)\left(\frac{\pi}{180}\right) = 0.7194$$

PROBLEM 3. The radius of a sphere is measured to be 4 cm with an error of $\pm.01$ cm. Use differentials to approximate the error in the surface area.

Answer: Now it's time for the other differential formula. The formula for the surface area of a sphere is:

$$S = 4\pi r^2$$

The formula says that $dS = S'dr$, so first, we find the derivative of the surface area ($S' = 8\pi r$) and plug away:

$$dS = 8\pi r \, dr = 8\pi(4)(\pm.01) = \pm 1.0053$$

This looks like a big error, but given that the surface area of a sphere with radius 4 is approximately 201 cm², the error is quite small.

PRACTICE PROBLEM SET 18

Use the differential formulas in this chapter to solve these problems. The answers are in Chapter 21.

1. Approximate $\sqrt{25.02}$.

2. Approximate $\sqrt[3]{63.97}$.

3. Approximate $\tan 61°$.

4. Approximate $(9.99)^3$.

5. The side of a cube is measured to be 6 in. with an error of ± 0.02 in. Estimate the error in the volume of the cube.

6. When a spherical ball bearing is heated, its radius increases by 0.01 mm. Estimate the change in volume of the ball bearing when the radius is 5 mm.

7. A side of an equilateral triangle is measured to be 10 cm. Estimate the change in the area of the triangle when the side shrinks to 9.8 cm.

8. A cylindrical tank is constructed to have a diameter of 5 meters and a height of 20 meters. Find the error in the volume if:

(a) the diameter is exact, but the height is 20.1 meters; and

(b) the height is exact, but the diameter is 5.1 meters.

LOGARITHMIC DIFFERENTIATION

There's one last topic in differential calculus that you BC students need to know: logarithmic differentiation. It's a very simple and handy technique used to find the derivatives of expressions that involve a lot of algebra. By employing the rules of logarithms, we can find the derivatives of expressions that would otherwise require a messy combination of the Chain Rule, the Product Rule, and the Quotient Rule.

First, let's review a couple of rules of logarithms (remember, when we refer to a logarithm in calculus, we mean the natural log (base e), not the common log):

$$\ln A + \ln B = \ln(AB)$$

$$\ln A - \ln B = \ln\left(\frac{A}{B}\right)$$

$$\ln A^B = B \ln A$$

For example, we can rewrite $\ln(x + 3)^5$ as $5\ln(x + 3)$.
As a quick review exercise, how could you rewrite:

$$\ln \frac{x^2}{(x+1)^2}$$

Answer: $2\ln x - 2\ln(x + 1)$.

The other important thing to remember from Chapter 9 is:

$$\frac{d}{dx}\ln u = \frac{1}{u}\frac{du}{dx}$$

Bearing these in mind, we can use these rules to find the derivative of a complicated expression without using all that mind-bending algebra. Instead, take the log of both sides of an expression and then use the rules of logarithms to simplify it before finding the derivative.

Example 1: Find the derivative of $y = \dfrac{x+3}{2x-5}$

The Quotient Rule works here just fine, but check this out instead. Take the log of both sides:

$$\ln y = \ln \frac{x+3}{2x-5}$$

Using log rules, you can rewrite the expression this way:

$$\ln y = \ln(x+3) - \ln(2x-5)$$

Now take the derivative of both sides:

$$\frac{1}{y}\frac{dy}{dx} = \frac{1}{x+3} - \frac{2}{2x-5}$$

Multiply both sides by y, and you get the following:

$$\frac{dy}{dx} = y\left(\frac{1}{x+3} - \frac{2}{2x-5}\right)$$

Finally, substitute for y:

$$\frac{dy}{dx} = \left(\frac{x+3}{2x-5}\right)\left(\frac{1}{x+3} - \frac{2}{2x-5}\right)$$

You might be thinking, "Why go through the hassle?" After all, you could have done this with the Quotient Rule and it would have involved less work. But, as you'll see, this technique comes in very handy when the algebra is especially messy. Also, we don't usually substitute back for the y term. Instead, just leave it in the derivative (unless it needs to be defined only in terms of x).

Example 2: Find the derivative of y, where $y^2 = (x+4)^3 (x-2)^5$.

Take the log of both sides:

$$\ln y^2 = \ln\left[(x+4)^3 (x-2)^5\right]$$

Next, use those log rules to get:

$$2 \ln y = 3 \ln(x+4) + 5 \ln(x-2)$$

Take the derivative of both sides:

$$\frac{2}{y}\frac{dy}{dx} = \frac{3}{x+4} + \frac{5}{x-2}$$

Finally, multiply both sides by $\dfrac{y}{2}$:

$$\frac{dy}{dx} = \frac{y}{2}\left[\frac{3}{x+4} + \frac{5}{x-2}\right]$$

That's it. Now, wasn't that easier? Substitute back for y only if you have to.

Example 3: Find the derivative of $y = \sqrt{\dfrac{x+3}{x-5}} \sqrt[3]{\dfrac{2x+7}{5x-1}}$.

Holy cripes! What a problem! Watch how using logs will save you. Take the log of both sides:

$$\ln y = \ln\left(\sqrt{\frac{x+3}{x-5}} \sqrt[3]{\frac{2x+7}{5x-1}}\right)$$

Now you can simplify using log rules:

$$\ln y = \frac{1}{2}\Big[\ln(x+3) - \ln(x-5)\Big] + \frac{1}{3}\Big[\ln(2x+7) - \ln(5x-1)\Big]$$

Take the derivative:

$$\frac{1}{y}\frac{dy}{dx} = \frac{1}{2}\left[\frac{1}{x+3} - \frac{1}{x-5}\right] + \frac{1}{3}\left[\frac{2}{2x+7} - \frac{5}{5x-1}\right]$$

And then multiply by y:

$$\frac{dy}{dx} = \frac{y}{2}\left[\frac{1}{x+3} - \frac{1}{x-5}\right] + \frac{y}{3}\left[\frac{2}{2x+7} - \frac{5}{5x-1}\right]$$

Example 4: Find the derivative of $y = \sqrt{\dfrac{x+3}{5-x}}$

Take the log of both sides:

$$\ln y = \ln\left(\sqrt{\frac{x+3}{5-x}}\right)$$

Simplify using the log rules:

$$\ln y = \frac{1}{2}\Big[\ln(x+3) - \ln(5-x)\Big]$$

Take the derivative:

$$\frac{1}{y}\frac{dy}{dx} = \frac{1}{2}\left[\frac{1}{x+3} + \frac{1}{5-x}\right]$$

Multiply by y:

$$\frac{dy}{dx} = \frac{y}{2}\left[\frac{1}{x+3} + \frac{1}{5-x}\right]$$

And you're done.

That's all there is to logarithmic differentiation. It's a really helpful tool for simplifying complicated derivatives. There's generally one question on the AP exam that uses logarithmic differentiation, and it's usually not that complicated.

Try these solved problems on your own. Cover the answers first, then check your work.

PROBLEM 1. Use logarithmic differentiation to find $\frac{dy}{dx}$ if $y = \frac{x^2\sqrt{1-x^3}}{\left(x^2+1\right)^2}$.

Answer: Take the log of both sides:

$$\ln y = \ln\left[\frac{x^2\sqrt{1-x^3}}{\left(x^2+1\right)^2}\right]$$

Next, use the log rules to simplify the expression:

$$\ln y = \ln x^2 + \ln\sqrt{1-x^3} - \ln\left(x^2+1\right)^2$$

$$\ln y = 2\ln x + \frac{1}{2}\ln\left(1-x^3\right) - 2\ln\left(x^2+1\right)$$

Taking the derivative of both sides, you should get:

$$\frac{1}{y}\frac{dy}{dx} = \frac{2}{x} - \frac{3x^2}{2\left(1-x^3\right)} - \frac{4x}{x^2+1}$$

Then get the derivative by itself by multiplying both sides by y:

$$\frac{dy}{dx} = y\left[\frac{2}{x} - \frac{3x^2}{2\left(1-x^3\right)} - \frac{4x}{x^2+1}\right]$$

PROBLEM 2. Use logarithmic differentiation to find $\frac{dy}{dx}$ if $y = \frac{\left(x^2-5x\right)\cos^2 x}{\left(x^3+1\right)^5}$.

Answer: The four-step process should be second nature by now. Take the log of both sides:

$$\ln y = \ln\left[\frac{\left(x^2-5x\right)\cos^2 x}{\left(x^3+1\right)^5}\right]$$

Simplify the expression using log rules:

$$\ln y = \ln(x^2 - 5x) + \ln(\cos^2 x) - \ln(x^3 + 1)^5$$

$$\ln y = \ln(x^2 - 5x) + 2\ln(\cos x) - 5\ln(x^3 + 1)$$

Take the derivative of both sides:

$$\frac{1}{y}\frac{dy}{dx} = \frac{2x - 5}{x^2 - 5x} - \frac{2\sin x}{\cos x} - \frac{15x^2}{x^3 + 1}$$

$$\frac{1}{y}\frac{dy}{dx} = \frac{2x - 5}{x^2 - 5x} - 2\tan x - \frac{15x^2}{x^3 + 1}$$

And multiply by y:

$$\frac{dy}{dx} = y\left[\frac{2x - 5}{x^2 - 5x} - 2\tan x - \frac{15x^2}{x^3 + 1}\right]$$

One more time.

PROBLEM 3. Use logarithmic differentiation to find $\dfrac{dy}{dx}$ if $y = \sqrt{\dfrac{\sec x}{(4 - x^3)^5}}$.

Answer: Take the log of both sides:

$$\ln y = \ln\sqrt{\frac{\sec x}{(4 - x^3)^5}}$$

Simplify:

$$\ln y = \frac{1}{2}\left[\ln(\sec x) - 5\ln(4 - x^3)\right]$$

Take the derivative:

$$\frac{1}{y}\frac{dy}{dx} = \frac{1}{2}\left[\frac{\sec x \ \tan x}{\sec x} + \frac{15x^2}{4 - x^3}\right]$$

$$\frac{1}{y}\frac{dy}{dx} = \frac{1}{2}\left[\tan x + \frac{15x^2}{4 - x^3}\right]$$

Multiply both sides by y:

$$\frac{dy}{dx} = \frac{y}{2}\left[\tan x + \frac{15x^2}{4 - x^3}\right]$$

PRACTICE PROBLEM SET 19

Use logarithmic differentiation to find the derivative of each of the following problems. The answers are in Chapter 21.

1. $y = x\left(\sqrt[4]{1-x^3}\right)$

2. $y = \sqrt{\dfrac{1+x}{1-x}}$

3. $y = \dfrac{\left(x^3+5\right)^{\frac{3}{2}} \sqrt[3]{4-x^2}}{x^4-x^2+6}$

4. $y = \dfrac{\sin x \, \cos x}{\sqrt{x^3-4}}$

5. $y = \dfrac{\left(4x^2-8x\right)^3 \left(5-3x^4+7x\right)^4}{\left(x^2+x\right)^3}$

6. $y = \dfrac{x-1}{x \tan x}$

7. $y = \left(x-x^2\right)^2 \left(x^3+x^4\right)^3 \left(x^6-x^5\right)^4$

8. $y = \sqrt[4]{\dfrac{x(1-x)(1+x)}{(x^2-1)(5-x)}}$

11

The Integral

Welcome to the other half of calculus! This, unfortunately, is the more difficult half, but don't worry: We'll get you through it. In differential calculus, you learned all of the fun things that you can do with the derivative. Now you'll learn to do the reverse: how to take an integral. As you might imagine, there's a bunch of new fun things that you can do with integrals, too.

It's also time for a new symbol $\int$, which stands for integration. An integral actually serves several different purposes, but the first, and most basic, is that of the antiderivative.

THE ANTIDERIVATIVE

An antiderivative is a derivative in reverse. Therefore, we're going to reverse some of the rules we learned with derivatives and apply them to integrals. For example, we know that the derivative of x^2 is $2x$. We use antidifferentiation if we're given the derivative of a function and we have to figure out the original function. Thus, the antiderivative of $2x$ is x^2. (Actually, the answer is slightly more complicated than that, but we'll get into that in a few moments.)

Now we need to add some info here to make sure that you get this absolutely correct. First, as far as notation goes, it is traditional to write the antiderivative of a function using its upper case letter, so the antiderivative of $f(x)$ is $F(x)$, the antiderivative of $g(x)$ is $G(x)$, and so on.

The second idea is very important: Each function has more than one antiderivative. In fact, there are an infinite number of antiderivatives of a function. Let's go back to our example to help illustrate this.

Remember that the antiderivative of $2x$ is x^2? Well, consider: If you take the derivative of $x^2 + 1$, you get $2x$. The same is true for $x^2 + 2$, $x^2 - 1$, and so on. In fact, if *any* constant is added to x^2, the derivative is still $2x$ because the derivative of a constant is zero.

Because of this, we write the antiderivative of $2x$ as $x^2 + C$; where C stands for any constant.

Finally, whenever you take the integral (or antiderivative) of a function of x, you always add the term dx (or dy if it's a function of y, etc.) to the integrand (the thing inside the integral). You'll learn why later.

For now, just remember that you must always use the dx symbol, and teachers love to take points off for forgetting the dx. Don't ask why, but they do!

Here is the **Power Rule** for antiderivatives:

$$\text{If } f(x) = x^n, \text{ then } \int f(x)dx = \frac{x^{n+1}}{n+1} + C \text{ (except when } n = -1\text{).}$$

Example 1: Find $\int x^3 dx$.

Using the Power Rule, we get:

$$\int x^3 dx = \frac{x^4}{4} + C$$

Don't forget the constant C, or your teachers will take points off for that, too!

Example 2: Find $\int x^{-3} dx$.

The Power Rule works with negative exponents, too:

$$\int x^{-3} dx = \frac{x^{-2}}{-2} + C$$

Not terribly hard, is it? Now it's time for a few more rules that look remarkably similar to the rules for derivatives that we saw in Chapter 4:

$$\int kf(x)dx = k\int f(x)dx$$

$$\int \left[f(x) + g(x) \right] dx = \int f(x)dx + \int g(x)dx$$

$$\int k\,dx = kx + C$$

Here are a few more examples to make you an expert:

Example 3: $\int 5 dx = 5x + C$

Example 4: $\int 7x^3 dx = \dfrac{7x^4}{4} + C$

Example 5: $\int (3x^2 + 2x) dx = x^3 + x^2 + C$

Example 6: $\int \sqrt{x}\, dx = \dfrac{x^{\frac{3}{2}}}{\frac{3}{2}} + C = \dfrac{2x^{\frac{3}{2}}}{3} + C$

INTEGRALS OF TRIG FUNCTIONS

The integrals of some trigonometric functions follow directly from the derivative formulas in Chapter 4:

$$\int \sin\, ax\, dx = -\frac{\cos\, ax}{a} + C$$

$$\int \cos ax\, dx = \frac{\sin ax}{a} + C$$

$$\int \sec ax \tan ax\, dx = \frac{\sec ax}{a} + C$$

$$\int \sec^2 ax\, dx = \frac{\tan ax}{a} + C$$

$$\int \csc ax \cot ax\, dx = -\frac{\csc ax}{a} + C$$

$$\int \csc^2 ax\, dx = -\frac{\cot\, ax}{a} + C$$

We didn't mention the integrals of tangent, cotangent, secant, and cosecant, because you need to know some rules about logarithms to figure them out. We'll get to them in a few chapters. Notice also that each of the answers is divided by a constant. This is to account for the Chain Rule. Let's do some examples.

Example 7: Check the integral $\int \sin 5x\, dx = -\dfrac{\cos 5x}{5} + C$ by differentiating the answer.

$$\frac{d}{dx}\left[-\frac{\cos 5x}{5} + C\right] = -\frac{1}{5}(-\sin 5x)(5) = \sin 5x$$

Notice how the constant is accounted for in the answer?

Example 8: $\int \sec^2 3x\, dx = \dfrac{\tan 3x}{3} + C$

Example 9: $\int \cos \pi x\, dx = \dfrac{\sin \pi x}{\pi} + C$

Example 10: $\int \sec\left(\dfrac{x}{2}\right)\tan\left(\dfrac{x}{2}\right)dx = 2\sec\left(\dfrac{x}{2}\right) + C$

If you're not sure if you have the correct answer when you take an integral, you can always check by differentiating the answer and seeing if you get what you started with. Try to get in the habit of doing that at the beginning, because it'll help you build confidence in your ability to find integrals properly. You'll see that, although you can differentiate just about any expression that you'll normally encounter, you won't be able to integrate many of the functions you see.

ADDITION AND SUBTRACTION

By using the rules for addition and subtraction, we can integrate most polynomials.

Example 11: Find $\int \left(x^3 + x^2 - x\right) dx$.

We can break this into separate integrals, which gives us:

$$\int x^3 dx + \int x^2 dx - \int x\, dx$$

Now you can integrate each of these individually:

$$\frac{x^4}{4} + C + \frac{x^3}{3} + C - \frac{x^2}{2} + C$$

You can combine the constants into one constant (it doesn't matter how many C's we use, because their sum is one collective constant whose derivative is zero):

$$\frac{x^4}{4} + \frac{x^3}{3} - \frac{x^2}{2} + C$$

Sometimes you'll be given information about the function you're seeking that will enable you to solve for the constant. Often, this is an "initial value," which is the value of the function when the variable is zero. As we've seen, normally there are an infinite number of solutions for an integral, but when we solve for the constant, there's only one.

Example 12: Find the equation of y where $\dfrac{dy}{dx} = 3x + 5$ and $y = 6$ when $x = 0$.

Let's put this in integral form:

$$y = \int (3x + 5) \, dx$$

Integrating, we get:

$$y = \frac{3x^2}{2} + 5x + C$$

Now we can solve for the constant because we know that $y = 6$ when $x = 0$:

$$6 = \frac{3(0)^2}{2} + 5(0) + C$$

Therefore, $C = 6$ and the equation is:

$$y = \frac{3x^2}{2} + 5x + 6$$

Example 13: Find $f(x)$ if $f'(x) = \sin x - \cos x$ and $f(\pi) = 3$.

Integrate $f'(x)$:

$$f(x) = \int (\sin x - \cos x) \, dx = -\cos x - \sin x + C$$

Now solve for the constant:

$$3 = -\cos(\pi) - \sin(\pi) + C$$

$$C = 2$$

Therefore, the equation becomes:

$$f(x) = -\cos x - \sin x + 2$$

Now we've covered the basics of integration. However, integration is a very sophisticated topic and there are many types of integrals that will cause you trouble. We will need several techniques to learn how to evaluate these integrals. The first and most important is called *u*-substitution, which we will cover in the second half of this chapter.

In the meantime, here are some solved problems. Do each problem, covering the answer first, then check your answer.

PROBLEM 1. Evaluate $\int x^{\frac{3}{5}} dx$.

Answer: Here's the Power Rule again:

$$\int x^n dx = \frac{x^{n+1}}{n+1} + C$$

Using the rule:

$$\int x^{\frac{3}{5}} dx = \frac{x^{\frac{8}{5}}}{\frac{8}{5}} + C$$

You can rewrite it as $\dfrac{5x^{\frac{8}{5}}}{8} + C$.

PROBLEM 2. Evaluate $\int \left(5x^3 + x^2 - 6x + 4\right) dx$.

Answer: We can break this up into several integrals:

$$\int \left(5x^3 + x^2 - 6x + 4\right) dx = \int 5x^3 dx + \int x^2 dx - \int 6x\, dx + 4\int dx$$

Each of these can be integrated according to the Power Rule:

$$\frac{5x^4}{4} + C + \frac{x^3}{3} + C - \frac{6x^2}{2} + C + 4x + C$$

This can be rewritten:

$$\frac{5x^4}{4} + \frac{x^3}{3} - 3x^2 + 4x + C$$

Notice that we combine the constant terms into one constant term C.

PROBLEM 3. Evaluate $\int \left(3-x^2\right)^2 dx$.

Answer: First, expand the integrand:

$$\int \left(9-6x^2+x^4\right) dx$$

Break this up into several integrals:

$$\int 9dx - 6\int x^2 dx + \int x^4 dx$$

And integrate according to the Power Rule:

$$9x - 2x^3 + \frac{x^5}{5} + C$$

PROBLEM 4. Evaluate $\int \left(4\sin x - 3\cos x\right) dx$.

Answer: Break this problem into two integrals:

$$4\int \sin x \, dx - 3\int \cos x \, dx$$

Each of these trig integrals can be evaluated according to its rule:

$$-4\cos x - 3\sin x + C$$

PROBLEM 5. $\int \left(2\sec^2 x - 5\csc^2 x\right) dx$

Answer: Break the integral in two:

$$2\int \sec^2 x \, dx - 5\int \csc^2 x \, dx$$

Each of these trig integrals can be evaluated according to its rule:

$$2\tan x + 5\cot x + C$$

PRACTICE PROBLEM SET 20

Now evaluate the following integrals. The answers are in Chapter 21.

1. $\int \dfrac{1}{x^4} dx$

2. $\int \dfrac{5}{\sqrt{x}} dx$

3. $\int \dfrac{x^5 + 7}{x^2} dx$

4. $\int \left(5x^4 - 3x^2 + 2x + 6\right) dx$

5. $\int \left(3x^{-3} - 2x^{-2} + x^4 + 16x^7\right) dx$

6. $\int \left(1 + x^2\right)(x - 2) dx$

7. $\int x^{\frac{1}{3}} (2 + x) dx$

8. $\int \left(x^3 + x\right)^2 dx$

9. $\int \dfrac{x^6 - 2x^4 + 1}{x^2} dx$

10. $\int x(x - 1)^3 dx$

11. $\int (\cos x - 5 \sin x) dx$

12. $\int \sec x (\sec x + \tan x) dx$

13. $\int \left(\sec^2 x + x\right) dx$

14. $\int \dfrac{\sin x}{\cos^2 x} dx$

15. $\int \dfrac{\cos^3 x + 4}{\cos^2 x} dx$

16. $\int \dfrac{\sin 2x}{\cos x} dx$

17. $\int \left(1 + \cos^2 x \sec x\right) dx$

18. $\int \left(\tan^2 x\right) dx$

19. $\int \dfrac{1}{\csc x} dx$

20. $\int \left(x - \dfrac{2}{\cos^2 x}\right) dx$

U-SUBSTITUTION

When we discussed differentiation, one of the most important techniques we mastered was the Chain Rule. Now, you'll learn the integration corollary of the Chain Rule (called *u*-substitution), which we use when the integrand is a composite function. All you do is replace the function with *u*, and then you can integrate the simpler function using the Power Rule (as shown below):

$$\int u^n du = \frac{u^{n+1}}{n+1} + C$$

Suppose you have to integrate $\int (x - 4)^{10} dx$. You could expand out this function and integrate each term, but that'll take a while. Instead, you can follow these four steps:

Step 1: Let $u = x - 4$. Then $\dfrac{du}{dx} = 1$ (rearrange this to get $du = dx$).

Step 2: Substitute $u = x - 4$ and $du = dx$ into the integrand:

$$\int u^{10} du$$

Step 3: Integrate:

$$\int u^{10} du = \frac{u^{11}}{11} + C$$

Step 4: Substitute back for *u*:

$$\frac{(x - 4)^{11}}{11} + C$$

That's *u*-substitution. The main difficulty you'll have will be picking the appropriate function to set equal to *u*. The best way to get better is to practice. The object is to pick a function and replace it with *u*, then take the derivative of *u* to find *du*. If we can't replace *all* of the terms in the integrand, we *can't* do the substitution.

Let's do some examples.

Example 1: $\int 10x\left(5x^2 - 3\right)^6 dx =$

Once again, you could expand this out and integrate each term, but that would be difficult. Use *u*-substitution.

Let $u = 5x^2 - 3$. Then $\dfrac{du}{dx} = 10x$ and $du = 10x\, dx$. Now substitute:

$$\int u^6 du$$

And integrate:

$$\int u^6 du = \frac{u^7}{7} + C$$

Substituting back gives you:

$$\frac{\left(5x^2 - 3\right)^7}{7} + C$$

Confirm that this is the integral by differentiating $\dfrac{\left(5x^2 - 3\right)^7}{7} + C$:

$$\frac{d}{dx}\left[\frac{\left(5x^2 - 3\right)^7}{7} + C\right] = \frac{7\left(5x^2 - 3\right)^6}{7}(10x) = \left(5x^2 - 3\right)^6 (10x)$$

Example 2: $\int 2x\sqrt{x^2 - 5}\, dx =$

If $u = x^2 - 5$, then $\dfrac{du}{dx} = 2x$ and $du = 2x\, dx$. Substitute *u* into the integrand:

$$\int u^{\frac{1}{2}}\, du$$

Integrate:

$$\int u^{\frac{1}{2}}\, du = \frac{u^{\frac{3}{2}}}{\frac{3}{2}} + C = \frac{2u^{\frac{3}{2}}}{3} + C$$

And substitute back:

$$\frac{2\left(x^2-5\right)^{\frac{3}{2}}}{3}+C$$

Note: From now on, we're not going to rearrange $\frac{du}{dx}$; we'll go directly to "$du =$" format. You should be able to do that step on your own.

Example 3: $\int 3\sin\left(3x-1\right)dx =$

Let $u = 3x - 1$. Then $du = 3dx$. Substitute the u in the integral:

$$\int \sin u \, du$$

Figure out the integral:

$$\int \sin u \, du = -\cos u + C$$

And throw the x's back in:

$$-\cos(3x - 1) + C$$

So far, this is only the simplest kind of u-substitution; naturally, the process can get worse when the substitution isn't as easy. Usually, you'll have to insert a constant term to put the integrand into a workable form. For example:

Example 4: $\int \left(5x+7\right)^{20} dx =$

Let $u = 5x + 7$. Then $du = 5dx$. Notice that we can't do the substitution immediately because we need to substitute for dx and we have $5dx$. No problem: Because 5 is a constant, just solve for dx:

$$\frac{1}{5}du = dx$$

Now you can substitute:

$$\int \left(5x+7\right)^{20} dx = \int u^{20}\left(\frac{1}{5}\right)du$$

Rearrange the integral and solve:

$$\int u^{20}\left(\frac{1}{5}\right)du = \frac{1}{5}\int u^{20}du = \frac{1}{5}\frac{u^{21}}{21}+C = \frac{u^{21}}{105}+C$$

And now it's time to substitute back:

$$\frac{u^{21}}{105} + C = \frac{(5x+7)^{21}}{105} + C$$

Example 5: $\int x \cos(3x^2 + 1) dx =$

Let $u = 3x^2 + 1$. Then $du = 6x\, dx$. We need to substitute for $x\, dx$, so we can rearrange the du term:

$$\frac{1}{6} du = x\, dx$$

Now substitute:

$$\int \frac{1}{6} \cos u\, du$$

Evaluate the integral:

$$\int \frac{1}{6} \cos u\, du = \frac{1}{6} \sin u + C$$

And substitute back:

$$\frac{1}{6} \sin u + C = \frac{1}{6} \sin(3x^2 + 1) + C$$

Example 6: $\int x \sec^2(x^2) dx =$

Let $u = x^2$. Then $du = 2x\, dx$ and $\frac{1}{2} du = x\, dx$.
Substitute:

$$\int \frac{1}{2} \sec^2 u\, du$$

Evaluate the integral:

$$\int \frac{1}{2} \sec^2 u\, du = \frac{1}{2} \tan u + C$$

Now the original function goes back in:

$$\frac{1}{2} \tan(x^2) + C$$

This is a good technique to master, so practice on the following solved problems. Do each problem, covering the answer first, then check your answer.

PROBLEM 1. Evaluate $\int \sec^2 3x\ dx$.

Answer: Let $u = 3x$ and $du = 3dx$. Then $\dfrac{1}{3} du = dx$.
Substitute and integrate:

$$\frac{1}{3}\int \sec^2 u\ du = \frac{1}{3}\tan u + C$$

Then substitute back:

$$\frac{1}{3}\tan 3x + C$$

PROBLEM 2. Evaluate $\int \sqrt{5x - 4}\ dx$.

Answer: Let $u = 5x - 4$ and $du = 5dx$. Then $\dfrac{1}{5} du = dx$.

Substitute and integrate:

$$\frac{1}{5}\int u^{\frac{1}{2}}\ du = \frac{2}{15}u^{\frac{3}{2}} + C$$

Then substitute back:

$$\frac{2}{15}\left(5x - 4\right)^{\frac{3}{2}} + C$$

PROBLEM 3. Evaluate $\int x\left(4x^2 - 7\right)^{10} dx$.

Answer: Let $u = 4x^2 - 7$ and $du = 8xdx$. Then $\dfrac{1}{8} du = x\ dx$.

Substitute and integrate:

$$\frac{1}{8}\int u^{10}\ du = \frac{1}{88}u^{11} + C$$

Then substitute back:

$$\frac{1}{88}\left(4x^2 - 7\right)^{11} + C$$

PROBLEM 4. Evaluate $\int \tan \dfrac{x}{3} \sec^2 \dfrac{x}{3} \, dx$.

Answer: Let $u = \tan \dfrac{x}{3}$ and $du = \dfrac{1}{3}\sec^2 \dfrac{x}{3} \, dx$. Then $3\,du = \sec^2 \dfrac{x}{3} \, dx$.

Substituting, we get:

$$3\int u \, du = \frac{3}{2}u^2 + C$$

Then substitute back:

$$\frac{3}{2}\tan^2 \frac{x}{3} + C$$

PRACTICE PROBLEM SET 21

Now evaluate the following integrals. The answers are in Chapter 21.

1. $\displaystyle\int \sin 2x \cos 2x \, dx$

2. $\displaystyle\int \dfrac{3x \, dx}{\sqrt[3]{10 - x^2}}$

3. $\displaystyle\int x^3 \sqrt{5x^4 + 20} \, dx$

4. $\displaystyle\int \dfrac{dx}{(x-1)^2}$

5. $\displaystyle\int (x^2 + 1)(x^3 + 3x)^{-5} \, dx$

6. $\displaystyle\int \dfrac{1}{\sqrt{x}} \sin \sqrt{x} \, dx$

7. $\displaystyle\int x^2 \sec^2 x^3 \, dx$

8. $\displaystyle\int \dfrac{\cos\left(\dfrac{3}{x}\right)}{x^2} \, dx$

9. $\displaystyle\int \dfrac{\sin 2x}{(1 - \cos 2x)^3} \, dx$

10. $\displaystyle\int \sin(\sin x) \cos x \, dx$

12

Definite Integrals

AREA UNDER A CURVE

It's time to learn one of the most important uses of the integral. We've already discussed how integration can be used to "antidifferentiate" a function; now you'll see that you can also use it to find the area under a curve. First, here's a little background about how to find the area without using integration.

Suppose you have to find the area under the curve $y = x^2 + 2$ from $x = 1$ to $x = 3$. The graph of the curve looks like this:

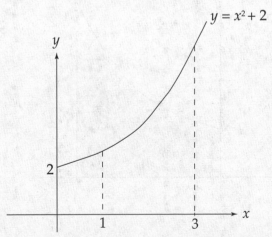

Don't panic yet. Nothing you've learned in geometry thus far has taught you how to find the area of something like this. You have learned how to find the area of a rectangle, though, and we're going to use rectangles to approximate the area between the curve and the x-axis.

Let's divide the region into two rectangles, one from $x = 1$ to $x = 2$ and one from $x = 2$ to $x = 3$, where the top of each rectangle comes just under the curve. It looks like this:

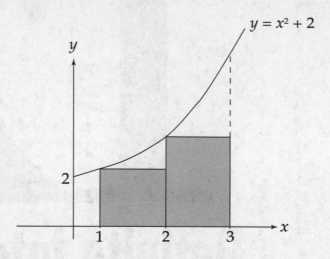

Notice that the width of each rectangle is 1. The height of the left rectangle is found by plugging 1 into the equation $y = x^2 + 2$ (yielding 3); the height of the right rectangle is found by plugging 2 into the same equation (yielding 6). The combined area of the two rectangles is (1)(3) + (1)(6) = 9. So we could say that the area under the curve is approximately 9 square units.

Naturally, this is a pretty rough approximation that significantly underestimates the area. Look at how much of the area we missed by using two rectangles! How do you suppose we could make the approximation better? Divide the region into more, thinner rectangles.

This time, cut up the region into four rectangles, each with width of $\dfrac{1}{2}$. It looks like this:

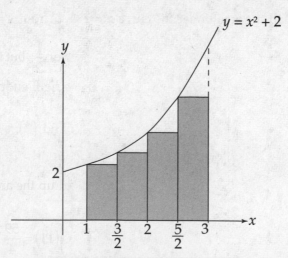

Now find the height of each rectangle the same way as before. Notice that the values we use are the left endpoints of each rectangle. The heights of the rectangles are, respectively:

$$(1)^2 + 2 = 3; \quad \left(\frac{3}{2}\right)^2 + 2 = \frac{17}{4}; \quad (2)^2 + 2 = 6 \text{ and } \left(\frac{5}{2}\right)^2 + 2 = \frac{33}{4}$$

Now, multiply each height by the width of $\frac{1}{2}$ and add up the areas:

$$\left(\frac{1}{2}\right)(3) + \left(\frac{1}{2}\right)\left(\frac{17}{4}\right) + \left(\frac{1}{2}\right)(6) + \left(\frac{1}{2}\right)\left(\frac{33}{4}\right) = \frac{43}{4}$$

This is a much better approximation of the area, but there's still a lot of space that isn't accounted for. We're still underestimating the area. The rectangles need to be thinner. But before we do that, let's do something else.

Notice how each of the rectangles is inscribed in the region. Suppose we used circumscribed rectangles instead—that is, we could determine the height of each rectangle by the higher of the two y-values, not the lower. Then the region would look like this:

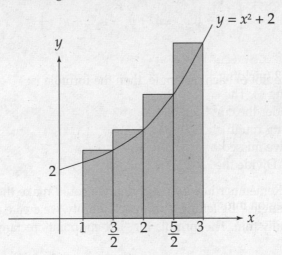

To find the area of the rectangles, we would still use the width of $\frac{1}{2}$, but the heights would change.

The heights of each rectangle are now found by plugging in the right endpoint of each rectangle:

$$\left(\frac{3}{2}\right)^2 + 2 = \frac{17}{4}; (2)^2 + 2 = 6; \left(\frac{5}{2}\right)^2 + 2 = \frac{33}{4}; \text{ and } (3)^2 + 2 = 11$$

Once again, multiply each height by the width of $\frac{1}{2}$ and add up the areas:

$$\left(\frac{1}{2}\right)\left(\frac{17}{4}\right) + \left(\frac{1}{2}\right)(6) + \left(\frac{1}{2}\right)\left(\frac{33}{4}\right) + \left(\frac{1}{2}\right)(11) = \frac{59}{4}$$

The area under the curve using four left end point rectangles is $\frac{43}{4}$, and the area using four right end point rectangles is $\frac{59}{4}$, so why not average the two? This gives us $\frac{51}{4}$, which is a better approximation of the area.

Now that we've found the area using the rectangles a few times, let's turn the method into a formula. Call the left endpoint of the interval a and the right endpoint of the interval b, and set the number of rectangles we use equal to n. Then the width of each rectangle is $\frac{b-a}{n}$. The height of the first inscribed rectangle is y_0, the height of the second rectangle is y_1, the height of the third rectangle is y_2, and so on, up to the last rectangle, which is y_{n-1}. If we use the left endpoint of each rectangle, the area under the curve is thus:

$$\left(\frac{b-a}{n}\right)\left[y_0 + y_1 + y_2 + y_3 \cdots + y_{n-1}\right]$$

If we use the right endpoint of each rectangle, then the formula is:

$$\left(\frac{b-a}{n}\right)\left[y_1 + y_2 + y_3 \cdots + y_n\right]$$

Now for the fun part. Remember how we said that we could make the approximation better by making more, thinner rectangles? By letting n approach infinity, we create an infinite number of rectangles that are infinitesimally thin. The formula for "left-endpoint" rectangles becomes:

$$\lim_{n\to\infty}\left(\frac{b-a}{n}\right)\left[y_0 + y_1 + y_2 + y_3 \cdots + y_{n-1}\right]$$

For "right-endpoint" rectangles, the formula becomes:

$$\lim_{n\to\infty}\left(\frac{b-a}{n}\right)\left[y_1 + y_2 + y_3 \cdots + y_n\right]$$

Note: Sometimes these are called "inscribed" and "circumscribed" rectangles, but that restricts the use of the formula. It's more exact to evaluate these rectangles using right and left endpoints.

We could also find the area using the midpoint of each interval. Let's once again use the above example, dividing the region into four rectangles. The region would look like this:

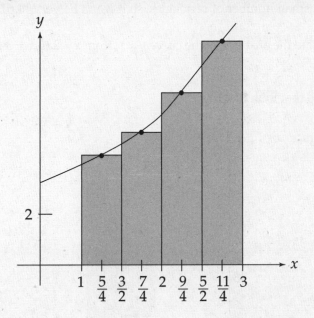

To find the area of the rectangles, we would still use the width of $\frac{1}{2}$, but the heights would now be found by plugging the midpoint of each interval into the equation:

$$\left(\frac{5}{4}\right)^2 + 2 = \frac{57}{16} ; \left(\frac{7}{4}\right)^2 + 2 = \frac{81}{16} ; \left(\frac{9}{4}\right)^2 + 2 = \frac{113}{16} ; \left(\frac{11}{4}\right)^2 + 2 = \frac{153}{16}$$

Once again, multiply each height by the width of $\frac{1}{2}$ and add up the areas:

$$\left(\frac{1}{2}\right)\left(\frac{57}{16}\right) + \left(\frac{1}{2}\right)\left(\frac{81}{16}\right) + \left(\frac{1}{2}\right)\left(\frac{113}{16}\right) + \left(\frac{1}{2}\right)\left(\frac{153}{16}\right) = \frac{404}{32} = \frac{101}{8} = 12.625$$

The general formula for approximating the area under a curve using midpoints is:

$$\left(\frac{b-a}{n}\right)\left[y_{\frac{1}{2}} + y_{\frac{3}{2}} + y_{\frac{5}{2}} + \ldots + y_{\frac{2n-1}{2}} \right]$$

(Note: The fractional subscript means to evaluate the function at the number halfway between each integral pair of values of n.)

When you take the limit of this infinite sum, you get the integral. (You knew the integral had to show up sometime, didn't you?) Actually, we write the integral like this:

$$\int_1^3 \left(x^2 + 2\right) dx$$

It is called a **definite integral**, and it means that we're finding the area under the curve $x^2 + 2$ from $x = 1$ to $x = 3$. (We'll discuss how to evaluate this in a moment.) On the AP exam, you'll only be asked to divide the region into a small number of rectangles, so it won't be very hard. Let's do an example.

Example 1: Approximate the area under the curve $y = x^3$ from $x = 2$ to $x = 3$ using four left-endpoint rectangles.

Draw four rectangles that look like this:

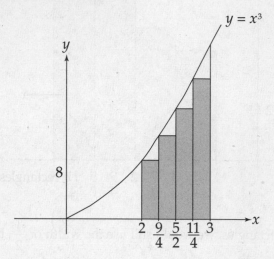

The width of each rectangle is $\dfrac{1}{4}$. The heights of the rectangles are:

$$2^3, \left(\frac{9}{4}\right)^3, \left(\frac{5}{2}\right)^3, \text{ and } \left(\frac{11}{4}\right)^3$$

Therefore, the area is:

$$\left(\frac{1}{4}\right)(2^3) + \left(\frac{1}{4}\right)\left(\frac{9}{4}\right)^3 + \left(\frac{1}{4}\right)\left(\frac{5}{2}\right)^3 + \left(\frac{1}{4}\right)\left(\frac{11}{4}\right)^3 = \frac{893}{64} \approx 13.953$$

Example 2: Repeat Example 1 using four right-endpoint rectangles.

Now draw four rectangles that look like this:

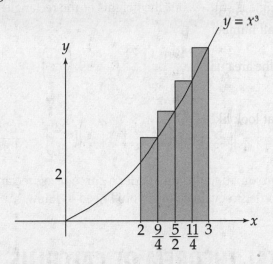

The width of each rectangle is still $\dfrac{1}{4}$, but the heights of the rectangles are now:

$$\left(\frac{9}{4}\right)^3, \ \left(\frac{5}{2}\right)^3, \ \left(\frac{11}{4}\right)^3, \text{ and } \left(3^3\right)$$

The area is now:

$$\left(\frac{1}{4}\right)\left(\frac{9}{4}\right)^3 + \left(\frac{1}{4}\right)\left(\frac{5}{2}\right)^3 + \left(\frac{1}{4}\right)\left(\frac{11}{4}\right)^3 + \left(\frac{1}{4}\right)\left(3^3\right) = \frac{1197}{64} \approx 18.703$$

Example 3: Repeat Example 1 using four midpoint rectangles.
Now draw four rectangles that look like this:

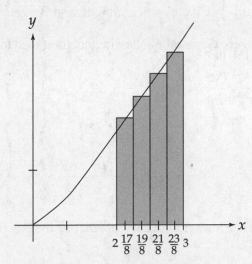

The width of each rectangle is still $\frac{1}{4}$, but the heights of the rectangles are now:

$$\left(\frac{17}{8}\right)^3, \left(\frac{19}{18}\right)^3, \left(\frac{21}{8}\right)^3, \text{ and } \left(\frac{23}{8}\right)^3$$

The area is now:

$$\left(\frac{1}{4}\right)\left(\frac{17}{8}\right)^3 + \left(\frac{1}{4}\right)\left(\frac{19}{8}\right)^3 + \left(\frac{1}{4}\right)\left(\frac{21}{8}\right)^3 + \left(\frac{1}{4}\right)\left(\frac{23}{8}\right)^3 = \frac{2075}{128} \approx 16.211$$

That's all there is to approximating the area under a curve using rectangles. Now, let's learn how to find the area exactly. In order to evaluate this, you'll need to know. . .

THE FUNDAMENTAL THEOREM OF CALCULUS

Before, we said that if you create an infinite number of infinitely thin rectangles, you'll get the area under the curve, which is an integral. For the example above, the integral is:

$$\int_2^3 x^3 dx$$

There is a rule to evaluating this integral. The rule is called the **Fundamental Theorem of Calculus**, and it says:

$$\int_a^b f(x)dx = F(b) - F(a) \text{ ; where } F(x) \text{ is the antiderivative of } f(x).$$

Using this rule, you can find $\int_2^3 x^3 dx$ by integrating it, and we get $\frac{x^4}{4}$. Now all you do is plug in 3 and 2 and take the difference. We use the following notation to symbolize this:

$$\left. \frac{x^4}{4} \right|_2^3$$

Thus we have:

$$\frac{3^4}{4} - \frac{2^4}{4} = \frac{81}{4} - \frac{16}{4} = \frac{65}{4}$$

Since $\frac{65}{4} = 16.25$, you can see how close we were with our three earlier approximations.

Example 4: Find $\int_1^3 \left(x^2 + 2\right) dx$.

Using the Fundamental Theorem of Calculus:

$$\int_1^3 \left(x^2 + 2\right) dx = \left.\left(\frac{x^3}{3} + 2x\right)\right|_1^3$$

If we evaluate this, we get:

$$\left(\frac{3^3}{3} + 2(3)\right) - \left(\frac{1^3}{3} + 2(1)\right) = \frac{38}{3}$$

This is the first function for which we found the approximate area by using inscribed rectangles. Our final estimate, where we averaged the inscribed and circumscribed rectangles, was $\frac{51}{4}$, and as you can see, that was very close (off by $\frac{1}{12}$). When we used the midpoints, we were off by $\frac{1}{24}$.

We're only going to do a few approximations using rectangles, because it's not a big part of the AP exam. On the other hand, definite integrals are a big part of the rest of this book.

Example 5: $\int_1^5 \left(x^2 - x\right) dx = \left.\left(\frac{x^3}{3} - \frac{x^2}{2}\right)\right|_1^5 = \left(\frac{125}{3} - \frac{25}{2}\right) - \left(\frac{1}{3} - \frac{1}{2}\right) = \frac{88}{3}$

Example 6: $\int_0^{\frac{\pi}{2}} \sin x \, dx = \left.\left(-\cos x\right)\right|_0^{\frac{\pi}{2}} = \left(-\cos\frac{\pi}{2}\right) - \left(-\cos 0\right) = 1$

Example 7: $\int_0^{\frac{\pi}{4}} \sec^2 x \, dx = \left.\tan x\right|_0^{\frac{\pi}{4}} = \tan\frac{\pi}{4} - \tan 0 = 1$

THE TRAPEZOID RULE

There's another approximation method that's even better than the rectangle method. Essentially, all you do is divide the region into trapezoids instead of rectangles. Let's use the problem that we did at the beginning of the chapter.

We get a picture that looks like this:

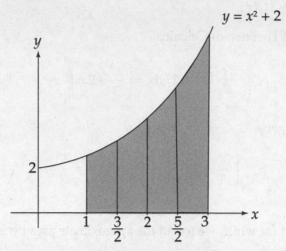

$$y = x^2 + 2$$

As you should recall from geometry, the formula for the area of a trapezoid is:

$$\frac{1}{2}(b_1 + b_2)h$$

(Note: b_1 and b_2 are the two bases of the trapezoid.) Notice that each of the shapes is a trapezoid on its side, so the height of each trapezoid is the length of the interval, $\frac{1}{2}$, and the bases are the y-values that correspond to each x-value. We found these earlier in the rectangle example; they are, in order: $3, \frac{17}{4}, 6, \frac{33}{4}$, and 11. We can find the area of each trapezoid and add them up:

$$\frac{1}{2}\left(3 + \frac{17}{4}\right)\left(\frac{1}{2}\right) + \frac{1}{2}\left(\frac{17}{4} + 6\right)\left(\frac{1}{2}\right) + \frac{1}{2}\left(6 + \frac{33}{4}\right)\left(\frac{1}{2}\right) + \frac{1}{2}\left(\frac{33}{4} + 11\right)\left(\frac{1}{2}\right) = \frac{51}{4}, \text{ or } 12.75$$

Recall that the actual value of the area is $\frac{38}{3}$ or 12.67; the Trapezoid Rule gives a pretty good approximation.

Notice how each trapezoid shares a base with the trapezoid next to it, except for the end ones. This enables us to simplify the formula for using the Trapezoid Rule. Each trapezoid has a height equal to the length of the interval divided by the number of trapezoids we use. If the interval is from $x = a$ to $x = b$, and the number of trapezoids is n, then the height of each trapezoid is $\frac{b-a}{n}$. Then our formula is:

$$\left(\frac{1}{2}\right)\left(\frac{b-a}{n}\right)\left[y_0 + 2y_1 + 2y_2 + 2y_3 \ldots + 2y_{n-2} + 2y_{n-1} + y_n\right]$$

This is all you need to know about the Trapezoid Rule. Just follow the formula and you won't have any problems. Let's do one more example.

Example 8: Approximate the area under the curve $y = x^3$ from $x = 2$ to $x = 3$ using four inscribed trapezoids.

Following the rule, the height of each trapezoid is $\dfrac{3-2}{4} = \dfrac{1}{4}$. Thus, the approximate area is:

$$\left(\frac{1}{2}\right)\left(\frac{1}{4}\right)\left[2^3 + 2\left(\frac{9}{4}\right)^3 + 2\left(\frac{5}{2}\right)^3 + 2\left(\frac{11}{4}\right)^3 + 3^3\right] = \frac{1045}{64}$$

Compare this answer to the actual value we found earlier—it's pretty close!

PROBLEM 1. Approximate the area under the curve $y = 4 - x^2$ from $x = -1$ to $x = 1$ with $n = 4$ inscribed rectangles.

Answer: Draw four rectangles that look like this:

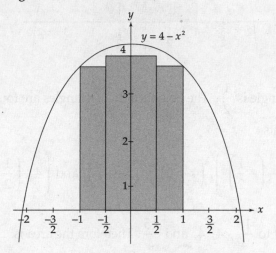

The width of each rectangle is $\dfrac{1}{2}$. The heights of the rectangles are found by evaluating $y = 4 - x^2$ at the appropriate endpoints:

$$\left(4 - (-1)^2\right), \left(4 - \left(-\frac{1}{2}\right)^2\right), \left(4 - \left(\frac{1}{2}\right)^2\right), \text{ and } \left(4 - (1)^2\right)$$

These can be simplified to $3, \dfrac{15}{4}, \dfrac{15}{4}$, and 3. Therefore the area is:

$$\left(\frac{1}{2}\right)(3) + \left(\frac{1}{2}\right)\left(\frac{15}{4}\right) + \left(\frac{1}{2}\right)\left(\frac{15}{4}\right) + \left(\frac{1}{2}\right)(3) = \frac{27}{4}$$

PROBLEM 2. Find the area under the curve $y = 4 - x^2$ from $x = -1$ to $x = 1$ with $n = 4$ circumscribed rectangles.

Answer: Draw four rectangles that look like this:

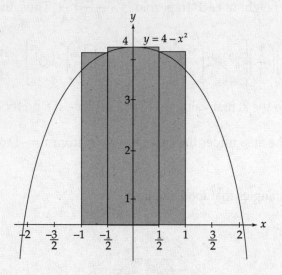

The width of each rectangle is $\dfrac{1}{2}$. The heights of the rectangles are found by evaluating $y = 4 - x^2$ at the appropriate endpoints:

$$\left(4 - \left(-\frac{1}{2}\right)^2\right), \ \left(4 - (0)^2\right), \ \left(4 - (0)^2\right), \text{ and } \left(4 - \left(\frac{1}{2}\right)^2\right)$$

These can be simplified to $\dfrac{15}{4}$, 4, 4, and $\dfrac{15}{4}$. Therefore the area is:

$$\left(\frac{1}{2}\right)\left(\frac{15}{4}\right) + \left(\frac{1}{2}\right)(4) + \left(\frac{1}{2}\right)(4) + \left(\frac{1}{2}\right)\left(\frac{15}{4}\right) = \frac{31}{4}$$

PROBLEM 3. Find the area under the curve $y = 4 - x^2$ from $x = -1$ to $x = 1$ using the Trapezoid Rule with $n = 4$.

Answer: Draw four trapezoids that look like this:

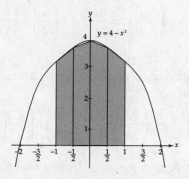

The width of each trapezoid is $\dfrac{1}{2}$. Evaluate the bases of the trapezoid by calculating $y = 4 - x^2$ at the appropriate endpoints. Following the rule, we get that the area is approximately:

$$\left(\frac{1}{2}\right)\left(\frac{1}{2}\right)\left[\left(4-(1)^2\right)+2\left(4-\left(-\frac{1}{2}\right)^2\right)+2\left(4-(0)^2\right)+2\left(4-\left(\frac{1}{2}\right)^2\right)+\left(4-(1)^2\right)\right]=$$

$$\left(\frac{1}{2}\right)\left(\frac{1}{2}\right)\left[3+\frac{15}{2}+8+\frac{15}{2}+3\right]=\frac{29}{4}$$

PROBLEM 4. Find the area under the curve $y = 4 - x^2$ from $x = -1$ to $x = 1$ using the Midpoint Formula with $n = 4$.

Answer: Draw four rectangles that look like this:

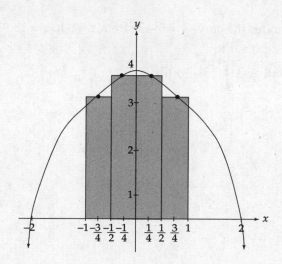

The width of each rectangle is $\dfrac{1}{2}$. The heights of the rectangles are found by evaluating $y = 4 - x^2$ at the appropriate points:

$$4 - \left(-\frac{3}{4}\right)^2 = \frac{55}{16}; \quad 4 - \left(-\frac{1}{4}\right)^2 = \frac{63}{16}; \quad 4 - \left(\frac{1}{4}\right)^2 = \frac{63}{16}; \quad 4 - \left(\frac{3}{4}\right)^2 = \frac{55}{16}$$

Multiply each height by the width of $\dfrac{1}{2}$ and add up the areas:

$$\left(\frac{1}{2}\right)\left(\frac{55}{16}\right) + \left(\frac{1}{2}\right)\left(\frac{63}{16}\right) + \left(\frac{1}{2}\right)\left(\frac{63}{16}\right) + \left(\frac{1}{2}\right)\left(\frac{55}{16}\right) = \frac{59}{8}$$

PROBLEM 5. Find the area under the curve $y = 4 - x^2$ from $x = -1$ to $x = 1$.
Answer: Now we can use the definite integral by evaluating:

$$\int_{-1}^{1} \left(4 - x^2\right) dx$$

This can be rewritten as:

$$\left(4x - \frac{x^3}{3}\right)\Bigg|_{-1}^{1}$$

Follow the Fundamental Theorem of Calculus:

$$\left(4 - \frac{1}{3}\right) - \left(4(-1) - \frac{(-1)^3}{3}\right) = \frac{22}{3}$$

PROBLEM 6. Find the area under the curve $y = 5 - 3x$ from $x = 0$ to $x = 1$.

Answer: Evaluate the integral $\displaystyle\int_{0}^{1} \left(5 - 3x\right) dx$:

$$\left(5x - \frac{3x^2}{2}\right)\Bigg|_{0}^{1} = \left(5 - \frac{3}{2}\right) - 0 = \frac{7}{2}$$

PRACTICE PROBLEM SET 22

Here's a great opportunity to practice finding the area beneath a curve and evaluating integrals. The answers are in Chapter 21.

1. Find the area under the curve $y = 2x - x^2$ from $x = 1$ to $x = 2$ with $n = 4$ left-endpoint rectangles.

2. Find the area under the curve $y = 2x - x^2$ from $x = 1$ to $x = 2$ with $n = 4$ right-endpoint rectangles.

3. Find the area under the curve $y = 2x - x^2$ from $x = 1$ to $x = 2$ using the Trapezoid Rule with $n = 4$.

4. Find the area under the curve $y = 2x - x^2$ from $x = 1$ to $x = 2$ using the Midpoint Formula with $n = 4$.

5. Find the area under the curve $y = 2x - x^2$ from $x = 1$ to $x = 2$.

6. Evaluate $\int_{-\frac{\pi}{2}}^{\frac{\pi}{2}} \cos x \, dx$.

7. Evaluate $\int_{1}^{9} 2x\sqrt{x} \, dx$.

8. Evaluate $\int_{0}^{1} \left(x^4 - 5x^3 + 3x^2 - 4x - 6\right) dx$.

9. Evaluate $\int_{-4}^{4} |x| \, dx$.

10. Evaluate $\int_{-\frac{\pi}{2}}^{\frac{\pi}{2}} \sin x \, dx$.

THE MEAN VALUE THEOREM FOR INTEGRALS

As you recall, we did the Mean Value Theorem once before, in Chapter 6, but this time we'll apply it to integrals, not derivatives. In fact, some books refer to it as the "Mean Value Theorem for Integrals" or MVTI. The most important aspect of the MVTI is that it enables you to find the average value of a function. In fact, the AP exam will often ask you to find the average value of a function, which is just its way of testing your knowledge of the MVTI.

Here's the theorem:

If $f(x)$ is continuous on a closed interval $[a, b]$, then at some point c in the interval $[a, b]$:

$$\int_a^b f(x)dx = f(c)(b-a)$$

This tells you that the area under the curve of $f(x)$ on the interval $[a, b]$ is equal to the value of the function at some value c (between a and b) times the length of the interval. If you look at this graphically, you can see that you're finding the area of a rectangle whose base is the interval and whose height is some value of $f(x)$ that creates a rectangle with the same area as the area under the curve.

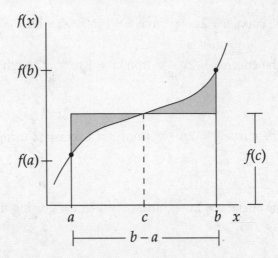

The number $f(c)$ gives us the average value of f on $[a, b]$. Thus, if we rearrange the theorem, we get the formula for finding the average value of $f(x)$ on $[a, b]$:

$$f(c) = \frac{1}{b-a} \int_a^b f(x)dx$$

There's all you need to know about finding average values. Try some examples.

Example 1: Find the average value of $f(x) = x^2$ from $x = 2$ to $x = 4$.

Evaluate the integral $\dfrac{1}{4-2} \displaystyle\int_2^4 x^2 dx$:

$$\frac{1}{4-2} \int_2^4 x^2 dx = \frac{1}{2}\left[\frac{x^3}{3}\bigg|_2^4\right] = \frac{1}{2}\left(\frac{64}{3} - \frac{8}{3}\right) = \frac{28}{3}$$

Example 2: Find the average value of $f(x) = \sin x$ on $[0,\pi]$.

Evaluate $\dfrac{1}{\pi-0} \displaystyle\int_0^\pi \sin x \, dx$:

$$\frac{1}{\pi-0} \int_0^\pi \sin x \, dx = \frac{1}{\pi}\left(-\cos x\right)\bigg|_0^\pi = \frac{1}{\pi}\left(-\cos \pi + \cos 0\right) = \frac{2}{\pi}$$

THE SECOND FUNDAMENTAL THEOREM OF CALCULUS

As you saw in the last chapter, we've only half-learned the theorem. It has two parts, often referred to as the First and Second Fundamental Theorems of Calculus:

The First Fundamental Theorem of Calculus (which you've already seen):

If $f(x)$ is continuous at every point of $[a, b]$, and $F(x)$ is an antiderivative of $f(x)$ on $[a, b]$, then $\int_a^b f(x)dx = F(b) - F(a)$.

The Second Fundamental Theorem of Calculus:

If $f(x)$ is continuous on $[a, b]$, then the derivative of the function $F(x) = \int_a^x f(t)dt$ is:

$$\frac{dF}{dx} = \frac{d}{dx}\int_a^x f(t)dt = f(x)$$

(Some books give the theorems in reverse order.)

We've already made use of the first theorem in evaluating definite integrals. In fact, we use the first Fundamental Theorem every time we evaluate a definite integral, so we're not going to give you any examples of that here. There is one aspect of the first Fundamental Theorem, however, that involves the area between curves (we'll discuss that in Chapter 14).

But for now, you should know this:

If we have a point c in the interval $[a, b]$, then:

$$\int_a^c f(x)dx + \int_c^b f(x)\, dx = \int_a^b f(x)dx$$

In other words, we can divide up the region into parts, add them up, and the result is the area of the region. We'll get back to this in the chapter on the area between two curves.

The second theorem tells us how to find the derivative of an integral.

Example 3: Find $\dfrac{d}{dx}\displaystyle\int_1^x \cos t\, dt$.

The second Fundamental Theorem says that the derivative of this integral is just $\cos x$.

Example 4: Find $\dfrac{d}{dx}\displaystyle\int_2^x \left(1-t^3\right)\,dt$.

Here, the theorem says that the derivative of this integral is just $(1 - x^3)$.

Isn't this easy? Let's add a couple of nuances. First, the constant term in the limits of integration is a "dummy term." Any constant will give the same answer. For example:

$$\frac{d}{dx}\int_2^x \left(1-t^3\right)\,dt = \frac{d}{dx}\int_{-2}^x \left(1-t^3\right)dt = \frac{d}{dx}\int_\pi^x \left(1-t^3\right)dt = 1-x^3$$

In other words, all we're concerned with is the variable term.

Second, if the upper limit is a function of x, instead of just plain x, we multiply the answer by the derivative of that term. For example:

$$\frac{d}{dx}\int_2^{x^2} \left(1-t^3\right)\,dt = \left[1-\left(x^2\right)^3\right](2x) = \left(1-x^6\right)(2x)$$

Example 5: Find $\dfrac{d}{dx}\displaystyle\int_0^{3x^4} \left(t+4t^2\right)dt = \left[3x^4 + 4(3x^4)^2\right]\left(12x^3\right).$

Try these solved problems on your own. You know the drill.

PROBLEM 1. Find the average value of $f(x) = \dfrac{1}{x^2}$ on the interval $[1, 3]$.

Answer: According to the Mean Value Theorem, the average value is found by evaluating:

$$\frac{1}{3-1}\int_1^3 \frac{dx}{x^2}$$

Your result should be:

$$\frac{1}{2}\left(-\frac{1}{x}\right)\Big|_1^3 = \frac{1}{2}\left(-\frac{1}{3}+1\right) = \frac{1}{3}$$

PROBLEM 2. Find the average value of $f(x) = \sin x$ on the interval $\left[-\pi, \pi\right]$.

Answer: According to the Mean Value Theorem, the average value is found by evaluating:

$$\frac{1}{2\pi}\left(\int_{-\pi}^\pi \sin x\,dx\right)$$

Integrating, we get:

$$\frac{1}{2\pi}\left(-\cos x\right)\Big|_{-\pi}^\pi = \frac{1}{2\pi}\left(-\cos\pi + \cos(-\pi)\right) = 0$$

PROBLEM 3. Find $\dfrac{d}{dx}\displaystyle\int_1^x \dfrac{dt}{1-\sqrt[3]{t}}$.

Answer: According to the Second Fundamental Theorem of Calculus:

$$\frac{d}{dx}\int_1^x \frac{dt}{1-\sqrt[3]{t}} = \frac{1}{1-\sqrt[3]{x}}$$

PROBLEM 4. Find $\dfrac{d}{dx}\displaystyle\int_1^{x^2} \dfrac{t\,dt}{\sin t}$.

Answer: According to the Second Fundamental Theorem of Calculus:

$$\frac{d}{dx}\int_1^{x^2} \frac{t\,dt}{\sin t} = \frac{x^2}{\sin\left(x^2\right)}(2x) = \frac{2x^3}{\sin x^2}$$

PRACTICE PROBLEM SET 23

Now try these problems. The answers are in Chapter 21.

1. Find the average value of $f(x) = 4x\cos x^2$ on the interval $\left[0, \sqrt{\dfrac{\pi}{2}}\right]$.

2. Find the average value of $f(x) = \sqrt{x}$ on the interval $[0, 16]$.

3. Find the average value of $f(x) = \sqrt{1-x}$ on the interval $[-1, 1]$.

4. Find the average value of $f(x) = 2|x|$ on the interval $[-1, 1]$.

5. Find $\dfrac{d}{dx}\displaystyle\int_1^x \sin^2 t\,dt$.

6. Find $\dfrac{d}{dx}\displaystyle\int_5^{3x} \left(t^2-t\right)dt$.

7. Find $\dfrac{d}{dx}\displaystyle\int_0^{x^2} |t|\,dt$.

8. Find $\dfrac{d}{dx}\displaystyle\int_1^x -2\cos t\,dt$.

13

Exponential and Logarithmic Functions, Part Two

You've learned how to integrate polynomials and some of the trig functions (there are more of them to come), and you have the first technique of integration: *u*-substitution. Now it's time to learn how to integrate some other functions—namely, exponential and logarithmic functions. Yes, the long-awaited second part of Chapter 9. The first integral is the natural logarithm:

$$\int \frac{du}{u} = \ln|u| + C$$

Notice the absolute value in the logarithm. This ensures that you aren't taking the logarithm of a negative number. If you know that the term you're taking the log of is positive (for example, $x^2 + 1$), we can dispense with the absolute value marks. Let's do some examples.

Example 1: Find $\displaystyle\int \frac{5dx}{x+3}$.

Whenever an integrand contains a fraction, check to see if the integral is a logarithm. Usually, the process involves u-substitution. Let $u = x + 3$ and $du = dx$. Then:

$$\int \frac{5dx}{x+3} = 5\int \frac{du}{u} = 5\ln|u| + C$$

Substituting back, the final result is:

$$5\ln|x+3| + C$$

Example 2: Find $\displaystyle\int \frac{2x\ dx}{x^2 + 1}$.

Let $u = x^2 + 1\ du = 2xdx$ and substitute into the integrand:

$$\int \frac{2x\ dx}{x^2 + 1} = \int \frac{du}{u} = \ln|u| + C$$

Then substitute back:

$$\ln\left(x^2 + 1\right) + C$$

MORE INTEGRALS OF TRIG FUNCTIONS

Remember when we started antiderivatives and we didn't do the integral of tangent, cotangent, secant, and cosecant? Well, their time has come.

Example 3: Find $\displaystyle\int \tan x\ dx$.

First, rewrite this integral as

$$\int \frac{\sin x}{\cos x}\ dx$$

Now we let $u = \cos x$ and $du = -\sin x\ dx$ and substitute:

$$\int -\frac{du}{u}$$

Now, integrate and re-substitute:

$$\int -\frac{du}{u} = -\ln|u| = -\ln|\cos x| + C$$

Thus, $\int \tan x \, dx = -\ln|\cos x| + C$.

Example 4: Find $\int \cot x \, dx$.

Just as before, rewrite this integral in terms of sine and cosine:

$$\int \frac{\cos x}{\sin x} \, dx$$

Now we let $u = \sin x$ and $du = \cos x \, dx$ and substitute:

$$\int \frac{du}{u}$$

Now, integrate:

$$\ln|u| + C = \ln|\sin x| + C$$

Therefore, $\int \cot x \, dx = \ln|\sin x| + C$. This looks a lot like the previous example, doesn't it?

Example 5: Find $\int \sec x \, dx$.

You could rewrite this integral as:

$$\int \frac{1}{\cos x} \, dx$$

However, if you try u-substitution at this point, it won't work. So what should you do? You'll probably never guess, so we'll show you: Multiply the sec x by $\dfrac{\sec x + \tan x}{\sec x + \tan x}$. This gives you:

$$\int \sec x \, dx = \int \sec x \frac{\sec x + \tan x}{\sec x + \tan x} \, dx = \int \frac{\sec^2 x + \sec x \tan x}{\sec x + \tan x} \, dx$$

Now you can do u-substitution. Let $u = \sec x + \tan x \quad du = (\sec x \tan x + \sec^2 x) \, dx$. Then rewrite the integral as:

$$\int \frac{du}{u}$$

Pretty slick, huh?

The rest goes according to plan as you integrate:

$$\int \frac{du}{u} = \ln |u| + C = \ln |\sec x + \tan x| + C$$

Therefore, $\int \sec x \, dx = \ln |\sec x + \tan x| + C$.

Example 6: Find $\int \csc x \, dx$.

You guessed it! Multiply $\csc x$ by $\dfrac{\csc x + \cot x}{\csc x + \cot x} \, dx$. This gives you:

$$\int \csc x \, \frac{\csc x + \cot x}{\csc x + \cot x} \, dx = \int \frac{\csc^2 x + \csc x \cot x}{\csc x + \cot x} \, dx$$

Let $u = \csc x + \cot x$ and $du = (-\csc x \cot x - \csc^2 x) \, dx$. And, just as in Example 5, you can rewrite the integral as:

$$\int -\frac{du}{u}$$

And integrate:

$$\int -\frac{du}{u} = -\ln |u| + C = -\ln |\csc x + \cot x| + C$$

Therefore, $\int \csc x \, dx = -\ln |\csc x + \cot x| + C$.

As we do more integrals, the natural log will turn up over and over. It's important that you get good at recognizing when integrating requires the use of the natural log.

INTEGRATING e^x AND a^x

Now let's learn how to find the integral of e^x. Remember that $\dfrac{d}{dx} e^x = e^x$? Well, you should be able to predict the formula below:

$$\int e^u \, du = e^u + C$$

As with the natural logarithm, most of these integrals use u-substitution.

Example 7: Find $\int e^{7x}dx$.

Let $u = 7x$, $du = 7dx$, and $\frac{1}{7}du = dx$. Then you have:

$$\int e^{7x}dx = \frac{1}{7}\int e^u du = \frac{1}{7}e^u + C$$

Substituting back, you get:

$$\frac{1}{7}e^{7x} + C$$

In fact, whenever you see $\int e^{kx}dx$, where k is a constant, the integral is:

$$\int e^{kx}dx = \frac{1}{k}e^{kx} + C$$

Example 8: Find $\int xe^{3x^2+1}\,dx$.

Let $u = 3x^2 + 1$, $du = 6x\,dx$, and $\frac{1}{6}\,du = x\,dx$. The result is:

$$\int xe^{3x+1}\,dx = \frac{1}{6}\int e^u du = \frac{1}{6}e^u + C$$

Now it's time to put the x's back in:

$$\frac{1}{6}e^{3x^2+1} + C$$

Example 9: Find $\int e^{\sin x}\cos x\,dx$.

Let $u = \sin x$ and $du = \cos x\,dx$. The substitution here couldn't be simpler:

$$\int e^u du = e^u + C = e^{\sin x} + C$$

As you can see, these integrals are pretty straightforward. The key is to use u-substitution to transform nasty-looking integrals into simple ones.

There's another type of exponential function whose integral you'll have to find occasionally:

$$\int a^u du$$

As you should recall from your rules of logarithms and exponents, the term a^u can be written as $e^{u \ln a}$. Because $\ln a$ is a constant, we can transform $\int a^u du$ into $\int e^{u \ln a} du$. If you integrate this, you'll get:

$$\int e^{u \ln a} du = \frac{1}{\ln a} e^{u \ln a} + C$$

Now substituting back a^u for $e^{u \ln a}$:

$$\int a^u du = \frac{1}{\ln a} a^u + C$$

Example 10: Find $\int 5^x dx$.

Follow the rule we just derived:

$$\int 5^x dx = \frac{1}{\ln 5} 5^x + C$$

Because these integrals don't show up too often on the AP exam, this is the last you'll see of them in this book. You should, however, be able to integrate them using the rule, or by converting them into a form of $\int e^u du$.

Try these on your own. Do each problem with the answers covered, then check your answer.

PROBLEM 1. Evaluate $\int \frac{dx}{3x}$.

Answer: Move the constant term outside of the integral, like this:

$$\frac{1}{3} \int \frac{dx}{x}$$

Now you can integrate:

$$\frac{1}{3} \int \frac{dx}{x} = \frac{1}{3} \ln|x| + C$$

PROBLEM 2. Evaluate $\int \dfrac{3x^2 dx}{x^3 - 1}$.

Answer: Let $u = x^3 - 1$ and $du = 3x^2\, dx$, and substitute:

$$\int \frac{du}{u}$$

Now integrate:

$$\ln |u| + C$$

And substitute back:

$$\ln |x^3 - 1| + C$$

PROBLEM 3. Evaluate $\int e^{5x} dx$.

Answer: Let $u = 5x$ and $du = 5dx$. Then $\dfrac{1}{5}\, du = dx$. Substitute in:

$$\frac{1}{5} \int e^u du$$

Integrate:

$$\frac{1}{5} e^u + C$$

And substitute back:

$$\frac{1}{5} e^{5x} + C$$

PROBLEM 4. Evaluate $\int 2^{3x} dx$.

Answer: Let $u = 3x$ and $du = 3dx$. Then $\dfrac{1}{3}\, du = dx$. Make the substitution:

$$\frac{1}{3} \int 2^u du$$

Integrate according to the rule. Your result should be:

$$\frac{1}{3\ln 2} 2^u + C$$

Now get back to the expression as a function of x:

$$\frac{1}{3\ln 2} 2^{3x} + C = \frac{1}{\ln 8} 2^{3x} + C$$

PRACTICE PROBLEM SET 24

Evaluate the following integrals. The answers are in Chapter 21.

1. $\displaystyle\int \frac{\sec^2 x}{\tan x}\,dx$

2. $\displaystyle\int \frac{\cos x}{1-\sin x}\,dx$

3. $\displaystyle\int \frac{1}{x\ln x}\,dx$

4. $\displaystyle\int \frac{1}{x}\cos(\ln x)\,dx$

5. $\displaystyle\int \frac{\sin x - \cos x}{\cos x}\,dx$

6. $\displaystyle\int \frac{dx}{\sqrt{x}\left(1+2\sqrt{x}\right)}$

7. $\displaystyle\int \frac{e^x\,dx}{1+e^x}$

8. $\displaystyle\int x e^{5x^2-1}\,dx$

9. $\displaystyle\int e^x \cos\left(2+e^x\right)dx$

10. $\displaystyle\int \frac{e^x + e^{-x}}{e^x - e^{-x}}\,dx$

11. $\displaystyle\int x 4^{-x^2}\,dx$

12. $\displaystyle\int 7^{\sin x} \cos x\,dx$

14

The Area Between Two Curves

These next two units discuss some of the most difficult topics you'll encounter in AP calculus. For some reason, students have terrible trouble setting up these problems, and ETS knows it. Believe it or not, ETS actually only asks relatively simple versions of these problems on the exam.

Unfortunately, this unit and the next are always on the AP. We'll try to make them as simple as possible. You've already learned that if you want to find the area under a curve, you can integrate the function of the curve by using the endpoints as limits. So far, though, we've only talked about the area between a curve and the *x*-axis. What if you have to find the area between two curves?

VERTICAL SLICES

Suppose you wanted to find the area between the curve $y = x$ and the curve $y = x^2$ from $x = 2$ to $x = 4$. First, sketch the curves:

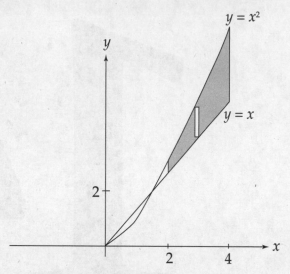

You can find the area by slicing up the region vertically, into a bunch of infinitely thin strips, and adding up the areas of all the strips. The height of each strip is $x^2 - x$, and the width of each strip is dx. Add up all the strips by using the integral:

$$\int_2^4 \left(x^2 - x\right) dx$$

Then, evaluate it:

$$\left(\frac{x^3}{3} - \frac{x^2}{2}\right)\Bigg|_2^4 = \left(\frac{64}{3} - \frac{16}{2}\right) - \left(\frac{8}{3} - \frac{4}{2}\right) = \frac{38}{3}$$

That wasn't so hard, was it? Don't worry. The process gets more complicated, but the idea remains the same. Now let's generalize this and come up with a rule:

> If a region is bounded by $f(x)$ above and $g(x)$ below at all points of the interval $[a, b]$, then the area of the region is given by:
>
> $$\int_a^b [f(x) - g(x)] dx$$

Example 1: Find the area of the region between the parabola $y = 1 - x^2$ and the line $y = 1 - x$.

First, make a sketch of the region:

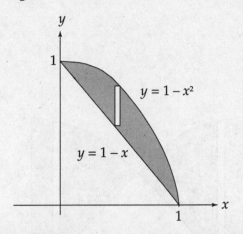

To find the points of intersection of the graphs, set the two equations equal to each other and solve for x:

$$1 - x^2 = 1 - x$$
$$x^2 - x = 0$$
$$x(x - 1) = 0$$
$$x = 0, 1$$

The left-hand edge of the region is $x = 0$ and the right-hand edge is $x = 1$, so the limits of integration are from 0 to 1.

Next, note that the top curve is always $y = 1 - x^2$ and the bottom curve is always $y = 1 - x$. (If the region has a place where the top and bottom curve switch, you need to make two integrals, one for each region. Fortunately, that's not the case here.) Thus, we need to evaluate:

$$\int_0^1 \left[\left(1 - x^2\right) - \left(1 - x\right) \right] dx$$

$$\int_0^1 \left[\left(1 - x^2\right) - \left(1 - x\right) \right] dx = \int_0^1 \left(-x^2 + x\right)\, dx = \left(-\frac{x^3}{3} + \frac{x^2}{2} \right)\Bigg|_0^1 = \frac{1}{6}$$

Sometimes you're given the endpoints of the region; sometimes you have to find them on your own.

Example 2: Find the area of the region between the curve $y = \sin x$ and the curve $y = \cos x$ from 0 to $\dfrac{\pi}{2}$.

First, sketch the region:

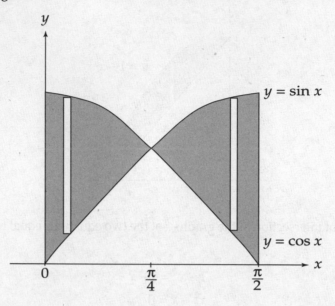

Notice that $\cos x$ is on top between 0 and $\dfrac{\pi}{4}$, then $\sin x$ is on top between $\dfrac{\pi}{4}$ and $\dfrac{\pi}{2}$. The point where they cross is $\dfrac{\pi}{4}$, so you have to divide the area into two integrals: one from 0 to $\dfrac{\pi}{4}$, and the other from $\dfrac{\pi}{4}$ to $\dfrac{\pi}{2}$. In the first region, $\cos x$ is above $\sin x$, so the integral to evaluate is:

$$\int_0^{\frac{\pi}{4}} (\cos x - \sin x)\, dx$$

The integral of the second region is a little different, because $\sin x$ is above $\cos x$:

$$\int_{\frac{\pi}{4}}^{\frac{\pi}{2}} (\sin x - \cos x)\, dx$$

If you add the two integrals, you'll get the area of the whole region:

$$\int_0^{\frac{\pi}{4}} (\cos x - \sin x)\, dx = (\sin x + \cos x)\Big|_0^{\frac{\pi}{2}} = \sqrt{2} - 1$$

$$\int_{\frac{\pi}{4}}^{\frac{\pi}{2}} (\sin x - \cos x)\, dx = (-\cos x - \sin x)\Big|_{\frac{\pi}{4}}^{\frac{\pi}{2}} = \sqrt{2} - 1$$

Adding these, we get that the area is $2\sqrt{2} - 2$.

HORIZONTAL SLICES

Now for the fun part. We can slice a region vertically when one function is at the top of our section and a different function is at the bottom. But what if the same function is both the top and the bottom of the slice (what we call a double-valued function)? You have to slice the region horizontally.

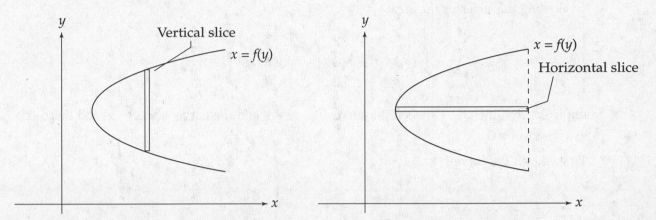

If we were to slice vertically, as in the left-hand picture, we'd have a problem. But if we were to slice horizontally, as in the right-hand picture, we don't have a problem. Instead of integrating an equation $f(x)$ with respect to x, we need to integrate an equation $f(y)$ with respect to y. As a result, our area formula changes a little:

> If a region is bounded by $f(y)$ on the right and $g(y)$ on the left at all points of the interval $[c, d]$, then the area of the region is given by:
>
> $$\int_c^d \left[f(y) - g(y) \right] dy$$

Example 3: Find the area of the region between the curve $x = y^2$ and the curve $x = y + 6$ from $y = 0$ to $y = 3$.

First, sketch the region.

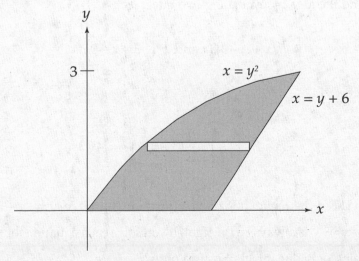

When you slice up the area horizontally, the right end of each section is the curve $x = y + 6$, and the left end of each section is always the curve $x = y^2$. Now set up our integral:

$$\int_0^3 \left(y + 6 - y^2\right)dy$$

Evaluating this gives us the area:

$$\int_0^3 \left(y + 6 - y^2\right)dy = \left(\frac{y^2}{2} + 6y - \frac{y^3}{3}\right)\Bigg|_0^3 = \frac{27}{2}$$

Example 4: Find the area between the curve $y = \sqrt{x+3}$ and the curve $y = \sqrt{3-x}$ and the x-axis from $x = -3$ to $x = 3$.

First, sketch the curves:

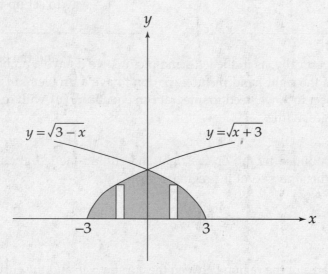

From $x = -3$ to $x = 0$, if you slice the region vertically, the curve $y = \sqrt{x+3}$ is on top, and the x-axis is on the bottom; from $x = 0$ to $x = 3$, the curve $y = \sqrt{3-x}$ is on top and the x-axis is on the bottom. Therefore, you can find the area by evaluating two integrals:

$$\int_{-3}^0 \left(\sqrt{x+3} - 0\right)dx \text{ and } \int_0^3 \left(\sqrt{3-x} - 0\right)dx$$

Your results should be:

$$\frac{2}{3}(x+3)^{\frac{3}{2}}\Bigg|_{-3}^0 + \left(-\frac{2}{3}(3-x)^{\frac{3}{2}}\right)\Bigg|_0^3 = 4\sqrt{3}$$

Let's suppose you sliced the region horizontally instead. The curve $y = \sqrt{x+3}$ is always on the left, and the curve $y = \sqrt{3-x}$ is always on the right. If you solve each equation for x in terms of y, you save some time by using only one integral instead of two.

The two equations are $x = y^2 - 3$ and $x = 3 - y^2$. We also have to change the limits of integration from x-limits to y-limits. The two curves intersect at $y = \sqrt{3}$, so our limits of integration are from $y = 0$ to $y = \sqrt{3}$. The new integral is:

$$\int_0^{\sqrt{3}} \left[(3 - y^2) - (y^2 - 3)\right] dy = \int_0^{\sqrt{3}} (6 - 2y^2) dy = 6y - \frac{2y^3}{3}\Big|_0^{\sqrt{3}} = 4\sqrt{3}$$

You get the same answer no matter which way you integrate (as long as you do it right!). The challenge of area problems is determining which way to integrate, and converting the equation to different terms. Unfortunately, there's no simple rule for how to do this. You have to look at the region and figure out its endpoints, as well as where the curves are with respect to each other.

Once you can do that, then the actual set-up of the integral(s) isn't that hard. Sometimes, evaluating the integrals isn't easy; however, if the integral of an AP question is difficult to evaluate, you'll only be required to set it up, not to evaluate it.

Here are some sample problems. On each, decide the best way to set up the integrals, and then evaluate them. Then check your answer.

PROBLEM 1. Find the area of the region between the curve $y = 3 - x^2$ and the line $y = 1 - x$ from $x = 0$ to $x = 2$.

Answer: First, make a sketch:

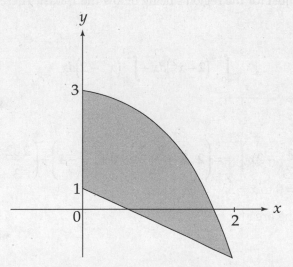

Because the curve $y = 3 - x^2$ is always above $y = 1 - x$ within the interval, you have to evaluate the following integral:

$$\int_0^2 \left[(3 - x^2) - (1 - x)\right] dx = \int_0^2 (2 + x - x^2) dx$$

Therefore, the area of the region is:

$$\left(2x + \frac{x^2}{2} - \frac{x^3}{3}\right)\Big|_0^2 = \frac{10}{3}$$

PROBLEM 2. Find the area between the x-axis and the curve $y = 2 - x^2$ from $x = 0$ to $x = 2$.

Answer: First, sketch the graph over the interval:

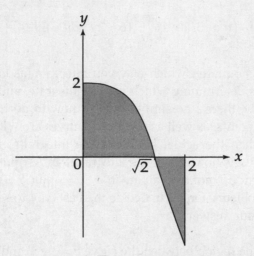

Because the curve crosses the x-axis at $\sqrt{2}$, you have to divide the region into two parts: from $x = 0$ to $x = \sqrt{2}$ and from $x = \sqrt{2}$ to $x = 2$. In the latter region, you'll need to i ntegrate $y = -\left(2 - x^2\right) = x^2 - 2$ to adjust for the region's being below the x-axis. Therefore, we can find the area by evaluating:

$$\int_0^{\sqrt{2}} \left(2 - x^2\right)dx + \int_{\sqrt{2}}^2 \left(x^2 - 2\right)dx$$

Integrating, we get:

$$\left(2x + -\frac{x^3}{3}\right)\Bigg|_0^{\sqrt{2}} + \left(\frac{x^3}{3} - 2x\right)\Bigg|_{\sqrt{2}}^2 = \left(2\sqrt{2} - \frac{2\sqrt{2}}{3}\right) - 0 + \left(\frac{8}{3} - 4\right) - \left(\frac{2\sqrt{2}}{3} - 2\sqrt{2}\right) = \frac{8\sqrt{2} - 4}{3}$$

PROBLEM 3. Find the area of the region between the curve $x = y^2 - 4y$ and the line $x = y$.

Answer: First, sketch the graph over the interval:

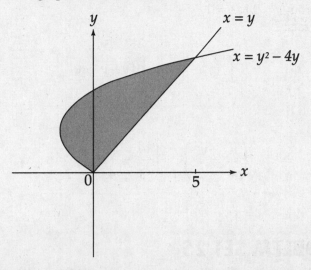

You don't have the endpoints this time, so you need to find where the two curves intersect. If you set them equal to each other, they intersect at $y = 0$ and at $y = 5$. The curve $x = y^2 - 4y$ is always to the left of $x = y$ over the interval we just found, so we can evaluate the following integral:

$$\int_0^5 \left[y - \left(y^2 - 4y \right) \right] dy = \int_0^5 \left(5y - y^2 \right) dy$$

The result of the integration should be:

$$\left(\frac{5y^2}{2} - \frac{y^3}{3} \right)\Bigg|_0^5 = \frac{125}{6}$$

PROBLEM 4. Find the area between the curve $x = y^3 - y$ and the line $x = 0$ (the y-axis).

Answer: First, sketch the graph over the interval:

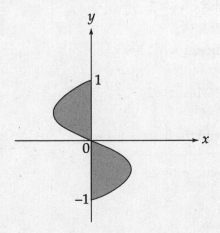

Next, find where the two curves intersect. By setting $y^3 - y = 0$, you'll find that they intersect at $y = -1$, $y = 0$, and $y = 1$. Notice that the curve is to the right of the y-axis from $y = -1$ to $y = 0$ and to the left of the y-axis from $y = 0$ to $y = 1$. Thus, the region must be divided into two parts: from $y = -1$ to $y = 0$ and from $y = 0$ to $y = 1$.

Set up the two integrals:

$$\int_{-1}^{0} \left(y^3 - y\right) dy + \int_{0}^{1} \left(y - y^3\right) dy$$

And integrate them:

$$\left(\frac{y^4}{4} - \frac{y^2}{2}\right)\Bigg|_{-1}^{0} + \left(\frac{y^2}{2} - \frac{y^4}{4}\right)\Bigg|_{0}^{1} = \frac{1}{2}$$

PRACTICE PROBLEM SET 25

Find the area of the region between the two curves in each problem, and be sure to sketch each one. (We only gave you endpoints in one of them.) The answers are in Chapter 21.

1. The curve $y = x^2 - 2$ and the line $y = 2$.

2. The curve $y = x^2$ and the curve $y = 4x - x^2$.

3. The curve $y = x^3$ and the curve $y = 3x^2 - 4$.

4. The curve $y = x^2 - 4x - 5$ and the curve $y = 2x - 5$.

5. The curve $y = x^3$ and the x-axis, from $x = -1$ to $x = 2$.

6. The curve $x = y^2$ and the line $x = y + 2$.

7. The curve $x = y^2$ and the curve $x = 3 - 2y^2$.

8. The curve $x = y^3 - y^2$ and the line $x = 2y$.

9. The curve $x = y^2 - 4y + 2$ and the line $x = y - 2$.

10. The curve $x = y^{\frac{2}{3}}$ and the curve $x = 2 - y^4$.

15

The Volume of a Solid of Revolution

Does the chapter title leave you in a cold sweat? Don't worry. You're not alone. This chapter covers a topic widely seen as one of the most difficult on the AP exam. There is *always* a volume question on the test. The good news is that you're almost never asked to evaluate the integral—you usually only have to set it up. The difficulty with this chapter, as with Chapter 14, is that there aren't any simple rules to follow. You have to draw the picture and figure it out.

In this chapter we're going to take the region between two curves, rotate it around a line (usually the *x*- or *y*-axis), and find the volume of the region. There are two methods of doing this: the **washers method** and the **cylindrical shells method**. Sometimes you'll hear the washers method called the **disk method**, but a disk is only a washer without a hole in the middle.

WASHERS AND DISKS

Let's look at the region between the curve $y = \sqrt{x}$ and the x-axis (the curve $y = 0$), from $x = 0$ to $x = 1$, and revolve it about the x-axis. The picture looks like this:

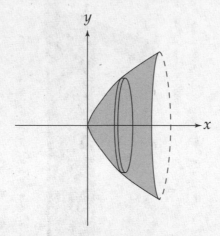

If you slice the resulting solid perpendicular to the x-axis, each cross-section of the solid is a circle, or disk (hence the phrase "disk method"). The radii of each disk vary from one value of x to the next, but you can find each radius by plugging it into the equation for y: Each radius is $\sqrt{x}$. The area of each disk is therefore:

$$\pi\left(\sqrt{x}\right)^2 = \pi x$$

Each disk is infinitesimally thin, so its thickness is dx; if you add up the volumes of all the disks, you'll get the entire volume. The way to add these up is by using the integral, with the endpoints of the interval as the limits of integration. Therefore, to find the volume, evaluate the integral:

$$\int_0^1 \pi x \, dx$$

Now, let's generalize this. If you have a region whose area is bounded by the curve $y = f(x)$ and the x-axis on the interval $[a, b]$, each disk has a radius of $f(x)$, and the area of each disk will be:

$$\pi\left[f(x)\right]^2$$

To find the volume, evaluate the integral:

$$\pi\int_a^b \left[f(x)\right]^2 dx$$

This is the formula for finding the volume using disks.

Example 1: Find the volume of the solid that results when the region between the curve $y = x$ and the x-axis, from $x = 0$ to $x = 1$, is revolved about the x-axis.

As always, sketch the region to get a better look at the problem:

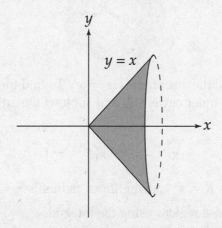

When you slice vertically, the top curve is $y = x$ and the limits of integration are from $x = 0$ to $x = 1$. Using our formula, we evaluate the integral:

$$\pi \int_0^1 x^2 dx$$

The result is:

$$\pi \int_0^1 x^2 dx = \pi \frac{x^3}{3}\bigg|_0^1 = \frac{\pi}{3}$$

By the way, did you notice that the solid in the problem is a cone with a height and radius of 1? The formula for the volume of a cone is $\frac{1}{3}\pi r^2 h$, so you should expect to get $\frac{\pi}{3}$.

Now, let's figure out how to find the volume of the solid that results when we revolve a region that does not touch the x-axis. Consider the region bounded above by the curve $y = x^3$ and below by the curve $y = x^2$, from $x = 2$ to $x = 4$, which is revolved about the x-axis. Sketch the region first:

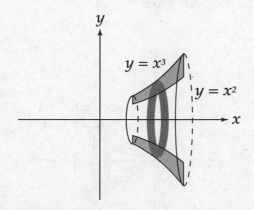

If you slice this region vertically, each cross-section looks like a washer (hence the phrase "washer method"):

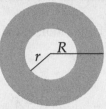

The outer radius is $R = x^3$ and the inner radius is $r = x^2$. To find the area of the region between the two circles, take the area of the outer circle, πR^2, and subtract the area of the inner circle, πr^2.

We can simplify this to:

$$\pi R^2 - \pi r^2 = \pi\left(R^2 - r^2\right)$$

Because the outer radius is $R = x^3$ and the inner radius is $r = x^2$, the area of each region is $\pi\left(x^6 - x^4\right)$. You can sum up these regions using the integral:

$$\pi \int_2^4 \left(x^6 - x^4\right)dx$$

Here's the general idea: In a region whose area is bounded above by the curve $y = f(x)$ and below by the curve $y = g(x)$, on the interval $[a, b]$, then each washer will have an area of:

$$\pi\left[f(x)^2 - g(x)^2\right]$$

To find the volume, evaluate the integral:

$$\pi\int_a^b \left[f(x)^2 - g(x)^2\right]dx$$

This is the formula for finding the volume using washers when the region is rotated around the x-axis.

Example 2: Find the volume of the solid that results when the region bounded by $y = x$ and $y = x^2$, from $x = 0$ to $x = 1$, is revolved about the x-axis.

Sketch it first:

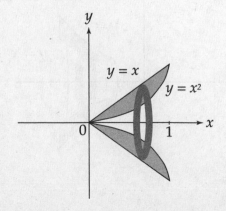

The top curve is $y = x$ and the bottom curve is $y = x^2$ throughout the region. Then our formula tells us that we evaluate the integral:

$$\pi \int_0^1 (x^2 - x^4)\,dx$$

The result is:

$$\pi \int_0^1 (x^2 - x^4)\,dx = \pi \left(\frac{x^3}{3} - \frac{x^5}{5} \right) \bigg|_0^1 = \frac{2\pi}{15}$$

Suppose the region we're interested in is revolved around the y-axis instead of the x-axis. Now, to find the volume, you have to slice the region horizontally instead of vertically. We discussed how to do this in the previous unit on area.

Now, if you have a region whose area is bounded on the right by the curve $x = f(y)$ and on the left by the curve $x = g(y)$, on the interval $[c, d]$, then each washer has an area of:

$$\pi \left[f(y)^2 - g(y)^2 \right]$$

To find the volume, evaluate the integral:

$$\pi \int_c^d \left[f(y)^2 - g(y)^2 \right] dy$$

This is the formula for finding the volume using washers when the region is rotated around the y-axis.

Example 3: Find the volume of the solid that results when the region bounded by the curve $x = y^2$ and the curve $x = y^3$, from $y = 0$ to $y = 1$ is revolved about the y-axis.

Sketch away:

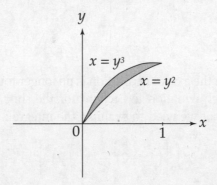

Since $x = y^2$ is always on the outside and $x = y^3$ is always on the inside, you have to evaluate the integral:

$$\pi \int_0^1 (y^4 - y^6)\,dy$$

Here's what you should get:

$$\pi\int_0^1\left(y^4-y^6\right)dx=\pi\left[\frac{y^5}{5}-\frac{y^7}{7}\right]_0^1=\frac{2\pi}{35}$$

There's only one more nuance to cover. Sometimes you'll have to revolve the region about a line instead of one of the axes. If so, this will affect the radii of the washers; you'll have to adjust the integral to reflect the shift. Once you draw a picture, it usually isn't too hard to see the difference.

Example 4: Find the volume of the solid that results when the area bounded by the curve $y=x^2$ and the curve $y=4x$ is revolved about the line $y=-2$. <u>Set up but do not evaluate the integral</u>. (This is how the AP exam will say it!)

You're not given the limits of integration here, so you need to find where the two curves intersect by setting the equations equal to each other:

$$x^2=4x$$

$$x^2-4x=0$$

$$x=0,4$$

These will be our limits of integration. Next, sketch the curve:

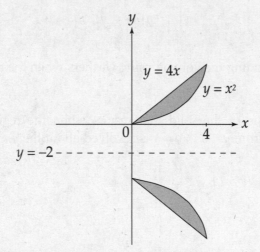

Notice that the distance from the axis of revolution is no longer found by just using each equation. Now, you need to add 2 to each equation to account for the shift in the axis. Thus, the radii are x^2+2 and $4x+2$. This means that we need to evaluate the integral:

$$\pi\int_0^4\left[\left(4x+2\right)^2-\left(x^2+2\right)^2\right]dx$$

Suppose instead that the region was revolved about the line $x = -2$. Sketch the region again:

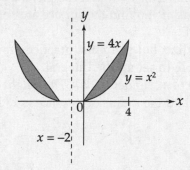

You'll have to slice the region horizontally this time; this means you're going to solve each equation for x in terms of y: $x = \sqrt{y}$ and $x = \dfrac{y}{4}$. We also need to find the y-coordinates of the intersection of the two curves: $y = 0, 16$.

Notice also that, again, each radius is going to be increased by 2 to reflect the shift in the axis of revolution. Thus we will have to evaluate the integral:

$$\pi \int_0^{16} \left[\left(\sqrt{y} + 2\right)^2 - \left(\frac{y}{4} + 2\right)^2 \right] dy$$

Finding the volumes isn't that hard, once you've drawn a picture, figured out whether you need to slice vertically or horizontally, and determined whether the axis of revolution has been shifted. Sometimes, though, there will be times when you want to slice vertically yet revolve around the y-axis (or slice horizontally yet revolve around the x-axis). Here's the method for finding volumes in this way.

CYLINDRICAL SHELLS

Let's examine the region bounded above by the curve $y = 2 - x^2$ and below by the curve $y = x^2$, from $x = 0$ to $x = 1$. Suppose you had to revolve the region about the y-axis instead of the x-axis:

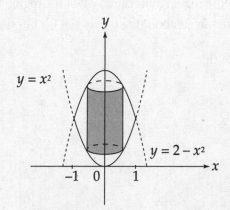

If you slice the region vertically and revolve the slice, you won't get a washer; you'll get a cylinder instead. Because each slice is an infinitesimally thin rectangle, the cylinder's "thickness" is also very, very thin, but real nonetheless. Thus, if you find the surface area of each cylinder and add them up, you'll get the volume of the region.

We know it's difficult to visualize, but you must practice drawing these pictures. If you can't draw the picture, you won't be able to set up the integral.

The formula for the surface area of a cylinder is $2\pi rh$. The height of the cylinder is the length of the vertical slice, $(2 - x^2) - x^2 = 2 - 2x^2$ and the radius of the slice is x. Thus, evaluate the integral:

$$2\pi \int_0^1 x\left(2 - 2x^2\right) dx$$

The math goes like this:

$$2\pi \int_0^1 x\left(2 - 2x^2\right) dx = 2\pi \int_0^1 \left(2x - 2x^3\right) dx = 2\pi \left(x^2 - \frac{x^4}{2} \right) \Bigg|_0^1 = \pi$$

Suppose you tried to slice the region horizontally and use washers. You'd have to convert each equation and find the new limits of integration. Because the region is not bounded by the same pair of curves throughout, you would have to evaluate the region using several integrals. The cylindrical shells method was invented precisely so you can avoid this.

From a general standpoint: If we have a region whose area is bounded above by the curve $y = f(x)$ and below by the curve $y = g(x)$, on the interval $[a, b]$, then each cylinder will have a height of $f(x) - g(x)$, a radius of x, and an area of $2\pi x\left[f(x) - g(x)\right]$.

To find the volume, evaluate the integral:

$$2\pi \int_a^b x\left[f(x) - g(x)\right] dx$$

This is the formula for finding the volume using cylindrical shells when the region is rotated around the y-axis.

Example 5: Find the volume of the region that results when the region bounded by the curve $y = \sqrt{x}$, the x-axis, and the line $x = 9$ is revolved about the y-axis. <u>Set up but do not evaluate the integral</u>.

Your sketch should look like this:

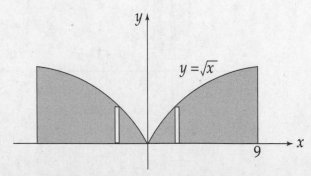

Notice that the limits of integration are from $x = 0$ to $x = 9$, and that each vertical slice is bounded from above by the curve $y = \sqrt{x}$ and from below by the x-axis ($y = 0$). We need to evaluate the integral:

$$2\pi\int_0^9 x\left(\sqrt{x} - 0\right)dx = 2\pi\int_0^9 x\left(\sqrt{x}\right)dx$$

Example 6: Find the volume that results when the region in Example 5 is revolved about the line $x = -1$. <u>Set up but do not evaluate the integral.</u>

Sketch the figure:

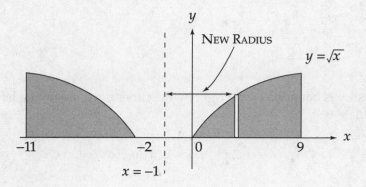

If you slice the region vertically, the height of the shell doesn't change because of the shift in axis of revolution, but you have to add 1 to each radius.

Our integral thus becomes:

$$2\pi\int_0^9 (x+1)\left(\sqrt{x}\right)dx$$

The last formula you need to learn involves slicing the region horizontally and revolving it about the x-axis. As you probably guessed, you'll get a cylindrical shell:

If you have a region whose area is bounded on the right by the curve $x = f(y)$ and on the left by the curve $x = g(y)$, on the interval $[c, d]$, then each cylinder will have a height of $f(y) - g(y)$, a radius of y, and an area of $2\pi y\big[f(y) - g(y)\big]$.

To find the volume, evaluate the integral:

$$2\pi\int_c^d y\big[f(y) - g(y)\big]dy$$

This is the formula for finding the volume using cylindrical shells when the region is rotated around the x-axis.

Example 7: Find the volume of the region that results when the region bounded by the curve $x = y^3$ and the line $x = y$, from $y = 0$ to $y = 1$, is rotated about the x-axis. <u>Set up but do not evaluate the integral</u>.

Let your sketch be your guide:

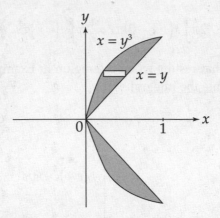

Each horizontal slice is bounded on the right by the curve $x = y$ and on the left by the line $x = y^3$. The integral to evaluate is:

$$2\pi \int_0^1 y\left(y - y^3\right) dy$$

Suppose that you had to revolve this region about the line $y = -1$ instead. Now the region looks like this:

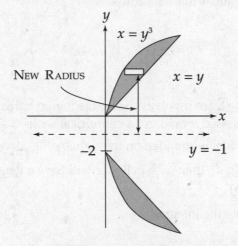

The radius of each cylinder is increased by 1 because of the shift in the axis of revolution, so the integral looks like this:

$$2\pi \int_0^1 (y + 1)\left(y - y^3\right) dy$$

Wasn't this fun? Volumes of Solids of Revolution require you to sketch the region carefully and to decide whether it'll be easier to slice the region vertically or horizontally. Once you figure out the slices' boundaries and the limits of integration (and you've adjusted for an axis of revolution, if necessary), it's just a matter of plugging into the integral. Usually, you won't be asked to evaluate the integral unless it's a simple one. Once you've conquered this topic, you're ready for anything.

VOLUMES OF SOLIDS WITH KNOWN CROSS-SECTIONS

There is one other type of volume that you need to be able to find. Sometimes, you will be given an object where you know the shape of the base and where perpendicular cross-sections are all the same regular, planar geometric shape. These sound hard, but are actually quite straightforward. This is easiest to explain through an example.

Example 8: Suppose we are asked to find the volume of a solid whose base is the circle $x^2 + y^2 = 4$, and where cross-sections perpendicular to the x-axis are all squares whose sides lie on the base of the circle. How would we find the volume?

First, make a drawing of the circle:

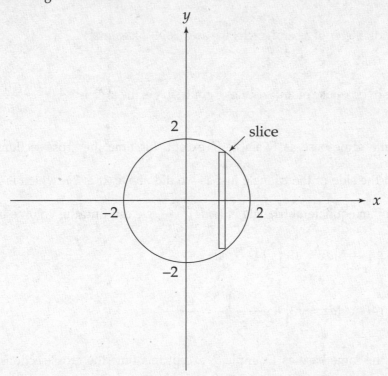

What this problem is telling us is that every time we make a vertical slice, the slice is the length of the base of a square. If we want to find the volume of the solid, all we have to do is integrate the area of the square, from one endpoint of the circle to the other.

The side of the square is the vertical slice whose length is $2y$, which we can find by solving the equation of the circle for y and multiplying by 2. We get $y = \sqrt{4 - x^2}$. Then the length of a side of the square is $2\sqrt{4 - x^2}$. Because the area of a square is $side^2$, we can find the volume by: $\int_{-2}^{2}(16 - 4x^2)dx$.

Let's perform the integration, although on some problems you will be permitted to find the answer with a calculator.

$$\int_{-2}^{2}\left(16-4x^2\right)dx = \left(16x - \frac{x^3}{3}\right)\Bigg|_{-2}^{2} = \left(32 - \frac{32}{3}\right) - \left(-32 + \frac{32}{3}\right)$$

$$= 64 - \frac{64}{3} = \frac{128}{3}$$

As you can see, the technique is very simple. First you find the side of the cross-section in terms of y. This will involve a vertical slice. Then you plug the side into the equation for the area of the cross-section. Then integrate the area from one endpoint of the base to the other. On the AP exam, cross-sections will be squares, equilateral triangles, circles or semi-circles, or maybe isosceles right triangles. So here are some handy formulae to know.

Given the side of an equilateral triangle, the area is: $A = (side)^2 \frac{\sqrt{3}}{4}$

Given the diameter of a semi-circle, the area is: $A = (diameter)^2 \frac{\pi}{8}$

Given the hypotenuse of an isosceles right triangle, the area is: $A = \frac{(hypotenuse)^2}{4}$

Example 9: Use the same base as Example 8, except this time the cross-sections are equilateral triangles. We find the side of the triangle just as we did above. It is $2y$, which is $2\sqrt{4-x^2}$. Now, because the area of an equilateral triangle is $(side)^2 \frac{\sqrt{3}}{4}$, we can find the volume by evaluating the integral $\frac{\sqrt{3}}{4}\int_{-2}^{2}(4)(4-x^2)dx = \sqrt{3}\int_{-2}^{2}(4-x^2)dx$.

We get: $\sqrt{3}\int_{-2}^{2}(4-x^2)dx = \sqrt{3}\left(4x - \frac{x^3}{3}\right)\Bigg|_{-2}^{2} = \frac{32\sqrt{3}}{3}$

Example 10: Use the same base as Example 8, except this time the cross-sections are semi-circles whose diameters lie on the base. We find the side of the semi-circle just as we did above. It is $2y$, which is $2\sqrt{4-x^2}$. Now, because the area of a semi-circle is $(diameter)^2 \frac{\pi}{8}$, we can find the volume by evaluating the integral $\frac{\pi}{8}\int_{-2}^{2}(4)(4-x^2)dx = \frac{\pi}{2}\int_{-2}^{2}(4-x^2)dx$.

We get: $\dfrac{\pi}{2}\displaystyle\int_{-2}^{2}\left(4-x^2\right)dx = \dfrac{\pi}{2}\left(4x-\dfrac{x^3}{3}\right)\Bigg|_{-2}^{2} - \dfrac{16\pi}{3}$

Here are some solved problems. Do each problem, covering the answer first, then check your answer.

PROBLEM 1. Find the volume of the solid that results when the region bounded by the curve $y = 16 - x^2$ and the curve $y = 16 - 4x$ is rotated about the x-axis. Use the washer method and <u>set up but do not evaluate the integral.</u>

Answer: First, sketch the region:

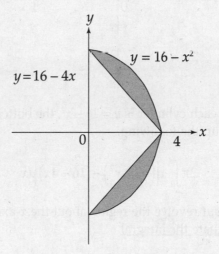

Next, find where the curves intersect by setting the two equations equal to each other:

$$16 - x^2 = 16 - 4x$$
$$x^2 = 4x$$
$$x^2 - 4x = 0$$
$$x = 0,\, 4$$

Slicing vertically, the top curve is always $y = 16 - x^2$ and the bottom is always $y = 16 - 4x$, so the integral looks like this:

$$\pi\int_{0}^{4}\left[\left(16-x^2\right)^2 - \left(16-4x\right)^2\right]dx$$

PROBLEM 2. Repeat Problem 1, but revolve the region about the y-axis and use the cylindrical shells method. <u>Set up but do not evaluate the integral</u>.

Answer: Sketch the situation:

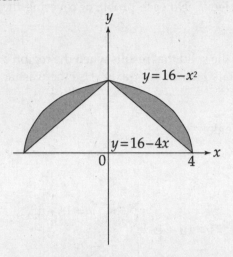

Slicing vertically, the top of each cylinder is $y = 16 - x^2$, the bottom is $y = 16 - 4x$, and the radius is x. Therefore, you should set up the following:

$$2\pi \int_0^4 x\left[\left(16 - x^2\right) - \left(16 - 4x\right)\right]dx$$

PROBLEM 3. Repeat Problem 1 but revolve the region about the x-axis and use the cylindrical shells method. <u>Set up but do not evaluate the integral</u>.

Answer: Sketch it like this:

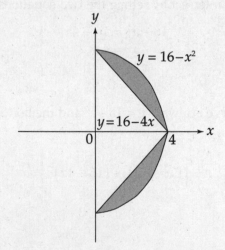

To slice horizontally, you have to solve each equation for x in terms of y and find the limits of integration with respect to y. First, solve for x in terms of y:

$$y = 16 - x^2 \text{ becomes } x = \sqrt{16-y}$$

and

$$y = 16 - 4x \text{ becomes } x = \frac{16-y}{4}$$

Next, determine the limits of integration: They're from $y = 0$ to $y = 16$. Slicing horizontally, the curve $x = \sqrt{16-y}$ is always on the right and the curve $x = \dfrac{16-y}{4}$ is always on the left. The radius is y, so we evaluate:

$$2\pi \int_0^{16} y\left[\left(\sqrt{16-y}\right) - \left(\frac{16-y}{4}\right)\right] dy$$

PROBLEM 4. Repeat Problem 1 but revolve the region about the y-axis and use the washers method. <u>Set up but do not evaluate the integral.</u>

Answer: Sketch.

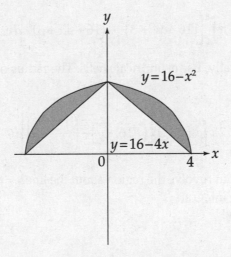

Slicing horizontally, the curve $x = \sqrt{16-y}$ is always on the right and the curve $x = \dfrac{16-y}{4}$ is always on the left. Therefore, your integral should look like this:

$$\pi \int_0^{16}\left[\left(\sqrt{16-y}\right)^2 - \left(\frac{16-y}{4}\right)^2\right] dy$$

PROBLEM 5. Repeat Problem 1, but revolve the region about the line $y = -3$. You may use either method. <u>Set up but do not evaluate the integral</u>.

Answer: Your sketch should resemble the one below (note that it's not drawn exactly to scale):

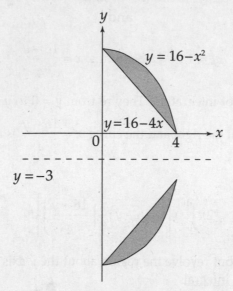

If you were to slice the region vertically, you would use washers. You'll need to add 3 to each radius to adjust for the axis of revolution. The integral to evaluate is:

$$\pi \int_0^4 \left[\left(16 - x^2 + 3\right)^2 - \left(16 - 4x + 3\right)^2 \right] dx$$

To slice the region horizontally, use cylindrical shells. The radius of each shell would increase by 3, and you would evaluate:

$$2\pi \int_0^{16} (y + 3) \left[\left(\sqrt{16 - y}\right) - \left(\frac{16 - y}{4}\right) \right] dy$$

PROBLEM 6. Repeat Problem 1, but revolve the region about the line $x = 8$. You may use either method. <u>Set up but do not evaluate the integral</u>.
Warning! This one is tricky!

Answer: First, sketch the region.

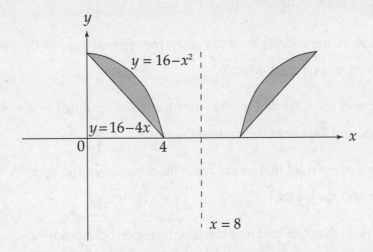

If you choose cylindrical shells, slice the region vertically; you'll need to adjust for the axis of revolution. Each radius can be found by subtracting x from 8. (Not 8 from x. That was the tricky part, in case you missed it.) The integral to evaluate is:

$$2\pi \int_0^4 (8-x)\left[(16-x^2)-(16-4x)\right]dx$$

If you choose washers, slice the region horizontally. The radius of each washer is found by subtracting each equation from 8. Notice also that the curve $x = \dfrac{16-y}{4}$ is now the outer radius of the washer, and the curve $x = \sqrt{16-y}$ is the inner radius. The integral looks like:

$$\pi \int_0^{16}\left[\left(8-\left(\frac{16-y}{4}\right)\right)^2 - \left(8-\left(\sqrt{16-y}\right)\right)^2\right]dy$$

PROBLEM 7: Find the volume of a solid whose base is the region between the x-axis and the curve $y = 4 - x^2$, and whose cross-sections perpendicular to the x-axis are equilateral triangles with a side that lies on the base.

Answer: The curve $y = 4 - x^2$ intersects the x-axis at $x = -2$ and $x = 2$. The side of the triangle is $4 - x^2$, so all that we have to do is evaluate $\dfrac{\sqrt{3}}{4}\int_{-2}^2 \left(4 - x^2\right)^2 dx$.

Expand the integrand to get:

$$\frac{\sqrt{3}}{4}\int_{-2}^2 \left(16 - 8x^2 + x^4\right)dx$$

Then integrate, which gives you:

$$\frac{\sqrt{3}}{4}\left(16x - \frac{8x^3}{3} + \frac{x^5}{5}\right)\Bigg|_{-2}^2 = \frac{128\sqrt{3}}{15} \approx 14.780$$

PRACTICE PROBLEM SET 26

Calculate the volumes below. The answers are in Chapter 21.

1. Find the volume of the solid that results when the region bounded by $y = \sqrt{9 - x^2}$ and the x-axis is revolved around the x-axis.

2. Find the volume of the solid that results when the region bounded by $y = \sec x$ and the x-axis from $x = -\dfrac{\pi}{4}$ to $x = \dfrac{\pi}{4}$ is revolved around the x-axis.

3. Find the volume of the solid that results when the region bounded by $x = 1 - y^2$ and the y-axis is revolved around the y-axis.

4. Find the volume of the solid that results when the region bounded by $x = \sqrt{5}y^2$ and the y-axis from $y = -1$ to $y = 1$ is revolved around the y-axis.

5. Find the volume of the solid that results when the region bounded by $y = x^3$, $x = 2$, and the x-axis is revolved around the line $x = 2$.

6. Use the method of cylindrical shells to find the volume of the solid that results when the region bounded by $y = x$, $x = 2$, and $y = -\dfrac{x}{2}$ is revolved around the y-axis.

7. Use the method of cylindrical shells to find the volume of the solid that results when the region bounded by $y = \sqrt{x}$, $y = 2x - 1$, and $x = 0$ is revolved around the y-axis.

8. Use the method of cylindrical shells to find the volume of the solid that results when the region bounded by $y = x^2$, $y = 4$, and $x = 0$ is revolved around the x-axis.

9. Use the method of cylindrical shells to find the volume of the solid that results when the region bounded by $y = 2\sqrt{x}$, $x = 4$, and $y = 0$ is revolved around the y-axis.

10. Use the method of cylindrical shells to find the volume of the solid that results when the region bounded by $y^2 = 8x$ and $x = 2$ is revolved around the line $x = 4$.

11. Find the volume of the solid whose base is the region between the semi-circle $y = \sqrt{16 - x^2}$ and the x-axis, and whose cross-sections perpendicular to the x-axis are squares with a side on the base.

12. Find the volume of the solid whose base is the region between $y = x^2$ and $y = 4$ and whose perpendicular cross-sections are isosceles right triangles with the hypotenuse on the base.

16

Integration By Parts

This chapter is about one of the most important and powerful techniques of integral calculus. This always shows up on the AP exam. You'll often find that an integral that otherwise seems to be undoable is simple once you use integration by parts.

THE FORMULA

Remember the Product Rule? It looks like this:

$$\frac{d}{dx}(uv) = u\frac{dv}{dx} + v\frac{du}{dx}$$

If we write this in differential form (i.e., eliminate the dx), we get $d(uv) = u\,dv + v\,du$. Rearranging, we get the following: $u\,dv = d(uv) - v\,du$. Integrating both sides, we obtain the integration by parts formula.

$$\int u\,dv = uv - \int v\,du$$

This formula allows you to write one integral in terms of another integral. This will often help you turn a difficult integral into an easy one.

Example 1: Find $\int x \sin x\,dx$.

Upon first glance, we've got a problem. If you try u-substitution, neither term is even close to the derivative of the other. Thus, you can't substitute. What do you do? (Hint: look at the title of the chapter.)

Let $u = x$ and $dv = \sin x\,dx$. Then $du = dx$ and $v = -\cos x$. If you plug these parts into the formula, you get:

$$\int x \sin x\,dx = -x \cos x + \int \cos x\,dx$$

Now we've turned the difficult left-side integral into an easy right-side integral:

$$\int x \sin x\,dx = -x \cos x + \sin x + C$$

Notice that we let $u = x$ and $dv = \sin x\,dx$. If we had let $u = \sin x$ and $dv = x\,dx$, we would have calculated that:

$$du = \cos x\,dx \text{ and } v = \frac{x^2}{2}$$

The formula would have been:

$$\int x \sin x\,dx = \frac{x^2 \sin x}{2} - \int \frac{x^2 \cos x}{2}dx$$

This not only doesn't fix our problem, it makes it worse! This leads us to a general rule:

If one of the terms is a power of x, let that term be u and the other term be dv. (The main exception to this rule is when the other term is ln x.)

Let's assure ourselves that the formula works. If $\int x \sin x\,dx = -x \cos x + \sin x + C$, and you differentiate the right-hand side, the result is:

$$-x(-\sin x) + (-1) \cos x + \cos x = x \sin x$$

As you can see, integration by parts is the Product Rule in reverse.

Example 2: Find $\int x^2 \sin x \, dx$.

As with Example 1, we let $u = x^2$ and $dv = \sin x \, dx$. Therefore:

$$du = 2x \, dx \text{ and } v = -\cos x$$

Now plug these into the formula:

$$\int x^2 \sin x \, dx = -x^2 \cos x + 2 \int x \cos x \, dx$$

Guess what you have to do now. You have to integrate by parts a second time!
Let $u = x$ and $dv = \cos x \, dx$, so $du = dx$ and $v = \sin x$. Now you have:

$$\int x^2 \sin x \, dx = -x^2 \cos x + 2x \sin x - 2 \int \sin x \, dx$$

The final integral becomes:

$$\int x^2 \sin x \, dx = -x^2 \cos x + 2x \sin x + 2 \cos x + C$$

Often, you'll have to do integration by parts twice. Good news: The AP exam never asks you to do it three times.

Example 3: Find $\int \ln x \, dx$.

Let $u = \ln x$ and $dv = dx$. (Yes, we're allowed to do this!) Then $du = \frac{1}{x} \, dx$ and $v = x$.

Plugging into the formula, you get:

$$\int \ln x \, dx = x \ln x - \int dx$$

Now the right side becomes:

$$\int \ln x \, dx = x \ln x - x + C$$

You should add this integral to the others you've memorized or are comfortable with deriving:

$$\int \ln x \, dx = x \ln x - x + C$$

There's one last type of integration by parts technique you need to know for the AP exam. It requires you to perform two rounds of integration by parts (followed by some simple algebra), and it helps you solve for an unknown integral.

Example 4: Find $\int e^x \cos x \, dx$.

First, we let $u = e^x$ and $dv = \cos x \, dx$. Then, $du = e^x \, dx$ and $v = \sin x$. When you plug this information into the formula, you get:

$$\int e^x \cos x \, dx = e^x \sin x - \int e^x \sin x \, dx$$

Now do integration by parts again. This time we let $u = e^x$ and $dv = \sin x \, dx$, so that $du = e^x \, dx$ and $v = -\cos x$. Now the formula looks like this:

$$\int e^x \cos x \, dx = e^x \sin x - \left(-e^x \cos x + \int e^x \cos x \, dx \right) = e^x \sin x + e^x \cos x - \int e^x \cos x \, dx$$

It looks as if you're back to square one, but notice that the unknown integral is on both the left- and right-hand sides of the equation. If you now add $\int e^x \cos x \, dx$ to both sides (isn't algebra wonderful?), you get:

$$2\int e^x \cos x \, dx = e^x \sin x + e^x \cos x$$

Now, all you do is divide both sides by 2 and throw in the constant:

$$\int e^x \cos x \, dx = \frac{e^x \sin x + e^x \cos x}{2} + C$$

This is why integration by parts is so powerful. You can evaluate a difficult integral by repeatedly rewriting it in terms of integrals you do know.

The AP exam always has integration by parts problems, and they're generally just like these. In fact, if you can do all of the examples and problems in this chapter, you should be able to do any integration by parts problem that will appear on the test.

PROBLEM 1. Evaluate $\int x \ln x \, dx$.

Answer: If you let $u = \ln x$ and $dv = x \, dx$, then $du = \dfrac{1}{x} dx$ and $v = \dfrac{x^2}{2}$. Notice that this is an exception to our rule about setting the x-term equal to u.

Now you have:

$$\int x \ln x \, dx = \left(\frac{x^2}{2} \right) \ln x - \int \frac{x^2}{2} \frac{1}{x} \, dx = \frac{x^2 \ln x}{2} - \frac{1}{2} \int x \, dx$$

Now you can evaluate the right-hand integral:

$$\int x \ln x \, dx = \frac{x^2 \ln x}{2} - \frac{x^2}{4} + C$$

PROBLEM 2. Evaluate $\int x^2 e^x \, dx$.

Answer: Let $u = x^2$ and $dv = e^x \, dx$. Then $du = 2x \, dx$ and $v = e^x$. The formula becomes:

$$\int x^2 e^x \, dx = x^2 e^x - 2\int x e^x dx$$

We need to use integration by parts a second time to evaluate the right-hand integral. Let $u = x$ and $dv = e^x \, dx$, so $du = dx$ and $v = e^x$. Now it looks like this:

$$\int x^2 e^x \, dx = x^2 e^x - 2\left[x e^x - \int e^x dx \right]$$

Now evaluate the right-hand integral:

$$\int x^2 e^x \, dx = x^2 e^x - 2x e^x + 2e^x + C$$

PROBLEM 3. Evaluate $\int \sin x \; e^{-x} dx$.

Answer: Let $u = \sin x$ and $dv = e^{-x} \, dx$. Then du = cos $x \, dx$ and $v = -e^{-x}$. Now the integral looks like this:

$$\int \sin x \; e^{-x} dx = -\sin x e^{-x} + \int \cos x e^{-x} dx$$

It's time for another round of integration by parts to evaluate the right-hand integral. Let $u = \cos x$ and $dv = e^{-x} dx$. Then $du = -\sin x \, dx$ and $v = -e^{-x}$. This gives you:

$$\int \sin x e^{-x} dx = -\sin x e^{-x} - \cos x e^{-x} - \int \sin x e^{-x} dx$$

Now add $\int \sin x e^{-x} dx$ to both sides:

$$2\int \sin x e^{-x} dx = -\sin x e^{-x} - \cos x e^{-x} + C$$

Therefore:

$$\int \sin x e^{-x} dx = \frac{-\sin x e^{-x}}{2} - \frac{\cos x e^{-x}}{2} + C$$

PRACTICE PROBLEM SET 27

Evaluate each of the following integrals. The answers are in Chapter 21.

1. $\int x \csc^2 x \, dx$

2. $\int x e^{2x} \, dx$

3. $\int \frac{\ln x}{x^2} \, dx$

4. $\int x^2 \cos x \, dx$

5. $\int x^2 \ln x \, dx$

6. $\int x \sin 2x \, dx$

7. $\int \ln^2 x \, dx$

8. $\int x \sec^2 x \, dx$

17

Trig Functions

INVERSE TRIG FUNCTIONS

In this unit, you'll learn a broader set of integration techniques. So far, you only know how to do a few types of integrals: polynomials, some trig functions, and logs. Now we'll turn our attention to a set of integrals that result in **inverse trigonometric functions**. But first, we need to go over the derivatives of the inverse trigonometric functions. (You might want to refer back to Chapter 10 on derivatives of inverse functions.)

Suppose you have the equation $\sin y = x$. If you differentiate both sides with respect to x, you get:

$$\cos y \frac{dy}{dx} = 1$$

Now divide both sides by $\cos y$:

$$\frac{dy}{dx} = \frac{1}{\cos y}$$

Because $\sin^2 y + \cos^2 y = 1$, we can replace $\cos y$ with $\sqrt{1 - \sin^2 y}$:

$$\frac{dy}{dx} = \frac{1}{\sqrt{1 - \sin^2 y}}$$

Finally, because $x = \sin y$, replace $\sin y$ with x. The derivative equals:

$$\frac{1}{\sqrt{1 - x^2}}$$

Now go back to the original equation $\sin y = x$ and solve for y in terms of x: $y = \sin^{-1} x$. If you differentiate both sides with respect to x, you get:

$$\frac{dy}{dx} = \frac{d}{dx} \sin^{-1} x$$

Replace $\frac{dy}{dx}$, and you get the final result:

$$\frac{d}{dx} \sin^{-1} x = \frac{1}{\sqrt{1 - x^2}}$$

This is the derivative of inverse sine. By similar means, you can find the derivatives of all six inverse trig functions. They're not difficult to derive, and they're also not difficult to memorize. The choice is yours. We use u instead of x to account for the Chain Rule.

$$\frac{d}{dx}\left(\sin^{-1} u\right) = \frac{1}{\sqrt{1 - u^2}} \frac{du}{dx}; \quad -1 < u < 1 \qquad \frac{d}{dx}\left(\cos^{-1} u\right) = \frac{-1}{\sqrt{1 - u^2}} \frac{du}{dx}; \quad -1 < u < 1$$

$$\frac{d}{dx}\left(\tan^{-1} u\right) = \frac{1}{1 + u^2} \frac{du}{dx} \qquad\qquad \frac{d}{dx}\left(\cot^{-1} u\right) = \frac{-1}{1 + u^2} \frac{du}{dx}$$

$$\frac{d}{dx}\left(\sec^{-1} u\right) = \frac{1}{|u|\sqrt{u^2 - 1}} \frac{du}{dx}; \quad |u| > 1 \qquad \frac{d}{dx}\left(\csc^{-1} u\right) = \frac{-1}{|u|\sqrt{u^2 - 1}} \frac{du}{dx}; \quad |u| > 1$$

Notice the domain restrictions for inverse sine, cosine, secant, and cosecant.

Example 1: $\dfrac{d}{dx}\sin^{-1}x^2 = \dfrac{2x}{\sqrt{1-\left(x^2\right)^2}} = \dfrac{2x}{\sqrt{1-x^4}}$

Example 2: $\dfrac{d}{dx}\tan^{-1}5x = \dfrac{5}{1+\left(5x\right)^2} = \dfrac{5}{1+25x^2}$

Example 3: $\dfrac{d}{dx}\sec^{-1}\left(x^2-x\right) = \dfrac{2x-1}{\left|x^2-x\right|\sqrt{\left(x^2-x\right)^2-1}} = \dfrac{2x-1}{\left|x^2-x\right|\sqrt{x^4-2x^3+x^2-1}}$

Finding the derivatives of inverse trig functions is just a matter of following the formulas. They're very rarely tested on the AP in this form and are not terribly important. In addition, the AP exam almost always tests only inverse sine and tangent, and then usually only as integrals, not as derivatives.

Therefore, it's time to learn the integrals. The derivative formulas lead directly to the integral formulas, but because the only difference between the derivatives of inverse sine, tangent, and secant and those of inverse cosine, cotangent, and cosecant is the negative sign, only the former functions are generally used.

$$\int \frac{du}{\sqrt{1-u^2}} = \sin^{-1}u + C \qquad \left(\text{valid for } u^2 < 1\right)$$

$$\int \frac{du}{1+u^2} = \tan^{-1}u + C$$

$$\int \frac{du}{u\sqrt{u^2-1}} = \sec^{-1}u + C \qquad \left(\text{valid for } u^2 > 1\right)$$

The first two always show up on the AP exam, so you should learn to recognize the pattern. Most of the time, the integration requires some sticky algebra to get the integral into the proper form.

Example 4: $\displaystyle\int \frac{x\,dx}{\sqrt{1-x^4}} =$

Don't forget about u-substitution. Let $u = x^2$ and $du = 2x\,dx$. Therefore, $\dfrac{1}{2}du = x\,dx$. Substituting and integrating, we get:

$$\frac{1}{2}\int \frac{du}{\sqrt{1-u^2}} = \frac{1}{2}\sin^{-1}u + C$$

Now substitute back:

$$\frac{1}{2}\sin^{-1}(x^2)+C$$

Example 5: $\displaystyle\int \frac{dx}{\sqrt{4-x^2}} =$

Anytime you see an integral where you have the square root of a constant minus a function, try to turn it into an inverse sine. You can do that here with a little simple algebra:

$$\int \frac{dx}{\sqrt{4-x^2}} = \int \frac{dx}{\sqrt{4\left(1-\frac{x^2}{4}\right)}} = \frac{1}{2}\int \frac{dx}{\sqrt{1-\frac{x^2}{4}}}$$

Now use u-substitution: let $u = \dfrac{x}{2}$ and $du = \dfrac{1}{2}dx$, so $2du = dx$, and substitute:

$$\frac{1}{2}\int \frac{dx}{\sqrt{1-\frac{x^2}{4}}} = \frac{1}{2}\int \frac{2du}{\sqrt{1-u^2}} = \sin^{-1}u + C$$

When you substitute back, you get:

$$\sin^{-1}\frac{x}{2}+C$$

Example 6: $\displaystyle\int \frac{e^x dx}{1+e^{2x}} =$

Again, use u-substitution. Let $u = e^x$ and $du = e^x\,dx$, and substitute in:

$$\int \frac{du}{1+u^2} = \tan^{-1}u + C$$

Then substitute back:

$$\tan^{-1}e^x + C$$

Let's do one last type that's slightly more difficult. For this one, you need to remember how to complete the square.

Example 7: $\displaystyle\int \frac{dx}{x^2+4x+5} =$

Complete the square in the denominator (your algebra teacher warned you about this):

$$x^2 + 4x + 5 = (x + 2)^2 + 1$$

Now rewrite the integral:

$$\int \frac{dx}{1+(x+2)^2}$$

Using u-substitution, let $u = x + 2$ and $du = dx$. Then do the substitution:

$$\int \frac{du}{1+u^2} = \tan^{-1}u + C$$

When you put the function of x back in to the integral, it reads:

$$\tan^{-1}(x + 2) + C$$

Evaluating these integrals involves looking for a particular pattern. If it's there, all you have to do is use algebra and u-substitution to make the integrand conform to the pattern. Once that's accomplished, the rest is easy. These integrals will show up again when we do partial fractions. Otherwise, as far as the AP exam is concerned, this is all you need to know.

Try these solved problems and don't forget to look for those patterns. Get out your index card and cover the answers while you work.

PROBLEM 1. Find the derivative of $y = \sin^{-1}\left(\dfrac{x}{2}\right)$.

Answer: The rule is:

$$\frac{d}{dx}\left(\sin^{-1}u\right) = \frac{1}{\sqrt{1-u^2}}\frac{du}{dx}$$

The algebra looks like this:

$$\frac{d}{dx}\left(\sin^{-1}\left(\frac{x}{2}\right)\right) = \frac{1}{\sqrt{1-\left(\frac{x}{2}\right)^2}}\frac{1}{2} = \frac{1}{2}\left(\frac{1}{\sqrt{1-\frac{x^2}{4}}}\right) = \frac{1}{2}\left(\frac{1}{\sqrt{\frac{4-x^2}{4}}}\right) = \frac{1}{2}\left(\frac{2}{\sqrt{4-x^2}}\right) = \frac{1}{\sqrt{4-x^2}}$$

PROBLEM 2. Evaluate $\int \dfrac{dx}{4+x^2}$.

Answer: First, you need to do a little algebra. Factor 4 out of the denominator to obtain this:

$$\int \dfrac{dx}{4\left(1+\dfrac{x^2}{4}\right)}$$

Next, rewrite the integrand as:

$$\frac{1}{4}\int \dfrac{dx}{\left(1+\left(\dfrac{x}{2}\right)^2\right)}$$

Now you can use u-substitution. Let $u=\dfrac{x}{2}$ and $du=\dfrac{1}{2}dx$, so $2du=dx$:

$$\frac{1}{2}\int \dfrac{du}{1+u^2}$$

Now integrate it:

$$\frac{1}{2}\tan^{-1}u+C$$

And re-substitute:

$$\frac{1}{2}\tan^{-1}\frac{x}{2}+C$$

PROBLEM 3. Evaluate $\int \dfrac{dx}{\sqrt{-x^2+4x-3}}$.

Answer: This time, you need to use some algebra by completing the square of the polynomial under the square root sign:

$$-x^2+4x-3=-\left(x^2-4x+3\right)=-\left[(x-2)^2-1\right]=\left[1-(x-2)^2\right]$$

Now rewrite the integrand as:

$$\int \dfrac{dx}{\sqrt{1-(x-2)^2}}$$

And use *u*-substitution. Let $u = x - 2$ and $du = dx$:

$$\int \frac{du}{\sqrt{1 - u^2}}$$

Now, this looks familiar. Once you integrate, you get:

$$\sin^{-1} u + C$$

After you substitute back it becomes:

$$\sin^{-1} (x - 2) + C$$

PRACTICE PROBLEM SET 28

Here is some more practice work on derivatives and integrals of inverse trig functions. The answers are in Chapter 21.

1. Find the derivative of $\frac{1}{4} \tan^{-1} \left(\frac{x}{4} \right)$.

2. Find the derivative of $\sin^{-1} \left(\frac{1}{x} \right)$.

3. Find the derivative of $\tan^{-1} \left(e^x \right)$.

4. Evaluate $\int \frac{dx}{x \sqrt{x^2 - \pi}}$.

5. Evaluate $\int \frac{dx}{7 + x^2}$.

6. Evaluate $\int \frac{dx}{x \left(1 + \ln^2 x \right)}$.

7. Evaluate $\int \frac{\sec^2 x \, dx}{\sqrt{1 - \tan^2 x}}$.

8. Evaluate $\int \frac{dx}{\sqrt{9 - 4x^2}}$.

9. Evaluate $\int \frac{e^{3x} dx}{1 + e^{6x}}$.

ADVANCED INTEGRALS OF TRIG FUNCTIONS

In Chapter 11, you learned how to find the integrals of some of the trigonometric functions. Now it's time to figure out how to find the integrals of some of the more complicated trig expressions. First, recall some of the basic trigonometric integrals:

$$\int \sin x \, dx = -\cos x + C \qquad \int \cos x \, dx = \sin x + C$$

$$\int \sec^2 x \, dx = \tan x + C \qquad \int \csc^2 \, dx = -\cot x + C$$

$$\int \sec x \tan x \, dx = \sec x + C \qquad \int \csc x \cot x \, dx = -\csc x + C$$

$$\int \tan x \, dx = -\ln |\cos x| + C \qquad \int \cot x \, dx = \ln |\sin x| + C$$

$$\int \sec x \, dx = \ln |\sec x + \tan x| + C \qquad \int \csc x \, dx = -\ln |\csc x + \cot x| + C$$

Some of these were derived by reversing differentiation, others by u-substitution.

Example 1: Evaluate $\int \sin^2 x \, dx$.

You can start by replacing $\sin^2 x$ with $\dfrac{1 - \cos 2x}{2}$. This comes from taking the Double Angle formula $\cos 2x = 1 - 2 \sin^2 x$ and solving for $\sin^2 x$. After you make that replacement, the integral looks like this:

$$\int \frac{1 - \cos 2x}{2} \, dx = \frac{1}{2} \int dx - \frac{1}{2} \int \cos 2x \, dx = \frac{x}{2} - \frac{\sin 2x}{4} + C$$

Remember this substitution:

$$\sin^2 x = \frac{1 - \cos 2x}{2}$$

You could use the substitution:

$$\cos^2 x = \frac{1 + \cos 2x}{2}$$

(Note: This comes from taking the Double Angle formula $\cos 2x = 2 \cos^2 x - 1$ and solving for $\cos^2 x$.) You can also use the substitution to find $\int \cos^2 x \, dx$.

Now let's do some variations.

Example 2: Evaluate $\int \sin^2 x \cos x \, dx$.

Here, use some simple u-substitution. Let $u = \sin x$ and $du = \cos x \, dx$ and substitute:

$$\int \sin^2 x \cos x \, dx = \int u^2 \, du = \frac{u^3}{3} + C$$

When you substitute back, you get:

$$\frac{\sin^3 x}{3} + C$$

In fact, you can do any integral of the form $\int \sin^n x \cos x \, dx$ using u-substitution, and the result will be:

$$\frac{\sin^{n+1} x}{n+1} + C$$

Similarly:

$$\int \cos^n x \sin x \, dx = -\frac{\cos^{n+1} x}{n+1} + C$$

How about higher powers of sine and cosine?

Example 3: Evaluate $\int \sin^3 x \, dx$.

First, break the integrand into this:

$$\int (\sin x)(\sin^2 x) \, dx$$

Next, using trig substitution, you get:

$$\int (\sin x)(\sin^2 x) \, dx = \int (\sin x)(1 - \cos^2 x) \, dx$$

You can turn this into two integrals:

$$\int \sin x \, dx - \int (\sin x \cos^2 x) \, dx$$

You can do both of these integrals:

$$-\cos x + \frac{\cos^3 x}{3} + C$$

Example 4: Evaluate $\int \sin^3 x \cos^2 x \, dx$.

Here, break the integrand into:

$$\int (\sin x)(\sin^2 x)(\cos^2 x) \, dx$$

Next, using trig substitution, you get:

$$\int (\sin x)(\sin^2 x)(\cos^2 x) \, dx = \int (\sin x)(1 - \cos^2 x)(\cos^2 x) \, dx$$

Now you can use u-substitution. Let $u = \cos x$, $du = -\sin x \, dx$, and substitute:

$$-\int (1 - u^2)u^2 \, du = \int (u^4 - u^2) du = \frac{u^5}{5} - \frac{u^3}{3} + C$$

Now substitute back, and you're done:

$$\frac{\cos^5 x}{5} - \frac{\cos^3 x}{3} + C$$

As you can see, these integrals all require you to know trig substitutions and u-substitution. The AP doesn't ask too many variations on these integrals, but let's do just a few other types, just in case.

Example 5: Evaluate $\int \tan^2 x \, dx$.

First, use the trigonometric substitution $\tan^2 x = \sec^2 x - 1$:

$$\int \tan^2 x \, dx = \int (\sec^2 x - 1) dx$$

Now break this into two integrals that are easy to evaluate:

$$\int \sec^2 x \, dx - \int dx$$

And integrate:

$$\tan x - x + C$$

Example 6: Evaluate $\int \tan^3 x \, dx$.

Recognize what to do here? Right! Break up the integrand!

$$\int (\tan x)\left(\tan^2 x\right) dx$$

Next, use the trig substitution $\tan^2 x = \sec^2 x - 1$ in the expression:

$$\int (\tan x)\left(\sec^2 x - 1\right) dx$$

Break this into two integrals:

$$\int \tan x \sec^2 x \, dx - \int \tan x \, dx$$

Tackle the first integral using u-substitution. Let $u = \tan x$, $du = \sec^2 x \, dx$:

$$\int u \, du = \frac{u^2}{2} + C$$

Substituting back gives you:

$$\frac{\tan^2 x}{2} + C$$

We've done the second integral before:

$$\int \tan x \, dx = \int \frac{\sin x}{\cos x} \, dx = -\ln \left| \cos x \right| + C$$

Thus the integral is:

$$\frac{\tan^2 x}{2} - \ln \left| \cos x \right| + C$$

Example 7: Evaluate $\displaystyle\int \sec^3 x \, dx$.

Now it's time for integration by parts. Let $u = \sec x$ and $dv = \sec^2 x \, dx$. Therefore, $du = \sec x \tan x \, dx$ and $v = \tan x$. Plug these into the formula, and you get:

$$\int \sec^3 x \, dx = \sec x \tan x - \int \tan^2 x \sec x \, dx$$

Next, substitute $\tan^2 x = \sec^2 x - 1$:

$$\int \tan^2 x \sec x \, dx = \int \left(\sec^2 x - 1\right)(\sec x) \, dx = \int \sec^3 x \, dx - \int \sec x \, dx$$

So, the integral has become:

$$\int \sec^3 x \, dx = \sec x \tan x - \int \sec^3 x \, dx + \int \sec x \, dx$$

Now, add $\int \sec^3 x \, dx$ to both sides:

$$2\int \sec^3 x \, dx = \sec x \tan x + \int \sec x \, dx$$

Finally, recall that the integral on the right is:

$$\int \sec x \, dx = \ln |\sec x + \tan x| + C$$

The combined integral is:

$$2\int \sec^3 x \, dx = \sec x \tan x + \ln |\sec x + \tan x| + C$$

When you divide by 2, you get your final answer:

$$\int \sec^3 x \, dx = \frac{\sec x \tan x + \ln |\sec x + \tan x|}{2} + C$$

Whew! This is about as difficult as the AP exam ever gets. Believe it or not, trigonometric integrals can get even more complicated, involving higher powers or more difficult combinations of trig functions. Thankfully, the AP tends to limit itself to the simpler ones.

If you can integrate any power of a trig function up to 4, as well as some of the basic combinations, you'll be able to handle any trigonometric integral that appears on the AP exam.

Walk yourself through the step-by-step process by trying some solved problems below. Cover each answer first, then check your answer.

PROBLEM 1. $\int \cos^2 x \, dx$

Answer: Use the substitution $\dfrac{1 + \cos 2x}{2}$. Now the integral looks like this:

$$\int \frac{1 + \cos 2x}{2} \, dx$$

Divide this into two integrals:

$$\int \frac{1}{2} \, dx + \int \frac{\cos 2x}{2} \, dx$$

When you evaluate each one separately, you get:

$$\frac{x}{2} + \frac{\sin 2x}{4} + C$$

PROBLEM 2. $\int \cos^3 x \, dx$

Answer: Here, split $\cos^3 x$ into $\cos x \cos^2 x$ and replace the second term with $(1 - \sin^2 x)$:

$$\int \cos x \left(1 - \sin^2 x\right) dx$$

This can be rewritten as:

$$\int \cos x \, dx - \int \sin^2 x \cos x \, dx$$

The left-hand integral is $\sin x$. Do the right-hand integral using u-substitution. Let $u = \sin x$ and $du = \cos x \, dx$. You get:

$$\int u^2 du = \frac{u^3}{3}$$

When you substitute back, the second integral becomes:

$$\frac{\sin^3 x}{3} + C$$

Thus, the complete answer is:

$$\sin x - \frac{\sin^3 x}{3} + C$$

PROBLEM 3. $\int \tan^2 x \sec^2 x \, dx$

Answer: This won't take long. Use u-substitution, by letting $u = \tan x$ and $du = \sec^2 x \, dx$:

$$\int u^2 du = \frac{u^3}{3}$$

The final result when you substitute back is:

$$\frac{\tan^3 x}{3} + C$$

PROBLEM 4. $\int (\tan x + \sec x)^2 dx$

Answer: First, expand the integrand:

$$\int \left(\tan^2 x + 2 \sec x \tan x + \sec^2 x\right) dx$$

Next, use the trig substitution $\tan^2 x = \sec^2 x - 1$ to get:

$$\int \left(\sec^2 x - 1 + 2\sec x \tan x + \sec^2 x\right) dx = \int \left(2\sec^2 x - 1 + 2\sec x \tan x\right) dx$$

Separate this into three (yes, three) integrals, all of which you know how to evaluate:

$$\int 2\sec^2 x \, dx - \int dx + \int 2\sec x \tan x \, dx = 2\tan x - x + 2\sec x + C$$

PRACTICE PROBLEM SET 29

Evaluate the following integrals. The answers are in Chapter 21.

1. $\displaystyle\int \sin^4 x \, dx$

2. $\displaystyle\int \cos^4 x \, dx$

3. $\displaystyle\int \cos^4 x \sin x \, dx$

4. $\displaystyle\int \sin^3 x \cos^5 x \, dx$

5. $\displaystyle\int \sin^2 x \cos^2 x \, dx$

6. $\displaystyle\int \tan^3 x \sec^2 x \, dx$

7. $\displaystyle\int \tan^5 x \, dx$

8. $\displaystyle\int \cot^2 x \sec x \, dx$

18

Other Applications of The Integral

Each of the three topics discussed in this chapter appears only on the BC exam. If you're in an AB course, move on to Chapter 19.

LENGTH OF A CURVE

Another way to apply integrals is to find the length of the graph. It's usually a pretty simple problem. All you have to do is use a formula.

Suppose you want to find the length of the graph of a function $y = f(x)$ from $x = a$ to $x = b$. Call this length L. You could divide L into a set of line segments, Δl, add up the lengths of each of them, and you would find L. The formula for the length of each line segment can be found with the Pythagorean theorem:

$$\Delta l = \sqrt{(\Delta x)^2 + (\Delta y)^2}$$

If we make Δl, Δx, and Δy infinitesimally small, they become dx and dy. If we then add up all of these line segments, we get:

$$L = \int_a^b dl = \int_a^b \sqrt{dx^2 + dy^2}$$

$$= \int_{x_1}^{x_2} \sqrt{1 + \left(\frac{dy}{dx}\right)^2}\, dx$$

$$= \int_{y_1}^{y_2} \sqrt{1 + \left(\frac{dx}{dy}\right)^2}\, dy$$

Here's the rule:

If the function $f(x)$ is continuous and differentiable on $[a, b]$, then the length of the curve $y = f(x)$ from a to b is:

$$L = \int_a^b \sqrt{1 + \left(\frac{dy}{dx}\right)^2}\, dx$$

Example 1: Find the length of the curve $y = x^{\frac{3}{2}}$ from $x = 0$ to $x = 4$.

First, find the first derivative of the function: $\dfrac{dy}{dx} = \dfrac{3}{2}x^{\frac{1}{2}}$.

Next, plug into the formula:

$$L = \int_0^4 \sqrt{1 + \left(\frac{3}{2}x^{\frac{1}{2}}\right)^2}\, dx$$

Now evaluate the integral:

$$L = \int_0^4 \sqrt{1 + \left(\frac{3}{2}x^{\frac{1}{2}}\right)^2}\, dx = \int_0^4 \sqrt{1 + \frac{9}{4}x}\, dx$$

Using u-substitution, let $u = 1 + \dfrac{9x}{4}$, $du = \dfrac{9}{4}dx$, and $\dfrac{4}{9}du = dx$. Then substitute:

$$\frac{4}{9}\int u^{\frac{1}{2}}du = \frac{8}{27}u^{\frac{3}{2}}$$

Once you substitute back, the result is: $\dfrac{8}{27}\left(1 + \dfrac{9}{4}x\right)^{\frac{3}{2}}\Bigg|_0^4 = \dfrac{8}{27}\left(10^{\frac{3}{2}} - 1\right)$

As you can see, the formula isn't terribly difficult, but it can often lead to a really ugly integral. Fortunately, the AP will either give you a curve where the integral works out easily, as it did here, or you'll only be asked to set up the integral, not to evaluate it.

Sometimes you'll be given the curve as a function of y instead of as a function of x. Then the formula for the length of the curve $x = f(y)$ on the interval $[c, d]$ is:

$$L = \int_c^d \sqrt{1 + \left(\frac{dx}{dy}\right)^2}\, dy$$

Example 2: Find the length of the curve $x = \sin y$, from $y = 0$ to $y = \dfrac{\pi}{2}$. <u>Set up but do not evaluate the integral.</u>

Since $\dfrac{dx}{dy} = \cos y$, we can plug it into the formula: $L = \displaystyle\int_0^{\frac{\pi}{2}} \sqrt{1 + \cos^2 y}\, dy$.

PARAMETRIC FUNCTIONS

Sometimes the curve will be defined parametrically, usually in terms of t (for time). Then the formula for the length of the curve from $t = a$ to $t = b$ is:

$$L = \int_a^b \sqrt{\left(\frac{dx}{dt}\right)^2 + \left(\frac{dy}{dt}\right)^2}\, dt$$

Example 3: Find the length of the curve defined by $x = \sin t$ and $y = \cos t$, from $t = 0$ to $t = \pi$.

Take the derivatives of the two t-functions: $\dfrac{dx}{dt} = \cos t$ and $\dfrac{dy}{dt} = \sin t$. Then use the formula:

$$L = \int_0^\pi \sqrt{\cos^2 t + \sin^2 t}\, dt$$

If you evaluate the integral, you get:

$$L = \int_0^\pi \sqrt{1}\, dt = \int_0^\pi dt = \pi$$

That's all there is to finding the length of a curve. As you've seen, many applications of the integral involve simple formulas. All you have to do is to plug in and evaluate the integral. If the integral is a difficult one, you probably just have to set it up.

Try these solved problems. Do each problem, covering the answer first, then check your answer.

PROBLEM 1. Find the length of the curve $y = \dfrac{1}{3}(x^2 + 2)^{\frac{3}{2}}$ from $x = 0$ to $x = 3$.

Answer: First, we find the first derivative $\dfrac{dy}{dx} = \dfrac{1}{3} \cdot \dfrac{3}{2}(x^2 + 2)^{\frac{1}{2}}(2x) = x(x^2 + 2)^{\frac{1}{2}}$

Next, plug into the formula:

$$L = \int_a^b \sqrt{1 + \left(\dfrac{dy}{dx}\right)^2}\, dx = \int_0^3 \sqrt{1 + x^2(x^2 + 2)}\, dx$$

Now you just have to evaluate the integral:

$$L = \int_0^3 \sqrt{1 + x^4 + 2x^2}\, dx = \int_0^3 \sqrt{(x^2 + 1)^2}\, dx = \left(\dfrac{x^3}{3} + x\right)\Bigg|_0^3 = 12$$

PROBLEM 2. Find the length of the curve $x = \dfrac{y^4}{4} + \dfrac{1}{8y^2}$ from $y = 1$ to $y = 2$.

Answer: Here, you have x in terms of y, so first we find $\dfrac{dx}{dy}$:

$$\dfrac{dx}{dy} = y^3 - \dfrac{1}{4y^3}$$

Next, find $\left(\dfrac{dx}{dy}\right)^2$:

$$\left(\dfrac{dx}{dy}\right)^2 = \left(y^3 - \dfrac{1}{4y^3}\right)^2 = y^6 - \dfrac{1}{2} + \dfrac{1}{16y^6}$$

Plug this into the formula:

$$L = \int_c^d \sqrt{1 + \left(\frac{dx}{dy}\right)^2}\, dy = \int_1^2 \sqrt{1 + \left(y^6 - \frac{1}{2} + \frac{1}{16y^6}\right)}\, dy = \int_1^2 \sqrt{y^6 + \frac{1}{2} + \frac{1}{16y^6}}\, dy$$

And evaluate the integral:

$$L = \int_1^2 \sqrt{y^6 + \frac{1}{2} + \frac{1}{16y^6}}\, dy = \int_1^2 \sqrt{\left(y^3 + \frac{1}{4y^3}\right)^2}\, dy = \left(\frac{y^4}{4} - \frac{1}{8y^2}\right)\bigg|_1^2 = \frac{123}{32}$$

PROBLEM 3. Find the length of the curve $x = \tan t$ and $y = \sec t$ from $t = 0$ to $t = \frac{\pi}{4}$. Set up but do not evaluate the integral.

Answer:

$$L = \int_a^b \sqrt{\left(\frac{dx}{dt}\right)^2 + \left(\frac{dy}{dt}\right)^2}\, dt$$

To use the above formula, you need to determine that $\frac{dx}{dt} = \sec^2 t$ and $\frac{dy}{dt} = \sec t \tan t$.

Plug these into the formula:

$$L = \int_0^{\frac{\pi}{4}} \sqrt{\sec^4 t + \sec^2 t \tan^2 t}\, dt$$

PRACTICE PROBLEM SET 30

Find the length of the following curves between the specified intervals. Evaluate the integrals unless the directions state otherwise. The answers are in Chapter 21.

1. $y = \dfrac{x^3}{12} + \dfrac{1}{x}$ from $x = 1$ to $x = 2$

2. $y = \tan x$ from $x = -\dfrac{\pi}{6}$ to $x = 0$ (<u>Set up but do not evaluate the integral.</u>)

3. $y = \sqrt{1 - x^2}$ from $x = 0$ to $x = \dfrac{1}{4}$ (<u>Set up but do not evaluate the integral.</u>)

4. $x = \dfrac{y^3}{18} + \dfrac{3}{2y}$ from $y = 2$ to $y = 3$

5. $x = \sqrt{1-y^2}$ from $y = -\dfrac{1}{2}$ to $y = \dfrac{1}{2}$ (Set up but do not evaluate the integral.)

6. $x = \sin y - y \cos y$ from $y = 0$ to $y = \pi$ (Set up but do not evaluate the integral.)

7. $x = \cos t$ and $y = \sin t$ from $t = \dfrac{\pi}{6}$ to $t = \dfrac{\pi}{3}$

8. $x = \sqrt{t}$ and $y = \dfrac{1}{t^3}$ from $t = 1$ to $t = 4$ (Set up but do not evaluate the integral.)

9. $x = 3t^2$ and $y = 2t$ from $t = 1$ to $t = 2$ (Set up but do not evaluate the integral.)

THE METHOD OF PARTIAL FRACTIONS

This is the last technique you'll learn to evaluate integrals. There are many, many more types of integrals and techniques to learn; in fact, there are courses in college primarily concerned with integrals and their uses! Fortunately for you, they're not on the AP exam (and therefore, not in this book). The BC exam usually has a partial fractions integral or two, and the concept isn't terribly hard.

We use the method of partial fractions to evaluate certain types of integrals that contain rational expressions. First, let's discuss the type of algebra you'll be doing.

If you wanted to add the expressions $\dfrac{3}{x-1}$ and $\dfrac{5}{x+2}$, you would do the following:

$$\frac{3}{x-1} + \frac{5}{x+2} = \frac{3(x+2) + 5(x-1)}{(x-1)(x+2)} = \frac{8x+1}{(x-1)(x+2)}$$

Now, suppose you had to do this in reverse; you were given the fraction on the right and you wanted to determine what two fractions were added to give you that fraction. Another way of asking this is: What constants A and B exist, such that $\dfrac{A}{x-1} + \dfrac{B}{x+2} = \dfrac{8x+1}{(x-1)(x+2)}$?

How do you go about solving for A and B? First, multiply through by $(x-1)(x+2)$ to clear the denominator:

$$A(x + 2) + B(x - 1) = 8x + 1$$

Next, simplify the left side:

$$Ax + 2A + Bx - B = 8x + 1$$

Now, if you group the terms on the left, you get:

$$(A + B)x + (2A - B) = 8x + 1$$

Therefore, $A + B = 8$ and $2A - B = 1$.

If you solve this pair of simultaneous equations, you get $A = 3$ and $B = 5$. Surprised? We hope not. Why would you need to know this method? Suppose you wanted to find:

$$\int \frac{8x+1}{(x-1)(x+2)}dx$$

You now know you can rewrite this integral as:

$$\int \frac{3}{x-1}dx + \int \frac{5}{x-2}dx$$

These integrals are easily evaluated:

$$\int \frac{3}{x-1}dx + \int \frac{5}{x-2}dx = 3\ln|x-1| + 5\ln|x-2| + C$$

Example 1: Evaluate $\int \frac{x+18}{(3x+5)(x+4)}dx$.

You need to find A and B such that:

$$\frac{A}{3x+5} + \frac{B}{x+4} = \frac{x+18}{(3x+5)(x+4)}$$

First, multiply through by $(3x + 5)(x + 4)$:

$$A(x + 4) + B(3x + 5) = x + 18$$

Next, simplify and group the terms:

$$Ax + 4A + 3Bx + 5B = x + 18$$

$$(A + 3B)x + (4A + 5B) = x + 18$$

You now have two simultaneous equations: $A + 3B = 1$ and $4A + 5B = 18$. If we solve the equations, we get $A = 7$ and $B = -2$. Thus, you can rewrite the integral as:

$$\int \frac{7}{3x+5}dx - \int \frac{2}{x+4}dx$$

These are both logarithmic integrals. The solution is:

$$\frac{7}{3}\ln\left|x+\frac{5}{3}\right| - 2\ln|x+4| + C$$

There are three main types of partial fractions that appear on the AP exam. You've just seen the first type: one with two linear factors in the denominator. The second type has a repeated linear term in the denominator.

Example 2: Evaluate $\displaystyle\int \frac{2x+4}{(x-1)^2}\,dx$.

Now you need to find two constants A and B, such that:

$$\frac{A}{x-1} + \frac{B}{(x-1)^2} = \frac{2x+4}{(x-1)^2}$$

Multiplying through by $(x-1)^2$, we get: $A(x-1) + B = 2x + 4$. Now simplify:

$$Ax - A + B = 2x + 4$$

$$Ax + (B - A) = 2x + 4$$

Thus, $A = 2$ and $B - A = 4$, so $B = 6$. Now we can rewrite the integral as:

$$\int \frac{2}{x-1}\,dx + \int \frac{6}{(x-1)^2}\,dx$$

The solution is:

$$2\ln|x-1| - \frac{6}{x-1} + C$$

The third type has an irreducible quadratic factor in the denominator.

Example 3: Evaluate $\displaystyle\int \frac{3x+5}{\left(x^2+1\right)(x+2)}\,dx$.

For a quadratic factor, you need to find A, B, and C such that:

$$\frac{Ax+B}{x^2+1} + \frac{C}{x+2} = \frac{3x+5}{\left(x^2+1\right)(x+2)}$$

Now you have a term $Ax + B$ over the quadratic term. Whenever you have a quadratic factor, you need to use a linear numerator, not a constant numerator.

Multiply through by $(x^2 + 1)(x + 2)$ and you get:

$$(Ax + B)(x + 2) + C(x^2 + 1) = 3x + 5$$

Simplify and group the terms:

$$Ax^2 + 2Ax + Bx + 2B + Cx^2 + C = 3x + 5$$

$$(A + C)x^2 + (2A + B)x + (2B + C) = 3x + 5$$

This gives you three equations:

$$A + C = 0$$

$$2A + B = 3$$

$$2B + C = 5$$

If you solve these three equations, the values are:

$$A = \frac{1}{5}, \ B = \frac{13}{5}, \text{ and } C = -\frac{1}{5}$$

Now you can rewrite the integral:

$$\int \frac{\frac{1}{5}x + \frac{13}{5}}{x^2 + 1} dx - \int \frac{\frac{1}{5}}{x+2} dx$$

Break the first integral into two integrals:

$$\frac{1}{5} \int \frac{x}{x^2 + 1} dx + \frac{13}{5} \int \frac{dx}{x^2 + 1} - \frac{1}{5} \int \frac{1}{x+2} dx$$

You can evaluate the first integral using u-substitution; the second integral is inverse tangent, and the third integral is a natural logarithm:

$$\frac{1}{10} \ln \left| x^2 + 1 \right| + \frac{13}{5} \tan^{-1}(x) - \frac{1}{5} \ln \left| x + 2 \right| + C$$

Notice how all of these integrals contained a natural logarithm term? That's typical of a partial fractions integral. Now try these solved problems. Do each problem, covering the answer first, then check your answer.

PROBLEM 1. Evaluate $\int \frac{4}{x^2 - 6x + 5} dx$.

Answer: First, factor the denominator:

$$\int \frac{4}{(x-1)(x-5)} dx$$

Find A and B such that:

$$\frac{A}{x-5} + \frac{B}{x-1} = \frac{4}{(x-5)(x-1)}$$

First, multiply through by $(x-5)(x-1)$:

$$A(x-1) + B(x-5) = 4$$

Next, simplify and group the terms:

$$Ax - A + Bx - 5B = 4$$

$$(A+B)x + (-A - 5B) = 4$$

You now have two simultaneous equations: $A + B = 0$ and $-A - 5B = 4$. If you solve the equations, you get $A = 1$ and $B = -1$. Thus, we can rewrite the integral as:

$$\int \frac{1}{x-5}dx - \int \frac{1}{x-1}dx$$

These are both logarithmic integrals. The solution is: $\ln|x-5| - \ln|x-1| + C$.

PROBLEM 2. Evaluate $\int \frac{(x+1)dx}{x(x^2+1)}$.

Answer: You need to find A, B, and C, such that:

$$\frac{A}{x} + \frac{Bx+C}{x^2+1} = \frac{x+1}{x(x^2+1)}$$

Multiply through by $x(x^2 + 1)$:

$$A(x^2 + 1) + (Bx + C)(x) = x + 1$$

Simplify and group the terms:

$$Ax^2 + A + Bx^2 + Cx = x + 1$$

$$(A + B)x^2 + Cx + A = x + 1$$

Now you have three equations:

$$A + B = 0$$

$$C = 1$$

$$A = 1$$

You only have to solve for B: Since $A = 1$, $B = -1$. Now rewrite the integral as:

$$\int \frac{1}{x}dx + \int \frac{-x+1}{x^2+1}dx$$

Break this into:

$$\int \frac{1}{x}dx - \int \frac{x\,dx}{x^2+1} + \int \frac{1}{x^2+1}dx$$

The first integral is a natural logarithm, the second integral requires u-substitution, and the third integral is an inverse tangent. The answer is:

$$\ln|x| - \frac{1}{2}\ln\left(x^2+1\right) + \tan^{-1}(x) + C$$

Problem 3. Evaluate $\int \dfrac{6x^2 - 17x + 25}{(x-1)(x-2)(x-3)}\, dx$.

Answer: You need to find A, B, and C such that:

$$\frac{A}{x-1} + \frac{B}{x-2} + \frac{C}{x-3} = \frac{6x^2 - 17x + 25}{(x-1)(x-2)(x-3)}$$

First, multiply through by $(x-1)(x-2)(x-3)$:

$$A(x-2)(x-3) + B(x-1)(x-3) + C(x-1)(x-2) = 6x^2 - 17x + 25$$

Next, simplify and group the terms:

$$A(x^2 - 5x + 6) + B(x^2 - 4x + 3) + C(x^2 - 3x + 2) = 6x^2 - 17x + 25$$

$$(A + B + C)x^2 + (-5A - 4B - 3C)x + (6A + 3B + 2C) = 6x^2 - 17x + 25$$

Now you have three simultaneous equations:

$$A + B + C = 6$$

$$-5A - 4B - 3C = -17$$

$$6A + 3B + 2C = 25$$

The three constants become: $A = 7$, $B = -15$, and $C = 14$. Thus, you can rewrite the integral as:

$$\int \frac{7}{x-1}\,dx - \int \frac{15}{x-2}\,dx + \int \frac{14}{x-3}\,dx$$

These are all logarithmic integrals. The solution is:

$$7\ln\left|x-1\right| - 15\ln\left|x-2\right| + 14\ln\left|x-3\right| + C$$

PRACTICE PROBLEM SET 31

Evaluate the following integrals. The answers are in Chapter 21.

1. $\displaystyle\int \frac{x+4}{(x-1)(x+6)}\,dx$

2. $\displaystyle\int \frac{x}{(x-3)(x+1)}\,dx$

3. $\displaystyle\int \frac{1}{x^3 + x^2 - 2x}\,dx$

4. $\displaystyle\int \frac{2x+1}{x^2 - 7x + 12}\,dx$

5. $\int \dfrac{2x-1}{(x-1)^2}\,dx$

6. $\int \dfrac{1}{(x+1)(x^2+1)}\,dx$

7. $\int \dfrac{2x+1}{(x+1)(x^2+2)}\,dx$

8. $\int \dfrac{x^2+3x-1}{x^3-1}\,dx$

IMPROPER INTEGRALS

There's one last type of integral that shows up on the BC exam. These are improper integrals, which are integrals evaluated over an open interval, rather than a closed one. More formally, an integral is improper if: (a) its integrand becomes infinite at one or more points in the interval of integration; or (b) one or both of the limits of integration is infinite.

We integrate an improper integral by evaluating the integral for a constant (a) and then taking the limit of the resulting integral as a approaches the limit in question. If the limit exists, the integral **converges** and the value of the integral is the limit. If the limit doesn't exist, the integral **diverges** and the integral cannot be evaluated there.

Confusing, huh? Let's clear the air with an example.

Example 1: Evaluate $\displaystyle\int_0^4 \sqrt{\dfrac{4+x}{4-x}}\,dx$.

At $x = 4$, the denominator is zero and the integrand is undefined. Therefore, replace the 4 in the limit of the integral with a and evaluate:

$$\lim_{a\to 4-}\int_0^a \sqrt{\dfrac{4+x}{4-x}}\,dx$$

Multiply the numerator and the denominator of the integrand by $\sqrt{4+x}$:

$$\int \sqrt{\dfrac{4+x}{4-x}}\,\dfrac{\sqrt{4+x}}{\sqrt{4+x}}\,dx = \int \dfrac{4+x}{\sqrt{16-x^2}}\,dx = \int \dfrac{4}{\sqrt{16-x^2}}\,dx + \int \dfrac{x}{\sqrt{16-x^2}}\,dx$$

Evaluate the first integral by factoring 16 out of the denominator:

$$\int \dfrac{4\,dx}{4\sqrt{1-\left(\dfrac{x}{4}\right)^2}} = \int \dfrac{dx}{\sqrt{1-\left(\dfrac{x}{4}\right)^2}}$$

Next, use u-substitution. Let $u = \dfrac{x}{4}$ and $du = \dfrac{1}{4}dx$:

$$\int \frac{4du}{\sqrt{1-u^2}} = 4\sin^{-1}u = 4\sin^{-1}\left(\frac{x}{4}\right)$$

Evaluate the second integral with u-substitution. Let $u = 16 - x^2$ and $du = -2x\,dx$:

$$-\frac{1}{2}\int u^{-\frac{1}{2}}du = -u^{\frac{1}{2}} = -\sqrt{16-x^2}$$

The final result is:

$$\int \frac{4}{\sqrt{16-x^2}}dx + \int \frac{x\,dx}{\sqrt{16-x^2}} = 4\sin^{-1}\frac{x}{4} - \sqrt{16-x^2}$$

Now you have to evaluate the integral at the limits of integration:

$$4\sin^{-1}\frac{x}{4} - \sqrt{16-x^2}\,\Big|_0^a = \left(4\sin^{-1}\frac{a}{4} - \sqrt{16-a^2}\right) + (4)$$

Finally, take the limit as a tends to 4:

$$\lim_{a\to 4^-}\left(\left(4\sin^{-1}\frac{a}{4} - \sqrt{16-a^2}\right) + (4)\right) = \left(\left(4\sin^{-1}(1)\right) + (4)\right) = 2\pi + 4$$

This may look complicated, but it was actually a very straightforward process. Because the integrand didn't exist at $x = 4$, replace 4 with a and then integrate. When you evaluated the limits of integration using a instead of 4, you then took the limit as a tends to 4.

Example 2: Evaluate $\displaystyle\int_0^\infty \frac{dx}{1+x^2}$.

Replace the upper limit of integration with a and take the limit as a tends to infinity:

$$\lim_{a\to\infty}\int_0^a \frac{dx}{1+x^2}$$

Integrate:

$$\int_0^a \frac{dx}{1+x^2} = \tan^{-1}x\,\Big|_0^a = \tan^{-1}a$$

Now, take the limit:

$$\lim_{a\to\infty}\tan^{-1}a = \frac{\pi}{2}$$

Let's do an integral that becomes undefined in the middle of the limits of integration.

Example 3: Evaluate $\int_0^2 \dfrac{dx}{\sqrt[3]{x-1}}$.

Note that this integral becomes undefined at $x = 1$. Because of this, you have to divide the integral into two parts: one for $x < 1$ and one for $x > 1$:

$$\lim_{a\to 1^-} \int_0^a \frac{dx}{\sqrt[3]{x-1}} \text{ and } \lim_{b\to 1^+} \int_b^2 \frac{dx}{\sqrt[3]{x-1}}$$

If either of these limits fails to exist, then the integral from 0 to 2 diverges. Evaluate them both:

$$\lim_{a\to 1^-}\left[\frac{3}{2}(x-1)^{\frac{2}{3}}\Big|_0^a\right] + \lim_{b\to 1^+}\left[\frac{3}{2}(x-1)^{\frac{2}{3}}\Big|_b^2\right]$$

$$= \lim_{a\to 1^-}\left[\frac{3}{2}(a-1)^{\frac{2}{3}} - \frac{3}{2}\right] + \lim_{b\to 1^+}\left[\frac{3}{2} - (b-1)^{\frac{2}{3}}\right] = -\frac{3}{2} + \frac{3}{2} = 0$$

Because both limits exist and are finite, the integral converges and the value is 0.

There are several other facets of evaluating improper integrals that we won't explore here because they don't appear on the AP exam. You'll only have to do the most simple of these, usually one with infinity as a limit of integration.

Evaluate these integrals and check your work.

PROBLEM 1. Evaluate $\int_1^\infty \dfrac{dx}{x}$.

Answer: First, evaluate the integral:

$$\int_1^a \frac{dx}{x} = \ln x\Big|_1^a = \ln a$$

Next, we evaluate the limit: $\lim_{a\to\infty} \ln a = \infty$

Therefore $\int_1^\infty \dfrac{dx}{x} = \infty$, and the integral diverges.

PROBLEM 2. Evaluate $\int_1^\infty \dfrac{dx}{x^2}$.

Answer: Evaluate the integral:

$$\int_1^a \frac{dx}{x^2} = -\frac{1}{x}\Big|_1^a = -\frac{1}{a} + 1$$

Next, evaluate the limit:

$$\lim_{a \to \infty}\left(-\frac{1}{a}+1\right)=1$$

Therefore $\int_1^\infty \frac{dx}{x^2}=1$, and the integral converges.

PROBLEM 3. Evaluate $\int_0^1 \frac{dx}{\sqrt{1-x^2}}$.

Answer: Evaluate the integral:

$$\int_0^a \frac{dx}{\sqrt{1-x^2}}=\sin^{-1}x\Big|_0^a=\sin^{-1}(a)-\sin^{-1}(0)=\sin^{-1}(a)$$

Next evaluate:

$$\lim_{a \to 1^-}\left(\sin^{-1}a\right)=\frac{\pi}{2}$$

Therefore $\int_0^1 \frac{dx}{\sqrt{1-x^2}}=\frac{\pi}{2}$, and the integral converges.

PROBLEM 4. Evaluate $\int_{-2}^2 \frac{dx}{x^2}$.

Answer: The integrand becomes undefined at $x=0$, so you have to divide the integral into:

$$\lim_{a \to 0^-}\int_{-2}^a \frac{dx}{x^2} \text{ and } \lim_{b \to 0^+}\int_b^2 \frac{dx}{x^2}$$

Now, evaluating both integrals:

$$\lim_{a \to 0^-}\left[-\frac{1}{x}\Big|_{-2}^a\right]+\lim_{b \to 0^+}\left[-\frac{1}{x}\Big|_b^2\right]=\lim_{a \to 0^-}\left[-\frac{1}{a}-\frac{1}{2}\right]+\lim_{b \to 0^+}\left[-\frac{1}{2}+\frac{1}{b}\right]=\infty$$

The integral diverges.

PRACTICE PROBLEM SET 32

Evaluate the following integrals. The answers are in Chapter 21.

1. $\displaystyle\int_0^1 \frac{dx}{\sqrt{x}}$

2. $\displaystyle\int_{-1}^1 \frac{dx}{x^{\frac{2}{3}}}$

3. $\displaystyle\int_{-\infty}^0 e^x dx$

4. $\displaystyle\int_{-\infty}^{\frac{\pi}{2}} \tan\theta\, d\theta$

5. $\displaystyle\int_1^4 \frac{dx}{1-x}$

6. $\displaystyle\int_0^1 \frac{x+1}{\sqrt{x^2+2x}}\, dx$

7. $\displaystyle\int_{-\infty}^0 \frac{dx}{(2x-1)^3}$

8. $\displaystyle\int_{-\infty}^{\infty} x^3 dx$

9. $\displaystyle\int_0^3 \frac{dx}{x-2}$

10. $\displaystyle\int_{-1}^8 \frac{dx}{\sqrt[3]{x}}$

CALCULUS OF POLAR CURVES

The topic of polar curves usually only shows up as one multiple-choice problem on the BC exam. However, we will cover the two most typical aspects of the calculus of polar curves. We expect that you had a full treatment of polar coordinates and curves in precalculus, so we won't cover them here.

SLOPE

The slope of a polar curve $r = f(\theta)$ is $\dfrac{dy}{dx}$. Because x and y are defined parametrically, we need to derive $\dfrac{dy}{dx}$ in terms of r and θ. Remember, in polar coordinates, that $x = r\cos\theta = f(\theta)\cos\theta$ and $y = r\sin\theta = f(\theta)\sin\theta$.

Note that: $\dfrac{dy}{dx} = \dfrac{\dfrac{dy}{d\theta}}{\dfrac{dx}{d\theta}}$

We substitute for x and y: $\dfrac{\dfrac{dy}{d\theta}}{\dfrac{dx}{d\theta}} = \dfrac{\dfrac{d}{d\theta}\left[f(\theta)\sin\theta\right]}{\dfrac{d}{d\theta}\left[f(\theta)\cos\theta\right]}$

Using the Product Rule, we get: $\dfrac{dy}{dx} = \dfrac{f'(\theta)\sin\theta + f(\theta)\cos\theta}{f'(\theta)\cos\theta - f(\theta)\sin\theta}$

This is the formula for finding the slope of a polar curve $r = f(\theta)$.

Example 1: Find the slope of the tangent line to the curve $r = 2 + 4\sin\theta$.

First, let's find $f'(\theta)$: $f'(\theta) = 4\cos\theta$
This gives us:

$$\frac{dy}{dx} = \frac{4\cos\theta\sin\theta + (2 + 4\sin\theta)\cos\theta}{4\cos\theta\cos\theta - (2 + 4\sin\theta)\sin\theta} = \frac{2\cos\theta + 8\sin\theta\cos\theta}{4\cos^2\theta - 4\sin^2\theta - 2\sin\theta} = \frac{2\cos\theta + 4\sin 2\theta}{4\cos 2\theta - 2\sin\theta}$$

Area in Polar Coordinates:

We are not going to derive the formula for you. If we want to find the area of a region between the origin and the curve $r = f(\theta)$, $a \le \theta \le b$, we use the formula: $Area = \displaystyle\int_a^b \frac{1}{2}r^2 d\theta$.

Example 2: Find the area of the region in the plane enclosed by the cardioid $r = 4 + 4\sin\theta$.

First, let's graph the curve:

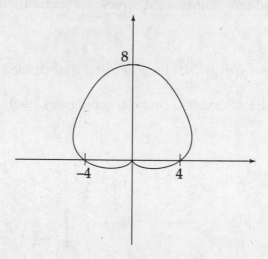

Because r sweeps out the region as θ goes from 0 to 2π, these are our limits of integration. Plug into the formula for area:

$$A = \int_0^{2\pi} \frac{1}{2}(4 + 4\sin\theta)^2 \, d\theta$$

Evaluate the integral:

$$A = \int_0^{2\pi} \frac{1}{2}(4 + 4\sin\theta)^2 \, d\theta = \int_0^{2\pi} \left(8 + 16\sin\theta + 8\sin^2\theta\right) d\theta$$

Use the trig identity $\sin^2\theta = \dfrac{1 - \cos 2\theta}{2}$ to rewrite the integrand:

$$\int_0^{2\pi} \left(8 + 16\sin\theta + 4 - 4\cos 2\theta\right) d\theta = \int_0^{2\pi} \left(12 + 16\sin\theta - 4\cos 2\theta\right) d\theta$$

Evaluate the integral:

$$\int_0^{2\pi} \left(12 + 16\sin\theta - 4\cos 2\theta\right) d\theta = \left(12\theta - 16\cos\theta - 2\sin 2\theta\right)\Big|_0^{2\pi} = (24\pi - 16) - (-16) = 24\pi$$

Example 3: Find the area inside the smaller loop of the limaçon $r = 1 + 2\cos\theta$.

First, let's graph the curve:

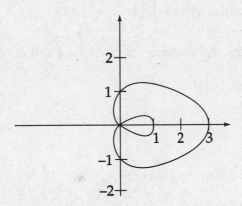

Because in the inner loop, r sweeps out the region as θ goes from $\dfrac{2\pi}{3}$ to $\dfrac{4\pi}{3}$, these are our limits of integration.

Plug into the formula for area:

$$A = \int_{\frac{2\pi}{3}}^{\frac{4\pi}{3}} \frac{1}{2}(1+2\cos\theta)^2\, d\theta$$

Evaluate the integral:

$$A = \int_{\frac{2\pi}{3}}^{\frac{4\pi}{3}} \frac{1}{2}(1+2\cos\theta)^2\, d\theta = \frac{1}{2}\int_{\frac{2\pi}{3}}^{\frac{4\pi}{3}} \left(1+4\cos\theta+4\cos^2\theta\right)d\theta$$

Use the trig identity $\cos^2\theta = \dfrac{1+\cos 2\theta}{2}$ to rewrite the integrand:

$$\frac{1}{2}\int_{\frac{2\pi}{3}}^{\frac{4\pi}{3}} \left(1+4\cos\theta+2+2\cos 2\theta\right)d\theta = \frac{1}{2}\int_{\frac{2\pi}{3}}^{\frac{4\pi}{3}} \left(3+4\cos\theta+2\cos 2\theta\right)d\theta$$

Evaluate the integral:

$$\frac{1}{2}\int_{\frac{2\pi}{3}}^{\frac{4\pi}{3}} \left(3+4\cos\theta+2\cos 2\theta\right)d\theta = \frac{1}{2}\left(3\theta+4\sin\theta+\sin 2\theta\right)\Big|_{\frac{2\pi}{3}}^{\frac{4\pi}{3}} = \frac{1}{2}\left(4\pi-2\sqrt{3}+\frac{\sqrt{3}}{2}\right)-\frac{1}{2}\left(2\pi+2\sqrt{3}-\frac{\sqrt{3}}{2}\right)=\pi-\frac{3}{2}\sqrt{3}$$

Area between two polar curves: Again, we are not going to derive the formula for you. If we want to find the area of a region between the curves $r_1 = f_1(\theta)$ and $r_2 = f_2(\theta)$, with $0 \leq r_1(\theta) \leq r_2(\theta)$ and $a \leq \theta \leq b$, we use the formula: $Area = \int_a^b \frac{1}{2}\left(r_2{}^2 - r_1{}^2\right)d\theta$.

Example 4: Find the area of the region inside the circle $r = 4$ and outside $r = 4 - \cos\theta$.

First, let's graph the region:

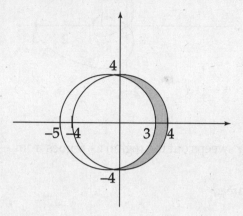

Because r sweeps out the region as θ goes from $-\dfrac{\pi}{2}$ to $\dfrac{\pi}{2}$, these are our limits of integration. Here,

because of symmetry, instead of evaluating $A = \dfrac{1}{2}\displaystyle\int_{-\frac{\pi}{2}}^{\frac{\pi}{2}}\left(r_2{}^2 - r_1{}^2\right)d\theta$, we can evaluate $A = \displaystyle\int_0^{\frac{\pi}{2}}\left(r_2{}^2 - r_1{}^2\right)d\theta$.

Plug into the formula for area:

$$A = \int_0^{\frac{\pi}{2}}\left[(4)^2 - (4 - \cos\theta)^2\right]d\theta = \int_0^{\frac{\pi}{2}}\left[8\cos\theta - \cos^2\theta\right]d\theta$$

Use the trig identity $\cos^2\theta = \dfrac{1 + \cos 2\theta}{2}$ to rewrite the integrand:

$$\int_0^{\frac{\pi}{2}}\left[8\cos\theta - \cos^2\theta\right]d\theta = \int_0^{\frac{\pi}{2}}\left(8\cos\theta - \frac{1 + \cos 2\theta}{2}\right)d\theta = \int_0^{\frac{\pi}{2}}\left(8\cos\theta - \frac{1}{2} - \frac{\cos 2\theta}{2}\right)d\theta$$

Evaluate the integral:

$$\int_0^{\frac{\pi}{2}}\left(8\cos\theta - \frac{1}{2} - \frac{\cos 2\theta}{2}\right)d\theta = \left(8\sin\theta - \frac{\theta}{2} - \frac{\sin 2\theta}{4}\right)\Bigg|_0^{\frac{\pi}{2}} = 8 - \frac{\pi}{4}$$

PRACTICE PROBLEM SET 33

Do the following problems on your own. The answers are in Chapter 21.

1. Find the slope of the curve $r = 2\cos 4\theta$.

2. Find the slope of the curve $r = 2 - 3\sin\theta$ at $(2, \pi)$.

3. Find the area inside the limaçon $r = 4 + 2\cos\theta$.

4. Find the area inside one loop of the lemniscate $r^2 = 4\cos 2\theta$.

5. Find the area inside $r = 2\cos\theta$ and outside $r = 1$.

6. Find the area inside the lemniscate $r^2 = 6\cos 2\theta$ and outside the circle $r = \sqrt{3}$.

19

Differential Equations

There are many types of differential equations, but only a very small number of them appear on the AP exam. There are courses devoted to learning how to solve a wide variety of differential equations, but AP calculus provides only a very basic introduction to the topic.

SEPARATION OF VARIABLES

If you're given an equation in which the derivative of a function is equal to some other function, you can determine the original function by integrating both sides of the equation and then solving for the constant term.

Example 1: If $\dfrac{dy}{dx} = \dfrac{4x}{y}$ and $y(0) = 5$, find an equation for y in terms of x.

The first step in solving these is to put all of the terms that contain y on the left side of the equals sign and all of the terms that contain x on the right side. We then have: $y\,dy = 4x\,dx$. The second step is to integrate both sides:

$$\int y\,dy = \int 4x\,dx$$

And then you integrate:

$$\frac{y^2}{2} = 2x^2 + C$$

You're not done yet. The final step is to solve for the constant by plugging in $x = 0$ and $y = 5$:

$$\frac{5^2}{2} = 2\left(0^2\right) + C, \text{ so } C = \frac{25}{2}$$

The solution is $\dfrac{y^2}{2} = 2x^2 + \dfrac{25}{2}$.

That's all there is to it. Separate the variables, integrate both sides, and solve for the constant.

Often, the equation will involve a logarithm. Let's do an example.

Example 2: If $\dfrac{dy}{dx} = 3x^2y$ and $y(0) = 2$, find an equation for y in terms of x.

First, put the y terms on the left and the x terms on the right:

$$\frac{dy}{y} = 3x^2dx$$

Next, integrate both sides:

$$\int \frac{dy}{y} = \int 3x^2dx$$

The result is: $\ln y = x^3 + C$.

It's customary to solve this equation for y. You can do this by putting both sides into exponential form:

$$y = e^{x^3 + C}$$

This can be rewritten as $y = e^{x^3}e^c$ and, because e^c is a constant, the equation becomes:

$$y = Ce^{x^3}$$

This is the preferred form of the equation. Now, solve for the constant. Plug in $x = 0$ and $y = 2$, and you get $2 = Ce^0$.

Because $e^0 = 1$, $C = 2$. The solution is $y = 2e^{x^3}$.

This is the typical differential equation that you'll see on the AP exam. The other common problem type involves position, velocity, and acceleration. We did several problems of this type in Chapter 8, before you knew how to use integrals. In a sample problem, you're given the velocity and acceleration and told to find distance (the reverse of what we did before).

Example 3: If the acceleration of a particle is given by $a(t) = -32$ ft/sec², and the velocity of the particle is 64 ft/sec and the height of the particle is 32 ft at time $t = 0$, find: (a) the equation of the particle's velocity at time t; (b) the equation for the particle's height, h, at time t; and (c) the maximum height of the particle.

Part A: Because acceleration is the rate of change of velocity with respect to time, you can write that $\dfrac{dv}{dt} = -32$. Now separate the variables and integrate both sides:

$$\int dv = \int -32\, dt$$

Integrating this expression, we get $v = -32t + C$. Now we can solve for the constant by plugging in $t = 0$ and $v = 64$. We get: $64 = -32(0) + C$ and $C = 64$. Thus, velocity is $v = -32t + 64$.

Part B: Because velocity is the rate of change of displacement with respect to time, you can write that:

$$\frac{dh}{dt} = -32t + 64$$

Separate the variables and integrate both sides:

$$\int dh = \int (-32t + 64)\, dt$$

Integrate the expression: $h = -16t^2 + 64t + C$. Now solve for the constant by plugging in $t = 0$ and $h = 32$:

$$32 = -16\left(0^2\right) + 64(0) + C \text{ and } C = 32$$

Thus, the equation for height is $h = -16t^2 + 64t + 32$.

Part C: In order to find the maximum height, you need to take the derivative of the height with respect to time and set it equal to zero. Notice that the derivative of height with respect to time is the velocity; just set the velocity equal to zero and solve for t:

$$-32t + 64 = 0, \text{ so } t = 2$$

Thus, at time $t = 2$, the height of the particle is a maximum. Now, plug $t = 2$ into the equation for height:

$$h = -16(2)^2 + 64(2) + 32 = 96$$

Therefore, the maximum height of the particle is 96 feet.

Here are some solved problems. Do each problem, covering the answer first, then check your answer.

PROBLEM 1. If $\dfrac{dy}{dx} = \dfrac{3x}{2y}$ and $y(0) = 10$, find an equation for y in terms of x.

Answer: First, separate the variables:

$$2y\, dy = 3x\, dx$$

Then, we take the integral of both sides:

$$\int 2y\, dy = \int 3x\, dx$$

Next, integrate both sides:

$$y^2 = \frac{3x^2}{2} + C$$

Finally, solve for the constant:

$$10^2 = \frac{3(0)^2}{2} + C \text{ so } C = 100$$

The solution is $y^2 = \dfrac{3x^2}{2} + 100$.

PROBLEM 2. If $\dfrac{dy}{dx} = 4xy^2$ and $y(0) = 1$, find an equation for y in terms of x.

Answer: First, separate the variables: $\dfrac{dy}{y^2} = 4x\, dx$ and take the integral of both sides:

$$\int \frac{dy}{y^2} = \int 4x\, dx$$

Next, integrate both sides: $-\dfrac{1}{y} = 2x^2 + C$. You can rewrite this as: $y = -\dfrac{1}{2x^2 + C}$.

Finally, solve for the constant:

$$1 = -\frac{1}{2(0)^2 + C} = \frac{-1}{C}, \text{ so } C = -1$$

The solution is $y = -\dfrac{1}{2x^2 - 1}$.

PROBLEM 3. If $\dfrac{dy}{dx} = \dfrac{y^2}{x}$ and $y(1) = \dfrac{1}{3}$, find an equation for y in terms of x.

Answer: This time, separating the variables gives us this: $\dfrac{dy}{y^2} = \dfrac{dx}{x}$.

Then, take the integral of both sides: $\displaystyle\int \dfrac{dy}{y^2} = \int \dfrac{dx}{x}$.

Next, integrate both sides: $-\dfrac{1}{y} = \ln x + C$ and rearrange:

$$y = \dfrac{-1}{\ln x + C}$$

Finally, solve for the constant: $\dfrac{1}{3} = \dfrac{-1}{C}$, so $C = -3$. The solution is $y = \dfrac{-1}{\ln x - 3}$.

PROBLEM 4. A city had a population of 10,000 in 1980 and 13,000 in 1990. Assuming an exponential growth rate, estimate the city's population in 2000.

Answer: The phrase "exponential growth rate" means that $\dfrac{dy}{dt} = ky$, where k is a constant. Take the integral of both sides:

$$\int \dfrac{dy}{y} = \int k\, dt$$

Then, integrate both sides: $(\ln y = kt + C)$ and put both sides in exponential form:

$$y = e^{kt+c} = Ce^{kt}$$

Next, use the information about the population to solve for the constants. If you treat 1980 as $t = 0$ and 1990 as $t = 10$, then:

$$10{,}000 = Ce^{k(0)} \text{ and } 13{,}000 = Ce^{k(10)}$$

So, $C = 10{,}000$ and $k = \dfrac{1}{10}\ln 1.3 \approx .0262$.

The equation for population growth is approximately $y = 10{,}000e^{.0262t}$. We can estimate that the population in 2000 will be:

$$y = 10{,}000e^{.0262(20)} = 16{,}900$$

EULER'S METHOD

You are going to use your calculator to find an approximate answer to a differential equation. The method is quite simple. First, you need a starting point and an initial slope.

Next, we use increments of h to come up with approximations. Each new approximation will use the following rules:

$$x_n = x_{n-1} + h$$

$$y_n = y_{n-1} + h\left(y'_{n-1}\right)$$

Repeat for $n = 1, 2, 3, \ldots$

This is much easier to understand if we do an example.

Example 1: Use Euler's Method, with $h = 0.2$, to estimate $y(1)$ if $y' = y - 2$ and $y(0) = 4$.

We are given that the curve goes through the point $(0, 4)$. We will call the coordinates of this point $x_0 = 0$ and $y_0 = 4$. The slope is found by $y_0 = 4$ plugging into $y' = y - 2$, so we have an initial slope of $y'_0 = 4 - 2 = 2$.

Now we need to find the next set of points.

Step 1: Increase x_0 by h to get x_1:

$$x_1 = 0.2$$

Step 2: Multiply h by y'_0 and add to y_0 to get y_1:

$$y_1 = 4 + 0.2(2) = 4.4$$

Step 3: Find y'_1 by plugging y_1 into the equation for y':

$$y'_1 = 4.4 - 2 = 2.4$$

Repeat until you get to the desired point (in this case $x = 1$).

Step 1: Increase x_1 by h to get x_2:

$$x_2 = 0.4$$

Step 2: Multiply h by y'_1 and add to y_1 to get y_2:

$$y_2 = 4.4 + 0.2(2.4) = 4.88$$

Step 3: Find y'_2 by plugging y_2 into the equation for y':

$$y'_2 = 4.88 - 2 = 2.88$$

Step 1: $x_3 = x_2 + h$:

$$x_3 = 0.6$$

Step 2: $y_3 = y_2 + h(y_2')$:

$$y_3 = 4.88 + 0.2(2.88) = 5.456$$

Step 3: $y_3' = y_3 - 2$:

$$y_3' = 5.456 - 2 = 3.456$$

Step 1: $x_4 = x_3 + h$:

$$x_4 = 0.8$$

Step 2: $y_4 = y_3 + h(y_3')$:

$$y_4 = 5.456 + 0.2(3.456) = 6.1472$$

Step 3: $y_4' = y_4 - 2$:

$$y_4' = 6.1472 - 2 = 4.1472$$

Step 1: $x_5 = x_4 + h$:

$$x_5 = 1.0$$

Step 2: $y_5 = y_4 + h(y_4')$:

$$y_5 = 6.1472 + 0.2(4.1472) = 6.97664$$

We don't need to go any further because we are asked for the value of y when $x = 1$.

The answer is $y = 6.97664$

Let's do another example.

Example 2: Use Euler's Method, with $h = 0.1$, to estimate $y(0.5)$ if $y' = y - 1$ and $y(0) = 3$.

We start with $x_0 = 0$ and $y_0 = 3$. The slope is found by plugging $y_0 = 3$ into $y' = y - 1$, so we have an initial slope of $y_0' = 3 - 1 = 2$.

Step 1: Increase x_0 by h to get x_1:

$$x_1 = 0.1$$

Step 2: Multiply h by y_0' and add to y_0 to get y_1:

$$y_1 = 3 + 0.1(2) = 3.2$$

Step 3: Find y_1' by plugging y_1 into the equation for y':

$$y_1' = 3.2 - 1 = 2.2$$

Step 1: $x_2 = x_1 + h$:

$$x_2 = 0.2$$

Step 2: $y_2 = y_1 + h(y_1')$:

$$y_2 = 3.2 + 0.1(2.2) = 3.42$$

Step 3: $y_2' = y_2 - 1$:

$$y_2' = 3.42 - 1 = 2.42$$

Step 1: $x_3 = x_2 + h$:

$$x_3 = 0.3$$

Step 2: $y_3 = y_2 + h(y_2')$:

$$y_3 = 3.42 + 0.1(2.42) = 3.662$$

Step 3: $y_3' = y_3 - 1$:

$$y_3' = 3.662 - 1 = 2.662$$

Step 1: $x_4 = x_3 + h$:

$$x_4 = 0.4$$

Step 2: $y_4 = y_3 + h(y_3')$:

$$y_4 = 3.662 + 0.1(2.662) = 3.9282$$

Step 3: $y_4' = y_4 - 1$:

$$y_4' = 3.9282 - 1 = 2.9282$$

Step 1: $x_5 = x_4 + h$:

$$x_5 = 0.5$$

Step 2: $y_5 = y_4 + h(y_4')$:

$$y_5 = 3.9282 + 0.1(2.9282) = 4.22102$$

The answer is $y = 4.22102$.

Now try these on your own. Do each problem first with the answer covered, then check your answer.

Problem 1: Use Euler's Method, with $h = 0.2$, to estimate $y(2)$ if $y' = 2y + 1$ and $y(1) = 5$.

We start with $x_0 = 1$ and $y_0 = 5$. The slope is found by plugging $y_0 = 5$ into $y' = 2y + 1$, so we have an initial slope of $y_0' = 2(5) + 1 = 11$.

Step 1: Increase x_0 by h to get x_1:

$$x_1 = 1.2$$

Step 2: Multiply h by y_0' and add to y_0 to get y_1:

$$y_1 = 5 + .2(11) = 7.2$$

Step 3: Find y_1' by plugging y_1 into the equation for y':

$$y_1' = 2(7.2) + 1 = 15.4$$

Step 1: $x_2 = x_1 + h$:

$$x_2 = 1.4$$

Step 2: $y_2 = y_1 + h(y_1')$:

$$y_2 = 7.2 + 0.2(15.4) = 10.28$$

Step 3: $y_2' = 2y_2 + 1$:

$$y_2' = 2(10.28) + 1 = 21.56$$

Step 1: $x_3 = x_2 + h$:

$$x_3 = 1.6$$

Step 2: $y_3 = y_2 + h(y_2')$:

$$y_3 = 10.28 + 0.2(21.56) = 14.592$$

Step 3: $y_3' = 2y_3 + 1$:

$$y_3' = 2(14.592) + 1 = 30.184$$

Step 1: $x_4 = x_3 + h$:

$$x_4 = 1.8$$

Step 2: $y_4 = y_3 + h(y_3')$:

$$y_4 = 14.592 + 0.2(30.184) = 20.6288$$

Step 3: $y_4' = 2y_4 + 1$:

$$y_4' = 2(20.6288) + 1 = 42.2576$$

Step 1: $x_5 = x_4 + h$:

$$x_5 = 2$$

Step 2: $y_5 = y_4 + h(y_4')$:

$$y_5 = 20.6288 + 0.2(42.2576) = 29.08032$$

The answer is $y = 29.08032$.

Problem 2: Use Euler's Method, with $h = 0.1$, to estimate $y(0.5)$ if $y' = y^2 + 1$ and $y(0) = 0$.

We start with $x_0 = 0$ and $y_0 = 0$. The slope is found by plugging $y_0 = 0$ into $y' = y^2 + 1$, so we have an initial slope of $y_0' = 1$.

Step 1: Increase x_0 by h to get x_1:

$$x_1 = 0.1$$

Step 2: Multiply h by y_0' and add to y_0 to get y_1:

$$y_1 = 0 + 0.1(1) = 0.1$$

Step 3: Find y_1' by plugging y_1 into the equation for y':

$$y_1' = (0.1)^2 + 1 = 1.01$$

Step 1: $x_2 = x_1 + h$:

$$x_2 = 0.2$$

Step 2: $y_2 = y_1 + h(y_1')$:

$$y_2 = 0.1 + 0.1(1.01) = 0.201$$

Step 3: $y_2' = (y_2)^2 + 1$:

$$y_2' = (0.201)^2 + 1 = 1.040$$

Step 1: $x_3 = x_2 + h$:

$$x_3 = 0.3$$

Step 2: $y_3 = y_2 + h(y_2')$:

$$y_3' = 0.0201 + 0.1(1.040) = 0.305$$

Step 3: $y_3' = (y_3)^2 + 1$:

$$y_3' = (0.305)^2 + 1 = 1.093$$

Step 1: $x_4 = x_3 + h$:

$$x_4 = 0.4$$

Step 2: $y_4 = y_3 + h(y_3')$:

$$y_4 = 0.305 + 0.1(1.093) = 0.414$$

Step 3: $y_4' = (y_4)^2 + 1$:

$$y_4' = (0.414)^2 + 1 = 1.171$$

Step 1: $x_5 = x_4 + h$:

$$x_5 = 0.5$$

Step 2: $y_5 = y_4 + h(y_4')$:

$$y_5 = 0.414 + 0.1(1.171) = 0.531$$

The answer is $y = 0.531$.

SLOPE FIELDS

Slope fields, also known as **direction fields**, were recently introduced into the AP calculus BC curriculum and have been on the AB test since 2004. Many students have commented that they find the topic difficult, so we will try to simplify it as much as possible.

The idea behind slope fields is to make a graphical representation of the <u>slope</u> of a function at various points in the plane. We are given a differential equation, but not the equation itself. So how do we do this? Well, it's always easiest to start with an example.

Example 1: Given $\dfrac{dy}{dx} = x$, sketch the slope field of the function.

What does this mean? Look at the equation. It gives us the derivative of the function, which is the *slope* of the tangent line to the curve at any point x. In other words, the equation tells us that the slope of the curve at any point x is the x value at that point.

For example, the slope of the curve at $x = 1$ is 1. The slope of the curve at $x = 2$ is 2. The slope of the curve at the origin is 0. The slope of the curve at $x = -1$ is -1. We will now represent these different slopes by drawing small segments of the tangent lines at those points. Let's make a sketch:

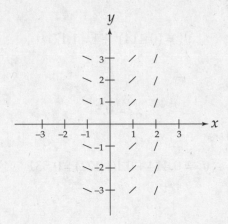

See how all of these slopes are independent of the y values, so for each value of x, the slope is the same vertically, but is different horizontally. Compare this slope field to the next example.

Example 2: Given $\dfrac{dy}{dx} = y$, sketch the slope field of the function.

Here, the slope of the curve at $y = 1$ is 1. The slope of the curve at $y = 2$ is 2. The slope of the curve at the origin is 0. The slope of the curve at $y = -1$ is -1. Let's make a sketch.

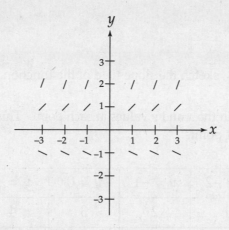

See how all of these slopes are independent of the x values, so for each value of y, the slope is the same horizontally, but is different vertically.

Now let's do a slightly harder example.

Example 3: Given $\dfrac{dy}{dx} = xy$, sketch the slope field of the function.

Now, we have to think about both the x and y values at each point. Let's calculate a few slopes.

At $(0,0)$, the slope is $(0)(0) = 0$.

At $(1,0)$, the slope is $(1)(0) = 0$.

At $(2,0)$, the slope is $(2)(0) = 0$.

At $(0,1)$, the slope is $(0)(1) = 0$.

At $(0,2)$, the slope is $(0)(2) = 0$.

So the slope will be zero at any point on the coordinate axes.

At $(1,1)$, the slope is $(1)(1) = 1$.

At $(1,2)$, the slope is $(1)(2) = 2$.

At $(1,-1)$, the slope is $(1)(-1) = -1$.

At $(1,-2)$, the slope is $(1)(-2) = -2$.

So the slope at any point where $x = 1$ will be the y value. Similarly, you should see that the slope at any point where $y = 1$ will be the x value. As we move out the coordinate axes, slopes will get steeper—whether positive or negative.

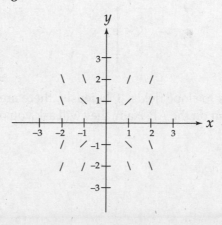

Let's do one more example.

Example 4: Given $\dfrac{dy}{dx} = y - x$, sketch the slope field of the function.

We have to think about both the x and y values at each point. This time, let's make a table of the values of the slope at different points.

	$y = -3$	$y = -2$	$y = -1$	$y = 0$	$y = 1$	$y = 2$	$y = 3$
$x = -3$	0	1	2	3	4	5	6
$x = -2$	–1	0	1	2	3	4	5
$x = -1$	–2	–1	0	1	2	3	4
$x = 0$	–3	–2	–1	0	1	2	3
$x = 1$	–4	–3	–2	–1	0	1	2
$x = 2$	–5	–4	–3	–2	–1	0	1
$x = 3$	–6	–5	–4	–3	–2	–1	0

Now, let's make a sketch of the slope field. Notice that the slopes are zero along the line $y = x$ and that the slopes get steeper as we move away from the line in either direction.

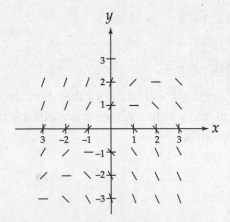

That's really all that there is to slope fields. Obviously, there are more complicated slope fields that one could come up with, but on the AP exam, they will ask you only to sketch the simplest ones.

PRACTICE PROBLEM SET 34

Now try these problems. The answers are in Chapter 21.

1. If $\dfrac{dy}{dx} = \dfrac{7x^2}{y^3}$ and $y(3) = 2$, find an equation for y in terms of x.

2. If $\dfrac{dy}{dx} = 5x^2\, y$ and $y(0) = 6$, find an equation for y in terms of x.

3. If $\dfrac{dy}{dx} = \dfrac{1}{y + x^2 y}$ and $y(0) = 2$, find an equation for y in terms of x.

4. If $\dfrac{dy}{dx} = \dfrac{e^x}{y^2}$ and $y(0) = 1$, find an equation for y in terms of x.

5. If $\dfrac{dy}{dx} = \dfrac{y^2}{x^3}$ and $y(1) = 2$, find an equation for y in terms of x.

6. If $\dfrac{dy}{dx} = \dfrac{\sin x}{\cos y}$ and $y(0) = \dfrac{3\pi}{2}$, find an equation for y in terms of x.

7. A colony of bacteria grows exponentially and the colony's population is 4,000 at time $t = 0$ and 6,500 at time $t = 3$. How big is the population at time $t = 10$?

8. A rock is thrown upward with an initial velocity, $v(t)$, of 18 m/s from a height, $h(t)$, of 45 m. If the acceleration of the rock is a constant –9 m/s², find the height of the rock at time $t = 4$.

9. The rate of growth of the volume of a sphere is proportional to its volume. If the volume of the sphere is initially 36π ft³, and expands to 90π ft³ after 1 second, find the volume of the sphere after 3 seconds.

10. A radioactive element decays exponentially proportionally to its mass. One-half of its original amount remains after 5,750 years. If 10,000 grams of the element are present initially, how much will be left after 1,000 years?

11. Use Euler's Method, with $h = 0.25$, to estimate $y(1)$ if $y' = y - x$ and $y(0) = 2$.

12. Use Euler's Method, with $h = 0.2$, to estimate $y(1)$ if $y' = -y$ and $y(0) = 1$.

13. Use Euler's Method, with $h = 0.1$, to estimate $y(0.5)$ if $y' = 4x^3$ and $y(0) = 0$.

14. Sketch the slope field for $\dfrac{dy}{dx} = 2x$.

15. Sketch the slope field for $\dfrac{dy}{dx} = -\dfrac{x}{y}$.

16. Sketch the slope field for $\dfrac{dy}{dx} = \dfrac{x}{y}$.

20

Infinite Series

SEQUENCES AND SERIES

First, let's learn some terminology. A **sequence** of numbers is an infinite succession of numbers that

follow a pattern: For example: $1, 2, 3, 4, \ldots$; or $\dfrac{1}{2}, \dfrac{1}{3}, \dfrac{1}{4} \ldots$; or $1, -1, 1, -1 \ldots$.

Terms in a sequence are usually denoted with a subscript; the first term of a sequence is a_1, the second term of a sequence is a_2, the nth term of a sequence is a_n, and so on.

Usually, the terms in a sequence are generated by a formula. For example, the sequence $a_n = \dfrac{n-1}{n}$ beginning with $n = 1$ is: $0, \dfrac{1}{2}, \dfrac{2}{3}, \dfrac{3}{4}, \ldots$. This is found by plugging in 1 for n, then 2, then 3, and so on. Notice that n is always an integer.

A sequence converges to a number if, as n gets bigger, the terms get closer to a certain number; that number is the limit of the sequence.

Here's the official math jargon:

> A sequence has a limit L if, for any $\varepsilon > 0$ there is an associated positive integer N such that $|a_n - L| < \varepsilon$ for all $n \geq N$. If so, the sequence **converges** to L and we write: $\lim_{n \to \infty} a_n = L$.

If the sequence has no finite limit, it **diverges**.

For example: the sequence $a_n = \dfrac{n-1}{n}$ converges, because $\lim_{n \to \infty} \dfrac{n-1}{n} = 1$. As n gets bigger, the terms of the sequence get closer and closer to 1. The sequence $a_n = 2^n$ diverges, because $\lim_{n \to \infty} 2^n = \infty$. As n gets bigger, the terms of the sequence get bigger.

Now that we've defined a sequence, we can define a series. A **series** is an expression of the form $a_1 + a_2 + a_3 + a_4 + \ldots a_n + \ldots$. If the series stops at some final term a_n, the series is finite. If the series continues indefinitely, it's an infinite series. These are the ones that primarily show up on the AP. Since a series is the sum of all the terms of a sequence, we often use sigma notation like this:

$$\sum_{n=1}^{\infty} a_n$$

The Harmonic Series, for example, looks like this:

$$\sum_{n=1}^{\infty} \frac{1}{n} = 1 + \frac{1}{2} + \frac{1}{3} + \frac{1}{4} + \ldots$$

> A **partial sum** of a series is the sum of the series up to a particular value of n. If the sequence of partial sums of a series converges to a limit L, then the series is said to converge to that limit L, and we write:
>
> $$\sum_{n=1}^{\infty} a_n = L$$

If there is no such limit, (like the Harmonic series, for example) then the series diverges.

Example 1: Does the series $\displaystyle\sum_{n=1}^{\infty} \frac{1}{3^n}$ converge and, if so, to what value?

The nth partial sum of this series is $\dfrac{1}{3} + \dfrac{1}{3^2} + \dfrac{1}{3^3} + \ldots \dfrac{1}{3^n}$. You can figure out the limit using the following method. First, write it out:

$$S_n = \frac{1}{3} + \frac{1}{3^2} + \frac{1}{3^3} + \ldots \frac{1}{3^n}$$

Next, multiply through by $\frac{1}{3}$:

$$\frac{1}{3}S_n = \frac{1}{3^2} + \frac{1}{3^3} + ... \frac{1}{3^{n+1}}$$

If you now subtract the second expression from the first, you get:

$$\frac{2}{3}S_n = \frac{1}{3} - \frac{1}{3^{n+1}}$$

Now, multiply through by $\frac{3}{2}$:

$$S_n = \frac{3}{2}\left(\frac{1}{3} - \frac{1}{3^{n+1}}\right)$$

Finally, take the limit:

$$\lim_{n \to \infty} \frac{3}{2}\left(\frac{1}{3} - \frac{1}{3^{n+1}}\right) = \frac{3}{2}\left(\frac{1}{3} - 0\right) = \frac{1}{2}$$

The series converges to $\frac{1}{2}$.

GEOMETRIC SERIES

The problem above contains an example of a series called a geometric series. Generally, this series takes the following form:

$$a + ar + ar^2 + ar^3 + ... + ar^{n-1} + ... = \sum_{n=1}^{\infty} ar^{n-1}$$

These series often show up on the AP exam. You're usually asked to determine whether the series converges or diverges, and if it converges, to what limit. The test for convergence of a geometric series is very simple:

If $|r| < 1$ the series converges.

If $|r| \geq 1$, the series diverges.

So, for example, the series $\frac{1}{2} + \frac{1}{2^2} + \frac{1}{2^3} + ...$ converges, whereas the series $2 + 2^2 + 2^3 + ...$ diverges.

If a geometric series converges, you can always figure out its sum by doing the following:

Let $S_n = a + ar + ar^2 + ar^3 + \ldots ar^{n-1}$

Multiply the expression by r:

$$rS_n = ar + ar^2 + ar^3 + \ldots ar^n$$

Now subtract the second expression from the first:

$$S_n - rS_n = a - ar^n$$

Factor S out of the left side:

$$S_n(1 - r) = a - ar^n$$

Divide through by $1 - r$:

$$S_n = \frac{a - ar^n}{(1-r)} = \frac{a\left(1-r^n\right)}{(1-r)}$$

Thus, if we want to find the sum of the first n terms of a geometric series, we use the following formula:

$$S_n = \frac{a\left(1-r^n\right)}{(1-r)}$$

For example, the sum of the first four terms of the series in Example 1 is:

$$S_4 = \frac{\frac{1}{3}\left(1-\left(\frac{1}{3}\right)^4\right)}{\left(1-\frac{1}{3}\right)} = \frac{40}{81}$$

For an infinite geometric series, if it converges, $\lim\limits_{n\to\infty} r^n = 0$, and its sum is found this way:

$$S = \frac{a}{1-r}$$

In Example 1 above, the first term is $a = \dfrac{1}{3}$ and $r = \dfrac{1}{3}$. The sum is: $\dfrac{\frac{1}{3}}{1-\frac{1}{3}} = \dfrac{1}{2}$.

Many students find it is easier to work through the derivation of the sum than to actually memorize the formula. Either way, you should always be able to find the sum of an infinite geometric series.

Example 2: Find the limit to which the series $2 + \dfrac{2}{5} + \dfrac{2}{25} + \dfrac{2}{125} + \ldots$ converges.

The first term is $a = 2$ and $r = \dfrac{1}{5}$, so the limit is $\dfrac{2}{1 - \dfrac{1}{5}} = \dfrac{5}{2}$.

The AP's treatment of series doesn't get very complicated, and the exam usually confines itself to finding the limit of an infinite geometric series. Just remember that if $|r| \geq 1$, the geometric series diverges and it has no limit. No exceptions.

THE RATIO TEST

Sometimes you'll simply be asked to determine whether a series converges. With a geometric series, you already know what to do. If the series isn't a geometric one, you can usually use the Ratio Test:

Let $\sum a_n$ be a series where all of the terms are positive, and suppose that

$$\lim_{n \to \infty} \frac{a_{n+1}}{a_n} = \rho$$

Then:

(a) If $\rho < 1$, the series converges.

(b) If $\rho > 1$, the series diverges.

(c) If $\rho = 1$, the test provides insufficient information and the series might converge or diverge.

Example 3: Determine whether the series $\displaystyle\sum_{n=1}^{\infty} \dfrac{n}{3^n}$ converges.

Use the ratio test:

$$\rho = \lim_{n \to \infty} \frac{\dfrac{n+1}{3^{n+1}}}{\dfrac{n}{3^n}} = \lim_{n \to \infty} \frac{n+1}{3^{n+1}} \left(\frac{3^n}{n} \right) = \lim_{n \to \infty} \frac{n+1}{n} \left(\frac{3^n}{3^{n+1}} \right) = \frac{1}{3}$$

Because $\rho < 1$, the series converges. Notice that it does *not* converge to the limit $\dfrac{1}{3}$. That value simply tells us that the series is a convergent one.

Example 4: Determine whether the series $\displaystyle\sum_{n=1}^{\infty} \dfrac{1}{3n}$ converges.

By the ratio test, you discover that:

$$\rho = \lim_{n \to \infty} \frac{\dfrac{1}{3(n+1)}}{\dfrac{1}{3n}} = \lim_{n \to \infty} \frac{1}{3(n+1)} \left(\frac{3n}{1} \right) = \lim_{n \to \infty} \frac{3n}{3(n+1)} = 1$$

Because $\rho = 1$, the test is insufficient and we don't know whether the series converges or diverges.

ALTERNATING SERIES

The next type of series to concern yourself with is the alternating series. This is a series whose terms are alternately positive and negative. For example:

$$1 - \frac{1}{2} + \frac{1}{3} - \frac{1}{4} + \dots \frac{(-1)^{n+1}}{n} + \dots$$

Usually, you'll be asked to determine whether such a series converges. First, test the following:

The series $\displaystyle\sum_{n=1}^{\infty} (-1)^{n+1} b_n$ converges if all three of the following conditions are satisfied:

(a) $b_n > 0$ (which means that the terms must alternate in sign)

(b) $b_n > b_{n+1}$ for all n

(c) $b_n \to 0$ as $n \to \infty$

Example 5: Determine whether the series $1 - \dfrac{1}{2} + \dfrac{1}{3} - \dfrac{1}{4} + \dots \dfrac{(-1)^{n+1}}{n} + \dots$ converges.

Let's check the criteria:

   (a)   Each of the b_n's is positive.

   (b)   Each b_n is greater than its succeeding b_{n+1}.

   (c)   The b_n's are tending to zero as n approaches infinity.

Therefore, the series converges. This series is called the Alternating Harmonic series. Notice that this series converges, whereas the Harmonic series diverges.

Usually, you'll be asked to determine whether a series converges "absolutely."

A series $\sum a_n$ *converges absolutely* if the corresponding series $\sum |a_n|$ converges.

INTEGRAL TEST

Another test that you can use to determine whether a series converges or diverges is the Integral Test, which says:

If f is positive, continuous, and decreasing for $x \geq 1$, and $a_n = f(n)$, then:

$$\sum_{n=1}^{\infty} a_n \text{ and } \int_1^{\infty} f(x)dx$$

Either both converge or both diverge.

In other words, if you want to test convergence for a series with positive terms, evaluate the integral and see if the integral converges.

Example 6: Does $\displaystyle\sum_{n=1}^{\infty} \frac{6n^2}{n^3+1}$ converge?

In order to determine whether this converges, we can evaluate the integral, replacing n with x.

Evaluate $\displaystyle\int_1^{\infty} \frac{6x^2}{x^3+1}dx$.

First, we replace the improper integral with a proper one and a limit. We get: $\displaystyle\lim_{a\to\infty} \int_1^a \frac{6x^2}{x^3+1}dx$.

Use u-substitution. Let $u = x^3 + 1$ and $du = 3x^2\,dx$.

We get: $\displaystyle\lim_{a\to\infty} 2\int_2^{a^3+1} \frac{du}{u} = \lim_{a\to\infty} 2(\ln u)\Big|_2^{a^3+1} = \lim_{a\to\infty} 2\big(\ln(a^3+1) - \ln 2\big) = \infty$.

Therefore, because the integral diverges, the series diverges.

Example 7: Does $\displaystyle\sum_{n=1}^{\infty} e^{-n}$ converge?

In order to determine whether this converges, we can evaluate the integral, replacing n with x.

Evaluate $\displaystyle\int_1^{\infty} e^{-x}dx$.

First, we replace the improper integral with a proper one and a limit. We get: $\displaystyle\lim_{a\to\infty} \int_1^a e^{-x}dx$.

Evaluate the integral. We get: $\lim_{a \to \infty} \int_1^a e^{-x}\,dx = \lim_{a \to \infty}\left(-e^{-x}\right)\Big|_1^a = \lim_{a \to \infty}\left(-e^{-a} + e^{-1}\right) = \frac{1}{e}$.

Therefore, because the integral converges, the series converges. Note that the series does *not* necessarily converge to $\frac{1}{e}$.

COMPARISON TEST

Another test for convergence is the Comparison Test (also known as the Direct Comparison Test), which says:

> Let $0 \le a_n \le b_n$ for all n.
>
> 1) If $\displaystyle\sum_{n=1}^{\infty} b_n$ converges, then $\displaystyle\sum_{n=1}^{\infty} a_n$ converges.
>
> 2) If $\displaystyle\sum_{n=1}^{\infty} a_n$ diverges, then $\displaystyle\sum_{n=1}^{\infty} b_n$ diverges.

In other words, if all of the terms of a series are less than those of a convergent series, then it too converges. And, if all of the terms of a series are greater than those of a divergent series, then it too diverges.

Example 8: Does $\displaystyle\sum_{n=1}^{\infty} \frac{1}{5+2^n}$ converge?

We know that $\frac{1}{2^n}$ converges because it is a geometric series with $|r| < 1$.

Compare the series in question with $\frac{1}{2^n}$. Each term of $\frac{1}{5+2^n}$ is less than $\frac{1}{2^n}$, so $\displaystyle\sum_{n=1}^{\infty} \frac{1}{5+2^n}$ converges by comparison.

Example 9: Does $\displaystyle\sum_{n=2}^{\infty} \frac{1}{n-1}$ converge?

We know that $\frac{1}{n}$ diverges because it is the Harmonic series.

Compare the series in question with $\frac{1}{n}$. Each term of $\frac{1}{n-1}$ is greater than $\frac{1}{n}$, so $\displaystyle\sum_{n=2}^{\infty} \frac{1}{n-1}$ diverges by comparison.

POWER SERIES

The most important type of series, and the one that the AP concentrates on, is the Power series, which takes the form:

$$\sum_{n=0}^{\infty} c_n x^n = c_0 + c_1 x + c_2 x^2 + c_3 x^3 + \ldots + c_n x^n + \ldots.$$

Notice that we're now going from $n = 0$ to $n = \infty$, rather than from $n = 1$ to $n = \infty$. This is because the first term is a constant.

You'll be asked to determine whether a power series converges. The test is as follows:

For any Power series in x, exactly one of the following is true:

(a) The series converges only for $x = 0$;

(b) The series converges absolutely for all x; or

(c) The series converges absolutely for all x in some open interval $(-R, R)$, and diverges if $x < -R$ or $x > R$. The series may converge or diverge at the endpoints of the interval.

For case (c), the number R is called the **radius of convergence**. In case (a), the radius of convergence is zero; in case (b) the radius is all x. The set of all values of x in the interval $(-R, R)$ is called the **interval of convergence**.

Example 10: Find the radius and interval of convergence for the Power series $\sum_{n=0}^{\infty} x^n$.

This is a geometric series with $r = x$; thus, it converges if $r < 1$.
Therefore, the radius of convergence is $R = 1$, and the interval of convergence is $(-1, 1)$.

Example 11: Find the radius and interval of convergence for the Power series $\sum_{n=0}^{\infty} \dfrac{x^n}{n!}$.

In order to determine convergence, apply the ratio test for absolute convergence:

$$\rho = \lim_{n \to \infty} \left| \frac{x^{n+1}}{(n+1)!} \frac{n!}{x^n} \right| = \lim_{n \to \infty} \left| \frac{x}{n+1} \right| = 0$$

Because $\rho = 0$ for all x, the series converges absolutely for all x. Therefore, the radius of convergence is $R = \infty$ and the interval of convergence is $(-\infty, \infty)$.

TAYLOR SERIES AND POLYNOMIALS

The final, and most important, topic in infinite series is the Taylor series. The power series and the Taylor series are the most frequent question topics on infinite series on the AP exam. A Taylor series expansion about a point $x = a$ is a power series expansion that's useful to approximate the function in the neighborhood of the point $x = a$.

If a function f has derivatives of all orders at a, then the Taylor series for f about $x = a$ is:

$$\sum_{k=0}^{\infty} \frac{f^{(k)}(a)}{k!}(x-a)^k = f(a) + f'(a)(x-a) + \frac{f''(a)}{2!}(x-a)^2 + \dots + \frac{f^{(n)}(a)}{n!}(x-a)^n + \dots$$

The special case of the Taylor series for $a = 0$ is called the **Maclaurin series:**

$$\sum_{k=0}^{\infty} \frac{f^{(k)}(0)}{k!}(x)^k = f(0) + f'(0)x + \frac{f''(0)}{2!}x^2 + \dots + \frac{f^{(n)}(0)}{n!}x^n + \dots$$

The AP usually asks for a Taylor series at $x = 0$. Note that this is the same thing as the Maclaurin series. Let's do an example to see what one of these looks like.

Example 12: Find the Taylor series about $a = 1$ generated by $f(x) = \frac{1}{x}$.

First, find the derivatives of $\frac{1}{x}$ and compute their values at $x = 1$:

$$f(x) = x^{-1} \qquad\qquad f(1) = 1$$
$$f'(x) = -x^{-2} \qquad\qquad f'(1) = -1$$
$$f''(x) = 2x^{-3} \qquad\qquad f''(1) = 2 = 2!$$
$$f'''(x) = -6x^{-4} \qquad\qquad f'''(1) = -6 = -3!$$
$$f^{(4)}(x) = 24x^{-5} \qquad\qquad f^{(4)}(1) = 24 = 4!$$
$$f^{(n)}(x) = (-1)^n \frac{n!}{x^{n+1}} \qquad f^{(n)}(1) = (-1)^n n!$$

Next, plug into the formula to generate the Taylor series:

$$1 - (x-1) + (x-1)^2 + \dots = \sum_{k=0}^{\infty} (-1)^k (x-1)^k$$

Example 13: Find the Taylor series about $a = 0$ generated by $f(x) = e^x$.

First, find the derivatives of e^x and compute their values at $x = 0$.

$$f(x) = e^x \qquad\qquad f(0) = 1$$
$$f'(x) = e^x \qquad\qquad f'(0) - 1$$
$$f''(x) = e^x \qquad\qquad f''(0) = 1$$
$$f'''(x) = e^x \qquad\qquad f'''(0) = 1$$
$$f^{(4)}(x) = e^x \qquad\qquad f^{(4)}(0) = 1$$
$$f^{(n)}(x) = e^x \qquad\qquad f^{(n)}(0) = 1$$

Next, plug into the formula to generate the Taylor series:

$$\sum_{k=0}^{\infty} \frac{x^k}{k!} = 1 + x + \frac{x^2}{2!} + \frac{x^3}{3!} + \frac{x^4}{4!} + \dots$$

This is a very important expansion to know. Memorize it and be able to use it on the exam. You're permitted to write the Taylor series expansion for e^x without explaining how to generate it.

That's all you need to know about Taylor series. There are four expansions you should prepare for on the AP. We already discussed the expansion for e^x. You'll also need to know the expansions for $\sin x$, $\cos x$, and $\ln(1 + x)$.

We'll give you the Taylor series expansions here, and you'll derive them in the problems.

$$e^x = 1 + x + \frac{x^2}{2!} + \frac{x^3}{3!} + \dots = \sum_{k=0}^{\infty} \frac{x^k}{k!}$$

$$\sin x = x - \frac{x^3}{3!} + \frac{x^5}{5!} + \dots = \sum_{k=0}^{\infty} (-1)^k \frac{x^{2k+1}}{(2k+1)!}$$

$$\cos x = 1 - \frac{x^2}{2!} + \frac{x^4}{4!} + \dots = \sum_{k=0}^{\infty} (-1)^k \frac{x^{2k}}{(2k)!}$$

$$\ln(1+x) = x - \frac{x^2}{2} + \frac{x^3}{3} - \frac{x^4}{4} \dots = \sum_{k=0}^{\infty} (-1)^k \frac{x^{k+1}}{k+1}$$

Taylor series can also be used to approximate the value of a function at a particular value. All you have to do is to plug that value into the Taylor series expansion for the function. The highest power term that you use is the degree of the Taylor polynomial. This is easier to see with an example.

Example 14: Use a third degree Taylor polynomial to estimate $e^{0.2}$.

All that we have to do is to plug 0.2 into the Taylor expansion up to the third power term.

We get: $e^{0.2} \approx 1 + 0.2 + \dfrac{0.2^2}{2!} + \dfrac{0.2^3}{3!} = 1.22133$. If we evaluate $e^{0.2}$ with a calculator, we get 1.22140.

As you can see, this is a pretty good approximation.

Sometimes you will be asked to find the "error bound" of a Taylor polynomial. This is also sometimes referred to as the "Lagrange error." The proof for the rule is quite difficult, so we will simply tell you the rule. If you are finding an nth degree Taylor polynomial, a good approximation to the error bound is the next nonzero term in a decreasing series. For example, if we wanted to find the error in the above example, we know that it's less than the fourth term evaluated at 0.2, which is $\frac{0.2^4}{4!} = 0.000066\overline{6}$.

PROBLEM 1. Find the sum of the series $4 + \frac{4}{3} + \frac{4}{9} + \frac{4}{27} + \ldots + \frac{4}{3^6}$.

Answer: This is a geometric series where $a = 4$, $r = \frac{1}{3}$, and $n = 7$. According to the formula, the sum is:

$$S_n = \frac{a(1-r^n)}{(1-r)}$$

Plugging in, you should get:

$$S_7 = \frac{4\left(1-\left(\frac{1}{3}\right)^7\right)}{\left(1-\frac{1}{3}\right)} = 5.997$$

PROBLEM 2. Find the limit to which the series $4 + \frac{4}{3} + \frac{4}{9} + \frac{4}{27} + \ldots$ converges.

Answer: This is the same series, but now you want the limit at infinity, so use the formula:

$$S = \frac{a}{1-r}$$

The result is:

$$S = \frac{4}{1-\frac{1}{3}} = 6$$

PROBLEM 3. Determine whether the series $\sum_{n=1}^{\infty} \frac{n-1}{5^n}$ converges.

Answer: By the Ratio Test:

$$\rho = \lim_{n \to \infty} \frac{\frac{n}{5^{n+1}}}{\frac{n-1}{5^n}} = \lim_{n \to \infty} \frac{n}{5^{n+1}}\left(\frac{5^n}{n-1}\right) = \lim_{n \to \infty} \frac{n}{n-1}\left(\frac{5^n}{5^{n+1}}\right) = \frac{1}{5}$$

Because $\rho < 1$, the series converges.

PROBLEM 4. Find the Taylor series about $a = 0$ generated by $f(x) = \sin x$.

Answer: First, find the derivatives of $\sin x$ and compute their values at $x = 0$.

$$
\begin{aligned}
f(x) &= \sin x & f(0) &= 0 \\
f'(x) &= \cos x & f'(0) &= 1 \\
f''(x) &= -\sin x & f''(0) &= 0 \\
f'''(x) &= -\cos x & f'''(0) &= -1 \\
f^{(4)}(x) &= \sin x & f^{(4)}(0) &= 0 \\
f^{(5)}(x) &= \cos x & f^{(5)}(0) &= 1
\end{aligned}
$$

As you've seen us do before, plug into the formula to generate the Taylor series:

$$
x - \frac{x^3}{3!} + \frac{x^5}{5!} + \ldots = \sum_{k=0}^{\infty} (-1)^k \frac{x^{2k+1}}{(2k+1)!}
$$

PROBLEM 5. Find the radius and interval of convergence for the series $\displaystyle\sum_{n=1}^{\infty} \frac{x^n}{1+n^2}$.

Answer: In order to determine convergence, apply the Ratio Test for absolute convergence:

$$
\rho = \lim_{n \to \infty} \left| \frac{x^{n+1}}{1+(n+1)^2} \left(\frac{1+n^2}{x^n} \right) \right| = \lim_{n \to \infty} \left| x \frac{(1+n^2)}{(1+(n+1)^2)} \right| = |x|
$$

Thus, if $|x| < 1$, then $\rho < 1$ and the series converges.

If $|x| > 1$, then $\rho > 1$ and the series diverges.

If $x = 1$, then $\displaystyle\sum_{n=0}^{\infty} \frac{x^n}{1+n^2} = \sum_{n=0}^{\infty} \frac{1}{1+n^2}$ (which converges).

If $x = -1$, then $\displaystyle\sum_{n=0}^{\infty} \frac{x^n}{1+n^2} = \sum_{n=0}^{\infty} \frac{(-1)^n}{1+n^2}$ (which converges).

Therefore, the radius of convergence is 1 and the interval of convergence is $[-1, 1]$.

PRACTICE PROBLEM SET 35

Now try these problems involving the series we've discussed in this chapter. The answers are in Chapter 21.

1. Find the sum of the series $2 + \dfrac{2}{5} + \dfrac{2}{25} + \ldots + \dfrac{2}{5^4}$.

2. Find the sum of the series $8 + \dfrac{8}{7} + \dfrac{8}{49} + \dfrac{8}{343} + \dfrac{8}{7^4} + \ldots$.

3. Does the series $\displaystyle\sum_{n=1}^{\infty} \dfrac{5^n}{(n-1)!}$ converge or diverge?

4. Does the series $\displaystyle\sum_{n=1}^{\infty} \dfrac{5^n}{n^2}$ converge or diverge?

5. Find the Taylor series about $a = 0$ generated by $f(x) = \cos x$.

6. Find the Taylor series about $a = 0$ generated by $f(x) = \ln(1 + x)$.

7. Find the Taylor series about $a = 0$ generated by $f(x) = e^{-x}$.

8. Find the first three nonzero terms of the Taylor series about $a = \dfrac{\pi}{3}$ generated by $f(x) = \sin x$.

9. Find the radius and interval of convergence for the series $\displaystyle\sum_{n=0}^{\infty} 3^n x^n$.

10. Find the radius and interval of convergence for the series $\displaystyle\sum_{n=0}^{\infty} (-1)^n \dfrac{x^{2n}}{(2n)!}$.

11. Estimate $\cos(.2)$ using a fourth degree Taylor polynomial about $a = 0$ and find the error bound.

12. Estimate $\ln(1.3)$ using a third degree Taylor polynomial about $a = 0$ and find the error bound.

13. Determine whether $\displaystyle\sum_{n=2}^{\infty} \dfrac{1}{n \ln n}$ converges.

14. Determine whether $\displaystyle\sum_{n=1}^{\infty} \dfrac{1}{n\sqrt[4]{n}}$ converges.

15. Determine whether $\displaystyle\sum_{n=2}^{\infty} \dfrac{\ln n}{n+1}$ converges.

16. Determine whether $\displaystyle\sum_{n=0}^{\infty} \dfrac{1}{n!}$ converges.

21

Answers to Practice Problem Sets

SOLUTIONS TO PRACTICE PROBLEM SET 1

1. 13

   To find the limit, we simply plug in 8 for x: $\lim\limits_{x \to 8}\left(x^2 - 5x - 11\right) = \left(8^2 - (5)(8) - 11\right) = 13$.

2. $\dfrac{4}{5}$

   To find the limit, we simply plug in 5 for x: $\lim\limits_{x \to 5}\left(\dfrac{x+3}{x^2-15}\right) = \dfrac{5+3}{5^2-15} = \dfrac{8}{10} = \dfrac{4}{5}$.

3. π^2

   To find the limit, we would plug in π for x, but there is no x in the limit. So the limit is simply π^2.

4. 4

   If we plug in 3 for x, we get $\dfrac{0}{0}$, which is indeterminate. When this happens, we try

   to factor the expression in order to get rid of the problem terms. Here we factor the

   top and get: $\lim\limits_{x \to 3}\left(\dfrac{x^2 - 2x - 3}{x-3}\right) = \dfrac{(x-3)(x+1)}{x-3}$. Now we can cancel the term $x-3$ to

   get $\lim\limits_{x \to 3}(x+1)$. Notice that we are allowed to cancel the terms because x is not 3 but

   very close to 3. Now we can plug in 3 for x: $\lim\limits_{x \to 3}(x+1) = 3 + 1 = 4$.

5. 0

   Here we are finding the limit as x goes to infinity. We divide

   the top and bottom by the highest power of x in the expression:

   $\lim\limits_{x \to \infty}\left(\dfrac{10x^2 + 25x + 1}{x^4 - 8}\right) = \lim\limits_{x \to \infty}\left(\dfrac{\dfrac{10x^2}{x^4} + \dfrac{25x}{x^4} + \dfrac{1}{x^4}}{\dfrac{x^4}{x^4} - \dfrac{8}{x^4}}\right)$. Next, simplify the top and bottom:

   $\lim\limits_{x \to \infty}\left(\dfrac{\dfrac{10}{x^2} + \dfrac{25}{x^3} + \dfrac{1}{x^4}}{1 - \dfrac{8}{x^4}}\right)$. Now, if we take the limit as x goes to infinity, we get:

   $\lim\limits_{x \to \infty}\left(\dfrac{\dfrac{10}{x^2} + \dfrac{25}{x^3} + \dfrac{1}{x^4}}{1 - \dfrac{8}{x^4}}\right) = \dfrac{0+0+0}{1+0} = 0$.

6. $+\infty$

Here we are finding the limit as x goes to infinity. We divide the top

and bottom by the highest power of x in the expression, which is x^4 :

$$\lim_{x \to \infty}\left(\frac{x^4 - 8}{10x^2 + 25x + 1}\right) = \lim_{x \to \infty}\left(\frac{\dfrac{x^4}{x^4} - \dfrac{8}{x^4}}{\dfrac{10x^2}{x^4} + \dfrac{25x}{x^4} + \dfrac{1}{x^4}}\right)$$. Next, simplify the top and bottom:

$$\lim_{x \to \infty}\left(\frac{1 - \dfrac{8}{x^4}}{\dfrac{10}{x^2} + \dfrac{25}{x^3} + \dfrac{1}{x^4}}\right)$$. Now, if we take the limit as x goes to infinity, we get:

$$\lim_{x \to \infty}\left(\frac{1 - \dfrac{8}{x^4}}{\dfrac{10}{x^2} + \dfrac{25}{x^3} + \dfrac{1}{x^4}}\right) = \frac{1 + 0}{0 + 0 + 0} = \infty .$$

7. $\dfrac{1}{10}$

Here we are finding the limit as x goes to infinity. We divide the top

and bottom by the highest power of x in the expression, which is x^4 :

$$\lim_{x \to \infty}\left(\frac{x^4 - 8}{10x^4 + 25x + 1}\right) = \lim_{x \to \infty}\left(\frac{\dfrac{x^4}{x^4} - \dfrac{8}{x^4}}{\dfrac{10x^4}{x^4} + \dfrac{25x}{x^4} + \dfrac{1}{x^4}}\right)$$. Next, simplify the top and bottom:

$$\lim_{x \to \infty}\left(\frac{1 - \dfrac{8}{x^4}}{10 + \dfrac{25}{x^3} + \dfrac{1}{x^4}}\right)$$. Now, if we take the limit as x goes to infinity, we get:

$$\lim_{x \to \infty}\left(\frac{1 - \dfrac{8}{x^4}}{10 + \dfrac{25}{x^3} + \dfrac{1}{x^4}}\right) = \frac{1 + 0}{10 + 0 + 0} = \frac{1}{10} .$$

8. $\sqrt{5}$

Here we are finding the limit as x goes to infinity. We divide the top and bottom by

the highest power of x in the expression, which is x^2. Notice that, under the radical,

we divide by x^4 because $\sqrt{x^4} = x^2$: $\lim_{x \to \infty}\left(\dfrac{\sqrt{5x^4 + 2x}}{x^2}\right) = \lim_{x \to \infty}\left(\dfrac{\sqrt{\dfrac{5x^4}{x^4} + \dfrac{2x}{x^4}}}{\dfrac{x^2}{x^2}}\right)$. Next,

simplify the top and bottom: $\lim_{x \to \infty}\left(\dfrac{\sqrt{5 + \dfrac{2}{x^3}}}{1}\right)$. Now, if we take the limit as x goes to

infinity, we get: $\lim_{x \to \infty}\left(\dfrac{\sqrt{5 + \dfrac{2}{x^3}}}{1}\right) = \dfrac{\sqrt{5 + 0}}{1} = \sqrt{5}$.

9. $+\infty$

Here we have to think about what happens when we plug in a value that is very

close to 6, but a little bit more. The top expression will approach 8. The bottom

expression will approach 0, but will be a little bit bigger. Thus, the limit will be $\dfrac{8}{0^+}$,

which is $+\infty$.

10. $-\infty$

Here we have to think about what happens when we plug in a value that is very

close to 6, but a little bit less. The top expression will approach 8. The bottom

expression will approach 0, but will be a little bit less. Thus, the limit will be $\dfrac{8}{0^-}$,

which is $-\infty$.

11. The limit *Does Not Exist*.

In order to evaluate the limit as x approaches 6, we find the limit as it approaches 6^+ (from the right) and the limit as it approaches 6^- (from the left). If the two limits approach the same value, or both approach positive infinity or both approach negative infinity, then the limit is that value, or the appropriately signed infinity. If the two limits do not agree, the limit "Does Not Exist." Here, if we look at the solutions to problems 9 and 10, we find that as x approaches 6^+, the limit is $+\infty$, but as x approaches 6^-, the limit is $-\infty$. Because the two limits are *not* the same, the limit *Does Not Exist*.

12. 1

Here we have to think about what happens when we plug in a value that is very close to 0, but a little bit more. The top and bottom expressions will both be positive and the same value, so we get: $\lim\limits_{x \to 0^+} \dfrac{x}{|x|} = \dfrac{0^+}{0^+} = 1$.

13. −1

Here we have to think about what happens when we plug in a value that is very close to 0, but a little bit less. The top expression will be negative, and the bottom expression will be positive, so we get: $\lim\limits_{x \to 0^-} \dfrac{x}{|x|} = \dfrac{0^-}{0^+} = -1$.

14. $+\infty$

Here we have to think about what happens when we plug in a value that is very close to 7, but a little bit more. The top expression will approach 7. The bottom expression will approach 0, but will be a little bit positive. Thus, the limit will be $\dfrac{7}{0^+}$, which is $+\infty$.

15. The limit *Does Not Exist*.

In order to evaluate the limit as x approaches 7, we find the limit as it approaches 7^+ (from the right) and the limit as it approaches 7^- (from the left). If the two limits approach the same value, or both approach positive infinity or both approach negative infinity, then the limit is that value, or the appropriately signed infinity. If the two limits do not agree, the limit "Does Not Exist." Here, if we look at the solutions to problem 14, we see that as x approaches 7^+, the limit is $+\infty$. As x approaches 7^-, the top expression will approach 7. The bottom will approach 0, but will be a little bit negative. Thus, the limit will be $\dfrac{7}{0^-}$, which is $-\infty$. Because the two limits are *not* the same, the limit *Does Not Exist*.

16. $+\infty$

In order to evaluate the limit as x approaches 7, we find the limit as it approaches 7^+ (from the right) and the limit as it approaches 7^- (from the left). If the two limits approach the same value, or both approach positive infinity or both approach negative infinity, then the limit is that value, or the appropriately-signed infinity. If the two limits do not agree, the limit "Does Not Exist." Here, we see that as x approaches 7^+, the top expression will approach 7. The bottom expression will approach 0, but will be a little bit positive. Thus the limit will be $\dfrac{7}{0^+}$, which is $+\infty$. As x approaches 7^-, the top expression will again approach 7. The bottom will approach 0, but will be a little bit positive. Thus, the limit will be $\dfrac{7}{0^+}$, which is $+\infty$. Because the two limits are the same, the limit is $+\infty$.

17. (a) 4; (b) 5; (c) The limit *Does Not Exist.*

(a) Notice that $f(x)$ is a piecewise function, which means that we use the function

$f(x) = x^2 - 5$ for all values of x less than or equal to 3. Thus, $\lim\limits_{x \to 3^-} f(x) = 3^2 - 5 = 4$.

(b) Here we use the function $f(x) = x + 2$ for all values of x greater than 3. Thus,

$\lim\limits_{x \to 3^+} f(x) = 3 + 2 = 5$.

(c) In order to evaluate the limit as x approaches 3, we find the limit as it

approaches 3^+ (from the right) and the limit as it approaches 3^- (from the left). If

the two limits approach the same value, or both approach positive infinity or both

approach negative infinity, then the limit is that value, or the appropriately signed

infinity. If the two limits do not agree, the limit "Does Not Exist." Here, if we refer

to the solutions in parts (a) and (b), we see that $\lim\limits_{x \to 3^-} f(x) = 4$ and $\lim\limits_{x \to 3^+} f(x) = 5$.

Because the two limits are *not* the same, the limit *Does Not Exist.*

18. (a) 4; (b) 4; (c) 4

(a) Notice that $f(x)$ is a piecewise function, which means that we use the function

$f(x) = x^2 - 5$ for all values of x less than or equal to 3. Thus, $\lim\limits_{x \to 3^-} f(x) = 3^2 - 5 = 4$.

(b) Here we use the function $f(x) = x + 1$ for all values of x greater than 3. Thus,

$\lim\limits_{x \to 3^+} f(x) = 3 + 1 = 4$.

(c) In order to evaluate the limit as x approaches 3, we find the limit as it

approaches 3^+ (from the right) and the limit as it approaches 3^- (from the left). If

the two limits approach the same value, or both approach positive infinity or both

approach negative infinity, then the limit is that value, or the appropriately signed

infinity. If the two limits do not agree, the limit "Does Not Exist." Here, if we refer

to the solutions in parts (a) and (b), we see that $\lim\limits_{x \to 3^-} f(x) = 4$ and $\lim\limits_{x \to 3^+} f(x) = 4$.

Because the two limits are the same, the limit is 4.

19. $\dfrac{3}{\sqrt{2}}$

Here, if we plug in $\dfrac{\pi}{4}$ for x, we get: $\lim\limits_{x \to \frac{\pi}{4}} 3\cos x = 3\cos\dfrac{\pi}{4} = \dfrac{3}{\sqrt{2}}$.

20. 0

Here, if we plug in 0 for x, we get: $\lim\limits_{x \to 0} 3\dfrac{x}{\cos x} = 3\dfrac{0}{\cos 0} = 3\dfrac{0}{1} = 0$.

21. 3

Remember rule number 1 on page 7, which says that $\lim\limits_{x \to 0} \dfrac{\sin x}{x} = 1$. If we want to

find the limit of its reciprocal, we can write this as $\lim\limits_{x \to 0} \dfrac{1}{\frac{\sin x}{x}} = \dfrac{1}{\lim\limits_{x \to 0} \frac{\sin x}{x}} = \dfrac{1}{1} = 1$.

Here, if we plug in 0 for x, we get: $\lim\limits_{x \to 0} \left(3\dfrac{x}{\sin x} \right) = (3)(1) = 3$.

22. $\dfrac{3}{8}$

Remember rule number 4, on page 8, which says that $\lim\limits_{x \to 0} \dfrac{\sin ax}{\sin bx} = \dfrac{a}{b}$. Here,

$\lim\limits_{x \to 0} \dfrac{\sin 3x}{\sin 8x} = \dfrac{3}{8}$. If we want to evaluate the limit the long way, first we divide the

numerator and the denominator of the expression by x: $\lim\limits_{x \to 0} \dfrac{\frac{\sin 3x}{x}}{\frac{\sin 8x}{x}}$. Next, we

multiply the numerator and the denominator of the top expression by 3 and the

numerator and the denominator of the bottom expression by 8. We get: $\lim\limits_{x \to 0} \dfrac{\frac{3\sin 3x}{3x}}{\frac{8\sin 8x}{8x}}$.

Now, we can evaluate the limit: $\lim\limits_{x \to 0} \dfrac{\frac{3\sin 3x}{3x}}{\frac{8\sin 8x}{8x}} = \dfrac{(3)(1)}{(8)(1)} = \dfrac{3}{8}$.

23. $\dfrac{7}{5}$

Here, we can rewrite the expression as

$$\lim_{x \to 0} \frac{\tan 7x}{\sin 5x} = \lim_{x \to 0} \frac{\dfrac{\sin 7x}{\cos 7x}}{\sin 5x} = \lim_{x \to 0} \frac{\sin 7x}{(\cos 7x)(\sin 5x)}.$$ Remember rule number 4, on page 8,

which says that $\lim\limits_{x \to 0} \dfrac{\sin ax}{\sin bx} = \dfrac{a}{b}$. Here, $\lim\limits_{x \to 0} \dfrac{\sin 7x}{(\cos 7x)(\sin 5x)} = \dfrac{7}{(1)(5)} = \dfrac{7}{5}$. If we want to

evaluate the limit the long way, we first divide the numerator and the denominator

of the expression by x: $\lim\limits_{x \to 0} \dfrac{\left(\dfrac{\sin 7x}{x}\right)}{(\cos 7x)\left(\dfrac{\sin 5x}{x}\right)}$. Next, we multiply the numerator

and the denominator of the top expression by 7 and the numerator and the

denominator of the bottom expression by 5. We get: $\lim\limits_{x \to 0} \dfrac{\left(\dfrac{7\sin 7x}{7x}\right)}{(\cos 7x)\left(\dfrac{5\sin 5x}{5x}\right)}$. Now,

we can evaluate the limit: $\lim\limits_{x \to 0} \dfrac{(7)(1)}{(1)(5)(1)} = \dfrac{7}{5}$.

24. The limit *Does Not Exist*.

The value of $\sin x$ oscillates between -1 and 1. Thus, as x approaches infinity, $\sin x$ does not approach a specific value. Therefore, the limit *Does Not Exist*.

25. 0

Here, as x approaches infinity, $\dfrac{1}{x}$ approaches 0. Thus, $\lim\limits_{x \to \infty} \sin \dfrac{1}{x} = \sin 0 = 0$.

26. 0

Here, use the trigonometric identity $\sin^2 x = 1 - \cos^2 x$ to rewrite the bottom expression:

$\lim\limits_{x \to 0} \dfrac{x^2 \sin x}{\sin^2 x}$. Next, we can break up the limit into $\lim\limits_{x \to 0} \left(\dfrac{x}{\sin x} \dfrac{x}{\sin x} \sin x \right)$. Remember

rule number 1 on page 7, which says that $\lim\limits_{x \to 0} \dfrac{\sin x}{x} = 1$. If we want to find, it

will simply be $\lim\limits_{x \to 0} \dfrac{1}{\dfrac{\sin x}{x}} = \dfrac{1}{\lim\limits_{x \to 0} \dfrac{\sin x}{x}} = \dfrac{1}{1} = 1$. Now we can evaluate the limit:

$\lim\limits_{x \to 0} \left(\dfrac{x}{\sin x} \dfrac{x}{\sin x} \sin x \right) = (1)(1)(0) = 0$.

27. $\dfrac{49}{121}$

We can break up the limit into $\lim\limits_{x \to 0} \dfrac{\sin 7x}{\sin 11x} \dfrac{\sin 7x}{\sin 11x}$. Remember rule number 4, on

page 8, which says that $\lim\limits_{x \to 0} \dfrac{\sin ax}{\sin bx} = \dfrac{a}{b}$. Here, $\lim\limits_{x \to 0} \dfrac{\sin 7x}{\sin 11x} \dfrac{\sin 7x}{\sin 11x} = \dfrac{7}{11} \cdot \dfrac{7}{11} = \dfrac{49}{121}$.

If we want to evaluate the limit the long way, we first divide the numerator

and the denominator of the expressions by x: $\lim\limits_{x \to 0} \left(\dfrac{\dfrac{\sin 7x}{x}}{\dfrac{\sin 11x}{x}} \dfrac{\dfrac{\sin 7x}{x}}{\dfrac{\sin 11x}{x}} \right)$. Next,

we multiply the numerator and the denominator of the top expression

by 7 and the numerator and the denominator of the bottom expression

by 11. We get: $\lim\limits_{x \to 0} \left(\dfrac{\dfrac{7 \sin 7x}{7x}}{\dfrac{11 \sin 11x}{11x}} \dfrac{\dfrac{7 \sin 7x}{7x}}{\dfrac{11 \sin 11x}{11x}} \right)$. Now, we can evaluate the limit:

$\lim\limits_{x \to 0} \left(\dfrac{\dfrac{7 \sin 7x}{7x}}{\dfrac{11 \sin 11x}{11x}} \dfrac{\dfrac{7 \sin 7x}{7x}}{\dfrac{11 \sin 11x}{11x}} \right) = \dfrac{(7)(1)}{(11)(1)} \dfrac{(7)(1)}{(11)(1)} = \left(\dfrac{7}{11} \right) \left(\dfrac{7}{11} \right) = \dfrac{49}{121}$.

28. 6

Notice that if we plug in 0 for h, we get $\dfrac{0}{0}$, which is indeterminate. If we expand the

expression in the numerator, we get: $\displaystyle\lim_{h\to 0}\frac{9+6h+h^2-9}{h}$. This simplifies to $\displaystyle\lim_{h\to 0}\frac{6h+h^2}{h}$.

Next, factor h out of the top expression: $\displaystyle\lim_{h\to 0}\frac{h(6+h)}{h}$. Now we can cancel the h and

evaluate the limit to get: $\displaystyle\lim_{h\to 0}\frac{h(6+h)}{h}=\lim_{h\to 0}(6+h)=6+0=6$.

29. $\cos x$

Notice that if we plug in 0 for h, we get $\dfrac{0}{0}$, which is indeterminate. Recall that the

trigonometric formula $\sin(A+B)=\sin A\cos B+\cos A\sin B$. Here, we can rewrite

the top expression as: $\displaystyle\lim_{h\to 0}\frac{\sin(x+h)-\sin x}{h}=\lim_{h\to 0}\frac{\sin x\cos h-\cos x\sin h-\sin x}{h}$. We

can break up the limit into: $\displaystyle\lim_{h\to 0}\frac{\sin x\cos h-\sin x}{h}-\frac{\cos x\sin h}{h}$. Next factor $\sin x$ out

of the top of the left-hand expression: $\displaystyle\lim_{h\to 0}\frac{\sin x(\cos h-1)}{h}-\frac{\cos x\sin h}{h}$. Now we can

break this into separate limits: $\displaystyle\lim_{h\to 0}\frac{\sin x(\cos h-1)}{h}-\lim_{h\to 0}\frac{\cos x\sin h}{h}$. The left-hand

limit is: $\displaystyle\lim_{h\to 0}\frac{\sin x(\cos h-1)}{h}=\sin x\lim_{-h\to 0}\frac{(\cos h-1)}{h}=\sin x\cdot 0=0$. The right-hand limit is:

$\displaystyle\cos x\lim_{h\to 0}\frac{\sin h}{h}=\cos x\cdot 1=\cos x$. Therefore, the limit is $\cos x$.

30. $-\dfrac{1}{x^2}$

Notice that if we plug in 0 for h, we get $\dfrac{0}{0}$, which is indeterminate. If we

combine the two expressions on top with a common denominator, we get:

$$\lim_{h\to0}\dfrac{\dfrac{1}{x+h}-\dfrac{1}{x}}{h}=\lim_{h\to0}\dfrac{\dfrac{x}{x(x+h)}-\dfrac{x+h}{x(x+h)}}{h}=\lim_{h\to0}\dfrac{\dfrac{x-(x+h)}{x(x+h)}}{h}.$$ We can simplify the top

expression, leaving us with: $\lim_{h\to0}\dfrac{\dfrac{-h}{x(x+h)}}{h}$. Next simplify the expression into:

$$\lim_{h\to0}\dfrac{\dfrac{-h}{x(x+h)}}{h}=\lim_{h\to0}\dfrac{-h}{hx(x+h)}.$$ We can cancel the h to get: $\lim_{h\to0}\dfrac{-1}{x(x+h)}$. Now if we

evaluate the limit we get: $\lim_{h\to0}\dfrac{-1}{x(x+h)}=\dfrac{-1}{x(x)}=-\dfrac{1}{x^2}$.

SOLUTIONS TO PRACTICE PROBLEM SET 2

1. Yes. It satisfies all three conditions.

   In order for a function $f(x)$ is continuous at a point $x = c$, it must fulfill *all three* of the following conditions:

   Condition 1: $f(c)$ exists.

   Condition 2: $\lim_{x \to c} f(x)$ exists.

   Condition 3: $\lim_{x \to c} f(x) = f(c)$

   Let's test each condition.

   $f(2) = 9$, which satisfies condition 1.

   $\lim_{x \to 2^-} f(x) = 9$ and $\lim_{x \to 2^+} f(x) = 9$, so $\lim_{x \to 2} f(x) = 9$, which satisfies condition 2.

   $\lim_{x \to 2} f(x) = 9 = f(2)$, which satisfies condition 3. Therefore, $f(x)$ is continuous at $x = 2$.

2. No. It fails condition 3.

   In order for a function $f(x)$ is continuous at a point $x = c$, it must fulfill *all three* of the following conditions:

   Condition 1: $f(c)$ exists.

   Condition 2: $\lim_{x \to c} f(x)$ exists.

   Condition 3: $\lim_{x \to c} f(x) = f(c)$

   Let's test each condition.

   $f(3) = 29$, which satisfies condition 1.

   $\lim_{x \to 3^-} f(x) = 30$ and $\lim_{x \to 3^+} f(x) = 30$, so $\lim_{x \to 3} f(x) = 30$, which satisfies condition 2.

   But, $\lim_{x \to 3} f(x) \neq f(3)$. Therefore $f(x)$ is not continuous at $x = 3$ because it fails condition 3.

3. No. It fails condition 1.

    In order for a function $f(x)$ is continuous at a point $x = c$, it must fulfill *all three* of the following conditions:

    Condition 1: $f(c)$ exists.

    Condition 2: $\lim_{x \to c} f(x)$ exists.

    Condition 3: $\lim_{x \to c} f(x) = f(c)$

    Notice that the function is not defined at $f(3)$. Therefore $f(x)$ is not continuous at $x = 3$ because it fails condition 1.

4. No. It is discontinuous at any odd integral multiple of $\dfrac{\pi}{2}$.

    Recall that $\sec x = \dfrac{1}{\cos x}$. This means that $\sec x$ is undefined at any value where $\cos x = 0$, which are the odd multiples of $\dfrac{\pi}{2}$. Therefore, $\sec x$ is not continuous everywhere.

5. No. It is discontinuous at the endpoints of the interval.

    Recall that $\sec x = \dfrac{1}{\cos x}$. This means that $\sec x$ is undefined at any value where $\cos x = 0$. Also recall that $\cos \dfrac{\pi}{2} = 0$ and $\cos\left(-\dfrac{\pi}{2}\right) = 0$. Therefore, $\sec x$ is not continuous everywhere on the interval $\left[-\dfrac{\pi}{2}, \dfrac{\pi}{2}\right]$.

6. Yes.

    Recall that $\sec x = \dfrac{1}{\cos x}$. This means that $\sec x$ is undefined at any value where $\cos x = 0$. Also recall that $\cos \dfrac{\pi}{2} = 0$ and $\cos\left(-\dfrac{\pi}{2}\right) = 0$. Therefore $\sec x$ is continuous everywhere on the interval $\left(-\dfrac{\pi}{2}, \dfrac{\pi}{2}\right)$ because the interval does not include the endpoints.

7. The function is continuous for $k = \dfrac{9}{16}$.

In order for a function $f(x)$ is continuous at a point $x = c$, it must fulfill *all three* of the following conditions:

Condition 1: $f(c)$ exists.

Condition 2: $\lim\limits_{x \to c} f(x)$ exists.

Condition 3: $\lim\limits_{x \to c} f(x) = f(c)$

We will need to find a value, or values, of k that enables $f(x)$ to satisfy each condition.

Condition 1: $f(4) = 0$

Condition 2: $\lim\limits_{x \to 4^-} f(x) = 0$ and $\lim\limits_{x \to 4^+} f(x) = 16k - 9$. In order for the limit to exist, the

two limits must be the same. If we solve $16k - 9 = 0$, we get $k = \dfrac{9}{16}$.

Condition 3: If we now let $k = \dfrac{9}{16}$, $\lim\limits_{x \to 4} f(x) = 0 = f(4)$. Therefore, the solution is

$k = \dfrac{9}{16}$

8. The function is continuous for $k = 6$ or $k = -1$.

In order for a function $f(x)$ is continuous at a point $x = c$, it must fulfill *all three* of the following conditions:

Condition 1: $f(c)$ exists.

Condition 2: $\lim\limits_{x \to c} f(x)$ exists.

Condition 3: $\lim\limits_{x \to c} f(x) = f(c)$

We will need to find a value, or values, of k that enables $f(x)$ to satisfy each condition.

Condition 1: $f(-3) = k^2 - 5k$

Condition 2: $\lim\limits_{x \to -3^-} f(x) = 6$ and $\lim\limits_{x \to -3^+} f(x) = 6$, so $\lim\limits_{x \to -3} f(x) = 6$.

Condition 3: Now we need to find a value, or values, of k such that

$$\lim_{x \to -3} f(x) = 6 = f(3). \text{ If we set } k^2 - 5k = 6, \text{ we obtain the solutions } k = 6 \text{ and } k = -1.$$

9. The removable discontinuity is at $\left(3, \dfrac{11}{5}\right)$.

A *removable discontinuity* occurs when you have a rational expression with common

factors in the numerator and denominator. Because these factors can be cancelled,

the discontinuity is "removable." In practical terms, this means that the removable

occurs where there is a "hole" in the graph. If we factor $f(x) = \dfrac{x^2 + 5x - 24}{x^2 - x - 6}$ we get:

$f(x) = \dfrac{(x+8)(x-3)}{(x+2)(x-3)}$. If we cancel the common factor, we get: $f(x) = \dfrac{(x+8)}{(x+2)}$. Now,

if we plug in $x = 3$, we get $f(x) = \dfrac{11}{5}$. Therefore, the removable discontinuity is at

$\left(3, \dfrac{11}{5}\right)$.

10. (a) 0; (b) 0; (c) 1; (d) 1; (e) $f(3)$ *Does Not Exist.* (f) a jump discontinuity at $x = -3$; a

removable discontinuity at $x = 3$; and an essential discontinuity at $x = 5$.

(a) If we look at the graph, we can see that $\lim_{x \to -\infty} f(x) = 0$.

(b) If we look at the graph, we can see that $\lim_{x \to \infty} f(x) = 0$.

(c) If we look at the graph, we can see that $\lim_{x \to 3^-} f(x) = 1$.

(d) If we look at the graph, we can see that $\lim_{x \to 3^+} f(x) = 1$.

(e) $f(3)$ Does Not Exist.

(f) There are three discontinuities: (1) a jump discontinuity at $x = -3$; (2) a

removable discontinuity at $x = 3$; and (3) an essential discontinuity at $x = 5$.

SOLUTIONS TO PRACTICE PROBLEM SET 3

1. 5

    We find the derivative of a function, $f(x)$, using the definition of the derivative,

    which is: $f'(x) = \lim_{h \to 0} \dfrac{f(x+h) - f(x)}{h}$. Here, $f(x) = 5x$ and $x = 3$. This means that

    $f(3) = 5(3) = 15$ and $f(3+h) = 5(3+h) = 15 + 5h$. If we now plug these into the

    definition of the derivative, we get: $f'(3) = \lim_{h \to 0} \dfrac{f(3+h) - f(3)}{h} = \lim_{h \to 0} \dfrac{15 + 5h - 15}{h}$.

    This simplifies to $f'(3) = \lim_{h \to 0} \dfrac{5h}{h} = \lim_{h \to 0} 5 = 5$.

    If you noticed that the function is simply the equation of a line, then you would
    have seen that the derivative is simply the slope of the line, which is 5 everywhere.

2. 4

    We find the derivative of a function, $f(x)$, using the definition of the

    derivative, which is: $f'(x) = \lim_{h \to 0} \dfrac{f(x+h) - f(x)}{h}$. Here, $f(x) = 4x$ and $x = -8$.

    This means that $f(-8) = 4(-8) = -32$ and $f(-8+h) = 4(-8+h) = -32 + 4h$. If

    we now plug these into the definition of the derivative, we get:

    $f'(-8) = \lim_{h \to 0} \dfrac{f(-8+h) - f(-8)}{h} = \lim_{h \to 0} \dfrac{-32 + 4h + 32}{h}$. This simplifies to

    $f'(-8) = \lim_{h \to 0} \dfrac{4h}{h} = \lim_{h \to 0} 4 = 4$.

    If you noticed that the function is simply the equation of a line, then you would
    have seen that the derivative is simply the slope of the line, which is 4 everywhere.

3. 20

We find the derivative of a function, $f(x)$, using the definition of the derivative,

which is: $f'(x) = \lim_{h \to 0} \dfrac{f(x+h) - f(x)}{h}$. Here, $f(x) = 2x^2$ and $x = 5$. This means

that $f(5) = 2(5)^2 = 50$ and $f(5+h) = 2(5+h)^2 = 2(25+10h+h^2) = 50+20h+2h^2$.

If we now plug these into the definition of the derivative, we get:

$f'(5) = \lim_{h \to 0} \dfrac{f(5+h) - f(5)}{h} = \lim_{h \to 0} \dfrac{50+20h+2h^2 - 50}{h}$. This simplifies to

$f'(5) = \lim_{h \to 0} \dfrac{20h+2h^2}{h}$. Now we can factor out the h from the numerator and cancel

it with the h in the denominator: $f'(5) = \lim_{h \to 0} \dfrac{h(20+2h)}{h} = \lim_{h \to 0}(20+2h)$. Now we take

the limit to get: $f'(5) = \lim_{h \to 0}(20+2h) = 20$.

4. −10

We find the derivative of a function, $f(x)$, using the definition of the derivative,

which is: $f'(x) = \lim_{h \to 0} \dfrac{f(x+h) - f(x)}{h}$. Here, $f(x) = 5x^2$ and $x = -1$. This means

that $f(-1) = 5(-1)^2 = 5$ and $f(-1+h) = 5(-1+h)^2 = 5(1-2h+h^2) = 5-10h+5h^2$.

If we now plug these into the definition of the derivative, we get:

$f'(-1) = \lim_{h \to 0} \dfrac{f(-1+h) - f(-1)}{h} = \lim_{h \to 0} \dfrac{5-10h+5h^2 - 5}{h}$. This simplifies to

$f'(-1) = \lim_{h \to 0} \dfrac{-10h+5h^2}{h}$. Now we can factor out the h from the numerator and

cancel it with the h in the denominator: $f'(-1) = \lim_{h \to 0} \dfrac{h(-10+5h)}{h} = \lim_{h \to 0}(-10+5h)$.

Now we take the limit to get: $f'(-1) = \lim_{h \to 0}(-10+5h) = -10$.

5. $16x$

We find the derivative of a function, $f(x)$, using the definition of

the derivative, which is: $f'(x) = \lim\limits_{h \to 0} \dfrac{f(x+h)-f(x)}{h}$. Here $f(x) = 8x^2$

and $f(x+h) = 8(x+h)^2 = 8(x^2 + 2xh + h^2) = 8x^2 + 16xh + 8h^2$

. If we now plug these into the definition of the derivative, we get:

$f'(x) = \lim\limits_{h \to 0} \dfrac{f(x+h)-f(x)}{h} = \lim\limits_{h \to 0} \dfrac{8x^2 + 16xh + 8h^2 - 8x^2}{h}$. This simplifies to

$f'(x) = \lim\limits_{h \to 0} \dfrac{16xh + 8h^2}{h}$. Now we can factor out the h from the numerator and cancel

it with the h in the denominator: $f'(x) = \lim\limits_{h \to 0} \dfrac{h(16x + 8h)}{h} = \lim\limits_{h \to 0}(16x + 8h)$. Now we

take the limit to get: $f'(x) = \lim\limits_{h \to 0}(16x + 8h) = 16x$.

6. $-20x$

We find the derivative of a function, $f(x)$, using the definition of the

derivative, which is: $f'(x) = \lim\limits_{h \to 0} \dfrac{f(x+h)-f(x)}{h}$. Here $f(x) = -10x^2$

and $f(x+h) = -10(x+h)^2 = -10(x^2 + 2xh + h^2) = -10x^2 - 20xh - 10h^2$.

If we now plug these into the definition of the derivative, we get:

$f'(x) = \lim\limits_{h \to 0} \dfrac{f(x+h)-f(x)}{h} = \lim\limits_{h \to 0} \dfrac{-10x^2 - 20xh - 10h^2 + 10x^2}{h}$. This simplifies to

$f'(x) = \lim\limits_{h \to 0} \dfrac{-20xh - 10h^2}{h}$. Now we can factor out the h from the numerator and

cancel it with the h in the denominator: $f'(x) = \lim\limits_{h \to 0} \dfrac{h(-20x - 10h)}{h} = \lim\limits_{h \to 0}(-20x - 10h)$.

Now we take the limit to get: $f'(x) = \lim\limits_{h \to 0}(-20x - 10h) = -20x$.

7. 40a

We find the derivative of a function, $f(x)$, using the definition of the derivative,

which is: $f'(x) = \lim\limits_{h \to 0} \dfrac{f(x+h) - f(x)}{h}$. Here, $f(x) = 20x^2$ and $x = a$. This means

that $f(a) = 20a^2$ and $f(a+h) = 20(a+h)^2 = 20(a^2 + 2ah + h^2) = 20a^2 + 40ah + 20h^2$.

If we now plug these into the definition of the derivative, we get:

$f'(a) = \lim\limits_{h \to 0} \dfrac{f(a+h) - f(a)}{h} = \lim\limits_{h \to 0} \dfrac{20a^2 + 40ah + 20h^2 - 20a^2}{h}$. This simplifies to

$f'(a) = \lim\limits_{h \to 0} \dfrac{40ah + 20h^2}{h}$. Now we can factor out the h from the numerator and

cancel it with the h in the denominator: $f'(a) = \lim\limits_{h \to 0} \dfrac{h(40a + 20h)}{h} = \lim\limits_{h \to 0}(40a + 20h)$.

Now we take the limit to get: $f'(a) = \lim\limits_{h \to 0}(40a + 20h) = 40a$.

8. 54

We find the derivative of a function, $f(x)$, using the definition

of the derivative, which is: $f'(x) = \lim\limits_{h \to 0} \dfrac{f(x+h) - f(x)}{h}$. Here,

$f(x) = 2x^3$ and $x = -3$. This means that $f(-3) = 2(-3)^3 = -54$ and

$f(-3+h) = 2(-3+h)^3 = 2\left((-3)^3 + 3(-3)^2 h + 3(-3)h^2 + h^3\right) = -54 + 54h - 18h^2 + 2h^3$.

If we now plug these into the definition of the derivative, we get:

$f'(-3) = \lim\limits_{h \to 0} \dfrac{f(-3+h) - f(-3)}{h} = \lim\limits_{h \to 0} \dfrac{-54 + 54h - 18h^2 + 2h^3 + 54}{h}$. This

simplifies to $f'(-3) = \lim\limits_{h \to 0} \dfrac{54h - 18h^2 + 2h^3}{h}$. Now we can factor out the

h from the numerator and cancel it with the h in the denominator:

$$f'(-3) = \lim_{h \to 0} \frac{h\left(54 - 18h + 2h^2\right)}{h} = \lim_{h \to 0}\left(54 - 18h + 2h^2\right).$$ Now we take the limit to get:

$$f'(-3) = \lim_{h \to 0}\left(54 - 18h + 2h^2\right) = 54.$$

9. $-9x^2$

We find the derivative of a function, $f(x)$, using the definition of the derivative,

which is: $f'(x) = \lim_{h \to 0} \dfrac{f(x+h) - f(x)}{h}$. Here, $f(x) = -3x^3$. This means that

$$f(x+h) = -3(x+h)^3 = -3\left(x^3 + 3x^2h + 3xh^2 + h^3\right) = -3x^3 - 9x^2h - 9xh^2 - 3h^3.$$

If we now plug these into the definition of the derivative, we get:

$$f'(x) = \lim_{h \to 0} \frac{f(x+h) - f(x)}{h} = \lim_{h \to 0} \frac{-3x^3 - 9x^2h - 9xh^2 - 3h^3 + 3x^3}{h}.$$ This

simplifies to $f'(x) = \lim_{h \to 0} \dfrac{-9x^2h - 9xh^2 - 3h^3}{h}$. Now we can factor out the

h from the numerator and cancel it with the h in the denominator:

$$f'(x) = \lim_{h \to 0} \frac{h\left(-9x^2 - 9xh - 3h^2\right)}{h} = \lim_{h \to 0}\left(-9x^2 - 9xh - 3h^2\right).$$ Now we take the limit to

get: $f'(x) = \lim_{h \to 0}\left(-9x^2 - 9xh - 3h^2\right) = -9x^2$.

10. $4x^3$

We find the derivative of a function, $f(x)$, using the definition of

the derivative, which is: $f'(x) = \lim_{h \to 0} \dfrac{f(x+h) - f(x)}{h}$. Here, $f(x) = x^4$.

This means that $f(x+h) = (x+h)^4 = \left(x^4 + 4x^3h + 6x^2h^2 + 4xh^3 + h^4\right)$.

If we now plug these into the definition of the derivative, we get:

$$f'(x) = \lim_{h \to 0} \frac{f(x+h) - f(x)}{h} = \lim_{h \to 0} \frac{x^4 + 4x^3h + 6x^2h^2 + 4xh^3 + h^4 - x^4}{h}.$$ This

simplifies to $f'(x) = \lim_{h \to 0} \dfrac{4x^3h + 6x^2h^2 + 4xh^3 + h^4}{h}$. Now we can factor out

the h from the numerator and cancel it with the h in the denominator:

$$f'(x) = \lim_{h \to 0} \frac{h\left(4x^3 + 6x^2h + 4xh^2 + h^3\right)}{h} = \lim_{h \to 0} \left(4x^3 + 6x^2h + 4xh^2 + h^3\right).$$ Now we take the

limit to get: $f'(x) = \lim_{h \to 0} \left(4x^3 + 6x^2h + 4xh^2 + h^3\right) = 4x^3$.

11. $5x^4$

We find the derivative of a function, $f(x)$, using the definition of the

derivative, which is: $f'(x) = \lim_{h \to 0} \dfrac{f(x+h) - f(x)}{h}$. Here, $f(x) = x^5$. This

means that $f(x+h) = (x+h)^5 = \left(x^5 + 5x^4h + 10x^3h^2 + 10x^2h^3 + 5xh^4 + h^5\right)$.

If we now plug these into the definition of the derivative, we get:

$$f'(x) = \lim_{h \to 0} \frac{f(x+h) - f(x)}{h} = \lim_{h \to 0} \frac{x^5 + 5x^4h + 10x^3h^2 + 10x^2h^3 + 5xh^4 + h^5 - x^5}{h}.$$ This

simplifies to $f'(x) = \lim_{h \to 0} \dfrac{5x^4h + 10x^3h^2 + 10x^2h^3 + 5xh^4 + h^5}{h}$. Now we can factor

out the h from the numerator and cancel it with the h in the denominator:

$$f'(x) = \lim_{h \to 0} \frac{h\left(5x^4 + 10x^3h + 10x^2h^2 + 5xh^3 + h^4\right)}{h} = \lim_{h \to 0} \left(5x^4 + 10x^3h + 10x^2h^2 + 5xh^3 + h^4\right).$$

Now we take the limit to get: $f'(x) = \lim_{h \to 0} \left(5x^4 + 10x^3h + 10x^2h^2 + 5xh^3 + h^4\right) = 5x^4$.

12. $\dfrac{1}{3}$

We find the derivative of a function, $f(x)$, using the definition of the derivative,

which is: $f'(x) = \lim\limits_{h \to 0} \dfrac{f(x+h) - f(x)}{h}$. Here, $f(x) = 2\sqrt{x}$ and $x = 9$. This means that

$f(9) = 2\sqrt{9} = 6$ and $f(9+h) = 2\sqrt{9+h}$. If we now plug these into the definition

of the derivative, we get: $f'(9) = \lim\limits_{h \to 0} \dfrac{f(9+h) - f(9)}{h} = \lim\limits_{h \to 0} \dfrac{2\sqrt{9+h} - 6}{h}$. Notice that

if we now take the limit, we get the indeterminate form $\dfrac{0}{0}$. With polynomials,

we merely simplify the expression to eliminate this problem. In any derivative

of a square root, we first multiply the top and the bottom of the expression by

the conjugate of the numerator and then we can simplify. Here, the conjugate

is $2\sqrt{9+h} + 6$. We get: $f'(9) = \lim\limits_{h \to 0} \dfrac{2\sqrt{9+h} - 6}{h} \bullet \dfrac{2\sqrt{9+h} + 6}{2\sqrt{9+h} + 6}$. This simplifies to:

$f'(9) = \lim\limits_{h \to 0} \dfrac{4(9+h) - 36}{h\left(2\sqrt{9+h} + 6\right)} = \lim\limits_{h \to 0} \dfrac{36 + 4h - 36}{h\left(2\sqrt{9+h} + 6\right)} = \lim\limits_{h \to 0} \dfrac{4h}{h\left(2\sqrt{9+h} + 6\right)}$. Now we can

cancel the h in the numerator and the denominator to get $f'(9) = \lim\limits_{h \to 0} \dfrac{4}{\left(2\sqrt{9+h} + 6\right)}$.

Now, we take the limit: $f'(9) = \lim\limits_{h \to 0} \dfrac{4}{\left(2\sqrt{9+h} + 6\right)} = \dfrac{4}{\left(2\sqrt{9} + 6\right)} = \dfrac{1}{3}$.

13. $\dfrac{5}{4}$

We find the derivative of a function, $f(x)$, using the definition of the derivative,

which is: $f'(x) = \lim\limits_{h \to 0} \dfrac{f(x+h) - f(x)}{h}$. Here, $f(x) = 5\sqrt{2x}$ and $x = 8$. This

means that $f(8) = 5\sqrt{16} = 20$ and $f(8+h) = 5\sqrt{2(8+h)} = 5\sqrt{16+2h}$.

If we now plug these into the definition of the derivative, we get:

$f'(8) = \lim\limits_{h \to 0} \dfrac{f(8+h) - f(8)}{h} = \lim\limits_{h \to 0} \dfrac{5\sqrt{16+2h} - 20}{h}$. Notice that if we now take

the limit, we get the indeterminate form $\dfrac{0}{0}$. With polynomials, we merely

simplify the expression to eliminate this problem. In any derivative of a square

root, we first multiply the top and the bottom of the expression by the

conjugate of the numerator and then we simplify. Here, the conjugate is

$5\sqrt{16+2h} + 20$. We get: $f'(8) = \lim\limits_{h \to 0} \dfrac{5\sqrt{16+2h} - 20}{h} \bullet \dfrac{5\sqrt{16+2h} + 20}{5\sqrt{16+2h} + 20}$. This simplifies

to: $f'(8) = \lim\limits_{h \to 0} \dfrac{25(16+2h) - 400}{h\left(5\sqrt{16+2h} + 20\right)} = \lim\limits_{h \to 0} \dfrac{400 + 50h - 400}{h\left(5\sqrt{16+2h} + 20\right)} = \lim\limits_{h \to 0} \dfrac{50h}{h\left(5\sqrt{16+2h} + 20\right)}$.

Now we can cancel the h in the numerator and the denominator

to get $f'(8) = \lim\limits_{h \to 0} \dfrac{50}{\left(5\sqrt{16+2h} + 20\right)}$. Now, we take the limit:

$f'(8) = \lim\limits_{h \to 0} \dfrac{50}{\left(5\sqrt{16+2h} + 20\right)} = \dfrac{50}{(20+20)} = \dfrac{5}{4}$.

14. $\dfrac{1}{2}$

We find the derivative of a function, $f(x)$, using the definition

of the derivative, which is: $f'(x) = \lim\limits_{h \to 0} \dfrac{f(x+h) - f(x)}{h}$. Here,

$f(x) = \sin x$ and $x = \dfrac{\pi}{3}$. This means that $f\left(\dfrac{\pi}{3}\right) = \sin\dfrac{\pi}{3} = \dfrac{\sqrt{3}}{2}$ and

$f\left(\dfrac{\pi}{3} + h\right) = \sin\left(\dfrac{\pi}{3} + h\right)$. If we now plug these into the definition of the

derivative, we get: $f'\left(\dfrac{\pi}{3}\right) = \lim\limits_{h \to 0} \dfrac{f\left(\dfrac{\pi}{3} + h\right) - f\left(\dfrac{\pi}{3}\right)}{h} = \lim\limits_{h \to 0} \dfrac{\sin\left(\dfrac{\pi}{3} + h\right) - \dfrac{\sqrt{3}}{2}}{h}$.

Notice that if we now take the limit, we get the indeterminate form $\dfrac{0}{0}$. We

cannot eliminate this problem merely by simplifying the expression the

way that we did with a polynomial. Recall that the trigonometric formula

$\sin(A + B) = \sin A \cos B + \cos A \sin B$. Here, we can rewrite the top expression as:

$f'\left(\dfrac{\pi}{3}\right) = \lim\limits_{h \to 0} \dfrac{\sin\left(\dfrac{\pi}{3} + h\right) - \dfrac{\sqrt{3}}{2}}{h} = \lim\limits_{h \to 0} \dfrac{\sin\dfrac{\pi}{3}\cos h + \cos\dfrac{\pi}{3}\sin h - \dfrac{\sqrt{3}}{2}}{h}$. We can break up

the limit into: $\lim\limits_{h \to 0} \dfrac{\sin\dfrac{\pi}{3}\cos h - \dfrac{\sqrt{3}}{2}}{h} + \dfrac{\cos\dfrac{\pi}{3}\sin h}{h} = \lim\limits_{h \to 0} \dfrac{\dfrac{\sqrt{3}}{2}\cos h - \dfrac{\sqrt{3}}{2}}{h} + \dfrac{\left(\dfrac{1}{2}\right)\sin h}{h}$. Next,

factor $\dfrac{\sqrt{3}}{2}$ out of the top of the left-hand expression: $\lim\limits_{h \to 0} \dfrac{\dfrac{\sqrt{3}}{2}(\cos h - 1)}{h} + \dfrac{\left(\dfrac{1}{2}\right)\sin h}{h}$. Now

we can break this into separate limits: $\lim\limits_{h \to 0} \dfrac{\dfrac{\sqrt{3}}{2}(\cos h - 1)}{h} + \lim\limits_{h \to 0} \dfrac{\left(\dfrac{1}{2}\right)\sin h}{h}$. The left-hand limit is: $\lim\limits_{h \to 0} \dfrac{\dfrac{\sqrt{3}}{2}(\cos h - 1)}{h} = \dfrac{\sqrt{3}}{2}\lim\limits_{h \to 0}\dfrac{(\cos h - 1)}{h} = \dfrac{\sqrt{3}}{2} \cdot 0 = 0$. The right-hand limit

is: $\dfrac{1}{2}\lim\limits_{h \to 0}\dfrac{\sin h}{h} = \dfrac{1}{2} \cdot 1 = \dfrac{1}{2}$. Therefore, the limit is $\dfrac{1}{2}$.

15. $-\sin x$

We find the derivative of a function, $f(x)$, using the definition of the

derivative, which is: $f'(x) = \lim\limits_{h \to 0}\dfrac{f(x+h) - f(x)}{h}$. Here, $f(x) = \cos x$ and

that $f(x+h) = \cos(x+h)$. If we now plug these into the definition of the

derivative, we get: $f'(x) = \lim\limits_{h \to 0}\dfrac{f(x+h) - f(x)}{h} = \lim\limits_{h \to 0}\dfrac{\cos(x+h) - \cos x}{h}$. Notice

that if we now take the limit, we get the indeterminate form $\dfrac{0}{0}$. We cannot

eliminate this problem merely by simplifying the expression the way

that we did with a polynomial. Recall that the trigonometric formula

$\cos(A+B) = \cos A \cos B - \sin A \sin B$. Here, we can rewrite the top expression as:

$f'(x) = \lim\limits_{h \to 0}\dfrac{\cos(x+h) - \cos x}{h} = \lim\limits_{h \to 0}\dfrac{\cos x \cos h - \sin x \sin h - \cos x}{h}$. We can break up

the limit into: $\lim\limits_{h \to 0}\dfrac{\cos x \cos h - \cos x}{h} - \dfrac{\sin x \sin h}{h}$. Next factor $\cos x$ out of the top

of the left-hand expression: $\lim\limits_{h \to 0}\dfrac{\cos x(\cos h - 1)}{h} - \dfrac{\sin x \sin h}{h}$. Now we can break

this into separate limits: $\lim\limits_{h \to 0}\dfrac{\cos x(\cos h - 1)}{h} - \lim\limits_{h \to 0}\dfrac{\sin x \sin h}{h}$. The left-hand limit is:

$\lim\limits_{h \to 0}\dfrac{\cos x(\cos h - 1)}{h} = \cos x \lim\limits_{h \to 0}\dfrac{(\cos h - 1)}{h} = \cos x \cdot 0 = 0$. The right-hand limit is:

$\sin x \lim\limits_{h \to 0}\dfrac{\sin h}{h} = \sin x \cdot 1 = \sin x$. Therefore, the limit is $-\sin x$.

16. $2x+1$

We find the derivative of a function, $f(x)$, using the definition

of the derivative, which is: $f'(x) = \lim\limits_{h \to 0} \dfrac{f(x+h) - f(x)}{h}$. Here,

$f(x) = x^2 + x$ and that $f(x+h) = (x+h)^2 + (x+h) = x^2 + 2xh + h^2 + x + h$.

If we now plug these into the definition of the derivative, we get:

$f'(x) = \lim\limits_{h \to 0} \dfrac{f(x+h) - f(x)}{h} = \lim\limits_{h \to 0} \dfrac{x^2 + 2xh + h^2 + x + h - (x^2 + x)}{h}$. This

simplifies to $f'(x) = \lim\limits_{h \to 0} \dfrac{2xh + h^2 + h}{h}$. Now we can factor out the h

from the numerator and cancel it with the h in the denominator:

$f'(x) = \lim\limits_{h \to 0} \dfrac{2xh + h^2 + h}{h} = \lim\limits_{h \to 0} \dfrac{h(2x + h + 1)}{h} = \lim\limits_{h \to 0}(2x + h + 1)$. Now we take the limit to

get: $f'(x) = \lim\limits_{h \to 0}(2x + h + 1) = 2x + 1$.

17. $3x^2 + 3$

We find the derivative of a function, $f(x)$, using the definition of the

derivative, which is: $f'(x) = \lim\limits_{h \to 0} \dfrac{f(x+h) - f(x)}{h}$. Here, $f(x) = x^3 + 3x + 2$

and that $f(x+h) = (x+h)^3 + 3(x+h) + 2 = x^3 + 3x^2h + 3xh^2 + h^3 + 3x + 3h + 2$.

If we now plug these into the definition of the derivative, we get:

$f'(x) = \lim\limits_{h \to 0} \dfrac{f(x+h) - f(x)}{h} = \lim\limits_{h \to 0} \dfrac{x^3 + 3x^2h + 3xh^2 + h^3 + 3x + 3h + 2 - (x^3 + 3x + 2)}{h}$.

This simplifies to $f'(x) = \lim\limits_{h \to 0} \dfrac{3x^2h + 3xh^2 + h^3 + 3h}{h}$. Now we can factor out

the h from the numerator and cancel it with the h in the denominator:

$$f'(x) = \lim_{h \to 0} \frac{3x^2h + 3xh^2 + h^3 + 3h}{h} \lim_{h \to 0} \frac{h(3x^2 + 3xh + h^2 + 3)}{h} = \lim_{h \to 0} (3x^2 + 3xh + h^2 + 3).$$

Now we take the limit to get: $f'(x) = \lim_{h \to 0} (3x^2 + 3xh + h^2 + 3) = 3x^2 + 3$.

18. $-\dfrac{1}{x^2}$

We find the derivative of a function, $f(x)$, using the definition of the

derivative, which is: $f'(x) = \lim_{h \to 0} \dfrac{f(x+h) - f(x)}{h}$. Here, $f(x) = \dfrac{1}{x}$ and that

$f(x+h) = \dfrac{1}{x+h}$. If we now plug these into the definition of the derivative,

we get: $f'(x) = \lim_{h \to 0} \dfrac{f(x+h) - f(x)}{h} = \lim_{h \to 0} \dfrac{\frac{1}{x+h} - \frac{1}{x}}{h}$. Notice that if we now take

the limit, we get the indeterminate form $\dfrac{0}{0}$. We cannot eliminate this problem

merely by simplifying the expression the way that we did with a polynomial.

Here, we combine the two terms in the numerator of the expression to get:

$$f'(x) = \lim_{h \to 0} \frac{\frac{1}{x+h} - \frac{1}{x}}{h} = \lim_{h \to 0} \frac{\frac{x}{x(x+h)} - \frac{x+h}{x(x+h)}}{h} = \lim_{h \to 0} \frac{\frac{-h}{x(x+h)}}{h}.$$ This simplifies to

$$f'(x) = \lim_{h \to 0} \frac{\frac{-h}{x(x+h)}}{h} = \lim_{h \to 0} \frac{-h}{x(x+h)h}.$$ Now we can cancel the factor h in the

numerator and the denominator to get $f'(x) = \lim_{h \to 0} \dfrac{-h}{x(x+h)h} = \lim_{h \to 0} \dfrac{-1}{x(x+h)}$. Now, we

take the limit: $f'(x) = \lim_{h \to 0} \dfrac{-1}{x(x+h)} = -\dfrac{1}{x^2}$.

19. $2ax + b$

We find the derivative of a function, $f(x)$, using the definition of the

derivative, which is: $f'(x) = \lim\limits_{h \to 0} \dfrac{f(x+h) - f(x)}{h}$. Here, $f(x) = ax^2 + bx + c$

and that $f(x+h) = a(x+h)^2 + b(x+h) + c = ax^2 + 2axh + ah^2 + bx + bh + c$.

If we now plug these into the definition of the derivative, we get:

$$f'(x) = \lim\limits_{h \to 0} \frac{f(x+h) - f(x)}{h} = \lim\limits_{h \to 0} \frac{ax^2 + 2axh + ah^2 + bx + bh + c - \left(ax^2 + bx + c\right)}{h}.$$

This simplifies to $f'(x) = \lim\limits_{h \to 0} \dfrac{2axh + ah^2 + bh}{h}$. Now we can factor out

the h from the numerator and cancel it with the h in the denominator:

$f'(x) = \lim\limits_{h \to 0} \dfrac{2axh + ah^2 + bh}{h} = \lim\limits_{h \to 0} \dfrac{h(2ax + ah + b)}{h} = \lim\limits_{h \to 0}(2ax + ah + b)$. Now we take the

limit to get: $f'(x) = \lim\limits_{h \to 0}(2ax + ah + b) = 2ax + b$.

20. $-\dfrac{2}{x^3}$

We find the derivative of a function, $f(x)$, using the definition of the

derivative, which is: $f'(x) = \lim\limits_{h \to 0} \dfrac{f(x+h) - f(x)}{h}$. Here, $f(x) = \dfrac{1}{x^2}$ and that

$f(x+h) = \dfrac{1}{(x+h)^2}$. If we now plug these into the definition of the derivative,

we get: $f'(x) = \lim\limits_{h \to 0} \dfrac{f(x+h) - f(x)}{h} = \lim\limits_{h \to 0} \dfrac{\dfrac{1}{(x+h)^2} - \dfrac{1}{x^2}}{h}$. Notice that if we now take the limit, we get the indeterminate form $\frac{0}{0}$. We cannot eliminate this problem

merely by simplifying the expression the way that we did with a polynomial.

Here, we combine the two terms in the numerator of the expression to get:

$$f'(x) = \lim_{h \to 0} \frac{\dfrac{1}{(x+h)^2} - \dfrac{1}{x^2}}{h} = \lim_{h \to 0} \frac{\dfrac{x^2}{x^2(x+h)^2} - \dfrac{(x+h)^2}{x^2(x+h)^2}}{h} = \lim_{h \to 0} \frac{\dfrac{x^2 - (x+h)^2}{x^2(x+h)^2}}{h} \cdot \text{This}$$

simplifies to $f'(x) = \lim_{h \to 0} \dfrac{\dfrac{x^2 - (x^2 + 2xh + h^2)}{x^2(x+h)^2}}{h} = \lim_{h \to 0} \dfrac{\dfrac{-2xh - h^2}{x^2(x+h)^2}}{h} = \lim_{h \to 0} \dfrac{-2xh - h^2}{x^2(x+h)^2 h}.$

Now we can cancel the h in the numerator and the denominator to

get $f'(x) = \lim_{h \to 0} \dfrac{h(-2x - h)}{x^2(x+h)^2 h} = \lim_{h \to 0} \dfrac{(-2x - h)}{x^2(x+h)^2}$. Now, we take the limit:

$$f'(x) = \lim_{h \to 0} \frac{(-2x - h)}{x^2(x+h)^2} = \frac{-2x}{x^2(x^2)} = -\frac{2}{x^3}.$$

SOLUTIONS TO PRACTICE PROBLEM SET 4

1. $64x^3 + 16x$

   First, expand $(4x^2 + 1)^2$ to get $16x^4 + 8x^2 + 1$. Now, use the Power Rule to take the derivative of each term. The derivative of $16x^4 = 16(4x^3) = 64x^3$. The derivative of $8x^2 = 8(2x) = 16x$. The derivative of $1 = 0$ (because the derivative of a constant is zero). Therefore, the derivative is: $64x^3 + 16x$.

2. $10x^9 + 36x^5 + 18x$

   First, expand $(x^5 + 3x)^2$ to get $x^{10} + 6x^6 + 9x^2$. Now, use the Power Rule to take the derivative of each term. The derivative of $x^{10} = 10x^9$. The derivative of $6x^6 = 6(6x^5) = 36x^5$. The derivative of $9x^2 = 9(2x) = 18x$. Therefore, the derivative is: $10x^9 + 36x^5 + 18x$.

3. $77x^6$

   Simply use the Power Rule. The derivative is $11x^7 = 11(7x^6) = 77x^6$.

4. $80x^9$

   Simply use the Power Rule. The derivative is $8x^{10} = 8(10x^9) = 80x^9$.

5. $54x^2 + 12$

   Use the Power Rule to take the derivative of each term. The derivative of $18x^3 = 18(3x^2) = 54x^2$. The derivative of $12x = 12$. The derivative of $11 = 0$ (because the derivative of a constant is zero). Therefore, the derivative is: $54x^2 + 12$.

6. $6x^{11}$

   Use the Power Rule to take the derivative of each term. The derivative of $x^{12} = 12x^{11}$. The derivative of $17 = 0$ (because the derivative of a constant is zero). Therefore, the derivative is: $\frac{1}{2}(12x^{11}) = 6x^{11}$.

7. $-3x^8 - 2x^2$

Use the Power Rule to take the derivative of each term. The derivative of $x^9 = 9x^8$. The derivative of $2x^3 = 2(3x^2) = 6x^2$. The derivative of $9 = 0$ (because the derivative of a constant is zero). Therefore, the derivative is: $-\dfrac{1}{3}(9x^8 + 6x^2) = -3x^8 - 2x^2$.

8. 0

Don't be fooled by the power. π^5 is a constant so the derivative is zero.

9. $\dfrac{2}{ab}x - \dfrac{2}{a^2} + \dfrac{d}{ax^2}$

Use the Power Rule to take the derivative of each term. The derivative of

$\dfrac{1}{b}x^2 = \dfrac{1}{b}(2x) = \dfrac{2}{b}x$. The derivative of $\dfrac{2}{a}x = \dfrac{2}{a}$. The derivative of $\dfrac{d}{x} = -\dfrac{d}{x^2}$

(remember the shortcut that we showed you on page 37). Therefore, the derivative

is: $\dfrac{1}{a}\left(\dfrac{2}{b}x - \dfrac{2}{a} + \dfrac{d}{x^2}\right) = \dfrac{2}{ab}x - \dfrac{2}{a^2} + \dfrac{d}{ax^2}$.

10. $64x^{-9} + \dfrac{6}{\sqrt{x}}$

Use the Power Rule to take the derivative of each term. The derivative of

$-8x^{-8} = -8(-8x^{-9}) = 64x^{-9}$. The derivative of $12\sqrt{x} = \dfrac{12}{2\sqrt{x}} = \dfrac{6}{\sqrt{x}}$ (remember the

shortcut that we showed you on page 37). Therefore, the derivative is: $64x^{-9} + \dfrac{6}{\sqrt{x}}$.

11. $-42x^{-8} - \dfrac{2}{\sqrt{x}}$

Use the Power Rule to take the derivative of each term. The derivative of

$6x^{-7} = 6(-7x^{-8}) = -42x^{-8}$. The derivative of $4\sqrt{x} = \dfrac{4}{2\sqrt{x}} = \dfrac{2}{\sqrt{x}}$ (remember the

shortcut that we showed you on page 37). Therefore, the derivative is: $-42x^{-8} - \dfrac{2}{\sqrt{x}}$.

12. $\dfrac{-5}{x^6} - \dfrac{8}{x^9}$

Use the Power Rule to take the derivative of each term. The derivative of $x^{-5} = -5x^{-6}$.

To find the derivative of $\dfrac{1}{x^8}$, we first rewrite it as x^{-8}. The derivative of $x^{-8} = -8x^{-9}$.

Therefore, the derivative is: $-5x^{-6} - 8x^{-9} = \dfrac{-5}{x^6} - \dfrac{8}{x^9}$.

13. $\dfrac{1}{2\sqrt{x}} - \dfrac{3}{x^4}$

Use the Power Rule to take the derivative of each term. The derivative of

$\sqrt{x} = \dfrac{1}{2\sqrt{x}}$ (remember the shortcut that we showed you on page 37). To find the

derivative of $\dfrac{1}{x^3}$, we first rewrite it as x^{-3}. The derivative of $x^{-3} = -3x^{-4}$. Therefore,

the derivative is: $\dfrac{1}{2\sqrt{x}} - 3x^{-4} = \dfrac{1}{2\sqrt{x}} - \dfrac{3}{x^4}$.

14. $216x^2 - 48x + 36$

First, expand $\left(6x^2 + 3\right)\left(12x - 4\right)$ to get $72x^3 - 24x^2 + 36x - 12$. Now, use the Power

Rule to take the derivative of each term. The derivative of $72x^3 = 72\left(3x^2\right) = 216x^2$.

The derivative of $24x^2 = 24\left(2x\right) = 48x$. The derivative of $36x = 36$. The derivative of

$12 = 0$ (because the derivative of a constant is zero). Therefore, the derivative is:

$216x^2 - 48x + 36$.

15. $-6 - 36x^2 + 12x^3 - 5x^4 - 14x^6$

First, expand $(3 - x - 2x^3)(6 + x^4)$ to get $18 - 6x - 12x^3 + 3x^4 - x^5 - 2x^7$. Now, use the

Power Rule to take the derivative of each term. The derivative of $18 = 0$ (because

the derivative of a constant is zero). The derivative of $6x = 6$. The derivative of

$12x^3 = 12(3x^2) = 36x^2$. The derivative of $3x^4 = 3(4x^3) = 12x^3$. The derivative of

$x^5 = 5x^4$. The derivative of $2x^7 = 2(7x^6) = 14x^6$. Therefore, the derivative is:

$-6 - 36x^2 + 12x^3 - 5x^4 - 14x^6$.

16. 0

Don't be fooled by the powers. Each term is a constant so the derivative is zero.

17. $-\dfrac{16}{x^5} + \dfrac{10}{x^6} + \dfrac{36}{x^7}$

First, expand $\left(\dfrac{1}{x} + \dfrac{1}{x^2}\right)\left(\dfrac{4}{x^3} - \dfrac{6}{x^4}\right)$ to get $\dfrac{4}{x^4} - \dfrac{6}{x^5} + \dfrac{4}{x^5} - \dfrac{6}{x^6} = \dfrac{4}{x^4} - \dfrac{2}{x^5} - \dfrac{6}{x^6}$. Next,

rewrite the terms as: $4x^{-4} - 2x^{-5} - 6x^{-6}$. Now, use the Power Rule to take the

derivative of each term. The derivative of $4x^{-4} = 4(-4x^{-5}) = -16x^{-5}$. The derivative

of $2x^{-5} = 2(-5x^{-6}) = -10x^{-6}$. The derivative of $6x^{-6} = -36x^{-7}$. Therefore, the

derivative is: $-16x^{-5} + 10x^{-6} + 36x^{-7} = -\dfrac{16}{x^5} + \dfrac{10}{x^6} + \dfrac{36}{x^7}$.

18. $\dfrac{1}{2\sqrt{x}}$

Use the Power Rule to take the derivative of each term. The derivative of $\sqrt{x} = \dfrac{1}{2\sqrt{x}}$

(remember the shortcut that we showed you on page 37). The derivative of $\dfrac{1}{\sqrt{3}} = 0$

(because the derivative of a constant is zero). Therefore, the derivative is: $\dfrac{1}{2\sqrt{x}}$.

19. $-\dfrac{16}{x^2}+\dfrac{14}{x^3}-\dfrac{24}{x^4}+\dfrac{16}{x^5}$

First, expand $\left(x^2+8x-4\right)\left(2x^{-2}+x^{-4}\right)$ to get $2+16x^{-1}-7x^{-2}+8x^{-3}-4x^{-4}$.

Now, use the Power Rule to take the derivative of each term. The derivative

of $2=0$ (because the derivative of a constant is zero). The derivative of

$16x^{-1}=16\left(-1x^{-2}\right)=-16x^{-2}$. The derivative of $7x^{-2}=7\left(-2x^{-3}\right)=-14x^{-3}$. The

derivative of $8x^{-3}=8\left(-3x^{-4}\right)=-24x^{-4}$. The derivative of $4x^{-4}=4\left(-4x^{-5}\right)=-16x^{-5}$.

Therefore, the derivative is: $-16x^{-2}+14x^{-3}-24x^{-4}+16x^{-5}=-\dfrac{16}{x^2}+\dfrac{14}{x^3}-\dfrac{24}{x^4}+\dfrac{16}{x^5}$.

20. 0

The derivative of a constant is zero.

21. $3x^2+6x+3$

First, expand $(x+1)^3$ to get x^3+3x^2+3x+1. Now, use the Power Rule to

take the derivative of each term. The derivative of $x^3=3x^2$. The derivative of

$3x^2=3(2x)=6x$. The derivative of $3x=3$. The derivative of $1=0$ (because the

derivative of a constant is zero). Therefore, the derivative is: $3x^2+6x+3$.

22. $\dfrac{1}{2\sqrt{x}}+\dfrac{1}{3\sqrt[3]{x^2}}+\dfrac{2}{3\sqrt[3]{x}}$

Use the Power Rule to take the derivative of each term. The derivative of

$\sqrt{x}=\dfrac{1}{2\sqrt{x}}$ (remember the shortcut that we showed you on page 37). Rewrite $\sqrt[3]{x}$

as $x^{\frac{1}{3}}$ and $\sqrt[3]{x^2}$ as $x^{\frac{2}{3}}$. The derivative of $x^{\frac{1}{3}}=\dfrac{1}{3}x^{-\frac{2}{3}}$. The derivative of $x^{\frac{2}{3}}=\dfrac{2}{3}x^{-\frac{1}{3}}$.

Therefore, the derivative is: $\dfrac{1}{2\sqrt{x}}+\dfrac{1}{3}x^{-\frac{2}{3}}+\dfrac{2}{3}x^{-\frac{1}{3}}=\dfrac{1}{2\sqrt{x}}+\dfrac{1}{3\sqrt[3]{x^2}}+\dfrac{2}{3\sqrt[3]{x}}$.

23. $6x^2 + 6x - 14$

First, expand $x(2x+7)(x-2)$ to get $x(2x^2 + 3x - 14) = 2x^3 + 3x^2 - 14x$. Now, use the Power Rule to take the derivative of each term. The derivative of $2x^3 = 2(3x^2) = 6x^2$. The derivative of $3x^2 = 3(2x) = 6x$. The derivative of $14x = 14$ Therefore, the derivative is: $6x^2 + 6x - 14$.

24. $\dfrac{5}{6\sqrt[6]{x}} + \dfrac{7}{10\sqrt[10]{x^3}}$

First, rewrite the terms as $x^{\frac{1}{2}}\left(x^{\frac{1}{3}} + x^{\frac{1}{5}} \right)$. Next, distribute to get:

$x^{\frac{1}{2}}\left(x^{\frac{1}{3}} + x^{\frac{1}{5}} \right) = x^{\frac{5}{6}} + x^{\frac{7}{10}}$. Now, use the Power Rule to take the derivative of each

term. The derivative of $x^{\frac{5}{6}} = \dfrac{5}{6}x^{-\frac{1}{6}}$. The derivative of $x^{\frac{7}{10}} = \dfrac{7}{10}x^{-\frac{3}{10}}$. Therefore, the

derivative is: $\dfrac{5}{6}x^{-\frac{1}{6}} + \dfrac{7}{10}x^{-\frac{3}{10}} = \dfrac{5}{6\sqrt[6]{x}} + \dfrac{7}{10\sqrt[10]{x^3}}$.

25. $5ax^4 + 4bx^3 + 3cx^2 + 2dx + e$

Use the Power Rule to take the derivative of each term. The derivative of

$ax^5 = a(5x^4) = 5ax^4$. The derivative of $bx^4 = b(4x^3) = 4bx^3$. The derivative of

$cx^3 = c(3x^2) = 3cx^2$. The derivative of $dx^2 = d(2x) = 2dx$. The derivative of $ex = e$.

The derivative of $f = 0$ (because the derivative of a constant is zero). Therefore, the

derivative is: $5ax^4 + 4bx^3 + 3cx^2 + 2dx + e$.

SOLUTIONS TO PRACTICE PROBLEM SET 5

1. $\dfrac{-80x^9 + 75x^8 + 12x^2 - 6x}{\left(5x^7 + 1\right)^2}$

   We find the derivative using the Quotient Rule (page 41), which says that if $f(x) = \dfrac{u}{v}$, then

   $f'(x) = \dfrac{v\dfrac{du}{dx} - u\dfrac{dv}{dx}}{v^2}$. Here $f(x) = \dfrac{4x^3 - 3x^2}{5x^7 + 1}$, so $u = 4x^3 - 3x^2$ and $v = 5x^7 + 1$. Using the

   Quotient Rule, we get: $f'(x) = \dfrac{\left(5x^7 + 1\right)\left(12x^2 - 6x\right) - \left(4x^3 - 3x^2\right)\left(35x^6\right)}{\left(5x^7 + 1\right)^2}$. This can be

   simplified to $f'(x) = \dfrac{-80x^9 + 75x^8 + 12x^2 - 6x}{\left(5x^7 + 1\right)^2}$.

2. $3x^2 - 6x - 1$

   We find the derivative using the Product Rule (page 40),

   which says that if $f(x) = uv$, then $f'(x) = u\dfrac{dv}{dx} + v\dfrac{du}{dx}$. Here

   $f(x) = \left(x^2 - 4x + 3\right)(x + 1)$, so $u = x^2 - 4x + 3$ and $v = x + 1$. Using the Product

   Rule, we get: $f'(x) = \left(x^2 - 4x + 3\right)(1) + (x + 1)(2x - 4)$. This can be simplified to

   $f'(x) = 3x^2 - 6x - 1$.

3. $10(x + 1)^9$

   We find the derivative using the Chain Rule (page 42), which says that if

   $y = f(g(x))$, then $y' = \left(\dfrac{df(g(x))}{dg}\right)\left(\dfrac{dg}{dx}\right)$. Here, $f(x) = (x + 1)^{10}$. Using the Chain

   Rule, we get: $f'(x) = 10(x + 1)^9(1) = 10(x + 1)^9$.

4. $\dfrac{16x^2 - 32}{\sqrt{(x^2 - 4)}}$

We find the derivative using the Chain Rule (page 42), which says that if

$y = f\big(g(x)\big)$, then $y' = \left(\dfrac{df\big(g(x)\big)}{dg}\right)\left(\dfrac{dg}{dx}\right)$. Here, $f(x) = 8\sqrt{(x^4 - 4x^2)}$, which

can be written as $f(x) = 8\big(x^4 - 4x^2\big)^{\frac{1}{2}}$. Using the Chain Rule, we get:

$f'(x) = 8\left(\dfrac{1}{2}\right)\big(x^4 - 4x^2\big)^{-\frac{1}{2}}\big(4x^3 - 8x\big)$. This can be simplified to $f'(x) = \dfrac{16x^2 - 32}{\sqrt{(x^2 - 4)}}$.

5. $\dfrac{3x^2 - 3x^4}{\big(x^2 + 1\big)^4}$

Here, we will find the derivative using the Chain Rule. We will also need the

Quotient Rule to take the derivative of the expression inside the parentheses. The

Chain Rule (page 42) says that if $y = f\big(g(x)\big)$, then $y' = \left(\dfrac{df\big(g(x)\big)}{dg}\right)\left(\dfrac{dg}{dx}\right)$, and

the Quotient Rule says that if $f(x) = \dfrac{u}{v}$, then $f'(x) = \dfrac{v\dfrac{du}{dx} - u\dfrac{dv}{dx}}{v^2}$. We get:

$f'(x) = 3\left(\dfrac{x}{x^2 + 1}\right)^2\left(\dfrac{\big(x^2 + 1\big)(1) - x(2x)}{\big(x^2 + 1\big)^2}\right)$. This can be simplified to $f'(x) = \dfrac{3x^2 - 3x^4}{\big(x^2 + 1\big)^4}$.

6. $\dfrac{1}{4}\left(\dfrac{2x-5}{5x+2}\right)^{-\frac{3}{4}}\left(\dfrac{29}{(5x+2)^2}\right)$

Here, we will find the derivative using the Chain Rule. We will also need the

Quotient Rule to take the derivative of the expression inside the parentheses.

The Chain Rule (page 42) says that if $y = f\big(g(x)\big)$, then $y' = \left(\dfrac{df\big(g(x)\big)}{dg}\right)\left(\dfrac{dg}{dx}\right)$,

and the Quotient Rule says that if $f(x) = \dfrac{u}{v}$, then $f'(x) = \dfrac{v\dfrac{du}{dx} - u\dfrac{dv}{dx}}{v^2}$. We

get: $f'(x) = \dfrac{1}{4}\left(\dfrac{2x-5}{5x+2}\right)^{-\frac{3}{4}}\left(\dfrac{(5x+2)(2)-(2x-5)(5)}{(5x+2)^2}\right)$. This can be simplified to

$f'(x) = \dfrac{1}{4}\left(\dfrac{2x-5}{5x+2}\right)^{-\frac{3}{4}}\left(\dfrac{29}{(5x+2)^2}\right)$.

7. $\dfrac{32x^{11}+7x^{\frac{7}{2}}}{16x^8}$

We find the derivative using the Quotient Rule (page 41),

which says that if $f(x) = \dfrac{u}{v}$, then $f'(x) = \dfrac{v\dfrac{du}{dx} - u\dfrac{dv}{dx}}{v^2}$. Here

$f(x) = \dfrac{4x^8 - \sqrt{x}}{8x^4}$, so $u = 4x^8 - \sqrt{x}$ and $v = 8x^4$. Using the Quotient Rule, we

get: $f'(x) = \dfrac{\left(8x^4\right)\left(32x^7 - \dfrac{1}{2\sqrt{x}}\right) - \left(4x^8 - \sqrt{x}\right)\left(32x^3\right)}{\left(8x^4\right)^2}$. This can be simplified to

$f'(x) = \dfrac{32x^{11} + 7x^{\frac{7}{2}}}{16x^8}$.

8. $3x^2 + 1 + \dfrac{1}{x^2} + \dfrac{3}{x^4}$

We have two ways that we could solve this. We could expand the expression

first and then take the derivative of each term, or we could find the derivative

using the Product Rule. Let's do both methods just to see that they both give

us the same answer. First, let's use the Product Rule (page 40), which says

that if $f(x) = uv$, then $f'(x) = u\dfrac{dv}{dx} + v\dfrac{du}{dx}$. Here $f(x) = \left(x + \dfrac{1}{x}\right)\left(x^2 - \dfrac{1}{x^2}\right)$,

so $u = \left(x + \dfrac{1}{x}\right)$ and $v = \left(x^2 - \dfrac{1}{x^2}\right)$. Using the Product Rule, we get:

$$f'(x) = \left(x + \dfrac{1}{x}\right)\left(2x - (-2)x^{-3}\right) + \left(x^2 - \dfrac{1}{x^2}\right)\left(1 - \dfrac{1}{x^2}\right) = \left(x + \dfrac{1}{x}\right)\left(2x + \dfrac{2}{x^3}\right) + \left(x^2 - \dfrac{1}{x^2}\right)\left(1 - \dfrac{1}{x^2}\right)$$

This can be simplified to

$$f'(x) = \left(2x^2 + \dfrac{2}{x^2} + 2 + \dfrac{2}{x^4}\right) + \left(x^2 - 1 - \dfrac{1}{x^2} + \dfrac{1}{x^4}\right) = 3x^2 + 1 + \dfrac{1}{x^2} + \dfrac{3}{x^4}.$$

The other way we could find the derivative is to expand the expression first and then

take the derivative. We get: $f(x) = \left(x + \dfrac{1}{x}\right)\left(x^2 - \dfrac{1}{x^2}\right) = x^3 - \dfrac{1}{x} + x - \dfrac{1}{x^3}$. Now, we can take

the derivative of each term. We get: $f'(x) = 3x^2 + \dfrac{1}{x^2} + 1 - (-3)x^{-4} = 3x^2 + \dfrac{1}{x^2} + 1 + \dfrac{3}{x^4}$. As

we can see, the second method is a little quicker and they both give the same result.

9. $\dfrac{4x^3}{(x+1)^5}$

Here, we will find the derivative using the Chain Rule. We will also need the

Quotient Rule to take the derivative of the expression inside the parentheses.

The Chain Rule (page 42) says that if $y = f(g(x))$, then $y' = \left(\dfrac{df(g(x))}{dg}\right)\left(\dfrac{dg}{dx}\right)$,

and the Quotient Rule says that if $f(x) = \dfrac{u}{v}$, then $f'(x) = \dfrac{v\dfrac{du}{dx} - u\dfrac{dv}{dx}}{v^2}$.

We get: $f'(x) = 4\left(\dfrac{x}{x+1}\right)^3\left(\dfrac{(x+1)(1) - (x)(1)}{(x+1)^2}\right)$. This can be simplified to

$f'(x) = 4\left(\dfrac{x}{x+1}\right)^3\left(\dfrac{1}{(x+1)^2}\right) = \dfrac{4x^3}{(x+1)^5}$.

10. $100(x^2 + x)^{99}(2x + 1)$

Here, we will find the derivative using the Chain Rule. The Chain Rule

(page 42) says that if $y = f(g(x))$, then $y' = \left(\dfrac{df(g(x))}{dg}\right)\left(\dfrac{dg}{dx}\right)$. We get:

$f'(x) = 100(x^2 + x)^{99}(2x + 1)$.

11. $\dfrac{-2x}{\left(x^2+1\right)^{\frac{1}{2}}\left(x^2-1\right)^{\frac{3}{2}}}$

Here, we will find the derivative using the Chain Rule. We will also need the

Quotient Rule to take the derivative of the expression inside the parentheses.

The Chain Rule (page 42) says that if $y = f\big(g(x)\big)$, then $y' = \left(\dfrac{df\big(g(x)\big)}{dg}\right)\left(\dfrac{dg}{dx}\right)$,

and the Quotient Rule says that if $f(x) = \dfrac{u}{v}$, then $f'(x) = \dfrac{v\dfrac{du}{dx} - u\dfrac{dv}{dx}}{v^2}$. We get:

$f'(x) = \dfrac{1}{2}\left(\dfrac{x^2+1}{x^2-1}\right)^{-\frac{1}{2}}\left(\dfrac{\left(x^2-1\right)(2x)-\left(x^2+1\right)(2x)}{(x-1)^2}\right)$. This can be simplified to

$f'(x) = \dfrac{1}{2}\left(\dfrac{x^2+1}{x^2-1}\right)^{-\frac{1}{2}}\left(\dfrac{-4x}{(x-1)^2}\right) = \dfrac{-2x}{\left(x^2+1\right)^{\frac{1}{2}}\left(x^2-1\right)^{\frac{3}{2}}}$.

12. $\dfrac{9}{64}$

We find the derivative using the Quotient Rule (page 41), which says that if

$f(x) = \dfrac{u}{v}$, then $f'(x) = \dfrac{v\dfrac{du}{dx} - u\dfrac{dv}{dx}}{v^2}$. Here $f(x) = \dfrac{(x+4)(x-8)}{(x+6)(x-6)}$, so $u = (x+4)(x-8)$

and $v = (x+6)(x-6)$. Before we take the derivative, we can simplify the numerator

and denominator of the expression: $f(x) = \dfrac{(x+4)(x-8)}{(x+6)(x-6)} = \dfrac{x^2-4x-32}{x^2-36}$. Now, using the Quotient Rule, we get: $f(x) = \dfrac{\left(x^2 - 36\right)\left(2x - 4\right) - \left(x^2 - 4x - 32\right)\left(2x\right)}{\left(x^2 - 36\right)^2}$.

Now, we don't simplify. We simply plug in $x = 2$ to get:

$$f(x) = \frac{\left((2)^2 - 36\right)\left(2(2) - 4\right) - \left((2)^2 - 4(2) - 32\right)\left(2(2)\right)}{\left((2)^2 - 36\right)^2} = \frac{(-32)(0) - (-36)(4)}{(-32)^2} = \frac{9}{64}.$$

13. 106

We find the derivative using the Quotient Rule (page 41), which

says that if $f(x) = \dfrac{u}{v}$, then $f'(x) = \dfrac{v\dfrac{du}{dx} - u\dfrac{dv}{dx}}{v^2}$. We will also need

the Chain Rule to take the derivative of the expression in the

denominator. The Chain Rule (page 42) says that if $y = f\big(g(x)\big)$, then

$y' = \left(\dfrac{df\big(g(x)\big)}{dg}\right)\left(\dfrac{dg}{dx}\right)$, here $f(x) = \dfrac{x^6 + 4x^3 + 6}{\left(x^4 - 2\right)^2}$, so $u = x^6 + 4x^3 + 6$ and

$v = \left(x^4 - 2\right)^2$. We get: $f(x) = \dfrac{\left(x^4 - 2\right)^2\left(6x^5 + 12x^2\right) - \left(x^6 + 4x^3 + 6\right)2\left(x^4 - 2\right)\left(4x^3\right)}{\left(x^4 - 2\right)^4}$.

Now, we don't simplify. We simply plug in $x = 1$ to get:

$$f(x) = \frac{\left((1)^4 - 2\right)^2\left(6(1)^5 + 12(1)^2\right) - \left((1)^6 + 4(1)^3 + 6\right)2\left((1)^4 - 2\right)\left(4(1)^3\right)}{\left((1)^4 - 2\right)^4} =$$

$\dfrac{(1)(18) - (11)2(-1)(4)}{(-1)^4} = 106$

14. 0

Here, we will find the derivative using the Chain Rule. We will also need the

Quotient Rule to take the derivative of the expression inside the parentheses.

The Chain Rule (page 42) says that if $y = f(g(x))$, then $y' = \left(\dfrac{df(g(x))}{dg}\right)\left(\dfrac{dg}{dx}\right)$,

and the Quotient Rule says that if $f(x) = \dfrac{u}{v}$, then $f'(x) = \dfrac{v\dfrac{du}{dx} - u\dfrac{dv}{dx}}{v^2}$.

We get: $f'(x) = 2\left(\dfrac{x - \sqrt{x}}{x + \sqrt{x}}\right)\left(\dfrac{\left(x + \sqrt{x}\right)\left(1 - \dfrac{1}{2\sqrt{x}}\right) - \left(x - \sqrt{x}\right)\left(1 + \dfrac{1}{2\sqrt{x}}\right)}{\left(x + \sqrt{x}\right)^2}\right)$.

Now, we don't simplify. We simply plug in $x = 1$ to get:

$$f'(x) = 2\left(\frac{1 - \sqrt{1}}{1 + \sqrt{1}}\right)\left(\frac{\left(1 + \sqrt{1}\right)\left(1 - \dfrac{1}{2\sqrt{1}}\right) - \left(1 - \sqrt{1}\right)\left(1 + \dfrac{1}{2\sqrt{1}}\right)}{\left(1 + \sqrt{1}\right)^2}\right) = 0.$$

15. $\dfrac{x^2 - 6x + 3}{(x - 3)^2}$

We find the derivative using the Quotient Rule (page 41), which says that if

$f(x) = \dfrac{u}{v}$, then $f'(x) = \dfrac{v\dfrac{du}{dx} - u\dfrac{dv}{dx}}{v^2}$. Here $f(x) = \dfrac{x^2 - 3}{x - 3}$, so $u = x^2 - 3$ and $v = x - 3$.

Using the Quotient Rule, we get: $f'(x) = \dfrac{(x - 3)(2x) - (x^2 - 3)(1)}{(x - 3)^2}$. This can be

simplified to $f'(x) = \dfrac{x^2 - 6x + 3}{(x - 3)^2}$.

16. 6

We find the derivative using the Product Rule (page 40),

which says that if $f(x) = uv$, then $f'(x) = u\dfrac{dv}{dx} + v\dfrac{du}{dx}$. Here

$f(x) = (x^4 - x^2)(2x^3 + x)$, so $u = x^4 - x^2$ and $v = 2x^3 + x$. Using the Product

Rule, we get: $f'(x) = (x^4 - x^2)(6x^2 + 1) + (2x^3 + x)(4x^3 - 2x)$.

Now, we don't simplify. We simply plug in $x = 1$ to get:

$f'(x) = ((1)^4 - (1)^2)(6(1)^2 + 1) + (2(1)^3 + (1))(4(1)^3 - 2(1)) = 6$.

17. $-\dfrac{7}{4}$

We find the derivative using the Quotient Rule (page 41),

which says that if $f(x) = \dfrac{u}{v}$, then $f'(x) = \dfrac{v\dfrac{du}{dx} - u\dfrac{dv}{dx}}{v^2}$. Here

$f(x) = \dfrac{x^2 + 2x}{x^4 - x^3}$, so $u = x^2 + 2x$ and $v = x^4 - x^3$. Using the Quotient

Rule, we get: $f'(x) = \dfrac{(x^4 - x^3)(2x + 2) - (x^2 + 2x)(4x^3 - 3x^2)}{(x^4 - x^3)^2}$.

Now, we don't simplify. We simply plug in $x = 2$ to get:

$f'(x) = \dfrac{((2)^4 - (2)^3)(2(2) + 2) - ((2)^2 + 2(2))(4(2)^3 - 3(2)^2)}{((2)^4 - (2)^3)^2} = -\dfrac{7}{4}$.

18. $\dfrac{2x^2+1}{\sqrt{x^2+1}}$

We find the derivative using the Chain Rule (page 42), which says that if

$$y = f\big(g(x)\big), \text{ then } y' = \left(\frac{df\big(g(x)\big)}{dg}\right)\left(\frac{dg}{dx}\right). \text{ Here, } f(x) = \sqrt{x^4+x^2} = \left(x^4+x^2\right)^{\frac{1}{2}}. \text{ Using}$$

the Chain Rule, we get: $f'(x) = \dfrac{1}{2}\left(x^4+x^2\right)^{-\frac{1}{2}}\left(4x^3+2x\right)$. This can be simplified to

$$f'(x) = \frac{2x^2+1}{\sqrt{x^2+1}}.$$

19. $-\dfrac{1}{4}$

We find the derivative using the Quotient Rule (page 41), which says that if

$$f(x) = \frac{u}{v}, \text{ then } f'(x) = \frac{v\dfrac{du}{dx} - u\dfrac{dv}{dx}}{v^2}. \text{ We will also need the Chain Rule to take the}$$

derivative of the expression in the denominator. The Chain Rule (page 42) says

that if $y = f\big(g(x)\big)$, then $y' = \left(\dfrac{df\big(g(x)\big)}{dg}\right)\left(\dfrac{dg}{dx}\right)$. Here $f(x) = \dfrac{x}{\left(1+x^2\right)^2}$, so $u = x$ and

$v = \left(1+x^2\right)^2$. We get: $f(x) = \dfrac{\left(1+x^2\right)^2(1) - (x)2\left(1+x^2\right)(2x)}{\left(1+x^2\right)^4}$. Now, we don't simplify.

We simply plug in $x = 1$ to get: $f(x) = \dfrac{\left(1+\left(1\right)^2\right)^2(1) - (1)2\left(1+\left(1\right)^2\right)(2(1))}{\left(1+\left(1\right)^2\right)^4} = -\dfrac{1}{4}$.

20. $-\dfrac{2}{(x-1)^3}$

We find the derivative using the Chain Rule that appeared on page 44,

which says that if $y = y(v)$ and $v = v(x)$, then $\dfrac{dy}{dx} = \dfrac{dy}{dv}\dfrac{dv}{dx}$. Here $\dfrac{dy}{du} = 2u$ and

$\dfrac{du}{dx} = -1(x-1)^{-2} = -\dfrac{1}{(x-1)^2}$. Thus, $\dfrac{dy}{dx} = (2u)\dfrac{-1}{(x-1)^2}$ and because $u = \dfrac{1}{x-1}$,

$\dfrac{dy}{dx} = \left(\dfrac{2}{x-1}\right)\left(\dfrac{-1}{(x-1)^2}\right) = -\dfrac{2}{(x-1)^3}$.

21. -24

We find the derivative using the Chain Rule that appeared on page 44, which says

that if $y = y(v)$ and $v = v(x)$, then $\dfrac{dy}{dx} = \dfrac{dy}{dv}\dfrac{dv}{dx}$. Here $\dfrac{dy}{dt} = \dfrac{(t^2-2)(2t)-(t^2+2)(2t)}{(t^2-2)^2}$

and $\dfrac{dt}{dx} = 3x^2$. Now, we plug $x = 1$ into the derivative. Note that, where $x = 1$,

$t = (1)^3 = 1$. We get: $\dfrac{dy}{dt} = \dfrac{\left((1)^2-2\right)(2(1))-\left((1)^2+2\right)(2(1))}{\left((1)^2-2\right)^2} = -8$ and $\dfrac{dt}{dx} = 3(1)^2 = 3$.

Thus, $\dfrac{dy}{dx} = \dfrac{dy}{dt}\dfrac{dt}{dx} = (-8)(3) = -24$.

22. $\left(t^3 - 6t^{\frac{5}{2}}\right)\left(5 + \dfrac{1}{2\sqrt{t}}\right) + \left(5t + \sqrt{t}\right)\left(3t^2 - 15t^{\frac{3}{2}}\right)$

Here, the solution will be much simpler if we first substitute $x = \sqrt{t}$ into the

expression for y. We get: $y = \left(t^3 - 6t^{\frac{5}{2}}\right)\left(5t + \sqrt{t}\right)$. Now, we find the derivative using

the Product Rule (page 40), which says that if $f(x) = uv$, then $f'(x) = u\dfrac{dv}{dx} + v\dfrac{du}{dx}$.

Here $y = \left(t^3 - 6t^{\frac{5}{2}}\right)\left(5t + \sqrt{t}\right)$, so $u = t^3 - 6t^{\frac{5}{2}}$ and $v = 5t + \sqrt{t}$. Using the Product Rule,

we get: $\dfrac{dy}{dt} = \left(t^3 - 6t^{\frac{5}{2}}\right)\left(5 + \dfrac{1}{2\sqrt{t}}\right) + \left(5t + \sqrt{t}\right)\left(3t^2 - 15t^{\frac{3}{2}}\right)$.

23. $-\dfrac{7\sqrt{2}}{16\sqrt{3}}$

We find the derivative using the Chain Rule that appeared on page 44, which says

that if $y = y(v)$ and $v = v(x)$, then $\dfrac{dy}{dx} = \dfrac{dy}{dv}\dfrac{dv}{dx}$. Here $\dfrac{du}{dx} = \dfrac{1}{2}\left(x^3 + x^2\right)^{-\frac{1}{2}}\left(3x^2 + 2x\right)$

and $\dfrac{dx}{dv} = -\dfrac{1}{v^2}$. Now, we plug $v = 2$ into the derivative. Note that, where $v = 2$,

$x = \dfrac{1}{2}$. We get: $\dfrac{du}{dx} = \dfrac{1}{2}\left(\left(\dfrac{1}{2}\right)^3 + \left(\dfrac{1}{2}\right)^2\right)^{-\frac{1}{2}}\left(3\left(\dfrac{1}{2}\right)^2 + 2\left(\dfrac{1}{2}\right)\right) = \dfrac{7}{8}\left(\dfrac{3}{8}\right)^{-\frac{1}{2}}$ and $\dfrac{dx}{dv} = -\dfrac{1}{4}$, so

$\dfrac{du}{dv} = \dfrac{7}{8}\left(\dfrac{3}{8}\right)^{-\frac{1}{2}}\left(-\dfrac{1}{4}\right) = -\dfrac{7\sqrt{2}}{16\sqrt{3}}$.

24. 2

We find the derivative using the Chain Rule that appeared on page 44, which says

that if $y = y(v)$ and $v = v(x)$, then $\dfrac{dy}{dx} = \dfrac{dy}{dv}\dfrac{dv}{dx}$. Here $\dfrac{dy}{du} = \dfrac{(1+u^2)(1)-(1+u)(2u)}{(1+u^2)^2}$

and $\dfrac{du}{dx} = 2x$. Now, we plug $x = 1$ into the derivative. Note that, where $x = 1$, $u = 0$.

We get: $\dfrac{dy}{du} = \dfrac{(1+0)(1)-(1+0)(0)}{(1+0)^2} = 1$ and $\dfrac{du}{dx} = 2$, so $\dfrac{dy}{dx} = (1)(2) = 2$.

25. $\dfrac{48v^5}{(v^2+8)^4}$

We find the derivative using the Chain Rule that appeared on page 44,

which says that if $y = y(v)$ and $v = v(x)$, then $\dfrac{dy}{dx} = \dfrac{dy}{dv}\dfrac{dv}{dx}$, although in this

case we have $u(y)$, $y(x)$, and $x(v)$, so we will find $\dfrac{du}{dv}$ by $\dfrac{du}{dv} = \dfrac{du}{dy}\dfrac{dy}{dx}\dfrac{dx}{dv}$.

Here $\dfrac{du}{dy} = 3y^2$, $\dfrac{dy}{dx} = \dfrac{(x+8)(1)-(x)(1)}{(x+8)^2} = \dfrac{8}{(x+8)^2}$, and $\dfrac{dx}{dv} = 2v$. Next,

$\dfrac{du}{dv} = \dfrac{du}{dy}\dfrac{dy}{dx}\dfrac{dx}{dv} = (3y^2)\left(\dfrac{8}{(x+8)^2}\right)(2v)$. Now, because $x = v^2$ and $y = \dfrac{x}{x+8} = \dfrac{v^2}{v^2+8}$,

we get: $\dfrac{du}{dv} = \left(3\dfrac{(v^2)^2}{(v^2+8)^2}\right)\left(\dfrac{8}{(v^2+8)^2}\right)(2v) = \dfrac{48v^5}{(v^2+8)^4}$.

SOLUTIONS TO PRACTICE PROBLEM SET 6

1. $2\sin x \cos x = \sin 2x$

   Recall that $\dfrac{d}{dx}(\sin x) = \cos x$. Here, we use the Chain Rule to find the derivative:

   $\dfrac{dy}{dx} = 2(\sin x)(\cos x)$. If you recall your trigonometric identities, $2\sin x \cos x = \sin 2x$.

   Either answer is acceptable.

2. $-2x\sin(x^2)$

   Recall that $\dfrac{d}{dx}(\cos x) = -\sin x$. Here, we use the Chain Rule to find the derivative:

   $\dfrac{dy}{dx} = \left(-\sin(x^2)\right)(2x) = -2x\sin(x^2)$.

3. $2\sec^3 x - \sec x$

   Recall that $\dfrac{d}{dx}(\tan x) = \sec^2 x$ and that $\dfrac{d}{dx}(\sec x) = \sec x \tan x$. Using the Product

   Rule, we get: $\dfrac{dy}{dx} = (\tan x)(\sec x \tan x) + (\sec x)(\sec^2 x)$. This can be simplified to

   $\sec^3 x + \sec x \tan^2 x = 2\sec^3 x - \sec x$.

4. $-4\csc^2(4x)$

   Recall that $\dfrac{d}{dx}(\cot x) = -\csc^2 x$. Here, we use the Chain Rule to find the derivative:

   $\dfrac{dy}{dx} = \left(-\csc^2 4x\right)(4) = -4\csc^2(4x)$.

5. $\dfrac{3\cos 3x}{2\sqrt{\sin 3x}}$

   Recall that $\dfrac{d}{dx}(\sin x) = \cos x$. Here, we use the Chain Rule to find the derivative:

   $\dfrac{dy}{dx} = \dfrac{1}{2}(\sin 3x)^{-\frac{1}{2}}(\cos 3x)(3)$. This can be simplified to $\dfrac{dy}{dx} = \dfrac{3\cos 3x}{2\sqrt{\sin 3x}}$.

6. $\dfrac{2\cos x}{\left(1-\sin x\right)^2}$

Recall that $\dfrac{d}{dx}\left(\sin x\right)=\cos x$. Here, we use the Quotient Rule to find the derivative:

$\dfrac{dy}{dx}=\dfrac{\left(1-\sin x\right)\left(\cos x\right)-\left(1+\sin x\right)\left(-\cos x\right)}{\left(1-\sin x\right)^2}$. This can be simplified to $\dfrac{2\cos x}{\left(1-\sin x\right)^2}$.

7. $-4x\csc^2\left(x^2\right)\cot\left(x^2\right)$

Recall that $\dfrac{d}{dx}\left(\csc x\right)=-\csc x\cot x$. Here, we use the Chain Rule to find the

derivative: $\dfrac{dy}{dx}=\left(2\csc x^2\right)\left(-\csc x^2\cot x^2\right)\left(2x\right)=-4x\csc^2\left(x^2\right)\cot\left(x^2\right)$.

8. $6\cos 3x\cos 4x-8\sin 3x\sin 4x$

Recall that $\dfrac{d}{dx}\left(\sin x\right)=\cos x$ and that $\dfrac{d}{dx}\left(\cos x\right)=-\sin x$. Here, we use the Product

Rule to find the derivative: $\dfrac{dy}{dx}=2\left[\left(\sin 3x\right)\left(-\sin 4x\right)\left(4\right)+\left(\cos 4x\right)\left(\cos 3x\right)\left(3\right)\right]$. This

can be simplified to $\dfrac{dy}{dx}=6\cos 3x\cos 4x-8\sin 3x\sin 4x$.

9. $16\sin 2x$

Recall that $\dfrac{d}{dx}\left(\sin x\right)=\cos x$ and that $\dfrac{d}{dx}\left(\cos x\right)=-\sin x$. Here, we will use the

Chain Rule four times to find the fourth derivative.

The first derivative is: $\dfrac{dy}{dx}=\left(\cos 2x\right)\left(2\right)=2\cos 2x$.

The second derivative is: $\dfrac{d^2y}{dx^2}=2\left(-\sin 2x\right)\left(2\right)=-4\sin 2x$.

The third derivative is: $\dfrac{d^3y}{dx^3}=-4\left(\cos 2x\right)\left(2\right)=-8\cos 2x$.

And the fourth derivative is: $\dfrac{d^4y}{dx^4}=-8\left(-\sin 2x\right)\left(2\right)=16\sin 2x$.

10. $\left[\cos\left(1+\cos^2 x\right)+\sin\left(1+\cos^2 x\right)\right]\left(-2\sin x\cos x\right)$

Recall that $\dfrac{d}{dx}\left(\sin x\right)=\cos x$ and that $\dfrac{d}{dx}\left(\cos x\right)=-\sin x$. Here, we will use

the Chain Rule to find the derivative: $\dfrac{dy}{dt}=\cos t-\left(-\sin t\right)=\cos t+\sin t$ and

$\dfrac{dt}{dx}=2\left(\cos x\right)\left(-\sin x\right)=-2\sin x\cos x$. Next, because $\dfrac{dy}{dx}=\dfrac{dy}{dt}\dfrac{dt}{dx}$ and $t=1+\cos^2 x$, we

get: $\dfrac{dy}{dx}=\left(\cos t+\sin t\right)\left(-2\sin x\cos x\right)=\left[\cos\left(1+\cos^2 x\right)+\sin\left(1+\cos^2 x\right)\right]\left(-2\sin x\cos x\right)$.

11. $\dfrac{2\tan x\sec^2 x}{\left(1-\tan x\right)^3}$

Recall that $\dfrac{d}{dx}\left(\tan x\right)=\sec^2 x$. Using the Quotient Rule and the Chain Rule, we get:

$\dfrac{dy}{dx}=2\left(\dfrac{\tan x}{1-\tan x}\right)\dfrac{\left(1-\tan x\right)\left(\sec^2 x\right)-\left(\tan x\right)\left(-\sec^2 x\right)}{\left(1-\tan x\right)^2}$. This simplifies to $\dfrac{2\tan x\sec^2 x}{\left(1-\tan x\right)^3}$.

12. $\left(\sec\theta\right)\left(\sec^2\left(2\theta\right)\right)\left(2\right)+\left(\tan 2\theta\right)\left(\sec\theta\tan\theta\right)$

Recall that $\dfrac{d}{dx}\left(\tan x\right)=\sec^2 x$ and that $\dfrac{d}{dx}\left(\sec x\right)=\sec x\tan x$. Using the Product

Rule and the Chain Rule, we get: $\dfrac{dr}{d\theta}=\left(\sec\theta\right)\left(\sec^2\left(2\theta\right)\right)\left(2\right)+\left(\tan 2\theta\right)\left(\sec\theta\tan\theta\right)$.

13. $-\left[\sin\left(1+\sin\theta\right)\right]\left(\cos\theta\right)$

Recall that $\dfrac{d}{dx}\left(\sin x\right)=\cos x$ and that $\dfrac{d}{dx}\left(\cos x\right)=-\sin x$. Using the Chain Rule, we

get: $\dfrac{dr}{d\theta}=-\left[\sin\left(1+\sin\theta\right)\right]\left(\cos\theta\right)$.

14. $\dfrac{\sec\theta(\tan\theta-1)}{(1+\tan\theta)^2}$

Recall that $\dfrac{d}{dx}(\tan x)=\sec^2 x$ and that $\dfrac{d}{dx}(\sec x)=\sec x\tan x$. Using the Quotient

Rule, we get: $\dfrac{dr}{d\theta}=\dfrac{(1+\tan\theta)(\sec\theta\tan\theta)-(\sec\theta)(\sec^2\theta)}{(1+\tan\theta)^2}$. This can be simplified

(using trigonometric identities) to $\dfrac{\sec\theta(\tan\theta-1)}{(1+\tan\theta)^2}$.

15. $-\dfrac{\left(\dfrac{4}{x^2}\right)\left(\csc^2\left(\dfrac{2}{x}\right)\right)}{\left(1+\cot\left(\dfrac{2}{x}\right)\right)^3}$

Recall that $\dfrac{d}{dx}(\cot x)=-\csc^2 x$. Here, we use the Chain Rule to find the derivative:

$$\frac{dy}{dx}=-2\left(1+\cot\left(\frac{2}{x}\right)\right)^{-3}\left(-\csc^2\left(\frac{2}{x}\right)\right)\left(\frac{-2}{x^2}\right)=-\frac{\left(\dfrac{4}{x^2}\right)\left(\csc^2\left(\dfrac{2}{x}\right)\right)}{\left(1+\cot\left(\dfrac{2}{x}\right)\right)^3}.$$

16. $\cos\left(\cos\left(\sqrt{x}\right)\right)\left(-\sin\sqrt{x}\right)\left(\dfrac{1}{2\sqrt{x}}\right)$

Recall that $\dfrac{d}{dx}(\sin x)=\cos x$ and that $\dfrac{d}{dx}(\cos x)=-\sin x$. Using the Chain Rule, we

get: $\dfrac{dy}{dx}=\cos\left(\cos\left(\sqrt{x}\right)\right)\left(-\sin\sqrt{x}\right)\left(\dfrac{1}{2\sqrt{x}}\right)$.

SOLUTIONS TO PRACTICE PROBLEM SET 7

1. $\dfrac{3x^2}{1+3y^2}$

We take the derivative of each term with respect to x:

$$\left(3x^2\right)\left(\frac{dx}{dx}\right)-\left(3y^2\right)\left(\frac{dy}{dx}\right)=(1)\left(\frac{dy}{dx}\right).$$

Next, because $\dfrac{dx}{dx}=1$ we can eliminate that term, we get:

$$\left(3x^2\right)-\left(3y^2\right)\left(\frac{dy}{dx}\right)=\left(\frac{dy}{dx}\right).$$

Next, group the terms containing $\dfrac{dy}{dx}:(3x^2)=\left(\dfrac{dy}{dx}\right)+(3y^2)\left(\dfrac{dy}{dx}\right).$

Factor out the term $\dfrac{dy}{dx}:(3x^2)=\left(\dfrac{dy}{dx}\right)(1+3y^2).$ Now we can isolate $\dfrac{dy}{dx}$:

$$\frac{dy}{dx}=\frac{3x^2}{1+3y^2}.$$

2. $\dfrac{8y-x}{y-8x}$

We take the derivative of each term with respect to x:

$$(2x)\left(\frac{dx}{dx}\right)-16\left[(x)\left(\frac{dy}{dx}\right)+(y)\left(\frac{dx}{dx}\right)\right]+(2y)\left(\frac{dy}{dx}\right)=0.$$

Next, because $\dfrac{dx}{dx}=1$ we can eliminate that term and we can distribute the -16

to get: $2x-16x\left(\dfrac{dy}{dx}\right)-16y+2y\left(\dfrac{dy}{dx}\right)=0.$

Next, group the terms containing $\dfrac{dy}{dx}$ on one side of the equal sign and the other

terms on the other side: $-16x\left(\dfrac{dy}{dx}\right)+2y\left(\dfrac{dy}{dx}\right)=16y-2x.$

Factor out the term $\dfrac{dy}{dx}:\left(\dfrac{dy}{dx}\right)(2y-16x)=16y-2x.$ Now we can isolate $\dfrac{dy}{dx}$:

$\dfrac{dy}{dx}=\dfrac{16y-2x}{2y-16x}$, which can be reduced to $\dfrac{dy}{dx}=\dfrac{8y-x}{y-8x}$

3. $\dfrac{1}{2}$

First, cross-multiply so that we don't have to use the quotient rule: $x + y = 3x - 3y$.

Next, simplify: $4y = 2x$, which reduces to $y = \dfrac{1}{2}x$. Now we can take the derivative: $\dfrac{dy}{dx} = \dfrac{1}{2}$. Note that just because a problem has the x's and y's mixed together doesn't mean that we need to use implicit differentiation to solve it!

4. $-\dfrac{\sin x + \cos x}{\sin y + \cos y}$

We take the derivative of each term with respect to x:

$$\left(-\sin y\right)\left(\frac{dy}{dx}\right) - \left(\cos x\right)\left(\frac{dx}{dx}\right) = \left(\cos y\right)\left(\frac{dy}{dx}\right) - \left(-\sin x\right)\left(\frac{dx}{dx}\right).$$

Next, because $\dfrac{dx}{dx} = 1$ we can eliminate that term to get:

$$\left(-\sin y\right)\left(\frac{dy}{dx}\right) - \cos x = \left(\cos y\right)\left(\frac{dy}{dx}\right) + \sin x.$$

Next, group the terms containing $\dfrac{dy}{dx}$ on one side of the equal sign and the

other terms on the other side: $\left(-\sin y\right)\left(\dfrac{dy}{dx}\right) - \left(\cos y\right)\left(\dfrac{dy}{dx}\right) = \sin x + \cos x$.

Factor out the term $\dfrac{dy}{dx}$: $\left(-\sin y - \cos y\right)\left(\dfrac{dy}{dx}\right) = \sin x + \cos x$. Now, we can isolate

$\dfrac{dy}{dx}$: $\dfrac{dy}{dx} = \dfrac{\sin x + \cos x}{-\sin y - \cos y}$, which can be simplified to $\dfrac{dy}{dx} = -\dfrac{\sin x + \cos x}{\sin y + \cos y}$.

5. $\dfrac{8}{7}$

We take the derivative of each term with respect to x:

$$(32x)\left(\dfrac{dx}{dx}\right) - 16\left[(x)\left(\dfrac{dy}{dx}\right) + (y)\left(\dfrac{dx}{dx}\right)\right] + (2y)\left(\dfrac{dy}{dx}\right) = 0.$$

Next, because $\dfrac{dx}{dx} = 1$ we can eliminate that term to get:

$32x - 16x\left(\dfrac{dy}{dx}\right) - 16y + 2y\left(\dfrac{dy}{dx}\right) = 0$. Next, don't simplify. Plug in $(1,1)$ for x and y:

$32(1) - 16(1)\left(\dfrac{dy}{dx}\right) - 16(1) + 2(1)\left(\dfrac{dy}{dx}\right) = 0$, which simplifies to $16 - 14\left(\dfrac{dy}{dx}\right) = 0$.

Finally, we can solve for $\dfrac{dy}{dx} : \dfrac{dy}{dx} = \dfrac{8}{7}$.

6. $\dfrac{1}{7}$

We take the derivative of each term with respect to x:

$$\left(\dfrac{1}{2}x^{-\frac{1}{2}}\right)\left(\dfrac{dx}{dx}\right) + \left(\dfrac{1}{2}y^{-\frac{1}{2}}\right)\left(\dfrac{dy}{dx}\right) = (4y)\left(\dfrac{dy}{dx}\right).$$

Next, because $\dfrac{dx}{dx} = 1$ we can eliminate that term to get:

$\dfrac{1}{2}x^{-\frac{1}{2}} + \left(\dfrac{1}{2}y^{-\frac{1}{2}}\right)\left(\dfrac{dy}{dx}\right) = (4y)\left(\dfrac{dy}{dx}\right)$. Next, don't simplify. Plug in $(1,1)$ for x and y,

$\dfrac{1}{2}(1)^{-\frac{1}{2}} + \left(\dfrac{1}{2}(1)^{-\frac{1}{2}}\right)\left(\dfrac{dy}{dx}\right) = 4(1)\left(\dfrac{dy}{dx}\right)$, which simplifies to $\dfrac{1}{2} + \left(\dfrac{1}{2}\right)\left(\dfrac{dy}{dx}\right) = 4\left(\dfrac{dy}{dx}\right)$.

Finally, we can solve for $\dfrac{dy}{dx} : \dfrac{dy}{dx} = \dfrac{1}{7}$.

7. −1

We take the derivative of each term with respect to x:

$$(x\cos y)\left(\frac{dy}{dx}\right)+(\sin y)\left(\frac{dx}{dx}\right)+(y\cos x)\left(\frac{dx}{dx}\right)+(\sin x)\left(\frac{dy}{dx}\right)=0.$$

Next, because $\dfrac{dx}{dx}=1$ we can eliminate that term to get:

$(x\cos y)\left(\dfrac{dy}{dx}\right)+\sin y+y\cos x+(\sin x)\left(\dfrac{dy}{dx}\right)=0$. Next, don't simplify. Plug in $\left(\dfrac{\pi}{4},\dfrac{\pi}{4}\right)$

for x and y: $\left(\dfrac{\pi}{4}\cos\dfrac{\pi}{4}\right)\left(\dfrac{dy}{dx}\right)+\sin\dfrac{\pi}{4}+\dfrac{\pi}{4}\cos\dfrac{\pi}{4}+\left(\sin\dfrac{\pi}{4}\right)\left(\dfrac{dy}{dx}\right)=0$, which simplifies to

$\left(\dfrac{\pi}{4}\dfrac{1}{\sqrt{2}}\right)\left(\dfrac{dy}{dx}\right)+\dfrac{1}{\sqrt{2}}+\dfrac{\pi}{4}\dfrac{1}{\sqrt{2}}+\dfrac{1}{\sqrt{2}}\left(\dfrac{dy}{dx}\right)=0$. If we multiply through by $\sqrt{2}$ we get:

$$\frac{\pi}{4}\frac{dy}{dx}+1+\frac{\pi}{4}+\frac{dy}{dx}=0$$

Finally, we can solve for $\dfrac{dy}{dx}$: $\dfrac{dy}{dx}=-1$.

8. $-\dfrac{1}{16y^3}$

We take the derivative of each term with respect to x: $(2x)\left(\dfrac{dx}{dx}\right)+(8y)\left(\dfrac{dy}{dx}\right)=0$.

Next, because $\dfrac{dx}{dx}=1$ we can eliminate that term to get:

$2x+(8y)\left(\dfrac{dy}{dx}\right)=0$. Next, we can isolate $\dfrac{dy}{dx}$: $\dfrac{dy}{dx}=-\dfrac{x}{4y}$. Now, we take the

derivative again: $\dfrac{d^2y}{dx^2}=-\dfrac{(4y)\left(\dfrac{dx}{dx}\right)-(x)\left(4\dfrac{dy}{dx}\right)}{16y^2}$. Next, because $\dfrac{dx}{dx}=1$

and $\dfrac{dy}{dx} = -\dfrac{x}{4y}$ we get: $\dfrac{d^2y}{dx^2} = -\dfrac{4y - 4x\left(-\dfrac{x}{4y}\right)}{16y^2}$. This can be simplified to

$$\dfrac{d^2y}{dx^2} = -\dfrac{4y + \dfrac{x^2}{y}}{16y^2} = -\dfrac{4y^2 + x^2}{16y^3} = -\dfrac{1}{16y^3}\,.$$

9. $\dfrac{\sin x \sin^2 y - \cos y \cos^2 x}{\sin^3 y}$

We take the derivative of each term with respect to x: $(\cos x)\left(\dfrac{dx}{dx}\right) = (-\sin y)\left(\dfrac{dy}{dx}\right)$.

Next, because $\dfrac{dx}{dx} = 1$ we can eliminate that term to get: $\cos x = (-\sin y)\left(\dfrac{dy}{dx}\right)$.

Next, we can isolate $\dfrac{dy}{dx}$: $\dfrac{dy}{dx} = -\dfrac{\cos x}{\sin y}$. Now, we take the derivative again:

$\dfrac{d^2y}{dx^2} = \dfrac{(\sin y)(\sin x)\left(\dfrac{dx}{dx}\right) + (\cos x)(\cos y)\left(\dfrac{dy}{dx}\right)}{\sin^2 y}$. Next, because $\dfrac{dx}{dx} = 1$ and

$\dfrac{dy}{dx} = -\dfrac{\cos x}{\sin y}$ we get: $\dfrac{d^2y}{dx^2} = \dfrac{(\sin y)(\sin x) + (\cos x)(\cos y)\left(-\dfrac{\cos x}{\sin y}\right)}{\sin^2 y}$. This can be

simplified to $\dfrac{d^2y}{dx^2} = \dfrac{\sin x \sin^2 y - \cos y \cos^2 x}{\sin^3 y}$.

10. 1

We can easily isolate y in this equation: $y = \dfrac{1}{2}x^2 - 2x + 1$. We take the derivative:

$\dfrac{dy}{dx} = x - 2$. And we take the derivative again: $\dfrac{d^2y}{dx^2} = 1$. Note that just because a

problem has the x's and y's mixed together doesn't mean that we need to use

implicit differentiation to solve it!

SOLUTIONS TO PRACTICE PROBLEM SET 8

1. $y - 2 = 5(x - 1)$

    Remember that the equation of a line through a point (x_1, y_1) with slope m is

    $y - y_1 = m(x - x_1)$. We find the y-coordinate by plugging $x = 1$ into the equation

    $y = 3x^2 - x$, and we find the slope by plugging $x = 1$ into the derivative of the

    equation.

    First, we find the y-coordinate, $y_1 : y = 3(1)^2 - 1 = 2$. This means that the line

    passes through the point $(1, 2)$.

    Next, we take the derivative: $\dfrac{dy}{dx} = 6x - 1$. Now we can find the slope, m:

    $\dfrac{dy}{dx}\bigg|_{x=1} = 6(1) - 1 = 5$. Finally, we plug in the point $(1, 2)$ and the slope $m = 5$ to get

    the equation of the tangent line: $y - 2 = 5(x - 1)$.

2. $y - 18 = 24(x - 3)$

    Remember that the equation of a line through a point (x_1, y_1) with slope m is

    $y - y_1 = m(x - x_1)$. We find the y-coordinate by plugging $x = 3$ into the equation

    $y = x^3 - 3x$, and we find the slope by plugging $x = 3$ into the derivative of the

    equation.

    First, we find the y-coordinate, $y_1 : y = (3)^3 - 3(3) = 18$. This means that the line

    passes through the point $(3, 18)$.

    Next, we take the derivative: $\dfrac{dy}{dx} = 3x^2 - 3$. Now we can find the slope, m:

    $\dfrac{dy}{dx}\bigg|_{x=3} = 3(3)^2 - 3 = 24$. Finally, we plug in the point $(3, 18)$ and the slope $m = 24$ to

    get the equation of the tangent line: $y - 18 = 24(x - 3)$.

3. $y - 4 = -(x - 2)$

Remember that the equation of a line through a point (x_1, y_1) with slope m is $y - y_1 = m(x - x_1)$. We find the y-coordinate by plugging $x = 2$ into the equation $y = \sqrt{8x}$ and we find the slope by plugging $x = 2$ into the derivative of the equation.

First, we find the y-coordinate, y_1: $y = \sqrt{8(2)} = 4$. This means that the line passes through the point $(2, 4)$.

Next, we take the derivative: $\dfrac{dy}{dx} = \dfrac{4}{\sqrt{8x}}$. Now we can find the slope, m:

$\left. \dfrac{dy}{dx} \right|_{x=2} = \dfrac{4}{\sqrt{8(2)}} = 1$. However, this is the slope of the *tangent* line. The *normal* line is perpendicular to the tangent line, so its slope will be the negative reciprocal of the tangent line's slope. In this case, the slope of the normal line is $\dfrac{-1}{1} = -1$. Finally, we plug in the point $(2, 4)$ and the slope $m = -1$ to get the equation of the normal line:

$y - 4 = -(x - 2)$.

4. $y - \dfrac{1}{4} = -\dfrac{3}{64}(x - 3)$

Remember that the equation of a line through a point (x_1, y_1) with slope m is $y - y_1 = m(x - x_1)$. We find the y-coordinate by plugging $x = 3$ into the equation $y = \dfrac{1}{\sqrt{x^2 + 7}}$, and we find the slope by plugging $x = 3$ into the derivative of the equation.

First, we find the y-coordinate, y_1: $y = \dfrac{1}{\sqrt{(3)^2 + 7}} = \dfrac{1}{4}$. This means that the line passes through the point $\left(3, \dfrac{1}{4}\right)$.

Next, we take the derivative: $\dfrac{dy}{dx} = -\dfrac{1}{2}(x^2+7)^{-\frac{3}{2}}(2x) = -\dfrac{x}{\left(\sqrt{x^2+7}\right)^3}$. Now we can

find the slope, m: $\left.\dfrac{dy}{dx}\right|_{x=3} = -\dfrac{3}{\left(\sqrt{(3)^2+7}\right)^3} = -\dfrac{3}{64}$. Finally, we plug in the point $\left(3, \dfrac{1}{4}\right)$

and the slope $m = -\dfrac{3}{64}$ to get the equation of the tangent line: $y - \dfrac{1}{4} = -\dfrac{3}{64}(x-3)$.

5. $y - 7 = \dfrac{1}{6}(x-4)$

Remember that the equation of a line through a point (x_1, y_1) with slope m is

$y - y_1 = m(x - x_1)$. We find the y-coordinate by plugging $x = 4$ into the equation

$y = \dfrac{x+3}{x-3}$ and we find the slope by plugging $x = 4$ into the derivative of the

equation.

First, we find the y-coordinate, y_1: $y = \dfrac{4+3}{4-3} = 7$. This means that the line passes

through the point $(4, 7)$.

Next, we take the derivative: $\dfrac{dy}{dx} = \dfrac{(x-3)(1)-(x+3)(1)}{(x-3)^2} = -\dfrac{6}{(x-3)^2}$. Now we can

find the slope, m: $\left.\dfrac{dy}{dx}\right|_{x=4} = -\dfrac{6}{(4-3)^2} = -6$. However, this is the slope of the *tangent*

line. The *normal* line is perpendicular to the tangent line, so its slope will be the

negative reciprocal of the tangent line's slope. In this case, the slope of the normal

line is $\dfrac{-1}{-6} = \dfrac{1}{6}$. Finally, we plug in the point $(4, 7)$ and the slope $m = \dfrac{1}{6}$ to get the

equation of the normal line: $y - 7 = \dfrac{1}{6}(x-4)$.

6. $y = -3x + 4$

Remember that the equation of a line through a point (x_1, y_1) with slope m is $y - y_1 = m(x - x_1)$. We find the slope by plugging $x = 0$ into the derivative of the equation $y = 4 - 3x - x^2$. First, we take the derivative: $\dfrac{dy}{dx} = -3 - 2x$. Now we can find the slope, m: $\dfrac{dy}{dx}\bigg|_{x=0} = -3 - 3(0) = -3$. Finally, we plug in the point $(0, 4)$ and the slope $m = -3$ to get the equation of the tangent line: $y - 4 = -3(x - 0)$ or $y = -3x + 4$.

7. $y = 0$

Remember that the equation of a line through a point (x_1, y_1) with slope m is $y - y_1 = m(x - x_1)$. We find the y-coordinate by plugging $x = 2$ into the equation $y = 2x^3 - 3x^2 - 12x + 20$, and we find the slope by plugging $x = 2$ into the derivative of the equation.

First, we find the y-coordinate, y_1: $y = 2(2)^3 - 3(2)^2 - 12(2) + 20 = 0$. This means that the line passes through the point $(2, 0)$.

Next, we take the derivative: $\dfrac{dy}{dx} = 6x^2 - 6x - 12$. Now we can find the slope, m: $\dfrac{dy}{dx}\bigg|_{x=2} = 6(2)^2 - 6(2) - 12 = 0$. Finally, we plug in the point $(2, 0)$ and the slope $m = 0$ to get the equation of the tangent line: $y - 0 = 0(x - 2)$ or $y = 0$.

8. $y + 29 = -39(x - 5)$

Remember that the equation of a line through a point (x_1, y_1) with slope m is $y - y_1 = m(x - x_1)$. We find the y-coordinate by plugging $x = 5$ into the equation $y = \dfrac{x^2 + 4}{x - 6}$ and we find the slope by plugging $x = 5$ into the derivative of the equation.

First, we find the y-coordinate, y_1: $y = \dfrac{(5)^2 + 4}{(5) - 6} = -29$. This means that the line

passes through the point $(5, -29)$.

Next, we take the derivative: $\dfrac{dy}{dx} = \dfrac{(x-6)(2x) - (x^2+4)(1)}{(x-6)^2} = \dfrac{x^2 - 12x - 4}{(x-6)^2}$. Now

we can find the slope, m: $\dfrac{dy}{dx}\bigg|_{x=5} = \dfrac{(5)^2 - 12(5) - 4}{(5-6)^2} = -39$. Finally, we plug in the

point $(5, -29)$ and the slope $m = -39$ to get the equation of the tangent line:

$y + 29 = -39(x - 5)$.

9. $y - 7 = \dfrac{24}{7}(x - 4)$

Remember that the equation of a line through a point (x_1, y_1) with

slope m is $y - y_1 = m(x - x_1)$. We find the slope by plugging $x = 4$ into

the derivative of the equation $y = \sqrt{x^3 - 15}$. First, we take the derivative:

$\dfrac{dy}{dx} = \dfrac{1}{2}(x^3 - 15)^{-\frac{1}{2}}(3x^2) = \dfrac{3x^2}{2\sqrt{x^3 - 15}}$. Now we can find the slope, m:

$\dfrac{dy}{dx}\bigg|_{x=4} = \dfrac{3(4)^2}{2\sqrt{(4)^3 - 15}} = \dfrac{24}{7}$. Finally, we plug in the point $(4, 7)$ and the slope $m = \dfrac{24}{7}$

to get the equation of the tangent line: $y - 7 = \dfrac{24}{7}(x - 4)$.

10. $y = 0$

Remember that the equation of a line through a point (x_1, y_1) with slope m is $y - y_1 = m(x - x_1)$. We find the y-coordinate by plugging $x = -2$ into the equation $y = (x^2 + 4x + 4)^2$, and we find the slope by plugging $x = -2$ into the derivative of the equation.

First, we find the y-coordinate, y_1: $y = ((-2)^2 + 4(-2) + 4)^2 = 0$. This means that the line passes through the point $(-2, 0)$.

Next, we take the derivative: $\dfrac{dy}{dx} = 2(x^2 + 4x + 4)(2x + 4)$. Now we can find the slope, m: $\dfrac{dy}{dx}\Big|_{x=-2} = 2((-2)^2 + 4(-2) + 4)(2(-2) + 4) = 0$. Finally, we plug in the point $(-2, 0)$ and the slope $m = 0$ to get the equation of the tangent line: $y - 0 = 0(x + 2)$ or $y = 0$.

11. $x = \pm\sqrt{\dfrac{3}{2}}$

The slope of the line $y = x$ is 1, so we want to know where the slope of the tangent line is equal to 1. We find the slope of the tangent line by taking the derivative:

$\dfrac{dy}{dx} = 6x^2 - 8$. Now we set the derivative equal to 1: $6x^2 - 8 = 1$. If we solve for x, we get: $x = \pm\sqrt{\dfrac{3}{2}}$.

12. $y - 7 = \dfrac{1}{2}(x - 3)$

Remember that the equation of a line through a point (x_1, y_1) with slope m is $y - y_1 = m(x - x_1)$. We find the y-coordinate by plugging $x = 3$ into the equation $y = \dfrac{3x + 5}{x - 1}$, and we find the slope by plugging $x = 3$ into the derivative of the equation.

First, we find the y-coordinate, $y_1: y = \dfrac{3(3)+5}{(3)-1} = 7$. This means that the line

passes through the point $(3,7)$.

Next, we take the derivative: $\dfrac{dy}{dx} = \dfrac{(x-1)(3)-(3x+5)(1)}{(x-1)^2} = \dfrac{-8}{(x-1)^2}$. Now we can

find the slope, m: $\left.\dfrac{dy}{dx}\right|_{x=3} = \dfrac{-8}{(3-1)^2} = -2$. However, this is the slope of the *tangent* line.

The *normal* line is perpendicular to the tangent line, so its slope will be the negative

reciprocal of the tangent line's slope. In this case, the slope of the normal line is

$\dfrac{-1}{-2} = \dfrac{1}{2}$. Finally, we plug in the point $(3,7)$ and the slope $m = \dfrac{1}{2}$ to get the equation

of the normal line: $y - 7 = \dfrac{1}{2}(x-3)$.

13. $x = 9$

A line that is parallel to the y-axis has an infinite (or undefined) slope. In order to

find where the normal line has an infinite slope, we first take the derivative to find

the slope of the tangent line: $\dfrac{dy}{dx} = 2(x-9)(1) = 2x - 18$. Next, because the normal

line is perpendicular to the tangent line, the slope of the normal line is the negative

reciprocal of the slope of the tangent line: $m = \dfrac{-1}{2x-18}$. Now, we need to find where

the slope is infinite. This is simply where the denominator of the slope is zero:

$x = 9$.

14. $\left(-\dfrac{3}{2}, \dfrac{41}{4}\right)$

A line that is parallel to the x-axis has a zero slope. In order to find where the

tangent line has a zero slope, we first take the derivative: $\dfrac{dy}{dx} = -3 - 2x$. Now, we

need to find where the slope is zero. The derivative $-3 - 2x = 0$ at $x = -\dfrac{3}{2}$. Now, we

need to find the y-coordinate, which we get by plugging $x = -\dfrac{3}{2}$ into the equation

for y: $8 - 3\left(-\dfrac{3}{2}\right) - \left(-\dfrac{3}{2}\right)^2 = \dfrac{41}{4}$. Therefore, the answer is $\left(-\dfrac{3}{2}, \dfrac{41}{4}\right)$.

15. $a = 1$, $b = 0$, and $c = 1$.

The two equations will have a common tangent line where they have the same

slope, which we find by taking the derivative of each equation. The derivative

of the first equation is: $\dfrac{dy}{dx} = 2x + a$. The derivative of the second equation is

$\dfrac{dy}{dx} = c + 2x$. Setting the two derivatives equal to each other, we get: $a = c$. Each

equation will pass through the point $(-1, 0)$. If we plug $(-1, 0)$ into the first

equation, we get: $0 = (-1)^2 + a(-1) + b$, which simplifies to: $a - b = 1$. If we plug

$(-1, 0)$ into the second equation, we get: $0 = c(-1) + (-1)^2$, which simplifies to $c = 1$.

Now we can find the values for a, b, and c. We get: $a = 1$, $b = 0$, and $c = 1$.

SOLUTIONS TO PRACTICE PROBLEM SET 9

1. $c = 0$

    The mean value theorem says that: If $f(x)$ is continuous on the interval $[a, b]$ and

    is differentiable everywhere on the interval (a, b), then there exists at least one

    number c on the interval (a, b) such that $\dfrac{f(b) - f(a)}{b - a} = f'(c)$. Here, the function is

    $f(x) = 3x^2 + 5x - 2$ and the interval is $[-1, 1]$. Thus, the mean value theorem says that

    $\dfrac{\left(3(1)^2 + 5(1) - 2\right) - \left(3(-1)^2 + 5(-1) - 2\right)}{(1+1)} = f'(c)$. This simplifies to $f'(c) = 5$. Next, we

    need to find $f'(c)$. The derivative of $f(x)$ is $f'(x) = 6x + 5$, so $f'(c) = 6c + 5$. Now we

    can solve for c: $6c + 5 = 5$ and $c = 0$. Note that 0 is in the interval $(-1, 1)$, just as we

    expected.

2. $c = \dfrac{4}{\sqrt{3}}$

    The mean value theorem says that: If $f(x)$ is continuous on the interval $[a, b]$ and

    is differentiable everywhere on the interval (a, b), then there exists at least one

    number c on the interval (a, b) such that $\dfrac{f(b) - f(a)}{b - a} = f'(c)$. Here, the function is

    $f(x) = x^3 + 24x - 16$ and the interval is $[0, 4]$. Thus, the mean value theorem says that

    $\dfrac{\left((4)^3 + 24(4) - 16\right) - \left((0)^3 + 24(0) - 16\right)}{(4 - 0)} = f'(c)$. This simplifies to $f'(c) = 40$. Next, we

    need to find $f'(c)$. The derivative of $f(x)$ is $f'(x) = 3x^2 + 24$, so $f'(c) = 3c^2 + 24$. Now

    we can solve for c: $3c^2 + 24 = 40$ and $c = \pm\dfrac{4}{\sqrt{3}}$. Note that $\dfrac{4}{\sqrt{3}}$ is in the interval $(0, 4)$, but $-\dfrac{4}{\sqrt{3}}$ is *not* in the interval. Thus, the answer is only $c = \dfrac{4}{\sqrt{3}}$. It's *very* important

to check that the answers you get for c fall in the given interval when doing mean

value theorem problems.

3. $c = \dfrac{-12 + 8\sqrt{3}}{3} \approx 0.62$

The mean value theorem says that: If $f(x)$ is continuous on the interval $[a, b]$ and

is differentiable everywhere on the interval (a, b), then there exists at least one

number c on the interval (a, b) such that $\dfrac{f(b) - f(a)}{b - a} = f'(c)$. Here, the function is

$f(x) = x^3 + 12x^2 + 7x$ and the interval is $[-4, 4]$. Thus, the mean value theorem says

that $\dfrac{\left((4)^3 + 12(4)^2 + 7(4) \right) - \left((-4)^3 + 12(-4)^2 + 7(-4) \right)}{(4 + 4)} = f'(c)$. This simplifies to

$f'(c) = 23$. Next, we need to find $f'(c)$. The derivative of $f(x)$ is $f'(x) = 3x^2 + 24x + 7$,

so $f'(c) = 3c^2 + 24c + 7$. Now we can solve for c: $3c^2 + 24c + 7 = 23$ and $c = \dfrac{-12 \pm 8\sqrt{3}}{3}$.

Note that $c = \dfrac{-12 + 8\sqrt{3}}{3}$ is in the interval $(-4, 4)$, but $\dfrac{-12 - 8\sqrt{3}}{3}$ is *not* in the

interval. Thus, the answer is only $c = \dfrac{-12 + 8\sqrt{3}}{3} \approx 0.62$. It's *very* important to check

that the answers you get for c fall in the given interval when doing mean value

theorem problems.

4. $c = \sqrt{2}$

The mean value theorem says that: If $f(x)$ is continuous on the interval $[a, b]$ and

is differentiable everywhere on the interval (a,b), then there exists at least one

number c on the interval (a, b) such that $\dfrac{f(b) - f(a)}{b - a} = f'(c)$. Here, the function

is $f(x) = \dfrac{6}{x} - 3$ and the interval is $[1, 2]$. Thus, the mean value theorem says that

$\dfrac{\left(\dfrac{6}{2} - 3\right) - \left(\dfrac{6}{1} - 3\right)}{(2 - 1)} = f'(c)$. This simplifies to $f'(c) = -3$. Next, we need to find $f'(c)$.

The derivative of $f(x)$ is $f'(x) = -\dfrac{6}{x^2}$, so $f'(c) = -\dfrac{6}{c^2}$. Now we can solve for c:

$-\dfrac{6}{c^2} = -3$ and $c = \pm\sqrt{2}$. Note that $c = \sqrt{2}$ is in the interval $(1, 2)$, but $-\sqrt{2}$ is *not* in

the interval. Thus, the answer is only $c = \sqrt{2}$. It's *very* important to check that the

answers you get for c fall in the given interval when doing mean value theorem

problems.

5. *No Solution.*

The mean value theorem says that: If $f(x)$ is continuous on the interval $[a, b]$ and

is differentiable everywhere on the interval (a, b), then there exists at least one

number c on the interval (a, b) such that $\dfrac{f(b) - f(a)}{b - a} = f'(c)$. Here, the function is

$f(x) = \dfrac{6}{x} - 3$ and the interval is $[-1, 2]$. Note that the function is *not* continuous on

the interval. It has an essential discontinuity (vertical asymptote) at $x = 0$. Thus, the

mean value theorem does not apply on the interval and there is no solution.

Suppose that we were to apply the theorem anyway. We would get:

$\dfrac{\left(\dfrac{6}{2} - 3\right) - \left(\dfrac{6}{-1} - 3\right)}{(2 + 1)} = f'(c)$. This simplifies to $f'(c) = 3$. Next, we need to find $f'(c)$.

The derivative of $f(x)$ is $f'(x) = -\dfrac{6}{x^2}$, so $f'(c) = -\dfrac{6}{c^2}$. Now we can solve for c:

$-\dfrac{6}{c^2} = 3$. This has no real solutions. Therefore, remember that it's *very* important to

check that the function is continuous and differentiable everywhere on the given

interval (it does not have to be differentiable at the endpoints) when doing mean

value theorem problems. If it is not, then the theorem does not apply.

6. $c = 4$

Rolle's theorem says that: If $f(x)$ is continuous on the interval $[a, b]$ and is differentiable everywhere on the interval (a, b), and if $f(a) = f(b) = 0$, then there exists at least one number c on the interval (a, b) such that $f'(c) = 0$. Here, the function is $f(x) = x^2 - 8x + 12$ and the interval is $[2, 6]$. First, we check if the function is equal to zero at both of the endpoints: $f(6) = (6)^2 - 8(6) + 12 = 0$ and $f(2) = (2)^2 - 8(2) + 12 = 0$. Next, we take the derivative to find $f'(c)$: $f'(x) = 2x - 8$, so $f'(c) = 2c - 8$. Now we can solve for c: $2c - 8 = 0$ and $c = 4$. Note that 4 is in the interval $(2, 6)$, just as we expected.

7. $c = \pm \dfrac{1}{\sqrt{3}}$

Rolle's theorem says that: If $f(x)$ is continuous on the interval $[a, b]$ and is

differentiable everywhere on the interval (a, b), and if $f(a) = f(b) = 0$, then there

exists at least one number c on the interval (a, b) such that $f'(c) = 0$. Here, the

function is $f(x) = x^3 - x$ and the interval is $[-1, 1]$. First, we check if the function is

equal to zero at both of the endpoints: $f(-1) = (-1)^3 - (-1) = 0$ and $f(1) = (1)^3 - (1) = 0$.

Next, we take the derivative to find $f'(c)$: $f'(x) = 3x^2 - 1$, so $f'(c) = 3c^2 - 1$. Now we

can solve for c: $3c^2 - 1 = 0$ and $c = \pm \dfrac{1}{\sqrt{3}}$. Note that $\pm \dfrac{1}{\sqrt{3}}$ are both in the interval

$(-1, 1)$, just as we expected.

8. $c = \dfrac{1}{2}$

Rolle's theorem says that: If $f(x)$ is continuous on the interval $[a, b]$ and is

differentiable everywhere on the interval (a, b), and if $f(a) = f(b) = 0$, then there

exists at least one number c on the interval (a, b) such that $f'(c) = 0$. Here, the

function is $f(x) = x(1 - x)$ and the interval is $[0, 1]$. First, we check if the function is

equal to zero at both of the endpoints: $f(0) = (0)(1 - 0) = 0$ and $f(1) = (1)(1 - 1) = 0$.

Next, we take the derivative to find $f'(c)$: $f'(x) = 1 - 2x$, so $f'(c) = 1 - 2c$. Now we

can solve for c: $1 - 2c = 0$ and $c = \dfrac{1}{2}$. Note that $\dfrac{1}{2}$ is in the interval $(0, 1)$, just as we

expected.

9. *No Solution.*

Rolle's theorem says that: If $f(x)$ is continuous on the interval $[a, b]$ and is

differentiable everywhere on the interval (a, b), and if $f(a) = f(b) = 0$, then there

exists at least one number c on the interval (a, b) such that $f'(c) = 0$. Here, the

function is $f(x) = 1 - \dfrac{1}{x^2}$ and the interval is $[-1, 1]$. Note that the function is *not*

continuous on the interval. It has an essential discontinuity (vertical asymptote) at

$x = 0$. Thus, Rolle's theorem does not apply on the interval and there is no solution.

Suppose we were to apply the heorem anyway. First, we check if the function is

equal to zero at both of the endpoints: $f(1) = 1 - \dfrac{1}{(1)^2} = 0$ and $f(-1) = 1 - \dfrac{1}{(-1)^2} = 0$.

Next, we take the derivative to find $f'(c)$: $f'(x) = \dfrac{2}{x^3}$, so $f'(c) = \dfrac{2}{c^3}$. This has no

solution.

Therefore, remember that it's *very* important to check that the function is

continuous and differentiable everywhere on the given interval (it does not have

to be differentiable at the endpoints) when doing Rolle's theorem problems. If it is

not, then the theorem does not apply.

10. $c - \dfrac{1}{8}$

Rolle's theorem says that: If $f(x)$ is continuous on the interval $[a, b]$ and is differentiable

everywhere on the interval (a, b), and if $f(a) = f(b) = 0$, then there exists at least one

number c on the interval (a, b) such that $f'(c) = 0$. Here, the function is $f(x) = x^{\frac{2}{3}} - x^{\frac{1}{3}}$

and the interval is $[0, 1]$. First, we check if the function is equal to zero at both of the

endpoints: $f(0) = (0)^{\frac{2}{3}} - (0)^{\frac{1}{3}} = 0$ and $f(1) = (1)^{\frac{2}{3}} - (1)^{\frac{1}{3}} = 0$. Next, we take the derivative

to find $f'(c)$ $f(x) = \dfrac{2}{3}x^{-\frac{1}{3}} - \dfrac{1}{3}x^{-\frac{2}{3}} = \dfrac{2}{3\sqrt[3]{x}} - \dfrac{1}{3\sqrt[3]{x^2}}$, so $f(c) = \dfrac{2}{3\sqrt[3]{c}} - \dfrac{1}{3\sqrt[3]{c^2}}$. Now we can

solve for c: $\dfrac{2}{3\sqrt[3]{c}} - \dfrac{1}{3\sqrt[3]{c^2}} = 0$ and $c = \dfrac{1}{8}$. Note that $\dfrac{1}{8}$ is in the interval $(0, 1)$, just as we

expected.

SOLUTIONS TO PRACTICE PROBLEM SET 10

1. The area is 32.

    First, let's draw a picture:

    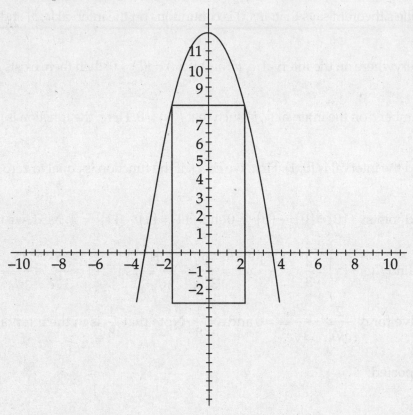

    The rectangle can be expressed as a function of x, where the height is $12 - x^2$

    and the base is $2x$. Then the area is: $A = 2x\,(12 - x^2) = 24x - 2x^3$. Now we take the

    derivative: $\dfrac{dA}{dx} = 24 - 6x^2$. Next we set the derivative equal to zero: $24 - 6x^2 = 0$. If

    we solve this for x, we get: $x = \pm 2$. A negative answer doesn't make any sense in the

    case, so we use the solution $x = 2$. We can then find the area by plugging in $x = 2$

    to get: $A = 24(2) - 2(2)^3 = 32$. We can verify that this is a maximum by taking the

    second derivative: $\dfrac{d^2A}{dx^2} = -12x$. Next, we plug in $x = 2$: $\dfrac{d^2A}{dx^2} = -12(2) = -24$. Because

    the value of the second derivative is negative, according to the second derivative

    test (see page 81), the area is a maximum at $x = 2$.

2. $x = \dfrac{7 - \sqrt{13}}{2} \approx 1.697$ inches

First, let's draw a picture:

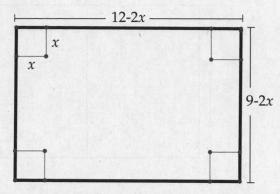

After we cut out the squares of side x and fold up the sides, the dimensions of the

box will be: width: $9 - 2x$; length: $12 - 2x$; depth: x.

   Using the formula for the volume of a rectangular prism, we can get an equation

for the volume of the box in terms of x: $V = x(9 - 2x)(12 - 2x) = 108x - 42x^2 + 4x^3$.

   Now we take the derivative: $\dfrac{dV}{dx} = 108 - 84x + 12x^2$. Next, we set the

derivative equal to zero: $108x - 84x + 12x^2 = 0$. If we solve this for x, we get:

$x = \dfrac{7 \pm \sqrt{13}}{2} \approx 5.303,\ 1.697$. We can't cut two squares of length 5.303 inches from a

side of length 9 inches, so we can get rid of that answer and so the answer must

be $x = \dfrac{7 - \sqrt{13}}{2} \approx 1.697$ inches. We can verify that this is a maximum by taking the

second derivative: $\dfrac{d^2V}{dx^2} = -84 + 24x$. Next, we plug in $x = 1.697$ to get approximately

$\dfrac{d^2V}{dx^2} = -84 + 24(1.697) = -43.272$. Because the value of the second derivative is

negative, according to the second derivative test (see page 81), the volume is a

maximum at $x = \dfrac{7 - \sqrt{13}}{2} \approx 1.697$ inches.

3. 16 meters by 24 meters

First, let's draw a picture:

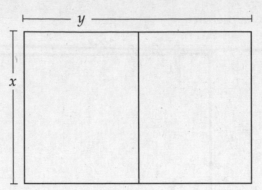

If we call the length of the plot y and the width x, the area of the plot is

$A = xy = 384$. The perimeter is $P = 3x + 2y$. So, if we want to minimize the length

of the fence, we need to minimize the perimeter of the plot. If we solve the

area equation for y, we get: $y = \dfrac{384}{x}$. Now, we can substitute this for y in the

perimeter equation: $P = 3x + 2\left(\dfrac{384}{x}\right) = 3x + \dfrac{768}{x}$. Now we take the derivative of

P: $\dfrac{dP}{dx} = 3 - \dfrac{768}{x^2}$. If we solve this for x, we get $x = \pm16$. A negative answer

doesn't make any sense in the case, so we use the solution $x = 16$ meters. Now we

can solve for y: $y = \dfrac{384}{16} = 24$ meters.

We can verify that this is a minimum by taking the second derivative:

$\dfrac{d^2P}{dx^2} = \dfrac{1536}{x^3}$. Next, we plug in $x = 16$ to get $\dfrac{d^2P}{dx^2} = \dfrac{1536}{16^3} = \dfrac{3}{8}$. Because the value of the

second derivative is positive, according to the second derivative test (see page 81),

the perimeter is a minimum at $x = 16$.

4. Radius is $\sqrt[3]{\dfrac{256}{\pi}}$ inches.

First, let's draw a picture:

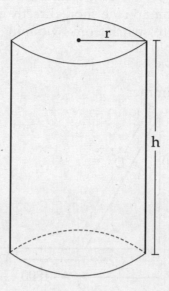

The volume of a cylinder is $V = \pi r^2 h = 512$. The material for the can is the surface

area of the cylinder (don't forget the ends!) $S = 2\pi rh + 2\pi r^2$. If we solve the volume

equation for h, we get: $h = \dfrac{512}{\pi r^2}$. Now we can substitute this for h in the surface

area equation: $S = 2\pi r \left(\dfrac{512}{\pi r^2} \right) + 2\pi r^2 = \dfrac{1024}{r} + 2\pi r^2$. Now we take the derivative of

$S: S = -\dfrac{1024}{r^2} + 4\pi r$. If we solve this for r, we get: $r = \sqrt[3]{\dfrac{256}{\pi}}$ inches. We can verify

that this is a minimum by taking the second derivative: $\dfrac{d^2 S}{dx^2} = \dfrac{2048}{r^3} + 4\pi$. Next, we

plug in $\sqrt[3]{\dfrac{256}{\pi}}$ and we can see that the value of the second derivative is positive.

Therefore, according to the second derivative test (see page 81), the perimeter is a

minimum at $r = \sqrt[3]{\dfrac{256}{\pi}}$.

5. 1352.786 meters

Let's think about the situation. If the swimmer swims the whole distance to the cottage, she will be traveling the entire time at her slowest speed. If she swims straight to shore first, minimizing her swimming distance, she will be maximizing her running distance. Therefore there should be a point, somewhere between the cottage and the point on the shore directly opposite her, where the swimmer should come on land to switch from swimming to running to get to the cottage in the shortest time.

Let's draw a picture.

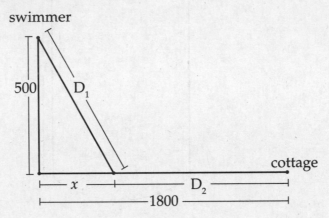

We'll call the distance x from the point on the shore directly opposite the swimmer to the point where she comes on land. We have two distances to consider. The first is the diagonal distance that the swimmer swims. This distance, which we'll call D_1 is $D_1 = \sqrt{500^2 + x^2} = \sqrt{250000 + x^2}$. The second distance, which we'll call D_2, is simply $D_2 = 1800 - x$. Remember that *rate × time = distance*? We'll use this formula to find the total time that the swimmer needs. The time for the swimmer to travel D_1 is $T_1 = \dfrac{D_1}{4} = \dfrac{\sqrt{250000 + x^2}}{4}$ (because she swims at 4 *m/s*) and the time for the swimmer to travel D_2 is $T_2 = \dfrac{D_2}{6} = \dfrac{1800 - x}{6} = 300 - \dfrac{x}{6}$. Therefore, the total time is $T = \dfrac{\sqrt{250000 + x^2}}{4} + 300 - \dfrac{x}{6}$. Now we simply take the derivative:

$\dfrac{dT}{dx} = \dfrac{1}{4}\left(\dfrac{1}{2}\right)\left(250000 + x^2\right)^{-\frac{1}{2}}(2x) - \dfrac{1}{6} = \dfrac{x}{4\sqrt{250000 + x^2}} - \dfrac{1}{6}$. Next, we set this equal to

zero and solve: $\dfrac{x}{4\sqrt{250000 + x^2}} - \dfrac{1}{6} = 0$. The best way to solve this is to move the $\dfrac{1}{6}$

to the other side of the equals sign and cross-multiply:

$$\dfrac{x}{4\sqrt{250000 + x^2}} = \dfrac{1}{6}$$

$$6x = 4\sqrt{250000 + x^2}\ .$$

Next we square both sides: $36x^2 = 16(250000 + x^2)$.
Simplify: $20x^2 = 4000000$.
Solve for x: $x = \pm 447.214\ m$. (We can ignore the negative answer.) Therefore, she should land $1800 - 447.214 = 1352.786$ meters from the cottage. We could verify that this is a minimum by taking the second derivative but that will be messy. It is simpler to use the calculator to check the sign of the derivative at a point on either side of the answer, or to graph the equation for the time.

6. $\left(\dfrac{2}{\sqrt{5}}, \dfrac{1}{\sqrt{5}}\right)$

First, let's draw a picture.

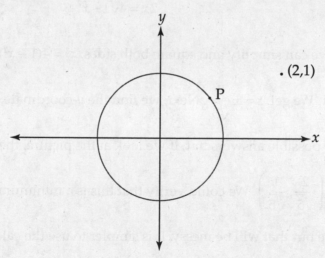

We need to find an expression for the distance from the point P to the point $(2, 1)$ and then minimize the distance. If we call the coordinates of $P(x, y)$ then we can find the distance to $(2, 1)$ using the distance formula: $D^2 = (x - 2)^2 + (y - 1)^2$. Next, just as we did in sample problem 4 (page 89), we can let $L = D^2$ and minimize L:

$$L = (x - 2)^2 + (y - 0)^2 = x^2 - 4x + 4 + y^2 - 2y + 1.$$

Because $x^2 + y^2 = 1$, we can substitute for y to get:

$L = x^2 - 4x + 4 + (1 - x^2) - 2\sqrt{1 - x^2} + 1$, which simplifies to: $L = -4x + 6 - 2\sqrt{1 - x^2}$.

Next, we take the derivative: $\dfrac{dL}{dx} = -4 - 2\left(\dfrac{1}{2}\right)(1 - x^2)^{-\frac{1}{2}}(-2x) = -4 + \dfrac{2x}{\sqrt{1 - x^2}}$. Next,

we set the derivative equal to zero: $-4 + \dfrac{2x}{\sqrt{1 - x^2}} = 0$. The best way to solve this is to

move the 4 to the other side of the equals sign and cross-multiply:

$$\frac{2x}{\sqrt{1 - x^2}} = 4$$

$$2x = 4\sqrt{1 - x^2}$$

Next we can simplify and square both sides: $x^2 = 4(1 - x^2)$. Now we can solve

this easily. We get: $x = \pm\dfrac{2}{\sqrt{5}}$. Next, we find the y-coordinate: $y = \pm\dfrac{1}{\sqrt{5}}$. There are

thus four possible answers but, if we look at the picture, the answer is obviously

the point $\left(\dfrac{2}{\sqrt{5}}, \dfrac{1}{\sqrt{5}}\right)$. We could verify that this is a minimum by taking the second

derivative but that will be messy. It is simpler to use the calculator to check the sign

of the derivative at a point on either side of the answer, or to graph the equation for

the distance.

7. $r = \dfrac{288}{4+\pi}$ inches

First, let's draw a picture.

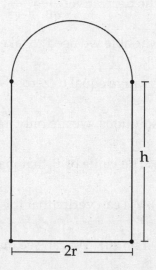

Call the width of the window $2r$. Notice that this is the diameter of the semicircle.

Call the height of the window h. The area of the rectangular portion of the window

is $2rh$ and the perimeter is $2r + 2h$. The area of the semicircular portion of the

window is $\dfrac{\pi r^2}{2}$ and the perimeter is $\dfrac{2\pi r}{2} = \pi r$. Therefore, the area of the window

is $A = 2rh + \dfrac{\pi r^2}{2}$ and the perimeter is $2r + 2h + \pi r = 288$. We can use the equation

for the perimeter to eliminate a variable from the equation for the area. Let's

isolate h: $h = 144 - r - \dfrac{\pi r}{2}$. Now we can substitute for h in the equation for the area:

$A = 2r\left(144 - r - \dfrac{\pi r}{2}\right) + \dfrac{\pi r^2}{2} = 288r - 2r^2 - \dfrac{\pi r^2}{2}$. Next, we can take the derivative:

$\dfrac{dA}{dr} = 288 - 4r - \pi r$. If we set this equal to zero and solve for r, we get: $r = \dfrac{288}{4+\pi}$

inches. We can verify that this is a maximum by taking the second derivative:

$\dfrac{d^2A}{dr^2} = -4 - \pi$. We can see that the value of the second derivative is negative.

Therefore, according to the second derivative test (see page 81), the area is a

maximum at $r = \dfrac{288}{4+\pi}$ inches.

8. $\theta = \dfrac{\pi}{4}$ radians (or 45 degrees)

Here, we simply take the derivative: $\dfrac{dR}{d\theta} = \dfrac{v_0^2}{g}\left(2\cos 2\theta\right)$. Note that v_0 and g are

constants, so the only variable we need to take the derivative with respect to is

θ. Now we set the derivative equal to zero: $\dfrac{v_0^2}{g}\left(2\cos 2\theta\right) = 0$. Although this has

an infinite number of solutions, we are only interested in values of θ between 0

and $\dfrac{\pi}{2}$ radians (why?). The value of θ that makes the derivative zero is $\theta = \dfrac{\pi}{4}$

radians (or 45 degrees). We can verify that this is a maximum by taking the second

derivative: $\dfrac{d^2R}{d\theta^2} = \dfrac{v_0^2}{g}\left(-4\sin 2\theta\right)$. We can see that the value of the second derivative

is negative at $\theta = \dfrac{\pi}{4}$. Therefore, according to the second derivative test (see page

81), the area is a maximum at $\theta = \dfrac{\pi}{4}$ radians.

9. $15 billion dollars.

Here, we simply take the derivative: $\dfrac{dP}{dx} = 3x^2 - 96x + 720$. Now we set the

derivative equal to zero: $3x^2 - 96x + 720 = 0$. The solutions to this are $x = 12$ and

$x = 20$. Note, however, that the function is bounded by $x = 0$ and $x = 40$.

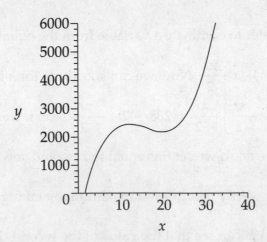

Thus, in order to find the maximum profit, we need to plug all four values of x into the profit equation to find which gives the greatest value. We get:

$P(0) = -1000$

$P(12) = (12)^3 - 48(12)^2 + 720(12) - 1000 = 2456$

$P(20) = (20)^3 - 48(20)^2 + 720(20) - 1000 = 2200$

$P(40) = (40)^3 - 48(40)^2 + 720(40) - 1000 = 15000$

Thus, even though we have a relative maximum at $x = 12$, the absolute maximum profit occurs when $x = 40$. The profit at that value is 15000, or $15 billion dollars.

If we look at a graph of the profit function, we can see that the critical points gave us relative maximum and minimum, but not the absolute maximum or minimum. This is why it is always important to check the endpoints of a function in any max/min problem.

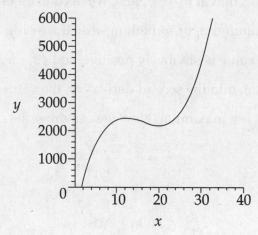

SOLUTIONS TO PRACTICE PROBLEM SET 11

1. Minimum at $\left(\sqrt{3}, -6\sqrt{3}-6\right)$; Maximum at $\left(-\sqrt{3}, 6\sqrt{3}-6\right)$; Point of inflection at $(0, 6)$.

   First, let's find the y-intercept. We set $x = 0$ to get: $y = (0)^3 - 9(0) - 6 = -6$. Therefore, the y-intercept is $(0, -6)$. Next, we find any critical points using the first derivative. The derivative is: $\frac{dy}{dx} = 3x^2 - 9$. If we set this equal to zero and solve for x, we get $x = \pm\sqrt{3}$. Plug $x = \sqrt{3}$ and $x = -\sqrt{3}$ into the original equation to find the y-coordinates of the critical points: When $x = \sqrt{3}$, $y = \left(\sqrt{3}\right)^3 - 9\left(\sqrt{3}\right) - 6 = -6\sqrt{3} - 6$. When $x = -\sqrt{3}$, $y = \left(-\sqrt{3}\right)^3 - 9\left(-\sqrt{3}\right) - 6 = 6\sqrt{3} - 6$. Thus, we have critical points at $\left(\sqrt{3}, -6\sqrt{3}-6\right)$ and $\left(-\sqrt{3}, 6\sqrt{3}-6\right)$. Next, we take the second derivative to find any points of inflection. The second derivative is: $\frac{d^2y}{dx^2} = 6x$, which is equal to zero at $x = 0$. Note that this is the y-intercept $(0, -6)$, which we already found, so there is a point of inflection at $(0, -6)$. Next, we need to determine if each critical point is maximum, minimum, or something else. If we plug $x = \sqrt{3}$ into the second derivative, the value is obviously positive, so $\left(\sqrt{3}, -6\sqrt{3}-6\right)$ is a minimum. If we plug $x = -\sqrt{3}$ into the second derivative, the value is obviously negative, so $\left(-\sqrt{3}, 6\sqrt{3}-6\right)$ is a maximum. Now we can draw the curve. It looks like this:

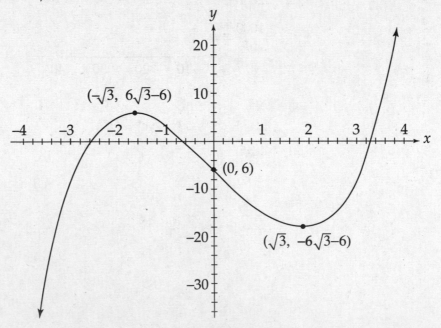

2. Minimum at (–3, –4); Maximum at (–1, 0); Point of inflection at (–2, –2).

First, let's find the y-intercept. We set $x = 0$ to get: $y = -(0)^3 - 6(0)^2 - 9(0) - 4 = -4$. Therefore, the y-intercept is (0, –4). Next, we find any critical points using the first derivative. The derivative is: $\frac{dy}{dx} = -3x^2 - 12x - 9$. If we set this equal to zero and solve for x, we get $x = -1$ and $x = -3$. Plug $x = -1$ and $x = -3$ into the original equation to find the y-coordinates of the critical points: When $x = -1$, $y = -(-1)^3 - 6(-1)^2 - 9(-1) - 4 = 0$. When $x = -3$, $y = -(-3)^3 - 6(-3)^2 - 9(-3) - 4 = -4$. Thus, we have critical points at (–1, 0) and (–3, –4). Next, we take the second derivative to find any points of inflection. The second derivative is: $\frac{d^2y}{dx^2} = -6x - 12$, which is equal to zero at $x = -2$. Plug $x = -2$ into the original equation to find the y-coordinate: $y = -(-2)^3 - 6(-2)^2 - 9(-2) - 4 = -2$, so there is a point of inflection at (–2, –2). Next, we need to determine if each critical point is maximum, minimum, or something else. If we plug $x = -1$ into the second derivative, the value is negative, so (–1, 0) is a maximum. If we plug $x = -3$ into the second derivative, the value is positive, so (–3, –4) is a minimum. Now we can draw the curve. It looks like this:

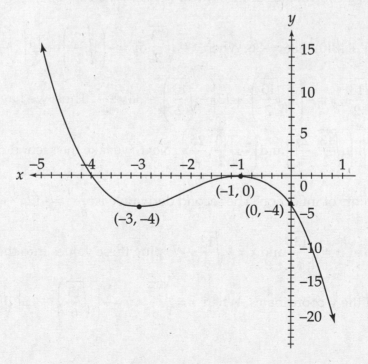

3. Minimum at $(0, -36)$; Maxima at $\left(\dfrac{\sqrt{13}}{2}, \dfrac{25}{4}\right)$ and $\left(-\dfrac{\sqrt{13}}{2}, \dfrac{25}{4}\right)$; points of inflection at $\left(\dfrac{\sqrt{13}}{6}, -\dfrac{451}{36}\right)$ and $\left(-\dfrac{\sqrt{13}}{6}, -\dfrac{451}{36}\right)$.

First, we can easily see that the graph has x-intercepts at $x = \pm 2$ and $x = \pm 3$. Next,

before we take the derivative, let's multiply the two terms so we don't have to

use the product rule. We get: $y = -x^4 + 13x^2 - 36$. Now we can take the derivative:

$\dfrac{dy}{dx} = -4x^3 + 26x$. Next we set the derivative equal to zero to find the critical points.

There are three solutions: $x = 0$, $x = \sqrt{\dfrac{13}{2}}$, and $x = -\sqrt{\dfrac{13}{2}}$.

We plug these values into the original equation to

find the y-coordinates of the critical points: When $x = 0$,

$y = -(0)^4 + 13(0)^2 - 36 = -36$. When $x = \sqrt{\dfrac{13}{2}}$, $y = -\left(\sqrt{\dfrac{13}{2}}\right)^4 + 13\left(\sqrt{\dfrac{13}{2}}\right)^2 - 36 = \dfrac{25}{4}$. When

$x = -\sqrt{\dfrac{13}{2}}$, $y = -\left(-\sqrt{\dfrac{13}{2}}\right)^4 + 13\left(-\sqrt{\dfrac{13}{2}}\right)^2 - 36 = \dfrac{25}{4}$. Thus, we have critical points at

$(0, -36)$, $\left(\sqrt{\dfrac{13}{2}}, \dfrac{25}{4}\right)$ and $\left(-\sqrt{\dfrac{13}{2}}, \dfrac{25}{4}\right)$. Next, we take the second derivative to find

any points of inflection. The second derivative is: $\dfrac{d^2y}{dx^2} = -12x^2 + 26$, which is equal

to zero at $x = \sqrt{\dfrac{13}{6}}$ and $x = -\sqrt{\dfrac{13}{6}}$. We plug these values into the original equation

to find the y-coordinates. When $x = \sqrt{\dfrac{13}{6}}$: $y = -\left(\sqrt{\dfrac{13}{6}}\right)^4 + 13\left(\sqrt{\dfrac{13}{6}}\right)^2 - 36 = -\dfrac{451}{36}$.

When $x = -\sqrt{\dfrac{13}{6}} : y = -\left(-\sqrt{\dfrac{13}{6}}\right)^4 + 13\left(-\sqrt{\dfrac{13}{6}}\right)^2 - 36 = -\dfrac{451}{36}$. So there are points

of inflection at $\left(\dfrac{\sqrt{13}}{6}, -\dfrac{451}{36}\right)$ and $\left(-\dfrac{\sqrt{13}}{6}, -\dfrac{451}{36}\right)$. Next, we need to determine

if each critical point is maximum, minimum, or something else. If we plug $x = 0$

into the second derivative, the value is positive, so $(0, -36)$ is a minimum. If we

plug $x = \sqrt{\dfrac{13}{2}}$ into the second derivative, the value is negative, so $\left(\sqrt{\dfrac{13}{2}}, \dfrac{25}{4}\right)$ is a

maximum. If we plug $x = -\sqrt{\dfrac{13}{2}}$ into the second derivative, the value is negative,

so $\left(-\sqrt{\dfrac{13}{2}}, \dfrac{25}{4}\right)$ is a maximum. Now we can draw the curve. It looks like this:

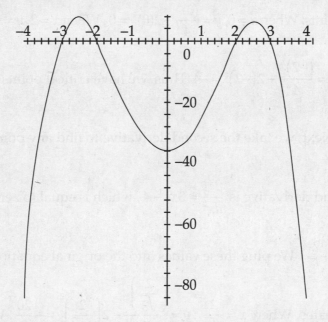

4. Maximum at $(0, 0)$; Minima at $(2, -4)$ and $(-2, -4)$; Points of inflection at $\left(\dfrac{2}{\sqrt{3}}, -\dfrac{20}{9}\right)$ and $\left(-\dfrac{2}{\sqrt{3}}, -\dfrac{20}{9}\right)$.

First, we can easily see that the graph has x-intercepts at $x = 0$ and $x = \pm\sqrt{8}$. Next, we take the derivative: $\dfrac{dy}{dx} = x^3 - 4x$. Next we set the derivative equal to zero to find the critical points. There are three solutions: $x = 0$, $x = 2$, and $x = -2$.

We plug these values into the original equation to find the y-coordinates of the critical points: When $x = 0$, $y = \dfrac{(0)^4}{4} - 2(0)^2 = 0$. When $x = 2$, $y = \dfrac{(2)^4}{4} - 2(2)^2 = -4$. When $x = -2$, $y = \dfrac{(-2)^4}{4} - 2(-2)^2 = -4$. Thus, we have critical points at $(0, 0)$, $(2, -4)$ and $(-2, -4)$. Next, we take the second derivative to find any points of inflection.

The second derivative is: $\dfrac{d^2y}{dx^2} = 3x^2 - 4$, which is equal to zero at $x = \dfrac{2}{\sqrt{3}}$ and $x = -\dfrac{2}{\sqrt{3}}$. We plug these values into the original equation to find the y-coordinates. When $x = \dfrac{2}{\sqrt{3}}$: $y = \dfrac{\left(\dfrac{2}{\sqrt{3}}\right)^4}{4} - 2\left(\dfrac{2}{\sqrt{3}}\right)^2 = -\dfrac{20}{9}$. When $x = -\dfrac{2}{\sqrt{3}}$: $y = \dfrac{\left(-\dfrac{2}{\sqrt{3}}\right)^4}{4} - 2\left(-\dfrac{2}{\sqrt{3}}\right)^2 = -\dfrac{20}{9}$. So there are points of inflection at $\left(\dfrac{2}{\sqrt{3}}, -\dfrac{20}{9}\right)$ and $\left(-\dfrac{2}{\sqrt{3}}, -\dfrac{20}{9}\right)$. Next, we need to determine if each critical point is maximum, minimum, or something else. If we plug $x = 0$ into the second derivative, the value

is negative, so $(0,0)$ is a maximum. If we plug $x = 2$ into the second derivative,

the value is positive, so $(2, -4)$ is a minimum. If we plug $x = -2$ into the second

derivative, the value is negative, so $(-2, -4)$ is a minimum. Now we can draw the

curve. It looks like this:

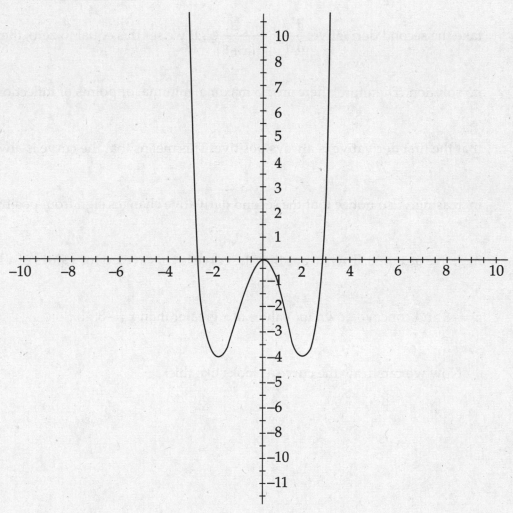

5. Vertical asymptote at $x = -8$; Horizontal asymptote at $y = 1$; No maxima, minima, or points of inflection.

First, notice that there is an x-intercept at $x = 3$ and that the y-intercept is $\left(0, -\dfrac{3}{8}\right)$.

Next, we take the derivative: $\dfrac{dy}{dx} = \dfrac{(x+8)(1)-(x-3)(1)}{(x+8)^2} = \dfrac{11}{(x+8)^2}$. Next we set the

derivative equal to zero to find the critical points. There is no solution. Next, we

take the second derivative: $\dfrac{d^2y}{dx^2} = -\dfrac{22}{(x+8)^3}$. If we set this equal to zero, there is also

no solution. Therefore, there are no maxima, minima, or points of inflection. Note

that the first derivative is always positive. This means that the curve is always

increasing. Also notice that the second derivative changes sign from positive to

negative at $x = -8$. This means that the curve is concave up for values of x less than

$x = -8$ and concave down for values of x greater than $x = -8$.

Now we can draw the curve. It looks like this:

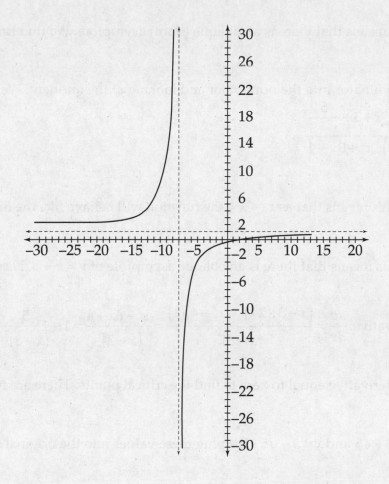

6.   Vertical asymptote at $x = 3$; Oblique asymptote of $y = x + 3$; Maximum at

$\left(3+\sqrt{5}, 6+2\sqrt{5}\right)$; Minimum at $\left(3-\sqrt{5}, 6-2\sqrt{5}\right)$; No points of inflection.

First, notice that there are x-intercepts at $x = \pm 2$ and that the y-intercept is $\left(0, \dfrac{4}{3}\right)$.

There is a vertical asymptote at $x = 3$. There is no horizontal asymptote but notice

that the degree of the numerator of the function is 1 greater than the denominator.

This means that there is an oblique (slant) asymptote. We find this by dividing the

denominator into the numerator and looking at the quotient. We get:

$$x-3 \overline{\smash{\big)}\ x^2+0x-4} \quad x+3+\dfrac{5}{x-3}$$

This means that as $x \to \pm\infty$, the function will behave like the function $y = x +$

3. This means that there is an oblique asymptote of $y = x + 3$. Next, we take the

derivative: $\dfrac{dy}{dx} = \dfrac{(x-3)(2x)-(x^2-4)(1)}{(x-3)^2} = \dfrac{x^2-6x+4}{(x-3)^2} = 1 - \dfrac{5}{(x-3)^2}$. Next we set

the derivative equal to zero to find the critical points. There are two solutions:

$x = 3 + \sqrt{5}$ and $x = 3 - \sqrt{5}$. We plug these values into the original equation to find

the y-coordinates of the critical points: When $x = 3 + \sqrt{5}$, $y = \dfrac{\left(3+\sqrt{5}\right)^2 - 4}{\left(3+\sqrt{5}\right)-3} = 6 + 2\sqrt{5}$.

When $x = -\sqrt{35}$, $y = \dfrac{\left(3-\sqrt{5}\right)^2 - 4}{\left(3-\sqrt{5}\right)-3} = 6 - 2\sqrt{5}$. Thus, we have critical points at

$\left(3+\sqrt{5}, 6+2\sqrt{5}\right)$ and $\left(3-\sqrt{5}, 6-2\sqrt{5}\right)$. Next, we take the second derivative:

$\dfrac{d^2y}{dx^2} = \dfrac{10}{(x-3)^3}$. If we set this equal to zero, there is no solution. Therefore, there

is no point of inflection. But notice that the second derivative changes sign from

negative to positive at $x = 3$. This means that the curve is concave down for values

of x less than $x = 3$ and concave up for values of x greater than $x = 3$. Next, we need to determine if each critical point is maximum, minimum, or something

else. If we plug $x = 3 + \sqrt{5}$ into the second derivative, the value is positive, so

$\left(3 + \sqrt{5}, 6 + 2\sqrt{5}\right)$ is a minimum. If we plug $x = -\sqrt{35}$ into the second derivative, the

value is positive, so $\left(3 - \sqrt{5}, 6 - 2\sqrt{5}\right)$ is a maximum.

Now we can draw the curve. It looks like this:

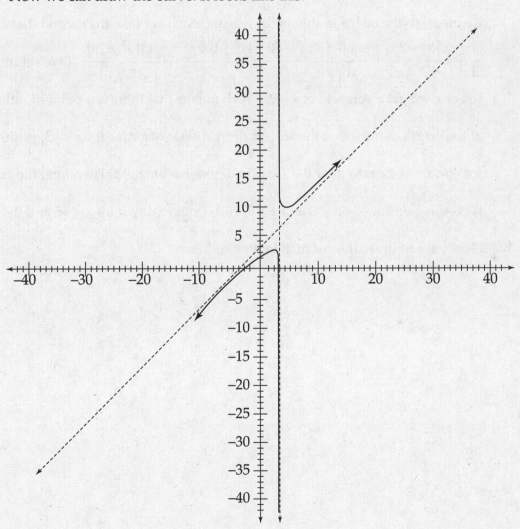

7. Vertical asymptotes at $x = 5$ and $x = -5$; Horizontal asymptote at $y = 0$ (x-axis); No maxima or minima; Point of inflection at $(0, 0)$.

First, notice that the curve goes through the origin. There are vertical asymptotes at $x = 5$ and $x = -5$. There is a horizontal asymptote at $y = 0$ (x-axis). Next, we take the derivative: $\dfrac{dy}{dx} = \dfrac{(x^2 - 25)(2) - (2x)(2x)}{(x^2 - 25)^2} = \dfrac{-2x^2 - 50}{(x^2 - 25)^2}$. Next we set the derivative equal to zero to find any critical points. There is no solution. Therefore, there are no maxima or minima. Note also that the function is always negative (where it is defined), so the curve is always decreasing. Next we take the second derivative: $\dfrac{d^2y}{dx^2} = \dfrac{(x^2 - 25)^2(-4x) - (-2x^2 - 50)(4x^3 - 100x)}{(x^2 - 25)^3} = \dfrac{(4x)(x^2 + 75)}{(x^2 - 25)^2}$. If we set this equal to zero, we get a solution at $x = 0$, which means that there is a point of inflection at the origin. Notice that the second derivative is negative for $x < -5$, positive for $-5 < x < 0$, negative for $0 < x < 5$, and positive for $x > 5$. Therefore, the curve is concave up for $-5 < x < 0$ and $x > 5$, and concave down for $x < -5$ and $0 < x < 5$.

Now we can draw the curve. It looks like this:

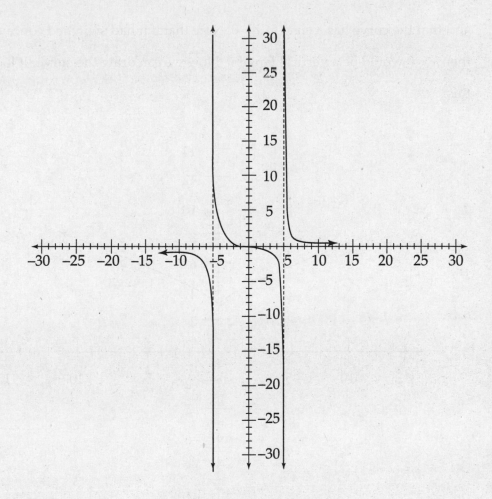

8. No maxima, minima, or points of inflection; Cusp at (0, 3).

First, notice that the function is always positive. There is a y-intercept at $(0, 3)$. There is no x-intercept. Next, we take the derivative: $\dfrac{dy}{dx} = \dfrac{2}{3}x^{-\frac{1}{3}}$. If we set the derivative equal to zero, there is no solution. *But,* notice that the derivative is not defined at $x = 0$. This means that the function has either a vertical tangent or a cusp at $x = 0$. We'll be able to determine which after we take the second derivative. Notice also that the derivative is negative for $x < 0$ and positive for $x > 0$. Therefore, the curve is decreasing for $x < 0$ and increasing for $x > 0$. Next, we take the second derivative: $\dfrac{dy}{dx} = -\dfrac{2}{9}x^{-\frac{4}{3}}$. If we set this equal to zero, there is no solution. The second derivative is always negative which tells us that the curve is always concave down and that the curve has a cusp at $x = 0$. Note that if it had switched concavity there, then $x = 0$ would be a vertical tangent. Now we can draw the curve. It looks like this:

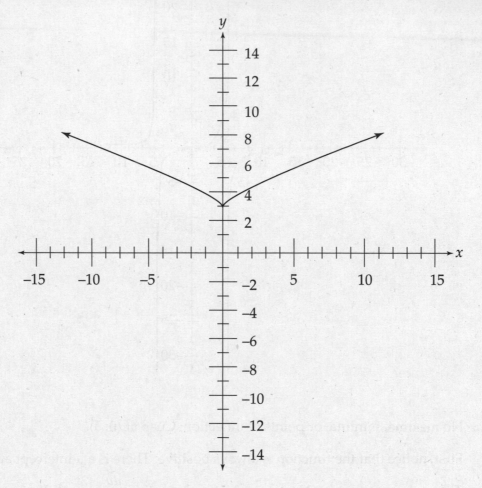

9. Maximum at (1, 1); No point of inflection; Cusp at (0, 0).

First, we notice that the curve has x-intercepts at $x = 0$ and $x = \dfrac{27}{8}$, and that there is a y-intercept at (0, 0). Before we take the derivative let's expand the expression. That way, we won't have to use the product rule. We get: $y = 3x^{\frac{2}{3}} - 2x$. Next we take the derivative: $\dfrac{dy}{dx} = 2x^{-\frac{1}{3}} - 2$. Next we set the derivative equal to zero to find the critical points. There is one solution: $x = 1$. We plug this value into the original equation to find the y-coordinate of the critical point: When $x = 1$, $y = 3(1)^{\frac{2}{3}} - 2(1) = 1$. Thus, we have a critical point at (1, 1). *But*, notice that the derivative is not defined at $x = 0$. This means that the function has either a vertical tangent or a cusp at $x = 0$. We'll be able to determine which after we take the second derivative. Notice also that the derivative is negative for $x < 0$ and for $x > 1$ and positive for $0 < x < 1$. Therefore, the curve is decreasing for $x < 0$ and for $x > 1$, and increasing for $0 < x < 1$. Next, we take the second derivative: $\dfrac{d^2y}{dx^2} = -\dfrac{2}{3}x^{-\frac{4}{3}}$. If we set this equal to zero, there is no solution. Therefore, there is no point of inflection. The second derivative is always negative which tells us that the curve is always concave down and that the curve has a cusp at $x = 0$. Note that if it had switched concavity there, then $x = 0$ would be a vertical tangent. Next, we need to determine if each critical point is maximum, minimum, or something else. If we plug $x = 1$ into the second derivative, the value is negative, so $(1, 1)$ is a maximum. Now we can draw the curve. It looks like this:

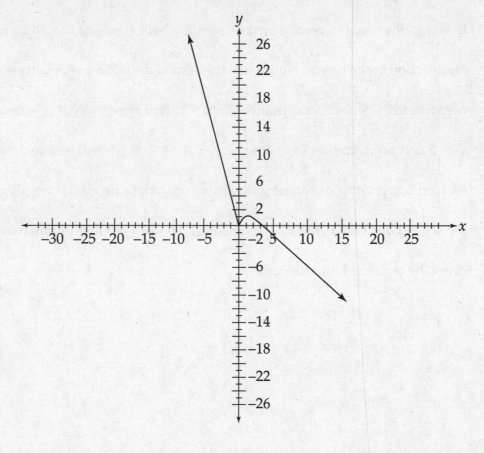

10. Maximum at (0, 0); Vertical asymptotes at $x = 2$ and $x = -2$; Horizontal asymptote at $y = 3$; No point of inflection.

First, notice that the curve goes through the origin. There are vertical asymptotes at $x = 2$ and $x = -2$. There is a horizontal asymptote at $y = 3$. Next, we take the derivative: $\dfrac{dy}{dx} = \dfrac{(x^2 - 4)(6x) - (3x^2)(2x)}{(x^2 - 4)^2} = \dfrac{-24x}{(x^2 - 4)^2}$. Next we set the derivative equal to zero to find any critical points. There is a solution at $x = 0$, which means that there is a critical point at (0, 0). Note also that the function is positive for $x < 0$ and negative for $x > 0$, so the curve is increasing for $x < 0$ and decreasing for $x > 0$. Next we take the second derivative: $\dfrac{d^2y}{dx^2} = \dfrac{\left(x^2 - 4\right)^2 (-24) - (-24x)\left(4x^3 - 16x\right)}{\left(x^2 - 4\right)^4} = \dfrac{72x^2 + 96}{\left(x^2 - 4\right)^3}$.

If we set this equal to zero, we get no solution, which means that there is no point of inflection at the origin. Notice that the second derivative is positive for $x < -2$, negative for $-2 < x < 2$, and positive for $x > 2$. Therefore, the curve is concave up for $x < -2$ and $x > 2$, and concave down for $-2 < x < 2$. Next, we need to determine if each critical point is maximum, minimum, or something else. If we plug $x = 0$ into the second derivative, the value is negative, so (0, 0) is a maximum. Now we can draw the curve. It looks like this:

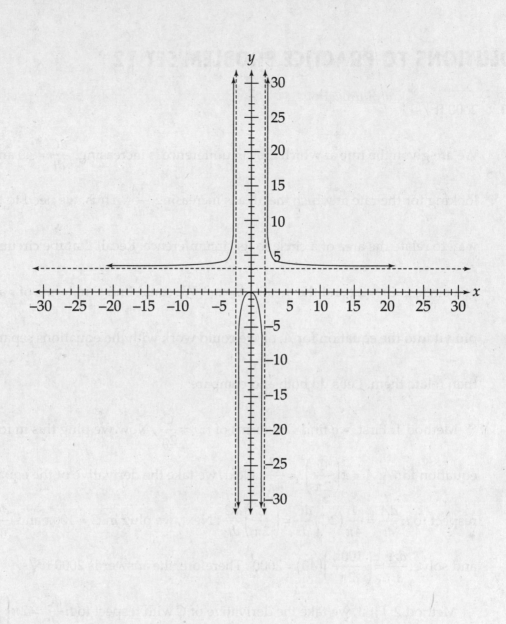

SOLUTIONS TO PRACTICE PROBLEM SET 12

1. 2000 ft²/s

    We are given the rate at which the circumference is increasing, $\dfrac{dC}{dt} = 40$ and are

    looking for the rate at which the area is increasing, $\dfrac{dA}{dt}$. Thus, we need to find a

    way to relate the area of a circle to its circumference. Recall that the circumference

    of a circle is $Cr = 2\pi$ and the area is $A = \pi r^2$. We could find C in terms of r and then

    plug it into the equation for A, or we could work with the equations separately and

    then relate them. Let's do both and compare:

    Method 1: First, we find C in terms of r: $r = \dfrac{C}{2\pi}$. Now we plug this in for r in the

    equation for A: $A = \pi \left(\dfrac{C}{2\pi}\right)^2 = \dfrac{C^2}{4\pi}$. Next, we take the derivative of the equation with

    respect to t: $\dfrac{dA}{dt} = \dfrac{1}{4\pi}(2C)\dfrac{dC}{dt} = \left(\dfrac{C}{2\pi}\right)\dfrac{dC}{dt}$. Next, we plug in $C = 100\pi$ and $\dfrac{dC}{dt} = 40$,

    and solve: $\dfrac{dA}{dt} = \left(\dfrac{100\pi}{2\pi}\right)(40) = 2000$. Therefore, the answer is 2000 ft²/s.

    Method 2: First, we take the derivative of C with respect to t: $\dfrac{dC}{dt} = 2\pi\left(\dfrac{dr}{dt}\right)$.

    Next, we plug in $\dfrac{dC}{dt} = 40$ and solve for $\dfrac{dr}{dt}$: $40 = 2\pi\left(\dfrac{dr}{dt}\right)$, so $\dfrac{dr}{dt} = \dfrac{20}{\pi}$. Next, we

    take the derivative of A with respect to t: $\dfrac{dA}{dt} = 2\pi r \dfrac{dr}{dt}$. Now we can plug in for

    $\dfrac{dr}{dt}$ and r and solve for $\dfrac{dA}{dt}$. Note that when the circumference is 100π, $r = 50$:

    $\dfrac{dA}{dt} = 2\pi(50)\left(\dfrac{20}{\pi}\right) = 2000$. Therefore, the answer is 2000 ft²/s.

Which method is better? In this case they are about the same. Method 1 is going to be more efficient if it is easy to solve for one variable in terms of the other and it is also easy to take the derivative of the resulting expression. Otherwise, we will prefer to use Method 2 (See Example 3 on page 107).

2. $\dfrac{3}{4}$ in/s

We are given the rate at which the volume is increasing, $\dfrac{dV}{dt} = 27\pi$ and are looking for the rate at which the radius is increasing, $\dfrac{dr}{dt}$. Thus, we need to find a way to relate the volume of a sphere to its radius. Recall that the volume of a sphere is $V = \dfrac{4}{3}\pi r^3$. All we have to do is take the derivative of the equation with respect to t: $\dfrac{dV}{dt} = \dfrac{4}{3}\pi\left(3r^2\right)\left(\dfrac{dr}{dt}\right) = 4\pi r^2 \dfrac{dr}{dt}$. Now we substitute $\dfrac{dV}{dt} = 27\pi$ and $r = 3$: $27\pi = 4\pi(3)^2 \dfrac{dr}{dt}$. If we solve for $\dfrac{dr}{dt}$, we get: $\dfrac{dr}{dt} = \dfrac{3}{4}$ in/s.

3. 100 km/hr

We are given the rate at which the Car A is moving south, $\dfrac{dA}{dt} = 80$ and the rate at which Car B is moving west, $\dfrac{dB}{dt} = 60$, and are looking for the rate at which the distance between them is increasing, which we'll call $\dfrac{dC}{dt}$. Note that the directions south and west are at right angles to each other. Thus, the distance that car A is from the starting point, which we'll call A, and the distance that car B is from the starting point, which we'll call B, are the lets of a right triangle, with C as the hypotenuse. We can relate the three distances using the Pythagorean theorem. Here, because A and B are the legs and C is the hypotenuse, $A^2 + B^2 = C^2$. Now, we take the derivative of the equation with respect to t: $2A\dfrac{dA}{dt} + 2B\dfrac{dB}{dt} = 2C\dfrac{dC}{dt}$. This simplifies to: $A\dfrac{dA}{dt} + B\dfrac{dB}{dt} = C\dfrac{dC}{dt}$. We know that Car A has been driving for 3 hours at 80 km/hr and Car B has been driving for 3 hours at 60 km/hr, so $A = 240$ and $B = 180$. Using the Pythagorean theorem, $240^2 + 180^2 = C^2$, so $C = 300$. Now we can substitute into our derivative equation: $(240)(80) + (180)(60) = (300)\dfrac{dC}{dt}$. If we solve for C, we get: $C = 100$ km/hr.

4. 3 m/s

We are given the rate at which the volume of the fluid is increasing, $\dfrac{dV}{dt} = 108\pi$

and are looking for the rate at which the height of the fluid is increasing, $\dfrac{dh}{dt}$. Thus,

we need to find a way to relate the volume of a cylinder to its height. We know

that the volume of a cylinder is $V = \pi r^2 h$. We will want to take the derivative of

the equation with respect to t. Note that the radius of the tank doesn't change as

the volume changes, therefore r is a constant in this problem, not a variable. We

get: $\dfrac{dV}{dt} = \pi r^2 \dfrac{dh}{dt}$. If we had not recognized that r is a constant and had taken the

derivative of it as well, we would have had terms with (Product Rule!). Because r is

not changing, $\dfrac{dr}{dt} = 0$, and we would have ended up with the same derivative.

Now we can plug in $\dfrac{dV}{dt} = 108\pi$ and $r = 6$, and solve for $\dfrac{dh}{dt}$. We get:

$108\pi = \pi(6)^2 \dfrac{dh}{dt}$. Thus, $\dfrac{dh}{dt} = 3$ m/s.

5. $243\sqrt{3}$ in^2/s

We are given the rate at which the sides of the triangle are increasing, $\dfrac{ds}{dt} = 27$

and are looking for the rate at which the area is increasing, $\dfrac{dA}{dt}$. Thus, we need to find a way to relate the area of an equilateral triangle to the length of a side. We

know that the area of an equilateral triangle in terms of its sides is $A = \dfrac{s^2\sqrt{3}}{4}$. (If

you don't know this formula, memorize it! It will come in very handy in future

math problems.) Now we take the derivative of this equation with respect to t:

$\dfrac{dA}{dt} = \dfrac{\sqrt{3}}{4}(2s)\left(\dfrac{ds}{dt}\right)$. Next, we plug $\dfrac{ds}{dt} = 27$ and $s = 18$ into the derivative and we

get: $\dfrac{dA}{dt} = \dfrac{\sqrt{3}}{4}(36)(27) = 243\sqrt{3}$ in^2/s.

6. $-\dfrac{5}{7}$ in/s

We are given the rate at which the water is flowing out of the container, $\dfrac{dV}{dt} = -35\pi$

(Why is it negative?), and are looking for the rate at which the depth of the water

is dropping, $\dfrac{dh}{dt}$. Thus, we need to find a way to relate the volume of a cone to

its height. We know that the volume of a cone is $V = \dfrac{1}{3}\pi r^2 h$. Notice that we have

a problem. We have a third variable, r in the equation. We cannot treat it as a

constant the way we did in problem 4 because as the volume of a cone changes,

both its height and radius change. But, we also know that, in any cone, the ratio

of the radius to the height is a constant. Here, when the radius is 21 (because the

diameter is 42), the height is 15. Thus, $\dfrac{r}{h} = \dfrac{21}{15} = \dfrac{7}{5}$. We can now isolate r in this

equation: $r = \dfrac{7h}{5}$. Now we can plug it into the volume formula to get rid of r:

$V = \dfrac{1}{3}\pi\left(\dfrac{7h}{5}\right)^2 h$ This simplifies to: $V = \dfrac{49\pi}{75}h^3$. Now we can take the derivative of this equation with respect to t: $\dfrac{dV}{dt} = \dfrac{49\pi}{75}\left(3h^2\right)\dfrac{dh}{dt}$. Next, we plug $\dfrac{dV}{dt} = -35\pi$ and

$h = 5$ into the derivative and we get: $-35\pi = \dfrac{49\pi}{75}\left(3(5)^2\right)\dfrac{dh}{dt}$. Now we can solve for

$\dfrac{dh}{dt}$: $\dfrac{dh}{dt} = -\dfrac{5}{7}$ in/s.

7.　$-\dfrac{25}{6}$ ft/s

We are given the rate at which the length of the rope, R, is changing, $\dfrac{dR}{dt} = -4$ and

are looking for the rate at which the boat, B, is approaching the dock, $\dfrac{dB}{dt}$. The key

to this problem is to realize that the vertical distance from the dock to the bow, the

distance from the boat to the dock, and the length of the rope form a right triangle.

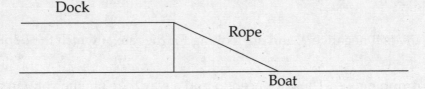

Dock

Rope

Boat

The vertical distance from the dock to the bow is always 7, so, using the

Pythagorean Theorem, we get: $7^2 + B^2 = R^2$. Now we can take the derivative of this

equation with respect to t: $2B\dfrac{dB}{dt} = 2R\dfrac{dR}{dt}$, which simplifies to: $B\dfrac{dB}{dt} = R\dfrac{dR}{dt}$. We

know that $R = 25$ and can use the Pythagorean theorem to find B: $7^2 + B^2 = 25^2$, so

$B = 24$. Now we plug $\dfrac{dR}{dt} = -4$, $R = 25$, and $B = 24$ into the derivative and we get:

$24\dfrac{dB}{dt} = 25(-4)$. Now we can solve for $\dfrac{dB}{dt}$: $\dfrac{dB}{dt} = -\dfrac{25}{6}$ ft/s.

8. $\dfrac{4}{3}$ ft/s

We are given the rate at which the woman is walking away from the street lamp and are looking for the rate at which the length of her shadow is changing. Here, it helps to draw a picture of the situation:

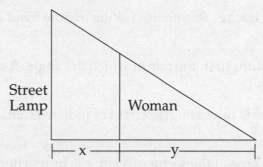

If we label the distant between the woman and the street lamp, x, and the length of the woman's shadow, y, we can use similar triangles to get: $\dfrac{y}{6} = \dfrac{x+y}{24}$. We can cross-multiply and simplify:

$24y = 6x + 6y$

$3y = x$

Next, we take the derivative of the equation with respect to t: $3\dfrac{dy}{dt} = \dfrac{dx}{dt}$. Now we can plug $\dfrac{dx}{dt} = 4$ into the derivative and solve: $\dfrac{dy}{dt} = \dfrac{4}{3}$ ft/s .

9. 380 volts/s

We are given the rate at which the current is decreasing, $\dfrac{dI}{dt} = -4$, and the rate at which the resistance is increasing, $\dfrac{dR}{dt} = 20$, and are looking for the rate at which the voltage is changing. We are also given an equation that relates the three variables: $V = IR$. So, we simply take the derivative of the equation with respect to t (Product Rule!): $\dfrac{dV}{dt} = I\dfrac{dR}{dt} + R\dfrac{dI}{dt}$. Now we can use our equation to find R, which we will need to plug into the derivative equation: $100 = 20R$, so $R = 5$.

Next, we plug $\dfrac{dI}{dt} = -4$, $\dfrac{dR}{dt} = 20$, $I = 20$, and $R = 5$ into the derivative equation:

$\dfrac{dV}{dt} = (20)(20) + (5)(-4) = 380$ volts/s.

10. $\dfrac{3\pi}{5}$ in^2/min

We know that it takes 60 minutes for the minute hand of a clock to make one

complete revolution, so the rate at which the angle, θ, formed by the minute

hand and noon is increasing, in terms of radians/min, is $\dfrac{d\theta}{dt} = \dfrac{2\pi}{60} = \dfrac{\pi}{30}$. Next, we

know that the area of the sector of a circle is proportional to its central angle, so

$\dfrac{\theta}{2\pi} = \dfrac{S}{\pi r^2}$, which can be simplified to $S = \dfrac{1}{2}r^2\theta$.

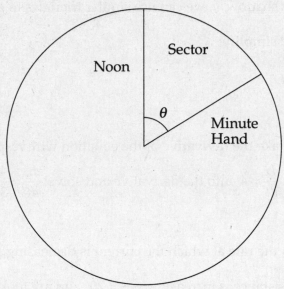

Note that the radius is 6 (the length of the minute hand) and is a constant. Next,

we take the derivative of the equation with respect to t: $\dfrac{dS}{dt} = \dfrac{1}{2}r^2\dfrac{d\theta}{dt}$.

Next we substitute $\dfrac{d\theta}{dt} = \dfrac{\pi}{30}$ into the derivative: $\dfrac{dS}{dt} = \dfrac{1}{2}(6)^2\left(\dfrac{\pi}{30}\right) = \dfrac{3\pi}{5}$ in^2/s.

SOLUTIONS TO PRACTICE PROBLEM SET 13

1. $v(t) = 3t^2 - 18t + 24$; $a(t) = 6t - 18$

   In order to find the velocity function of the particle, we simply take the derivative
   of the position function with respect to t: $\dfrac{dx}{dt} = v(t) = 3t^2 - 18t + 24$. In order to
   find the acceleration function of the particle, we simply take the derivative of the
   velocity function with respect to t: $\dfrac{dv}{dt} = 6t - 18$.

2. $v(t) = 2\cos(2t) - \sin(t)$; $a(t) = -4\sin(2t) - \cos(t)$

   In order to find the velocity function of the particle, we simply take the derivative
   of the position function with respect to t: $\dfrac{dx}{dt} = v(t) = 2\cos(2t) - \sin(t)$. In order to
   find the acceleration function of the particle, we simply take the derivative of the
   velocity function with respect to t: $\dfrac{dv}{dt} = a(t) = -4\sin(2t) - \cos(t)$.

3. $t = 3$

   In order to find where the particle is changing direction, we need to find where

   the velocity of the particle changes sign. The velocity function of the particle is

   the derivative of the position function: $\dfrac{dx}{dt} = v(t) = \dfrac{(t^2 + 9)(1) - (t)(2t)}{(t^2 + 9)^2} = \dfrac{9 - t^2}{(t^2 + 9)^2}$.

   Next, we set the velocity equal to zero. The solutions are: $t = \pm 3$. We can ignore the

   negative solution because t must be positive. Next we check the sign of the velocity

   on either side of $t = 3$. When $0 < t < 3$, the velocity is positive, so the particle is

   moving to the right. When $t > 3$, the velocity is negative, so the particle is moving

   to the left. Therefore, the particle is changing direction at $t = 3$.

4. $t = \pi$ and $t = 3\pi$

In order to find where the particle is changing direction, we need to find where the velocity of the particle changes sign. The velocity function of the particle is the derivative of the position function: $\dfrac{dx}{dt} = v(t) = \dfrac{1}{2}\cos\left(\dfrac{t}{2}\right)$. Next, we set the velocity equal to zero. The solutions are: $t = \pi$ and $t = 3\pi$. Actually, there are an infinite number of solutions but remember that we are restricted to $0 < t < 4\pi$. Next we check the sign of the velocity on the intervals $0 < t < \pi$, $\pi < t < 3\pi$, and $3\pi < t < 4\pi$. When $0 < t < \pi$, the velocity is positive, so the particle is moving to the right. When $\pi < t < 3\pi$, the velocity is negative, so the particle is moving to the left. When $3\pi < t < 4\pi$, the velocity is positive, so the particle is moving to the right. Therefore, the particle is changing direction at $t = \pi$ and $t = 3\pi$.

5. The distance is 69.

In order to find the distance that the particle travels, we need to look at the position of the particle at $t = 2$ and at $t = 5$. We also need to see if the particle changes direction anywhere on the interval between the two times. If so, we will need to look at the particle's position at those "turning points" as well. The way to find out if the particle is changing direction is to look at the velocity of the particle, which we find by taking the derivative of the position function. We get: $\dfrac{dx}{dt} = v(t) = 6t + 2$. If we set the velocity equal to zero, we get $t = -\dfrac{1}{3}$, which is not in the time interval. This means that the velocity doesn't change sign and thus the particle does not change direction. Now we look at the position of the particle on the interval. At $t = 2$, the particle's position is: $x = 3(2)^2 + 2(2) + 4 = 20$. At $t = 5$, the particle's position is: $x = 3(5)^2 + 2(5) + 4 = 89$. Therefore, the particle travels a distance of 69.

6. The distance is 48.

    In order to find the distance that the particle travels, we need to look at the position

    of the particle at $t = 0$ and at $t = 4$. We also need to see if the particle changes

    direction anywhere on the interval between the two times. If so, we will need to

    look at the particle's position at those "turning points" as well. The way to find out

    if the particle is changing direction is to look at the velocity of the particle, which

    we find by taking the derivative of the position function. We get: $\dfrac{dx}{dt} = v(t) = 2t + 8$.

    If we set the velocity equal to zero, we get $t = -4$, which is not in the time interval.

    This means that the velocity doesn't change sign and thus the particle does not

    change direction. Now we look at the position of the particle on the interval. At

    $t = 0$, the particle's position is: $x = (0)^2 + 8(0) = 0$. At $t = 4$, the particle's position is:

    $x = (4)^2 + 8(4) = 48$. Therefore, the particle travels a distance of 48.

7. Velocity is 0; acceleration is 0.

    This should not be a surprise because $2\sin^2 t + 2\cos^2 t = 2$, so the position is a

    constant. This means that the particle is not moving and thus has a velocity and

    acceleration of 0.

8. $t = \dfrac{-8 + \sqrt{70}}{3} \approx 0.122$

    In order to find where the particle is changing direction, we need to find where

    the velocity of the particle changes sign. The velocity function of the particle is the

    derivative of the position function: $\dfrac{dx}{dt} = v(t) = 3t^2 + 16t - 2$. Next, we set the velocity

    equal to zero. The solutions are: $t = \dfrac{-8 + \sqrt{70}}{3}$ and $t = \dfrac{-8 - \sqrt{70}}{3}$. We can eliminate

    the second solution because it is negative and we are restricted to $t > 0$. Next we

    check the sign of the velocity on the intervals $0 < t < \dfrac{-8 + \sqrt{70}}{3}$ and $t > \dfrac{-8 + \sqrt{70}}{3}$.

When $0 < t < \dfrac{-8+\sqrt{70}}{3}$, the velocity is negative, so the particle is moving to the left.

When $t > \dfrac{-8+\sqrt{70}}{3}$, the velocity is positive, so the particle is moving to the right.

Therefore, the particle is changing direction at $t = \dfrac{-8+\sqrt{70}}{3}$.

9. The velocity is never 0, which means that it never changes sign and thus the particle does not change direction.

In order to find where the particle is changing direction, we need to find where the velocity of the particle changes sign. The velocity function of the particle is the derivative of the position function: $\dfrac{dx}{dt} = v(t) = 6t^2 - 12t + 12$. Next, we set the velocity equal to zero. There are no real solutions. If we try a few values, we can see that the velocity is always positive. Therefore, the particle does not change direction.

10. Distance is $2 + \sin^2 4 \approx 2.573$

In order to find the distance that the particle travels, we need to look at the position of the particle at $t = 0$ and at $t = 2$. We also need to see if the particle changes direction anywhere on the interval between the two times. If so, we will need to look at the particle's position at those "turning points" as well. The way to find out if the particle is changing direction is to look at the velocity of the particle, which we find by taking the derivative of the position function. We get: $\dfrac{dx}{dt} = v(t) = 4\sin(2t)\cos(2t)$. If we set the velocity equal to zero, we get $t = \dfrac{\pi}{4}$ and $t = \dfrac{\pi}{2}$. Actually, there are an infinite number of solutions, but remember that we are restricted to $0 < t < 2$. Next we check the sign of the velocity on the intervals

$0 < t < \dfrac{\pi}{4}$, $\dfrac{\pi}{4} < t < \dfrac{\pi}{2}$, and $\dfrac{\pi}{2} < t < 2$. When $0 < t < \dfrac{\pi}{4}$, the velocity is positive, so the particle is moving to the right. When $\dfrac{\pi}{4} < t < \dfrac{\pi}{2}$, the velocity is negative, so the particle is moving to the left. When $\dfrac{\pi}{2} < t < 2$, the velocity is positive, so the particle is moving to the right. Now we look at the position of the particle on the interval.

At $t = 0$, the particle's position is: $x = \sin^2(0) = 0$. At $t = \dfrac{\pi}{4}$, the particle's position is: $x = \sin^2\left(\dfrac{\pi}{2}\right) = 1$. At $t = \dfrac{\pi}{2}$, the particle's position is: $x = \sin^2(\pi) = 0$. And at $t = 2$, the particle's position is: $x = \sin^2(4)$. Therefore, the particle travels a distance of 1 on the interval $0 < t < \dfrac{\pi}{4}$, a distance of 1 in the other direction on the interval $\dfrac{\pi}{4} < t < \dfrac{\pi}{2}$, and a distance of $\sin^2(4)$ on the interval $\dfrac{\pi}{2} < t < 2$. Therefore, the total distance that the particle travels is $2 + \sin^2 4 \approx 2.573$.

SOLUTIONS TO PRACTICE PROBLEM SET 14

1. $f'(x) = \dfrac{4x^3}{x^4 + 8}$

   The rule for finding the derivative of $y = \ln u$ is $\dfrac{dy}{dx} = \dfrac{1}{u}\dfrac{du}{dx}$, where u is a function of x.

   Here, $u = x^4 + 8$. Therefore, the derivative is: $f'(x) = \dfrac{1}{x^4 + 8}(4x^3) = \dfrac{4x^3}{x^4 + 8}$.

2. $f'(x) = \dfrac{1}{x} + \dfrac{1}{6 + 2x}$

   The rule for finding the derivative of $y = \ln u$ is $\dfrac{dy}{dx} = \dfrac{1}{u}\dfrac{du}{dx}$, where u is a function

   of x. Before we find the derivative, we can use the laws of logarithms to

   expand the logarithm. This way, we won't have to use the product rule. We get:

   $\ln(3x\sqrt{3+x}) = \ln 3 + \ln x + \ln\sqrt{3+x} = \ln 3 + \ln x + \dfrac{1}{2}\ln(3+x)$. Now we can find the

   derivative: $f'(x) = 0 + \dfrac{1}{x} + \dfrac{1}{2}\dfrac{1}{3+x} = \dfrac{1}{x} + \dfrac{1}{6+2x}$.

3. $f'(x) = \csc x$

   The rule for finding the derivative of $y = \ln u$ is $\dfrac{dy}{dx} = \dfrac{1}{u}\dfrac{du}{dx}$, where u is a function of x.

   Here $u = \cot x - \csc x$. Therefore, the derivative is:

   $f'(x) = \dfrac{1}{\cot x - \csc x}(-\csc^2 x + \csc x \cot x)$. This can be simplified to:

   $f'(x) = \dfrac{(-\csc x + \cot x)(\csc x)}{\cot x - \csc x} = \csc x$.

4. $f'(x) = \ln(\cos 3x) - 3x \tan 3x - 3x^2$

   The rule for finding the derivative of $y = \ln u$ is $\dfrac{dy}{dx} = \dfrac{1}{u}\dfrac{du}{dx}$, where u is a function of x.

   Here we will use the Product Rule to find the derivative:

   $x\left(\dfrac{1}{\cos 3x}\right)(-3\sin 3x) + (1)\ln\cos 3x - 3x^2$. This simplifies to:

   $f'(x) = \ln(\cos 3x) - 3x \tan 3x - 3x^2$.

5. $f'(x) = \dfrac{2}{x} - \dfrac{x}{5 + x^2}$

The rule for finding the derivative of $y = \ln u$ is $\dfrac{dy}{dx} = \dfrac{1}{u}\dfrac{du}{dx}$, where u is a function of

x. Before we find the derivative, we can use the laws of logarithms to expand the

logarithm. This way, we won't have to use the Product Rule or the Quotient Rule.

We get: $\ln\left(\dfrac{5x^2}{\sqrt{5 + x^2}}\right) = \ln 5 + \ln x^2 - \ln\sqrt{5 + x^2} = \ln 5 + 2\ln x - \dfrac{1}{2}\ln\left(5 + x^2\right)$. Now we

can find the derivative: $f'(x) = 0 + 2\dfrac{1}{x} - \dfrac{1}{2}\dfrac{1}{5 + x^2}(2x) = \dfrac{2}{x} - \dfrac{x}{5 + x^2}$.

6. $f'(x) = e^{x\cos x}(\cos x - x\sin x)$

The rule for finding the derivative of $y = e^u$ is $\dfrac{dy}{dx} = e^u\dfrac{du}{dx}$, where u is a function

of x. Here we will use the Product Rule to find the derivative of the exponent:

$f'(x) = e^{x\cos x}(\cos x - x\sin x)$.

7. $f'(x) = -3e^{-3x}\sin 5x + 5e^{-3x}\cos 5x$

The rule for finding the derivative of $y = e^u$ is $\dfrac{dy}{dx} = e^u\dfrac{du}{dx}$, where u is a

function of x. Here we will use the Product Rule to find the derivative:

$f'(x) = e^{-3x}(-3)\sin 5x + e^{-3x}(5\cos 5x)$, which we can rearrange to

$f'(x) = -3e^{-3x}\sin 5x + 5e^{-3x}\cos 5x$.

8. $f'(x) = e^{\tan 4x}\dfrac{4x\sec^2 4x - 1}{4x^2}$

The rule for finding the derivative of $y = e^u$ is $\dfrac{dy}{dx} = e^u\dfrac{du}{dx}$, where u is a

function of x. Here we will use the Quotient Rule to find the derivative:

$f'(x) = \dfrac{(4x)\left(e^{\tan 4x}\right)\left(4\sec^2 4x\right) - \left(e^{\tan 4x}\right)(4)}{(4x)^2}$. This can be simplified to:

$f'(x) = e^{\tan 4x}\dfrac{4x\sec^2 4x - 1}{4x^2}$.

9. $f'(x) = \pi e^{\pi x} - \pi$

The rule for finding the derivative of $y = e^u$ is $\dfrac{dy}{dx} = e^u \dfrac{du}{dx}$, where u is a function of x

and the rule for finding the derivative of $y = \ln u$ is $\dfrac{dy}{dx} = \dfrac{1}{u}\dfrac{du}{dx}$, where u is a function

of x.

We get: $f'(x) = e^{\pi x}(\pi) - \dfrac{1}{e^{\pi x}}\pi e^{\pi x}$. This can be simplified to $f'(x) = \pi e^{\pi x} - \pi$. You

might have noticed that $\ln e^{\pi x} = \pi x$, which would have made the derivative a little

easier.

10. $f'(x) = \dfrac{3}{x \ln 12}$

The rule for finding the derivative of $y = \log_a u$ is $\dfrac{dy}{dx} = \dfrac{1}{u \ln a}\dfrac{du}{dx}$, where u is a

function of x. Before we find the derivative, we can use the laws of logarithms

to expand the logarithm. We get: $f(x) = \log_{12} x^3 = 3\log_{12} x$. Now we can find the

derivative: $f'(x) = \dfrac{3}{x \ln 12}$

11. $f'(x) = \dfrac{1}{\ln 6}\left(\dfrac{1}{x} + \dfrac{\sec^2 x}{\tan x}\right)$

The rule for finding the derivative of $y = \log_a u$ is $\dfrac{dy}{dx} = \dfrac{1}{u \ln a}\dfrac{du}{dx}$, where u is a

function of x. Before we find the derivative, we can use the laws of logarithms to

expand the logarithm. This way, we won't have to use the Product Rule or the

Quotient Rule. We get: $f(x) = \log_6(3x \tan x) = \log_6 3 + \log_6 x + \log_6 \tan x$. Now we

can find the derivative: $f'(x) = 0 + \dfrac{1}{x \ln 6} + \dfrac{1}{\tan x \ln 6}(\sec^2 x)$. This can be simplified

to: $f'(x) = \dfrac{1}{\ln 6}\left(\dfrac{1}{x} + \dfrac{\sec^2 x}{\tan x}\right)$.

12. $f'(x) = \dfrac{1}{xe^{4x}\ln 4} - \dfrac{4\log_4 x}{e^{4x}}$

The rule for finding the derivative of $y = \log_a u$ is $\dfrac{dy}{dx} = \dfrac{1}{u\ln a}\dfrac{du}{dx}$, and

the rule for finding the derivative of $y = e^u$ is $\dfrac{dy}{dx} = e^u \dfrac{du}{dx}$, where u is a

function of x. Here we will use the Quotient Rule to find the derivative:

$f'(x) = \dfrac{\left(e^{4x}\right)\left(\dfrac{1}{x\ln 4}\right) - \left(\log_4 x\right)\left(e^{4x}\right)\left(4\right)}{\left(e^{4x}\right)^2}$. This can be simplified to:

$f'(x) = \dfrac{1}{xe^{4x}\ln 4} - \dfrac{4\log_4 x}{e^{4x}}$.

13. $f'(x) = \dfrac{3}{2}$

The rule for finding the derivative of $y = \log_a u$ is $\dfrac{dy}{dx} = \dfrac{1}{u\ln a}\dfrac{du}{dx}$, and the rule

for finding the derivative of $y = a^u$ is $\dfrac{dy}{dx} = a^u\left(\ln a\right)\dfrac{du}{dx}$, where u is a function of x.

Before we find the derivative, we can use the laws of logarithms to simplify the

logarithm. Here we get: $f(x) = \dfrac{1}{2}\log 10^{3x}$. Now if you are alert, you will remember

that $\log 10^{3x} = 3x$, so this simplifies to $f(x) = \dfrac{1}{2}3x = \dfrac{3}{2}x$. The derivative is simply

$f'(x) = \dfrac{3}{2}$.

14. $f'(x) = \dfrac{2\ln x}{x\ln 10}$

The rule for finding the derivative of $y = \log_a u$ is $\dfrac{dy}{dx} = \dfrac{1}{u\ln a}\dfrac{du}{dx}$, and the rule for

finding the derivative of $y = \ln u$ is $\dfrac{dy}{dx} = \dfrac{1}{u}\dfrac{du}{dx}$, where u is a function of x. Here we

will use the Product Rule to find the derivative: $f'(x) = \left(\ln x\right)\left(\dfrac{1}{x\ln 10}\right) + \left(\log x\right)\left(\dfrac{1}{x}\right)$.

This can be simplified to $f'(x) = \dfrac{2\ln x}{x\ln 10}$.

15. $f'(x) = 3e^{3x} - 3^{ex}(e)(\ln 3)$

The rule for finding the derivative of $y = e^u$ is $\dfrac{dy}{dx} = e^u \dfrac{du}{dx}$, and the rule for finding

the derivative of $y = a^u$ is $\dfrac{dy}{dx} = a^u (\ln a) \dfrac{du}{dx}$, where u is a function of x. Here we get:

$f'(x) = 3e^{3x} - 3^{ex}(e)(\ln 3)$.

16. $f'(x) = 10^{\sin x}(\cos x)(\ln 10)$

The rule for finding the derivative of $y = a^u$ is $\dfrac{dy}{dx} = a^u (\ln a) \dfrac{du}{dx}$, where u is a

function of x. Here we get: $f'(x) = 10^{\sin x}(\cos x)(\ln 10)$.

17. $f'(x) = 5^{\tan x}(\sec^2 x)\ln 5$

The rule for finding the derivative of $y = a^u$ is $\dfrac{dy}{dx} = a^u (\ln a) \dfrac{du}{dx}$, where u is a

function of x. Here we get: $f'(x) = 5^{\tan x}(\sec^2 x)\ln 5$.

18. $f'(x) = \ln 10$

Before we find the derivative, we can use the laws of logarithms to simplify
the logarithm. We get: $f(x) = \ln(10^x) = x \ln 10$. Now the derivative is simply
$f'(x) = \ln 10$.

19. $f'(x) = x^4 5^x (5 + x \ln 5)$

The rule for finding the derivative of $y = a^u$ is $\dfrac{dy}{dx} = a^u (\ln a) \dfrac{du}{dx}$, where u is

a function of x. Here we will use the product rule to find the derivative:

$f'(x) = x^5 (5^x \ln 5) + (5^x)(5x^4)$, which simplifies to: $f'(x) = x^4 5^x (5 + x \ln 5)$.

SOLUTIONS TO PRACTICE PROBLEM SET 15

1. $\dfrac{16}{15}$

   First, we take the derivative of y: $\dfrac{dy}{dx} = 1 - \dfrac{1}{x^2}$. Next, we find the value of x where

   $y = \dfrac{17}{4} : \dfrac{17}{4} = x + \dfrac{1}{x}$.

   With a little algebra, you should get $x = 4$ or $x = \dfrac{1}{4}$. Because $x > 1$, we can ignore

   the second answer. Or, if you are permitted, use your calculator.

   Now we can use the formula for the derivative of the inverse of $f(x)$ (see page

   125): $\left. \dfrac{d}{dx} f^{-1}(x) \right|_{x=c} = \dfrac{1}{\left[\dfrac{d}{dy} f(y) \right]_{y=a}}$, where $f(a) = c$. This formula means that we find

   the derivative of the inverse of a function at a value a by taking the reciprocal of

   the derivative and plugging in the value of x that makes y equal to a.

   $\left. \dfrac{1}{\dfrac{dy}{dx}} \right|_{x=4} = \left. \dfrac{1}{1 - \dfrac{1}{x^2}} \right|_{x=4} = \dfrac{16}{15}$.

2. $-\dfrac{1}{12}$

   First, we take the derivative of y: $\dfrac{dy}{dx} = 3 - 15x^2$. Next, we find the value of x where

   $y = 2 : 2 = 3x - 5x^3$.

   With a little algebra, you should get $x = -1$. Or, if you are permitted, use your

   calculator.

Now we can use the formula for the derivative of the inverse of $f(x)$ (see page

125): $\dfrac{d}{dx}f^{-1}(x)\Big|_{x=c} = \dfrac{1}{\left[\dfrac{d}{dy}f(y)\right]_{y=a}}$, where $f(a)=c$. This formula means that we find

the derivative of the inverse of a function at a value a by taking the reciprocal of

the derivative and plugging in the value of x that makes y equal to a.

$$\dfrac{1}{\dfrac{dy}{dx}\Big|_{x=-1}} = \dfrac{1}{3-15x^2\Big|_{x=-1}} = -\dfrac{1}{12}.$$

3. $\dfrac{1}{e}$

First, we take the derivative of y: $\dfrac{dy}{dx}=e^x$. Next, we find the value of x where $y=e$:

$e=e^x$. It should be obvious that $x=1$.

Now we can use the formula for the derivative of the inverse of $f(x)$ (see page

125): $\dfrac{d}{dx}f^{-1}(x)\Big|_{x=c} = \dfrac{1}{\left[\dfrac{d}{dy}f(y)\right]_{y=a}}$, where $f(a)=c$. This formula means that we find

the derivative of the inverse of a function at a value a by taking the reciprocal of

the derivative and plugging in the value of x that makes y equal to a.

$$\dfrac{1}{\dfrac{dy}{dx}\Big|_{x=1}} = \dfrac{1}{e^x\Big|_{x=1}} = \dfrac{1}{e}.$$

4. $\dfrac{1}{3}$

First, we take the derivative of $f(x): f'(x) = 7x^6 - 10x^4 + 6x^2$. Next, we find the

value of x where $f(x) = 1: x^7 - 2x^5 + 2x^3 = 1$. You should be able to tell by inspection

that $x = 1$ is a solution. Or, if you are permitted, use your calculator. Remember that

the AP won't give you a problem where it is very difficult to solve for the inverse

value of y. If the algebra looks difficult, look for an obvious solution, such as $x = 0$

or $x = 1$ or $x = -1$.

Now we can use the formula for the derivative of the inverse of $f(x)$ (see page

125): $\dfrac{d}{dx} f^{-1}(x)\bigg|_{x=c} = \dfrac{1}{\left[\dfrac{d}{dy} f(y)\right]_{y=a}}$, where $f(a) = c$. This formula means that we find

the derivative of the inverse of a function at a value a by taking the reciprocal of

the derivative and plugging in the value of x that makes y equal to a.

$$\dfrac{1}{\dfrac{dy}{dx}\bigg|_{x=1}} = \dfrac{1}{7x^6 - 10x^4 + 6x^2\big|_{x=1}} = \dfrac{1}{3}.$$

5. $\dfrac{1}{4}$

First, we take the derivative of $y: \dfrac{dy}{dx} = 1 + 3x^2$. Next, we find the value of x where

$y = -2 : -2 = x + x^3$. You should be able to tell by inspection that $x = -1$ is a solution.

Or, if you are permitted, use your calculator. Remember that the AP won't give you

a problem where it is very difficult to solve for the inverse value of y. If the algebra

looks difficult, look for an obvious solution, such as $x = 0$ or $x = 1$ or $x = -1$.

Now we can use the formula for the derivative of the inverse of $f(x)$ (see page

125): $\dfrac{d}{dx}f^{-1}(x)\Big|_{x=c} = \dfrac{1}{\left[\dfrac{d}{dy}f(y)\right]_{y=a}}$, where $f(a)=c$. This formula means that we find

the derivative of the inverse of a function at a value a by taking the reciprocal of

the derivative and plugging in the value of x that makes y equal to a.

$$\dfrac{1}{\dfrac{dy}{dx}\Big|_{x=-1}} = \dfrac{1}{1+3x^2\Big|_{x=-1}} = \dfrac{1}{4}$$

6. 1

First, we take the derivative of y: $\dfrac{dy}{dx} = 4-3x^2$. Next, we find the value of x where

$y = 3 : 3 = 4x - x^3$. You should be able to tell by inspection that $x = 1$ is a solution.

Or, if you are permitted, use your calculator. Remember that the AP won't give you

a problem where it is very difficult to solve for the inverse value of y. If the algebra

looks difficult, look for an obvious solution, such as $x = 0$ or $x = 1$ or $x = -1$.

Now we can use the formula for the derivative of the inverse of $f(x)$ (see page

125): $\dfrac{d}{dx}f^{-1}(x)\Big|_{x=c} = \dfrac{1}{\left[\dfrac{d}{dy}f(y)\right]_{y=a}}$, where $f(a)=c$. This formula means that we find the derivative of the inverse of a function at a value a by taking the reciprocal of

the derivative and plugging in the value of x that makes y equal to a.

$$\dfrac{1}{\left.\dfrac{dy}{dx}\right|_{x=1}} = \left.\dfrac{1}{4-3x^2}\right|_{x=1} = 1$$

7. 1

First, we take the derivative of y: $\dfrac{dy}{dx} = \dfrac{1}{x}$. Next, we find the value of x where $y = 0$:

$\ln x = 0$. You should know that $x = 1$ is the solution. Now we can use the formula

for the derivative of the inverse of $f(x)$ (see page 125): $\left.\dfrac{d}{dx} f^{-1}(x)\right|_{x=c} = \dfrac{1}{\left[\dfrac{d}{dy} f(y)\right]_{y=a}}$,

where $f(a) = c$. This formula means that we find the derivative of the inverse of a

function at a value a by taking the reciprocal of the derivative and plugging in the

value of x that makes y equal to a.

$$\dfrac{1}{\left.\dfrac{dy}{dx}\right|_{x=1}} = \left.\dfrac{1}{\dfrac{1}{x}}\right|_{x=1} = 1$$

8. $\dfrac{15}{8}$

First, we take the derivative of y: $\dfrac{dy}{dx} = \dfrac{1}{3} x^{-\frac{2}{3}} + \dfrac{1}{5} x^{-\frac{4}{5}}$. Next, we find the value of x

where $y = 2$: $x^{\frac{1}{3}} + x^{\frac{1}{5}} = 2$. You should be able to tell by inspection that $x = 1$ is a

solution. Or, if you are permitted, use your calculator. Remember that the AP won't

give you a problem where it is very difficult to solve for the inverse value of y. If

the algebra looks difficult, look for an obvious solution, such as $x = 0$ or $x = 1$ or

$x = -1$.

Now we can use the formula for the derivative of the inverse of $f(x)$ (see page

125): $\dfrac{d}{dx} f^{-1}(x)\bigg|_{x=c} = \dfrac{1}{\left[\dfrac{d}{dy} f(y)\right]_{y=a}}$, where $f(a) = c$. This formula means that we find

the derivative of the inverse of a function at a value a by taking the reciprocal of

the derivative and plugging in the value of x that makes y equal to a.

$$\dfrac{1}{\dfrac{dy}{dx}\bigg|_{x=1}} = \dfrac{1}{\dfrac{1}{3}x^{-\frac{2}{3}} + \dfrac{1}{5}x^{-\frac{4}{5}}\bigg|_{x=1}} = \dfrac{15}{8}$$

SOLUTIONS TO PRACTICE PROBLEM SET 16

1. $x - y^2$

    Recall the trigonometric identity $1 + \tan^2\theta = \sec^2\theta$ (see page 867). We can rewrite this identity as $\tan^2\theta = \sec^2\theta - 1$. Here, we are given that $x = \sec^2 t - 1$ and $y = \tan t$. Using this identity and plugging in our parametric equations, we get the equation: $x = y^2$.

2. $y = \sqrt{1 - x^2}$

    Here we are given that $x = t$ and $y = \sqrt{1 - t^2}$. We can simply substitute x for t in the equation for y and we get: $y = \sqrt{1 - x^2}$.

3. $y = x^2 - 6x$

    Here we are given that $x = 4t + 3$ and $y = 16t^2 - 9$. If we take the equation for x and isolate $4t$, we get: $x - 3 = 4t$. Next, because $(4t)^2 = 16t^2$, we can substitute into the equation for y. We get: $y = (x - 3)^2 - 9$. This can be simplified to $y = x^2 - 6x$.

4. $y - 48 = \dfrac{2}{3}(x - 40)$

    We could first come up with an equation for y in terms of x by eliminating the parameter, but this is often more time-consuming than necessary. Instead, we first find the slope of the tangent line using the formula $\dfrac{dy}{dx} = \dfrac{\dfrac{dy}{dt}}{\dfrac{dx}{dt}}$. Taking the derivative of each equation with respect to t, we get: $\dfrac{dy}{dt} = 8$ and $\dfrac{dx}{dt} = 2t$. Therefore,

    $\dfrac{dy}{dx} = \dfrac{8}{2t} = \dfrac{4}{t}$. If we evaluate this at $t = 6$, we get: $\dfrac{dy}{dx} = \dfrac{4}{6} = \dfrac{2}{3}$.

    At $t = 6$, we know that $y = 48$ and $x = 40$. Now we can find the equation of the

    tangent line: $y - 48 = \dfrac{2}{3}(x - 40)$.

5. $y - 1 = \sqrt{2}\left(x - \sqrt{2}\right)$

We could first come up with an equation for y in terms of x by eliminating

the parameter, but this is often more time consuming than necessary. Instead,

we first find the slope of the tangent line using the formula $\dfrac{dy}{dx} = \dfrac{dy/dt}{dx/dt}$. Taking

the derivative of each equation with respect to t, we get: $\dfrac{dy}{dt} = \sec^2 t$ and

$\dfrac{dx}{dt} = \sec t \tan t$. Therefore, $\dfrac{dy}{dx} = \dfrac{\sec^2 t}{\sec t \tan t} = \dfrac{\sec t}{\tan t}$. If we evaluate this at $t = \dfrac{\pi}{4}$, we get:

$\dfrac{dy}{dx} = \dfrac{\sec \dfrac{\pi}{4}}{\tan \dfrac{\pi}{4}} = \dfrac{\sqrt{2}}{1} = \sqrt{2}$.

At $t = \dfrac{\pi}{4}$, we know that $y = \tan \dfrac{\pi}{4} = 1$ and $x = \sec \dfrac{\pi}{4} = \sqrt{2}$. Now we can find the

equation of the tangent line: $y - 1 = \sqrt{2}\left(x - \sqrt{2}\right)$.

6. $(-2, 7)$

The particle's direction will be horizontal when it is only moving in the x direction.

In other words, when $\dfrac{dy}{dt} = 0$. We take the derivative of y with respect to t:

$\dfrac{dy}{dt} = 3t^2 - 3$. If we set this equal to zero and solve, we get: $3t^2 - 3 = 0$ and $t = \pm 1$.

We can ignore the negative solution because t must be positive. Now, in order to

find the coordinates of the particle, we simply plug $t = 1$ into the equations of the

particle's position. We get: $x = -2(1)^2 = -2$ and $y = (1)^3 - 3(1) + 9 = 7$. Therefore, the

particle's position is $(-2, 7)$.

7. $\left(\ln 2, -4\right)$

The particle's direction will be horizontal when it is only moving in the x direction. In other words, when $\frac{dy}{dt} = 0$. We take the derivative of y with respect to t: $\frac{dy}{dt} = 2t - 4$. If we set this equal to zero and solve, we get: $2t - 4 = 0$ and $t = 2$. Now, in order to find the coordinates of the particle, we simply plug $t = 2$ into the equations of the particle's position. We get: $x = \ln 2$ and $y = \left(2\right)^2 - 4\left(2\right) = -4$. Therefore, the particle's position is $\left(\ln 2, -4\right)$.

8. $t = \dfrac{2\pi}{3}, \dfrac{4\pi}{3}$

We find the horizontal and vertical components of the particle's velocity by taking the derivative of each parametric equation with respect to t. We get: $x = 2\cos t$ and $y = \cos t - \dfrac{1}{2}$. If we set these equal to each other, we get: $\cos t - \dfrac{1}{2} = 2\cos t$, which can be simplified to $\cos t = -\dfrac{1}{2}$. If we solve this, we get: $t = \dfrac{2\pi}{3}, \dfrac{4\pi}{3}$. Note that there are actually an infinite number of solutions, but note that we are restricted to $0 \le t \le 2\pi$.

SOLUTIONS TO PRACTICE PROBLEM SET 17

1. $\dfrac{3}{4}$

   Recall L'Hôpital's Rule: If $f(c) = g(c) = 0$, or if $f(c) = g(c) = \infty$, and if $f'(c)$

   and $g'(c)$ exist, and if $g'(c) \neq 0$, then $\lim\limits_{x \to c} \dfrac{f(x)}{g(x)} = \lim\limits_{x \to c} \dfrac{f'(x)}{g'(x)}$ (page 134). Here,

   $f(x) = \sin 3x$ and $g(x) = \sin 4x$, and $\sin 0 = 0$. This means that we can use

   L'Hôpital's Rule to find the limit. We take the derivative of the numerator and

   the denominator: $\lim\limits_{x \to 0} \dfrac{\sin 3x}{\sin 4x} = \lim\limits_{x \to 0} \dfrac{3\cos 3x}{4\cos 4x}$. If we take the new limit, we get:

   $\lim\limits_{x \to 0} \dfrac{3\cos 3x}{4\cos 4x} = \dfrac{3\cos 0}{4\cos 0} = \dfrac{(3)(1)}{(4)(1)} = \dfrac{3}{4}$.

2. 1

   Recall L'Hôpital's Rule: If $f(c) = g(c) = 0$, or if $f(c) = g(c) = \infty$, and if $f'(c)$

   and $g'(c)$ exist, and if $g'(c) \neq 0$, then $\lim\limits_{x \to c} \dfrac{f(x)}{g(x)} = \lim\limits_{x \to c} \dfrac{f'(x)}{g'(x)}$ (page 134). Here,

   $f(x) = x - \pi$ and $g(x) = \sin x$. We can see that $x - \pi = 0$ when $x = \pi$, and that

   $\sin \pi = 0$. This means that we can use L'Hôpital's Rule to find the limit. We take the

   derivative of the numerator and the denominator: $\lim\limits_{x \to 0} \dfrac{x - \pi}{\sin x} = \lim\limits_{x \to 0} \dfrac{1}{\cos x}$. If we take

   the new limit, we get: $\lim\limits_{x \to 0} \dfrac{1}{\cos x} = \dfrac{1}{\cos 0} = \dfrac{1}{1} = 1$.

3. $\dfrac{1}{6}$

Recall L'Hôpital's Rule: If $f(c) = g(c) = 0$, or if $f(c) = g(c) = \infty$, and if $f'(c)$

and $g'(c)$ exist, and if $g'(c) \neq 0$, then $\lim\limits_{x \to c} \dfrac{f(x)}{g(x)} = \lim\limits_{x \to c} \dfrac{f'(x)}{g'(x)}$ (page 134). Here,

$f(x) = x - \sin x$ and $g(x) = x^3$. We can see that $x - \sin x = 0$ when $x = 0$, and that

$0^3 = 0$. This means that we can use L'Hôpital's Rule to find the limit. We take the

derivative of the numerator and the denominator: $\lim\limits_{x \to 0} \dfrac{x - \sin x}{x^3} = \lim\limits_{x \to 0} \dfrac{1 - \cos x}{3x^2}$.

If we take the new limit, we get: $\lim\limits_{x \to 0} \dfrac{1 - \cos x}{3x^2} = \dfrac{1 - \cos 0}{3(0)^2} = \dfrac{1 - 1}{0} = \dfrac{0}{0}$. But this is

still indeterminate, so what do we do? Use L'Hôpital's Rule again! We take the

derivative of the numerator and the denominator: $\lim\limits_{x \to 0} \dfrac{1 - \cos x}{3x^2} = \lim\limits_{x \to 0} \dfrac{\sin x}{6x}$. If

we take the limit, we get: $\lim\limits_{x \to 0} \dfrac{\sin x}{6x} = \dfrac{\sin 0}{6(0)} = \dfrac{0}{0}$. We need to use L'Hôpital's Rule

one more time. We get: $\lim\limits_{x \to 0} \dfrac{\sin x}{6x} = \lim\limits_{x \to 0} \dfrac{\cos x}{6}$. Now if we take the limit, we get:

$\lim\limits_{x \to 0} \dfrac{\cos x}{6} = \dfrac{\cos 0}{6} = \dfrac{1}{6}$. Notice that if L'Hôpital's Rule results in an indeterminate

form, we can use the rule again and again (but not infinitely often).

4. -2

Recall L'Hôpital's Rule: If $f(c) = g(c) = 0$, or if $f(c) = g(c) = \infty$, and if $f'(c)$

and $g'(c)$ exist, and if $g'(c) \neq 0$, then $\lim\limits_{x \to c} \dfrac{f(x)}{g(x)} = \lim\limits_{x \to c} \dfrac{f'(x)}{g'(x)}$ (page 134). Here,

$f(x) = e^{3x} - e^{5x}$ and $g(x) = x$. We can see that $e^{3x} - e^{5x} = 0$ when $x = 0$, and that the denominator is obviously zero at $x = 0$. This means that we can use

L'Hôpital's Rule to find the limit. We take the derivative of the numerator and

the denominator: $\lim\limits_{x \to 0} \dfrac{e^{3x} - e^{5x}}{x} = \lim\limits_{x \to 0} \dfrac{3e^{3x} - 5e^{5x}}{1}$. If we take the new limit, we get:

$\lim\limits_{x \to 0} \dfrac{3e^{3x} - 5e^{5x}}{1} = \dfrac{3e^0 - 5e^0}{1} = \dfrac{3(1) - 5(1)}{1} = -2$.

5. -2

Recall L'Hôpital's Rule: If $f(c) = g(c) = 0$, or if $f(c) = g(c) = \infty$, and if $f'(c)$

and $g'(c)$ exist, and if $g'(c) \ne 0$, then $\lim\limits_{x \to c} \dfrac{f(x)}{g(x)} = \lim\limits_{x \to c} \dfrac{f'(x)}{g'(x)}$ (page 134).

Here, $f(x) = \tan x - x$ and $g(x) = \sin x - x$. We can see that $\tan x - x = 0$

and $\sin x - x = 0$ when $x = 0$. This means that we can use L'Hôpital's

Rule to find the limit. We take the derivative of the numerator and the

denominator: $\lim\limits_{x \to 0} \dfrac{\tan x - x}{\sin x - x} = \lim\limits_{x \to 0} \dfrac{\sec^2 x - 1}{\cos x - 1}$. If we take the new limit, we get:

$\lim\limits_{x \to 0} \dfrac{\sec^2 x - 1}{\cos x - 1} = \dfrac{\sec^2(0) - 1}{\cos(0) - 1} = \dfrac{1 - 1}{1 - 1} = \dfrac{0}{0}$. But this is still indeterminate, so what do

we do? Use L'Hôpital's Rule again! We take the derivative of the numerator and the denominator: $\lim\limits_{x\to 0}\dfrac{\sec^2 x - 1}{\cos x - 1} = \lim\limits_{x\to 0}\dfrac{2\sec x(\sec x \tan x)}{\sin x} = \lim\limits_{x\to 0}\dfrac{2\sec^2 x \tan x}{-\sin x}$. If we

take the limit, we get: $\lim\limits_{x\to 0}\dfrac{2\sec^2(0)\tan(0)}{-\sin(0)} = \dfrac{0}{0}$. At this point you might be getting

nervous as the derivatives start to get messier. Let's try using trigonometric

identities to simplify the limit. If we rewrite the numerator in terms of $\sin x$

and $\cos x$, we get: $\dfrac{2\sec^2 x \tan x}{-\sin x} = \dfrac{2\left(\dfrac{1}{\cos^2 x}\right)\left(\dfrac{\sin x}{\cos x}\right)}{-\sin x}$. We can simplify this to:

$\dfrac{2\left(\dfrac{1}{\cos^2 x}\right)\left(\dfrac{\sin x}{\cos x}\right)}{-\sin x} = -2\dfrac{\dfrac{\sin x}{\cos^3 x}}{\sin x}$. This simplifies to: $-2\dfrac{\sin x}{\cos^3 x}\dfrac{1}{\sin x} = \dfrac{-2}{\cos^3 x}$. Now if we

take the limit: $\lim\limits_{x\to 0}\dfrac{-2}{\cos^3 x} = \dfrac{-2}{\cos^3(0)} = \dfrac{-2}{1^3} = -2$.

Note that we could have used trigonometric identities on either of the first two limits as well. Remember that when you have a limit that is an indeterminate form, you can sometimes use algebra or trigonometric identities (or both) to simplify the limit. Sometimes this will get rid of the problem.

6. 0

Recall L'Hôpital's Rule: If $f(c) = g(c) = 0$, or if $f(c) = g(c) = \infty$, and if $f'(c)$ and

$g'(c)$ exist, and if $g'(c) \neq 0$, then $\lim\limits_{x\to c}\dfrac{f(x)}{g(x)} = \lim\limits_{x\to c}\dfrac{f'(x)}{g'(x)}$ (page 134). Here, $f(x) = x^5$

and $g(x) = e^{5x}$. We can see that $x^5 = \infty$ when $x = \infty$, and that $e^\infty = \infty$. This means

that we can use L'Hôpital's Rule to find the limit. We take the derivative of the numerator and the denominator: $\lim\limits_{x\to\infty}\dfrac{x^5}{e^{5x}}=\lim\limits_{x\to\infty}\dfrac{5x^4}{5e^{5x}}=\lim\limits_{x\to\infty}\dfrac{x^4}{e^{5x}}$. If we take the

new limit, we get: $\lim\limits_{x\to 0}\dfrac{x^4}{e^{5x}}=\dfrac{\infty}{\infty}$. But this is still indeterminate, so what do we do?

Use L'Hôpital's Rule again! We take the derivative of the numerator and the

denominator: $\lim\limits_{x\to\infty}\dfrac{x^4}{e^{5x}}=\lim\limits_{x\to\infty}\dfrac{4x^3}{5e^{5x}}$. We are going to need to use L'Hôpital's Rule

again. In fact, we can see that each time we use the rule we are reducing the

power of the x in the numerator and that we are going to need to keep doing so

until the x term is gone. Let's take the derivative: $\lim\limits_{x\to\infty}\dfrac{4x^3}{5e^{5x}}=\lim\limits_{x\to\infty}\dfrac{12x^2}{25e^{5x}}$. And again:

$\lim\limits_{x\to\infty}\dfrac{12x^2}{25e^{5x}}=\lim\limits_{x\to\infty}\dfrac{24x}{125e^{5x}}$. And one more time: $\lim\limits_{x\to\infty}\dfrac{24x}{125e^{5x}}=\lim\limits_{x\to\infty}\dfrac{24}{625e^{5x}}$. Now if we

take the limit, we get: $\lim\limits_{x\to\infty}\dfrac{24}{625e^{5x}}=0$. Notice that if L'Hôpital's Rule results in an

indeterminate form, we can use the rule again and again (but not infinitely often).

7. $\dfrac{1}{7}$

Recall L'Hôpital's Rule: If $f(c)=g(c)=0$, or if $f(c)=g(c)=\infty$, and if $f'(c)$

and $g'(c)$ exist, and if $g'(c)\neq 0$, then $\lim\limits_{x\to c}\dfrac{f(x)}{g(x)}=\lim\limits_{x\to c}\dfrac{f'(x)}{g'(x)}$ (page 134). Here,

$f(x)=x^5+4x^3-8$ and $g(x)=7x^5-3x^2-1$. We can see that $x^5+4x^3-8=\infty$

and $7x^5-3x^2-1=\infty$ when $x=\infty$. This means that we can use L'Hôpital's

Rule to find the limit. We take the derivative of the numerator and the

denominator: $\lim\limits_{x\to\infty}\dfrac{x^5+4x^3-8}{7x^5-3x^2-1}=\lim\limits_{x\to\infty}\dfrac{5x^4+12x^2}{35x^4-6x}$. If we take the new limit, we gct: $\lim\limits_{x\to\infty}\dfrac{5x^4+12x^2}{35x^4-6x}=\dfrac{\infty}{\infty}$. But this is still indeterminate, so what do we do?

Use L'Hôpital's Rule again! We take the derivative of the numerator and the

denominator: $\lim\limits_{x\to\infty}\dfrac{5x^4+12x^2}{35x^4-6x}=\lim\limits_{x\to\infty}\dfrac{20x^3+24x}{140x^3-6}$. We are going to need to use

L'Hôpital's Rule again. In fact, we can see that each time we use the rule we are

reducing the power of the x terms in the numerator and denominator and that

we are going to need to keep doing so until the x terms are gone. Let's take the

derivative: $\lim\limits_{x\to\infty}\dfrac{20x^3+24x}{140x^3-6}=\lim\limits_{x\to\infty}\dfrac{60x^2+24}{420x^2}$. And again: $\lim\limits_{x\to\infty}\dfrac{60x^2+24}{420x^2}=\lim\limits_{x\to\infty}\dfrac{120x}{840x}$.

Now we can take the limit: $\lim\limits_{x\to\infty}\dfrac{120x}{840x}=\lim\limits_{x\to\infty}\dfrac{1}{7}=\dfrac{1}{7}$. Notice that if L'Hôpital's Rule

results in an indeterminate form, we can use the rule again and again (but not

infinitely often).

8.   1

Recall L'Hôpital's Rule: If $f(c)=g(c)=0$, or if $f(c)=g(c)=\infty$, and if $f'(c)$

and $g'(c)$ exist, and if $g'(c)\neq 0$, then $\lim\limits_{x\to c}\dfrac{f(x)}{g(x)}=\lim\limits_{x\to c}\dfrac{f'(x)}{g'(x)}$ (page 134). Here,

$f(x)=\ln(\sin x)$ and $g(x)=\ln(\tan x)$, and that both of these approach infinity

as x approaches 0 from the right. This means that we can use L'Hôpital's Rule to find the limit. We take the derivative of the numerator and the denominator:

$$\lim_{x \to 0^+} \frac{\ln(\sin x)}{\ln(\tan x)} = \lim_{x \to 0^+} \frac{\dfrac{\cos x}{\sin x}}{\dfrac{\sec^2 x}{\tan x}}$$. Let's use trigonometric identities to simplify the limit:

$$\frac{\dfrac{\cos x}{\sin x}}{\dfrac{\sec^2 x}{\tan x}} = \frac{\cos x}{\sin x} \frac{\tan x}{\sec^2 x} = \frac{\cos x}{\sin x} \frac{\dfrac{\sin x}{\cos x}}{\sec^2 x} = \frac{1}{\sec^2 x}$$. Now if we take the new limit, we get:

$$\lim_{x \to 0^+} \frac{1}{\sec^2 x} = 1 .$$

9. $\dfrac{1}{2}$

Recall L'Hôpital's Rule: If $f(c) = g(c) = 0$, or if $f(c) = g(c) = \infty$, and if $f'(c)$

and $g'(c)$ exist, and if $g'(c) \neq 0$, then $\lim_{x \to c} \dfrac{f(x)}{g(x)} = \lim_{x \to c} \dfrac{f'(x)}{g'(x)}$ (page 134). Here,

$f(x) = \cot 2x$ and $g(x) = \cot x$, and that both of these approach infinity as x

approaches 0 from the right. This means that we can use L'Hôpital's Rule to

find the limit. We take the derivative of the numerator and the denominator:

$$\lim_{x \to 0^+} \frac{\cot 2x}{\cot x} = \lim_{x \to 0^+} \frac{-2 \cot 2x \csc 2x}{-\cot x \csc x}$$. This seems to be worse than what we

started with. Instead, let's use trigonometric identities to simplify the limit:

$$\frac{\cot 2x}{\cot x} = \frac{\dfrac{\cos 2x}{\sin 2x}}{\dfrac{\cos x}{\sin x}} = \frac{\cos 2x}{\sin 2x} \frac{\sin x}{\cos x} = \frac{\cos^2 x - \sin^2 x}{2 \sin x \cos x} \frac{\sin x}{\cos x}$$. Notice that our problem

is with sin x as x approaches zero (because it becomes zero), not with cos x.

As long as we are multiplying the numerator and denominator by $\sin x$, we

are going to get an indeterminate form. So, thanks to trigonometric identities,

we can eliminate the problem term: $\dfrac{\cos^2 x - \sin^2 x}{2 \sin x \cos x} \dfrac{\sin x}{\cos x} = \dfrac{\cos^2 x - \sin^2 x}{2 \cos^2 x}$.

If we take the limit of this expression, it is not indeterminate. We get:

$\displaystyle\lim_{x \to 0^+} \dfrac{\cos^2 x - \sin^2 x}{2 \cos^2 x} = \dfrac{\cos^2 0 - \sin^2 0}{2 \cos^2 0} = \dfrac{1^2 - 0}{2(1^2)} = \dfrac{1}{2}$. Notice that we didn't need to

use L'Hôpital's Rule here. You should bear in mind that just because a limit is

indeterminate does not mean that the best way to evaluate it is with L'Hôpital's

Rule.

10. 1

Recall L'Hôpital's Rule: If $f(c) = g(c) = 0$, or if $f(c) = g(c) = \infty$, and if $f'(c)$ and

$g'(c)$ exist, and if $g'(c) \neq 0$, then $\displaystyle\lim_{x \to c} \dfrac{f(x)}{g(x)} = \lim_{x \to c} \dfrac{f'(x)}{g'(x)}$ (page 134). Here, $f(x) = x$

and $g(x) = \ln(x+1)$, and that both of these approach zero as x approaches 0 from

the right. This means that we can use L'Hôpital's Rule to find the limit. We take the

derivative of the numerator and the denominator: $\displaystyle\lim_{x \to 0^+} \dfrac{1}{\dfrac{1}{x+1}} = \lim_{x \to 0^+}(x+1)$. Now if we

take the new limit, we get: $\displaystyle\lim_{x \to 0^+}(x+1) = 1$.

SOLUTIONS TO PRACTICE PROBLEM SET 18

1. 5.002

    Recall the differential formula that we use for approximating the value of a

    function: $f(x + \Delta x) \approx f(x) + f'(x)\Delta x$ (page 139). Here, we want to approximate the

    value of $\sqrt{25.02}$, so we'll use $f(x) = \sqrt{x}$ with $x = 25$ and $\Delta x = .02$. First we need to

    find $f'(x)$: $f'(x) = \dfrac{1}{2\sqrt{x}}$. Now we plug into the formula: $f(x + \Delta x) \approx \sqrt{x} + \dfrac{1}{2\sqrt{x}} \Delta x$. If

    we plug in $x = 25$ and $\Delta x = .02$, we get: $\sqrt{25 + .02} \approx \sqrt{25} + \dfrac{1}{2\sqrt{25}}(.02)$. If we evaluate

    this, we get: $\sqrt{25.02} \approx 5 + \dfrac{1}{10}(.02) = 5.002$.

2. 3.999375

    Recall the differential formula that we use for approximating the value

    of a function: $f(x + \Delta x) \approx f(x) + f'(x)\Delta x$ (page 139). Here, we want to

    approximate the value of $\sqrt{63.97}$, so we'll use $f(x) = \sqrt[3]{x}$ with $x = 64$

    and $\Delta x = -.03$. First we need to find $f'(x)$: $f'(x) = \dfrac{1}{3}x^{-\frac{2}{3}} = \dfrac{1}{3\sqrt[3]{x^2}}$. Now we

    plug into the formula: $f(x + \Delta x) \approx \sqrt[3]{x} + \dfrac{1}{3\sqrt[3]{x^2}} \Delta x$. If we plug in $x = 64$ and

    $\Delta x = -.03$, we get: $\sqrt[3]{64 - .03} \approx \sqrt[3]{64} + \dfrac{1}{3\sqrt[3]{64^2}}(-.03)$. If we evaluate this, we get:

    $\sqrt[3]{63.97} \approx 4 + \dfrac{1}{48}(-.03) = 3.999375$.

3. 1.802

Recall the differential formula that we use for approximating the value of a

function: $f(x + \Delta x) \approx f(x) + f'(x)\Delta x$ (page 139). Here, we want to approximate

the value of tan61°. Be careful! Whenever we work with trigonometric

functions, it is *very* important to work with radians, *not* degrees! Remember

that $60° = \dfrac{\pi}{3}$ radians and $1° = \dfrac{\pi}{180}$ radians, so we'll use $f(x) = \tan x$ with $x = \dfrac{\pi}{3}$

and $\Delta x = \dfrac{\pi}{180}$. First we need to find $f'(x)$: $f'(x) = \sec^2 x$. Now we plug into

the formula: $f(x + \Delta x) \approx \tan x + \dfrac{1}{\sec^2 x}\Delta x$. If we plug in $x = \dfrac{\pi}{3}$ and $\Delta x = \dfrac{\pi}{180}$,

we get: $\tan\left(\dfrac{\pi}{3} + \dfrac{\pi}{180}\right) \approx \tan\left(\dfrac{\pi}{3}\right) + \sec^2\left(\dfrac{\pi}{3}\right)\left(\dfrac{\pi}{180}\right)$. If we evaluate this, we get:

$\tan\left(\dfrac{61\pi}{180}\right) \approx \sqrt{3} + (2)^2\left(\dfrac{\pi}{180}\right) \approx 1.802$.

4. 997
    Recall the differential formula that we use for approximating the value of a
    function: $f(x + \Delta x) \approx f(x) + f'(x)\Delta x$ (page 139). Here, we want to approximate the
    value of $(9.99)^3$, so we'll use $f(x) = x^3$ with $x = 10$ and $\Delta x = -.01$. First we need to find
    $f'(x)$: $f'(x) = 3x^2$. Now we plug into the formula: $f(x + \Delta x) \approx x^3 + 3x^2\Delta x$. If we plug in
    $x = 10$ and $\Delta x = -.01$, we get: $(10 - .01)^3 \approx (10)^3 + 3(10)^2(-.01)$. If we evaluate this, we
    get: $(9.99)^3 \approx 1000 + 3(10)^2(-.01) = 997$.

5. ±2.16 in³
    Recall the formula that we use when we want to approximate the error in a
    measurement: $dy = f'(x)dx$. Here we want to approximate the error in the volume of
    a cube when we know that it has a side of length 6 in. with an error of
    ±.02 in., where $V(x) = x^3$ (the volume of a cube of side x) with $dx = ±.02$. We find the
    derivative of the volume: $V'(x) = 3x^2$. Now we can plug into the formula:
    $dV = 3x^2dx$. If we plug in $x = 6$ and $dx = ±.02$, we get: $dV = 3(6)^2(±.02) = ±2.16$.

6. $\pi \approx 3.142$ mm^3

Recall the formula that we use when we want to approximate the error in a measurement: $dy = f'(x)dx$. Here we want to approximate the increase in the volume of a sphere when we know that it has a radius of length 5 mm with an increase of .01 mm, where $V(r) = \frac{4}{3}\pi r^3$ (the volume of a sphere of radius r) with $dr = .01$. We find the derivative of the volume: $V'(r) = \frac{4}{3}\pi(3r^2) = 4\pi r^2$. Now we can plug into the formula: $dV = 4\pi r^2 dr$. If we plug in $r = 5$ and $dr = .01$, we get:

$dV = 4\pi(5)^2(.01) = \pi \approx 3.142$.

7. -1.732 cm^2

Recall the formula that we use when we want to approximate the error in a measurement: $dy = f'(x)dx$. Here we want to approximate the decrease in the area of an equilateral triangle when we know that it has a side of length 10 cm with a decrease of .2 cm, where $A(x) = \frac{x^2\sqrt{3}}{4}$ (the area of an equilateral triangle of side x) with $dx = -.2$. We find the derivative of the area: $A'(x) = \frac{2x\sqrt{3}}{4} = \frac{x\sqrt{3}}{2}$. Now we can plug into the formula: $dA = \frac{x\sqrt{3}}{2} dx$. If we plug in $x = 10$ and $dx = -.2$, we get:

$dA = \frac{10\sqrt{3}}{2}(-.2) = -\sqrt{3} \approx -1.732$.

8. (a) 1.963 m^3;   (b) 15.708 m^3
    (a) Recall the formula that we use when we want to approximate the error in a measurement: $dy = f'(x)dx$. Here we want to approximate the error in the volume of a cylinder when we know that it has a diameter of length 5 m (which means that its radius is 2.5 m) and its height is 20 m, with an error in the height of .1 m, where $V = \pi r^2 h$ with $dh = .1$. Note that the radius is exact, so when we take the derivative we will only treat the height as a variable. We find the derivative of the volume: $V' = \pi r^2$. Now we can plug into the formula: $dV = \pi r^2 dh$. If we plug in $r = 2.5$, $h = 20$ and $dh = .1$, we get: $dV = \pi(2.5)^2(.1) = .625\pi \approx 1.963$.

(b) Here we want to approximate the error in the volume of a cylinder when we know that it has a diameter of length 5 m (which means that its radius is 2.5 m) and its height is 20 m, with an error in the diameter of .1 m (which means that the error in the radius is .05 m), where $V = \pi r^2 h$ with $dr = .05$. Note that the height is exact, so when we take the derivative we will only treat the radius as a variable. We find the derivative of the volume: $V' = 2\pi rh$. Now we can plug into the formula: $dV = 2\pi rhdh$. If we plug in $r = 2.5$, $h = 20$ and $dr = .05$, we get: $dV = 2\pi(2.5)(20)(.05) = 5\pi \approx 15.708$.

SOLUTIONS TO PRACTICE PROBLEM SET 19

1. $y\left[\dfrac{1}{x}-\dfrac{3x^2}{4\left(1-x^3\right)}\right]$

Anytime we are presented with finding the derivative of a complex expression, we

look to see if we can use logarithmic differentiation to simplify the problem. Often,

doing so means that we can avoid a messy expression involving the Product,

Quotient, or Chain Rules. We always do the same four steps:

Step One: Take the log of both sides: $\ln y = \ln\left(x\sqrt[4]{1-x^3}\right)$.

Step Two: Simplify the expression using Log Rules:

$\ln y = \ln x + \ln\left(\sqrt[4]{1-x^3}\right)$

$\ln y = \ln x + \dfrac{1}{4}\ln\left(1-x^3\right)$

Step Three: Take the derivative of both sides: $\dfrac{1}{y}\dfrac{dy}{dx}=\dfrac{1}{x}+\dfrac{1}{4}\dfrac{-3x^2}{1-x^3}=\dfrac{1}{x}-\dfrac{3x^2}{4\left(1-x^3\right)}$.

Step Four: Multiply both sides by y: $\dfrac{dy}{dx}=y\left[\dfrac{1}{x}-\dfrac{-3x^2}{4\left(1-x^3\right)}\right]$.

2. $\dfrac{y}{2}\left[\dfrac{1}{1+x}+\dfrac{1}{1-x}\right]$

Anytime we are presented with finding the derivative of a complex expression, we

look to see if we can use logarithmic differentiation to simplify the problem. Often, doing so means that we can avoid a messy expression involving the Product,

Quotient, or Chain Rules. We always do the same four steps:

Step One: Take the log of both sides: $\ln y = \ln \sqrt{\dfrac{1+x}{1-x}}$.

Step Two: Simplify the expression using Log Rules:

$\ln y = \dfrac{1}{2} \ln \left(\dfrac{1+x}{1-x} \right)$

$\ln y = \dfrac{1}{2} \left[\ln(1+x) - \ln(1-x) \right]$

Step Three: Take the derivative of both sides: $\dfrac{1}{y}\dfrac{dy}{dx} = \dfrac{1}{2}\left[\dfrac{1}{1+x} - \dfrac{1}{1-x} \right]$.

Step Four: Multiply both sides by y: $\dfrac{dy}{dx} = \dfrac{y}{2}\left[\dfrac{1}{1+x} - \dfrac{1}{1-x} \right]$.

3. $y\left[\dfrac{9x^2}{2(x^3+5)} - \dfrac{2x}{3(4-x^2)} - \dfrac{4x^3 - 2x}{(x^4 - x^2 + 6)} \right]$

Anytime we are presented with finding the derivative of a complex expression,

we look to see if we can use logarithmic differentiation to simplify the problem.

Often, doing so means that we can avoid a messy expression involving the

Product, Quotient, or Chain Rules. We always do the same four steps:

Step One: Take the log of both sides: $\ln y = \ln \dfrac{(x^3+5)^{\frac{3}{2}}\left(\sqrt[3]{4-x^2} \right)}{(x^4 - x^2 + 6)}$.

Step Two: Simplify the expression using Log Rules:

$\ln y = \ln\left(x^3+5\right)^{\frac{3}{2}} + \ln\left(\sqrt[3]{4-x^2} \right) - \ln\left(x^4 - x^2 + 6\right)$

$\ln y = \dfrac{3}{2}\ln\left(x^3+5\right) + \dfrac{1}{3}\ln\left(4-x^2\right) - \ln\left(x^4 - x^2 + 6\right)$

Step Three: Take the derivative of both sides:

$$\frac{1}{y}\frac{dy}{dx} = \frac{3}{2}\left(\frac{3x^2}{x^3+5}\right) + \frac{1}{3}\left(\frac{-2x}{4-x^2}\right) - \frac{4x^3-2x}{x^4-x^2+6} = \frac{9x^2}{2(x^3+5)} - \frac{2x}{3(4-x^2)} - \frac{4x^3-2x}{(x^4-x^2+6)}.$$

Step Four: Multiply both sides by y: $\dfrac{dy}{dx} = y\left[\dfrac{9x^2}{2(x^3+5)} - \dfrac{2x}{3(4-x^2)} - \dfrac{4x^3-2x}{(x^4-x^2+6)}\right].$

4. $y\left[\cot x - \tan x - \dfrac{3x^2}{2(x^3-4)}\right]$

Anytime we are presented with finding the derivative of a complex expression, we

look to see if we can use logarithmic differentiation to simplify the problem. Often,

doing so means that we can avoid a messy expression involving the Product,

Quotient, or Chain Rules. We always do the same four steps:

Step One: Take the log of both sides: $\ln y = \ln\dfrac{\sin x \cos x}{\sqrt{x^3-4}}$.

Step Two: Simplify the expression using Log Rules:

$\ln y = \ln\sin x + \ln\cos x - \ln\sqrt{x^3-4}$

$\ln y = \ln\sin x + \ln\cos x - \dfrac{1}{2}\ln\left(x^3-4\right)$

Step Three: Take the derivative of both sides:

$$\frac{1}{y}\frac{dy}{dx} = \frac{\cos x}{\sin x} + \frac{-\sin x}{\cos x} - \frac{1}{2}\frac{3x^2}{x^3-4} = \cot x - \tan x - \frac{3x^2}{2(x^3-4)}.$$

Step Four: Multiply both sides by y: $\dfrac{dy}{dx} = y\left[\cot x - \tan x - \dfrac{3x^2}{2(x^3-4)}\right].$

5. $y\left[\dfrac{6(x-1)}{(x^2-2x)}+\dfrac{4(-12x^3+7)}{(5-3x^4+7x)}-\dfrac{3(2x+1)}{(x^2+x)}\right]$

Anytime we are presented with finding the derivative of a complex expression, we

look to see if we can use logarithmic differentiation to simplify the problem. Often,

doing so means that we can avoid a messy expression involving the Product,

Quotient, or Chain Rules. We always do the same four steps:

Step One: Take the log of both sides: $\ln y = \ln \dfrac{\left(4x^2-8x\right)^3\left(5-3x^4+7x\right)^4}{\left(x^2+x\right)^3}$.

Step Two: Simplify the expression using Log Rules:

$\ln y = \ln(4x^2-8x)^3 + \ln(5-3x^4+7x)^4 - \ln(x^2+x)^3$

$\ln y = 3\ln(4x^2-8x) + 4\ln(5-3x^4+7x) - 3\ln(x^2+x)$

Step Three: Take the derivative of both sides:

$\dfrac{1}{y}\dfrac{dy}{dx} = 3\dfrac{8x-8}{4x^2-8x}+4\dfrac{-12x^3+7}{5-3x^4+7x}-3\dfrac{2x+1}{x^2+x}=\dfrac{3(2x-2)}{x^2-2x}+\dfrac{4(-12x^3+7)}{(5-3x^4+7x)}-\dfrac{3(2x+1)}{(x^2+x)}$.

Step Four: Multiply both sides by y: $\dfrac{dy}{dx}=y\left[\dfrac{6(x-1)}{(x^2-2x)}+\dfrac{4(-12x^3+7)}{(5-3x^4+7x)}-\dfrac{3(2x+1)}{(x^2+x)}\right]$.

6. $y\left[\dfrac{1}{x-1}-\dfrac{1}{x}-\sec x\csc x\right]$

Anytime we are presented with finding the derivative of a complex expression, we

look to see if we can use logarithmic differentiation to simplify the problem. Often, doing so means that we can avoid a messy expression involving the Product,

Quotient, or Chain Rules. We always do the same four steps:

Step One: Take the log of both sides: $\ln y = \ln \dfrac{x-1}{x \tan x}$.

Step Two: Simplify the expression using Log Rules:

$\ln y = \ln(x-1) - \ln x - \ln \tan x$

Step Three: Take the derivative of both sides:

$\dfrac{1}{y}\dfrac{dy}{dx} = \dfrac{1}{x-1} - \dfrac{1}{x} - \dfrac{\sec^2 x}{\tan x} = \dfrac{1}{x-1} - \dfrac{1}{x} - \sec x \csc x$.

Step Four: Multiply both sides by y: $\dfrac{dy}{dx} = y\left[\dfrac{1}{x-1} - \dfrac{1}{x} - \sec x \csc x \right]$.

7. $y\left[\dfrac{2(1-2x)}{(x-x^2)} + \dfrac{3(3x^2+4x^3)}{(x^3+x^4)} + \dfrac{4(6x^5-5x^4)}{(x^6-x^5)} \right]$

Anytime we are presented with finding the derivative of a complex expression, we

look to see if we can use logarithmic differentiation to simplify the problem. Often,

doing so means that we can avoid a messy expression involving the Product,

Quotient, or Chain Rules. We always do the same four steps:

Step One: Take the log of both sides: $\ln y = \ln\left[(x-x^2)^2 (x^3+x^4)^3 (x^6-x^5)^4 \right]$.

Step Two: Simplify the expression using Log Rules:

$\ln y = \ln(x-x^2)^2 + \ln(x^3+x^4)^3 + \ln(x^6-x^5)^4$

$\ln y = 2 \ln(x - x^2) + 3 \ln(x^3 + x^4) + 4 \ln(x^6 - x^5)$

Step Three: Take the derivative of both sides:

$$\frac{1}{y}\frac{dy}{dx} = 2\left(\frac{1-2x}{x-x^2}\right) + 3\left(\frac{3x^2+4x^3}{x^3+x^4}\right) + 4\left(\frac{6x^5-5x^4}{x^6-x^5}\right).$$

Step Four: Multiply both sides by y: $\dfrac{dy}{dx} = y\left[\dfrac{2(1-2x)}{(x-x^2)} + \dfrac{3(3x^2+4x^3)}{(x^3+x^4)} + \dfrac{4(6x^5-5x^4)}{(x^6-x^5)}\right].$

8. $\dfrac{y}{4}\left[\dfrac{1}{x} - \dfrac{1}{1-x} + \dfrac{1}{1+x} - \dfrac{2x}{x^2-1} + \dfrac{1}{5-x}\right]$

Anytime we are presented with finding the derivative of a complex expression, we

look to see if we can use logarithmic differentiation to simplify the problem. Often,

doing so means that we can avoid a messy expression involving the Product,

Quotient, or Chain Rules. We always do the same four steps:

Step One: Take the log of both sides: $\ln y = \ln \sqrt[4]{\dfrac{x(1-x)(1+x)}{(x^2-1)(5-x)}}.$

Step Two: Simplify the expression using Log Rules:

$\ln y = \dfrac{1}{4}\ln \dfrac{x(1-x)(1+x)}{(x^2-1)(5-x)}$

$\ln y = \dfrac{1}{4}\left[\ln x + \ln(1-x) + \ln(1+x) - \ln(x^2-1) - \ln(5-x)\right]$

Step Three: Take the derivative of both sides:

$$\frac{1}{y}\frac{dy}{dx} = \frac{1}{4}\left[\frac{1}{x} + \frac{1}{1-x} + \frac{1}{1+x} - \frac{2x}{x^2-1} + \frac{1}{5-x}\right].$$

Step Four: Multiply both sides by y: $\dfrac{dy}{dx} = \dfrac{y}{4}\left[\dfrac{1}{x} - \dfrac{1}{1-x} + \dfrac{1}{1+x} - \dfrac{2x}{x^2-1} + \dfrac{1}{5-x}\right].$

SOLUTIONS TO PRACTICE PROBLEM SET 20

1. $-\dfrac{1}{3x^3}+C$

   Here we will use the Power Rule (page 150), which says that $\int x^n dx = \dfrac{x^{n+1}}{n+1}+C$. The integral is: $\int \dfrac{1}{x^4}dx = \int x^{-4}dx = \dfrac{x^{-3}}{-3}+C = -\dfrac{1}{3x^3}+C$.

2. $10\sqrt{x}+C$

   Here we will use the Power Rule (page 150), which says that $\int x^n dx = \dfrac{x^{n+1}}{n+1}+C$. The integral is: $\int \dfrac{5}{\sqrt{x}}dx = 5\int x^{-\frac{1}{2}}dx = 5\dfrac{x^{\frac{1}{2}}}{\frac{1}{2}}+C = 10\sqrt{x}+C$.

3. $\dfrac{x^4}{4}-\dfrac{7}{x}+C$

   Here we will use the Power Rule (page 150), which says that $\int x^n dx = \dfrac{x^{n+1}}{n+1}+C$.

   First, let's simplify the integrand: $\int \dfrac{x^5+7}{x^2}dx = \int \left(\dfrac{x^5}{x^2}+\dfrac{7}{x^2}\right)dx = \int \left(x^3+7x^{-2}\right)dx$. Now we can evaluate the integral: $\int \left(x^3+7x^{-2}\right)dx = \dfrac{x^4}{4}+7\dfrac{x^{-1}}{-1}+C = \dfrac{x^4}{4}-\dfrac{7}{x}+C$.

4. $x^5-x^3+x^2+6x+C$

   Here we will use the Power Rule (page 150), which says that $\int x^n dx = \dfrac{x^{n+1}}{n+1}+C$. The integral is: $\int \left(5x^4-3x^2+2x+6\right)dx = 5\dfrac{x^5}{5}-3\dfrac{x^3}{3}+2\dfrac{x^2}{2}+6x+C = x^5-x^3+x^2+6x+C$.

5. $-\dfrac{3}{2x^2}+\dfrac{2}{x}+\dfrac{x^5}{5}+2x^8+C$

Here we will use the Power Rule (page 150), which says that $\displaystyle\int x^n dx = \dfrac{x^{n+1}}{n+1}+C$.

The integral is:

$$\int\left(3x^{-3}-2x^{-2}+x^4+16x^7\right)dx = 3\dfrac{x^{-2}}{-2}-2\dfrac{x^{-1}}{-1}+\dfrac{x^5}{5}+16\dfrac{x^8}{8}+C = -\dfrac{3}{2x^2}+\dfrac{2}{x}+\dfrac{x^5}{5}+2x^8+C.$$

6. $\dfrac{x^4}{4}-\dfrac{2x^3}{3}+\dfrac{x^2}{2}-2x+C$

Here we will use the Power Rule (page 150), which says that $\displaystyle\int x^n dx = \dfrac{x^{n+1}}{n+1}+C$.

First, let's simplify the integrand: $\int(1+x^2)(x-2)dx = \int(x^3-2x^2+x-2)dx$. Now we

can evaluate the integral: $\displaystyle\int\left(x^3-2x^2+x-2\right)dx = \dfrac{x^4}{4}-\dfrac{2x^3}{3}+\dfrac{x^2}{2}-2x+C$.

7. $\dfrac{3x^{\frac{4}{3}}}{2}+\dfrac{3x^{\frac{7}{3}}}{7}+C$

Here we will use the Power Rule (page 150), which says that $\displaystyle\int x^n dx = \dfrac{x^{n+1}}{n+1}+C$.

First, let's simplify the integrand: $\displaystyle\int x^{\frac{1}{3}}(2+x)dx = \int\left(2x^{\frac{1}{3}}+x^{\frac{4}{3}}\right)dx$. Now we can

evaluate the integral: $\displaystyle\int\left(2x^{\frac{1}{3}}+x^{\frac{4}{3}}\right)dx = 2\dfrac{x^{\frac{4}{3}}}{\frac{4}{3}}+\dfrac{x^{\frac{7}{3}}}{\frac{7}{3}}+C = \dfrac{3x^{\frac{4}{3}}}{2}+\dfrac{3x^{\frac{7}{3}}}{7}+C$.

8. $\dfrac{x^7}{7}+\dfrac{2x^5}{5}+\dfrac{x^3}{3}+C$

Here we will use the Power Rule (page 150), which says that $\displaystyle\int x^n dx = \dfrac{x^{n+1}}{n+1}+C$.

First, let's simplify the integrand: $\int(x^3+x)^2\,dx = \int(x^6+2x^4+x^2)dx$. Now we can

evaluate the integral: $\displaystyle\int\left(x^6+2x^4+x^2\right)dx = \dfrac{x^7}{7}+\dfrac{2x^5}{5}+\dfrac{x^3}{3}+C$.

9. $\dfrac{x^5}{5} - \dfrac{2x^3}{3} - \dfrac{1}{x} + C$

Here we will use the Power Rule (page 150), which says that $\int x^n dx = \dfrac{x^{n+1}}{n+1} + C$.

First, let's simplify the integrand:

$\displaystyle\int \dfrac{x^6 - 2x^4 + 1}{x^2} dx = \int \left(\dfrac{x^6}{x^2} - 2\dfrac{x^4}{x^2} + \dfrac{1}{x^2} \right) dx = \int \left(x^4 - 2x^2 + x^{-2} \right) dx$. Now we can evaluate

the integral: $\displaystyle\int \left(x^4 - 2x^2 + x^{-2} \right) dx = \dfrac{x^5}{5} - \dfrac{2x^3}{3} + \dfrac{x^{-1}}{-1} + C = \dfrac{x^5}{5} - \dfrac{2x^3}{3} - \dfrac{1}{x} + C$.

10. $\dfrac{x^5}{5} - \dfrac{3x^4}{4} + x^3 - \dfrac{x^2}{2} + C$

Here we will use the Power Rule (page 150), which says that $\int x^n dx = \dfrac{x^{n+1}}{n+1} + C$.

First, let's simplify the integrand:

$\int x(x-1)^3 dx = \int x(x^3 - 3x^2 + 3x - 1)dx = \int (x^4 - 3x^3 + 3x^2 - x)dx$.

Now we can evaluate the integral:

$\displaystyle\int \left(x^4 - 3x^3 + 3x^2 - x \right) dx = \dfrac{x^5}{5} - \dfrac{3x^4}{4} + \dfrac{3x^3}{3} - \dfrac{x^2}{2} + C = \dfrac{x^5}{5} - \dfrac{3x^4}{4} + x^3 - \dfrac{x^2}{2} + C$.

11. $\sin x + 5 \cos x + C$
Here we will use the Rules for the Integrals of Trig Functions (page 151), namely:
$\int \sin x dx = -\cos x + C$ and $\int \cos x dx = \sin x + C$. We get:
$\int \cos x - 5 \sin x dx = \sin x + 5 \cos x + C$.

12. $\tan x + \sec x + C$
Here we will use the Rules for the Integrals of Trig Functions (page 151),
namely: $\int \sec^2 x dx = \tan x + C$ and $\int (\sec x \tan x)dx = \sec x + C$. First, let's
expand the integrand: $\int \sec x (\sec x + \tan x)dx = \int (\sec^2 x + \sec x \tan x)\, dx$. We get:
$\int (\sec^2 x + \sec x \tan x)dx = \tan x + \sec x + C$.

13. $\tan x + \dfrac{x^2}{2} + C$

Here we will use the Rules for the Integrals of Trig Functions (page 151),

namely: $\int \sec^2 x dx = \tan x + C$ and the Power Rule (page 150), which says that

$\displaystyle\int x^n dx = \dfrac{x^{n+1}}{n+1} + C$. We get: $\displaystyle\int \left(\sec^2 x + x \right) dx = \tan x + \dfrac{x^2}{2} + C$.

14. $\sec x + C$

Here we will use the Rules for the Integrals of Trig Functions (page 151), namely:

$\int(\sec x \tan x)dx = \sec x + C$. First, we need to rewrite the integrand, using trig

identities: $\int \dfrac{\sin x}{\cos^2 x}dx = \int\left(\dfrac{1}{\cos x}\dfrac{\sin x}{\cos x}\right)dx = \int(\sec x \tan x)dx$. Now we can evaluate

the integral: $\int(\sec x \tan x)dx = \sec x + C$.

15. $\sin x + 4 \tan x + C$

Here we will use the Rules for the Integrals of Trig Functions (page 151), namely:

$\int \sec^2 x dx = \tan x + C$ and $\int \cos x dx = \sin x + C$.

First, we need to rewrite the integrand, using trig identities:

$\int \dfrac{\cos^3 x + 4}{\cos^2 x}dx = \int\left(\dfrac{\cos^3 x}{\cos^2 x} + \dfrac{4}{\cos^2 x}\right)dx = \int\left(\cos x + 4\sec^2 x\right)dx$. Now we can evaluate

the integral: $\int(\cos x + 4 \sec^2 x)dx = \sin x + 4 \tan x + C$.

16. $-2 \cos x + C$

Here we will use the Rules for the Integrals of Trig Functions (page 151), namely:

$\int \sin x dx = -\cos x + C$. First, we need to rewrite the integrand, using trig identities:

$\int \dfrac{\sin 2x}{\cos x}dx = \int \dfrac{2 \sin x \cos x}{\cos x}dx = \int 2 \sin x dx$. Now we can evaluate the integral:

$\int 2 \sin x dx = -2 \cos x + C$.

17. $x + \sin x + C$

Here we will use the Rules for the Integrals of Trig Functions (page 151), namely:

$\int \cos x dx = \sin x + C$. First, we need to rewrite the integrand, using trig identities:

$\int\left(1 + \cos^2 x \sec x\right)dx = \int\left(1 + \dfrac{\cos^2 x}{\cos x}\right)dx = \int(1 + \cos x)dx$. Now we can evaluate the

integral: $\int(1 + \cos x)dx = x \sin x + C$.

18. $\tan x - x + C$

Here we will use the Rules for the Integrals of Trig Functions (page 151), namely: $\int \sec^2 x\, dx = \tan x + C$. First, we need to rewrite the integrand, using trig identities: $\int (\tan^2 x)dx = \int (\sec^2 x - 1)dx$. Now we can evaluate the integral: $\int (\sec^2 x - 1)dx = \tan x - x + C$.

19. $-\cos x + C$

Here we will use the Rules for the Integrals of Trig Functions (page 151), namely:

$\int \sin x\, dx = -\cos x + C$. First, we need to rewrite the integrand, using trig identities:

$\int \dfrac{1}{\csc x}\, dx = \int \sin x\, dx$. Now we can evaluate the integral: $\int \sin x\, dx = -\cos x + C$.

20. $\dfrac{x^2}{2} - 2\tan x + C$

Here we will use the Rules for the Integrals of Trig Functions (page 151),

namely: $\int \sec^2 x\, dx = \tan x + C$. First, we need to rewrite the integrand, using trig

identities: $\int \left(x - \dfrac{2}{\cos^2 x} \right) dx = \int \left(x - 2\sec^2 x \right) dx$. Now we can evaluate the integral:

$\int \left(x - 2\sec^2 x \right) dx = \dfrac{x^2}{2} - 2\tan x + C$.

SOLUTIONS TO PRACTICE PROBLEM SET 21

1. $\dfrac{\sin^2 2x}{4} + C$

   If we let $u = \sin 2x$, then $du = 2\cos 2xdx$. We need to substitute for $\cos 2xdx$, so we

   can divide the du term by 2: $\dfrac{du}{2} = \cos 2xdx$. Now we can substitute into the integral:

   $\displaystyle \int \sin 2x \cos 2xdx = \frac{1}{2}\int udu$. Now we can integrate: $\dfrac{1}{2}\displaystyle\int udu = \frac{1}{2}\left(\frac{u^2}{2}\right) + c = \frac{u^2}{4} + C$.

   Last, we substitute back and get: $\dfrac{\sin^2 2x}{4} + C$.

2. $-\dfrac{9}{4}\left(10 - x^2\right)^{\frac{2}{3}} + C$

   First, pull the constant out of the integrand: $\displaystyle\int \frac{3xdx}{\sqrt[3]{10 - x^2}}dx = 3\int \frac{xdx}{\sqrt[3]{10 - x^2}}dx$.

   If we let $u = 10 - x^2$, then $du = -2xdx$. We need to substitute for xdx, so

   we can divide the du term by -2: $-\dfrac{du}{2} = xdx$. Now we can substitute

   into the integral: $3\displaystyle\int \frac{xdx}{\sqrt[3]{10 - x^2}}dx = -\frac{3}{2}\int u^{-\frac{1}{3}}du$. Now we can integrate:

   $-\dfrac{3}{2}\displaystyle\int u^{-\frac{1}{3}}du = -\frac{3}{2}\frac{u^{\frac{2}{3}}}{\frac{2}{3}} + C = -\frac{9}{4}u^{\frac{2}{3}} + C$. Last, we substitute back and get:

   $-\dfrac{9}{4}\left(10 - x^2\right)^{\frac{2}{3}} + C$.

3. $\dfrac{1}{30}\left(5x^4+20\right)^{\frac{3}{2}}+C$

If we let $u = 5x^4 + 20$, then $du = 20x^3dx$. We need to substitute for x^3dx,

so we can divide the du term by 20: $\dfrac{du}{20}=x^3dx$. Now we can substitute

into the integral: $\displaystyle\int x^3\sqrt{5x^4+20}\,dx=\dfrac{1}{20}\int u^{\frac{1}{2}}du$. Now we can integrate:

$\dfrac{1}{20}\displaystyle\int u^{\frac{1}{2}}du=\dfrac{1}{20}\dfrac{u^{\frac{3}{2}}}{\dfrac{3}{2}}+C=\dfrac{1}{30}u^{\frac{3}{2}}+C$. Last, we substitute back and get:

$\dfrac{1}{30}\left(5x^4+20\right)^{\frac{3}{2}}+C$.

4. $-\dfrac{1}{x-1}+C$

If we let $u = x - 1$, then $du = dx$. Now we can substitute into the integral:

$\displaystyle\int\dfrac{dx}{\left(x-1\right)^2}=\int u^{-2}du$. Now we can integrate: $\displaystyle\int u^{-2}du=\dfrac{u^{-1}}{-1}+C=-\dfrac{1}{u}+C$. Last, we

substitute back and get: $-\dfrac{1}{x-1}+C$.

5. $-\dfrac{1}{12\left(x^3+3x\right)^4}+C$

If we let $u = x^3 + 3x$, then $du = (3x^2 + 3)dx$. We need to substitute for $(x^2 + 1)dx$,

so we can divide the du term by 3: $\dfrac{du}{3}=\left(x^2+1\right)dx$. Now we can substitute

into the integral: $\displaystyle\int\left(x^2+1\right)\left(x^3+3x\right)^{-5}dx=\dfrac{1}{3}\int u^{-5}du$. Now we can integrate:

$\dfrac{1}{3}\displaystyle\int u^{-5}du=\dfrac{1}{3}\dfrac{u^{-4}}{-4}+C=-\dfrac{1}{12}\dfrac{1}{u^4}+C$. Last, we substitute back and get:

$-\dfrac{1}{12\left(x^3+3x\right)^4}+C$.

6. $-2\cos\sqrt{x}+C$

If we let $u=\sqrt{x}$, then $du=\dfrac{1}{2\sqrt{x}}dx$. We need to substitute for $\dfrac{1}{\sqrt{x}}dx$, so we can

multiply the du term by 2: $2du=\dfrac{1}{\sqrt{x}}dx$. Now we can substitute into the integral:

$\displaystyle\int\frac{1}{\sqrt{x}}\sin\sqrt{x}\,dx=2\int\sin u\,du$. Now we can integrate: $2\int\sin u\,du=-2\cos u+C$. Last,

we substitute back and get: $-2\cos\sqrt{x}+C$.

7. $\dfrac{1}{3}\tan\left(x^3\right)+C$

If we let $u=x^3$, then $du=3x^2dx$. We need to substitute for x^2dx, so we can

divide the du term by 3: $\dfrac{du}{3}=x^2dx$. Now we can substitute into the integral:

$\displaystyle\int x^2\sec^2\left(x^3\right)dx=\frac{1}{3}\int\sec^2 u\,du$. Now we can integrate: $\dfrac{1}{3}\displaystyle\int\sec^2 u\,du=\frac{1}{3}\tan u+C$. Last,

we substitute back and get: $\dfrac{1}{3}\tan\left(x^3\right)+C$.

8. $-\dfrac{1}{3}\sin\left(\dfrac{3}{x}\right)+C$

If we let $u=\dfrac{3}{x}$, then $du=-\dfrac{3}{x^2}dx$. We need to substitute for $\dfrac{1}{x^2}dx$, so we can

divide the du term by -3: $-\dfrac{du}{3}=\dfrac{1}{x^2}dx$. Now we can substitute into the integral:

$\displaystyle\int\frac{\cos\left(\dfrac{3}{x}\right)}{x^2}dx=-\frac{1}{3}\int\cos u\,du$. Now we can integrate: $-\dfrac{1}{3}\displaystyle\int\cos u\,du=-\frac{1}{3}\sin u+C$.

Last, we substitute back and get: $-\dfrac{1}{3}\sin\left(\dfrac{3}{x}\right)+C$.

9. $-\dfrac{1}{4}\left(1-\cos 2x\right)^{-2}+C$

If we let $u = 1 - \cos 2x$, then $du = 2\sin 2x\,dx$. We need to substitute for $\sin 2x\,dx$,

so we can divide the du term by 2: $\dfrac{du}{2} = \sin 2x\,dx$. Now we can substitute

into the integral: $\displaystyle\int \dfrac{\sin 2x}{\left(1-\cos 2x\right)^3}\,dx = \dfrac{1}{2}\int u^{-3}\,du$. Now we can integrate:

$\dfrac{1}{2}\displaystyle\int u^{-3}\,du = \dfrac{1}{2}\left(\dfrac{u^{-2}}{-2}\right)+C = -\dfrac{1}{4}\left(\dfrac{1}{u^2}\right)+C$. Last, we substitute back and get:

$-\dfrac{1}{4}\left(1-\cos 2x\right)^{-2}+C$.

10. $-\cos(\sin x) + C$
If we let $u = \sin x$, then $du = \cos x\,dx$. Now we can substitute into the integral:
$\int\sin(\sin x)\cos x\,dx = \int\sin u\,du$. Now we can integrate: $\int\sin u\,du = -\cos u + C$. Last, we
substitute back and get: $-\cos(\sin x) + C$.

SOLUTIONS TO PRACTICE PROBLEM SET 22

1. $\dfrac{25}{32}$

First let's draw a picture.

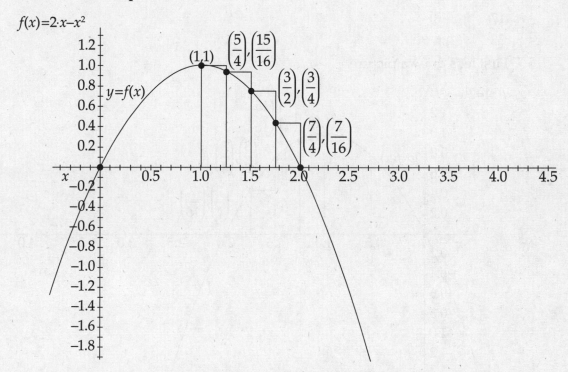

The width of each rectangle is found by taking the difference between the

endpoints and dividing by n. Here, the width of each rectangle is $\dfrac{2-1}{4} = \dfrac{1}{4}$.

We find the heights of the rectangles by evaluating $y = 2x - x^2$ at the appropriate

endpoints:

$$y(1) = 2(1) - (1)^2 = 1 \;;\quad y\left(\frac{5}{4}\right) = 2\left(\frac{5}{4}\right) - \left(\frac{5}{4}\right)^2 = \frac{15}{16} \;;\quad y\left(\frac{3}{2}\right) = 2\left(\frac{3}{2}\right) - \left(\frac{3}{2}\right)^2 = \frac{3}{4}$$

and $y\left(\dfrac{7}{4}\right) = 2\left(\dfrac{7}{4}\right) - \left(\dfrac{7}{4}\right)^2 = \dfrac{7}{16}$.

Therefore, the area is: $\left(\dfrac{1}{4}\right)\left(1 + \dfrac{15}{16} + \dfrac{3}{4} + \dfrac{7}{16}\right) = \dfrac{25}{32}$

2. $\dfrac{17}{32}$

First let's draw a picture.

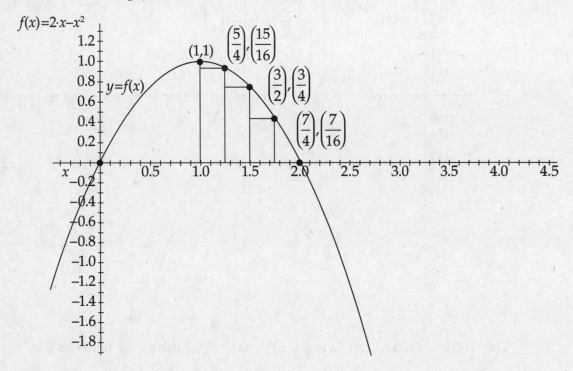

The width of each rectangle is found by taking the difference between the endpoints and dividing by n. Here, the width of each rectangle is $\dfrac{2-1}{4} = \dfrac{1}{4}$.

We find the heights of the rectangles by evaluating $y = 2x - x^2$ at the appropriate endpoints.

$y\left(\dfrac{5}{4}\right) = 2\left(\dfrac{5}{4}\right) - \left(\dfrac{5}{4}\right)^2 = \dfrac{15}{16}$; $\; y\left(\dfrac{3}{2}\right) = 2\left(\dfrac{3}{2}\right) - \left(\dfrac{3}{2}\right)^2 = \dfrac{3}{4}$; $\; y\left(\dfrac{7}{4}\right) = 2\left(\dfrac{7}{4}\right) - \left(\dfrac{7}{4}\right)^2 = \dfrac{7}{16}$;

and $y(2) = 2(2) - (2)^2 = 0$.

Therefore, the area is: $\left(\dfrac{1}{4}\right)\left(\dfrac{15}{16} + \dfrac{3}{4} + \dfrac{7}{16} + 0\right) = \dfrac{17}{32}$.

3. $\dfrac{21}{32}$

First let's draw a picture.

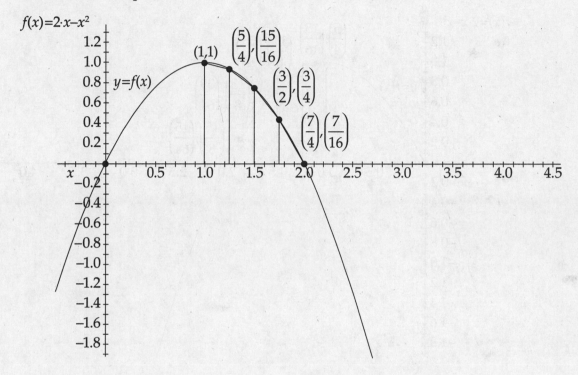

$f(x)=2 \cdot x - x^2$

The height of each trapezoid is found by taking the difference between the endpoints and dividing by n. Here, the width of each trapezoid is $\dfrac{2-1}{4}=\dfrac{1}{4}$.

We find the bases of the trapezoids by evaluating $y = 2x - x^2$ at the appropriate endpoints:

$y(1) = 2(1) - (1)^2 = 1$; $y\left(\dfrac{5}{4}\right)=2\left(\dfrac{5}{4}\right)-\left(\dfrac{5}{4}\right)^2=\dfrac{15}{16}$; $y\left(\dfrac{3}{2}\right)=2\left(\dfrac{3}{2}\right)-\left(\dfrac{3}{2}\right)^2=\dfrac{3}{4}$;

$y\left(\dfrac{7}{4}\right)=2\left(\dfrac{7}{4}\right)-\left(\dfrac{7}{4}\right)^2=\dfrac{7}{16}$; and $y(2) = 2(2) - (2)^2 = 0$.

Therefore, the area is: $\left(\dfrac{1}{2}\right)\left(\dfrac{1}{4}\right)\left[1+(2)\left(\dfrac{15}{16}\right)+(2)\left(\dfrac{3}{4}\right)+(2)\left(\dfrac{7}{16}\right)+0\right]=\dfrac{21}{32}$.

4. $\dfrac{43}{64}$

First let's draw a picture.

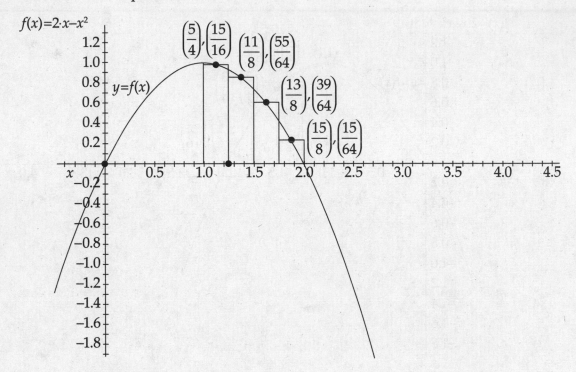

The height of each rectangle is found by taking the difference between the

endpoints and dividing by n. Here, the width of each rectangle is $\dfrac{2-1}{4} = \dfrac{1}{4}$.

We find the bases of the rectangles by evaluating $y = 2x - x^2$ at the appropriate

endpoints:

$$y\left(\frac{9}{8}\right) = 2\left(\frac{9}{8}\right) - \left(\frac{9}{8}\right)^2 = \frac{63}{64}; \quad y\left(\frac{11}{8}\right) = 2\left(\frac{11}{8}\right) - \left(\frac{11}{8}\right)^2 = \frac{55}{64};$$

$$y\left(\frac{13}{8}\right) = 2\left(\frac{13}{8}\right) - \left(\frac{13}{8}\right)^2 = \frac{39}{64}; \text{ and } y\left(\frac{15}{8}\right) = 2\left(\frac{15}{8}\right) - \left(\frac{15}{8}\right)^2 = \frac{15}{64}.$$

Therefore, the area is: $\left(\dfrac{1}{4}\right)\left(\dfrac{63}{64} + \dfrac{55}{64} + \dfrac{39}{64} + \dfrac{15}{64}\right) = \dfrac{43}{64}$.

5. $\dfrac{2}{3}$

We will find the exact area by evaluating the integral $\int\limits_{1}^{2}\left(2x-x^2\right)dx$. According to

the Fundamental Theorem of Calculus: $\int\limits_{1}^{2}\left(2x-x^2\right)dx=\left(\dfrac{2x^2}{2}-\dfrac{x^3}{3}\right)\bigg|_{1}^{2}=\left(x^2-\dfrac{x^3}{3}\right)\bigg|_{1}^{2}$. If

we evaluate the integral at the limits, we get: $\left[(2)^2-\left(\dfrac{2^3}{3}\right)\right]-\left[(1)^2-\left(\dfrac{1^3}{3}\right)\right]=\dfrac{2}{3}$.

6. 2

According to the Fundamental Theorem of Calculus:

$$\int\limits_{-\frac{\pi}{2}}^{\frac{\pi}{2}}\cos x\,dx=\sin x\bigg|_{-\frac{\pi}{2}}^{\frac{\pi}{2}}=\sin\frac{\pi}{2}-\sin\left(-\frac{\pi}{2}\right)=2.$$

7. $\dfrac{968}{5}$

First, let's rewrite the integrand: $\int\limits_{1}^{9}\left(2x\sqrt{x}\right)dx=\int\limits_{1}^{9}\left(2x^{\frac{3}{2}}\right)dx$.

Now, according to the Fundamental Theorem of Calculus:

$$\int\limits_{1}^{9}\left(2x^{\frac{3}{2}}\right)dx=\left(\dfrac{2x^{\frac{5}{2}}}{\dfrac{5}{2}}\right)\bigg|_{1}^{9}=\left(\dfrac{4x^{\frac{5}{2}}}{5}\right)\bigg|_{1}^{9}=\left(\dfrac{4(9)^{\frac{5}{2}}}{5}-\dfrac{4(1)^{\frac{5}{2}}}{5}\right)=\dfrac{968}{5}.$$

8. $-\dfrac{161}{20}$

According to the Fundamental Theorem of Calculus:

$$\int\limits_{0}^{1}\left(x^4-5x^3+3x^2-4x-6\right)dx=\left(\dfrac{x^5}{5}-5\dfrac{x^4}{4}+x^3-2x^2-6x\right)\bigg|_{0}^{1}=$$

$$\left(\dfrac{(1)^5}{5}-5\dfrac{(1)^4}{4}+(1)^3-2(1)^2-6(1)\right)-0=-\dfrac{161}{20}$$

9. 16

Recall that the absolute value function must be rewritten as a piecewise

function: $|x| = \begin{cases} x; x \geq 0 \\ -x; x < 0 \end{cases}$. Thus, we need to split the integral into two separate

integrals in order to evaluate it: $\int_{-4}^{4} |x|\,dx = \int_{-4}^{0} (-x)\,dx + \int_{0}^{4} x\,dx$. Now, according to the

Fundamental Theorem of Calculus: $\int_{-4}^{0} (-x)\,dx = \left(-\frac{x^2}{2} \right)\Big|_{-4}^{0} = (0) - \left(-\frac{(-4)^2}{2} \right) = 8$ and

$\int_{0}^{4} (x)\,dx = \left(\frac{x^2}{2} \right)\Big|_{0}^{4} = \left(\frac{(4)^2}{2} \right) - (0) = 8$. Therefore, the answer is 8 + 8 = 16.

10. 0

According to the Fundamental Theorem of Calculus:

$\int_{-\frac{\pi}{2}}^{\frac{\pi}{2}} \sin x\,dx = -\cos x \Big|_{-\frac{\pi}{2}}^{\frac{\pi}{2}} = -\cos\frac{\pi}{2} + \cos\left(-\frac{\pi}{2} \right) = 0$.

SOLUTIONS TO PRACTICE PROBLEM SET 23

1. $2\sqrt{\dfrac{2}{\pi}}$

We find the average value of the function, $f(x)$, on the interval $[a,b]$ using the

formula $f(c) = \dfrac{1}{b-a}\displaystyle\int_a^b f(x)\,dx$ (see page 178). Here we are looking for the

average value of $f(x) = 4x\cos x^2$ on the interval $\left[0, \sqrt{\dfrac{\pi}{2}}\right]$. Using the formula,

we need to find: $\dfrac{1}{\sqrt{\dfrac{\pi}{2}}-0}\displaystyle\int_0^{\sqrt{\frac{\pi}{2}}}\left(4x\cos x^2\right)dx = \sqrt{\dfrac{2}{\pi}}\displaystyle\int_0^{\sqrt{\frac{\pi}{2}}}\left(4x\cos x^2\right)dx$. We will need

to use u-substitution to evaluate the integral. Let $u = x^2$ and $du = 2x\,dx$. We

need to substitute for $4x\,dx$, so we multiply by 2 to get $2\,du = 4x\,dx$. Now

we can substitute into the integral: $\int(4x\cos x^2)dx = 2\int\cos u\,du = 2\sin u$.

If we substitute back, we get $2\sin x^2$. Now we can evaluate the integral:

$$\sqrt{\dfrac{2}{\pi}}\int_0^{\sqrt{\frac{\pi}{2}}}\left(4x\cos x^2\right)dx = \sqrt{\dfrac{2}{\pi}}\left(2\sin x^2\right)\Big|_0^{\sqrt{\frac{\pi}{2}}} = \sqrt{\dfrac{2}{\pi}}\left(2\sin\dfrac{\pi}{2} - 2\sin 0\right) = 2\sqrt{\dfrac{2}{\pi}}$$

2. $\dfrac{8}{3}$

We find the average value of the function, $f(x)$, on the interval $[a,b]$ using the

formula $f(c) = \dfrac{1}{b-a}\displaystyle\int_a^b f(x)\,dx$ (see page 178). Here we are looking for the average

value of $f(x) = \sqrt{x}$ on the interval $[0,16]$. Using the formula, we need to find:

$\dfrac{1}{16-0}\displaystyle\int_0^{16}\left(\sqrt{x}\right)dx$. We get: $\dfrac{1}{16}\displaystyle\int_0^{16}\left(\sqrt{x}\right)dx = \dfrac{1}{16}\left(\dfrac{x^{\frac{3}{2}}}{\dfrac{3}{2}}\right)\Bigg|_0^{16} = \dfrac{1}{24}\left(x^{\frac{3}{2}}\right)\Bigg|_0^{16} = \dfrac{1}{24}\left((16)^{\frac{3}{2}}-0\right) = \dfrac{8}{3}$

3. $\dfrac{2\sqrt{2}}{3}$

We find the average value of the function, $f(x)$, on the interval $[a,b]$ using the

formula $f(c) = \dfrac{1}{b-a}\displaystyle\int_a^b f(x)\,dx$ (see page 178). Here we are looking for the average

value of $f(x) = \sqrt{1-x}$ on the interval $[-1,1]$. Using the formula, we need to find:

$\dfrac{1}{1-(-1)}\displaystyle\int_{-1}^1\left(\sqrt{1-x}\right)dx$. We get:

$\dfrac{1}{2}\displaystyle\int_{-1}^1 (1-x)^{\frac{1}{2}}\,dx = \dfrac{1}{2}\left(-\dfrac{(1-x)^{\frac{3}{2}}}{\dfrac{3}{2}}\right)\Bigg|_{-1}^1 = -\dfrac{1}{3}(1-x)^{\frac{3}{2}}\Big|_{-1}^1 = -\dfrac{1}{3}\left(0-2^{\frac{3}{2}}\right) = \dfrac{2\sqrt{2}}{3}$.

4. 1

We find the average value of the function, $f(x)$, on the interval $[a,b]$ using the

formula $f(c) = \dfrac{1}{b-a}\displaystyle\int_a^b f(x)dx$ (see page 178). Here we are looking for the average

value of $f(x) = 2|x|$ on the interval $[-1,1]$. Using the formula, we need to find:

$\dfrac{1}{1-(-1)}\displaystyle\int_{-1}^1 (2|x|)dx$. Recall that the absolute value function must be rewritten as

a piecewise function: $|x| = \begin{cases} x; x \geq 0 \\ -x; x < 0 \end{cases}$. Thus, we need to split the integral into two

separate integrals in order to evaluate it: $\dfrac{1}{1-(-1)}\displaystyle\int_{-1}^1 (2|x|)dx = \int_{-1}^0 (-x)dx + \int_0^1 xdx$. We

get: $\displaystyle\int_{-1}^0 (-x)dx + \int_0^1 xdx = \left(-\dfrac{x^2}{2}\right)\Big|_{-1}^0 + \left(\dfrac{x^2}{2}\right)\Big|_{-1}^0 = \left(0 - \left(-\dfrac{1}{2}\right)\right) - \left(\dfrac{1}{2} - 0\right) = 1$.

5. $\sin^2 x$

We find the derivative of an integral using the Second Fundamental Theorem of

Calculus: $\dfrac{d}{dx}\displaystyle\int_a^x f(t)dt = f(x)$ (see page 179). We get: $\dfrac{d}{dx}\displaystyle\int_1^x \sin^2 t\, dt = \sin^2 x$.

6. $27x^2 - 9x$

We find the derivative of an integral using the Second Fundamental

Theorem of Calculus: $\dfrac{d}{dx}\displaystyle\int_a^x f(t)dt = f(x)$ (see page 179). We get:

$\dfrac{d}{dx}\displaystyle\int_1^{3x} (t^2 - t)\, dt = 3\left[(3x)^2 - (3x)\right] = 27x^2 - 9x$. Don't forget that because the upper

limit is a function, we need to multiply the answer by the derivative of that

function (see example 5, page 180).

7. $2x^3$

We find the derivative of an integral using the Second Fundamental Theorem

of Calculus: $\dfrac{d}{dx}\displaystyle\int_a^x f(t)\,dt = f(x)$ (see page 179). Normally we would need to

rewrite the absolute value function as a piecewise function, but notice that

we are evaluating the absolute value over an interval where all values will be

positive. Thus we can ignore the absolute value and rewrite the integral as:

$\dfrac{d}{dx}\displaystyle\int_0^{x^2} |t|\,dt = \dfrac{d}{dx}\displaystyle\int_0^{x^2} t\,dt$. We get: $\dfrac{d}{dx}\displaystyle\int_0^{x^2} t\,dt = \left(x^2\right)(2x) = 2x^3$. Don't forget that because the

upper limit is a function, we need to multiply the answer by the derivative of that

function (see example 5, page 180).

8. $-2\cos x$

We find the derivative of an integral using the Second Fundamental Theorem of

Calculus: $\dfrac{d}{dx}\displaystyle\int_a^x f(t)\,dt = f(x)$ (see p. 179). We get: $\dfrac{d}{dx}\displaystyle\int_1^x -2\cos t\,dt = -2\cos x$.

SOLUTIONS TO PRACTICE PROBLEM SET 24

1. $\ln |\tan x| + C$

   Whenever we have an integral in the form of a quotient, we check to see if the solution is a logarithm. A clue is whether the numerator is the derivative of the denominator, as it is here. Let's use u-substitution. If we let $u = \tan x$ then $du = \sec^2 x\,dx$. If we substitute into the integrand, we get: $\int \dfrac{\sec^2 x}{\tan x}\,dx = \int \dfrac{du}{u}$. Recall that $\int \dfrac{du}{u} = \ln|u| + C$ (see page 183). Substituting back, we get: $\int \dfrac{\sec^2 x}{\tan x}\,dx = \ln|\tan x| + C$.

2. $-\ln |1 - \sin x| + C$

   Whenever we have an integral in the form of a quotient, we check to see if the solution is a logarithm. A clue is whether the numerator is the derivative of the denominator, as it is here. Let's use u-substitution. If we let $u = 1 - \sin x$ then $du = -\cos x\,dx$. If we substitute into the integrand, we get: $\int \dfrac{\cos x}{1 - \sin x}\,dx = -\int \dfrac{du}{u}$. Recall that $\int \dfrac{du}{u} = \ln|u| + C$ (see page 183). Substituting back, we get: $\int \dfrac{\cos x}{1 - \sin x}\,dx = -\ln|1 - \sin x| + C$.

3. $\ln |\ln x| + C$

   Whenever we have an integral in the form of a quotient, we check to see if the solution is a logarithm. A clue is whether the numerator is the derivative of the denominator, as it is here. Let's use u-substitution. If we let $u = \ln x$ then $du = \dfrac{1}{x}\,dx$. If we substitute into the integrand, we get: $\int \dfrac{1}{x \ln x}\,dx = \int \dfrac{du}{u}$. Recall that $\int \dfrac{du}{u} = \ln|u| + C$ (see page 183). Substituting back, we get: $\int \dfrac{1}{x \ln x}\,dx = \ln|\ln x| + C$.

4. $\sin(\ln x) + C$

Recall that $\dfrac{d}{dx}\ln x = \dfrac{1}{x}$ (see page 118). Here, we can use u-substitution to get rid of the log in the integrand. If we let $u = \ln x$ then $du = \dfrac{1}{x}dx$. If we substitute into the integrand, we get: $\displaystyle\int\dfrac{1}{x}\cos(\ln x)dx = \int\cos u\,du = \sin u + C$. Substituting back we get: $\displaystyle\int\dfrac{1}{x}\cos(\ln x)dx = \sin(\ln x) + C$.

5. $-\ln|\cos x| - x + C$

First, let's rewrite the integrand:

$$\int\frac{\sin x - \cos x}{\cos x}dx = \int\left(\frac{\sin x}{\cos x} - \frac{\cos x}{\cos x}\right)dx = \int\left(\frac{\sin x}{\cos x} - 1\right)dx = \int\left(\frac{\sin x}{\cos x}\right)dx - \int dx.$$

Whenever we have an integral in the form of a quotient, we check to see if the solution is a logarithm. A clue is whether the numerator is the derivative of the denominator, as it is in the first integral. Let's use u-substitution. If we let $u = \cos x$ then $du = -\sin x\,dx$. If we substitute into the integrand, we get: $\displaystyle\int\left(\frac{\sin x}{\cos x}\right)dx = -\int\frac{du}{u}$.

Recall that $\displaystyle\int\frac{du}{u} = \ln|u| + C$ (see page 183). Substituting back, we get:

$\displaystyle\int\left(\frac{\sin x}{\cos x}\right)dx = -\ln|\cos x| + C$. The second integral is simply $\int dx = x + C$. Therefore,

the integral is $\displaystyle\int\left(\frac{\sin x}{\cos x}\right)dx - \int dx = -\ln|\cos x| - x + C$.

6. $\ln\left(1+2\sqrt{x}\right)+C$

Whenever we have an integral in the form of a quotient, we check to see if the solution is a logarithm. A clue is whether the numerator is the derivative of the denominator, as it is here. Let's use u-substitution. If we let $u = 1+2\sqrt{x}$ then $du = \dfrac{1}{\sqrt{x}}dx$. If we substitute into the integrand, we get: $\displaystyle\int \dfrac{1}{\sqrt{x}\left(1+2\sqrt{x}\right)}dx = \int \dfrac{du}{u}$.

Recall that $\displaystyle\int\dfrac{du}{u} = \ln|u|+C$ (see page 183). Substituting back, we get:

$\displaystyle\int\dfrac{1}{\sqrt{x}\left(1+2\sqrt{x}\right)}dx = \ln\left(1+2\sqrt{x}\right)+C$. Notice that we don't need the absolute value bars because $1+2\sqrt{x}$ is never negative.

7. $\ln(1 + e^x) + C$

Whenever we have an integral in the form of a quotient, we check to see if the solution is a logarithm. A clue is whether the numerator is the derivative of the denominator, as it is here. Let's use u-substitution. If we let $u = 1 + e^x$ then $du = e^x dx$. If we substitute into the integrand, we get: $\displaystyle\int\dfrac{e^x}{1+e^x}dx = \int\dfrac{du}{u}$. Recall that $\displaystyle\int\dfrac{du}{u} = \ln|u|+C$ (see page 183). Substituting back, we get: $\displaystyle\int\dfrac{e^x}{1+e^x}dx = \ln\left(1+e^x\right)+C$.

Notice that we don't need the absolute value bars because $1 + e^x$ is never negative.

8. $\dfrac{1}{10}e^{5x^2-1}+C$

Recall that $\int e^u du = e^u + C$ (see page 186). Let's use u-substitution. If we

let $u = 5x^2 - 1$ then $du = 10x\,dx$. But we need to substitute for $x\,dx$, so if

we divide du by 10, we get: $\dfrac{1}{10}du = x\,dx$. Now, if we substitute into the

integrand, we get: $\int xe^{5x^2-1}dx = \dfrac{1}{10}\int e^u du = \dfrac{1}{10}e^u + C$. Substituting back, we get:

$\int xe^{5x^2-1}dx = \dfrac{1}{10}e^{5x^2-1}+C$.

9. $\sin(2 + e^x) + C$
Recall that $\int e^u du = e^u + C$ (see page 186). Let's use u-substitution. If
we let $u = 2 + e^x$ then $du = e^x dx$. If we substitute into the integrand, we
get: $\int e^x \cos(2 + e^x)dx = \int \cos u\,du = \sin u + C$. Substituting back, we get:
$\int e^x \cos(2 + e^x)dx = \sin(2 + e^x) + C$.

10. $\ln\left|e^x - e^{-x}\right| + C$

Recall that $\int e^u du = e^u + C$ (see page 186). Let's use u-substitution. If we let

$u = e^x - e^{-x}$ then $du = e^x + e^{-x}dx$. If we substitute into the integrand, we get:

$\int \dfrac{e^x + e^{-x}}{e^x - e^{-x}}dx = \int \dfrac{du}{u}$. Recall that $\int \dfrac{du}{u} = \ln|u| + C$ (see page 183). Substituting back,

we get: $\int \dfrac{e^x + e^{-x}}{e^x - e^{-x}}dx = \ln\left|e^x - e^{-x}\right| + C$.

11. $-\dfrac{4^{-x^2}}{\ln 16} + C$

Recall that $\int a^u du = \dfrac{1}{\ln a} a^u + C$ (see page 188). Let's use u-substitution. If we

let $u = -x^2$ then $du = -2x dx$. But we need to substitute for $x dx$, so if we divide

du by -2, we get: $-\dfrac{1}{2} du = x dx$. Now, if we substitute into the integrand,

we get: $\int x 4^{-x^2} dx = -\dfrac{1}{2} \int 4^u du = -\dfrac{1}{2} \left(\dfrac{1}{\ln 4} \right) 4^u + C$. Substituting back, we get:

$\int x 4^{-x^2} dx = -\dfrac{1}{2} \left(\dfrac{1}{\ln 4} \right) 4^{-x^2} + C = -\dfrac{1}{\ln 16} 4^{-x^2} + C$.

12. $\dfrac{7^{\sin x}}{\ln 7} + C$

Recall that $\int a^u du = \dfrac{1}{\ln a} a^u + C$ (see page 188). Let's use u-substitution. If

we let $u = \sin x$ then $du = \cos x dx$. If we substitute into the integrand,

we get: $\int 7^{\sin x} \cos x dx = \int 7^u du = \dfrac{1}{\ln 7} 7^u + C$. Substituting back, we get:

$\int 7^{\sin x} \cos x dx = \dfrac{7^{\sin x}}{\ln 7} + C$.

SOLUTIONS TO PRACTICE PROBLEM SET 25

1. $\dfrac{32}{3}$

We find the area of a region bounded by $f(x)$ above and $g(x)$ below at all points

of the interval $[a,b]$ using the formula $\displaystyle\int_a^b \big[\,f(x)-g(x)\,\big]\,dx$. Here, $f(x)=2$ and

$g(x)=x^2-2$. First, let's make a sketch of the region:

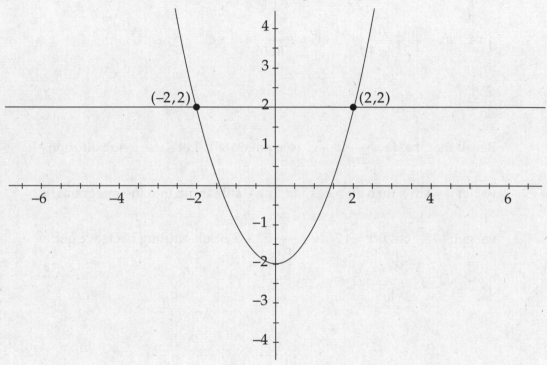

Next, we need to find where the two curves intersect, which will be the endpoints

of the region. We do this by setting the two curves equal to each other. We get:

$x^2 - 2 = 2$. The solutions are $(-2,0)$ and $(2,0)$. Therefore, in order to find the area of

the region, we need to evaluate the integral $\int_{-2}^{2}\left(2-\left(x^2-2\right)\right)dx = \int_{-2}^{2}\left(4-x^2\right)dx$. We get:

$$\int_{-2}^{2}\left(4-x^2\right)dx = \left(4x - \frac{x^3}{3}\right)\Bigg|_{-2}^{2} = \left(4(2) - \frac{(2)^3}{3}\right) - \left(4(-2) - \frac{(-2)^3}{3}\right) = \frac{32}{3}.$$

2. $\dfrac{8}{3}$

We find the area of a region bounded by $f(x)$ above and $g(x)$ below at all points

of the interval [a,b] using the formula $\int_{a}^{b}\left[f(x) - g(x)\right]dx$. Here, $f(x) = 4x - x^2$ and

$g(x) = x^2$.

First, let's make a sketch of the region:

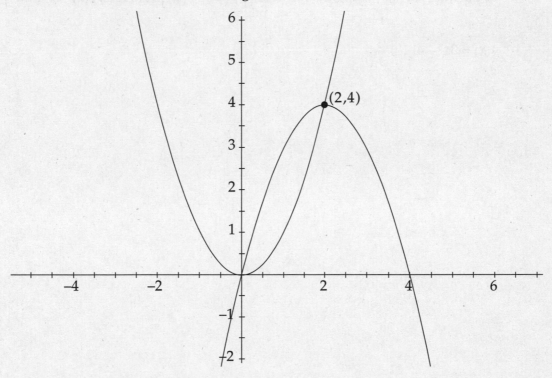

Next, we need to find where the two curves intersect, which will be the endpoints

of the region. We do this by setting the two curves equal to each other. We get:

$4x - x^2 = x^2$. The solutions are $(0,0)$ and $(2,4)$. Therefore, in order to find the area of

the region, we need to evaluate the integral $\int_0^2 \left(\left(4x - x^2\right) - x^2\right) dx = \int_0^2 \left(4x - 2x^2\right) dx$. We

get: $\int_0^2 \left(4x - 2x^2\right) dx = \left(2x^2 - \dfrac{2x^3}{3} \right)\Big|_0^2 = \left(2(2)^2 - \dfrac{2(2)^3}{3} \right) - 0 = \dfrac{8}{3}$.

3. $\dfrac{27}{4}$

We find the area of a region bounded by $f(x)$ above and $g(x)$ below at all points

of the interval $[a,b]$ using the formula $\int_a^b \left[f(x) - g(x) \right] dx$. Here, $f(x) = x^3$ and

$g(x) = 3x^2 - 4$.

First, let's make a sketch of the region:

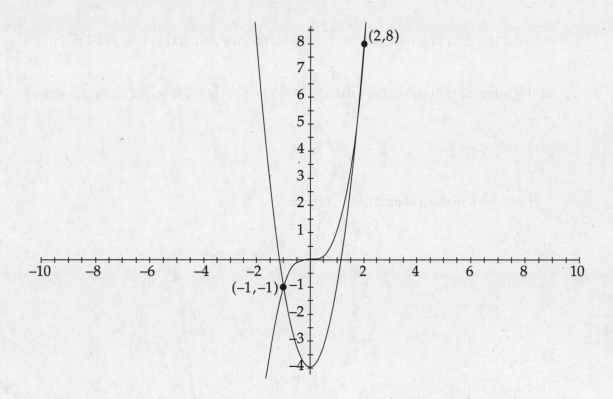

Next, we need to find where the two curves intersect, which will

be the endpoints of the region. We do this by setting the two curves

equal to each other. We get: $3x^2 - 4 = x^3$. The solutions are (-1, -1) and

(2, 8). Therefore, in order to find the area of the region, we need to

evaluate the integral $\int\limits_{-1}^{2}\left(x^3 - \left(3x^2 - 4\right)\right)dx = \int\limits_{-1}^{2}\left(x^3 - 3x^2 + 4\right)dx$. We get:

$$\int\limits_{-1}^{2}\left(x^3 - 3x^2 + 4\right)dx = \left(\frac{x^4}{4} - x^3 + 4x\right)\Bigg|_{-1}^{2} = \left(\frac{(2)^4}{4} - (2)^3 + 4(2)\right) - \left(\frac{(-1)^4}{4} - (-1)^3 + 4(-1)\right) = \frac{27}{4}$$

4.   36

We find the area of a region bounded by $f(x)$ above and $g(x)$ below at all points

of the interval $[a,b]$ using the formula $\int_a^b \left[f(x) - g(x) \right] dx$. Here, $f(x) = 2x - 5$ and

$g(x) = x^2 - 4x - 5$.

First, let's make a sketch of the region:

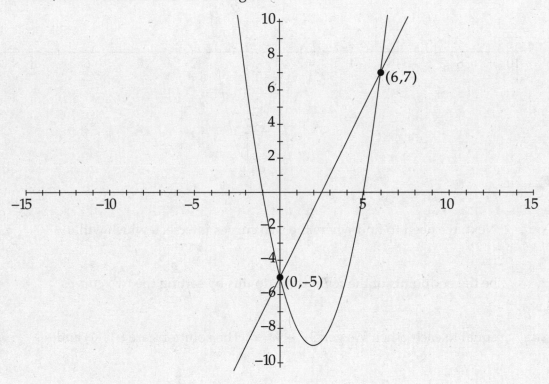

Next, we need to find where the two curves intersect, which will be the

endpoints of the region. We do this by setting the two curves equal to each other.

We get: $x^2 - 4x - 5 = 2x - 5$. The solutions are (0,-5) and (6,7). Therefore, in order to

find the area of the region, we need to evaluate the integral

$$\int_0^6 \left[(2x-5) - (x^2 - 4x - 5) \right] dx = \int_0^6 \left(-x^2 + 6x \right) dx. \text{ We get:}$$

$$\int_0^6 \left(-x^2 + 6x \right) dx = \left(-\frac{x^3}{3} + 3x^2 \right) \Bigg|_0^6 = \left(-\frac{(6)^3}{3} + 3(6)^2 \right) - 0 = 36.$$

5. $\dfrac{17}{4}$

We find the area of a region bounded by $f(x)$ above and $g(x)$ below at all points of

the interval $[a,b]$ using the formula $\displaystyle\int_a^b \left[f(x) - g(x) \right] dx$.

First, let's make a sketch of the region:

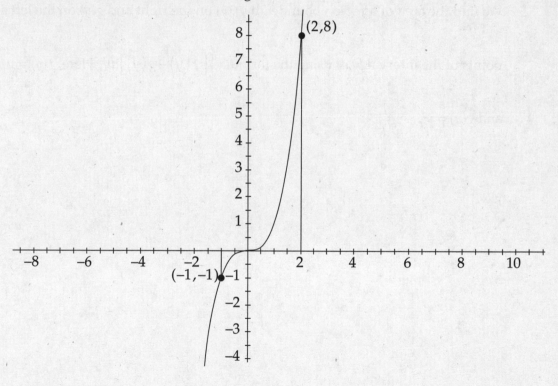

Notice that in the region from $x = -1$ to $x = 0$ the top curve is $f(x) = 0$ (the

x-axis) and the bottom curve is $g(x) = x^3$, but from $x = 0$ to $x = 2$ the situation is reversed, so the top curve is $f(x) = x^3$ and the bottom curve is $g(x) = 0$.

Thus, we split the region into two pieces and find the area by evaluating

two integrals and adding the answers: $\int\limits_{-1}^{0}(0-x^3)dx$ and $\int\limits_{0}^{2}(x^3-0)dx$. We get:

$$\int\limits_{-1}^{0}(0-x^3)dx = \left(-\frac{x^4}{4}\right)\Bigg|_{-1}^{0} = 0 - \left(-\frac{(-1)^4}{4}\right) = \frac{1}{4} \text{ and } \int\limits_{0}^{2}(x^3-0)dx = \left(\frac{x^4}{4}\right)\Bigg|_{0}^{2} = \frac{(2)^4}{4} - 0 = 4.$$

Therefore, the area of the region is $\dfrac{17}{4}$.

6. $\dfrac{9}{2}$

We find the area of a region bounded by $f(y)$ on the right and $g(y)$ on the left at all

points of the interval [c,d] using the formula $\int\limits_{c}^{d}\left[f(y)-g(y)\right]dy$. Here, $f(y) = y + 2$

and $g(y) = y^2$.

First, let's make a sketch of the region:

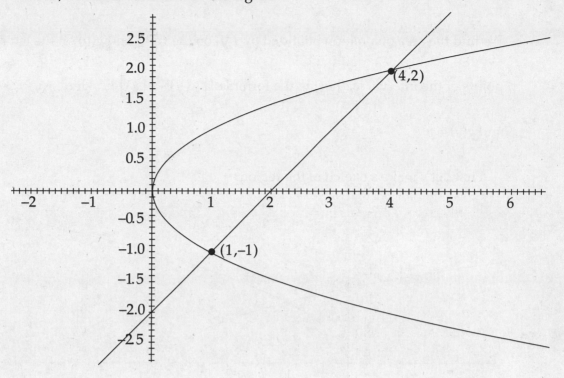

Next, we need to find where the two curves intersect, which will be the

endpoints of the region. We do this by setting the two curves equal to each other.

We get: $y^2 = y + 2$. The solutions are (4,2) and (1,–1). Therefore, in order to find

the area of the region, we need to evaluate the integral $\int_{-1}^{2}\left(y+2-y^2\right)dy$. We get:

$$\int_{-1}^{2}\left(y+2-y^2\right)dy = \left(\frac{y^2}{2}+2y-\frac{y^3}{3}\right)\Bigg|_{-1}^{2} = \left(\frac{(2)^2}{2}+2(2)-\frac{(2)^3}{3}\right)-\left(\frac{(-1)^2}{2}+2(-1)-\frac{(-1)^3}{3}\right) = \frac{9}{2}$$

7.   4

We find the area of a region bounded by $f(y)$ on the right and $g(y)$ on the left at all

points of the interval $[c,d]$ using the formula $\int_c^d \left[f(y) - g(y) \right] dy$. Here, $f(y) = 3 - 2y^2$

and $g(y) = y^2$.

First, let's make a sketch of the region:

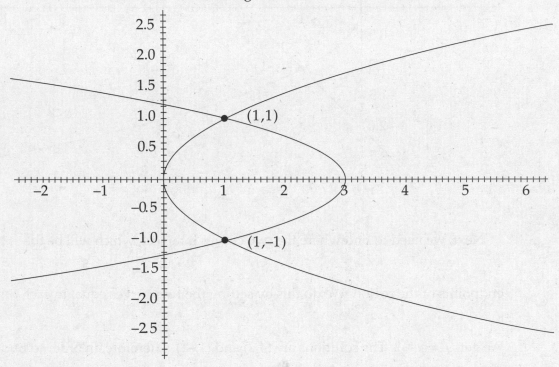

Next, we need to find where the two curves intersect, which will be the

endpoints of the region. We do this by setting the two curves equal to each other.

We get: $y^2 = 3 - 2y^2$. The solutions are $(1,1)$ and $(1, -1)$. Therefore, in order to find the

area of the region, we need to evaluate the integral $\int_{-1}^{1} \left(3 - 2y^2 - y^2 \right) dy = \int_{-1}^{1} \left(3 - 3y^2 \right) dy$.

We get: $\int_{-1}^{1} \left(3 - 3y^2 \right) dy = \left(3y - y^3 \right) \Big|_{-1}^{1} = \left(3(1) - (1)^3 \right) - \left(3(-1) - (-1)^3 \right) = 4$.

8. $\dfrac{37}{12}$

We find the area of a region bounded by $f(y)$ on the right and $g(y)$ on the left at all points of the interval $[c,d]$ using the formula $\int_{c}^{d}\left[f(y)-g(y)\right]dy$. Here, $f(y) = 3 - 2y^2$ and $g(y) = y^2$.

First, let's make a sketch of the region:

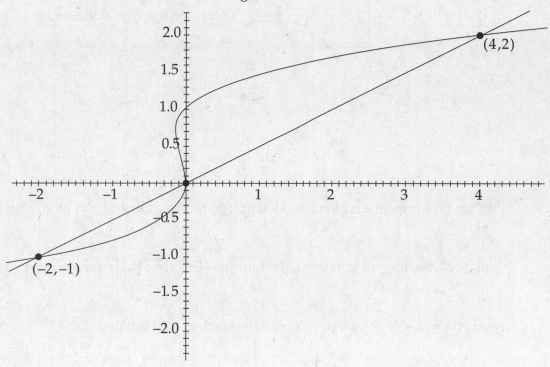

Next, we need to find where the two curves intersect, which will be the endpoints of the region. We do this by setting the two curves equal to each other. We get: $y^3 - y^2 = 2y$. The solutions are $(4,2)$, $(0,0)$ and $(-2,-1)$. Notice that in the region from $y = -1$ to $y = 0$ the right curve is $f(y) = y^3 - y^2$ and the left curve is $g(y) = 2y$, but from $y = 0$ to $y = 2$ the situation is reversed, so the right

curve is $f(y) = 2y$ and the left curve is $g(y) = y^3 - y^2$. Thus, we split the region

into two pieces and find the area by evaluating two integrals and adding the

answers: $\int_{-1}^{0}(y^3 - y^2 - 2y)dy$ and $\int_{0}^{2}(2y - (y^3 - y^2))dy = \int_{0}^{2}(2y - y^3 + y^2)dy$. We

get: $\int_{-1}^{0}(y^3 - y^2 - 2y)dy = \left(\frac{y^4}{4} - \frac{y^3}{3} - y^2\right)\Big|_{-1}^{0} = 0 - \left(\frac{(-1)^4}{4} - \frac{(-1)^3}{3} - (-1)^2\right) = \frac{5}{12}$ and

$\int_{0}^{2}(2y - y^3 + y^2)dy = \left(y^2 - \frac{y^4}{4} + \frac{y^3}{3}\right)\Big|_{0}^{2} = \frac{8}{3}$. Therefore, the area of the region is

$\frac{5}{12} + \frac{8}{3} = \frac{37}{12}$.

9. $\frac{9}{2}$

We find the area of a region bounded by $f(y)$ on the right and $g(y)$ on the left at all

points of the interval $[c,d]$ using the formula $\int_{c}^{d}\left[f(y) - g(y)\right]dy$. Here, $f(y) = y - 2$

and $g(y) = y^2 - 4y + 2$. First, let's make a sketch of the region:

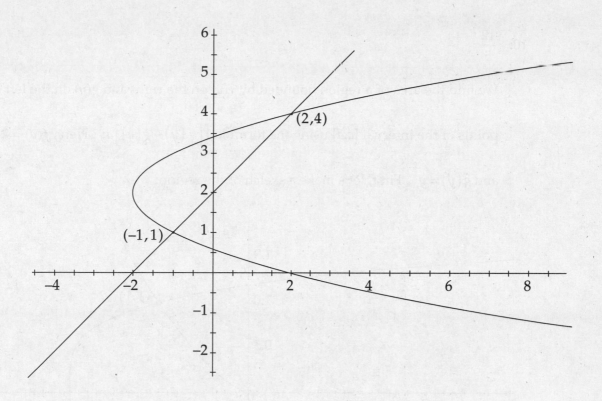

Next, we need to find where the two curves intersect, which will be the

endpoints of the region. We do this by setting the two curves equal to each

other. We get: $y^2 - 4y + 2 = y - 2$. The solutions are (2,4) and (−1,1). Therefore,

in order to find the area of the region, we need to evaluate the integral

$\int_1^4 \left[(y-2) - (y^2 - 4y + 2) \right] dy = \int_1^4 \left[(-y^2 + 5y - 4) \right] dy$. We get: $\int_1^4 \left[(-y^2 + 5y - 4) \right] dy =$

$\left(-\frac{y^3}{3} + \frac{5y^2}{2} - 4y \right) \Bigg|_1^4 = \left(-\frac{(4)^3}{3} + \frac{5(4)^2}{2} - 4(4) \right) - \left(-\frac{(1)^3}{3} + \frac{5(1)^2}{2} - 4(1) \right) = \frac{9}{2}$

10. $\dfrac{12}{5}$

We find the area of a region bounded by $f(y)$ on the right and $g(y)$ on the left at all

points of the interval $[c,d]$ using the formula $\displaystyle\int_{c}^{d}\left[f(y)-g(y)\right]dy$. Here, $f(y)=2-y^4$

and $g(y)=y^{\frac{2}{3}}$. First, let's make a sketch of the region:

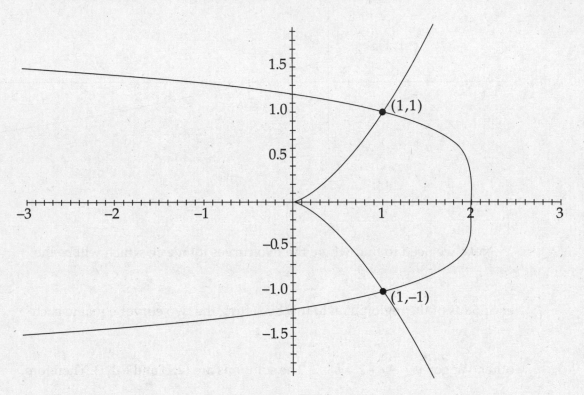

Next, we need to find where the two curves intersect, which will be the

endpoints of the region. We do this by setting the two curves equal to each other.

We get: $2-y^4=y^{\frac{2}{3}}$. The solutions are $(1,1)$ and $(1,-1)$. Therefore, in order to find

the area of the region, we need to evaluate the integral $\displaystyle\int_{-1}^{1}\left(2-y^4-y^{\frac{2}{3}}\right)dy$. We get:

$$\int_{-1}^{1}\left(2-y^4-y^{\frac{2}{3}}\right)dy=\left(2y-\frac{y^5}{5}-\frac{3}{5}y^{\frac{5}{3}}\right)\Bigg|_{-1}^{1}=\left(2(1)-\frac{(1)^5}{5}-\frac{3}{5}(1)^{\frac{5}{3}}\right)-\left(2(-1)-\frac{(-1)^5}{5}-\frac{3}{5}(-1)^{\frac{5}{3}}\right)=\frac{12}{5}$$

SOLUTIONS TO PRACTICE PROBLEM SET 26

1. $36\,\pi$

    When the region we are revolving is defined between a curve $f(x)$ and the x-axis, we can find the volume using disks. We use the formula $V = \pi\int_a^b \left[f(x)\right]^2 dx$ (see page 202). Here we have a region between $f(x) = \sqrt{9-x^2}$ and the x-axis. First, we need to find the endpoints of the region. We do this by setting $f(x) = \sqrt{9-x^2}$ equal to zero and solving for x. We get: $x = -3$ and $x = 3$. Thus, we will find the volume by evaluating $\pi\int_{-3}^3 \left(\sqrt{9-x^2}\right)^2 dx = \pi\int_{-3}^3 \left(9-x^2\right)dx$. We get:

    $$\pi\int_{-3}^3 \left(9-x^2\right)dx = \pi\left(9x - \frac{x^3}{3}\right)\Bigg|_{-3}^3 = 36\pi$$

2. $2\,\pi$

    When the region we are revolving is defined between a curve $f(x)$ and the x-axis, we can find the volume using disks. We use the formula $V = \pi\int_a^b \left[f(x)\right]^2 dx$ (see page 202). Here we have a region between $f(x) = \sec x$ and the x-axis. We are given the endpoints of the region: $x = -\frac{\pi}{4}$ and $x = \frac{\pi}{4}$. Thus, we will find the volume by evaluating $\pi\int_{-\frac{\pi}{4}}^{\frac{\pi}{4}} \sec^2 x\,dx$. We get: $\pi\int_{-\frac{\pi}{4}}^{\frac{\pi}{4}} \sec^2 x\,dx = \pi\left(\tan x\right)\Big|_{-\frac{\pi}{4}}^{\frac{\pi}{4}} = 2\pi$.

3. $\dfrac{16\pi}{15}$

When the region we are revolving is defined between a curve $f(y)$ and the y-axis,

we can find the volume using disks. We use the formula $V = \pi\displaystyle\int_a^b \left[f(y)\right]^2 dy$

(see page 205 and note that when $g(y) = 0$ we get disks instead of washers).

Here we have a region between $f(y) = 1 - y^2$ and the y-axis. First, we need

to find the endpoints of the region. We do this by setting $f(y) = 1 - y^2$ equal

to zero and solving for y. We get: $y = -1$ and $y = 1$. Thus, we will find

the volume by evaluating $\pi\displaystyle\int_{-1}^{1}\left(1 - y^2\right)^2 dy = \pi\displaystyle\int_{-1}^{1}\left(1 - 2y^2 + y^4\right)dy$. We get:

$$\pi\int_{-1}^{1}\left(1 - 2y^2 + y^4\right)dy = \pi\left(y - \frac{2y^3}{3} + \frac{y^5}{5}\right)\Bigg|_{-1}^{1} = \frac{16\pi}{15}.$$

4. 2π

When the region we are revolving is defined between a curve $f(y)$ and the y-axis, we can find the volume using disks. We use the formula $V = \pi\displaystyle\int_a^b \left[f(y)\right]^2 dy$ (See page 205 and note that when $g(y) = 0$ we get disks instead of washers). Here we have a region between $f(y) = \sqrt{5}y^2$ and the y-axis. We are given the endpoints of the region: $y = -1$ and $y = 1$. Thus, we will find the volume by evaluating

$\pi\displaystyle\int_{-1}^{1}\left(\sqrt{5}y^2\right)^2 dy = \pi\displaystyle\int_{-1}^{1}\left(5y^4\right)dy$. We get: $\pi\displaystyle\int_{-1}^{1}\left(5y^4\right)dy = \pi\left(y^5\right)\Big|_{-1}^{1} = 2\pi$.

5. $\dfrac{16\pi}{5}$

When the region we are revolving is defined between a curve $f(x)$ and

$g(x)$, we can find the volume using cylindrical shells. We use the formula

$V = 2\pi \int_{a}^{b} x \big[f(x) - g(x) \big] dx$ (see page 208). Here we have a region between

$f(x) = x^3$ and the line $x = 2$ that we are revolving around the line $x = 2$. If

we use vertical slices, then we will need to use cylindrical shells to find the

volume. If we use horizontal slices, then we will need to use washers to find

the volume. Here we will use cylindrical shells. (Try doing it yourself using

washers. You should get the same answer but it is much harder!) First, we

need to find the endpoints of the region. We get the left endpoint by setting

$f(x) = x^3$ equal to zero and solving for x. We get: $x = 0$. The right endpoint

is simply $x = 2$. Next, note that we are not revolving around the x-axis but

around the line $x = 2$. Thus, the radius of each shell is not x but rather $2 - x$.

The height of each shell is simply $f(x) - g(x) = x^3 - 0 = x^3$. Therefore, we will

find the volume by evaluating $2\pi \int_{0}^{2} \big[(2 - x)(x^3) \big] dx = 2\pi \int_{0}^{2} \left(2x^3 - x^4 \right) dx$. We get:

$2\pi \int_{0}^{2} \left(2x^3 - x^4 \right) dx = 2\pi \left(\dfrac{x^4}{2} - \dfrac{x^5}{5} \right) \Big|_{0}^{2} = \dfrac{16\pi}{5}$.

6. 8π

When the region we are revolving is defined between a curve $f(x)$ and

$g(x)$, we can find the volume using cylindrical shells. We use the formula

$V = 2\pi\int_a^b x\big[f(x)-g(x)\big]dx$ (see page 208). Here we have $f(x) = x$ and $g(x) = -\dfrac{x}{2}$.

Thus, the height of each shell is $f(x)-g(x) = x-\left(-\dfrac{x}{2}\right) = \dfrac{3x}{2}$ and the radius is

simply x. The endpoints of our region are $x = 0$ and $x = 2$. Therefore, we will find

the volume by evaluating: $2\pi\int_0^2\left(x\left(\dfrac{3x}{2}\right)\right)dx = 2\pi\int_0^2\left(\dfrac{3x^2}{2}\right)dx = 3\pi\int_0^2 x^2 dx$. We get:

$3\pi\int_0^2 x^2 dx = 3\pi\left(\dfrac{x^3}{3}\right)\Big|_0^2 = 8\pi$.

7. $\dfrac{7\pi}{15}$

When the region we are revolving is defined between a curve $f(x)$ and $g(x)$, we can find

the volume using cylindrical shells. We use the formula $V = 2\pi\int_a^b x\big[f(x)-g(x)\big]dx$

(see page 208). Here we have $f(x) = \sqrt{x}$ and $g(x) = 2x-1$. Thus, the height of each

shell is $f(x)-g(x) = \sqrt{x}-(2x-1) = \sqrt{x}-2x+1$ and the radius is simply x. The

left endpoint of our region is $x = 0$ and we find the right endpoint by finding

where $f(x) = \sqrt{x}$ intersects $g(x) = 2x-1$. We get $x = 1$. Therefore, we will find

the volume by evaluating: $2\pi\int_0^1\left(x\left(\sqrt{x}-2x+1\right)\right)dx = 2\pi\int_0^1\left(x^{\frac{3}{2}}-2x^2+x\right)dx$. We get:

$2\pi\int_0^1\left(x^{\frac{3}{2}}-2x^2+x\right)dx = 2\pi\left(\dfrac{2x^{\frac{5}{2}}}{5}-\dfrac{2x^3}{3}+\dfrac{x^2}{2}\right)\Big|_0^1 = \dfrac{7\pi}{15}$.

8. $\dfrac{128\pi}{5}$

When the region we are revolving is defined between a curve $f(y)$ and

$g(y)$, we can find the volume using cylindrical shells. We use the formula

$V = 2\pi \displaystyle\int_a^b y\left[f(y) - g(y) \right] dy$ (see page 208). Here we have $f(y) = \sqrt{y}$ (which we

get by solving $y = x^2$ for x) and $g(y) = 0$ (the y-axis). We can easily see that the top

endpoint is $y = 4$ and the bottom one is $y = 0$. Therefore, we will find the volume by

evaluating: $2\pi \displaystyle\int_0^4 \left(y\sqrt{y} \right) dy = 2\pi \displaystyle\int_0^4 \left(y^{\frac{3}{2}} \right) dy$. We get: $2\pi \displaystyle\int_0^4 \left(y^{\frac{3}{2}} \right) dy = 2\pi \left(\dfrac{2y^{\frac{5}{2}}}{5} \right) \Big|_0^4 = \dfrac{128\pi}{5}$.

9. $\dfrac{256\pi}{5}$

When the region we are revolving is defined between a curve $f(x)$ and

$g(x)$, we can find the volume using cylindrical shells. We use the formula

$V = 2\pi \displaystyle\int_a^b x\left[f(x) - g(x) \right] dx$ (See page 208). Here we have $f(x) = 2\sqrt{x}$ and $g(x) = 0$.

Thus, the height of each shell is $f(x) - g(x) = 2\sqrt{x}$ and the radius is simply x. We

can easily see that the left endpoint is $x = 0$ and that the right endpoint is $x = 4$.

Therefore, we will find the volume by evaluating: $2\pi \displaystyle\int_0^4 \left(x\left(2\sqrt{x} \right) \right) dx = 2\pi \displaystyle\int_0^4 \left(2x^{\frac{3}{2}} \right) dx$.

We get: $2\pi \displaystyle\int_0^4 \left(2x^{\frac{3}{2}} \right) dx = 4\pi \left(\dfrac{2x^{\frac{5}{2}}}{5} \right) \Big|_0^4 = \dfrac{256\pi}{5}$.

10. $\dfrac{896\pi}{15}$

When the region we are revolving is defined between a curve $f(x)$ and

$g(x)$, we can find the volume using cylindrical shells. We use the formula

$V = 2\pi\displaystyle\int_a^b x\big[f(x)-g(x)\big]dx$ (See page 208). Here we have $f(x)=2\sqrt{2x}$

(which we get by solving $y^2 = 8x$ for y and taking the top half above the

x-axis) and $g(x)=-2\sqrt{2x}$ (the bottom half). Thus the height of each

shell is $f(x)-g(x)=4\sqrt{2x}$. We can easily see that the left endpoint is

$x = 0$ and that the right endpoint is $x = 2$. Next, note that we are not

revolving around the x-axis but around the line $x = 4$. Thus, the radius

of each shell is not x but rather $4 - x$. Therefore, we will find the volume

by evaluating: $2\pi\displaystyle\int_0^2\Big[(4-x)4\sqrt{2x}\Big]dx = 8\pi\sqrt{2}\int_0^2\left(4x^{\frac{1}{2}}-x^{\frac{3}{2}}\right)dx$. We get:

$8\pi\sqrt{2}\displaystyle\int_0^2\left(4x^{\frac{1}{2}}-x^{\frac{3}{2}}\right)dx = 8\pi\sqrt{2}\left.\left(\dfrac{8x^{\frac{3}{2}}}{3}-\dfrac{2x^{\frac{5}{2}}}{5}\right)\right|_0^2 = \dfrac{896\pi}{15}$.

11. $\dfrac{256}{3}$

To find the volume of a solid with a cross-section of a square, we integrate the

area of the square ($side^2$) over the endpoints of the interval. Here, the sides of

the squares are found by $f(x) - g(x) = \sqrt{16 - x^2} - 0$ and the intervals are found

by setting $y = \sqrt{16 - x^2}$ equal to zero. We get: $x = -4$ and $x = 4$. Thus, we find

the volume by evaluating the integral $\int_{-4}^{4} \left(\sqrt{16 - x^2}\right)^2 dx = \int_{-4}^{4} (16 - x^2) dx$. We get:

$$\int_{-4}^{4} (16 - x^2) dx = \left(16x - \frac{x^3}{3}\right)\Bigg|_{-4}^{4} = \frac{256}{3}.$$

12. $\dfrac{128}{15}$

To find the volume of a solid with a cross-section of a square, we integrate

the area of the isosceles right triangle $\dfrac{hypotenuse^2}{4}$ over the endpoints

of the interval. Here, the hypotenuses of the triangles are found by

$f(x) - g(x) = 4 - x^2$ and the intervals are found by setting $y = x^2$ equal to

$y = 4$. We get: $x = -2$ and $x = 2$. Thus, we find the volume by evaluating

the integral $\int_{-2}^{2} \dfrac{(4 - x^2)^2}{4} dx = \int_{-2}^{2} \dfrac{(16 - 8x^2 + x^4)}{4} dx = \int_{-2}^{2} \left(4 - 2x^2 + \dfrac{x^4}{4}\right) dx$. We get:

$$\int_{-2}^{2} \left(4 - 2x^2 + \frac{x^4}{4}\right) dx = \left(4x - \frac{2x^3}{3} + \frac{x^5}{20}\right)\Bigg|_{-2}^{2} = \frac{128}{15}.$$

SOLUTIONS TO PRACTICE PROBLEM SET 27

1. $-x\cot x + \ln|\sin x| + C$

   Recall that *integration by parts* is a way of evaluating integrals of the form $\int u\,dv$, where both u and v are functions of x. The formula for evaluating the integral is: $\int u\,dv = uv - \int v\,du$ (see page 220). Here, if we let $u = x$ and $dv = \csc^2 x\,dx$, then we can find du by taking the derivative of u, and we can find v by taking the integral of dv. We get: $du = dx$ and $v = \int \csc^2 x\,dx = -\cot x$. Plugging into the formula, we get: $\int x\csc^2 x\,dx = -x\cot x - \int(-\cot x)\,dx = -x\cot x + \int \cot x\,dx$. Now we just have to find $\int \cot x\,dx$. We do this by rewriting the integrand in terms of $\sin x$ and $\cos x$: $\int \cot x\,dx = \int \dfrac{\cos x}{\sin x}\,dx = \ln|\sin x| + C$. Therefore, $\int x\csc^2 x\,dx = -x\cot x + \ln|\sin x| + C$.

2. $\dfrac{x}{2}e^{2x} - \dfrac{1}{4}e^{2x} + C$

   Recall that *integration by parts* is a way of evaluating integrals of the form $\int u\,dv$, where both u and v are functions of x. The formula for evaluating the integral is: $\int u\,dv = uv - \int v\,du$ (see page 220). Here, if we let $u = x$ and $dv = e^{2x}\,dx$, then we can find du by taking the derivative of u, and we can find v by taking the integral of dv. We get: $du = dx$ and $v = \int e^{2x}\,dx = \dfrac{1}{2}e^{2x}$. Plugging into the formula, we get: $\int xe^{2x}\,dx = x\left(\dfrac{1}{2}e^{2x}\right) - \dfrac{1}{2}\int e^{2x}\,dx$. Now we just have to find $\dfrac{1}{2}\int e^{2x}\,dx$:

   $\dfrac{1}{2}\int e^{2x}\,dx = \dfrac{1}{4}e^{2x} + C$. Therefore, $\int xe^{2x}\,dx = \dfrac{x}{2}e^{2x} - \dfrac{1}{4}e^{2x} + C$.

3. $-\dfrac{1}{x}\ln x - \dfrac{1}{x} + C$

Recall that *integration by parts* is a way of evaluating integrals of the form $\int u\,dv$,

where both u and v are functions of x. The formula for evaluating the integral is:

$\int u\,dv = uv - \int v\,du$ (see page 220). Here, if we let $u = \ln x$ and $dv = \dfrac{1}{x^2}\,dx$, then we

can find du by taking the derivative of u, and we can find v by taking the integral

of dv. We get: $du = \dfrac{1}{x}\,dx$ and $v = \int \dfrac{1}{x^2}\,dx = -\dfrac{1}{x}$. Plugging into the formula, we get:

$\int \dfrac{\ln x}{x^2}\,dx = -\dfrac{\ln x}{x} - \int \left(-\dfrac{1}{x}\right)\left(\dfrac{1}{x}\right)dx = -\dfrac{\ln x}{x} + \int x^{-2}dx$. Now we just have to find

$\int x^{-2}dx : \int x^{-2}dx = -\dfrac{1}{x} + C$. Therefore, $\int \dfrac{\ln x}{x^2}\,dx = -\dfrac{\ln x}{x} - \dfrac{1}{x} + C$.

4. $x^2 \sin x + 2x \cos x - 2 \sin x + C$

Recall that *integration by parts* is a way of evaluating integrals of the form $\int u\,dv$,

where both u and v are functions of x. The formula for evaluating the integral

is: $\int u\,dv = uv - \int v\,du$ (see page 220). Here, if we let $u = x^2$ and $dv = \cos dx$,

then we can find du by taking the derivative of u, and we can find v by taking

the integral of dv. We get: $du = 2x\,dx$ and $v = \int \cos x\,dx = \sin x$. Plugging into

the formula, we get: $\int x^2 \cos dx = x^2 \sin x - 2\int x \sin x\,dx$. Now we have to find

$\int x \sin x\,dx$. Once again we will have to use integration by parts. This

time, if we let $u = x$ and $dv = \sin x\,dx$, then $du = dx$ and $v = \int \sin x\,dx = -\cos x$.

Plugging into the formula, we get: $\int x \sin x\,dx = -x \cos x + \int \cos x\,dx$. Finally,

we have to find $\int \cos x\,dx = \sin x + C$. Putting everything together, we get:

$\int x^2 \cos dx = x^2 \sin x - 2\left(-x \cos x + \sin x\right) + C = x^2 \sin x + 2x \cos x - 2 \sin x + C$.

5. $\dfrac{x^3}{3}\ln x - \dfrac{x^3}{9} + C$

Recall that *integration by parts* is a way of evaluating integrals of the form $\int u\,dv$,

where both u and v are functions of x. The formula for evaluating the integral

is: $\int u\,dv = uv - \int v\,du$ (see page 220). Here, if we let $u = \ln x$ and $dv = x^2$, then we

can find du by taking the derivative of u, and we can find v by taking the integral

of dv. We get: $du = \dfrac{1}{x}dx$ and $v = \int x^2 dx = \dfrac{x^3}{3}$. Plugging into the formula, we get:

$\int x^2 \ln x\,dx = \dfrac{x^3}{3}\ln x - \int \dfrac{x^3}{3}\left(\dfrac{1}{x}\right)dx = x^3 \ln x - \dfrac{1}{3}\int x^2 dx$. Now we just have to find

$\dfrac{1}{3}\int x^2 dx = \dfrac{x^3}{9} + C$. Therefore, $\int x^2 \ln x\,dx = \dfrac{x^3}{3}\ln x - \dfrac{x^3}{9} + C$.

6. $-\dfrac{1}{2}x\cos 2x + \dfrac{1}{4}\sin 2x + C$

Recall that *integration by parts* is a way of evaluating integrals of the form $\int u\,dv$,

where both u and v are functions of x. The formula for evaluating the integral

is: $\int u\,dv = uv - \int v\,du$ (see page 220). Here, if we let $u = x$ and $du = \sin 2x\,dx$, then

we can find du by taking the derivative of u, and we can find v by taking the

integral of dv. We get: $du = dx$ and $v = \int \sin 2x\,dx = -\dfrac{1}{2}\cos 2x$. Plugging into the

formula, we get: $\int x\sin 2x\,dx = -\dfrac{1}{2}x\cos 2x + \dfrac{1}{2}\int \cos 2x\,dx$. Now we just have to find

$\dfrac{1}{2}\int \cos 2x\,dx = \dfrac{1}{4}\sin 2x + C$. Therefore, $\int x\sin 2x\,dx = -\dfrac{1}{2}x\cos 2x + \dfrac{1}{4}\sin 2x + C$.

7. $x\ln^2 x - 2x\ln x + 2x + C$

Recall that *integration by parts* is a way of evaluating integrals of the form

$\int udv$, where both u and v are functions of x. The formula for evaluating the

integral is: $\int udv = uv - \int vdu$ (see page 220). Here, if we let $u = \ln^2 x$ and $dv = dx$

then we can find du by taking the derivative of u, and we can find v by taking

the integral of dv. We get: $du = 2\ln x\left(\dfrac{1}{x}\right)dx$ and $v = \int dx = x$. Plugging into

the formula, we get: $\int \ln^2 xdx = x\ln^2 x - 2\int x\ln x\left(\dfrac{1}{x}\right)dx = x\ln^2 x - 2\int \ln xdx$.

Now we have to find $\int \ln xdx$. Once again we will have to use integration by

parts. This time, if we let $u = \ln x$ and $dv = dx$, then $du = \dfrac{1}{x}dx$ and $v = \int dx = x$.

Plugging into the formula, we get: $\int \ln xdx = x\ln x - \int x\left(\dfrac{1}{x}\right)dx = x\ln x - \int dx$.

Finally we have to find $\int x = x + C$. Putting everything together, we get:

$\int \ln^2 xdx = x\ln^2 x - 2(x\ln x - x) = x\ln^2 x - 2x\ln x + 2x + C$.

8. $x\tan x + \ln|\cos x| + C$

Recall that *integration by parts* is a way of evaluating integrals of the form $\int udv$,

where both u and v are functions of x. The formula for evaluating the integral

is: $\int udv = uv - \int vdu$ (see page 220). Here, if we let $u = x$ and $dv = \sec^2 xdx$ then

we can find du by taking the derivative of u, and we can find v by taking the

integral of dv. We get: $du = dx$ and $v = \int \sec^2 xdx = \tan x$. Plugging into the

formula, we get: $\int x\sec^2 xdx = x\tan x - \int \tan xdx$. Now we just have to find

$\int \tan xdx$. We do this by rewriting the integrand in terms of $\sin x$ and $\cos x$:

$\int \tan xdx = \int \dfrac{\sin x}{\cos x}dx = -\ln|\cos x| + C$. Therefore, $\int x\sec^2 xdx = x\tan x + \ln|\cos x| + C$.

SOLUTIONS TO PRACTICE PROBLEM SET 28

1. $\dfrac{1}{16+x^2}$

    We find the derivative of the inverse tangent using the formula

    $\dfrac{d}{dx}\left(\tan^{-1}u\right)=\dfrac{1}{1+u^2}\dfrac{du}{dx}$ (see page 226). Here, we have $u=\dfrac{x}{4}$, so $\dfrac{du}{dx}=\dfrac{1}{4}$. Therefore,

    $\dfrac{d}{dx}\left(\dfrac{1}{4}\tan^{-1}\dfrac{x}{4}\right)=\dfrac{1}{4}\dfrac{1}{1+\left(\dfrac{x}{4}\right)^2}\left(\dfrac{1}{4}\right)=\dfrac{1}{16}\dfrac{1}{1+\dfrac{x^2}{16}}=\dfrac{1}{16+x^2}$.

2. $\dfrac{-1}{|x|\sqrt{x^2-1}}$

    We find the derivative of the inverse sine using the formula

    $\dfrac{d}{dx}\left(\sin^{-1}u\right)=\dfrac{1}{\sqrt{1-u^2}}\dfrac{du}{dx}$ (see page 226). Here, we have $u=\dfrac{1}{x}$, so $\dfrac{du}{dx}=-\dfrac{1}{x^2}$.

    Therefore, $\dfrac{d}{dx}\sin^{-1}\left(\dfrac{1}{x}\right)=\dfrac{1}{\sqrt{1-\left(\dfrac{1}{x}\right)^2}}\left(-\dfrac{1}{x^2}\right)=\dfrac{-1}{\sqrt{1-\dfrac{1}{x^2}}}\left(\dfrac{1}{x^2}\right)=\dfrac{-1}{|x|\sqrt{x^2-1}}$.

3. $\dfrac{e^x}{1+e^{2x}}$

    We find the derivative of the inverse tangent using the formula

    $\dfrac{d}{dx}\left(\tan^{-1}u\right)=\dfrac{1}{1+u^2}\dfrac{du}{dx}$ (see page 226). Here, we have $u=e^x$, so $\dfrac{du}{dx}=e^x$. Therefore,

    $\dfrac{d}{dx}\left(\tan^{-1}e^x\right)=\dfrac{1}{1+\left(e^x\right)^2}\left(e^x\right)=\dfrac{e^x}{1+e^{2x}}$.

4. $\dfrac{1}{\sqrt{\pi}}\sec^{-1}\dfrac{x}{\sqrt{\pi}}+C$

Recall that $\displaystyle\int\dfrac{du}{u\sqrt{u^2-1}}=\sec^{-1}u+C$ (see page 227). Here we have $\displaystyle\int\dfrac{dx}{x\sqrt{x^2-\pi}}$ and

we just need to rearrange the integrand so that it is in the proper form to use

the integral formula. If we factor π out of the radicand we get: $\displaystyle\int\dfrac{dx}{x\sqrt{\pi}\sqrt{\dfrac{x^2}{\pi}-1}}$.

Next, we do u-substitution. Let $u=\dfrac{x}{\sqrt{\pi}}$ and $du=\dfrac{1}{\sqrt{\pi}}dx$. Multiply both by

$\sqrt{\pi}$ so that $u\sqrt{\pi}=x$ and $du\sqrt{\pi}=dx$. Substituting into the integrand we get:

$\displaystyle\int\dfrac{du\sqrt{\pi}}{\pi u\sqrt{u^2-1}}=\dfrac{1}{\sqrt{\pi}}\int\dfrac{du}{u\sqrt{u^2-1}}$. Now we get: $\dfrac{1}{\sqrt{\pi}}\displaystyle\int\dfrac{du}{u\sqrt{u^2-1}}=\dfrac{1}{\sqrt{\pi}}\sec^{-1}u+C$.

Substituting back we get: $\dfrac{1}{\sqrt{\pi}}\sec^{-1}\dfrac{x}{\sqrt{\pi}}+C$.

5. $\dfrac{1}{\sqrt{7}}\tan^{-1}\dfrac{x}{\sqrt{7}}+C$

Recall that $\displaystyle\int\dfrac{du}{1+u^2}=\tan^{-1}u+C$ (see page 227). Here we have $\displaystyle\int\dfrac{dx}{7+x^2}$ and

we just need to rearrange the integrand so that it is in the proper form to

use the integral formula. If we factor 7 out of the denominator we get:

$\int \dfrac{dx}{7\left(1+\dfrac{x^2}{7}\right)} = \dfrac{1}{7}\int \dfrac{dx}{\left(1+\left(\dfrac{x}{\sqrt{7}}\right)^2\right)}$. Next, we do u-substitution. Let $u = \dfrac{x}{\sqrt{7}}$ and

$du = \dfrac{1}{\sqrt{7}}dx$. Multiply du by $\sqrt{7}$ so that $du\sqrt{7} = dx$. Substituting into the

integrand we get: $\dfrac{1}{7}\int \dfrac{du\sqrt{7}}{1+u^2} = \dfrac{1}{\sqrt{7}}\int \dfrac{du}{1+u^2}$. Now we get: $\dfrac{1}{\sqrt{7}}\int \dfrac{du}{1+u^2} = \dfrac{1}{\sqrt{7}}\tan^{-1}u + C$.

Substituting back we get: $\dfrac{1}{\sqrt{7}}\tan^{-1}\dfrac{x}{\sqrt{7}} + C$.

6. $\tan^{-1}(\ln x) + C$

Recall that $\int \dfrac{du}{1+u^2} = \tan^{-1}u + C$ (see page 227). Here we have $\int \dfrac{dx}{x\left(1+\ln^2 x\right)}$ and

we will need to do u-substitution. Let $u = \ln x$ and $du = \dfrac{1}{x}dx$. Substituting into the

integrand we get: $\int \dfrac{du}{1+u^2} = \tan^{-1}u + C$. Substituting back we get: $\tan^{-1}\left(\ln x\right) + C$.

7. $\sin^{-1}(\tan x) + C$

Recall that $\int \dfrac{du}{\sqrt{1-u^2}} = \sin^{-1}u + C$ (see page 227). Here we have $\int \dfrac{\sec^2 x\,dx}{\sqrt{1-\tan^2 x}}$ and

we will need to do u-substitution. Let $u = \tan x$ and $du = \sec^2 x\,dx$. Substituting

into the integrand we get: $\int \dfrac{du}{\sqrt{1-u^2}} = \sin^{-1}u + C$. Substituting back we get:

$\sin^{-1}\left(\tan x\right) + C$.

8. $\dfrac{1}{2}\sin^{-1}\dfrac{2x}{3}+C$

Recall that $\displaystyle\int\dfrac{du}{\sqrt{1-u^2}}=\sin^{-1}u+C$ (see page 227). Here we have $\displaystyle\int\dfrac{dx}{\sqrt{9-4x^2}}$

and we just need to rearrange the integrand so that it is in the proper

form to use the integral formula. If we factor 9 out of the radicand we get:

$$\int\dfrac{dx}{3\sqrt{1-\dfrac{4x^2}{9}}}=\dfrac{1}{3}\int\dfrac{dx}{\sqrt{1-\left(\dfrac{2x}{3}\right)^2}}.$$ Next, we do u-substitution. Let $u=\dfrac{2x}{3}$ and

$du=\dfrac{2}{3}dx$. Multiply du by $\dfrac{3}{2}$ so that $\dfrac{3}{2}du=dx$. Substituting into the integrand we

get: $\dfrac{1}{3}\left(\dfrac{3}{2}\right)\displaystyle\int\dfrac{du}{\sqrt{1-u^2}}=\dfrac{1}{2}\sin^{-1}u+C$. Substituting back we get: $\dfrac{1}{2}\sin^{-1}\dfrac{2x}{3}+C$.

9. $\dfrac{1}{3}\tan^{-1}\left(e^{3x}\right)+C$

Recall that $\displaystyle\int\dfrac{du}{1+u^2}=\tan^{-1}u+C$ (see page 227). Here we have $\displaystyle\int\dfrac{e^{3x}dx}{1+e^{6x}}$

and we will need to do u-substitution. Let $u=e^{3x}$ and $du=3e^{3x}dx$. Divide

du by 3 so that $\dfrac{1}{3}du=e^{3x}dx$. Substituting into the integrand we get:

$\displaystyle\int\dfrac{e^{3x}dx}{1+e^{6x}}=\dfrac{1}{3}\int\dfrac{du}{1+u^2}=\dfrac{1}{3}\tan^{-1}u+C$. Substituting back we get: $\dfrac{1}{3}\tan^{-1}\left(e^{3x}\right)+C$.

SOLUTIONS TO PRACTICE PROBLEM SET 29

1. $\dfrac{3x}{8} - \dfrac{\sin 2x}{4} + \dfrac{\sin 4x}{32} + C$

Here we use the substitution $\sin^2 x = \dfrac{1 - \cos 2x}{2}$ into the integrand. We get:

$\displaystyle\int \sin^4 x\, dx = \int \left(\dfrac{1 - \cos 2x}{2}\right)^2 dx = \int \left(\dfrac{1 - 2\cos 2x + \cos^2 2x}{4}\right) dx$. We can break this into

three integrals: $\displaystyle\int \left(\dfrac{1 - 2\cos 2x + \cos^2 2x}{4}\right) dx = \dfrac{1}{4}\int dx - \dfrac{1}{2}\int \cos 2x\, dx + \dfrac{1}{4}\int \cos^2 2x\, dx$.

The first two integrals are easy: $\dfrac{1}{4}\displaystyle\int dx - \dfrac{1}{2}\int \cos 2x\, dx = \dfrac{x}{4} - \dfrac{\sin 2x}{4}$. For

the third integral, we use the substitution $\cos^2 x = \dfrac{1 + \cos 2x}{2}$. We get:

$\displaystyle\int \cos^2 2x\, dx = \int \dfrac{1 + \cos 4x}{2} dx = \dfrac{1}{2}\int dx + \dfrac{1}{2}\int \cos 4x\, dx$. Now we integrate these:

$\dfrac{1}{2}\displaystyle\int dx + \dfrac{1}{2}\int \cos 4x\, dx = \dfrac{1}{2}x + \dfrac{1}{8}\sin 4x + C$. Now we put everything together to get:

$\dfrac{x}{4} - \dfrac{\sin 2x}{4} + \dfrac{1}{4}\left(\dfrac{1}{2}x + \dfrac{1}{8}\sin 4x\right) + C = \dfrac{3x}{8} - \dfrac{\sin 2x}{4} + \dfrac{\sin 4x}{32} + C$.

2. $\dfrac{3x}{8} + \dfrac{\sin 2x}{4} + \dfrac{\sin 4x}{32} + C$

Here we use the substitution $\cos^2 x = \dfrac{1 + \cos 2x}{2}$ into the integrand. We get:

$\displaystyle\int \cos^4 x\, dx = \int \left(\dfrac{1 + \cos 2x}{2}\right)^2 dx = \int \left(\dfrac{1 + 2\cos 2x + \cos^2 2x}{4}\right) dx$. We can break this into

three integrals: $\displaystyle\int \left(\dfrac{1 + 2\cos 2x + \cos^2 2x}{4}\right) dx = \dfrac{1}{4}\int dx + \dfrac{1}{2}\int \cos 2x\, dx + \dfrac{1}{4}\int \cos^2 2x\, dx$.

The first two integrals are easy: $\dfrac{1}{4}\displaystyle\int dx + \dfrac{1}{2}\int \cos 2x\, dx = \dfrac{x}{4} + \dfrac{\sin 2x}{4}$. For the

third integral, we again use the substitution $\cos^2 x = \dfrac{1 + \cos 2x}{2}$. We get:

$\int \cos^2 2x dx = \int \dfrac{1+\cos 4x}{2} dx = \dfrac{1}{2}\int dx + \dfrac{1}{2}\int \cos 4x dx$. Now we integrate these:

$\dfrac{1}{2}\int dx + \dfrac{1}{2}\int \cos 4x dx = \dfrac{1}{2}x + \dfrac{1}{8}\sin 4x + C$. Now we put everything together to get:

$\dfrac{x}{4} + \dfrac{\sin 2x}{4} + \dfrac{1}{4}\left(\dfrac{1}{2}x + \dfrac{1}{8}\sin 4x\right) + C = \dfrac{3x}{8} + \dfrac{\sin 2x}{4} + \dfrac{\sin 4x}{32} + C$.

3. $-\dfrac{\cos^5 x}{5} + C$

Here we can use u-substitution. If we let $u = \cos x$ then $du = -\sin x dx$. Substituting into the integrand, we get: $\int \cos^4 x \sin x dx = -\int u^4 du = -\dfrac{u^5}{5} + C$. Now we substitute back: $\int \cos^4 x \sin x dx = -\dfrac{\cos^5 x}{5} + C$.

4. $-\dfrac{\cos^6 x}{6} + \dfrac{\cos^8 x}{8} + C$

Here, we first break up the $\sin^3 x$ in the integrand into $\sin x(\sin^2 x)$. Now we can rewrite the integrand as: $\int \sin^3 x \cos^5 x dx = \int \sin x\left(\sin^2 x\right)\cos^5 x dx$. Next, we use the trig identity $\sin^2 x = 1 - \cos^2 x$ and substitute into the integrand:

$\int \sin x\left(1 - \cos^2 x\right)\cos^5 x dx = \int \sin x\left(\cos^5 x - \cos^7 x\right)dx$. Now we can use u-substitution. If we let $u = \cos x$ then $du = -\sin x dx$. Substituting into the integrand, we get: $-\int\left(u^5 - u^7\right)du = -\dfrac{u^6}{6} + \dfrac{u^8}{8} + C$. Now we substitute back:

$\int \sin^3 x \cos^5 x dx = -\dfrac{\cos^6 x}{6} + \dfrac{\cos^8 x}{8} + C$.

5. $\dfrac{x}{8} - \dfrac{\sin 4x}{32} + C$

First, we use the trig identity $\sin^2 x = 1 - \cos^2 x$ and substitute into the integrand:

$\displaystyle \int \sin^2 x \cos^2 x\, dx = \int \left(1 - \cos^2 x\right)\cos^2 x\, dx = \int \left(\cos^2 x - \cos^4 x\right)dx$. Next, we use the

substitution $\cos^2 x = \dfrac{1 + \cos 2x}{2}$ into the integrand: $\displaystyle \int \left(\dfrac{1 + \cos 2x}{2}\right) - \left(\dfrac{1 + \cos 2x}{2}\right)^2 dx$.

We use a little algebra:

$$\int \left(\dfrac{1 + \cos 2x}{2}\right) - \left(\dfrac{1 + \cos 2x}{2}\right)^2 dx =$$

$$\int \left(\dfrac{1 + \cos 2x}{2}\right) - \left(\dfrac{1 + 2\cos 2x + \cos^2 2x}{2}\right) dx =$$

$$\int \left(\dfrac{1}{4} - \dfrac{\cos^2 2x}{4}\right) dx$$

Now we break this into two integrals: $\dfrac{1}{4}\displaystyle\int dx - \int \dfrac{\cos^2 2x}{4}\, dx$. The first integral

is easy: $\dfrac{1}{4}\displaystyle\int dx = \dfrac{x}{4}$. For the second integral, we again use the substitution

$\cos^2 x = \dfrac{1 + \cos 2x}{2}$ into the integrand: $\dfrac{1}{4}\displaystyle\int \dfrac{1 + \cos 2x}{2}\, dx = \dfrac{1}{8}\int dx + \dfrac{1}{8}\int \cos 4x\, dx$. These

are both easy to integrate: $\dfrac{1}{8}\displaystyle\int dx + \dfrac{1}{8}\int \cos 4x\, dx = \dfrac{x}{8} + \dfrac{\sin 4x}{32}$. Putting it all together,

we get: $\dfrac{x}{4} - \left(\dfrac{x}{8} + \dfrac{\sin 4x}{32}\right) = \dfrac{x}{8} - \dfrac{\sin 4x}{32} + C$.

There is another way to do this integral that is easier, but only if you

spot it. Recall that $\sin 2x = 2\sin x \cos x$. This means that we could rewrite

the integrand as: $\displaystyle \int \sin^2 x \cos^2 x\, dx = \int \left(\dfrac{\sin 2x}{2}\right)^2 dx = \dfrac{1}{4}\int \sin^2 2x\, dx$. Now,

we can use the substitution $\sin^2 x = \dfrac{1 - \cos 2x}{2}$ to rewrite the integrand:

$\frac{1}{4}\int \sin^2 2x dx = \frac{1}{4}\int \frac{1-\cos 4x}{2}dx = \frac{1}{8}\int (1-\cos 4x)dx$. This is easy to integrate:

$\frac{1}{8}\int (1-\cos 4x)dx = \frac{1}{8}\left(x - \frac{\sin 4x}{4}\right) = \frac{x}{8} - \frac{\sin 4x}{32} + C$. This is why you should know

your trigonometric identities really well before you take calculus!

6. $\dfrac{\tan^4 x}{4} + C$

Here we can use u-substitution. If we let $u = \tan x$, then $du = \sec^2 x dx$. Substituting

into the integrand, we get: $\int \tan^3 x \sec^2 x dx = \int u^3 du = \dfrac{u^4}{4} + C$. Now we substitute

back: $\int \tan^3 x \sec^2 x dx = \dfrac{\tan^4 x}{4} + C$.

7. $\dfrac{\tan^4 x}{4} - \dfrac{\tan^2 x}{2} - \ln|\cos x| + C$

Here, we first break up the $\tan^5 x$ in the integrand into

$\int \tan^5 x dx = \int \tan^3 x \left(\tan^2 x\right)dx$. Next, we use the trigonometric

identity $\tan^2 x = \sec^2 x - 1$ and rewrite the integrand:

$\int \left(\tan^3 x\right)\left(\sec^2 x - 1\right)dx = \int \left(\tan^3 x \sec^2 x - \tan^3 x\right)dx$. Now we break this into

two integrals: $\int \left(\tan^3 x \sec^2 x\right)dx - \int \tan^3 x dx$. Next, break up the integrand

of the second integral into $\int \tan^3 x dx = \int \tan x \left(\tan^2 x\right)dx$. Once again,

use the trigonometric identity $\tan^2 x = \sec^2 x - 1$ to rewrite the integrand:

$\int \tan x \left(\sec^2 x - 1\right)dx = \int \tan x \sec^2 x dx - \int \tan x dx$. Putting the integrals together,

we get: $\int \tan^3 x \sec^2 x dx - \int \tan x \sec^2 x dx + \int \tan x dx$. We can use u-substitution to

find the first two integrals. If we let $u = \tan x$, then $du = \sec^2 x dx$. Substituting into

the integrand, we get: $\int \tan^3 x \sec^2 x dx - \int \tan x \sec^2 x dx = \int u^3 du - \int u du = \dfrac{u^4}{4} - \dfrac{u^2}{2}$.

Substituting back, we get: $\int \tan^3 x \sec^2 x\,dx - \int \tan x \sec^2 x\,dx = \dfrac{\tan^4 x}{4} - \dfrac{\tan^2 x}{2}$. The last integral we have done before (see page 184): $\int \tan x\,dx = -\ln|\cos x|$. Therefore

$$\int \tan^5 x\,dx = \frac{\tan^4 x}{4} - \frac{\tan^2 x}{2} - \ln|\cos x| + C.$$

8. $-\csc x + C$

First, rewrite the integrand in terms of $\sin x$ and $\cos x$:

$$\int \cot^2 x \sec x\,dx = \int \frac{\cos^2 x}{\sin^2 x}\left(\frac{1}{\cos x}\right)dx = \int \frac{\cos x}{\sin^2 x}\,dx.$$ Next, we do u-substitution.

If we let $u = \sin x$, then $du = \cos x\,dx$. Substituting into the integrand,

we get: $\int \dfrac{\cos x}{\sin^2 x}\,dx = \int u^{-2}\,du = -\dfrac{1}{u} + C$. Substituting back, we get:

$$\int \frac{\cos x}{\sin^2 x}\,dx = -\frac{1}{\sin x} + C = -\csc x + C.$$

SOLUTIONS TO PRACTICE PROBLEM SET 30

1. $\dfrac{13}{12}$

   Recall that the length of the curve $y = f(x)$ from $x = a$ to $x = b$ is $L = \displaystyle\int_a^b \sqrt{1 + \left(\dfrac{dy}{dx}\right)^2}\, dx$

   (see page 240). Here we have $y = \dfrac{x^3}{12} + \dfrac{1}{x}$ from $x = 1$ to $x = 2$. First, we need to find

   the derivative: $\dfrac{dy}{dx} = \dfrac{x^2}{4} - \dfrac{1}{x^2}$. Now we plug this into the formula for the length:

   $\displaystyle\int_1^2 \sqrt{1 + \left(\dfrac{x^2}{4} - \dfrac{1}{x^2}\right)^2}\, dx$. Now we need to use some algebra to simplify the integrand:

   Get a common denominator: $\displaystyle\int_1^2 \sqrt{1 + \left(\dfrac{x^2}{4} - \dfrac{1}{x^2}\right)^2}\, dx = \int_1^2 \sqrt{1 + \left(\dfrac{x^4 - 4}{4x^2}\right)^2}\, dx$.

   Square the right-hand term: $\displaystyle\int_1^2 \sqrt{1 + \left(\dfrac{x^4 - 4}{4x^2}\right)^2}\, dx = \int_1^2 \sqrt{1 + \left(\dfrac{x^8 - 8x^4 + 16}{16x^4}\right)}\, dx$.

   Get a common denominator: $\displaystyle\int_1^2 \sqrt{1 + \left(\dfrac{x^8 - 8x^4 + 16}{16x^4}\right)}\, dx = \int_1^2 \sqrt{\left(\dfrac{x^8 + 8x^4 + 16}{16x^4}\right)}\, dx$.

   Factor the numerator: $\displaystyle\int_1^2 \sqrt{\left(\dfrac{x^8 + 8x^4 + 16}{16x^4}\right)}\, dx = \int_1^2 \sqrt{\dfrac{\left(x^4 + 4\right)^2}{16x^4}}\, dx$.

   Take the square root: $\displaystyle\int_1^2 \sqrt{\dfrac{\left(x^4 + 4\right)^2}{16x^4}}\, dx = \int_1^2 \dfrac{\left(x^4 + 4\right)}{4x^2}\, dx$.

   And break up the fraction: $\displaystyle\int_1^2 \dfrac{\left(x^4 + 4\right)}{4x^2}\, dx = \int_1^2 \left(\dfrac{x^2}{4} + \dfrac{1}{x^2}\right) dx$.

   Now we can integrate easily: $\displaystyle\int_1^2 \left(\dfrac{x^2}{4} + \dfrac{1}{x^2}\right) dx = \left(\dfrac{x^3}{12} - \dfrac{1}{x}\right)\Bigg|_1^2 = \dfrac{13}{12}$.

2. $\displaystyle\int_{-\frac{\pi}{6}}^{0} \sqrt{1 + \sec^4 x}\, dx$

Recall that the length of the curve $y = f(x)$ from $x = a$ to $x = b$ is $L = \displaystyle\int_{a}^{b} \sqrt{1 + \left(\dfrac{dy}{dx}\right)^2}\, dx$

(see page 240). Here we have $y = \tan x$ from $x = -\dfrac{\pi}{6}$ to $x = 0$. First, we need to

find the derivative: $\dfrac{dy}{dx} = \sec^2 x$. Now we plug this into the formula for the length:

$$L = \int_{-\frac{\pi}{6}}^{0} \sqrt{1 + \left(\sec^2 x\right)^2}\, dx = \int_{-\frac{\pi}{6}}^{0} \sqrt{1 + \sec^4 x}\, dx\,.$$

3. $\displaystyle\int_{0}^{\frac{1}{4}} \sqrt{\dfrac{1}{1 - x^2}}\, dx$

Recall that the length of the curve $y = f(x)$ from $x = a$ to $x = b$ is $L = \displaystyle\int_{a}^{b} \sqrt{1 + \left(\dfrac{dy}{dx}\right)^2}\, dx$

(see page 240). Here we have $y = \sqrt{1 - x^2}$ from $x = 0$ to $x = \dfrac{1}{4}$. First, we need to

find the derivative: $\dfrac{dy}{dx} = \dfrac{1}{2}\left(1 - x^2\right)^{-\frac{1}{2}}(-2x) = -\dfrac{x}{\sqrt{1 - x^2}}$. Now we plug this into the

formula for the length: $L = \displaystyle\int_{0}^{\frac{1}{4}} \sqrt{1 + \left(-\dfrac{x}{\sqrt{1 - x^2}}\right)^2}\, dx = \int_{0}^{\frac{1}{4}} \sqrt{1 + \dfrac{x^2}{1 - x^2}}\, dx = \int_{0}^{\frac{1}{4}} \sqrt{\dfrac{1}{1 - x^2}}\, dx\,.$

4. $\dfrac{47}{36}$

Recall that the length of the curve $x = f(y)$ from $y = c$ to $y = d$ is $L = \int_c^d \sqrt{1 + \left(\dfrac{dx}{dy}\right)^2}\, dy$

(see page 241). Here we have $x = \dfrac{y^3}{18} + \dfrac{3}{2y}$ from $y = 2$ to $y = 3$. First, we need to

find the derivative: $\dfrac{dx}{dy} = \dfrac{y^2}{6} - \dfrac{3}{2y^2}$. Now we plug this into the formula for the

length: $\int_2^3 \sqrt{1 + \left(\dfrac{y^2}{6} - \dfrac{3}{2y^2}\right)^2}\, dy$. Now we need to use some algebra to simplify the

integrand:

Get a common denominator: $\displaystyle\int_2^3 \sqrt{1 + \left(\dfrac{y^2}{6} - \dfrac{3}{2y^2}\right)^2}\, dy = \int_2^3 \sqrt{1 + \left(\dfrac{y^4 - 9}{6y^2}\right)^2}\, dy$.

Square the right-hand term: $\displaystyle\int_2^3 \sqrt{1 + \left(\dfrac{y^4 - 9}{6y^2}\right)^2}\, dy = \int_2^3 \sqrt{1 + \left(\dfrac{y^8 - 18y^4 + 81}{36y^4}\right)}\, dy$.

Get a common denominator: $\displaystyle\int_2^3 \sqrt{1 + \left(\dfrac{y^8 - 18y^4 + 81}{36y^4}\right)}\, dy = \int_2^3 \sqrt{\left(\dfrac{y^8 + 18y^4 + 81}{36y^4}\right)}\, dy$.

Factor the numerator: $\displaystyle\int_2^3 \sqrt{\left(\dfrac{y^8 + 18y^4 + 81}{36y^4}\right)}\, dy = \int_2^3 \sqrt{\dfrac{\left(y^4 + 9\right)^2}{36y^4}}\, dy$.

Take the square root: $\displaystyle\int_2^3 \sqrt{\dfrac{\left(y^4 + 9\right)^2}{36y^4}}\, dy = \int_2^3 \left(\dfrac{y^4 + 9}{6y^2}\right) dy$.

And break up the fraction: $\displaystyle\int_2^3 \left(\dfrac{y^4 + 9}{6y^2}\right) dy = \int_2^3 \left(\dfrac{y^2}{6} + \dfrac{3}{2} y^{-2}\right) dy$.

Now we can integrate easily: $\displaystyle\int_2^3 \left(\dfrac{y^2}{6} + \dfrac{3}{2} y^{-2}\right) dy = \left(\dfrac{y^3}{18} - \dfrac{3}{2y}\right)\Bigg|_2^3 = \dfrac{47}{36}$.

5. $\displaystyle\int_{-\frac{1}{2}}^{\frac{1}{2}} \sqrt{\frac{1}{1-y^2}}\,dy$

Recall that the length of the curve $x = f(y)$ from $y = c$ to $y = d$ is $L = \displaystyle\int_c^d \sqrt{1+\left(\frac{dx}{dy}\right)^2}\,dy$

(see page 241). Here we have $x = \sqrt{1-y^2}$ from $y = -\dfrac{1}{2}$ to $y = \dfrac{1}{2}$. First, we need to

find the derivative: $\dfrac{dx}{dy} = \dfrac{1}{2}\left(1-y^2\right)^{-\frac{1}{2}}(-2y) = -\dfrac{y}{\sqrt{1-y^2}}$. Now we plug this into the

formula for the length: $L = \displaystyle\int_{-\frac{1}{2}}^{\frac{1}{2}} \sqrt{1+\left(-\frac{y}{\sqrt{1-y^2}}\right)^2}\,dy = \int_{-\frac{1}{2}}^{\frac{1}{2}}\sqrt{1+\frac{y^2}{1-y^2}}\,dy = \int_{-\frac{1}{2}}^{\frac{1}{2}}\sqrt{\frac{1}{1-y^2}}\,dy$.

6. $\displaystyle\int_0^{\pi} \sqrt{1+y^2\sin^2 y}\,dy$

Recall that the length of the curve $x = f(y)$ from $y = c$ to $y = d$ is $L = \displaystyle\int_c^d \sqrt{1+\left(\frac{dx}{dy}\right)^2}\,dy$

(see page 241). Here we have $x = \sin y - y\cos y$ from $y = 0$ to $y = \pi$. First, we need

to find the derivative: $\dfrac{dx}{dy} = \cos y - \left(-y\sin y + \cos y\right) = y\sin y$. Now we plug this into

the formula for the length: $L = \displaystyle\int_0^{\pi} \sqrt{1+y^2\sin^2 y}\,dy$.

7. $\dfrac{\pi}{6}$

Recall that, if a curve is defined parametrically, in terms of t, from $t = a$ to

$t = b$, its length is found by: $\displaystyle\int_a^b \sqrt{\left(\frac{dx}{dt}\right)^2 + \left(\frac{dy}{dt}\right)^2}\,dt$. Here, we have $x = \cos t$ and

$y = \sin t$ from $t = \dfrac{\pi}{6}$ to $t = \dfrac{\pi}{3}$. First, we need to find the derivatives: $\dfrac{dx}{dt} = -\sin t$ and

$\dfrac{dy}{dt} = \cos t$. Now we plug this into the formula for the length: $\displaystyle\int_{\frac{\pi}{6}}^{\frac{\pi}{3}} \sqrt{\sin^2 t + \cos^2 t}\, dt$.

Next, we use the trigonometric identity $\sin^2 t + \cos^2 t = 1$ to rewrite the integrand:

$$\int_{\frac{\pi}{6}}^{\frac{\pi}{3}} \sqrt{\sin^2 t + \cos^2 t}\, dt = \int_{\frac{\pi}{6}}^{\frac{\pi}{3}} dt = \left(t\right)\Big|_{\frac{\pi}{6}}^{\frac{\pi}{3}} = \frac{\pi}{6}\,.$$

$$\int_1^4 \sqrt{\left(\frac{1}{2\sqrt{t}}\right)^2 + \left(\frac{-3}{t^4}\right)^2}\, dt = \int_1^4 \sqrt{\frac{1}{4t} + \frac{9}{t^8}}\, dt$$

8. $\dfrac{1}{2}\displaystyle\int_1^4 \dfrac{\sqrt{t^7 + 36}}{t^4}\, dt$

Recall that if a curve is defined parametrically, in terms of t, from $t = a$ to $t = b$,

its length is found by: $\displaystyle\int_a^b \sqrt{\left(\dfrac{dx}{dt}\right)^2 + \left(\dfrac{dy}{dt}\right)^2}\, dt$. Here, we have $x = \sqrt{t}$ and $y = \dfrac{1}{t^3}$

from $t = 1$ to $t = 4$. First, we need to find the derivatives: $\dfrac{dx}{dt} = \dfrac{1}{2\sqrt{t}}$ and $\dfrac{dy}{dt} = -\dfrac{3}{t^4}$.

Now we plug this into the formula for the length. With a little algebra, we get:

$$\int_1^4 \sqrt{\frac{1}{4t} + \frac{9}{t^8}}\, dt = \int_1^4 \sqrt{\frac{t^7 + 36}{4t^8}}\, dt = \frac{1}{2}\int_1^4 \frac{\sqrt{t^7 + 36}}{t^4}\, dt\,.$$

9. $2\displaystyle\int_1^2 \sqrt{9t^2 + 1}\, dt$

Recall that if a curve is defined parametrically, in terms of t, from $t = a$ to $t = b$, its

length is found by: $\displaystyle\int_a^b \sqrt{\left(\dfrac{dx}{dt}\right)^2 + \left(\dfrac{dy}{dt}\right)^2}\, dt$. Here, we have $x = 3t^2$ and $y = 2t$ from

$t = 1$ to $t = 2$. First, we need to find the derivatives: $\dfrac{dx}{dt} = 6t$ and $\dfrac{dy}{dt} = 2$. Now we

plug this into the formula for the length: $\displaystyle\int_1^2 \sqrt{\left(6t\right)^2 + 4}\, dt = \int_1^2 \sqrt{36t^2 + 4}\, dt = 2\int_1^2 \sqrt{9t^2 + 1}\, dt$

SOLUTIONS TO PRACTICE PROBLEM SET 31

1. $\dfrac{5}{7}\ln|x-1|+\dfrac{2}{7}\ln|x+6|+C$ $B=\dfrac{1}{4}$

    We need to find A and B such that $\dfrac{A}{x-1}+\dfrac{B}{x+6}=\dfrac{x+4}{(x-1)(x+6)}$. First, we multiply

    through by $(x-1)(x+6)$: $A(x+6)+B(x-1)=x+4$.

    Distribute: $Ax+6A+Bx-B=x+4$.

    Group the terms on the left side: $(A+B)x+(6A-B)=x+4$.

    Now we have two equations: $A+B=1$ and $6A-B=4$.

    If we solve for A and B, we get: $A=\dfrac{5}{7}$ and $B=\dfrac{2}{7}$. This means that we can

    rewrite the integral as: $\displaystyle\int\dfrac{x+4}{(x-1)(x+6)}\,dx=\dfrac{5}{7}\int\dfrac{A}{(x-1)}\,dx+\dfrac{2}{7}\int\dfrac{B}{(x+6)}\,dx$. We can

    easily integrate these: $\dfrac{5}{7}\ln|x-1|+\dfrac{2}{7}\ln|x+6|+C$.

2. $\dfrac{3}{4}\ln|x-3|+\dfrac{1}{4}\ln|x+1|+C$

    We need to find A and B such that $\dfrac{A}{x-3}+\dfrac{B}{x+1}=\dfrac{x}{(x-3)(x+1)}$. First, we multiply

    through by $(x-3)(x+1)$: $A(x+1)+B(x-3)=x$

    Distribute: $Ax+A+Bx-3B=x$.

    Group the terms on the left side: $(A+B)x+(A-3B)=x$.

    Now we have two equations: $A+B=1$ and $A-3B=0$.

If we solve for A and B, we get: $A = \dfrac{3}{4}$ and $B = \dfrac{1}{4}$. This means that we can

rewrite the integral as: $\displaystyle\int \dfrac{x}{(x-3)(x+1)}\,dx = \dfrac{3}{4}\int \dfrac{A}{(x-3)}\,dx + \dfrac{1}{4}\int \dfrac{B}{(x+1)}\,dx$. We can easily

integrate these: $\dfrac{3}{4}\ln|x-3| + \dfrac{1}{4}\ln|x+1| + C$.

3. $\quad -\dfrac{1}{2}\ln|x| + \dfrac{1}{6}\ln|x+2| + \dfrac{1}{3}\ln|x-1| + C$

First, we need to factor the denominator of the integrand:

$$\int \dfrac{1}{x^3 + x^2 - 2x}\,dx = \int \dfrac{1}{x(x^2 + x - 2)}\,dx = \int \dfrac{1}{x(x+2)(x-1)}\,dx.$$

Now, we need to find A, B, and C such that $\dfrac{A}{x} + \dfrac{B}{x+2} + \dfrac{C}{x-1} = \dfrac{1}{x(x+2)(x-1)}$.

We multiply through by $x(x + 2)(x - 1)$: $A(x + 2)(x - 1) + Bx(x - 1) + Cx(x + 2) = 1$.

Expand all of the terms: $A(x^2 + x - 2) + B(x^2 - x) + C(x^2 + 2x) = 1$.

Distribute: $Ax^2 + Ax - 2A + Bx^2 - Bx + Cx^2 + 2Cx = 1$.

Group the terms on the left side: $(A + B + C)x^2 + (A - B + 2C)x - 2A = 1$.

Now we have three equations: $A + B + C = 0$, $A - B + 2C = 0$, and $-2A = 1$.

If we solve for A, B, and C, we get: $A = -\dfrac{1}{2}$, $B = \dfrac{1}{6}$, and $C = \dfrac{1}{3}$. This means that

we can rewrite the integral as: $\displaystyle\int \dfrac{1}{x(x+2)(x-1)}\,dx = -\dfrac{1}{2}\int \dfrac{dx}{x} + \dfrac{1}{6}\int \dfrac{dx}{x+2} + \dfrac{1}{3}\int \dfrac{dx}{x-1}$.

We can easily integrate these: $-\dfrac{1}{2}\ln|x| + \dfrac{1}{6}\ln|x+2| + \dfrac{1}{3}\ln|x-1| + C$.

4. $-7\ln|x-3|+9\ln|x-4|+C$

First, we need to factor the denominator of the integrand:

$$\int\frac{2x+1}{x^2-7x+12}\,dx=\int\frac{2x+1}{(x-3)(x-4)}\,dx\,.$$

Now, we need to find A and B such that $\dfrac{A}{x-3}+\dfrac{B}{x-4}=\dfrac{2x+1}{(x-3)(x-4)}$.

We multiply through by $(x-3)(x-4)$: $A(x-4)+B(x-3)=2x+1$.

Distribute: $Ax-4A+Bx-3B=2x+1$.

Group the terms on the left side: $(A+B)x+(-4A-3B)=2x+1$.

Now we have two equations: $A+B=2$ and $-4A-3B=1$.

If we solve for A and B, we get: $A=-7$ and $B=9$.

This means that we can rewrite the integral as:

$$\int\frac{2x+1}{x^2-7x+12}\,dx=-7\int\frac{dx}{x-3}+9\int\frac{dx}{x-4}\,.$$ We can easily integrate these:

$-7\ln|x-3|+9\ln|x-4|+C\,.$

5. $2\ln|x-1|-\dfrac{1}{x-1}+C$

We need to find A and B such that $\dfrac{A}{x-1}+\dfrac{B}{(x-1)^2}=\dfrac{2x-1}{(x-1)^2}$.

We multiply through by $(x-1)^2$: $A(x-1)+B=2x-1$.

Distribute: $Ax-A+B=2x-1$.

Now we have two equations: $A=2$ and $-A+B=-1$.

If we solve for A and B, we get: $A=2$ and $B=1$.

This means that we can rewrite the integral as: $\displaystyle\int\frac{2x-1}{(x-1)^2}\,dx=2\int\frac{dx}{x-1}+\int\frac{dx}{(x-1)^2}\,.$

We can easily integrate these: $2\ln|x-1|-\dfrac{1}{x-1}+C\,.$

6. $\frac{1}{2}\ln|x+1|-\frac{1}{4}\ln(x^2+1)+\frac{1}{2}\tan^{-1}x+C$

We need to find A and $Bx+C$ such that $\dfrac{A}{x+1}+\dfrac{Bx+C}{x^2+1}=\dfrac{1}{(x+1)(x^2+1)}$.

We multiply through by $(x+1)(x^2+1)$: $A(x^2+1)+(Bx+C)(x+1)=1$.

Expand all of the terms: $Ax^2+A+Bx^2+Bx+Cx+C=1$.

Group the terms on the left side: $(A+B)x^2+(B+C)x+(A+C)=1$.

Now we have three equations: $A+B=0$, $B+C=0$, and $A+C=1$.

If we solve for A, B, and C, we get: $A=\dfrac{1}{2}$, $B=-\dfrac{1}{2}$, and $C=\dfrac{1}{2}$.

This means that we can rewrite the integral as:

$$\int\frac{1}{(x+1)(x^2+1)}\,dx=\frac{1}{2}\int\frac{dx}{x+1}-\frac{1}{2}\int\frac{x}{x^2+1}\,dx+\frac{1}{2}\int\frac{dx}{x^2+1}.$$

If we integrate these, we get: $\frac{1}{2}\ln|x+1|-\frac{1}{4}\ln(x^2+1)+\frac{1}{2}\tan^{-1}x+C$. If you had

trouble with these integrals, you should review the sections on logarithmic and

trigonometric integrals.

7. $-\frac{1}{3}\ln|x+1|+\frac{1}{6}\ln(x^2+2)+\frac{5\sqrt{2}}{6}\tan^{-1}\left(\frac{x}{\sqrt{2}}\right)+C$

We need to find A and $Bx+C$ such that $\dfrac{A}{x+1}+\dfrac{Bx+C}{x^2+2}=\dfrac{2x+1}{(x+1)(x^2+2)}$.

We multiply through by $(x+1)(x^2+2)$: $A(x^2+2)+(Bx+C)(x+1)=2x+1$.

Expand all of the terms: $Ax^2+2A+Bx^2+Bx+Cx+C=2x+1$.

Group the terms on the left side: $(A+B)x^2+(B+C)x+(2A+C)=2x+1$.

Now we have three equations: $A+B=0$, $B+C=2$, and $2A+C=1$.

If we solve for A, B, and C, we get: $A=-\dfrac{1}{3}$, $B=\dfrac{1}{3}$, and $C=\dfrac{5}{3}$.

This means that we can rewrite the integral as:

$$\int \frac{2x+1}{(x+1)(x^2+1)}dx = -\frac{1}{3}\int \frac{dx}{x+1}+\frac{1}{3}\int \frac{x}{x^2+2}dx+\frac{5}{3}\int \frac{dx}{x^2+2}.$$

If we integrate these, we get: $-\frac{1}{3}\ln|x+1|+\frac{1}{6}\ln(x^2+2)+\frac{5\sqrt{2}}{6}\tan^{-1}\left(\frac{x}{\sqrt{2}}\right)+C$.

If you had trouble with these integrals, you should review the sections on

logarithmic and trigonometric integrals.

8. $\ln|x-1|+\frac{4}{\sqrt{3}}\tan^{-1}\frac{2x+1}{\sqrt{3}}+C$

First, we need to factor the denominator of the integrand:

$$\int \frac{x^2+3x-1}{x^3-1}dx = \int \frac{x^2+3x-1}{(x-1)(x^2+x+1)}dx.$$

We need to find A and $Bx + C$ such that $\dfrac{A}{x-1}+\dfrac{Bx+C}{x^2+x+1}=\dfrac{x^2+3x-1}{(x-1)(x^2+x+1)}$.

We multiply through by $(x - 1)(x^2 + x + 1)$:

$A(x^2 + x +1) + (Bx + C)(x - 1) = x^2 + 3x -1$.

Expand all of the terms: $Ax^2 + Ax + A + Bx^2 - Bx + Cx - C = x^2 + 3x - 1$.

Group the terms on the left side: $(A + B)x^2 + (A - B + C)x + (A - C) = x^2 + 3x - 1$.

Now we have three equations: $A + B = 1$, $A - B + C = 3$, and $A - C = -1$.

If we solve for A, B, and C, we get: $A = 1$, $B = 0$, and $C = 2$.

This means that we can rewrite the integral as:

$\int \dfrac{x^2 + 3x - 1}{x^3 - 1} dx = \int \dfrac{dx}{x - 1} + 2 \int \dfrac{dx}{x^2 + x + 1}$. The first integral is easy: $\int \dfrac{dx}{x - 1} = \ln|x - 1|$.

The second takes a little work and will be a good test of your algebra. First,

complete the square to rewrite the denominator: $2 \int \dfrac{dx}{x^2 + x + 1} = 2 \int \dfrac{dx}{\left(x + \dfrac{1}{2}\right)^2 + \dfrac{3}{4}}$.

Next, multiply the top and bottom of the integrand by $\dfrac{4}{3}$:

$2 \int \dfrac{\dfrac{4}{3} dx}{\dfrac{4}{3}\left(x + \dfrac{1}{2}\right)^2 + 1} = \dfrac{8}{3} \int \dfrac{dx}{\dfrac{4}{3}\left(x + \dfrac{1}{2}\right)^2 + 1}$. This can be rewritten as: $\dfrac{8}{3} \int \dfrac{dx}{\left(\dfrac{2x + 1}{\sqrt{3}}\right)^2 + 1}$.

Now we do u-substitution. If we let $u = \dfrac{2x + 1}{\sqrt{3}}$, then $du = \dfrac{2}{\sqrt{3}} dx$. Multiply

du by $\dfrac{\sqrt{3}}{2}$: $\dfrac{\sqrt{3}}{2} du = dx$. Now we can substitute into the integrand:

$\dfrac{8}{3}\left(\dfrac{\sqrt{3}}{2}\right) \int \dfrac{du}{u^2 + 1} = \dfrac{4}{\sqrt{3}} \tan^{-1} u + C$. Substituting back, we get: $\dfrac{4}{\sqrt{3}} \tan^{-1}\left(\dfrac{2x + 1}{\sqrt{3}}\right) + C$.

Now we can put both integrals together: $\ln|x - 1| + \dfrac{4}{\sqrt{3}} \tan^{-1} \dfrac{2x + 1}{\sqrt{3}} + C$.

SOLUTIONS TO PRACTICE PROBLEM SET 32

1. 2

Notice that the integrand is undefined at the lower limit of integration $x = 0$.

We remedy this by replacing the lower limit with a and taking the limit of the

integral as a approaches 0: $\int_0^1 \dfrac{dx}{\sqrt{x}} = \lim_{a \to 0} \int_a^1 \dfrac{dx}{\sqrt{x}}$. Now we evaluate the integral:

$$\int_a^1 \dfrac{dx}{\sqrt{x}} = \left(\dfrac{x^{\frac{1}{2}}}{\dfrac{1}{2}} \right) \Bigg|_a^1 = \left(2\sqrt{x} \right) \Big|_a^1 = 2 - 2\sqrt{a}.$$ Finally, we take the limit: $\lim_{a \to 0} \left(2 - 2\sqrt{a} \right) = 2$.

2. 6

Notice that, although the integrand is defined at both limits of integration,

it is undefined between them at $x = 0$. We remedy this by, first, splitting the

integral into two parts at $x = 0$, $\int_{-1}^1 \dfrac{dx}{x^{\frac{2}{3}}} = \int_{-1}^0 \dfrac{dx}{x^{\frac{2}{3}}} + \int_0^1 \dfrac{dx}{x^{\frac{2}{3}}}$ and, second, replacing

the limit with a and taking the limit of the integral as a approaches 0,

$$\int_{-1}^0 \dfrac{dx}{x^{\frac{2}{3}}} + \int_0^1 \dfrac{dx}{x^{\frac{2}{3}}} = \lim_{a \to 0} \int_{-1}^a \dfrac{dx}{x^{\frac{2}{3}}} + \lim_{a \to 0} \int_a^1 \dfrac{dx}{x^{\frac{2}{3}}}.$$ Now we evaluate the integrals:

$$\int_{-1}^a \dfrac{dx}{x^{\frac{2}{3}}} = \left(3x^{\frac{1}{3}} \right) \Bigg|_{-1}^a = 3\sqrt[3]{a} + 3 \text{ and } \int_a^1 \dfrac{dx}{x^{\frac{2}{3}}} = \left(3x^{\frac{1}{3}} \right) \Bigg|_a^1 = 3 - 3\sqrt[3]{a}.$$

Finally, we take the limits: $\lim_{a \to 0} \left(3\sqrt[3]{a} + 3 \right) = 3$ and $\lim_{a \to 0} \left(3 - 3\sqrt[3]{a} \right) = 3$. Therefore, the

integral is $3 + 3 = 6$.

3. 1

We can't evaluate an integral where a limit of integration is infinity. We

remedy this by replacing the lower limit with a and taking the limit of the

integral as a approaches $-\infty$. $\int_{-\infty}^{0} e^x dx = \lim_{a \to -\infty} \int_{a}^{0} e^x dx$. Now we evaluate the integral:

$\int_{a}^{0} e^x dx = \left. \left(e^x \right) \right|_{a}^{0} = 1 - e^a$. Finally, we take the limit: $\lim_{a \to -\infty} \left(1 - e^a \right) = 1$.

4. Diverges

We can't evaluate an integral where a limit of integration is infinity. We remedy

this by replacing the lower limit with a and taking the limit of the integral as a

approaches $-\infty$. But we have a second problem: $\tan \dfrac{\pi}{2}$ is also undefined. We

remedy this by replacing the upper limit with b and taking the limit of the integral

as b approaches $\dfrac{\pi}{2}$. And we overcome the two limits difficulty by splitting the

integral into two parts at a value where we know that we can integrate and take

each limit separately. A simple place to split the integral is at $x = 0$. We get:

$\int_{-\infty}^{\frac{\pi}{2}} \tan \theta d\theta = \lim_{a \to -\infty} \int_{a}^{0} \tan \theta d\theta + \lim_{b \to \frac{\pi}{2}} \int_{0}^{b} \tan \theta d\theta$. Now we evaluate the integrals:

$\int_{a}^{0} \tan \theta d\theta = \left. \left(-\ln \left| \cos \theta \right| \right) \right|_{a}^{0} = \ln \left| \cos a \right|$

$\int_{0}^{b} \tan \theta d\theta = \left. \left(-\ln \left| \cos \theta \right| \right) \right|_{0}^{b} = -\ln \left| \cos b \right|$.

Finally, we take the limits: $\lim_{a \to -\infty} \ln \left| \cos a \right| = D.N.E.$ and $\lim_{b \to \frac{\pi}{2}} -\ln \left| \cos b \right| = D.N.E.$

Neither limit exists, so the integral diverges. As a general rule, a trigonometric

integral (but not an inverse trig one) is going to diverge if one of the limits of

integration is infinite.

5. Diverges

Notice that the integrand is undefined at the lower limit of integration $x = 1$.

We remedy this by replacing the lower limit with a and taking the limit of

the integral as a approaches 1: $\displaystyle\int_1^4 \frac{dx}{1-x} = \lim_{a \to 1} \int_a^4 \frac{dx}{1-x}$. Now we evaluate the

integral: $\displaystyle\int_a^4 \frac{dx}{1-x} = \left(-\ln|1-x|\right)\Big|_a^4 = -\ln 3 + \ln|1-a|$. Finally, we take the limit:

$\displaystyle\lim_{a \to 1}\left(-\ln 3 + \ln|1-a|\right) = D.N.E.$ Therefore, the integral diverges.

6. $\sqrt{3}$

Notice that the integrand is undefined at the lower limit of integration $x = 0$.

We remedy this by replacing the lower limit with a and taking the limit of the

integral as a approaches 0: $\displaystyle\int_0^1 \frac{x+1}{\sqrt{x^2+2x}}\,dx = \lim_{a \to 0} \int_a^1 \frac{x+1}{\sqrt{x^2+2x}}\,dx$. Now we evaluate the

integral. If we let $u = x^2 + 2x$, then $du = (2x + 2)dx$. If we divide du by 2, we get

$\frac{1}{2}du = (x+1)dx$. Now we can substitute into the integrand. Let's ignore the limits

of integration until we substitute back. We get: $\displaystyle\int \frac{x+1}{\sqrt{x^2+2x}}\,dx = \frac{1}{2}\int u^{-\frac{1}{2}}du = u^{\frac{1}{2}}$.

Now we substitute back and evaluate at the limits of integration:

$\left(\sqrt{x^2+2x}\right)\Big|_a^1 = \sqrt{3} - \sqrt{a^2+2a}$. Finally, we take the limit: $\displaystyle\lim_{a \to 0}\left[\sqrt{3} - \sqrt{a^2+2a}\right] = \sqrt{3}$.

7. $-\dfrac{1}{4}$

We can't evaluate an integral where a limit of integration is infinity. We remedy

this by replacing the lower limit with a and taking the limit of the integral as

a approaches $-\infty$: $\displaystyle\int_{-\infty}^0 \frac{dx}{(2x-1)^3} = \lim_{a \to -\infty} \int_a^0 \frac{dx}{(2x-1)^3}$. Now we evaluate the integral:

$$\int_a^0 \frac{dx}{(2x-1)^3} = \left(-\frac{1}{4(2x-1)^2}\right)\Bigg|_a^0 = -\frac{1}{4} + \frac{1}{4(2a-1)^2}$$. Finally, we take the limit:

$$\lim_{a\to-\infty}\left(-\frac{1}{4} + \frac{1}{4(2a-1)^2}\right) = -\frac{1}{4}.$$

8. Diverges

We can't evaluate an integral where a limit of integration is infinity. We remedy this by replacing the limit with a and taking the limit of the integral as a approaches ∞. We also need to split the integral into two parts where it is defined at one of the limits. A simple place to split the integral is at $x = 0$. We get:

$$\int_{-\infty}^{\infty} x^3 dx = \lim_{a\to\infty}\int_{-a}^{0} x^3 dx + \lim_{a\to\infty}\int_{0}^{a} x^3 dx$$. Now we evaluate the integrals:

$$\int_{-a}^{0} x^3 dx = \left(\frac{x^4}{4}\right)\Bigg|_{-a}^{0} = -\frac{a^4}{4}$$

$$\int_{0}^{a} x^3 dx = \left(\frac{x^4}{4}\right)\Bigg|_{0}^{a} = \frac{a^4}{4}.$$

Now we take the limits: $\lim_{a\to\infty}-\dfrac{a^4}{4} = -\infty$ and $\lim_{a\to\infty}\dfrac{a^4}{4} = \infty$. Therefore, the integral diverges. This is a tricky integral. Notice that if the limits of integration were finite and equal to each other, we would always get zero. It is easy to see this if we graph the function $y = x^3$ and look at the areas on each side of the y-axis. They will always cancel each other because of symmetry.

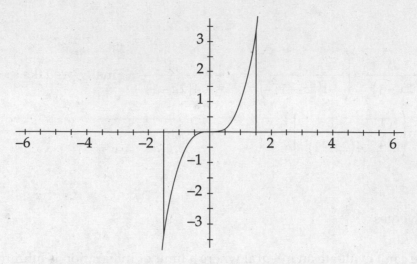

Thus, we would think that the integral will always be zero. But, because the limits of integration are infinite, the areas are infinite and we would be adding infinities, which do not necessarily cancel. In other words, the area from zero to infinity is infinite and the area from zero to minus infinity is infinite. We can't add two infinite quantities and get a finite one. Therefore, the integral is meaningless.

9. Diverges

Notice that, although the integrand is defined at both limits of integration,

it is undefined between them at $x = 2$. We remedy this by, first, splitting

the integral into two parts at $x = 2$, $\displaystyle\int_0^3 \frac{dx}{x-2} = \int_0^2 \frac{dx}{x-2} + \int_2^3 \frac{dx}{x-2}$ and, second,

replacing the limit with a and taking the limit of the integral as a approaches 2,

$\displaystyle\int_0^2 \frac{dx}{x-2} + \int_2^3 \frac{dx}{x-2} = \lim_{a\to 2}\int_0^a \frac{dx}{x-2} + \lim_{a\to 2}\int_2^3 \frac{dx}{x-2}$. Now we evaluate the integrals:

$\displaystyle\int_0^a \frac{dx}{x-2} = \left(\ln|x-2|\right)\Big|_0^a = \ln|a-2| - \ln 2$ and $\displaystyle\int_a^3 \frac{dx}{x-2} = \left(\ln|x-2|\right)\Big|_a^3 = -\ln|a-2|$.

Finally, we take the limits: $\displaystyle\lim_{a\to 2}\left(\ln|a-2| - \ln 2\right) = D.N.E.$ and

$\displaystyle\lim_{a\to 2}\left(-\ln|a-2|\right) = D.N.E.$

Therefore the integral diverges.

10. $\dfrac{9}{2}$

Notice that although the integrand is defined at both limits of integration,

it is undefined between them at $x = 0$. We remedy this by, first, splitting the

integral into two parts at $x = 0$, $\displaystyle\int_{-1}^{8}\dfrac{dx}{\sqrt[3]{x}} = \int_{-1}^{0}\dfrac{dx}{\sqrt[3]{x}} + \int_{0}^{8}\dfrac{dx}{\sqrt[3]{x}}$ and, second, replacing

the limit with a and taking the limit of the integral as a approaches 0,

$\displaystyle\int_{-1}^{0}\dfrac{dx}{\sqrt[3]{x}} + \int_{0}^{8}\dfrac{dx}{\sqrt[3]{x}} = \lim_{a\to 0}\int_{-1}^{a}\dfrac{dx}{\sqrt[3]{x}} + \lim_{a\to 0}\int_{a}^{8}\dfrac{dx}{\sqrt[3]{x}}$. Now we evaluate the integrals:

$\displaystyle\int_{-1}^{a}\dfrac{dx}{\sqrt[3]{x}} = \left(\dfrac{3x^{\frac{2}{3}}}{2}\right)\Bigg|_{-1}^{a} = \dfrac{3a^{\frac{2}{3}}}{2} - \dfrac{3}{2}$ and $\displaystyle\int_{a}^{8}\dfrac{dx}{\sqrt[3]{x}} = \left(\dfrac{3x^{\frac{2}{3}}}{2}\right)\Bigg|_{a}^{8} = 6 - \dfrac{3a^{\frac{2}{3}}}{2}$.

Finally, we take the limits: $\displaystyle\lim_{a\to 0}\left(\dfrac{3a^{\frac{2}{3}}}{2} - \dfrac{3}{2}\right) = -\dfrac{3}{2}$ and $\displaystyle\lim_{a\to 0}\left(6 - \dfrac{3a^{\frac{2}{3}}}{2}\right) = 6$. Therefore,

the integral is $-\dfrac{3}{2} + 6 = \dfrac{9}{2}$.

SOLUTIONS TO PRACTICE PROBLEM SET 33

1. $\dfrac{4\sin 4\theta \sin\theta - \cos 4\theta \cos\theta}{4\sin 4\theta \cos\theta + \cos 4\theta \sin\theta}$

Recall that the formula for the slope of a polar curve is $\dfrac{dy}{dx} = \dfrac{f'(\theta)\sin\theta + f(\theta)\cos\theta}{f'(\theta)\cos\theta - f(\theta)\sin\theta}$

(see page 255). Here we have $f(\theta) = 2\cos 4\theta$, so $f'(\theta) = -8\sin 4\theta$. Plugging into

the formula, we get: $\dfrac{dy}{dx} = \dfrac{-8\sin 4\theta \sin\theta + 2\cos 4\theta \cos\theta}{-8\sin 4\theta \cos\theta - 2\cos 4\theta \sin\theta}$, which can be reduced to

$\dfrac{4\sin 4\theta \sin\theta - \cos 4\theta \cos\theta}{4\sin 4\theta \cos\theta + \cos 4\theta \sin\theta}$.

2. $\dfrac{2}{3}$

Recall that the formula for the slope of a polar curve is $\dfrac{dy}{dx} = \dfrac{f'(\theta)\sin\theta + f(\theta)\cos\theta}{f'(\theta)\cos\theta - f(\theta)\sin\theta}$

(see page 255). Here we have $f(\theta) = 2 - 3\sin\theta$, so $f'(\theta) = -3\cos\theta$. Plugging into the

formula, we get: $\dfrac{dy}{dx} = \dfrac{-3\cos\theta \sin\theta + (2 - 3\sin\theta)\cos\theta}{-3\cos\theta \cos\theta - (2 - 3\sin\theta)\sin\theta}$. Now we evaluate the slope at

$(r,\theta) = (2,\pi): \dfrac{dy}{dx} = \dfrac{-3\cos\pi \sin\pi + (2 - 3\sin\pi)\cos\pi}{-3\cos\pi \cos\pi - (2 - 3\sin\pi)\sin\pi} = \dfrac{2}{3}$.

3. 18π

Recall that the formula for the area of between the origin and the curve $r = f(\theta)$

from $\theta = a$ to $\theta = b$ is $A = \displaystyle\int_a^b \frac{1}{2} r^2 d\theta$ (see page 255). Here, we have $r = 4 + 2\cos\theta$.

First, let's graph the curve:

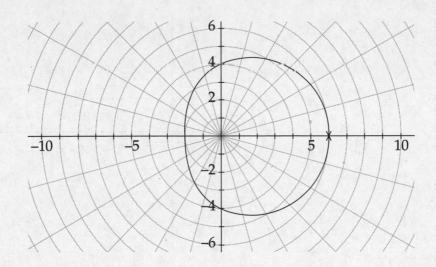

We can see that the loop runs from $\theta = 0$ to $\theta = 2\pi$. Plugging into the formula, we

get: $A = \dfrac{1}{2}\displaystyle\int_0^{2\pi}(4+2\cos\theta)^2\,d\theta = \dfrac{1}{2}\int_0^{2\pi}(16+16\cos\theta+4\cos^2\theta)d\theta = \int_0^{2\pi}(8+8\cos\theta+2\cos^2\theta)d\theta.$

We can break this into three integrals:

$\displaystyle\int_0^{2\pi}(8+8\cos\theta+2\cos^2\theta)d\theta = 8\int_0^{2\pi}d\theta+8\int_0^{2\pi}\cos\theta d\theta+2\int_0^{2\pi}\cos^2\theta d\theta.$ We can easily evaluate

the first two integrals: $8\displaystyle\int_0^{2\pi}d\theta = 8(\theta)\Big|_0^{2\pi} = 16\pi$ and $8\int_0^{2\pi}\cos\theta d\theta = 8(\sin\theta)\Big|_0^{2\pi} = 0$. The

third integral requires us to use the trigonometric substitution $\cos^2\theta = \dfrac{1+\cos 2\theta}{2}$

(see page 236): $2\displaystyle\int_0^{2\pi}\cos^2\theta d\theta = 2\int_0^{2\pi}\dfrac{1+\cos\theta}{2}d\theta = \int_0^{2\pi}(1+\cos 2\theta)d\theta = \left(\theta+\dfrac{1}{2}\sin 2\theta\right)\Big|_0^{2\pi} = 2\pi.$

Therefore, the area is 18π.

4. 2

Recall that the formula for the area of between the origin and the curve $r = f(\theta)$

from $\theta = a$ to $\theta = b$ is $A = \displaystyle\int_a^b \dfrac{1}{2}r^2 d\theta$ (see page 255). Here, we have $r^2 = 4\cos 2\theta$. First,

let's graph the curve:

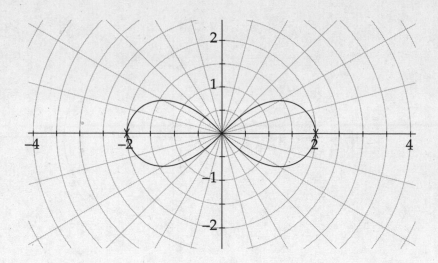

If we plot a few points, we can see that the loop runs from $\theta = -\dfrac{\pi}{4}$ to $\theta = \dfrac{\pi}{4}$.

Plugging into the formula, we get:

$$A = \frac{1}{2}\int_{-\frac{\pi}{4}}^{\frac{\pi}{4}}\left(4\cos 2\theta\right)d\theta = 2\int_{-\frac{\pi}{4}}^{\frac{\pi}{4}}\cos 2\theta\, d\theta = \left(\sin 2\theta\right)\Big|_{-\frac{\pi}{4}}^{\frac{\pi}{4}} = 2\,.$$

5. $\dfrac{\pi}{3} + \dfrac{\sqrt{3}}{2}$

Recall that the formula for the area between the two curves $r_1 = f_1(\theta)$ and $r_2 = f_2(\theta)$,

with $0 \le r_1(\theta) \le r_2(\theta)$ from $\theta = a$ to $\theta = b$ is $A = \int_a^b \dfrac{1}{2}\left(r_2^2 - r_1^2\right)d\theta$ (see page 258). Here,

we have $r_2 = 2\cos\theta$ and $r_1 = 1$. First, let's graph the curves:

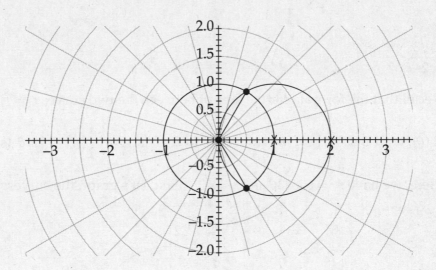

If we solve for the intersection of the two curves, we find that the

region runs from $\theta = -\dfrac{\pi}{3}$ to $\theta = \dfrac{\pi}{3}$. Plugging into the formula, we get:

$$A = \frac{1}{2}\int\limits_{-\frac{\pi}{3}}^{\frac{\pi}{3}}\left[\left(2\cos\theta\right)^2 - 1^2\right]d\theta = \frac{1}{2}\int\limits_{-\frac{\pi}{3}}^{\frac{\pi}{3}}\left(4\cos^2\theta - 1\right)d\theta = \int\limits_{-\frac{\pi}{3}}^{\frac{\pi}{3}}\left(2\cos^2\theta\right)d\theta - \frac{1}{2}\int\limits_{-\frac{\pi}{3}}^{\frac{\pi}{3}}d\theta.$$

The first integral requires us to use the trigonometric

substitution $\cos^2\theta = \dfrac{1 + \cos 2\theta}{2}$ (see page 236):

$$2\int\limits_{-\frac{\pi}{3}}^{\frac{\pi}{3}}\cos^2\theta\, d\theta = 2\int\limits_{-\frac{\pi}{3}}^{\frac{\pi}{3}}\frac{1 + \cos 2\theta}{2}d\theta = \int\limits_{-\frac{\pi}{3}}^{\frac{\pi}{3}}\left(1 + \cos 2\theta\right)d\theta = \left(\theta + \frac{1}{2}\sin 2\theta\right)\Bigg|_{-\frac{\pi}{3}}^{\frac{\pi}{3}} = \frac{2\pi}{3} + \frac{\sqrt{3}}{2}.$$ The

second integral is simply $\dfrac{1}{2}\int\limits_{-\frac{\pi}{3}}^{\frac{\pi}{3}}d\theta = \dfrac{1}{2}(\theta)\Big|_{-\frac{\pi}{3}}^{\frac{\pi}{3}} = \dfrac{\pi}{3}$. Therefore, the area is $\dfrac{\pi}{3} + \dfrac{\sqrt{3}}{2}$.

6. $\dfrac{3\sqrt{3}}{2} - \dfrac{\pi}{2}$

Recall that the formula for the area of between the two curves $r_1 = f_1(\theta)$ and $r_2 = f_2(\theta)$, with $0 \le r_1(\theta) \le r_2(\theta)$ from $\theta = a$ to $\theta = b$ is $A = \int_a^b \dfrac{1}{2}\left(r_2^2 - r_1^2\right)d\theta$ (see page 258).

Here, we have $r_2^2 = 6\cos 2\theta$ and $r_1 = \sqrt{3}$. First, let's graph the curves:

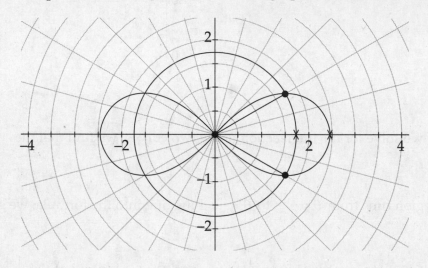

If we solve for the intersection of the two curves, we find that the

region runs from $\theta = -\dfrac{\pi}{6}$ to $\theta = \dfrac{\pi}{6}$. Plugging into the formula, we get:

$A = \dfrac{1}{2}\displaystyle\int_{-\frac{\pi}{6}}^{\frac{\pi}{6}} \left(6\cos 2\theta - 3\right)d\theta = 3\displaystyle\int_{-\frac{\pi}{6}}^{\frac{\pi}{6}} \left(\cos 2\theta\right)d\theta - \dfrac{3}{2}\displaystyle\int_{-\frac{\pi}{6}}^{\frac{\pi}{6}} d\theta$. Evaluating the integrals, we get:

$3\displaystyle\int_{-\frac{\pi}{6}}^{\frac{\pi}{6}} \left(\cos 2\theta\right)d\theta = \left(\dfrac{3\sin 2\theta}{2}\right)\Bigg|_{-\frac{\pi}{6}}^{\frac{\pi}{6}} = \dfrac{3\sqrt{3}}{2}$ and $\dfrac{3}{2}\displaystyle\int_{-\frac{\pi}{6}}^{\frac{\pi}{6}} d\theta = \dfrac{3}{2}(\theta)\Big|_{-\frac{\pi}{6}}^{\frac{\pi}{6}} = \dfrac{\pi}{2}$. Therefore, the area is

$\dfrac{3\sqrt{3}}{2} - \dfrac{\pi}{2}$.

SOLUTIONS TO PRACTICE PROBLEM SET 34

1. $y = \sqrt[4]{\dfrac{28x^3}{3} - 236}$

We solve this differential equation by separation of variables. We want to get all of the y variables on one side of the equals sign and all of the x variables on the other side. We can do this easily by cross multiplying. We get: $y^3 dy = 7x^2 dx$. Next, we integrate both sides:

$$\int y^3 dy = \int 7x^2 dx$$

$$\frac{y^4}{4} = 7\frac{x^3}{3} + C$$

$$y^4 = \frac{28x^3}{3} + C$$

Now we solve for C. We plug in $x = 3$ and $y = 2$:

$16 = 252 + C$

$C = -236$

Therefore, $y^4 = \dfrac{28x^3}{3} - 236$.

Now we isolate y. We get the equation: $y = \sqrt[4]{\dfrac{28x^3}{3} - 236}$.

2. $y = 6e^{\frac{5x^3}{3}}$

We solve this differential equation by separation of variables. We want to get all of

the y variables on one side of the equals sign and all of the x variables on the other

side. We can do this easily by dividing both sides by y and multiplying both sides

by dx. We get: $\dfrac{dy}{y} = 5x^2 dx$. Next, we integrate both sides:

$$\int \frac{dy}{y} = \int 5x^2 dx$$

$$\ln y = \frac{5x^3}{3} + C_0$$

Now we isolate y: $y = e^{\frac{5x^3}{3} + C}$. We can rewrite this as $y = e^{\frac{5x^3}{3}}\left(e^{C_0}\right) = Ce^{\frac{5x^3}{3}}$.

Note that we are using the letter C in the last equation. This is to distinguish it

from the C_0 in the first equation. Now we solve for C. We plug in $x = 0$ and $y = 6$:

$6 = Ce^0 = C$. Therefore, the equation is $y = 6e^{\frac{5x^3}{3}}$.

3. $y = \sqrt{2\tan^{-1}x + 4}$

We solve this differential equation by separation of variables. We want to get all of the y variables on one side of the equals sign and all of the x variables on the other side. First, we factor the y out of the denominator of the right hand expression:

$\dfrac{dy}{dx} = \dfrac{1}{y + x^2 y} = \dfrac{1}{y(1+x^2)}$. Next, we multiply both sides by y and by dx. We get:

$y\,dy = \dfrac{dx}{1+x^2}$. Next, we integrate both sides:

$\displaystyle\int y\,dy = \int \dfrac{dx}{1+x^2}$

$\dfrac{y^2}{2} = \tan^{-1}x + C$

Now we isolate y: $y^2 = 2\tan^{-1}x + C$

$y = \sqrt{2\tan^{-1}x + C}$

Now we solve for C. We plug in $x = 0$ and $y = 2$:

$2 = \sqrt{2\tan^{-1}0 + C}$

$C = 4$

Therefore, the equation is $y = \sqrt{2\tan^{-1}x + 4}$.

4. $y = \sqrt[3]{3e^x - 2}$

We solve this differential equation by separation of variables. We want to get all of the y variables on one side of the equals sign and all of the x variables on the other side. We can do this easily by cross multiplying. We get: $y^2 dy = e^x dx$. Next, we integrate both sides:

$\displaystyle\int y^2 dy = \int e^x dx$

$\dfrac{y^3}{3} = e^x + C$

Now we isolate y:

$$y^3 = 3e^x + C$$

$$y = \sqrt[3]{3e^x + C}$$

Now we solve for C. We plug in $x = 0$ and $y = 1$:

$$1 = \sqrt[3]{3e^0 + C}$$

$$C = -2$$

Therefore, the equation is $y = \sqrt[3]{3e^x - 2}$.

5. $y = 2x^2$

We solve this differential equation by separation of variables. We want to get all of the y variables on one side of the equals sign and all of the x variables on the other side. We can do this easily by dividing both sides by y^2 and multiplying both sides by dx. We get:

$$\frac{dy}{y^2} = \frac{dx}{x^3}.$$ Next, we integrate both sides:

$$\int \frac{dy}{y^2} = \int \frac{dx}{x^3}$$

$$-\frac{1}{y} = -\frac{1}{2x^2} + C$$

Now we isolate y:

$$\frac{1}{y} = \frac{1}{2x^2} + C$$

Now we solve for C. We plug in $x = 1$ and $y = 2$:

$$2 = 2(1)2 + C$$

$$C = 0$$

Therefore, the equation is $\dfrac{1}{y} = \dfrac{1}{2x^2} + C$, which can be rewritten as $y = 2x^2$.

6. $y = \sin^{-1}(-\cos x)$

We solve this differential equation by separation of variables. We want to get all of the y variables on one side of the equals sign and all of the x variables on the other side. We can do this easily by cross multiplying. We get: $\cos y dy = \sin x dx$. Next, we integrate both sides:

$$\int \cos y dy = \int \sin x dx$$

$\sin y = -\cos x + C$

Now we solve for C. We plug in $x = 0$ and $y = \dfrac{3\pi}{2}$:

$\sin \dfrac{3\pi}{2} = -\cos 0 + C$

$-1 = -1 + C$

$C = 0$

Now we isolate y to get the equation $y = \sin^{-1}(-\cos x)$.

7. 20,000 (approximately)

The phrase "exponential growth" means that we can represent the situation with the differential equation $\dfrac{dy}{dt} = ky$, where k is a constant and y is the population at a time t. Here we are also told that $y = 4{,}000$ at $t = 0$ and $y = 6{,}500$ at $t = 3$. We solve this differential equation by separation of variables. We want to get all of the y variables on one side of the equals sign and all of the t variables on the other side. We can do this easily by dividing both sides by y and multiplying both sides by dt. We get: $\dfrac{dy}{y} = kdt$. Next, we integrate both sides:

$$\int \dfrac{dy}{y} = \int kdt$$

$\ln y = =kt + C_0$

$y = Ce^{kt}$

Next, we plug in $y = 4{,}000$ and $t = 0$ to solve for C:

$4{,}000 = Ce^0$

$C = 4{,}000$

Now we have $y = 4{,}000^{kt}$. Next we plug in $y = 6{,}500$ and $t = 3$ to solve for k:

$6{,}500 = 4{,}000e^{3k}$

$k = \dfrac{1}{3}\ln\dfrac{13}{8} \approx .162$.

Therefore, our equation for the population of bacteria, y, at time, t, is

$y \approx 4000e^{.162t}$, or if we want an exact solution, it is $y = 4000\left(\dfrac{13}{8}\right)^{\frac{t}{3}}$. Finally,

we can solve for the population at time $t = 10$: $y \approx 4000e^{.162(10)} \approx 20212$ or

$y = 4000\left(\dfrac{13}{8}\right)^{\frac{10}{3}} \approx 20179$. (Notice how, even with an "exact" solution we still

have to round the answer. And, if we are concerned with significant figures, the

population can be written as 20,000.)

8. 45 m

Because acceleration is the derivative of velocity, we can write: $\dfrac{dv}{dt} = -9$. We are

also told that $v = 18$ and $h = 45$ when $t = 0$. We solve this differential equation by

separation of variables. We want to get all of the v variables on one side of the

equals sign and all of the t variables on the other side. We can do this easily by

multiplying both sides by

dt: $dv = -9dt$. Next, we integrate both sides:

$\int dv = \int -9dt$

$v = -9 + C_0$

Now we can solve for C_0C by plugging in $v = 18$ and $t = 0$: $18 = -9(0) + C_0$ so

$C_0 = 18$. Thus our equation for the velocity of the rock is $v = -9t + 18$. Next, because

the height of the rock is the derivative of the velocity, we can write $\dfrac{dh}{dt} = -9t + 18$.

We again separate the variables by multiplying both sides by dt: $dh = (-9t + 18)dt$.

We integrate both sides:

$$\int dh = \int (-9t + 18)\, dt$$

$$h = -\frac{9t^2}{2} + 18t + C_1$$

Next, we plug in $h = 45$ and $t = 0$ to solve for C_1:

$$45 = -\frac{9(0)^2}{2} + 18(0) + C_1, \text{ so } C_1 = 45$$

Therefore, the equation for the height of the rock, h, at time, t, is:

$$h = -\frac{9t^2}{2} + 18t + 45.$$

Finally, we can solve for the height of the rock at time $t = 4$: $h = -\dfrac{9t^2}{2} + 18t + 45$

$$h = -\frac{9(4)^2}{2} + 18(4) + 45 = 45\text{m}.$$

9. $\dfrac{1125\pi}{2} \approx 1800\text{ft}^3$

We can express this situation with the differential equation $\dfrac{dV}{dt} = kV$ where k

is a constant and V is the volume of the sphere at time t. We are also told that

$V = 36\pi$ when $t = 0$ and $V = 90\pi$ when $t = 1$. We solve this differential equation

by separation of variables. We want to get all of the V variables on one side of the

equals sign and all of the t variables on the other side. We can do this easily by

dividing both sides by V and multiplying both sides by dt. We get: $\dfrac{dV}{V} = kdt$. Next,

we integrate both sides:

$$\int \frac{dV}{V} = \int k\,dt$$

$$\ln V = kt + C_0$$

$$V = Ce^{kt}$$

Next, we plug in $V = 36\pi$ and $t = 0$ to solve for C: $36\pi = Ce^0$ so $C = 36\pi$. This

gives us the equation $V = 36\pi e^{kt}$. Next, we plug in $V = 90\pi$ and $t = 1$ to solve for k:

$90\pi = 36\pi e^k$

$k = \ln\dfrac{5}{2} \approx .916$

Therefore, the equation for the volume of the sphere, V, at time, t, is $V \approx 36\pi e^{.916t}$,

or if we want an exact solution, it is $V = 36\pi \dfrac{5}{2}^t$. Finally, we can solve for the

volume at time $t = 3$: $V \approx 36\pi e^{.916(3)} \approx 1766\text{ft}^3$ or $V = \dfrac{1125\pi}{2}\text{ft}^3$. (And, if we are

concerned with significant figures, the volume can be written as 1800.)

10. 8,900 grams (approximately)

We can express this situation with the differential equation $\dfrac{dm}{dt} = -km$, where m

is the mass at time t. We are also given that $m = 10,000$ when $t = 0$ and $m = 5,000$

when $t = 5,750$. We solve this differential equation by separation of variables. We

want to get all of the m variables on one side of the equals sign and all of the t

variables on the other side. We can do this easily by dividing both sides by m and

multiplying both sides by dt. We get: $\dfrac{dm}{m} = -kdt$. Next, we integrate both sides:

$\displaystyle\int \dfrac{dm}{m} = -\int kdt$

$\ln m = -kt + C_0$

$m = Ce^{-kt}$

Now we can solve for C by plugging in $m = 10,000$ and $t = 0$: $10,000 = Ce^0$, so

$C = 10,000$. This gives us the equation $m = 10,000e^{-kt}$. Next, we can solve for k by

plugging in $m = 5,000$ and $t = 5,750$:

$5000 = 10000e^{-5750k}$

$\dfrac{1}{2} = e^{-5750k}$

$-\dfrac{1}{5750}\ln\dfrac{1}{2} = k \approx .000121$

Therefore, the equation for the mass of the element, m, at

time, t, is $m \approx 10000e^{-.000121t}$, or if we want an exact solution, it is

$m = 10000\left(\dfrac{1}{2}\right)^{\frac{t}{5750}}$. Finally, we can solve for the mass of the element at time

$t = 1,000$: $m \approx 10000e^{-.000121(1000)} \approx 8860$gms or $m = 10000\left(\dfrac{1}{2}\right)^{\frac{1000}{5750}} \approx 8864$gms. (And, if

we are concerned with significant figures, the mass can be written as 8900.)

11. 4.441

We start with $x_0 = 0$ and $y_0 = 2$ and $h = 0.25$. The slope is found by plugging $x_0 = 0$
and $y_0 = 2$ into $y' = y - x$, so we have $y'_0 = 2 - 0 = 2$.
Step 1: Increase x_0 by h to get x_1: $x_1 = 0 + 0.25 = 0.25$
Step 2: Multiply h by y'_0 and add y_0 to get y_1: $y_1 = 2 + (0.25)(2) = 2.5$
Step 3: Find y'_1 by plugging y_1 and x_1 into the equation $y' = y -$:
$y'_1 = 2.5 - 0.25 = 2.25$
  Now we repeat until we get to $x = 1$:
Step 1: Increase x_1 by h to get x_2: $x_2 = 0.25 + 0.25 = 0.5$.
Step 2: Multiply h by y'_1 and add y_1 to get y_2: $y_2 = 2.5 + (0.25)(2.25) = 3.0625$
Step 3: Find y'_2 by plugging y_2 and x_2 into the equation $y' = y - x$:
$y'_2 = 3.0625 - .5 = 2.5625$
  Repeat:
Step 1: Increase x_2 by h to get x_3: $x_3 = 0.25 + 0.5 = 0.75$
Step 2: Multiply h by y'_2 and add y_2 to get y_3: $y_3 = 3.0625 + (0.25)(2.5625) = 3.703125$
Step 3: Find y'_3 by plugging y_3 and x_3 into the equation $y' = y - x$:
$y'_3 = 3.703125 - .75 = 2.953125$.
  Repeat one last time:
Step 1: Increase x_3 by h to get x_4: $x_4 = 0.25 + 0.75 = 1$
Step 2: Multiply h by y'_3 and add y_3 to get y_4:
$y_4 = 3.703125 + (0.25)(2.953125) = 4.441$

12. 0.328

We start with $x_0 = 0$ and $h = 0.2$. The slope is found by plugging $x_0 = 0$ and $y_0 = 0$
into $y' = -y$, so we have $y'_0 = -1$.
Step 1: Increase by h to get x_1: $x_1 = 0 + 0.2 = 0.2$
Step 2: Multiply h by y'_0 and add y_0 to get y_1: $y_1 = 1 + (0.2)(-1) = 0.8$
Step 3: Find y'_1 by plugging y_1 and x_1 into the equation $y' = -y$: $y'_1 = -0.8$

Now we repeat until we get to $x = 1$:

Step 1: Increase x_1 by h to get x_2: $x_2 = 0.2 + 0.2 = 0.4$

Step 2: Multiply h by y_1' and add y_1 to get y_2: $y_2 = 0.8 + (.2)(-0.8) = 0.64$

Step 3: Find y_2' by plugging y_2 and x_2 into the equation $y' = -y$: $y_2' = -0.64$

Repeat:

Step 1: Increase x_2 by h to get x_3: $x_3 = 0.2 + 0.4 = 0.6$

Step 2: Multiply h by y_2' and add y_2 to get y_3: $y_3 = 0.64 + (.2)(-0.64) = 0.512$

Step 3: Find y_3' by plugging y_3 and x_3 into the equation $y' = -y$: $y_3' = -0.512$.

Repeat:

Step 1: Increase x_3 by h to get x_4: $x_4 = 0.2 + 0.6 = 0.8$

Step 2: Multiply h by y_3' and add y_3 to get y_4: $y_4 = 0.512 + (0.2)(-0.512) = 0.4096$

Step 3: Find y_4' by plugging y_4 and x_4 into the equation $y' = -y$: $y_4' = -0.4096$

Repeat one last time:

Step 1: Increase x_4 by h to get x_5: $x_5 = 0.2 + 0.8 = 1$

Step 2: Multiply h by y_4' and add y_4 to get $y_0 = 1$ $y_5 = 0.4096 + (0.2)(-0.4096) = 0.328$.

13. 0.04

We start with $x_0 = 0$ and $y_0 = 0$ and $h = 0.2$. The slope is found by plugging $x_0 = 0$ and $y_0 = 0$ into $y' = 4x^3$, so we have $y_0' = 0$.

Step 1: Increase x_0 by h to get x_1: $x_1 = 0 + 0.4 = 0.1$

Step 2: Multiply h by y_0' and add y_0 to get y_1: $y_1 = 0 + (0.1)(0) = 0$

Step 3: Find y_1' by plugging y_1 and x_1 into the equation $y' = 4x^3$: $y_1' = 0.004$

Now we repeat until we get to $x = 0.5$:

Step 1: Increase x_1 by h to get x_2: $x_2 = 0.1 + 0.1 = 0.2$

Step 2: Multiply h by y_1' and add y_1 to get y_2: $y_2 = 0 + (.1)(.004) = 0.0004$

Step 3: Find y_2' by plugging y_2 and x_2 into the equation $y' = 4x^3$: $y_2' = 0.032$

Repeat:

Step 1: Increase x_2 by h to get x_3: $x_3 = 0.1 + 0.2 = 0.3$

Step 2: Multiply h by y_2' and add y_2 to get y_3: $y_3 = 0.0004 + (.1)(0.032) = 0.0036$

Step 3: Find y_3' by plugging y_3 and x_3 into the equation $y' = 4x^3$: $y_3' = 0.108$.

Repeat:

Step 1: Increase x_3 by h to get x_4: $x_4 = 0.1 + 0.3 = 0.4$

Step 2: Multiply h by y_3' and add y_3 to get y_4: $y_4 = 0.0036 + (0.1)(0.108) = .0144$

Step 3: Find y_4' by plugging y_4 and x_3 into the equation $y' = 4x^3$: $y_4' = 0.256$

Repeat one last time:

Step 1: Increase x_4 by h to get x_5: $x_5 = 0.1 + 0.4 = 0.5$

Step 2: Multiply h by y_4' and add y_4 to get y_5: $y_5 = 0.0144 + (0.1)(0.256) = 0.04$.

14.

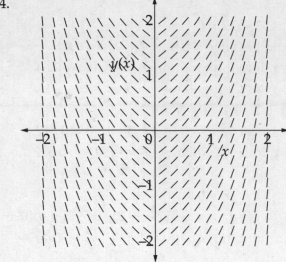

15.

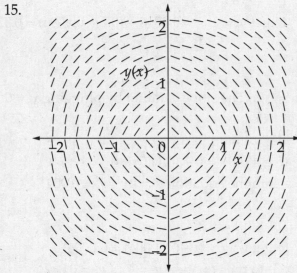

16.

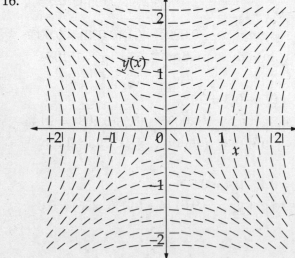

SOLUTIONS TO PRACTICE PROBLEM SET 35

1. Sum is 2.499

   This is a geometric series. We find the sum of the first n terms of a geometric series

   using the formula $S = \dfrac{a(1-r)^n}{(1-r)}$, where a is the first term of the series and r is the

   common ratio (see page 280). Here, the first term is $a = 2$ and the common ratio is

   $r = \dfrac{1}{5}$. Plugging into the formula, we get: $S = \dfrac{2\left(1-\left(\dfrac{1}{5}\right)^5\right)}{\left(1-\dfrac{1}{5}\right)} = 2.499$.

2. Sum is $\dfrac{28}{3}$

   This is an infinite geometric series. We find the sum of an infinite geometric

   series using the formula $S = \dfrac{a}{1-r}$, where a is the first term of the series and r is the

   common ratio (see page 280). Here, the first term is $a = 8$ and the common ratio is

   $r = \dfrac{1}{7}$. Plugging into the formula, we get: $S = \dfrac{8}{1-\dfrac{1}{7}} = \dfrac{28}{3}$.

3. Converges

   We can use the ratio test to determine whether the series converges. The test

   can be found on page 281. Here, we have $a_n = \dfrac{5^n}{(n-1)!}$ and $a_{n+1} = \dfrac{5^{n+1}}{n!}$. Plugging

   into the test, we get: $\lim\limits_{n\to\infty} \dfrac{\dfrac{5^{n+1}}{n!}}{\dfrac{5^n}{(n-1)!}} = \lim\limits_{n\to\infty}\left(\dfrac{5^{n+1}}{n!}\right)\left(\dfrac{(n-1)!}{5^n}\right) = \lim\limits_{n\to\infty}\left(\dfrac{5}{n}\right) = 0$. Therefore, the

   series converges.

4. Diverges

We can use the ratio test to determine whether the series converges. The test can be found on page 281. Here, we have $a_n = \dfrac{5^n}{n^2}$ and $a_{n+1} = \dfrac{5^{n+1}}{(n+1)^2}$. Plugging into the test, we get: $\displaystyle\lim_{n\to\infty} \dfrac{\dfrac{5^{n+1}}{(n+1)^2}}{\dfrac{5^n}{n^2}} = \lim_{n\to\infty}\left(\dfrac{5^{n+1}}{(n+1)^2}\right)\left(\dfrac{n^2}{5^n}\right) = \lim_{n\to\infty}(5)\left(\dfrac{n}{n+1}\right)^2 = 5$. Therefore, the series diverges.

5. $\cos x = 1 - \dfrac{x^2}{2!} + \dfrac{x^4}{4!} - \dfrac{x^6}{6!} + \ldots = \displaystyle\sum_{k=0}^{\infty} (-1)^k \dfrac{x^{2k}}{(2k)!}$

We find a Taylor Series by the formula

$$\sum_{k=0}^{\infty} \dfrac{f^{(k)}}{k!}(x-a)^k = f(a) + f'(a)(x-a) + \dfrac{f''(a)}{2!}(x-a)^2 + \ldots + \dfrac{f^{(n)}(a)}{n!}(x-a)^n + \ldots$$

First, let's find a few derivatives of $\cos x$ and evaluate them at $a = 0$:

$f(x) = \cos x;$ $f(0) = \cos 0 = 1$

$f'(x) = -\sin x;$ $f'(0) = -\sin 0 = 0$

$f''(x) = -\cos x;$ $f''(0) = -\cos 0 = -1$

$f'''(x) = \sin x;$ $f'''(0) = \sin 0 = 0$

$f^{(4)}(x) = \cos x;$ $f^{(4)}(0) = \cos 0 = 1$

$f^{(5)}(x) = -\sin x;$ $f^{(5)}(x) = -\sin 0 = 0$

$f^{(6)}(x) = -\cos x;$ $f^{(6)}(0) = -\cos 0 = -1$

Let's see if we find a pattern. Plugging into the formula, we get:

$$\cos x = 1 + 0 + \dfrac{(-1)}{2!}x^2 + 0 + \dfrac{1}{4!}x^4 + 0 - \dfrac{1}{6!}x^6.$$

We can see that the general formula is: $\cos x = 1 - \dfrac{x^2}{2!} + \dfrac{x^4}{4!} - \dfrac{x^6}{6!} + \ldots = \displaystyle\sum_{k=0}^{\infty} (-1)^k \dfrac{x^{2k}}{(2k)!}$.

You should memorize the Taylor series that are highlighted on page 287. The AP does not require you to derive them when you use them. You can simply state the formulas.

6. $\ln(1+x) = x - \dfrac{x^2}{2} + \dfrac{x^3}{3} - \dfrac{x^4}{4} + \ldots = \displaystyle\sum_{k=0}^{\infty} (-1)^k \dfrac{x^{k+1}}{k+1}$

We find a Taylor Series by the formula

$$\sum_{k=0}^{\infty} \frac{f^{(k)}}{k!}(x-a)^k = f(a) + f'(a)(x-a) + \frac{f''(a)}{2!}(x-a)^2 + \ldots + \frac{f^{(n)}(a)}{n!}(x-a)^n + \ldots$$

First, let's find a few derivatives of ln (1 + x) and evaluate them at $a = 0$:

$f(x) = \ln(1+x);$ $f(0) = \ln(1+0) = 0$

$f'(x) = \dfrac{1}{(1+x)};$ $f'(0) = \dfrac{1}{1+0} = 1$

$f''(x) = \dfrac{-1}{(1+x)^2};$ $f''(0) = \dfrac{-1}{(1+0)^2} = -1$

$f'''(x) = \dfrac{2}{(1+x)^2};$ $f'''(0) = \dfrac{2}{(1+0)^3} = 2$

$f^{(4)}(x) = \dfrac{-6}{(1+x)^3};$ $f^{(4)}(0) = \dfrac{-6}{(1+0)^3} = -6$

Let's see if we find a pattern. Plugging into the formula, we get:

$\ln(1+x) = 0 + (1)(x) + \left(\dfrac{-1}{2!}\right)(x^2) + \left(\dfrac{2}{3!}\right)(x^3) + \left(\dfrac{-6}{4!}\right)(x^4)$. This simplifies to

$\ln(1+x) = x - \dfrac{x^2}{2} + \dfrac{x^3}{3} - \dfrac{x^4}{4}$.

We can see that the general formula is:

$$\ln(1+x) = x - \frac{x^2}{2} + \frac{x^3}{3} - \frac{x^4}{4} + \ldots = \sum_{k=0}^{\infty} (-1)^k \frac{x^{k+1}}{k+1}$$

You should memorize the Taylor series that are highlighted on page 287. The AP does not require you to derive them when you use them. You can simply state the formulas.

7. $e^{-x} = 1 - x + \frac{x^2}{2!} - \frac{x^3}{3!} + \frac{x^4}{4!} + \ldots = \sum_{k=0}^{\infty} (-1)^k \frac{x^k}{k!}$

We find a Taylor series by the formula

$$\sum_{k=0}^{\infty} \frac{f^{(k)}}{k!} (x-a)^k = f(a) + f'(a)(x-a) + \frac{f''(a)}{2!}(x-a)^2 + \ldots + \frac{f^{(n)}(a)}{n!}(x-a)^n + \ldots$$

First, let's find a few derivatives of e^{-x} and evaluate them at $a = 0$:

$f(x) = e^{-x};$ $f(0) = e^0 = 1$

$f'(x) = -e^{-x};$ $f'(0) = -e^0 = -1$

$f''(x) = e^{-x};$ $f''(0) = e^0 = 1$

$f'''(x) = -e^{-x};$ $f'''(0) = -e^0 = -1$

$f^{(4)}(x) = e^{-x};$ $f^{(4)}(0) = e^0 = 1$

Let's see if we find a pattern. Plugging into the formula, we get:

$$e^{-x} = 1 - x + \frac{x^2}{2!} - \frac{x^3}{3!} + \frac{x^4}{4!}$$

We can see that the general formula is: $e^{-x} = 1 - x + \frac{x^2}{2!} - \frac{x^3}{3!} + \frac{x^4}{4!} + \ldots = \sum_{k=0}^{\infty} (-1)^k \frac{x^k}{k!}$

You should memorize the Taylor series that are highlighted on page 287. The AP does not require you to derive them when you use them. You can simply state the formulas.

8. $\dfrac{\sqrt{3}}{2}+\dfrac{1}{2}\left(x-\dfrac{\pi}{3}\right)-\dfrac{\sqrt{3}}{4}\left(x-\dfrac{\pi}{3}\right)^{2}$

We find a Taylor series by the formula

$$\sum_{k=0}^{\infty}\frac{f^{(k)}}{k!}(x-a)^{k}=f(a)+f'(a)(x-a)+\frac{f''(a)}{2!}(x-a)^{2}+...+\frac{f^{(n)}(a)}{n!}(x-a)^{n}+...$$

First, let's find a few derivatives of $\sin x$ and evaluate them at $a=\dfrac{\pi}{3}$:

$f(x)=\sin x;\qquad f\left(\dfrac{\pi}{3}\right)=\sin\dfrac{\pi}{3}=\dfrac{\sqrt{3}}{2}$

$f'(x)=\cos x;\qquad f'\left(\dfrac{\pi}{3}\right)=\cos\dfrac{\pi}{3}=\dfrac{1}{2}$

$f''(x)=-\sin x;\qquad f''\left(\dfrac{\pi}{3}\right)=-\sin\dfrac{\pi}{3}=-\dfrac{\sqrt{3}}{2}$

These should give us three non-zero terms. Let's plug into the formula. We get:

$\sin x=\dfrac{\sqrt{3}}{2}+\dfrac{1}{2}\left(x-\dfrac{\pi}{3}\right)-\dfrac{\sqrt{3}}{2}\dfrac{\left(x-\dfrac{\pi}{3}\right)^{2}}{2!}$, which simplifies to

$\dfrac{\sqrt{3}}{2}+\dfrac{1}{2}\left(x-\dfrac{\pi}{3}\right)-\dfrac{\sqrt{3}}{4}\left(x-\dfrac{\pi}{3}\right)^{2}$.

You should memorize the Taylor series that are highlighted on page 287. The AP does not require you to derive them when you use them. You can simply state the formulas.

9. The radius of convergence is $\dfrac{1}{3}$; the interval of convergence is $\left(-\dfrac{1}{3},\dfrac{1}{3}\right)$.

The interval of convergence of a series refers to those values of x where the series

converges. A geometric series converges when the common ratio of its terms is

$-1<r<1$. Here, we have the series $\displaystyle\sum_{k=0}^{\infty}3^{n}x^{n}=\sum_{k=0}^{\infty}(3x)^{n}$, so the common ratio is $3x$.

To find the interval of convergence, all we have to do is set $-1 < 3x < 1$ and solve

for x. We get: $-\dfrac{1}{3} < x < \dfrac{1}{3}$. Thus the interval of convergence is $\left(-\dfrac{1}{3}, \dfrac{1}{3}\right)$. The radius

of convergence is simply the distance from the center of the interval to either

endpoint, or half the width of the interval. In this case, the radius of convergence

is $\dfrac{1}{3}$.

10. The radius of convergence is ∞; the interval of convergence is $(-\infty, \infty)$.

The interval of convergence of a series refers to those values of x where the

series converges. Here we will apply the Ratio Test for absolute convergence:

$$p = \lim_{n \to \infty} \left| \frac{(-1)^{n+1}\left(\dfrac{x^{2n+2}}{(2n+2)!}\right)}{(-1)^{n}\left(\dfrac{x^{2n}}{(2n)!}\right)} \right| = \lim_{n \to \infty} \left| \left(\frac{x^{2n+2}}{(2n+2)!}\right)\left(\frac{(2n)!}{x^{2n}}\right) \right| = \lim_{n \to \infty} \frac{x^2}{(2n+2)(2n+1)} = 0.$$

This will converge if $p < 1$, which is true here for all values of x. Therefore, the

interval of convergence is $(-\infty, \infty)$. The radius of convergence is simply distance

from the center of the interval to either endpoint, or half the width of the interval.

In this case, the radius of convergence is ∞.

11. 0.980067; $8.\overline{8} \times 10^{-8}$

We find a Taylor series by the formula

$$\sum_{k=0}^{\infty} \frac{f^{(k)}}{k!}(x-a)^k = f(a) + f'(a)(x-a) + \frac{f''(a)}{2!}(x-a)^2 + \ldots + \frac{f^{(n)}(a)}{n!}(x-a)^n + \ldots$$

First, let's find a few derivatives of $\cos x$ and evaluate them at $a = 0$:

$f(x) = \cos x;$ $f(0) = \cos 0 = 1$

$f'(x) = -\sin x;$ $f'(0) = -\sin 0 = 0$

$f''(x) = -\cos x;$ $f''(0) = -\cos 0 = -1$

$f'''(x) = \sin x;$ $f'''(0) = -\sin 0 = 0$

$f^{(4)}(x) = \cos x;$ $f^{(4)}(0) = \cos 0 = 1$

Plugging into the formula, we get: $\cos x \approx 1 + 0 + \frac{(-1)}{2!}x^2 + 0 + \frac{1}{4!}x^4$. This is the

fourth degree Taylor polynomial. You should memorize the Taylor series that are

highlighted on page 287. The AP does not require you to derive them when you

use them. You can simply state the formulas. Now we simply plug $x = 0.2$ into

the polynomial. We get: $\cos x \approx 1 + 0 + \frac{(-1)}{2!}(0.2)^2 + 0 + \frac{1}{4!}(0.2)^4 \approx .980067$. To find

the error bound, we can simply use the next term of the polynomial. Here, the next

term is $\frac{x^6}{6!}$. If we plug in $x = 0.2$, we get: $8.\overline{8} \times 10^{-8}$.

12. 0.264; 0.002025

We find a Taylor series by the formula

$$\sum_{k=0}^{\infty} \frac{f^{(k)}}{k!}(x-a)^k = f(a) + f'(a)(x-a) + \frac{f''(a)}{2!}(x-a)^2 + \ldots + \frac{f^{(n)}(a)}{n!}(x-a)^n + \ldots$$

First, let's find a few derivatives of $\ln(1+x)$ and evaluate them at $a = 0$:

$$f(x) = \ln(1+x); \qquad f(0) = \ln(1+0) = 0$$

$$f'(x) = \frac{1}{(1+x)}; \qquad f'(0) = \frac{1}{1+0} = 1$$

$$f''(x) = \frac{-1}{(1+x)^2}; \qquad f''(0) = \frac{-1}{(1+0)^2} = -1$$

$$f'''(x) = \frac{2}{(1+x)^2}; \qquad f'''(0) = \frac{2}{(1+0)^3} = 2$$

Plugging into the formula, we get:

$$\ln(1+x) \approx 0 + (1)(x) + \left(\frac{-1}{2!}\right)(x^2) + \left(\frac{2}{3!}\right)(x^3).$$ This simplifies to $\ln(1+x) \approx x - \frac{x^2}{2} + \frac{x^3}{3}$.

This is the third degree Taylor polynomial.

You should memorize the Taylor series that are highlighted on page 287. The

AP does not require you to derive them when you use them. You can simply

state the formulas. Now we simply plug $x = 0.3$ into the polynomial. We get:

$$\ln(1+0.3) \approx (0.3) - \frac{(0.3)^2}{2} + \frac{(0.3)^3}{3} \approx 0.264.$$ To find the error bound, we can simply

use the next term of the polynomial. Here, the next term is $\frac{x^4}{4}$. If we plug in

$x = 0.3$, we get: 0.002025.

13. Diverges by the integral test.

There are a variety of tests for convergence of a series. If a series is not alternating and is not geometric, we usually look to see if we can use a comparison test, a ratio test, or an integral test. We can easily integrate this integral using u-substitution, so we will use the integral test. Here, the series is $\sum_{n=2}^{\infty} \frac{1}{n \ln n}$, so we need to see if $\int_{2}^{\infty}\left(\frac{1}{x \ln x}\right) dx$ converges. First, we replace the upper limit with a and take the limit as a goes to infinity. We get: $\int_{2}^{\infty}\left(\frac{1}{x \ln x}\right) dx = \lim_{a \to \infty} \int_{2}^{a}\left(\frac{1}{x \ln x}\right) dx$. Next, if we let $u = \ln x$, then $du = \frac{1}{x} dx$. Substituting into the integrand, we get: $\int\left(\frac{1}{x \ln x}\right) dx = \int \frac{du}{u} = \ln|u|$. Substituting back, we get: $\left(\ln|\ln x|\right)\Big|_{2}^{a} = \ln(\ln a) - \ln(\ln 2)$. Finally, we take the limit:

$\lim_{a \to \infty}\left[\ln(\ln a) - \ln(\ln 2)\right] = D.N.E.$ Therefore, the series diverges by the integral test.

14. Converges by the integral test.

There are a variety of tests for convergence of a series. If a series is not alternating and is not geometric, we usually look to see if we can use a comparison test, a ratio test, or an integral test. We can easily integrate this integral, so we will use the integral test. Here, the series is $\sum_{n=1}^{\infty} \frac{1}{n \sqrt[4]{n}}$, so we need to see if $\int_{1}^{\infty}\left(\frac{1}{x \sqrt[4]{x}}\right) dx = \int_{1}^{\infty} x^{-\frac{5}{4}} dx$ converges. First, we replace the upper limit with a and take the limit as a goes to infinity. We get: $\int_{1}^{\infty} x^{-\frac{5}{4}} dx = \lim_{a \to \infty} \int_{1}^{a} x^{-\frac{5}{4}} dx$. Next, we integrate:

$\int_{1}^{a} x^{-\frac{5}{4}} dx = \left(-4x^{-\frac{1}{4}}\right)\Big|_{1}^{a} = -4a^{-\frac{1}{4}} + 4$. Now, we take the limit: $\lim_{a \to \infty}\left(-4a^{-\frac{1}{4}} + 4\right) = 4$

Therefore, the series converges by the integral test.

15. Diverges by the comparison test.

There are a variety of tests for convergence of a series. If a series is not alternating and is not geometric, we usually look to see if we can use a comparison test, a ratio test, or an integral test. Here, the series is $\sum\limits_{n=2}^{\infty} \dfrac{\ln n}{n+1}$, which we can easily compare to the series $\sum\limits_{n=2}^{\infty} \dfrac{1}{n+1}$. The series $\sum\limits_{n=2}^{\infty} \dfrac{1}{n+1}$ is essentially the harmonic series (it's just missing the first two terms), which diverges. The series $\sum\limits_{n=2}^{\infty} \dfrac{\ln n}{n+1} > \sum\limits_{n=2}^{\infty} \dfrac{1}{n+1}$ for all terms. Therefore, the series diverges by the comparison test.

16. Converges by the comparison test.

There are a variety of tests for convergence of a series. If a series is not alternating and is not geometric, we usually look to see if we can use a comparison test, a ratio test, or an integral test. Here, the series is $\sum\limits_{n=4}^{\infty} \dfrac{1}{n!}$, which we can easily compare to the series $\sum\limits_{n=4}^{\infty} \dfrac{1}{n^2}$. The series $\sum\limits_{n=4}^{\infty} \dfrac{1}{n^2}$ converges and the series $\sum\limits_{n=4}^{\infty} \dfrac{1}{n!} < \sum\limits_{n=4}^{\infty} \dfrac{1}{n^2}$ for all terms. Therefore, the series converges by the comparison test.

22

The Princeton Review
AP Calculus AB
Practice Test 1

CALCULUS AB

SECTION I, Part A

Time—55 Minutes

Number of questions—28

A CALCULATOR MAY NOT BE USED ON THIS PART OF THE EXAMINATION

<u>Directions</u>: Solve each of the following problems, using the available space for scratchwork. After examining the form of the choices, decide which is the best of the choices given and fill in the corresponding oval on the answer sheet. No credit will be given for anything written in the test book. Do not spend too much time on any one problem.

<u>In this test</u>: Unless otherwise specified, the domain of a function f is assumed to be the set of all real numbers x for which $f(x)$ is a real number.

1. If $f(x) = 5x^{\frac{4}{3}}$, then $f'(8) =$

(A) 10   (B) $\dfrac{40}{3}$ (C) 40   (D) 80   (E) $\dfrac{160}{3}$

2. $\lim\limits_{x \to \infty} \dfrac{5x^2 - 3x + 1}{4x^2 + 2x + 5}$ is

(A) 0   (B) $\dfrac{4}{5}$ (C) $\dfrac{3}{11}$ (D) $\dfrac{5}{4}$ (E) ∞

GO ON TO THE NEXT PAGE

3. If $f(x) = \dfrac{3x^2 + x}{3x^2 - x}$ then $f'(x)$ is

(A) 1

(B) $\dfrac{6x^2 + 1}{6x^2 - 1}$

(C) $\dfrac{-6}{(3x - 1)^2}$

(D) $\dfrac{-2x^2}{(x^2 - x)^2}$

(E) $\dfrac{36x^3 - 2x}{(x^2 - x)^2}$

4. If the function f is continuous for all real numbers and if $f(x) = \dfrac{x^2 - 7x + 12}{x - 4}$ when $x \neq 4$, then $f(4) =$

(A) 1   (B) $\dfrac{8}{7}$ (C) -1 (D) 0   (E) undefined

GO ON TO THE NEXT PAGE

5. If $x^2 - 2xy + 3y^2 = 8$, then $\dfrac{dy}{dx} =$

(A) $\dfrac{8 + 2y - 2x}{6y - 2x}$

(B) $\dfrac{3y - x}{y - x}$

(C) $\dfrac{2x - 2y}{6y - 2x}$

(D) $\dfrac{1}{3}$

(E) $\dfrac{y - x}{3y - x}$

GO ON TO THE NEXT PAGE

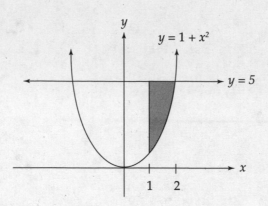

6. Which of the following integrals correctly corresponds to the area of the shaded region in the figure above ?

(A) $\int_1^2 (x^2 - 4)dx$

(B) $\int_1^2 (4 - x^2)dx$

(C) $\int_1^5 (x^2 - 4)dx$

(D) $\int_1^5 (x^2 + 4)dx$

(E) $\int_1^5 (4 - x^2)dx$

---

7. If $f(x) = \sec x + \csc x$, then $f'(x) =$

(A) 0

(B) $\sec^2 x + \csc^2 x$

(C) $\csc x - \sec x$

(D) $\sec x \tan x + \csc x \cot x$

(E) $\sec x \tan x - \csc x \cot x$

GO ON TO THE NEXT PAGE

8. An equation of the line normal to the graph of $y = \sqrt{(3x^2 + 2x)}$ at (2, 4) is

(A) $-4x + y = 20$ (B) $4x + 7y = 20$ (C) $-7x + 4y = 2$ (D) $7x + 4y = 30$ (E) $4x + 7y = 36$

---

9. $\int_{-1}^{1} \frac{4}{1+x^2}\, dx =$

(A) 0 (B) π (C) 1 (D) 2π (E) 2

---

10. If $f(x) = \cos^2 x$, then $f''(\pi) =$

(A) -2 (B) 0 (C) 1 (D) 2 (E) 2π

---

11. If $f(x) = \dfrac{5}{x^2 + 1}$ and $g(x) = 3x$, then $g(f(2)) =$

(A) -3 (B) $\dfrac{5}{37}$ (C) 3 (D) 5 (E) $\dfrac{37}{5}$

GO ON TO THE NEXT PAGE

12. $\int x\sqrt{5x^2 - 4}\ dx =$

(A) $\dfrac{1}{10}\left(5x^2 - 4\right)^{\frac{3}{2}} + C$

(B) $\dfrac{1}{15}\left(5x^2 - 4\right)^{\frac{3}{2}} + C$

(C) $-\dfrac{1}{5}\left(5x^2 - 4\right)^{-\frac{1}{2}} + C$

(D) $\dfrac{20}{3}\left(5x^2 - 4\right)^{\frac{3}{2}} + C$

(E) $\dfrac{3}{20}\left(5x^2 - 4\right)^{\frac{3}{2}} + C$

---

13. The slope of the line tangent to the graph of $3x^2 + 5\ln y = 12$ at $(2, 1)$ is

(A) $-\dfrac{12}{5}$ (B) $\dfrac{12}{5}$ (C) $\dfrac{5}{12}$ (D) 12   (E) -7

---

14. The equation $y = 2 - 3\sin\dfrac{\pi}{4}(x - 1)$ has a fundamental period of

(A) $\dfrac{1}{8}$ (B) $\dfrac{\pi}{4}$ (C) $\dfrac{4}{\pi}$ (D) 8   (E) 2π

GO ON TO THE NEXT PAGE

15. If $f(x) = \begin{cases} x^2 + 5 \text{ if } x < 2 \\ 7x - 5 \text{ if } x \geq 2 \end{cases}$, for all real numbers x, which of the following must be true?

    I. $f(x)$ is continuous everywhere.

    II. $f(x)$ is differentiable everywhere.

    III. $f(x)$ has a local minimum at $x = 2$.

(A) I only   (B) I and II only   (C) II and III only   (D) I and III only   (E) I, II, and III

---

16. For what value of x does the function $f(x) = x^3 - 9x^2 - 120x + 6$ have a local minimum?

(A) 10   (B) 4   (C) 3   (D) −4   (E) −10

---

17. The acceleration of a particle moving along the x-axis at time t is given by $a(t) = 4t - 12$. If the velocity is 10 when $t = 0$ and the position is 4 when $t = 0$, then the particle is changing direction at

(A) $t = 1$

(B) $t = 3$

(C) $t = 5$

(D) $t = 1$ and $t = 5$

(E) $t = 1$ and $t = 3$ and $t = 5$

GO ON TO THE NEXT PAGE

18. The average value of the function $f(x) = (x-1)^2$ on the interval from $x = 1$ to $x = 5$ is

(A) $-\dfrac{16}{3}$
(B) $\dfrac{16}{3}$
(C) $\dfrac{64}{3}$
(D) $\dfrac{66}{3}$
(E) $\dfrac{256}{3}$

---

19. $\displaystyle\int\left(e^{3\ln x} + e^{3x}\right)dx =$

(A) $3 + \dfrac{e^{3x}}{3} + C$

(B) $\dfrac{x^4}{4} + 3e^{3x} + C$

(C) $\dfrac{e^{x^4}}{4} + 3e^{3x} + C$

(D) $\dfrac{e^{x^4}}{4} + \dfrac{e^{3x}}{3} + C$

(E) $\dfrac{x^4}{4} + \dfrac{e^{3x}}{3} + C$

GO ON TO THE NEXT PAGE

20. If $f(x) = \sqrt{(x^3 + 5x + 121)}\,(x^2 + x + 11)$ then $f'(0) =$

(A) $\dfrac{5}{2}$ 　　　　(B) $\dfrac{27}{2}$ 　　　　(C) 22 　　　　(D) $22 + \dfrac{2}{\sqrt{5}}$ 　　　　(E) $\dfrac{247}{2}$

---

21. If $f(x) = 5^{3x}$ then $f'(x) =$

(A) $5^{3x}(\ln 125)$ 　　　(B) $\dfrac{5^{3x}}{3\ln 5}$ 　　　(C) $3(5^{2x})$ 　　　(D) $3(5^{3x})$ 　　　(E) $3x(5^{3x-1})$

---

22. A solid is generated when the region in the first quadrant enclosed by the graph of $y = (x^2 + 1)^3$, the line $x = 1$, the x-axis, and the y-axis is revolved about the x-axis. Its volume is found by evaluating which of the following integrals?

(A) $\pi \displaystyle\int_{1}^{8} \left(x^2 + 1\right)^3 dx$

(B) $\pi \displaystyle\int_{1}^{8} \left(x^2 + 1\right)^6 dx$

(C) $\pi \displaystyle\int_{0}^{1} \left(x^2 + 1\right)^3 dx$

(D) $\pi \displaystyle\int_{0}^{1} \left(x^2 + 1\right)^6 dx$

(E) $2\pi \displaystyle\int_{0}^{1} \left(x^2 + 1\right)^6 dx$

GO ON TO THE NEXT PAGE

23. $\displaystyle\lim_{x\to 0} 4\,\frac{\sin x \cos x - \sin x}{x^2} =$

(A) 2 (B) $\dfrac{40}{3}$ (C) ∞ (D) 0 (E) undefined

24. If $\dfrac{dy}{dx} = \dfrac{(3x^2+2)}{y}$ and $y = 4$ when $x = 2$, then when $x = 3$, $y =$

(A) 18 (B) $\pm\sqrt{66}$ (C) 58 (D) $\pm\sqrt{74}$ (E) $\pm\sqrt{58}$

25. $\displaystyle\int \frac{dx}{9+x^2} =$

(A) $3\tan^{-1}\left(\dfrac{x}{3}\right)+C$

(B) $\dfrac{1}{3}\tan^{-1}\left(\dfrac{x}{3}\right)+C$

(C) $\dfrac{1}{9}\tan^{-1}\left(\dfrac{x}{3}\right)+C$

(D) $\dfrac{1}{3}\tan^{-1}(x)+C$

(E) $\dfrac{1}{9}\tan^{-1}(x)+C$

GO ON TO THE NEXT PAGE

26. If $f(x) = \cos^3(x+1)$ then $f'(\pi) =$

(A) $-3\cos^2(\pi+1)\sin(\pi+1)$

(B) $3\cos^2(\pi+1)$

(C) $3\cos^2(\pi+1)\sin(\pi+1)$

(D) $3\pi\cos^2(\pi+1)$

(E) 0

27. $\displaystyle\int x\sqrt{x+3}\,dx =$

(A) $\dfrac{2}{3}(x)^{\frac{3}{2}} + 6(x)^{\frac{1}{2}} + C$

(B) $\dfrac{2(x+3)^{\frac{3}{2}}}{3} + C$

(C) $\dfrac{2}{5}(x+3)^{\frac{5}{2}} - 2(x+3)^{\frac{3}{2}} + C$

(D) $\dfrac{3(x+3)^{\frac{3}{2}}}{2} + C$

(E) $\dfrac{4x^2(x+3)^{\frac{3}{2}}}{3} + C$

GO ON TO THE NEXT PAGE

28. If $f(x) = \ln\big(\ln(1-x)\big)$, then $f'(x) =$

(A) $\quad -\dfrac{1}{\ln(1-x)}$

(B) $\quad \dfrac{1}{(1-x)\ln(1-x)}$

(C) $\quad \dfrac{1}{(1-x)^2}$

(D) $\quad -\dfrac{1}{(1-x)\ln(1-x)}$

(E) $\quad -\dfrac{1}{\ln(1-x)^2}$

STOP

END OF PART A SECTION I

IF YOU FINISH BEFORE TIME IS CALLED, YOU MAY CHECK YOUR WORK ON PART A ONLY.

DO NOT GO ON TO PART B UNTIL YOU ARE TOLD TO DO SO.

SECTION I, Part B

Time—50 Minutes

Number of questions—17

A GRAPHING CALCULATOR IS REQUIRED FOR SOME QUESTIONS ON THIS PART OF THE EXAMINATION

Directions: Solve each of the following problems, using the available space for scratchwork. After examining the form of the choices, decide which is the best of the choices given and fill in the corresponding oval on the answer sheet. No credit will be given for anything written in the test book. Do not spend too much time on any one problem.

In this test:

1. The **exact** numerical value of the correct answer does not always appear among the choices given. When this happens, select from among the choices the number that best approximates the exact numerical value.

2. Unless otherwise specified, the domain of a function f is assumed to be the set of all real numbers x for which $f(x)$ is a real number.

29. $\displaystyle\int_0^{\frac{\pi}{4}} \sin x \, dx + \int_{-\frac{\pi}{4}}^0 \cos x \, dx =$

(A) $-\sqrt{2}$ (B) -1 (C) 0 (D) 1 (E) $\sqrt{2}$

GO ON TO THE NEXT PAGE

30. Boats A and B leave the same place at the same time. Boat A heads due north at 12 km/hr. Boat B heads due east at 18 km/hr. After 2.5 hours, how fast is the distance between the boats increasing (in km/hr)?

(A) 21.63   (B) 31.20   (C) 75.00   (D) 9.84   (E) 54.08

---

31. $\lim\limits_{h \to 0} \dfrac{\tan\left(\dfrac{\pi}{6} + h\right) - \tan\left(\dfrac{\pi}{6}\right)}{h} =$

(A) $\dfrac{\sqrt{3}}{3}$ (B) $\dfrac{4}{3}$ (C) $\sqrt{3}$ (D) 0 (E) $\dfrac{3}{4}$

---

32. If $\displaystyle\int_{30}^{100} f(x)\,dx = A$ and $\displaystyle\int_{50}^{100} f(x)\,dx = B$, then $\displaystyle\int_{30}^{50} f(x)\,dx =$

(A) $A + B$ (B) $A - B$ (C) 0 (D) $B - A$ (E) 20

---

33. If $f(x) = 3x^2 - x$, and $g(x) = f^{-1}(x)$, then $g'(10)$ could be

(A) 59 (B) $\dfrac{1}{59}$ (C) $\dfrac{1}{10}$ (D) 11 (E) $\dfrac{1}{11}$

GO ON TO THE NEXT PAGE

34. The graph of $y = x^3 - 5x^2 + 4x + 2$ has a local minimum at

(A) (0.46, 2.87)   (B) (0.46, 0)   (C) (2.87, –4.06)   (D) (4.06, 2.87)   (E) (1.66, –0.59)

35. The volume generated by revolving about the y-axis the region enclosed by the graphs $y = 9 - x^2$ and $y = 9 - 3x$, for $0 \leq x \leq 2$, is

(A) -8π (B) 4π (C) 8π (D) 24π (E) 48π

36. The average value of the function $f(x) = \ln^2 x$ on the interval $[2, 4]$ is

(A) –1.204   (B) 1.204   (C) 2.159   (D) 2.408   (E) 8.636

37. $\dfrac{d}{dx} \displaystyle\int_0^{3x} \cos(t)\,dt =$

(A) $\sin 3x$ (B) $-3\sin 3x$ (C) $\cos 3x$ (D) $3\sin 3x$ (E) $3\cos 3x$

GO ON TO THE NEXT PAGE

38. If the definite integral $\int_1^3 (x^2 + 1)dx$ is approximated by using the Trapezoid Rule with $n = 4$, the error is

(A) 0   (B) $\dfrac{7}{3}$ (C) $\dfrac{1}{12}$ (D) $\dfrac{65}{6}$ (E) $\dfrac{97}{3}$

39. The radius of a sphere is increasing at a rate proportional to its radius. If the radius is 4 initially, and the radius is 10 after two seconds, what will the radius be after three seconds?

(A) 62.50   (B) 13.00   (C) 15.81   (D) 16.00   (E) 25.00

40. Use differentials to approximate the change in the volume of a sphere when the radius is increased from 10 to 10.02 cm.

(A) 4213.973   (B) 1261.669   (C) 1256.637   (D) 25.233   (E) 25.133

GO ON TO THE NEXT PAGE

41. $\displaystyle\int \ln 2x \ dx =$

(A) $\dfrac{\ln 2x}{x} + C$

(B) $\dfrac{\ln 2x}{2x} + C$

(C) $x \ln x - x + C$

(D) $x \ln 2x - x + C$

(E) $2x \ln 2x - 2x + C$

---

42. If the function $f(x)$ is differentiable and $f(x) = \begin{cases} ax^3 - 6x; & \text{if } x \le 1 \\ bx^2 + 4; & x > 1 \end{cases}$, then $a =$

(A) 0   (B) 1   (C) −14   (D) −24   (E) 26

---

43. Two particles leave the origin at the same time and move along the y-axis with their respective positions determined by the functions $y_1 = \cos 2t$ and $y_2 = 4\sin t$ for $0 < t < 6$. For how many values of t do the particles have the same acceleration?

(A) 0   (B) 1   (C) 2   (D) 3   (E) 4

GO ON TO THE NEXT PAGE

44. Find the distance traveled (to three decimal places) in the first four seconds, for a particle whose velocity is given by $v(t) = 7e^{-t^2}$; where t stands for time.

(A) 0.976   (B) 6.204   (C) 6.359   (D) 12.720   (E) 7.000

---

45. $\int \tan^6 x \sec^2 x \, dx =$

(A) $\dfrac{\tan^7 x}{7} + C$

(B) $\dfrac{\tan^7 x}{7} + \dfrac{\sec^3 x}{3} + C$

(C) $\dfrac{\tan^7 x \sec^3 x}{21} + C$

(D) $7\tan^7 x + C$

(E) $\dfrac{2}{7}\tan^7 x \sec x + C$

STOP

END OF PART B SECTION I

IF YOU FINISH BEFORE TIME IS CALLED, YOU MAY CHECK YOUR WORK ON PART B ONLY.

DO NOT GO ON TO SECTION II UNTIL YOU ARE TOLD TO DO SO.

You may wish to look over the problems before starting to work on them, since it is not expected that everyone will be able to complete all parts of all problems. All problems are given equal weight, but the parts of a particular problem are not necessarily given equal weight.

A GRAPHING CALCULATOR IS REQUIRED FOR SOME PROBLEMS OR PARTS OF PROBLEMS ON THIS SECTION OF THE EXAMINATION.

- You should write all work for each part of each problem in the space provided for that part in the booklet. Be sure to write clearly and legibly. If you make an error, you may save time by crossing it out rather than trying to erase it. Erased or crossed-out work will not be graded.

- Show all your work. You will be graded on the correctness and completeness of your methods as well as your answers. Correct answers without supporting work may not receive credit.

- Justifications require that you give mathematical (noncalculator) reasons and that you clearly identify functions, graphs, tables, or other objects you use.

- You are permitted to use your calculator to solve an equation, find the derivative of a function at a point, or calculate the value of a definite integral. However, you must clearly indicate the setup of your problem, namely the equation, function, or integral you are using. If you use other built-in features or programs, you must show the mathematical steps necessary to produce your results.

- Your work must be expressed in standard mathematical notation rather than calculator syntax.

  For example, $\int_{1}^{5} x^2 dx$ may not be written as fnInt (X^2, X, 1, 5).

- Unless otherwise specified, answers (numeric or algebraic) need not be simplified. If your answer is given as a decimal approximation, it should be correct to three places after the decimal point.

- Unless otherwise specified, the domain of a function f is assumed to be the set of all real numbers x for which $f(x)$ is a real number.

SECTION II, PART A
Time—45 minutes
Number of problems—3

A graphing calculator is required for some problems or parts of problems.

During the timed portion for Part A, you may work only on the problems in Part A.

On Part A, you are permitted to use your calculator to solve an equation, find the derivative of a function at a point, or calculate the value of a definite integral. However, you must clearly indicate the setup of your problem, namely the equation, function, or integral you are using. If you use other built-in features or programs, you must show the mathematical steps necessary to produce your results.

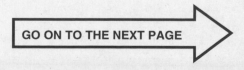
GO ON TO THE NEXT PAGE

1. Consider the equation $x^2 - 2xy + 4y^2 = 64$.

   (a) Write an expression for the slope of the curve at any point (x,y).

   (b) Find the equation of the tangent lines to the curve at the point $x = 2$.

   (c) Find $\dfrac{d^2y}{dx^2}$ at $(0,4)$.

---

2. A particle moves along the x-axis so that its acceleration at any time $t > 0$ is given by $a(t) = 12t - 18$. At time $t = 1$, the velocity of the particle is $v(1) = 0$ and the position is $x(1) = 9$.

   (a) Write an expression for the velocity of the particle $v(t)$.

   (b) At what values of t does the particle change direction?

   (c) Write an expression for the position $x(t)$ of the particle.

   (d) Find the total distance traveled by the particle from $t = \dfrac{3}{2}$ to $t = 6$.

---

3. Let R be the region enclosed by the graphs of $y = 2 \ln x$ and $y = \dfrac{x}{2}$, and the lines $x = 2$ and $x = 8$.

   (a) Find the area of R.
   (b) Set up, <u>but do not integrate</u>, an integral expression, in terms of a single variable, for the volume of the solid generated when R is revolved about the x-axis.
   (c) Set up, <u>but do not integrate</u>, an integral expression, in terms of a single variable, for the volume of the solid generated when R is revolved about the line $x = -1$.

No calculator is allowed for these problems.

During the timed portion for Part B, you may continue to work on the problems in Part A without the use of any calculator.

---

4. Water is draining at the rate of 48π ft³/second from the vertex at the bottom of a conical tank whose diameter at its base is 40 feet and whose height is 60 feet.

   (a) Find an expression for the volume of water in the tank in terms of its radius at the surface of the water.

   (b) At what rate is the radius of the water in the tank shrinking when the radius is 16 feet?

   (c) How fast is the height of the water in the tank dropping at the instant that the radius is 16 feet?

---

5. Let f be the function given by $f(x) = 2x^4 - 4x^2 + 1$.

   (a) Find an equation of the line tangent to the graph at $(-2,17)$.

   (b) Find the x- and y-coordinates of the relative maxima and relative minima. Verify your answer.

   (c) Find the x- and y-coordinates of the points of inflection. Verify your answer.

---

6. Let $F(x) = \int_0^x \left[\cos\left(\frac{t}{2}\right) + \left(\frac{3}{2}\right) \right] dt$ on the closed interval $[0, 4\pi]$.

   (a) Approximate $F(2\pi)$ using four inscribed rectangles.

   (b) Find $F'(2\pi)$.

   (c) Find the average value of $F'(x)$ on the interval $[0, 4\pi]$.

END OF EXAMINATION

ANSWER KEY TO SECTION I

1. B	11. C	21. A	31. B	41. D
2. D	12. B	22. D	32. B	42. C
3. C	13. A	23. D	33. E	43. D
4. A	14. D	24. E	34. C	44. B
5. E	15. A	25. B	35. C	45. A
6. B	16. A	26. A	36. B	
7. E	17. D	27. C	37. E	
8. E	18. B	28. D	38. C	
9. D	19. E	29. D	39. C	
10. A	20. B	30. A	40. E	

23

Answers and Explanations to AB Practice Test 1

ANSWERS AND EXPLANATIONS TO SECTION I

PROBLEM 1. If $f(x) = 5x^{\frac{4}{3}}$, then $f'(8) =$

We need to use basic differentiation to solve this problem.

Step 1: $f'(x) = \dfrac{4}{3}\left(5x^{\frac{1}{3}}\right)$

Step 2: Now all we have to do is plug in 8 for x and simplify.

$$\frac{4}{3}\left(5\left(8^{\frac{1}{3}}\right)\right) = \frac{4}{3}(5(2)) = \frac{40}{3}$$

The answer is (B).

PROBLEM 2. $\displaystyle\lim_{x\to\infty}\dfrac{5x^2 - 3x + 1}{4x^2 + 2x + 5}$ is

Step 1: To solve this problem, you need to remember how to evaluate limits. Always do limit problems on the first pass. Whenever we have a limit of a polynomial fraction where $x \to \infty$, we divide the numerator and the denominator, separately, by the highest power of x in the fraction.

$$\lim_{x\to\infty}\frac{5x^2 - 3x + 1}{4x^2 + 2x + 5} = \lim_{x\to\infty}\frac{\dfrac{5x^2}{x^2} - \dfrac{3x}{x^2} + \dfrac{1}{x^2}}{\dfrac{4x^2}{x^2} + \dfrac{2x}{x^2} + \dfrac{5}{x^2}}$$

Step 2: Simplify $\displaystyle\lim_{x\to\infty}\dfrac{5 - \dfrac{3}{x} + \dfrac{1}{x^2}}{4 + \dfrac{2}{x} + \dfrac{5}{x^2}}$.

Step 3: Now take the limit. Remember that the $\displaystyle\lim_{x\to\infty}\dfrac{k}{x^n} = 0$, if $n > 0$, where k is a constant. Thus we get:

$$\lim_{x\to\infty}\frac{5 - \dfrac{3}{x} + \dfrac{1}{x^2}}{4 + \dfrac{2}{x} + \dfrac{5}{x^2}} = \lim_{x\to\infty}\frac{5 - 0 + 0}{4 + 0 + 0} = \frac{5}{4}$$

The answer is (D).

PROBLEM 3. If $f(x) = \dfrac{3x^2 + x}{3x^2 - x}$ then $f'(x)$ is

Step 1: We need to use the Quotient Rule to evaluate this derivative. Remember, the derivative of $\dfrac{u}{v} = \dfrac{v\dfrac{du}{dx} - u\dfrac{dv}{dx}}{v^2}$. But before we take the derivative, we should factor an

x out of the top and bottom and cancel, simplifying the quotient:

$$f(x) = \frac{3x^2 + x}{3x^2 - x} = \frac{x(3x+1)}{x(3x-1)} = \frac{3x+1}{3x-1}$$

Step 2: Now take the derivative:

$$f'(x) = \frac{(3x-1)(3) - (3x+1)(3)}{(3x-1)^2}$$

Step 3: Simplify:

$$\frac{9x - 3 - 9x - 3}{(3x-1)^2} = \frac{-6}{(3x-1)^2}$$

The answer is (C).

PROBLEM 4. If the function f is continuous for all real numbers and if $f(x) = \dfrac{x^2 - 7x + 12}{x - 4}$ when $x \neq 4$, then $f(4) =$

This problem is testing your knowledge of continuity.

Step 1: Notice that if we plug 4 into the numerator and denominator we get $\dfrac{0}{0}$, which is undefined. So, the first thing that we should do is factor the numerator. What we are looking for is a common factor in the numerator and denominator. If we find a common factor, we can cancel the factors and simplify the problem.

We get $f(x) = \dfrac{x^2 - 7x + 12}{x - 4} = \dfrac{(x-3)(x-4)}{x-4} = (x-3)$.

Step 2: Now we plug in 4 for x and we get 1.

The answer is (A).

PROBLEM 5. If $x^2 - 2xy + 3y^2 = 8$, then $\dfrac{dy}{dx} =$

Whenever we have a polynomial where the x's and y's are not easily separated, we need to use implicit differentiation to find the derivative.

Step 1: Take the derivative of everything with respect to x:

$$2x\frac{dx}{dx} - 2\left(x\frac{dy}{dx} + y\frac{dx}{dx}\right) + 6y\frac{dy}{dx} = 0$$

Remember that $\dfrac{dx}{dx} = 1$!

Step 2: Simplify and then put all of the terms containing $\dfrac{dy}{dx}$ on one side, and all of the other terms on the other side:

$$2x - 2x\frac{dy}{dx} - 2y + 6y\frac{dy}{dx} = 0$$

$$-2x\frac{dy}{dx} + 6y\frac{dy}{dx} = 2y - 2x$$

Factor out the $\dfrac{dy}{dx}$, then isolate it:

$$\frac{dy}{dx}(6y - 2x) = 2y - 2x$$

$$\frac{dy}{dx} = \frac{2y - 2x}{(6y - 2x)} = \frac{y - x}{3y - x}$$

The answer is (E).

PROBLEM 6.

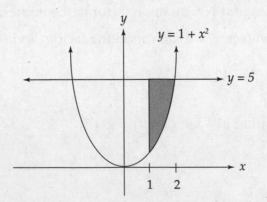

Which of the following integrals correctly corresponds to the area of the region in the figure above between the curve $y = 1 + x^2$ and the line $y = 5$ from $x = 1$ to $x = 2$?

We use integrals to find the area between two curves. If the top curve of a region is $f(x)$ and the bottom curve of a region is $g(x)$, from $x = a$ to $x = b$, then the area is found by the integral:

$$\int_a^b [f(x) - g(x)] dx$$

Step 1: The top curve here is the line $y = 5$, and the bottom curve is $y = 1 + x^2$, and the region extends from the line $x = 1$ to the line $x = 2$. Thus, the integral for the area is:

$$\int_1^2 \left[(5) - \left(1 + x^2\right)\right] dx = \int_1^2 \left(4 - x^2\right) dx$$

The answer is (B).

PROBLEM 7. If $f(x) = \sec x + \csc x$, then $f'(x) =$

This question is testing whether you know your derivatives of trigonometric functions. If you do, this is an easy problem.

Step 1: The derivative of $\sec x$ is $\sec x \tan x$ and the derivative of

$\csc x$ is $-\csc x \cot x$. That makes the derivative here $\sec x \tan x - \csc x \cot x$.

The answer is (E).

PROBLEM 8. An equation of the line normal to the graph of $y = \sqrt{\left(3x^2 + 2x\right)}$ at $(2, 4)$ is

Here we do everything that we normally do for finding the equations of tangent lines, except that we use the negative reciprocal of the slope to find the normal line. This is because the normal line is perpendicular to the tangent line.

Step 1: First, find the slope of the tangent line:

$$\frac{dy}{dx} = \frac{1}{2}\left(3x^2 + 2x\right)^{-\frac{1}{2}}(6x + 2)$$

Step 2: DON'T SIMPLIFY. Immediately plug in $x = 2$. We get:

$$\frac{dy}{dx} = \frac{1}{2}\left(3x^2 + 2x\right)^{-\frac{1}{2}}(6x + 2) = \frac{1}{2}\left(3(2)^2 + 2(2)\right)^{-\frac{1}{2}}(6(2) + 2) = \frac{1}{2}(16)^{-\frac{1}{2}}(14) = \frac{7}{4}$$

This means that the slope of the tangent line at $x = 2$ is $\frac{7}{4}$, so the slope of the normal line is $-\frac{4}{7}$.

Step 3: Then the equation of the tangent line is $(y - 4) = -\frac{4}{7}(x - 2)$.

Step 4: Multiply through by 7 and simplify.

$$7y - 28 = -4x + 8$$
$$4x + 7y = 36$$

The answer is (E).

PROBLEM 9. $\displaystyle\int_{-1}^{1} \frac{4}{1+x^2}\,dx =$

You should recognize this integral as one of the inverse trigonometric integrals.

Step 1: As you should recall, $\displaystyle\int \frac{dx}{1+x^2} = \tan^{-1}(x) + C$. The 4 is no big deal, just multiply the integral by 4 to get $4\tan^{-1}(x)$. Then we just have to evaluate the limits of integration.

Step 2: $4\tan^{-1}(x)\Big|_{-1}^{1} = 4\tan^{-1}(1) - 4\tan^{-1}(-1) = 4\left(\frac{\pi}{4}\right) - 4\left(-\frac{\pi}{4}\right) = 2\pi$

The answer is (D).

PROBLEM 10. If $f(x) = \cos^2 x$, then $f''(\pi) =$

This problem is just asking us to find a higher order derivative of a trigonometric function.

Step 1: The first derivative requires the Chain Rule:

$$f(x) = \cos^2 x$$
$$f'(x) = 2(\cos x)(-\sin x) = -2\cos x \sin x$$

Step 2: The second derivative requires the Product Rule:

$$f'(x) = -2\cos x \sin x$$
$$f''(x) = -2(\cos x \cos x - \sin x \sin x) = -2\left(\cos^2 x - \sin^2 x\right)$$

Step 3: Now we plug in π for x and simplify:

$$-2\left(\cos^2(\pi) - \sin^2(\pi)\right) = -2(1 - 0) = -2$$

The answer is (A).

PROBLEM 11. If $f(x) = \dfrac{5}{x^2 + 1}$ and $g(x) = 3x$ then $g(f(2)) =$

Step 1: To find $g(f(x))$, all you need to do is to replace all of the x's in $g(x)$ with $f(x)$'s:

$$g(f(x)) = 3f(x) = 3\left(\frac{5}{x^2 + 1}\right) = \frac{15}{x^2 + 1}$$

Step 2: Now all we have to do is plug in 2 for x:

$$g(f(2)) = \frac{15}{2^2 + 1} = 3$$

The answer is (C).

PROBLEM 12. $\displaystyle\int x\sqrt{5x^2 - 4}\, dx =$

Any time we have an integral with an x factor whose power is one less than another x factor, we can try to do the integral with u-substitution. This is our favorite technique for doing integration and the most important one to master.

Step 1: Let $u = 5x^2 - 4$ and $du = 10x\,dx$ and so $\dfrac{1}{10}du = x\,dx$.

Then we can rewrite the integral as:

$$\int x\sqrt{5x^2 - 4}\, dx = \frac{1}{10}\int u^{\frac{1}{2}} du$$

Step 2: Now this becomes a basic integral:

$$\frac{1}{10}\int u^{\frac{1}{2}} du = \frac{1}{10}\left(\frac{u^{\frac{3}{2}}}{\frac{3}{2}}\right) + C = \frac{1}{15}u^{\frac{3}{2}} + C$$

Step 3: Reverse the substitution and we get: $\dfrac{1}{15}\left(5x^2 - 4\right)^{\frac{3}{2}} + C$

The answer is (B).

PROBLEM 13. The slope of the line tangent to the graph of $3x^2 + 5\ln y = 12$ at $(2,1)$ is

This is another equation of a tangent line problem, combined with implicit differentiation. Often the AP exam has more than one tangent line problem, so make sure that you can do these well!

By the way, do you remember the derivative of $\ln(f(x))$? It is $\dfrac{f'(x)}{f(x)}$.

Step 1: First, we take the derivative of the equation:

$$6x\frac{dx}{dx} + \frac{5}{y}\frac{dy}{dx} = 0$$

Step 2: Next, we simplify and solve for $\dfrac{dy}{dx}$:

$$6x + \frac{5}{y}\frac{dy}{dx} = 0$$

$$\frac{dy}{dx} = \frac{-6xy}{5}$$

Step 3: Now we plug in 2 for x and 1 for y to get the slope of the tangent line:

$$\frac{dy}{dx} = \frac{-6(2)(1)}{5} = \frac{-12}{5}$$

The answer is (A).

PROBLEM 14. The equation $y = 2 - 3\sin\dfrac{\pi}{4}(x-1)$ has a fundamental period of

The AP people expect you to remember a lot of your trigonometry, so if you're rusty, review the unit in the Appendix.

Step 1: In an equation of the form $f(x) = A \sin B (x \pm C) \pm D$, you should know four components. The amplitude of the equation is $|A|$, the horizontal or phase shift is $\pm C$, the vertical shift is $\pm D$, and the fundamental period is $\dfrac{2\pi}{B}$.

The same is true for $f(x) = A \cos B (x \pm C) \pm D$.

Step 2: All we have to do is plug into the formula for the period:

$$\frac{2\pi}{B} = \frac{2\pi}{\dfrac{\pi}{4}} = 8$$

The answer is (D).

PROBLEM 15. If $f(x) = \begin{cases} x^2 + 5 & \text{if } x < 2 \\ 7x - 5 & \text{if } x \geq 2 \end{cases}$, for all real numbers x, which of the following must be true?

    I. $f(x)$ is continuous everywhere.

    II. $f(x)$ is differentiable everywhere.

    III. $f(x)$ has a local minimum at $x = 2$.

This problem is testing your knowledge of the rules of continuity and differentiability. While the more formal treatment is located in the unit on continuity, here we'll go directly to a shortcut to the right answer. This type of function is called a piecewise function because it is broken into two or more pieces, depending on the value of x that one is looking at.

Step 1: If a piecewise function is continuous at a point a, then when you plug a into each of the pieces of the function, you should get the same answer. The function consists of a pair of polynomials (remember that all polynomials are continuous!), where the only point that might be a problem is $x = 2$. So here we'll plug 2 into both pieces of the function to see if we get the same value. If we do, then the function is continuous. If we don't, then it's discontinuous. At $x = 2$, the upper piece is equal to 9 and the lower piece is also equal to 9. So the function is continuous everywhere, and **I** is true. You should then eliminate answer choice (C).

Step 2: If a piecewise function is differentiable at a point a, then when you plug a into each of the derivatives of the pieces of the function, you should get the same answer. It is the same idea as in Step 1. So here we will plug 2 into the derivatives of both pieces of the function to see if we get the same value. If we do, then the function is differentiable. If we don't, then it is non-differentiable at $x = 2$.

The derivative of the upper piece is $2x$, and at $x = 2$, the derivative is 4.

The derivative of the lower piece is 7 everywhere.

Because the two derivatives are not equal, the function is not differentiable everywhere and **II** is false. You should then eliminate answer choices (B) and (E).

Step 3: The slope of the function to the left of $x = 2$ is 4. The slope of the function to the right of $x = 2$ is 7. If the slope of a continuous function has the same sign on either side of a point then the function cannot have a local minimum or maximum at that point. So **III** is false because of what we found in Step 2. You should then eliminate answer choice (D).

The answer is (A).

PROBLEM 16. For what value of x does the function $f(x) = x^3 - 9x^2 - 120x + 6$ have a local minimum?

This problem requires you to know how to find maxima/minima. This is a part of curve sketching and is one of the most important parts of differential calculus. A function has *critical points* where the derivative is zero or undefined (which is never a problem when the function is an ordinary polynomial). After finding the critical points we test them to determine whether they are maxima or minima or something else.

Step 1: First, as usual, take the derivative and set it equal to zero:

$$f'(x) = 3x^2 - 18x - 120$$
$$3x^2 - 18x - 120 = 0$$

Step 2: Find the values of x that make the derivative equal to zero. These are the critical points:

$$3x^2 - 18x - 120 = 0$$
$$x^2 - 6x - 40 = 0$$
$$(x - 10)(x + 4) = 0$$
$$x = \{10, -4\}$$

Step 3: In order to determine whether a critical point is a maximum or a minimum, we need to take the second derivative:

$$f''(x) = 6x - 18$$

Step 4: Now we plug the critical points from Step 2 into the second derivative. If it yields a negative value, then the point is a maximum. If it yields a positive value, then the point is a minimum. If it yields zero, it is neither, and is most likely a point of inflection.

$$6(10) - 18 = 42$$
$$6(-4) - 18 = -42$$

Therefore 10 is a minimum.

The answer is (A).

PROBLEM 17. The acceleration of a particle moving along the x-axis at time t is given by $a(t) = 4t - 12$. If the velocity is 10 when $t = 0$ and the position is 4 when $t = 0$, then the particle is changing direction at

Step 1: Because acceleration is the derivative of velocity, if we know the acceleration of a particle, we can find the velocity by integrating the acceleration with respect to t:

$$\int (4t - 12)dt = 2t^2 - 12t + C$$

Next, because the velocity is 10 at $t = 0$, we can plug in 0 for t and solve for the constant:

$$2(0)^2 - 12(0) + C = 10.$$

Therefore $C = 10$ and the velocity, $v(t)$, is $2t^2 - 12t + 10$.

Step 2: In order to find when the particle is changing direction we need to know when the velocity is equal to zero, so we set $v(t) = 0$ and solve for t:

$$2t^2 - 12t + 10 = 0$$
$$t^2 - 6t + 5 = 0$$
$$(t - 5)(t - 1) = 0$$
$$t = \{1, 5\}$$

Now, provided that the acceleration is not also zero at $t = \{1, 5\}$, the particle will be changing direction at those times. The acceleration is found by differentiating the equation for velocity with respect to time: $a(t) = 4t - 12$. This is not zero at either $t = 1$ or $t = 5$. Therefore, the particle is changing direction when $t = 1$ and $t = 5$.

The answer is (D).

PROBLEM 18. The average value of the function $f(x) = (x - 1)^2$ on the interval from $x = 1$ to $x = 5$ is

Step 1: If you want to find the average value of $f(x)$ on an interval $[a, b,]$ you need to evaluate the integral $\dfrac{1}{b-a}\int_a^b f(x)\,dx$.

So here we would evaluate the integral $\dfrac{1}{5-1}\int_1^5 (x-1)^2\,dx$.

Step 2: $\dfrac{1}{5-1}\int_1^5 (x-1)^2\,dx = \dfrac{1}{4}\int_1^5 \left(x^2 - 2x + 1\right)dx$

$$= \dfrac{1}{4}\left(\dfrac{x^3}{3} - x^2 + x\right)\Bigg|_1^5 = \dfrac{1}{4}\left[\left(\dfrac{5^3}{3} - 5^2 + 5\right) - \left(\dfrac{1}{3} - 1 + 1\right)\right]$$

$$= \dfrac{1}{4}\left(\dfrac{125}{3} - 20 - \dfrac{1}{3}\right) = \dfrac{64}{12} = \dfrac{16}{3}$$

The answer is (B).

PROBLEM 19. $\int \left(e^{3\ln x} + e^{3x} \right) dx =$

This problem requires that you know your rules of exponential functions.

Step 1: First of all, $e^{3\ln x} = e^{\ln x^3} = x^3$. So we can rewrite the integral as:

$$\int \left(e^{3\ln x} + e^{3x} \right) dx = \int \left(x^3 + e^{3x} \right) dx$$

Step 2: The rule for the integral of an exponential function is $\int e^k dx = \frac{1}{k} e^{kx} + C$.

Now we can do this integral. $\int \left(x^3 + e^{3x} \right) dx = \frac{x^4}{4} + \frac{1}{3} e^{3x} + C$.

The answer is (E).

PROBLEM 20. If $f(x) = \sqrt{\left(x^3 + 5x + 121 \right)\left(x^2 + x + 11 \right)}$ then $f'(0) =$

This problem is just a complicated derivative, requiring you to be familiar with the Chain Rule and the Product Rule.

Step 1: $f'(x) = \frac{1}{2}\left(x^3 + 5x + 121 \right)^{-\frac{1}{2}}\left(3x^2 + 5 \right)\left(x^2 + x + 11 \right) + \left(x^3 + 5x + 121 \right)^{\frac{1}{2}}\left(2x + 1 \right)$

Step 2: Whenever a problem asks you to find the value of a complicated derivative at a particular point, NEVER simplify the derivative. Immediately plug in the value for x and do arithmetic instead of algebra:

$$f'(0) = \frac{1}{2}\left(0^3 + 5(0) + 121 \right)^{-\frac{1}{2}}\left(3(0)^2 + 5 \right)\left(0^2 + (0) + 11 \right) + \left((0)^3 + 5(0) + 121 \right)^{\frac{1}{2}}\left(2(0) + 1 \right)$$

$$= \frac{1}{2}(121)^{-\frac{1}{2}}(5)(11) + (121)^{\frac{1}{2}}(1) = \frac{5}{2} + 11 = \frac{27}{2}$$

The answer is (B).

PROBLEM 21. If $f(x) = 5^{3x}$ then $f'(x) =$

This problem requires you to know how to find the derivative of an exponential function. The rule is: If a function is of the form $a^{f(x)}$, its derivative is $a^{f(x)} (\ln a) f'(x)$. Now all we have to do is follow the rule!

Step 1: $f(x) = 5^{3x}$

$\quad\quad\quad f'(x) = 5^{3x} (\ln 5)(3)$

Step 2: If you remember your rules of logarithms, $3\ln 5 = \ln(5^3) = \ln 125$.

So we can rewrite the answer to $f'(x) = 5^{3x}(\ln 5)(3) = 5^{3x}\ln 125$.

The answer is (A).

PROBLEM 22. A solid is generated when the region in the first quadrant enclosed by the graph of $y = (x^2 + 1)^3$, the line $x = 1$, the y-axis and the x-axis, is revolved about the x-axis. Its volume is found by evaluating which of the following integrals? ·

This problem requires you to know how to find the volume of a solid of revolution. If you have a region between two curves, from $x = a$ to $x = b$, then the volume generated when the region is revolved around the x-axis is: $\pi \int_a^b \left[f(x)^2 - g(x)^2 \right] dx$, if $f(x)$ is above $g(x)$ throughout the region.

Step 1: First, we have to determine what the region looks like. The curve looks like this:

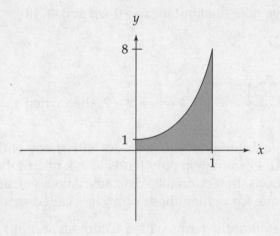

The shaded region is the part that we are interested in. Notice that the curve is always above the x-axis (which is $g(x)$). Now we just follow the formula:

$$\pi \int_0^1 \left[\left[\left(x^2+1\right)^3 \right]^2 - [0]^2 \right] dx = \pi \int_0^1 \left(x^2+1\right)^6 dx$$

The answer is (D).

PROBLEM 23. $\displaystyle\lim_{x\to 0} 4\,\frac{\sin x \cos x - \sin x}{x^2} =$

This problem requires us to evaluate the limit of a trigonometric function.

There are two important trigonometric limits to memorize:

$$\lim_{x\to 0}\frac{\sin x}{x}=1 \text{ and } \lim_{x\to 0}\frac{1-\cos x}{x}=0$$

Step 1: The first step that we always take when evaluating the limit of a trigonometric function is to rearrange the function so that it looks like some combination of the limits above. We can do this by factoring $\sin x$ out of the numerator.

Now we can break this into limits that we can easily evaluate:

$$\lim_{x\to 0} 4\,\frac{\sin x \cos x - \sin x}{x^2} = 4\lim_{x\to 0}\left(\frac{\sin x}{x}\right)\left(\frac{\cos x - 1}{x}\right)$$

$$\left(\text{Note that } \lim_{x\to 0}\frac{1-\cos x}{x}=-\lim_{x\to 0}\frac{\cos x - 1}{x}=0.\right)$$

Step 2: Now if we take the limit as $x\to 0$ we get: $4(1)(0) = 0$

The answer is (D).

PROBLEM 24. If $\displaystyle\frac{dy}{dx}=\frac{(3x^2+2)}{y}$ and $y=4$ when $x=2$, then when $x=3$, $y=$

This is a very basic differential equation. As with many of the more difficult topics in calculus, the AP examination only tends to ask us to solve very straightforward differential equations. In fact, on the AB examination, you are only going to need to know one technique for getting these right. It is called *separation of variables*.

Step 1: First, take all of the terms with a y in them and put them on the left side of the equal sign. Take all of the terms with an x in them and put them on the right side of the equal sign. Then we get:

$$ydy = (3x^2 + 2)dx$$

Step 2: Now integrate both sides:

$$\int ydy = \int (3x^2 + 2)dx$$

$$\frac{y^2}{2} = x^3 + 2x + C$$

Notice how we only use one constant. All we have to do now is solve for C. We do this by plugging in 2 for x and 4 for y.

$$\frac{16}{2} = 2^3 + 4 + C$$

$$C = -4$$

So we can rewrite the equation as $\dfrac{y^2}{2} = x^3 + 2x - 4$.

Step 3: Now if we plug in 3 for x, we will get y:

$$\frac{y^2}{2} = 27 + 6 - 4$$

$$y^2 = 58$$

$$y = \pm\sqrt{58}$$

The answer is (E).

PROBLEM 25. $\displaystyle\int \frac{dx}{9 + x^2} =$

This is another inverse trigonometric integral.

Step 1: We know that $\displaystyle\int \frac{dx}{1 + x^2} = \tan^{-1}(x) + C$.

(See problem 9 if you're not sure of this.) The trick here is to get the denominator of the fraction in the integrand to be of the correct form. If we factor 9 out of the denominator we get:

$$\int \frac{dx}{9 + x^2} = \int \frac{dx}{9\left(1 + \dfrac{x^2}{9}\right)} = \frac{1}{9}\int \frac{dx}{1 + \dfrac{x^2}{9}} = \frac{1}{9}\int \frac{dx}{1 + \left(\dfrac{x}{3}\right)^2}$$

Step 2: Now if we use u-substitution we will be able to evaluate this integral.

Let $u = \dfrac{x}{3}$ and $du = \dfrac{1}{3}dx$ or $3du = dx$. Then we have:

$$\frac{1}{9}\int \frac{dx}{1 + \left(\dfrac{x}{3}\right)^2} = \frac{1}{9}\int \frac{3du}{1 + u^2} = \frac{1}{3}\int \frac{du}{1 + u^2} = \frac{1}{3}\tan^{-1}(u) + C$$

Step 3: Now all we have to do is reverse the u-substitution and we're done:

$$\frac{1}{3}\tan^{-1}(u) + C = \frac{1}{3}\tan^{-1}\left(\frac{x}{3}\right) + C$$

The answer is (B).

PROBLEM 26. If $f(x) = \cos^3(x+1)$ then $f'(\pi) =$

Think of $\cos^3(x+1)$ as $[\cos(x+1)]^3$.

Step 1: First, we take the derivative of the outside function and ignore the inside functions. The derivative of u^3 is $3u^2$.

We get: $\dfrac{d}{dx}[u]^3 = 3[u]^2$.

Step 2: Next, we take the derivative of the cosine term and multiply. The derivative of $\cos u$ is $-\sin u$.

$$\frac{d}{dx}[\cos(u)]^3 = -3[\cos(u)]^2 \sin(u)$$

Step 3: Finally, we take the derivative of $x+1$ and multiply. The derivative of $x+1$ is 1:

$$\frac{d}{dx}[\cos(x+1)]^3 = -3[\cos(x+1)]^2 \sin(x+1)$$

The answer is (A).

PROBLEM 27. $\displaystyle\int x\sqrt{x+3}\, dx =$

We can do this integral with u-substitution.

Step 1: Let $u = x+3$. Then $du = dx$ and $u - 3 = x$.

Step 2: Substituting, we get:

$$\int x\sqrt{x+3}\, dx = \int (u-3)u^{\frac{1}{2}}\, du$$

Why is this better than the original integral, you might ask? Because now we can distribute and the integral becomes easy.

Step 3: When we distribute, we get:

$$\int (u-3)u^{\frac{1}{2}}\, du = \int \left(u^{\frac{3}{2}} - 3u^{\frac{1}{2}} \right) du$$

Step 4: Now we can integrate:

$$\int \left(u^{\frac{3}{2}} - 3u^{\frac{1}{2}} \right) du = \frac{2}{5} u^{\frac{5}{2}} - 3\left(\frac{2}{3} u^{\frac{3}{2}} \right) + C$$

Step 5: Substituting back, we get:

$$\frac{2}{5} u^{\frac{5}{2}} - 3\left(\frac{2}{3} u^{\frac{3}{2}} \right) + C = \frac{2}{5}(x+3)^{\frac{5}{2}} - 2(x+3)^{\frac{3}{2}} + C$$

The answer is (C).

PROBLEM 28. If $f(x) = \ln(\ln(1-x))$, then $f'(x) =$

Here, we use the Chain Rule.

Step 1: First, take the derivative of the outside function.

The derivative of $\ln u$ is $\dfrac{du}{u}$.

We get:

$$\frac{d}{dx} \ln(\ln(u)) = \frac{1}{\ln(u)}$$

Step 2: Now we take the derivative of the function in the denominator. Once again, the function is $\ln u$.

We get:

$$\frac{d}{dx} \ln(\ln(1-x)) = \frac{1}{\ln(1-x)}\left(\frac{-1}{1-x} \right) = -\frac{1}{(1-x)\ln(1-x)}$$

The answer is (D).

PROBLEM 29. $\displaystyle\int_0^{\frac{\pi}{4}} \sin x \ dx + \int_{-\frac{\pi}{4}}^0 \cos x \ dx =$

This is a pair of basic trigonometric integrals. You should have memorized several trigonometric integrals, particularly $\displaystyle\int \sin x \ dx = -\cos x + C$ and $\displaystyle\int \cos x \ dx = \sin x + C$.

Step 1: $\displaystyle\int_0^{\frac{\pi}{4}} \sin x \ dx + \int_{-\frac{\pi}{4}}^0 \cos x \ dx = -\cos x\Big|_0^{\frac{\pi}{4}} + \sin x\Big|_{-\frac{\pi}{4}}^0$

Step 2: Now we evaluate the limits of integration, and we're done:

$$-\cos x\Big|_0^{\frac{\pi}{4}} + \sin x\Big|_{-\frac{\pi}{4}}^{0} = \left[\left(-\cos\frac{\pi}{4}\right) - \left(-\cos(0)\right)\right] + \left[\left(\sin(0)\right) - \left(\sin\left(-\frac{\pi}{4}\right)\right)\right] = -\frac{1}{\sqrt{2}} + 1 + 0 + \frac{1}{\sqrt{2}} = 1$$

The answer is (D).

PROBLEM 30. Boats A and B leave the same place at the same time. Boat A heads due north at 12 km/hr. Boat B heads due east at 18 km/hr. After 2.5 hours, how fast is the distance between the boats increasing (in km/hr)?

Step 1: The boats are moving at right angles to each other and are thus forming a right triangle with the distance between them forming the hypotenuse. Whenever we see right triangles in related rates problems, we look to use the Pythagorean theorem. Call the distance that Boat A travels y, and the distance that Boat B travels x. Then the rate at which Boat A goes north is $\frac{dy}{dt}$, and the rate at which Boat B travels is $\frac{dx}{dt}$. The distance between the two boats is z, and we are looking for how fast z is growing, which is $\frac{dz}{dt}$. Now we can use the Pythagorean theorem to set up the relationship: $x^2 + y^2 = z^2$.

Step 2: Differentiating both sides we obtain:

$$2x\frac{dx}{dt} + 2y\frac{dy}{dt} = 2z\frac{dz}{dt} \quad \text{or} \quad x\frac{dx}{dt} + y\frac{dy}{dt} = z\frac{dz}{dt}$$

Step 3: After 2.5 hours, Boat A has traveled 30 km and Boat B has traveled 45 km. Because of the Pythagorean theorem, we also know that, when $y = 30$ and $x = 45$, $z = 54.08$.

Step 4: Now we plug everything into the equation from Step 2 and solve for $\frac{dz}{dt}$:

$$(45)(18) + (30)(12) = (54.08)\frac{dz}{dt}$$

$$1170 = (54.08)\frac{dz}{dt}$$

$$21.63 = \frac{dz}{dt}$$

The answer is (A).

PROBLEM 31. $\lim\limits_{h\to 0}\dfrac{\tan\left(\dfrac{\pi}{6}+h\right)-\tan\left(\dfrac{\pi}{6}\right)}{h}=$

This may *appear* to be a limit problem, but it is *actually* testing to see whether you know the definition of the derivative.

Step 1: You should recall that the definition of the derivative says:

$$\lim\limits_{h\to 0}\dfrac{f(x+h)-f(x)}{h}=f'(x)$$

Thus, if we replace $f(x)$ with tan (x), we can rewrite the problem as:

$$\lim\limits_{h\to 0}\dfrac{\tan(x+h)-\tan(x)}{h}=\left[\tan(x)\right]'$$

Step 2: The derivative of tan x is sec^2 x. Thus:

$$\lim\limits_{h\to 0}\dfrac{\tan\left(\dfrac{\pi}{6}+h\right)-\tan\left(\dfrac{\pi}{6}\right)}{h}=\sec^2\left(\dfrac{\pi}{6}\right)$$

Step 3: Because $\sec\left(\dfrac{\pi}{6}\right)=\dfrac{2}{\sqrt{3}}$, $\sec^2\left(\dfrac{\pi}{6}\right)=\dfrac{4}{3}$.

The answer is (B).

> **Note:** If you had trouble with this problem, you should review the units on the definition of the derivative and derivatives of trigonometric functions.

PROBLEM 32. If $\displaystyle\int_{30}^{100}f(x)dx=A$ and $\displaystyle\int_{50}^{100}f(x)dx=B$ then $\displaystyle\int_{30}^{50}f(x)dx=$

This question is testing your knowledge of the rules of definite integrals.

Step 1: Generally speaking, $\displaystyle\int_{a}^{b}f(x)dx+\int_{b}^{c}f(x)dx=\int_{a}^{c}f(x)dx$.

So here, $\displaystyle\int_{30}^{50}f(x)dx+\int_{50}^{100}f(x)dx=\int_{30}^{100}f(x)dx$.

If we substitute $\displaystyle\int_{30}^{100}f(x)dx=A$ and $\displaystyle\int_{50}^{100}f(x)dx=B$, we get $\displaystyle\int_{30}^{50}f(x)dx+B=A$.

The answer is (B).

PROBLEM 33. If $f(x) = 3x^2 - x$, and $g(x) = f^{-1}(x)$, then $g'(10)$ could be

This problem requires you to know how to find the derivative of an inverse function.

Step 1: The rule for finding the derivative of an inverse function is:

$$\text{If } y = f(x) \text{ and if } g(x) = f^{-1}(x) \text{ then } g'(x) = \frac{1}{f'(y)}$$

Step 2: In order to use the formula, we need to find the derivative of f and the value of x that corresponds to $y = 10$.

First, $f'(x) = 6x - 1$. Second, when $y = 10$ we get $10 = 3x^2 - x$.

If we solve this for x we get $x = 2$ (and $x = -\dfrac{5}{3}$, but we'll use 2. It's easier.).

Step 3: Plugging into the formula, we get $\dfrac{1}{f'(y)} = \dfrac{1}{(6)(2)-1} = \dfrac{1}{11}$.

The answer is (E).

> **Note:** There was another possible answer using $x = -\dfrac{5}{3}$, but that doesn't give us one of the answer choices. Generally, the AP examination sticks to the easier answer. They are testing whether you know what to do and usually NOT trying to trick you.

PROBLEM 34. The graph of $y = x^3 - 5x^2 + 4x + 2$ has a local minimum at

This is another maxima/minima question.

Step 1: Take the derivative of the function and set it equal to zero:

$$f'(x) = 3x^2 - 10x + 4 = 0$$

Step 2: Use the quadratic formula to solve for x. You should get $x = \{2.87, 0.46\}$.

Step 3: Now take the second derivative of the function:

$$f''(x) = 6x - 10$$

Step 4: Plug each of the critical values from Step 2 into the second derivative. If you get a positive value, the point is a minimum. If you get a negative value, the point is a maximum. If you get zero, the point is probably a point of inflection (don't worry about that here):

$$f''(2.87) = 7.21$$
$$f''(.46) = -7.21$$

So 2.87 is the *x*-coordinate of the minimum. To find the *y*-coordinate, just plug 2.87 into $f(x)$ and you get -4.06.

The answer is (C).

PROBLEM 35. The volume generated by revolving about the *y*-axis the region enclosed by the graphs $y = 9 - x^2$ and $y = 9 - 3x$, for $0 \le x \le 2$, is

This is another volume of a solid of revolution problem. As you should have noticed by now, these are very popular on the AP Examination and show up in both the Multiple-Choice section and in the Free-Response section. If you are not good at these, go back and review the unit carefully. You cannot afford to get these wrong on the AP! The good thing about *this* volume problem is that it is in the calculator part of the Multiple-Choice section, so you can use a graphing calculator to assist you.

Step 1: First, graph the two curves on the same set of axes. The graph should look like this:

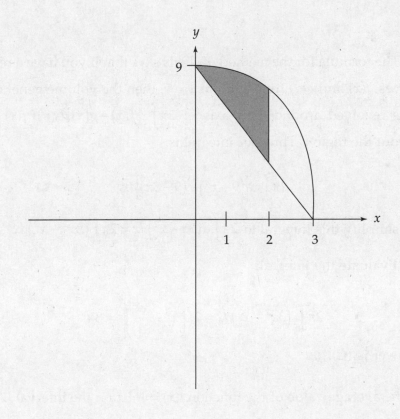

Step 2: We are being asked to rotate this region around the y-axis, and both of the functions are in terms of x, so we should use the method of shells. We use this method whenever we take a vertical slice of a region and rotate it around an axis parallel to the slice (review the unit if you are not sure what it means). This will give us a region that looks like this:

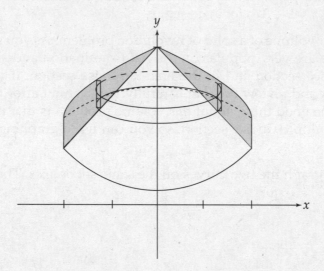

Step 3: The formula for the method of shells says that if you have a region between two curves, $f(x)$ and $g(x)$ from $x = a$ to $x = b$, then the volume generated when the region is revolved around the y-axis is: $2\pi \int_a^b x[f(x) - g(x)]dx$; if $f(x)$ is above $g(x)$ throughout the region. Thus our integral is:

$$2\pi \int_0^2 x[(9 - x^2) - (9 - 3x)]dx$$

We can simplify this integral to $2\pi \int_0^2 x(3x - x^2)dx = 2\pi \int_0^2 (3x^2 - x^3)dx$.

Step 4: Evaluate the integral:

$$2\pi \int_0^2 (3x^2 - x^3)dx = 2\pi \left(x^3 - \frac{x^4}{4} \right)\Bigg|_0^2 = 8\pi$$

The answer is (C).

PROBLEM 36.   The average value of the function $f(x) = \ln^2 x$ on the interval [2,4] is

This problem requires you to be familiar with the Mean Value Theorem for integrals which we use to find the average value of a function.

Step 1: If you want to find the average value of $f(x)$ on an interval $[a,b]$, you need to evaluate the integral $\dfrac{1}{b-a} \int_a^b f(x)dx$. So here we evaluate the integral $\dfrac{1}{2} \int_2^4 \ln^2 x \ dx$.

You have to do this integral on your calculator because you do not know how to evaluate this integral analytically unless you are very good with integration by parts!

Use **fnint**. Divide this by 2 and you will get 1.204.

The answer is (B).

PROBLEM 37. $\dfrac{d}{dx}\displaystyle\int_0^{3x}\cos(t)dt =$

This problem is testing your knowledge of the Second Fundamental Theorem of calculus. The theorem states that $\dfrac{d}{dx}\displaystyle\int_a^u f(t)dt = f(u)\dfrac{du}{dx}$, where a is a constant and u is a function of x. So all we have to do is follow the theorem: $\dfrac{d}{dx}\displaystyle\int_0^{3x}\cos(t)dt = 3\cos 3x$.

The answer is (E).

PROBLEM 38. If the definite integral $\displaystyle\int_1^3 \left(x^2 + 1\right)dx$ is approximated by using the Trapezoid Rule with $n = 4$, the error is

This problem will require you to be familiar with the Trapezoid Rule. This is very easy to do on the calculator, and some of you may even have written programs to evaluate this. Even if you haven't, the formula is easy. The area under a curve from $x = a$ to $x = b$, divided into n intervals, is approximated by the Trapezoid Rule and is

$$\left(\frac{1}{2}\right)\left(\frac{b-a}{n}\right)\left[y_0 + 2y_1 + 2y_2 + 2y_3 \ldots + 2y_{n-2} + 2y_{n-1} + y_n\right]$$

This formula may look scary, but it actually is quite simple, and the AP Examination never uses a very large value for n anyway.

Step 1: $\dfrac{b-a}{n} = \dfrac{3-1}{4} = \dfrac{1}{2}$. Plugging into the formula, we get:

$$\frac{1}{4}\left[\left(1^2 + 1\right) + 2\left(1.5^2 + 1\right) + 2\left(2^2 + 1\right) + 2\left(2.5^2 + 1\right) + \left(3^2 + 1\right)\right]$$

This is easy to plug into your calculator and you will get 10.75 or $\dfrac{43}{4}$.

Step 2: In order to find the error, we now need to know the actual value of the integral:

$$\int_1^3 \left(x^2 + 1\right)dx = \frac{x^3}{3} + x\Big|_1^3 = \frac{32}{3}$$

Step 3: The error is $\dfrac{43}{4} - \dfrac{32}{3} = \dfrac{1}{12}$.

The answer is (C).

PROBLEM 39. The radius of a sphere is increasing at a rate proportional to itself. If the radius is 4 initially, and the radius is 10 after two seconds, then what will the radius be after three seconds?

This is not a related rate problem; this is a differential equation! It just happens to involve a rate.

Step 1: If we translate the first sentence into an equation we get: $\dfrac{dR}{dt} = kR$.

Put all of the terms that contain an R on the left of the equals sign, and all of the terms that contain a t on the right hand side:

$$\frac{dR}{R} = kdt$$

Step 2: Integrate both sides:

$$\int \frac{dR}{R} = k \int dt$$

Step 3: If we solve this for R, we get $R = Ce^{kt}$ (see the unit on differential equations).

Now we need to solve for C and k. First we solve for C by plugging in the information that the radius is 4 initially. This means that $R = 4$ when $t = 0$.

If $4 = Ce^0$, then $C = 4$

Next we solve for k by plugging in the information that $R = 10$ when $t = 2$:

$$10 = 4e^{2k}$$

$$\frac{5}{2} = e^{2k}$$

$$\ln \frac{5}{2} = 2k$$

$$\frac{1}{2} \ln \frac{5}{2} = k$$

Step 4: Now we have our final equation: $R = 4e^{\left(\frac{1}{2} \ln \frac{5}{2}\right)t}$.

If we plug in $t = 3$ we get: $R = 4e^{\left(\frac{1}{2} \ln \frac{5}{2}\right)(3)} = 15.811$.

The answer is (C).

PROBLEM 40. Use differentials to approximate the change in the volume of a sphere when the radius is increased from 10 to 10.02 cm.

The volume of a sphere is $V = \frac{4}{3}\pi R^3$. Using differentials, the change will be:

$dV = 4\pi R^2 dR$.

Substitute in $R = 10$ and $dR = .02$, and we get:

$$dV = 4\pi(10^2)(.02)$$

$$dV = 8\pi \approx 25.133cm^3$$

The answer is (E).

PROBLEM 41. $\int \ln 2x \; dx =$

This is a simple integral that we do using integration by parts. The AB examination only has the simplest of these types of integrals, although the BC examination has harder ones. Furthermore, you should memorize that $\int \ln(ax) \, dx = x\ln(ax) - x + C$, which makes this integral easy.

Step 1: The formula for integration by parts is: $\int u\,dv = uv - \int v\,du$

The trick is that we have to let $dv = dx$:

$$\text{Let } u = \ln 2x \text{ and } dv = dx$$

$$du = \frac{2}{2x}dx = \frac{1}{x}dx \text{ and } v = x$$

Plugging in to the formula we get:

$$\int \ln 2x\,dx = x\ln 2x - \int dx = x\ln 2x - x + C.$$

The answer is (D).

PROBLEM 42. For the function $f(x) = \begin{cases} ax^3 - 6x; \text{ if } x \leq 1 \\ bx^2 + 4; x > 1 \end{cases}$ to be continuous and differentiable, a

This question is testing your knowledge of the rules of continuity, where we also discuss differentiability.

Step 1: If the function is continuous, then if we plug 1 into the top and bottom pieces of the function we should get the same answer:

$$a(1^3) - 6(1) = b(1^2) + 4$$
$$a - 6 = b + 4$$

Step 2: If the function is differentiable, then if we plug 1 into the derivatives of the top and bottom pieces of the function we should get the same answer:

$$3a(1^2) - 6 = 2b(1)$$
$$3a - 6 = 2b$$

Step 3: Now we have a pair of simultaneous equations. If we solve them, we get $a = -14$.

The answer is (C).

PROBLEM 43. Two particles leave the origin at the same time and move along the y-axis with their respective positions determined by the functions $y_1 = \cos 2t$ and $y_2 = 4\sin t$ for $0 < t < 6$. For how many values of t do the particles have the same acceleration?

If you want to find acceleration, all you have to do is take the second derivative of the position functions.

Step 1: $\dfrac{dy_1}{dx} = -2\sin 2t$ and $\dfrac{dy_2}{dx} = 4\cos t$

$\dfrac{d^2y_1}{dx^2} = -4\cos 2t$ and $\dfrac{d^2y_2}{dx^2} = -4\sin t$

Step 2: Now all we have to do is to graph both of these equations on the same set of axes on a calculator. You should make the window from $x = 0$ to $x = 7$ (leave yourself a little room so that you can see the whole range that you need). You should get a picture that looks like this:

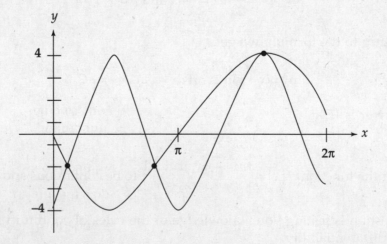

Where the graphs intersect, the acceleration is the same. There are three points of intersection.

The answer is (D).

PROBLEM 44. Find the distance traveled (to three decimal places) in the first four seconds, for a particle whose velocity is given by $v(t) = 7e^{-t^2}$, where t stands for time.

Step 1: If we want to find the distance traveled, we take the integral of velocity from the starting time to the finishing time. Therefore, we need to evaluate $\int_0^4 7e^{-t^2}\, dt$.

Step 2: But we have a problem! We can't take the integral of e^{-t^2}. This means that the AP exam wants you to find the answer using your calculator.

Rounded to three decimal places, the answer is 6.204.

The answer is (B).

PROBLEM 45. $\int \tan^6 x \sec^2 x\, dx =$

We can do this integral with u-substitution.

Step 1: Let $u = \tan x$. Then $du = \sec^2 x\, dx$.

Step 2: Substituting, we get: $\int \tan^6 x \sec^2 x\, dx = \int u^6 du$.

Step 3: This is an easy integral: $\int u^6 du = \dfrac{u^7}{7} + C$.

Step 4: Substituting back, we get: $\dfrac{\tan^7 x}{7} + C$.

The answer is (A).

ANSWERS AND EXPLANATIONS TO SECTION II

PROBLEM 1. Consider the equation $x^2 - 2xy + 4y^2 = 64$.

(a) Write an expression for the slope of the curve at any point (x,y).

Step 1: The slope of the curve is just the derivative. But, here, we have to use implicit differentiation to find the derivative. If we take the derivative of each term with respect to x, we get:

$$2x\frac{dx}{dx} - 2\left(x\frac{dy}{dx} + y\frac{dx}{dx}\right) + 8y\frac{dy}{dx} = 0$$

Remember that $\frac{dx}{dx} = 1$, which gives us:

$$2x - 2\left(x\frac{dy}{dx} + y\right) + 8y\frac{dy}{dx} = 0$$

Step 2: Now just simplify and solve for $\frac{dy}{dx}$.

$$2x - 2x\frac{dy}{dx} - 2y + 8y\frac{dy}{dx} = 0$$

$$x - x\frac{dy}{dx} - y + 4y\frac{dy}{dx} = 0$$

$$-x\frac{dy}{dx} + 4y\frac{dy}{dx} = y - x$$

$$(4y - x)\frac{dy}{dx} = y - x$$

$$\frac{dy}{dx} = \frac{y - x}{4y - x}$$

(b) Find the equation of the tangent lines to the curve at the point $x = 2$.

Step 1: We are going to use the point-slope form of a line, $y - y_1 = m(x - x_1)$, where (x_1, y_1) is a point on the curve, and the derivative at that point is the slope m. First, we need to know the value of y when $x = 2$. If we plug 2 for x into the original equation, we get:

$$4 - 4y + 4y^2 = 64$$

$$4y^2 - 4y - 60 = 0$$

Using the quadratic formula, we get:

$$y = \frac{1 \pm \sqrt{61}}{2} = 4.41, -3.41$$

Notice that there are two values of y when $x = 2$, which is why there are two tangent lines.

Step 2: Now that we have our points, we need the slope of the tangent line at $x = 2$:

$$\frac{dy}{dx} = \frac{y - x}{4y - x}$$

$$\text{At } y = 4.41, \frac{dy}{dx} = \frac{4.41 - 2}{4(4.41) - 2} = 0.15$$

$$\text{At } y = -3.41, \frac{dy}{dx} = \frac{-3.41 - 2}{4(-3.41) - 2} = 0.35$$

Step 3: Plugging into our equation for the tangent line, we get:

$$y - 4.41 = 0.15(x - 2)$$
$$y + 3.41 = 0.35(x - 2)$$

It is not necessary to simplify these equations.

(c) Find $\dfrac{d^2y}{dx^2}$ at $(0, 4)$.

Step 1: Once we have the first derivative, we have to differentiate again to find $\dfrac{d^2y}{dx^2}$.

But, we have to use implicit differentiation again:

$$\frac{dy}{dx} = \frac{y - x}{4y - x}$$

Using the quotient rule:

$$\frac{d^2y}{dx^2} = \frac{(4y - x)\left(\dfrac{dy}{dx} - \dfrac{dx}{dx}\right) - (y - x)\left(4\dfrac{dy}{dx} - \dfrac{dx}{dx}\right)}{(4y - x)^2}$$

Simplifying we get:

$$\frac{d^2y}{dx^2} = \frac{(4y-x)\left(\dfrac{dy}{dx}-1\right)-(y-x)\left(4\dfrac{dy}{dx}-1\right)}{(4y-x)^2}$$

Now, we plug in $\dfrac{y-x}{4y-x}$ for $\dfrac{dy}{dx}$, which gives us:

$$\frac{d^2y}{dx^2} = \frac{(4y-x)\left(\dfrac{y-x}{4y-x}-1\right)-(y-x)\left(4\dfrac{y-x}{4y-x}-1\right)}{(4y-x)^2}$$

Now we would have to use a lot of algebra to simplify this but, fortunately, we can just plug (0, 4) in immediately for x and y, and solve from there:

$$\frac{d^2y}{dx^2} = \frac{(16)\left(\dfrac{4}{16}-1\right)-(4)\left(4\dfrac{4}{16}-1\right)}{(16)^2} = \frac{-3}{64}$$

PROBLEM 2. A particle moves along the x-axis so that its acceleration at any time $t > 0$ is given by $a(t) = 12t - 18$. At time $t = 1$, the velocity of the particle is $v(1) = 0$ and the position is $x(1) = 9$.

(a) Write an expression for the velocity of the particle $v(t)$.

Step 1: We know that the derivative of velocity with respect to time is acceleration, so the integral of acceleration with respect to time is velocity:

$$\int a(t)\,dt = v(t)$$

$$\int 12t - 18\,dt = 6t^2 - 18t + C = v(t)$$

If we plug in the information that at time $t = 1$, $v(1) = 0$, we can solve for C.

$$6(1)^2 - 18(1) + C = 0$$
$$-12 + C = 0$$
$$C = 12$$

This means that the velocity of the particle is $6t^2 - 18t + 12$.

(b) At what values of t does the particle change direction?

When a particle is in motion, it changes direction at the time when its velocity is zero. (As long as acceleration is not also zero.) So all we have to do is set velocity equal to zero and solve for t.

$$6t^2 - 18t + 12 = 0$$
$$t^2 - 3t + 2 = 0$$
$$(t-2)(t-1) = 0$$
$$t = 1, 2$$

(c) Write an expression for the position $x(t)$ of the particle.

We know that the derivative of position with respect to time is velocity, so the integral of velocity with respect to time is position:

$$\int v(t)\,dt = x(t)$$

$$\int \left(6t^2 - 18t + 12\right)dt = 2t^3 - 9t^2 + 12t + C = x(t)$$

If we plug in the information that at time $t = 1$, $x(1) = 9$, we can solve for C:

$$2(1)^3 - 9(1)^2 + 12(1) + C = 9$$
$$5 + C = 9$$
$$C = 4 \text{ so } x(t) = 2t^3 - 9t^2 + 12t + 4$$

(d) Find the total distance traveled by the particle from $t = \dfrac{3}{2}$ to $t = 6$?

Step 1: Normally, all that we have to do to find the distance traveled is to integrate the velocity equation from the starting time to the ending time. But we have to watch out for whether the particle changes direction. If so, we have to break the integration into two parts—a positive integral for when it is traveling to the right, and a negative integral for when it is traveling to the left.

We know that the particle changes direction at $t = 1$ and at $t = 2$. We need to know which direction the particle is moving at time $t = \dfrac{3}{2}$. We can do this by plugging $\dfrac{3}{2}$ into the velocity and looking at its sign. $6\left(\dfrac{3}{2}\right)^2 - 18\left(\dfrac{3}{2}\right) + 12 = -\dfrac{3}{2}$.

This is negative, so the particle is moving to the left from $t = \dfrac{3}{2}$ to $t = 2$. And, because we know that the particle changes direction at $t = 2$, it must be moving to the right after that. Therefore we are going to need two integrals, one for $t = \dfrac{3}{2}$ to $t = 2$ and one for $t = 2$ to $t = 6$. So we need to evaluate:

$$\int_{\frac{3}{2}}^{2} -\left(6t^2 - 18t + 12\right)dt + \int_{2}^{6}\left(6t^2 - 18t + 12\right)dt$$

We already integrated these in part (c), $\int\left(6t^2 - 18t + 12\right)dt = 2t^3 - 9t^2 + 12t + C$, but now, instead of solving for the constant, we evaluate the equation at the limits of integration:

$$-\left(2t^3 - 9t^2 + 12t\right)\Big|_{\frac{3}{2}}^{2} + \left(2t^3 - 9t^2 + 12t\right)\Big|_{2}^{6}$$

$$= -\left(2(2)^3 - 9(2)^2 + 12(2)\right) + \left(2\left(\frac{3}{2}\right)^3 - 9\left(\frac{3}{2}\right)^2 + 12\left(\frac{3}{2}\right)\right) +$$

$$\left(2(6)^3 - 9(6)^2 + 12(6)\right) - \left(2(2)^3 - 9(2)^2 + 12(2)\right)$$

$$= -4 + 4.5 + 180 - 4 = 176.5 \text{ or } \frac{353}{2}$$

PROBLEM 3. Let R be the region enclosed by the graphs of $y = 2\ln x$ and $y = \frac{x}{2}$, and the lines $x = 2$ and $x = 8$.

(a) Find the area of R.

Step 1: If there are two curves, $f(x)$ and $g(x)$, where $f(x)$ is always above $g(x)$, on the interval $[a,b]$, then the area of the region between the two curves is found by:

$$\int_a^b \left(f(x) - g(x)\right)dx$$

In order to determine whether one of the curves is above the other, we can graph them on the calculator.

The graph looks like this:

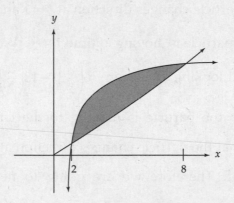

As we can see, the graph of $y = 2\ln x$ is above $y = \frac{x}{2}$ on the entire interval, so all we have to do is evaluate the integral $\int_2^8 \left(2\ln x - \frac{x}{2}\right)dx =$.

Step 2: We can do the integration one of two ways—on the calculator or analytically.

Calculator: Evaluate **fnint** $\left(\left(2\ln x - \left(\dfrac{x}{2}\right)\right), x, 2, 8\right) = 3.498$

Analytically: $\displaystyle\int_2^8\left(2\ln x - \frac{x}{2}\right)dx = 2\int_2^8 \ln x\,dx - \frac{1}{2}\int_2^8 x\,dx =$

$$= 2(x\ln x - x)\Big|_2^8 - \frac{1}{2}\left(\frac{x^2}{2}\right)\Big|_2^8 = 18.498 - 15 = 3.498$$

By the way, you should have memorized $\displaystyle\int \ln x\,dx = x\ln x - x$, or you can do it as one of the basic integration by parts integrals.

(b) Set up, but <u>do not integrate</u>, an integral expression, in terms of a single variable, for the volume of the solid generated when R is revolved about the *x-axis*.

Step 1: If there are two curves, $f(x)$ and $g(x)$, where $f(x)$ is always above $g(x)$, on the interval $[a,b]$, then the volume of the solid generated when the region is revolved about the *x*-axis is found by using the method of washers:

$$\pi\int_a^b\left[\left[f(x)\right]^2 - \left[g(x)\right]^2\right]dx$$

Here, we already know that $f(x)$ is above $g(x)$ on the interval, so the integral we need to evaluate is:

$$\pi\int_2^8\left[\left[2\ln x\right]^2 - \left[\frac{x}{2}\right]^2\right]dx$$

(c) Set up, but <u>do not integrate</u>, an integral expression, in terms of a single variable, for the volume of the solid generated when R is revolved about the line $x = -1$.

Step 1: Now we have to revolve the area around a <u>vertical</u> axis. If there are two curves, $f(x)$ and $g(x)$, where $f(x)$ is always above $g(x)$, on the interval $[a,b]$, then the volume of the solid generated when the region is revolved about the *y*-axis is found by using the method of shells:

$$2\pi\int_a^b x\left[f(x) - g(x)\right]dx$$

When we are rotating around a vertical axis, we use the same formula as when we rotate around the y-axis, but we have to account for the shift away from $x = 0$. Here we have a curve that is 1 unit farther away from the line $x = -1$ than it is from the y-axis, so we add 1 to the radius of the shell (for a more detailed explanation of shifting axes, see the unit on finding the volume of a solid of revolution). This gives us the equation:

$$2\pi \int_2^8 (x+1)\left[2\ln x - \frac{x}{2}\right] dx$$

PROBLEM 4. Water is draining at the rate of 48π ft³/sec from the vertex at the bottom of a conical tank whose diameter at its base is 40 feet and whose height is 60 feet.

(a) Find an expression for the volume of water (in ft³/sec) in the tank in terms of its radius.

The formula for the volume of a cone is: $V = \frac{1}{3}\pi R^2 H$, where R is the radius of the cone, and H is the height. The ratio of the height of a cone to its radius is constant at any point on the edge of the cone, so we also know that $\frac{H}{R} = \frac{60}{20} = 3$. (Remember that the radius is half the diameter.) If we solve this for H and substitute, we get:

$$H = 3R$$
$$V = \frac{1}{3}\pi R^2 (3R) = \pi R^3$$

(b) At what rate (in ft/sec) is the radius of the water in the tank shrinking when the radius is 16 feet?

Step 1: This is a related rates question. We now have a formula for the volume of the cone in terms of its radius, so if we differentiate it in terms of t we should be able to solve for the rate of change of the radius $\frac{dR}{dt}$.

We are given that the rate of change of the volume and the radius are, respectively:

$$\frac{dV}{dt} = -48\pi \text{ and } R = 16$$

Differentiating the formula for the v olume, we get: $\frac{dV}{dt} = 3\pi R^2 \frac{dR}{dt}$.

Now we plug in and get: $-48\pi = 3\pi 16^2 \frac{dR}{dt}$. Finally, if we solve for $\frac{dR}{dt}$, we get:

$$\frac{dR}{dt} = -\frac{1}{16} \text{ ft / sec}$$

(c) How fast (in ft/sec) is the height of the water in the tank dropping at the instant that the radius is 16 feet?

Step 1: This is the same idea as the previous problem, except that we want to solve for $\dfrac{dH}{dt}$. In order to do this, we need to go back to our ratio of height to radius and solve it for the radius:

$$\frac{H}{R} = 3 \quad \text{or} \quad \frac{H}{3} = R$$

Substituting for R in the original equation, we get: $V = \dfrac{1}{3}\pi\left(\dfrac{H}{3}\right)^2 H = \dfrac{\pi H^3}{27}$.

Step 2: Now we need to know what H is when R is 16. Using our ratio:

$$H = 3\,(16) = 48.$$

Step 3: Now if we differentiate we get:

$$\frac{dV}{dt} = \frac{\pi H^2}{9}\frac{dH}{dt}$$

Now we plug in and solve:

$$48\pi = \frac{\pi(48)^2}{9}\frac{dH}{dt}$$

$$\frac{dH}{dt} = -\frac{3}{16}$$

One should also note that, because $H = 3R$, $\dfrac{dH}{dt} = 3\dfrac{dR}{dt}$. Thus, after we found $\dfrac{dR}{dt}$ in part 2, we merely had to multiply it by 3 to find the answer for part 3.

PROBLEM 5. Let f be the function given by $y = f(x) = 2x^4 - 4x^2 + 1$.

(a) Find an equation of the line tangent to the graph at $(-2,17)$.

In order to find the equation of a tangent line at a particular point, we need to take the derivative of the function and plug in the x and y values at that point to give us the slope of the line.

Step 1: The derivative is: $f'(x) = 8x^3 - 8x$. If we plug in $x = -2$, we get:

$$f'(-2) = 8(-2)^3 - 8(-2) = -48$$

This is the slope m.

Step 2: Now we use the slope-intercept form of the equation of a line, $y - y_1 = m(x - x_1)$, and plug in the appropriate values of x, y, and m.

$$y - 17 = -48(x + 2)$$

If we simplify this we get $y = -48x - 79$.

(b) Find the x- and y-coordinates of the relative maxima and relative minima.

If we want to find the maxima/minima, we need to take the derivative and set it equal to zero. The values that we get are called critical points. We will then test each point to see if it is a maximum or a minimum.

Step 1: We already have the first derivative from part (a), so we can just set it equal to zero:

$$8x^3 - 8x = 0$$

If we now solve this for x we get:

$$8x(x^2 - 1) = 0 \quad 8x(x + 1)(x - 1) = 0 \quad x = 0, 1, -1$$

These are our critical points. In order to test if a point is a maximum or a minimum, we usually use the *second derivative test*. We plug each of the critical points into the second derivative. If we get a positive value, the point is a relative minimum. If we get a negative value, the point is a relative maximum. If we get zero, the point is a point of inflection.

Step 2: The second derivative is $f''(x) = 24x^2 - 8$. If we plug in the critical points we get:

$$f''(0) = 24(0)^2 - 8 = -8$$
$$f''(1) = 24(1)^2 - 8 = 16$$
$$f''(-1) = 24(-1)^2 - 8 = 16$$

So $x = 0$ is a relative maximum, and $x = 1, -1$ are relative minima.

Step 3: In order to find the y-coordinates, we plug the x values back into the original equation, and solve:

$$f(0) = 1$$
$$f(1) = -1$$
$$f(-1) = -1$$

And our points are:

(0,1) is a relative maximum

(1,-1) is a relative minimum

(-1,-1) is a relative minimum

(c) Find the x- and y- coordinates of the points of inflection.

If we want to find the points of inflection, we set the second derivative equal to zero. The values that we get are the x-coordinates of the points of inflection.

Step 1: We already have the second derivative from part (b), so all we have to do is set it equal to zero and solve for x:

$$24x^2 - 8 = 0 \qquad x^2 = \frac{1}{3} \qquad x = \pm\sqrt{\frac{1}{3}}$$

Step 2: In order to find the y-coordinates, we plug the x values back into the original equation, and solve:

$$f\left(\sqrt{\frac{1}{3}}\right) = 2\left(\sqrt{\frac{1}{3}}\right)^4 - 4\left(\sqrt{\frac{1}{3}}\right)^2 + 1 = \frac{2}{9} - \frac{4}{3} + 1 = -\frac{1}{9}$$

$$f\left(-\sqrt{\frac{1}{3}}\right) = 2\left(-\sqrt{\frac{1}{3}}\right)^4 - 4\left(-\sqrt{\frac{1}{3}}\right)^2 + 1 = \frac{2}{9} - \frac{4}{3} + 1 = -\frac{1}{9}$$

So the points of inflection are: $\left(\sqrt{\frac{1}{3}}, -\frac{1}{9}\right)$ and $\left(-\sqrt{\frac{1}{3}}, -\frac{1}{9}\right)$.

PROBLEM 6. Let $F(x) = \int_0^x \left[\cos\left(\frac{t}{2}\right) + \left(\frac{3}{2}\right)\right] dt$ on the closed interval $[0, 4\pi]$.

(a) Approximate $F(2\pi)$ using four inscribed rectangles.

This means that we need to find $\int_0^{2\pi} \left[\cos\left(\frac{t}{2}\right) + \left(\frac{3}{2}\right)\right] dt$.

Step 1: The graph of $\cos\left(\frac{t}{2}\right) + \left(\frac{3}{2}\right)$ from 0 to 2π, using four inscribed rectangles looks like:

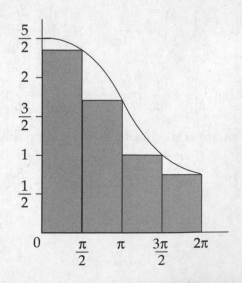

If we are cutting the interval $[0,2\pi]$ into 4 rectangles, the width of each rectangle is $\dfrac{\pi}{2}$.

The height of each rectangle depends on the x-coordinate.

Step 2: We can now set up the calculation for the area of the rectangles:

$$\text{Area} = \frac{\pi}{2}\left[\left(\cos\frac{\pi}{4}+\frac{3}{2}\right)+\left(\cos\frac{\pi}{2}+\frac{3}{2}\right)+\left(\cos\frac{3\pi}{4}+\frac{3}{2}\right)+\left(\cos\pi+\frac{3}{2}\right)\right]$$

$$= \frac{\pi}{2}\left[\left(\frac{3}{2}+\frac{1}{\sqrt{2}}\right)+\left(\frac{3}{2}\right)+\left(\frac{3}{2}-\frac{1}{\sqrt{2}}\right)+\left(\frac{1}{2}\right)\right] = \frac{5\pi}{2} \approx 7.854$$

(b) Find $F'(2\pi)$.

Step 1: The Second Fundamental Theorem of calculus says that if $f(x)$ is a continuous function, and a is a constant, then $\dfrac{d}{dx}\displaystyle\int_a^x f(t)\,dt = f(x)$.

So here we have: $\dfrac{d}{dx}\displaystyle\int_0^x\left[\cos\left(\frac{t}{2}\right)+\frac{3}{2}\right]dt = \cos\left(\frac{x}{2}\right)+\frac{3}{2}$

Step 2: Now we plug in 2π for x and we get $\cos\pi+\dfrac{3}{2}=\dfrac{1}{2}$.

(c) Find the average value of $F'(x)$ on the interval $[0,4\pi]$.

Step 1: The Mean Value Theorem for integrals says that if you want to find the average value of $f(x)$ on an interval $[a,b]$, you need to evaluate the integral $\dfrac{1}{b-a}\displaystyle\int_a^b f(x)\,dx$. So here we would evaluate the integral $\dfrac{1}{4\pi-0}\displaystyle\int_0^{4\pi}\left(\cos\left(\frac{x}{2}\right)+\frac{3}{2}\right)dx$:

$$\frac{1}{4\pi}\int_0^{4\pi}\left(\cos\left(\frac{x}{2}\right)+\frac{3}{2}\right)dx = \frac{1}{4\pi}\int_0^{4\pi}\cos\frac{x}{2}\,dx + \frac{3}{8\pi}\int_0^{4\pi}dx =$$

$$\frac{1}{4\pi}\,2\sin\frac{x}{2}\bigg|_0^{4\pi} + \frac{3}{8\pi}x\bigg|_0^{4\pi} = \frac{1}{2\pi}\sin\frac{x}{2}\bigg|_0^{4\pi} + \frac{3}{8\pi}x\bigg|_0^{4\pi}.$$

Step 2: Now we evaluate at the limits of integration and we get:

$$\frac{1}{2\pi}\sin\frac{x}{2}\bigg|_0^{4\pi} + \frac{3}{8\pi}x\bigg|_0^{4\pi} = \frac{1}{2\pi}(\sin 2\pi - \sin 0) + \frac{3}{8\pi}(4\pi) = \frac{3}{2}$$

24

The Princeton Review AP Calculus AB Practice Test 2

CALCULUS AB

SECTION I, Part A

Time—55 Minutes

Number of questions—28

A CALCULATOR MAY NOT BE USED ON THIS PART OF THE EXAMINATION

Directions: Solve each of the following problems, using the available space for scratchwork. After examining the form of the choices, decide which is the best of the choices given and fill in the corresponding oval on the answer sheet. No credit will be given for anything written in the test book. Do not spend too much time on any one problem.

In this test: Unless otherwise specified, the domain of a function f is assumed to be the set of all real numbers x for which $f(x)$ is a real number.

1. If $g(x) = \dfrac{1}{32}x^4 - 5x^2$, find $g'(4)$.

 (A) -72

 (B) -32

 (C) -24

 (D) 24

 (E) 32

2. The domain of the function $f(x) = \sqrt{4 - x^2}$ is

 (A) $x < -2$ or $x > 2$

 (B) $x \le -2$ or $x \ge 2$

 (C) $-2 < x < 2$

 (D) $-2 \le x \le 2$

 (E) $x \le 2$

GO ON TO THE NEXT PAGE

3. $\lim\limits_{x \to 5} \dfrac{x^2 - 25}{x - 5}$ is

(A) 0

(B) 10

(C) −10

(D) 5

(E) The limit does not exist.

---

4. If $f(x) = \dfrac{x^5 - x + 2}{x^3 + 7}$, find $f'(x)$.

(A) $\dfrac{\left(5x^4 - 1\right)}{\left(3x^2\right)}$

(B) $\dfrac{\left(5x^4 - 1\right) - \left(3x^2\right)}{\left(x^3 + 7\right)}$

(C) $\dfrac{\left(x^3 + 7\right)\left(5x^4 - 1\right) - \left(x^5 - x + 2\right)\left(3x^2\right)}{\left(x^3 + 7\right)}$

(D) $\dfrac{\left(x^5 - x + 2\right)\left(3x^2\right) - \left(x^3 + 7\right)\left(5x^4 - 1\right)}{\left(x^3 + 7\right)^2}$

(E) $\dfrac{\left(x^3 + 7\right)\left(5x^4 - 1\right) - \left(x^5 - x + 2\right)\left(3x^2\right)}{\left(x^3 + 7\right)^2}$

GO ON TO THE NEXT PAGE

5. Evaluate $\lim\limits_{h \to 0} \dfrac{5\left(\frac{1}{2}+h\right)^4 - 5\left(\frac{1}{2}\right)^4}{h}$.

(A) $\dfrac{5}{2}$

(B) $\dfrac{5}{16}$

(C) 40

(D) 160

(E) The limit does not exist.

---

6. $\displaystyle\int x\sqrt{3x}\,dx =$

(A) $\dfrac{2\sqrt{3}}{5}x^{\frac{5}{2}} + C$

(B) $\dfrac{5\sqrt{3}}{2}x^{\frac{5}{2}} + C$

(C) $\dfrac{\sqrt{3}}{2}x^{\frac{1}{2}} + C$

(D) $2\sqrt{3x} + C$

(E) $\dfrac{5\sqrt{3}}{2}x^{\frac{3}{2}} + C$

GO ON TO THE NEXT PAGE

7. Find k so that $f(x) = \begin{cases} \dfrac{x^2 - 16}{x - 4} & ; x \neq 4 \\ k & ; x = 4 \end{cases}$ is continuous for all x.

(A) All real values of k make $f(x)$ continuous for all x.

(B) 0

(C) 16

(D) 8

(E) There is no real value of k that makes $f(x)$ continuous for all x.

8. Which of the following integrals correctly gives the area of the region consisting of all points above the x-axis and below the curve $y = 8 + 2x - x^2$?

(A) $\displaystyle\int_{-2}^{4} (x^2 - 2x - 8)\, dx$

(B) $\displaystyle\int_{-4}^{2} (8 + 2x - x^2)\, dx$

(C) $\displaystyle\int_{-2}^{4} (8 + 2x - x^2)\, dx$

(D) $\displaystyle\int_{-4}^{2} (x^2 - 2x - 8)\, dx$

(E) $\displaystyle\int_{2}^{4} (8 + 2x - x^2)\, dx$

9. If $f(x) = x^2 \cos 2x$, find $f'(x)$.

(A) $2x \sin 2x$

(B) $-2x \cos 2x + 2x^2 \sin 2x$

(C) $-4x \sin 2x$

(D) $2x \cos 2x - 2x^2 \sin 2x$

(E) $2x - 2 \sin 2x$

GO ON TO THE NEXT PAGE

10. An equation of the line tangent to $y = 4x^3 - 7x^2$ at $x = 3$ is

(A) $y + 45 = 66(x + 3)$

(B) $y - 45 = 66(x - 3)$

(C) $y = 66x$

(D) $y = 66(x - 3)$

(E) $y - 45 = \dfrac{-1}{66}(x - 3)$

---

11. $\displaystyle\int_{0}^{\frac{1}{2}} \frac{2}{\sqrt{1-x^2}}\, dx =$

(A) $\dfrac{\pi}{6}$ (B) $\dfrac{\pi}{3}$ (C) $-\dfrac{\pi}{3}$ (D) $\dfrac{2\pi}{3}$ (E) $-\dfrac{2\pi}{3}$

---

12. Find a positive value c, for x, that satisfies the conclusion of the Mean Value Theorem for Derivatives for $f(x) = 3x^2 - 5x + 1$ on the interval $\left[2, 5\right]$.

(A) 1

(B) $\dfrac{13}{6}$

(C) $\dfrac{11}{6}$

(D) $\dfrac{23}{6}$

(E) $\dfrac{7}{2}$

GO ON TO THE NEXT PAGE

13. Given $f(x) = 2x^2 - 7x - 10$, find the absolute maximum of $f(x)$ on $[-1, 3]$.

(A) -1

(B) $\dfrac{7}{4}$

(C) -13

(D) $-\dfrac{129}{8}$

(E) 0

---

14. Find $\dfrac{dy}{dx}$ if $x^3y + xy^3 = -10$.

(A) $\left(3x^2 + 3xy^2\right)$

(B) $-\left(3x^2 + 3xy^2\right)$

(C) $\dfrac{\left(3x^2y + y^3\right)}{\left(3xy^2 + x^3\right)}$

(D) $-\dfrac{\left(3x^2y + y^3\right)}{\left(3xy^2 + x^3\right)}$

(E) $-\dfrac{\left(x^2y + y^3\right)}{\left(xy^2 + x^3\right)}$

GO ON TO THE NEXT PAGE

15. If $f(x) = \sqrt{1 + \sqrt{x}}$, find $f'(x)$.

(A) $\dfrac{-1}{4\sqrt{x}\sqrt{1+\sqrt{x}}}$

(B) $\dfrac{1}{2\sqrt{x}\sqrt{1+\sqrt{x}}}$

(C) $\dfrac{1}{4\sqrt{1+\sqrt{x}}}$

(D) $\dfrac{1}{4\sqrt{x}\sqrt{1+\sqrt{x}}}$

(E) $\dfrac{-1}{2\sqrt{x}\sqrt{1+\sqrt{x}}}$

16. $\displaystyle\int 7xe^{3x^2}\,dx =$

(A) $\dfrac{1}{42}e^{3x^2} + C$

(B) $\dfrac{6}{7}e^{3x^2} + C$

(C) $\dfrac{7}{6}e^{3x^2} + C$

(D) $7e^{3x^2} + C$

(E) $42e^{3x^2} + C$

GO ON TO THE NEXT PAGE

17. Find the equation of the tangent line to $9x^2 + 16y^2 = 52$ through $(2, -1)$.

   (A) $-9x + 8y - 26 = 0$

   (B) $9x - 8y - 26 = 0$

   (C) $9x - 8y - 106 = 0$

   (D) $8x + 9y - 17 = 0$

   (E) $9x + 16y - 2 = 0$

18. A particle's position is given by $s = t^3 - 6t^2 + 9t$. What is its acceleration at time $t = 4$?

   (A)   0

   (B)   9

   (C) -9

   (D) -12

   (E)   12

19. If $f(x) = 3^{\pi x}$, then $f'(x) =$

   (A) $\dfrac{3^{\pi x}}{\pi \ln 3}$

   (B) $\dfrac{3^{\pi x}}{\ln 3}$

   (C) $\dfrac{3^{\pi x}}{\pi}$

   (D) $\pi\left(3^{\pi x - 1}\right)$

   (E) $\pi \ln 3 \left(3^{\pi x}\right)$

GO ON TO THE NEXT PAGE

20. The average value of $f(x) = \dfrac{1}{x}$ from $x = 1$ to $x = e$ is

(A) $\dfrac{1}{e+1}$

(B) $\dfrac{1}{1-e}$

(C) $e-1$

(D) $1-\dfrac{1}{e^2}$

(E) $\dfrac{1}{e-1}$

21. If $f(x) = \sin^2 x$, find $f'''(x)$.

(A) $-\sin^2 x$

(B) $2\cos 2x$

(C) $\cos 2x$

(D) $-4\sin 2x$

(E) $-\sin 2x$

GO ON TO THE NEXT PAGE

22. Find the slope of the normal line to $y = x + \cos xy$ at $(0, 1)$.

   (A) 1
   (B) −1
   (C) 0
   (D) 2
   (E) Undefined

---

23. $\int e^x \left(e^{3x} \right) dx =$

   (A) $\dfrac{1}{3} e^{3x} + C$

   (B) $\dfrac{1}{4} e^{4x} + C$

   (C) $\dfrac{1}{4} e^{5x} + C$

   (D) $4e^{4x} + C$

   (E) $4e^{5x} + C$

---

24. $\displaystyle \lim_{x \to 0} \frac{\tan^3(2x)}{x^3} =$

   (A) −8
   (B) −2
   (C) 2
   (D) 8
   (E) The limit does not exist.

GO ON TO THE NEXT PAGE

25. A solid is generated when the region in the first quadrant bounded by the graph of $y = 1 + \sin^2 x$, the line $x = \dfrac{\pi}{2}$, the x-axis, and the y-axis is revolved about the x-axis. Its volume is found by evaluating which of the following integrals?

(A) $\pi \displaystyle\int_0^1 \left(1 + \sin^4 x\right) dx$

(B) $\pi \displaystyle\int_0^1 \left(1 + \sin^2 x\right)^2 dx$

(C) $\pi \displaystyle\int_0^{\frac{\pi}{2}} \left(1 + \sin^4 x\right) dx$

(D) $\pi \displaystyle\int_0^{\frac{\pi}{2}} \left(1 + \sin^2 x\right)^2 dx$

(E) $\pi \displaystyle\int_0^{\frac{\pi}{2}} \left(1 + \sin^2 x\right) dx$

26. If $y = \left(\dfrac{x^3 - 2}{2x^5 - 1}\right)^4$, find $\dfrac{dy}{dx}$ at $x = 1$.

(A) –52   (B) –28   (C) –13   (D) 13   (E) 52

GO ON TO THE NEXT PAGE

27. $\int x\sqrt{5-x}\ dx =$

(A) $-\dfrac{10}{3}(5-x)^{\frac{3}{2}}$

(B) $\sqrt{\dfrac{5x^2}{2}-\dfrac{x^3}{3}}+C$

(C) $\dfrac{10}{3}\sqrt{\dfrac{5x^2}{2}-\dfrac{x^3}{3}}+C$

(D) $10(5-x)^{\frac{1}{2}}+\dfrac{2}{3}(5-x)^{\frac{3}{2}}+C$

(E) $-\dfrac{10}{3}(5-x)^{\frac{3}{2}}+\dfrac{2}{5}(5-x)^{\frac{5}{2}}+C$

---

28. If $\dfrac{dy}{dx}=\dfrac{x^3+1}{y}$ and $y=2$ when $x=1$, then, when $x=2$, $y=$

(A) $\sqrt{\dfrac{27}{2}}$ (B) $\sqrt{\dfrac{27}{8}}$ (C) $\pm\sqrt{\dfrac{27}{8}}$ (D) $\pm\dfrac{3}{2}$ (E) $\pm\sqrt{\dfrac{27}{2}}$

STOP

END OF PART A SECTION I

IF YOU FINISH BEFORE TIME IS CALLED, YOU MAY CHECK YOUR WORK ON PART A ONLY.

DO NOT GO ON TO PART B UNTIL YOU ARE TOLD TO DO SO.

CALCULUS AB

SECTION I, Part B

Time—50 Minutes

Number of questions—17

A GRAPHING CALCULATOR IS REQUIRED FOR SOME QUESTIONS ON THIS PART OF THE EXAMINATION

Directions: Solve each of the following problems, using the available space for scratchwork. After examining the form of the choices, decide which is the best of the choices given and fill in the corresponding oval on the answer sheet. No credit will be given for anything written in the test book. Do not spend too much time on any one problem.

In this test:

1. The **exact** numerical value of the correct answer does not always appear among the choices given. When this happens, select from among the choices the number that best approximates the exact numerical value.

2. Unless otherwise specified, the domain of a function f is assumed to be the set of all real numbers x for which $f(x)$ is a real number.

29. The graph of $y = 5x^4 - x^5$ has an inflection point (or points) at

(A) $x = 0$ only
(B) $x = 3$ only
(C) $x = 0, 3$
(D) $x = -3$ only
(E) $x = 0, -3$

30. The average value of $f(x) = e^{4x^2}$ on the interval $\left[-\dfrac{1}{4}, \dfrac{1}{4}\right]$ is

(A) 0.272
(B) 0.545
(C) 1.090
(D) 2.180
(E) 4.360

GO ON TO THE NEXT PAGE

31. $\displaystyle\int_0^1 \tan x \, dx =$

(A) 0

(B) $\dfrac{\tan^2 1}{2}$

(C) $\ln(\cos(1))$

(D) $\ln(\sec(1))$

(E) $\ln(\sec(1)) - 1$

32. $\dfrac{d}{dx}\displaystyle\int_0^{x^2} \sin^2 t \, dt =$

(A) $x^2 \sin^2(x^2)$

(B) $2x \sin^2(x^2)$

(C) $\sin^2(x^2)$

(D) $x^2 \cos^2(x^2)$

(E) $2x \cos^2(x^2)$

GO ON TO THE NEXT PAGE

33. Find the value(s) of $\dfrac{dy}{dx}$ of $x^2y + y^2 = 5$ at $y = 1$.

(A) $-\dfrac{3}{2}$ only

(B) $-\dfrac{2}{3}$ only

(C) $\dfrac{2}{3}$ only

(D) $\pm\dfrac{2}{3}$

(E) $\pm\dfrac{3}{2}$

34. The graph of $y = x^3 - 2x^2 - 5x + 2$ has a local maximum at

(A) $(2.120, 0)$
(B) $(2.120, -8.061)$
(C) $(-0.786, 0)$
(D) $(-0.786, 4.209)$
(E) $(0.666, -1.926)$

35. Approximate $\displaystyle\int_0^1 \sin^2 x \, dx$ using the Trapezoid Rule with $n = 4$, to three decimal places.

(A) 0.277
(B) 0.273
(C) 0.555
(D) 1.109
(E) 2.219

GO ON TO THE NEXT PAGE

36. The volume generated by revolving about the x-axis the region above the curve $y = x^3$, below the line $y = 1$, and between $x=0$ and $x=1$ is

(A) $\dfrac{\pi}{42}$

(B) 0.143π

(C) $\dfrac{\pi}{7}$

(D) 0.643π

(E) $\dfrac{6\pi}{7}$

---

37. A 20 foot ladder slides down a wall at 5 ft/sec. At what speed is the bottom sliding out when the top is 10 feet from the floor (in ft/sec)?

(A) 0.346   (B) 2.887   (C) 0.224   (D) 5.774   (E) 4.472

---

38. $\displaystyle\int \dfrac{\ln x}{3x}\, dx =$

(A) $6\ln^2|x| + C$

(B) $\dfrac{1}{6}\ln(\ln|x|) + C$

(C) $\dfrac{1}{3}\ln^2|x| + C$

(D) $\dfrac{1}{6}\ln^2|x| + C$

(E) $\dfrac{1}{3}\ln|x| + C$

GO ON TO THE NEXT PAGE

39. Find two non-negative numbers x and y whose sum is 100 and for which x^2y is a maximum.

   (A) $x = 33.333$ and $y = 33.333$
   (B) $x = 50$ and $y = 50$
   (C) $x = 33.333$ and $y = 66.667$
   (D) $x = 100$ and $y = 0$
   (E) $x = 66.667$ and $y = 33.333$

---

40. Find the distance traveled (to three decimal places) from $t = 1$ to $t = 5$ seconds, for a particle whose velocity is given by $v(t) = t + \ln t$.

   (A) 6.000
   (B) 1.609
   (C) 16.047
   (D) 0.800
   (E) 148.413

GO ON TO THE NEXT PAGE

41. $\int \sin^5(2x)\cos(2x)\,dx =$

(A) $\dfrac{\sin^6 2x}{12} + C$

(B) $\dfrac{\sin^6 2x}{6} + C$

(C) $\dfrac{\sin^6 2x}{3} + C$

(D) $\dfrac{\cos^5 2x}{3} + C$

(E) $\dfrac{\cos^5 2x}{6} + C$

42. The volume of a cube is increasing at a rate proportional to its volume at any time t. If the volume is 8 ft^3 originally, and 12 ft^3 after 5 seconds, what is its volume at $t = 12$ seconds?

(A) 21.169
(B) 22.941
(C) 16.000
(D) 28.800
(E) 17.600

43. If $f(x) = \left(1 + \dfrac{x}{20}\right)^5$, find $f''(40)$.

(A) 0.068
(B) 1.350
(C) 5.400
(D) 6.750
(E) 540.000

GO ON TO THE NEXT PAGE

44. A particle's height at a time $t \geq 0$ is given by $h(t) = 100t - 16t^2$. What is its maximum height?

(A) 312.500   (B) 156.250   (C) 78.125   (D) 6.250   (E) 3.125

---

45. If $f(x)$ is continuous and differentiable and $f(x) = \begin{cases} ax^4 + 5x; \, x \leq 2 \\ bx^2 - 3x; \, x > 2 \end{cases}$, then $b=$

(A) 0.5
(B) 0
(C) 2
(D) 6
(E) There is no value of b.

STOP

END OF SECTION I

IF YOU FINISH BEFORE TIME IS CALLED, YOU MAY CHECK YOUR WORK ON PART B ONLY.

DO NOT GO ON TO SECTION II UNTIL YOU ARE TOLD TO DO SO.

SECTION II
GENERAL INSTRUCTIONS

You may wish to look over the problems before starting to work on them, since it is not expected that everyone will be able to complete all parts of all problems. All problems are given equal weight, but the parts of a particular problem are not necessarily given equal weight.

A GRAPHING CALCULATOR IS REQUIRED FOR SOME PROBLEMS OR PARTS OF PROBLEMS ON THIS SECTION OF THE EXAMINATION.

- You should write all work for each part of each problem in the space provided for that part in the booklet. Be sure to write clearly and legibly. If you make an error, you may save time by crossing it out rather than trying to erase it. Erased or crossed-out work will not be graded.

- Show all your work. You will be graded on the correctness and completeness of your methods as well as your answers. Cop‹çct answers without supporting work may not receive credit.

- Justifications require that you give mathematical (noncalculator) reasons and that you clearly identify functions, graphs, tables, or other objects you use.

- You are permitted to use your calculator to solve an equation, find the derivative of a function at a point, or calculate the value of a definite integral. However, you must clearly indicate the setup of your problem, namely the equation, function, or integral you are using. If you use other built-in features or programs, you must show the mathematical steps necessary to produce your results.

- Your work must be expressed in standard mathematical notation rather than calculator syntax.

  For example, $\int_1^5 x^2 dx$ may not be written as fnInt $(X^2, X, 1, 5)$.

- Unless otherwise specified, answers (numeric or algebraic) need not be simplified. If your answer is given as a decimal approximation, it should be correct to three places after the decimal point.

- Unless otherwise specified, the domain of a function f is assumed to be the set of all real numbers x for which $f(x)$ is a real number.

SECTION II, PART A
Time—45 minutes
Number of problems—3

A graphing calculator is required for some problems or parts of problems.

During the timed portion for Part A, you may work only on the problems in Part A.

On Part A, you are permitted to use your calculator to solve an equation, find the derivative of a function at a point, or calculate the value of a definite integral. However, you must clearly indicate the setup of your problem, namely the equation, function, or integral you are using. If you use other built-in features or programs, you must show the mathematical steps necessary to produce your results.

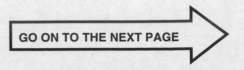
GO ON TO THE NEXT PAGE

1. Consider the curve defined by $y = x^4 + 4x^3$.

   (a) Find the equation of the tangent line to the curve at $x = -1$.

   (b) Find the coordinates of the absolute minimum.

   (c) Find the coordinates of the point(s) of inflection.

---

2. The temperature on New Year's Day in Hinterland was given by $T(H) = -A - B\cos\left(\dfrac{\pi H}{12}\right)$, where T is the temperature in degrees Fahrenheit and H is the number of hours from midnight ($0 \leq T < 24$).

   (a) The initial temperature at midnight was $-15°$ F, and at noon of New Year's Day was $5°$ F. Find A and B.

   (b) Find the average temperature for the first 10 hours.

   (c) Use the Trapezoid Rule with 4 equal subdivisions to estimate $\displaystyle\int_6^8 T(H)\,dH$.

   (d) Find an expression for the rate that the temperature is changing with respect to H.

---

3. Sea grass grows on a lake. The rate of growth of the grass is $\dfrac{dG}{dt} = kG$, where k is a constant.

   (a) Find an expression for G, the amount of grass in the lake (in tons), in terms of t, the number of years, if the amount of grass is 100 tons initially, and 120 tons after one year.

   (b) In how many years will the amount of grass available be 300 tons?

(c)   If fish are now introduced into the lake and consume a consistent 80 tons/year of sea grass, how long will it take for the lake to be completely free of sea grass?

PART B
Time—45 minutes
Number of problems—3

No calculator is allowed for these problems.

During the timed portion for Part B, you may continue to work on the problems in Part A without the use of any calculator.

4. Water is being poured into a hemispherical bowl of radius 6 inches at the rate of 4 in³/sec.

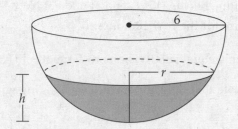

(a)   Given that the volume of the water in the spherical segment shown above is $V = \pi h^2\left(R - \dfrac{h}{3}\right)$, where R is the radius of the *sphere*, find the rate that the water level is rising when the water is 2 inches deep.

(b)   Find an expression for r, the radius of the *surface of the spherical segment* of water, in terms of h.

(c)   How fast is the circular area of the surface of the spherical segment of water growing (in in²/sec) when the water is 2 inches deep?

5. Let R be the region in the first quadrant bounded by $y^2 = x$ and $x^2 = y$.

(a)   Find the area of region R.

(b)   Find the volume of the solid generated when R is revolved about the x-axis.

(c)   The section of a certain solid cut by any plane perpendicular to the x-axis is a circle with the endpoints of its diameter lying on the parabolas $y^2 = x$ and $x^2 = y$. Find the volume of the solid.

6. An object moves with velocity $v(t) = t^2 - 8t + 7$.

    (a)   Write a polynomial expression for the position of the particle at any time t ≥ 0.

    (b)   At what time(s) is the particle changing direction?

    (c)   Find the total distance traveled by the particle from time $t = 0$ to $t = 4$.

END OF EXAMINATION

ANSWER KEY TO SECTION 1

1.	B	11.	B	21.	D	31.	D	41.	A
2.	D	12.	E	22.	B	32.	B	42.	A
3.	B	13.	A	23.	B	33.	D	43.	B
4.	E	14.	D	24.	D	34.	D	44.	B
5.	A	15.	D	25.	D	35.	A	45.	D
6.	A	16.	C	26.	A	36.	E		
7.	D	17.	B	27.	E	37.	B		
8.	C	18.	E	28.	E	38.	D		
9.	D	19.	E	29.	B	39.	E		
10.	B	20.	E	30.	C	40.	C		

25

Answers and Explanations to AB Practice Test 2

ANSWERS AND EXPLANATIONS TO SECTION I

PROBLEM 1. If $g(x) = \dfrac{1}{32}x^4 - 5x^2$, find $g'(4)$.

First, take the derivative:

$$g'(x) = \frac{1}{32}\left(4x^3\right) - 5(2x) = \frac{x^3}{8} - 10x$$

Now, plug in 4 for x:

$$\frac{(4)^3}{8} - 10(4) = 8 - 40 = -32$$

The answer is (B).

PROBLEM 2. The domain of the function $f(x) = \sqrt{4 - x^2}$ is

When you have a square root in a function, the domain will require that the expression under the radical (the "radicand") not be negative. Thus, the domain will be those values where $4 - x^2$ is not negative.

In other words, $4 - x^2 \geq 0$.

We solve this by, first, factoring the expression on the left: $(2 + x)(2 - x) \geq 0$

Next, we take the roots of the left side, which are –2 and 2, and put them on a number line:

Now, we pick a value in each of the three regions on the number line $x < -2$, $-2 < x < 2$, and $x > 2$. We plug the value into the expression $4 - x^2$ to see if we get a positive or negative value. If it's positive, then we include that region in the domain. If it's negative, then we exclude that region from the domain.

Let's try –3 for a value in the region $x < -2$.

We get: $4 - (-3)^2 = -5$, so we exclude the region $x < -2$ from the domain.

Now, we try 0 for a value in the region $-2 < x < 2$.

We get: $4 - (0)^2 = 4$, so we include the region $-2 < x < 2$ in the domain.

Finally, we try 3 for a value in the region $x > 2$.

We get: $4 - (3)^2 = -5$, so we exclude the region $x > 2$ from the domain.

Because the radicand is allowed to be zero, we include the endpoints in the domain. Therefore, the domain is $-2 \leq x \leq 2$.

The answer is (D).

PROBLEM 3. $\lim\limits_{x \to 5} \dfrac{x^2 - 25}{x - 5}$ is

Notice that if we plug 5 into the expressions in the numerator and the denominator, we get: $\dfrac{0}{0}$, which is undefined. Before we give up, we need to see if we can simplify the limit so that it can be evaluated. If we factor the expression in the numerator, we get: $\dfrac{(x+5)(x-5)}{(x-5)}$, which can be simplified to $x+5$.

<u>Now</u>, if we take the limit (by plugging in 5 for x), we get 10.

The answer is (B).

PROBLEM 4. If $f(x) = \dfrac{x^5 - x + 2}{x^3 + 7}$, find $f'(x)$.

We need to use the Quotient Rule, which is:

Given $f(x) = \dfrac{g(x)}{h(x)}$, then $f'(x) = \dfrac{h(x)g'(x) - g(x)h'(x)}{\left[h(x)\right]^2}$

Here, we have:

$$f'(x) = \dfrac{\left(x^3 + 7\right)\left(5x^4 - 1\right) - \left(x^5 - x + 2\right)\left(3x^2\right)}{\left(x^3 + 7\right)^2}$$

The answer is (E).

PROBLEM 5. Evaluate $\lim\limits_{h \to 0} \dfrac{5\left(\dfrac{1}{2} + h\right)^4 - 5\left(\dfrac{1}{2}\right)^4}{h}$.

Notice how this limit takes the form of the definition of the derivative, which is:

$$f'(x) = \lim\limits_{h \to 0} \dfrac{f(x+h) - f(x)}{h}$$

Here, if we think of $f(x)$ as $5x^4$, then this expression gives the derivative of $5x^4$ at the point $x = \dfrac{1}{2}$.

The derivative of $5x^4$ is $f'(x) = 20x^3$.

At $x = \dfrac{1}{2}$, we get $f'\left(\dfrac{1}{2}\right) = 20\left(\dfrac{1}{2}\right)^3 = \dfrac{5}{2}$.

The answer is (A).

PROBLEM 6. $\int x\sqrt{3x}\ dx =$

First, rewrite the integral as: $\int x\left(\sqrt{3}\right)x^{\frac{1}{2}}dx$.

Now we can simplify the integral to: $\sqrt{3}\int x^{\frac{3}{2}}\ dx$.

Using the power rule for integrals, which is: $\int x^n\ dx = \dfrac{x^{n+1}}{n+1}+C$

Then, we get: $\sqrt{3}\int x^{\frac{3}{2}}\ dx = \sqrt{3}\,\dfrac{x^{\frac{5}{2}}}{\frac{5}{2}}+C=\dfrac{2\sqrt{3}}{5}x^{\frac{5}{2}}+C$

The answer is (A).

PROBLEM 7. Find k so that $f(x)=\begin{cases} \dfrac{x^2-16}{x-4} & ;x\neq 4 \\ k & ;x=4 \end{cases}$ is continuous for all x.

In order for $f(x)$ to be continuous at a point c, there are three conditions that need to be fulfilled:

(1) $f(c)$ exists.

(2) $\lim\limits_{x\to c} f(x)$ exists.

(3) $\lim\limits_{x\to c} f(x)=f(c)$.

First, let's check condition (1): $f(4)$ exists; it's equal to k.

Next, let's check condition (2):

From the left side, we get:

$$\lim_{x\to 4^-}\frac{x^2-16}{x-4}=\lim_{x\to 4^-}\frac{(x-4)(x+4)}{x-4}=\lim_{x\to 4^-}(x+4)=8$$

From the right side, we get:

$$\lim_{x\to 4^+}\frac{x^2-16}{x-4}=\lim_{x\to 4^+}\frac{(x-4)(x+4)}{x-4}=\lim_{x\to 4^+}(x+4)=8$$

Therefore, the limit exists, and $\lim\limits_{x\to 4}\dfrac{x^2-16}{x-4}=8$.

Now, let's check condition (3). In order for this condition to be fulfilled, k must equal 8.

The answer is (D).

PROBLEM 8. Which of the following integrals correctly gives the area of the region consisting of all points above the x-axis and below the curve $y = 8 + 2x - x^2$?

The curve $y = 8 + 2x - x^2$ is an upside-down parabola and looks like this:

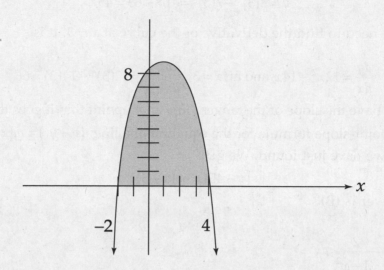

Notice that it crosses the x-axis at $x = -2$ and at $x = 4$.

The formula for the area of the region under the curve $f(x)$ and above the x-axis from $x = a$ to $x = b$ is: $\int_a^b f(x)\, dx$.

Thus, in order to find the area of the desired region, we need to evaluate the integral $\int_{-2}^4 \left(8 + 2x - x^2\right) dx$.

The answer is (C).

PROBLEM 9. If $f(x) = x^2 \cos 2x$, find $f'(x)$.

Here we need to use the Product Rule, which is:

If $f(x) = uv$, where u and v are both functions of x,

$$\text{then } f'(x) = u\frac{dv}{dx} + v\frac{du}{dx}$$

Here, we get:

$$f'(x) = x^2(-2\sin 2x) + 2x(\cos 2x)$$

The answer is (D).

PROBLEM 10. An equation of the line tangent to $y = 4x^3 - 7x^2$ at $x = 3$ is

If we want to find the equation of the tangent line, first we need to find the y-coordinate that corresponds to $x = 3$. It is:

$$y = 4(3)^3 - 7(3)^2 = 108 - 63 = 45$$

Next, we need to find the derivative of the curve at $x = 3$. It is:

$$\frac{dy}{dx} = 12x^2 - 14x \text{ and at } x = 3, \left.\frac{dy}{dx}\right|_{x=3} = 12(3)^2 - 14(3) = 66$$

Now we have the slope of the tangent line and a point that it goes through. We can use the point-slope formula for the equation of a line, $(y - y_1) = m(x - x_1)$, and plug in what we have just found. We get:

$$(y - 45) = 66(x - 3)$$

The answer is (B).

PROBLEM 11. $\displaystyle\int_0^{\frac{1}{2}} \frac{2}{\sqrt{1-x^2}}\, dx =$

This integral is of the form $\displaystyle\int \frac{dx}{\sqrt{a^2-x^2}} = \sin^{-1}\left(\frac{x}{a}\right) + C$, where $a = 1$.

Thus, we get:

$$\int_0^{\frac{1}{2}} \frac{2dx}{\sqrt{1-x^2}} = 2\sin^{-1}(x)\Big|_0^{\frac{1}{2}} = 2\left[\sin^{-1}\left(\frac{1}{2}\right) - \sin^{-1}(0)\right] = 2\left(\frac{\pi}{6} - 0\right) = \frac{\pi}{3}$$

The answer is (B).

PROBLEM 12. Find a positive value c, for x, that satisfies the conclusion of the Mean Value Theorem for derivatives for $f(x) = 3x^2 - 5x + 1$ on the interval $[2,5]$.

The Mean Value Theorem for derivatives says that, given a function $f(x)$ which is continuous and differentiable on $[a,b]$, then there exists some value c on (a,b) where

$$\frac{f(b) - f(a)}{b - a} = f'(c)$$

Here, we have $\displaystyle\frac{f(b) - f(a)}{b - a} = \frac{f(5) - f(2)}{5 - 2} = \frac{51 - 3}{3} = 16$

Plus, we have $f'(c) = 6c - 5$, so we simply set $6c - 5 = 16$

If we solve for c, we get: $c = \dfrac{7}{2}$

The answer is (E).

PROBLEM 13. Given $f(x) = 2x^2 - 7x - 10$ find the absolute maximum of $f(x)$ on $[-1,3]$.

First, let's take the derivative and then set it equal to zero to determine any critical points of the function:

$$f'(x) = 4x - 7$$

$$4x - 7 = 0$$

$$x = \frac{7}{4}$$

Now we can use the second derivative test to determine if this is a local minimum or maximum:

$$f''(x) = 4$$

Because the second derivative is always positive, the function is concave up everywhere and thus $x = \frac{7}{4}$ must be a local minimum.

How, then, do we find the absolute maximum? Anytime we are given a function that is defined on an interval, the endpoints of the interval are also critical points. Thus, all that we have to do now is to plug the endpoints into the function and see which one gives us the bigger value. That will be the absolute maximum:

$$f(-1) = 2(-1)^2 - 7(-1) - 10 = -1$$

$$f(3) = 2(3)^2 - 7(3) - 10 = -13$$

Therefore, the absolute maximum of $f(x)$ on the interval $[-1, 3]$ is -1.

The answer is (A).

PROBLEM 14. Find $\dfrac{dy}{dx}$ if $x^3y + xy^3 = -10$.

We need to use implicit differentiation to find $\dfrac{dy}{dx}$:

$$3x^2y + x^3\frac{dy}{dx} + y^3 + 3xy^2\frac{dy}{dx} = 0$$

Now, in order to isolate $\dfrac{dy}{dx}$, we move all of the terms that do not contain $\dfrac{dy}{dx}$ to the right side of the equals sign:

$$x^3\frac{dy}{dx} + 3xy^2\frac{dy}{dx} = -3x^2y - y^3$$

Factor out $\dfrac{dy}{dx}$:

$$\frac{dy}{dx}\left(x^3+3xy^2\right)=-3x^2y-y^3$$

And divide both sides by $\left(x^3+3xy^2\right)$ to isolate $\dfrac{dy}{dx}$:

$$\frac{dy}{dx}=-\frac{3x^2y+y^3}{x^3+3xy^2}$$

The answer is (D).

PROBLEM 15. If $f(x)=\sqrt{1+\sqrt{x}}$, find $f'(x)$.

First, rewrite the equation using fractional powers instead of radical signs:

$$f(x)=\left(1+x^{\frac{1}{2}}\right)^{\frac{1}{2}}$$

Now take the derivative:

$$f'(x)=\frac{1}{2}\left(1+x^{\frac{1}{2}}\right)^{-\frac{1}{2}}\left(\frac{1}{2}x^{-\frac{1}{2}}\right)$$

This can be rewritten as:

$$f'(x)=\frac{1}{4}\frac{1}{\sqrt{x}}\frac{1}{\sqrt{1+\sqrt{x}}}$$

The answer is (D).

PROBLEM 16. $\displaystyle\int 7xe^{3x^2}\,dx=$

We can use u-substitution to evaluate the integral.

Let $u=3x^2$ and $du=6x\,dx$. If we solve the second term for $x\,dx$, we get:

$$\frac{1}{6}du=x\,dx$$

Now we can rewrite the integral as:

$$\frac{7}{6}\int e^u\,du$$

Evaluate the integral to get:

$$\frac{7}{6}e^u + C$$

Now substitute back to get:

$$\frac{7}{6}e^{3x^2} + C$$

The answer is (C).

PROBLEM 17. Find the equation of the tangent line to $9x^2 + 16y^2 = 52$ through $(2,-1)$.

First, we need to find $\frac{dy}{dx}$. It's simplest to find it implicitly:

$$18x + 32y\frac{dy}{dx} = 0$$

Now solve for $\frac{dy}{dx}$:

$$\frac{dy}{dx} = -\frac{18x}{32y} = -\frac{9x}{16y}$$

Next, plug in $x = 2$ and $y = -1$ to get the slope of the tangent line at the point:

$$\frac{dy}{dx} = \frac{-18}{-16} = \frac{9}{8}$$

Now use the point-slope formula to find the equation of the tangent line:

$$(y+1) = \frac{9}{8}(x-2)$$

If we multiply through by 8, we get: $8y + 8 = 9x - 18$ or $9x - 8y - 26 = 0$.

The answer is (B).

PROBLEM 18. A particle's position is given by $s = t^3 - 6t^2 + 9t$. What is its acceleration at time $t = 4$?

Acceleration is the second derivative of position with respect to time (velocity is the first derivative).

The first derivative is: $v(t) = 3t^2 - 12t + 9$

The second derivative is: $a(t) = 6t - 12$

Now we simply plug in $t = 4$ and we get: $a(4) = 24 - 12 = 12$

The answer is (E).

PROBLEM 19. If $f(x) = 3^{\pi x}$, then $f'(x) =$

The derivative of an expression of the form a^u, where u is a function of x, is:

$$\frac{d}{dx}a^u = a^u (\ln a)\frac{du}{dx}$$

Here, we get:

$$\frac{d}{dx}3^{\pi x} = 3^{\pi x}(\ln 3)\pi$$

The answer is (E).

PROBLEM 20. The average value of $f(x) = \dfrac{1}{x}$ from $x = 1$ to $x = e$ is

In order to find the average value, we use the Mean Value Theorem for integrals, which says that the average value of $f(x)$ on the interval $[a,b]$ is $\dfrac{1}{b-a}\displaystyle\int_a^b f(x)\,dx$.

Here, we have $\dfrac{1}{e-1}\displaystyle\int_1^e \dfrac{1}{x}\,dx$.

Evaluating the integral, we get: $\ln x\big|_1^e = \ln e - \ln 1 = 1$. Therefore, the answer is $\dfrac{1}{e-1}$.

The answer is (E).

PROBLEM 21. If $f(x) = \sin^2 x$, find $f'''(x)$.

We just use the Chain Rule three times:

$$f'(x) = 2\sin x \cos x = \sin 2x$$

$$f''(x) = 2\cos 2x$$

$$f'''(x) = -4\sin 2x$$

The answer is (D).

PROBLEM 22. Find the slope of the normal line to $y = x + \cos xy$ at $(0,1)$.

First, we need to find $\dfrac{dy}{dx}$ using implicit differentiation:

$$\frac{dy}{dx} = 1 - \left(x\frac{dy}{dx} + y\right)\sin xy$$

Rather than simplifying this, simply plug in $(0,1)$ to find $\dfrac{dy}{dx}$.

We get: $\dfrac{dy}{dx} = 1$.

This means that the slope of the tangent line at $(0, 1)$ is 1, so the slope of the normal line at $(0, 1)$ is the negative reciprocal, which is –1.

The answer is (B).

PROBLEM 23. $\displaystyle\int e^x\left(e^{3x}\right)dx =$

First, add the exponents to get: $\displaystyle\int e^{4x}\,dx$

Evaluating the integral, we get: $\dfrac{1}{4}e^{4x} + C$

The answer is (B).

PROBLEM 24. $\displaystyle\lim_{x\to 0}\dfrac{\tan^3(2x)}{x^3} =$

We will need to use the fact that $\displaystyle\lim_{x\to 0}\dfrac{\sin x}{x} = 1$ to find the limit.

First, rewrite the limit as:

$$\lim_{x\to 0}\dfrac{\sin^3(2x)}{x^3\cos^3(2x)}$$

Next, break the fraction into:

$$\lim_{x\to 0}\left(\dfrac{\sin^3(2x)}{x^3}\dfrac{1}{\cos^3(2x)}\right)$$

Now, if we multiply the top and bottom of the first fraction by 8, we get:

$$\lim_{x\to 0}\dfrac{8\sin^3(2x)}{(2x)^3}\dfrac{1}{\cos^3(2x)}$$

Now, we can take the limit, which gives us: 8(1)(1) = 8

The answer is (D).

PROBLEM 25. A solid is generated when the region in the first quadrant bounded by the graph of $y = 1 + \sin^2 x$, the line $x = \dfrac{\pi}{2}$, the x-axis, and the y-axis is revolved about the x-axis. Its volume is found by evaluating which of the following integrals?

First, let's graph the curve:

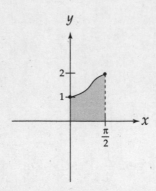

We can find the volume by taking a vertical slice of the region. The formula for the volume of a solid of revolution around the x-axis, using a vertical slice bounded from above by the curve $f(x)$ and from below by $g(x)$, on the interval $[a, b]$ is:

$$\pi \int_a^b \left[f(x)^2 - g(x)^2 \right] dx$$

Here, we get:

$$\pi \int_0^{\frac{\pi}{2}} \left(1 + \sin^2 x \right)^2 dx$$

The answer is (D).

PROBLEM 26. If $y = \left(\dfrac{x^3 - 2}{2x^5 - 1} \right)^4$, find $\dfrac{dy}{dx}$ at $x = 1$.

We use the Chain Rule and the Quotient Rule:

$$\frac{dy}{dx} = 4 \left(\frac{x^3 - 2}{2x^5 - 1} \right)^3 \left[\frac{\left(2x^5 - 1 \right)\left(3x^2 \right) - \left(x^3 - 2 \right)\left(10x^4 \right)}{\left(2x^5 - 1 \right)^2} \right]$$

If we plug in 1 for x, we get:

$$\frac{dy}{dx} = 4(-1)^3 \left[\frac{3 + 10}{1^2} \right] = -52$$

The answer is (A).

PROBLEM 27. $\int x\sqrt{5-x}\,dx =$

We can evaluate this integral using u-substitution.

Let $u = 5-x$ and $5-u = x$. Then $-du = dx$.

Substituting, we get:

$$-\int (5-u)u^{\frac{1}{2}}\,du$$

The integral can be rewritten as:

$$-\int\left(5u^{\frac{1}{2}} - u^{\frac{3}{2}}\right)du$$

Evaluating the integral, we get:

$$-5\frac{u^{\frac{3}{2}}}{\frac{3}{2}} + \frac{u^{\frac{5}{2}}}{\frac{5}{2}} + C$$

This can be simplified to:

$$-\frac{10}{3}u^{\frac{3}{2}} + \frac{2}{5}u^{\frac{5}{2}} + C$$

Finally, substituting back, we get:

$$-\frac{10}{3}(5-x)^{\frac{3}{2}} + \frac{2}{5}(5-x)^{\frac{5}{2}} + C$$

The answer is (E).

PROBLEM 28. If $\dfrac{dy}{dx} = \dfrac{x^3+1}{y}$ and $y = 2$ when $x = 1$, then, when $x = 2$, $y =$

This is a differential equation that can be solved using separation of variables. Put all of the terms containing y on the left and all of the terms containing x on the right. We get:

$$y\,dy = \left(x^3 + 1\right)dx$$

Next, we integrate both sides:

$$\int y\,dy = \int\left(x^3 + 1\right)dx$$

Evaluating the integrals, we get:

$$\frac{y^2}{2} = \frac{x^4}{4} + x + C$$

Next, we plug in $y = 2$ and $x = 1$ to solve for C. We get: $2 = \frac{1}{4} + 1 + C$ and so $C = \frac{3}{4}$. This gives us:

$$\frac{y^2}{2} = \frac{x^4}{4} + x + \frac{3}{4}$$

Now, if we substitute $x = 2$, we get:

$$\frac{y^2}{2} = 4 + 2 + \frac{3}{4} = \frac{27}{4}$$

Solving for y, we get:

$$y = \pm \sqrt{\frac{27}{2}}$$

The answer is (E).

PROBLEM 29. The graph of $y = 5x^4 - x^5$ has an inflection point (or points) at

In order to find the inflection point(s) of a polynomial, we need to find the values of x where its second derivative is zero.

First, we find the second derivative:

$$\frac{dy}{dx} = 20x^3 - 5x^4$$

$$\frac{d^2y}{dx^2} = 60x^2 - 20x^3$$

Now, let's set the second derivative equal to zero and solve for x:

$$60x^2 - 20x^3 = 0$$

$$20x^2(3 - x) = 0$$

$$x = 3$$

This is the point of inflection. $x = 0$ is not a point of inflection because $\frac{d^2y}{dx^2}$ does not change sign there. If you are unsure that these are correct, graph the second derivative with a calculator and look at the picture.

The answer is (B).

PROBLEM 30. The average value of $f(x) = e^{4x^2}$ on the interval $\left[-\dfrac{1}{4}, \dfrac{1}{4}\right]$ is

In order to find the average value, we use the Mean Value Theorem for Integrals, which says that the average value of $f(x)$ on the interval $[a,b]$ is $\dfrac{1}{b-a}\displaystyle\int_a^b f(x)\,dx$.

Here, we have:

$$\frac{1}{\dfrac{1}{4}+\dfrac{1}{4}}\int_{-\frac{1}{4}}^{\frac{1}{4}} e^{4x^2}\,dx = 2\int_{-\frac{1}{4}}^{\frac{1}{4}} e^{4x^2}\,dx$$

You can't evaluate this integral using any of the techniques that you have studied so far, so use the calculator to evaluate the integral numerically.

Remember this: Any integral on the AP exam that contains an e^{x^2} term that is not multiplied by x, must be integrated using the calculator.

You should get approximately 1.090. **The AP exam always expects you to round to three decimal places.**

The answer is (C).

PROBLEM 31. $\displaystyle\int_0^1 \tan x\,dx =$

First, rewrite the integral as $\displaystyle\int_0^1 \frac{\sin x}{\cos x}\,dx$.

Now, we can use u-substitution to evaluate the integral. Let $u = \cos x$. Then $du = -\sin x$. We can also change the limits of integration. The lower limit becomes $\cos 0 = 1$ and the upper limit becomes $\cos 1$, which we leave alone. Now we perform the substitution and we get:

$$-\int_1^{\cos 1} \frac{du}{u}$$

Evaluating the integral, we get: $-\ln u\Big|_1^{\cos 1} = -\ln(\cos 1) + \ln 1 = -\ln(\cos 1)$. This log is also equal to $\ln(\sec 1)$.

The answer is (D).

PROBLEM 32. $\dfrac{d}{dx}\displaystyle\int_0^{x^2} \sin^2 t\; dt =$

The Second Fundamental Theorem of calculus tells us how to find the derivative of an integral. It says that $\dfrac{d}{dx}\displaystyle\int_c^u f(t)\, dt = f(u)\dfrac{du}{dx}$, where c is a constant and u is a function of x.

Here we can use the theorem to get:

$$\frac{d}{dx}\int_0^{x^2} \sin^2 t\; dt = \left(\sin^2\left(x^2\right)\right)(2x) \text{ or } 2x\sin^2\left(x^2\right)$$

The answer is (B).

PROBLEM 33. Find the value(s) of $\dfrac{dy}{dx}$ of $x^2y + y^2 = 5$ at $y = 1$.

Here, we use implicit differentiation to find $\dfrac{dy}{dx}$:

$$2xy + x^2\frac{dy}{dx} + 2y\frac{dy}{dx} = 0$$

Now we plug $y = 1$ into the original equation to find its corresponding x values:

$$x^2 + 1 = 5$$

$$x^2 = 4$$

$$x = \pm 2$$

Now plug in the x and y values to find the value of $\dfrac{dy}{dx}$.

For $y = 1$ and $x = 2$, we get:

$$2(2)(1) + (2)^2\frac{dy}{dx} + 2(1)\frac{dy}{dx} = 0$$

Solving for $\dfrac{dy}{dx}$, we get:

$$4 + 6\frac{dy}{dx} = 0 \text{ and } \frac{dy}{dx} = -\frac{2}{3}$$

For $y = 1$ and $x = -2$, we get:

$$2(-2)(1) + (-2)^2\frac{dy}{dx} + 2(1)\frac{dy}{dx} = 0$$

Solving for $\dfrac{dy}{dx}$, we get:

$$-4 + 6\dfrac{dy}{dx} = 0 \text{ and } \dfrac{dy}{dx} = \dfrac{2}{3}$$

The answer is (D).

PROBLEM 34. The graph of $y = x^3 - 2x^2 - 5x + 2$ has a local maximum at

First, let's find $\dfrac{dy}{dx}$:

$$\dfrac{dy}{dx} = 3x^2 - 4x - 5$$

Next, set the derivative equal to zero and solve for x:

$$3x^2 - 4x - 5 = 0$$

Using the quadratic formula (or your calculator), we get:

$$x = \dfrac{4 \pm \sqrt{16 + 60}}{6} \approx 2.120, -0.786$$

Let's use the second derivative test to determine which is the maximum. We take the second derivative and then plug in the critical values that we found when we set the first derivative equal to zero. **If the sign of the second derivative at a critical value is positive, then the curve has a local minimum there. If the sign of the second derivative is negative, then the curve has a local maximum there.**

The second derivative is: $\dfrac{d^2y}{dx^2} = 6x - 4$. This is negative at $x = -0.786$, so the curve has a local maximum there. Now we plug $x = -0.786$ into the original equation to find the y-coordinate of the maximum. We get approximately 4.209. Therefore, the curve has a local maximum at $(-0.786, 4.209)$.

The answer is (D).

PROBLEM 35. Approximate $\displaystyle\int_0^1 \sin^2 x \, dx$ using the Trapezoid Rule with $n = 4$, to three decimal places.

The Trapezoid Rule enables us to approximate the area under a curve with a fair degree of accuracy. The rule says that the area between the x-axis and the curve $y = f(x)$, on the interval $[a, b]$, with n trapezoids, is:

$$\dfrac{1}{2}\dfrac{b-a}{n}\left[y_0 + 2y_1 + 2y_2 + 2y_3 + \ldots + 2y_{n-1} + y_n\right]$$

Using the rule here, with $n = 4$, $a = 0$, and $b = 1$, we get:

$$\frac{1}{2}\left(\frac{1}{4}\right)\left[\sin^2 0 + 2\sin^2\frac{1}{4} + 2\sin^2\frac{1}{2} + 2\sin^2\frac{3}{4} + \sin^2 1\right]$$

This is approximately 0.277.

The answer is (A).

PROBLEM 36. The volume generated by revolving about the *x*-axis the region above the curve $y = x^3$, below the line $y = 1$, and between $x=0$ and $x=1$ is

First, make a quick sketch of the region:

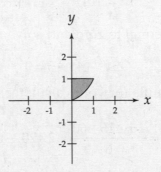

We can find the volume by taking a vertical slice of the region. The formula for the volume of a solid of revolution around the *x*-axis, using a vertical slice bounded from above by the curve $f(x)$ and from below by $g(x)$, on the interval $[a,b]$, is:

$$\pi\int_a^b\left[f(x)^2 - g(x)^2\right]dx$$

Here, we get:

$$\pi\int_0^1\left[(1)^2 - (x^3)^2\right]dx$$

Now we have to evaluate the integral. First, expand the integrand to get:

$$\pi\int_0^1(1 - x^6)dx$$

Next, integrate to get:

$$\pi\left(x - \frac{x^7}{7}\right)\bigg|_0^1 = \pi\left(1 - \frac{1}{7}\right) = \frac{6\pi}{7}$$

The answer is (E).

PROBLEM 37. A 20 foot ladder slides down a wall at 5 ft/sec. At what speed is the bottom sliding out when the top is 10 feet from the floor (in ft/sec)?

First, let's make a sketch of the situation:

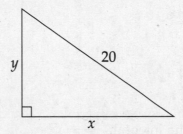

We are given that $\dfrac{dy}{dt} = -5$ (it's negative because the ladder is sliding down and its customary to make the upward direction positive), and we want to find $\dfrac{dx}{dt}$ when $y = 10$.

We can find a relationship between x and y using the Pythagorean Theorem. We get: $x^2 + y^2 = 400$.

Now, taking the derivative with respect to t, we get:

$$2x\frac{dx}{dt} + 2y\frac{dy}{dt} = 0, \text{ which can be simplified to } x\frac{dx}{dt} = -y\frac{dy}{dt}$$

Next, we need to find x when $y = 10$.

Using the Pythagorean Theorem:

$$x^2 + 10^2 = 400, \text{ so } x = \sqrt{300} \approx 17.321$$

Now, plug into the equation above to get:

$$17.321\frac{dx}{dt} = -10(-5) \text{ and } \frac{dx}{dt} \approx 2.887$$

The answer is (B).

PROBLEM 38. $\int \dfrac{\ln x}{3x}\, dx =$

We can evaluate the integral with u-substitution.

Let $u = \ln x$. Then $du = \dfrac{dx}{x}$.

Substituting, we get: $\dfrac{1}{3}\displaystyle\int u\, du$

Now, we can evaluate the integral: $\dfrac{1}{3}\dfrac{u^2}{2} + C$

Substituting back, we get: $\dfrac{\ln^2|x|}{6} + C$

The answer is (D).

PROBLEM 39. Find two nonnegative numbers x and y whose sum is 100 and for which $x^2 y$ is a maximum.

Let's set $P = x^2 y$. We want to maximize P, so we need to eliminate one of the variables. We are also given that $x + y = 100$, so we can solve this for y and substitute. $y = 100 - x$, so $P = x^2(100 - x) = 100x^2 - x^3$.

Now we can take the derivative.

$$\frac{dP}{dx} = 200x - 3x^2$$

Set the derivative equal to zero and solve for x:

$$200x - 3x^2 = 0$$

$$x(200 - 3x) = 0$$

$$x = 0 \text{ or } x = \frac{200}{3} \approx 66.667$$

Now we can use the second derivative to find the maximum. $\dfrac{d^2P}{dx^2} = 200 - 6x$.

If we plug in $x = 66.667$, the second derivative is negative, so P is a maximum at $x = 66.667$. Solving for y, we get $y \approx 33.333$.

The answer is (E).

PROBLEM 40. Find the distance traveled (to three decimal places) from $t = 1$ to $t = 5$ seconds, for a particle whose velocity is given by $v(t) = t + \ln t$.

The function $t + \ln t$ is always positive on the interval, so we can find the distance traveled by evaluating the integral:

$$\int_1^5 (t + \ln t)\, dt$$

We can evaluate the integral numerically using the calculator.

You should get approximately 16.047. **The AP exam always expects you to round to three decimal places.**

The answer is (C).

PROBLEM 41. $\int \sin^5(2x)\cos(2x)\, dx =$

We can evaluate this integral using u-substitution.

Let $u = \sin(2x)$. Then $du = 2\cos(2x)dx$, which we can rewrite as $\frac{1}{2}du = \cos(2x)dx$.

Substituting into the integrand, we get:

$$\frac{1}{2}\int u^5 du$$

Evaluating the integral gives us:

$$\frac{1}{2}\frac{u^6}{6} + C = \frac{u^6}{12} + C$$

Substituting back, we get:

$$\frac{\sin^6(2x)}{12} + C$$

The answer is (A).

PROBLEM 42. The volume of a cube is increasing at a rate proportional to its volume at any time t. If the volume is 8 ft³ originally, and 12 ft³ after 5 seconds, what is its volume at $t = 12$ seconds?

When we see a phrase where something is increasing at a rate "proportional to itself at any time t," this means that we set up the differential equation:

$$\frac{dV}{dt} = kV$$

(or whatever the appropriate variable is)

We solve this differential equation using separation of variables.

First, move the V to the left side and the dt to the right side, to get:

$$\frac{dV}{V} = k\,dt$$

Now, integrate both sides:

$$\int \frac{dV}{V} = k \int dt$$

$$\ln V = kt + C$$

Next, it's traditional to put the equation in terms of V. We do this by exponentiating both sides to the base e. We get:

$$V = e^{kt+C}$$

Using the rules of exponents, we can rewrite this as:

$$V = e^{kt} e^{C}$$

Finally, because e^C is a constant, we can rewrite the equation as:

$$V = Ce^{kt}$$

Now, we use the initial condition that $V = 8$ at time $t = 0$ to solve for C:

$$8 = Ce^0 = C(1) = C$$

This gives us:

$$V = 8e^{kt}$$

Next, we use the condition that $V = 12$ at time $t = 5$ to solve for k:

$$12 = 8e^{5k}$$

$$\frac{3}{2} = e^{5k}$$

$$\ln \frac{3}{2} = 5k$$

$$k = \frac{1}{5}\ln\frac{3}{2}$$

This gives us:

$$V = 8e^{\left(\frac{1}{5}\ln\frac{3}{2}\right)t}$$

Finally, we plug in $t = 12$ and solve for V:

$$V = 8e^{\left(\frac{1}{5}\ln\frac{3}{2}\right)(12)} \approx 21.169$$

The answer is (A).

PROBLEM 43. If $f(x) = \left(1 + \dfrac{x}{20}\right)^5$, find $f''(40)$.

The first derivative is:

$$f'(x) = 5\left(1 + \frac{x}{20}\right)^4 \left(\frac{1}{20}\right) = \frac{1}{4}\left(1 + \frac{x}{20}\right)^4$$

The second derivative is:

$$f''(x) = \frac{1}{4}(4)\left(1 + \frac{x}{20}\right)^3 \left(\frac{1}{20}\right) = \frac{1}{20}\left(1 + \frac{x}{20}\right)^3$$

Evaluating this at $x = 40$, we get:

$$f''(x) = \frac{1}{20}\left(1 + \frac{40}{20}\right)^3 = \frac{27}{20} = 1.350$$

The answer is (B).

PROBLEM 44. A particle's height at a time $t \geq 0$ is given by $h(t) = 100t - 16t^2$. What is its maximum height?

First, let's take the derivative: $h'(t) = 100 - 32t$

Now, we set it equal to zero and solve for t: $100 - 32t = 0$

$$t = \frac{100}{32}$$

Now, to solve for the maximum height, we simply plug $t = \dfrac{100}{32}$ back into the original equation for height:

$$h\left(\frac{100}{32}\right) = 100\left(\frac{100}{32}\right) - 16\left(\frac{100}{32}\right)^2 = 156.250$$

By the way, we know that this is a maximum not a minimum because the second derivative is -32, which means that the critical value will give us a maximum not a minimum.

The answer is (B).

PROBLEM 45. If $f(x)$ is continuous and differentiable and $f(x) = \begin{cases} ax^4 + 5x; x \le 2 \\ bx^2 - 3x; x > 2 \end{cases}$ then $b =$

In order to solve this for b, we need $f(x)$ to be continuous at $x = 2$.

If we plug $x = 2$ into both pieces of this piecewise function, we get:

$$f(x) = \begin{cases} 16a + 10; x \le 2 \\ 4b - 6; x > 2 \end{cases}$$

So, we need $16a + 10 = 4b - 6$.

Now, if we take the derivative of both pieces of this function and plug in $x = 2$ we get:

$$f'(x) = \begin{cases} 32a + 5; x \le 2 \\ 4b - 3; \ x > 2 \end{cases}, \text{ so we need } 32a + 5 = 4b - 3$$

Solving the simultaneous equations, we get $a = \dfrac{1}{2}$ and $b = 6$.

The answer is (D).

ANSWERS AND EXPLANATIONS TO SECTION II

PROBLEM 1. Consider the curve defined by $y = x^4 + 4x^3$.

(a) If we want to find the equation of the tangent line, first we need to find the y-coordinate that corresponds to $x = -1$.

It is:

$$y = (-1)^4 + 4(-1)^3 = 1 - 4 = -3$$

Next, we need to find the derivative of the curve at $x = -1$.

It is $\dfrac{dy}{dx} = 4x^3 + 12x^2$ and, at $x = -1$, $\dfrac{dy}{dx}\Big|_{x=-1} = 4(-1)^3 + 12(-1)^2 = 8$.

Now we have the slope of the tangent line and a point that it goes through. We can use the point-slope formula for the equation of a line, $(y - y_1) = m(x - x_1)$, and plug in what we have just found.

We get:

$$(y + 3) = 8(x + 1), \text{ which can be rewritten as } y = 8x + 5$$

(b) First, we set the derivative equal to zero and solve for x:

$$\frac{dy}{dx} = 4x^3 + 12x^2 = 0$$

$$4x^2(x + 3) = 0$$

$$x = 0 \text{ or } x = -3$$

Now, we can use the second derivative test to determine whether a critical value is the x-coordinate of a minimum or a maximum. The second derivative test is the following:

If c is a critical point, then:

c is the x-coordinate of a maximum if $f''(c) < 0$, and

c is the x-coordinate of a minimum if $f''(c) > 0$.

By the way, **c is the x-coordinate of a point of inflection if $f''(c) = 0$, and the second derivative changes sign at that point.**

So now we need to find the second derivative:

$$\frac{d^2y}{dx^2} = 12x^2 + 24x$$

If we plug in $x = -3$, we get:

$$\frac{d^2y}{dx^2} = 12(-3)^2 + 24(-3) = 36$$

So, the curve has a minimum at $x = -3$. Finally, to get the y-coordinate of the minimum, we plug $x = -3$ into the original equation and we get:

$$y = (-3)^4 + 4(-3)^3 = 81 - 108 = -27$$

Thus, the curve has an absolute minimum at $(-3, -27)$.

(c) In order to find points of inflection, we need to set the second derivative equal to zero. We have the second derivative from part (b) above.

$$12x^2 + 24x = 0$$
$$12x(x + 2) = 0$$
$$x = 0 \text{ or } x = -2$$

Next, we need to check if the second derivative changes sign at both of these points. We can do this by trying points on the number line in the different intervals created by these points. If we try a point to the left of $x = -2$, for example $x = -3$, and plug it into the second derivative, we get $\frac{d^2y}{dx^2} = 36$. If we then try a point between $x = 0$ and $x = -2$, for example $x = -1$, we get $\frac{d^2y}{dx^2} = -12$. Finally, if we try a point to the right of $x = 0$, for example $x = 1$, we get $\frac{d^2y}{dx^2} = 36$. The second derivative changes sign at both $x = 0$ and $x = -2$, so these are both the x-coordinates of points of inflection. To get the y-coordinates, simply plug $x = 0$ and $x = -2$ into the original equation: $y = x^4 + 4x^3$. We find that the points of inflection are $(0, 0)$ and $(-2, -16)$.

PROBLEM 2. The temperature on New Year's Day in Hinterland was given by $T(H) = -A - B\cos\left(\dfrac{\pi H}{12}\right)$, where T is the temperature in degrees Fahrenheit and H is the number of hours from midnight ($0 \le T < 24$).

(a) Simply plug in the temperature, -15, for T and the time, midnight ($T = 0$), for H into the equation. We get: $-15 = -A - B\cos 0$, which simplifies to $-15 = -A - B$.

Now plug the temperature, 5, for T and the time, noon ($H = 12$), for H into the equation. We get: $5 = -A - B\cos(\pi)$, which simplifies to $5 = -A + B$.

Now we can solve the pair of simultaneous equations for A and B, and we get $A = 5°F$ and $B = 10°F$.

(b) In order to find the average value, we use the Mean Value Theorem for integrals, which says that the average value of $f(x)$ on the interval $[a,b]$ is:

$$\frac{1}{b-a}\int_a^b f(x)\,dx$$

Here, we have: $\dfrac{1}{10-0}\displaystyle\int_0^{10}\left(-5 - 10\cos\left(\dfrac{\pi H}{12}\right)\right)dH$

Evaluating the integral, we get:

$$\frac{1}{10}\left[\left(-5H - \frac{120}{\pi}\sin\left(\frac{\pi H}{12}\right)\right)\right]\Bigg|_0^{10} = \frac{1}{10}\left[-50 - \frac{120}{\pi}\sin\left(\frac{5\pi}{6}\right)\right] = \frac{1}{10}\left(-50 - \frac{60}{\pi}\right) \approx -6.910°F$$

(c) The Trapezoid Rule enables us to approximate the area under a curve with a fair degree of accuracy. The rule says that the area between the x-axis and the curve $y = f(x)$, on the interval $[a, b]$, with n trapezoids, is:

$$\frac{1}{2}\frac{b-a}{n}\left[y_0 + 2y_1 + 2y_2 + 2y_3 + \ldots + 2y_{n-1} + y_n\right]$$

Using the rule here, with $n = 4$, $a = 6$, and $b = 8$, we get:

$$\frac{1}{2}\cdot\frac{1}{2}\left[\left(-5 - 10\cos\frac{6\pi}{12}\right) + 2\left(-5 - 10\cos\frac{13\pi}{24}\right) + 2\left(-5 - 10\cos\frac{7\pi}{12}\right) + 2\left(-5 - 10\cos\frac{15\pi}{24}\right) + \left(-5 - 10\cos\frac{8\pi}{12}\right)\right]$$

This is approximately $-4.890°F$.

(d) We simply take the derivative with respect to H:

$$\frac{dT}{dH} = -10\left(\frac{\pi}{12}\right)\left(-\sin\frac{\pi H}{12}\right) = \frac{5\pi}{6}\sin\frac{\pi H}{12}$$

PROBLEM 3. Sea grass grows on a lake. The rate of growth of the grass is $\dfrac{dG}{dt} = kG$, where k is a constant.

(a) We solve this differential equation using separation of variables.

First, move the G to the left side and the dt to the right side, to get: $\dfrac{dG}{G} = k\,dt$.

Now, integrate both sides:

$$\int \frac{dG}{G} = k \int dt$$
$$\ln G = kt + C$$

Next, solve for G by exponentiating both sides to the base e. We get: $G = e^{kt+C}$

Using the rules of exponents, we can rewrite this as: $G = e^{kt}e^C$. Finally, because e^C is a constant, we can rewrite the equation as: $G = Ce^{kt}$.

Now, we use the initial condition that $G = 100$ at time $t = 0$ to solve for C:

$$100 = Ce^0 = C(1) = C$$

This gives us $G = 100e^{kt}$.

Next, we use the condition that $G = 120$ at time $t = 1$ to solve for k:

$$120 = 100e^k$$

$$1.2 = e^k$$

$$\ln 1.2 = k \approx 0.1823$$

This gives us: $G = 100e^{0.1823t}$

(b) All we need to do is set G equal to 300 and solve for t:

$$300 = 100e^{0.1823t}$$

$$3 = e^{0.1823t}$$

$$\ln 3 = 0.1823t$$

$$t \approx 6.026 \text{ years}$$

(c) Now we have to account for the fish's consumption of the sea grass. So we have to evaluate the differential equation $\dfrac{dG}{dt} = kG - 80$.

First, separate the variables, to get:

$$\frac{dG}{kG - 80} = dt$$

Now, integrate both sides:

$$\int \frac{dG}{kG-80} = \int dt \text{ or } \int \frac{dG}{G-\frac{80}{k}} = k\int dt$$

$$\ln\left(G-\frac{80}{k}\right) = kt + C$$

Next, exponentiate both sides to the base e. We get:

$$G - \frac{80}{k} = Ce^{kt}$$

Solving for G, we get:

$$G = \left(G_0 - \frac{80}{k}\right)e^{kt} + \frac{80}{k}$$

Now, set $G = 0$. We get:

$$0 = \left(G_0 - \frac{80}{k}\right)e^{kt} + \frac{80}{k}$$

Now, set $G_0 = 300$ and solve for e^{kt}:

$$e^{kt} = \frac{\frac{-80}{k}}{300 - \frac{80}{k}} = \frac{80}{80 - 300k}$$

Take the log of both sides:

$$kt = \ln\left(\frac{80}{80 - 300k}\right)$$

and $t = \frac{1}{k}\ln\left(\frac{80}{80 - 300k}\right)$

Now, we plug in the value for k that we got in part (a) above and we get $t \approx 6.313$ years.

PROBLEM 4. Water is being poured into a hemispherical bowl of radius 6 inches at the rate of 4 in³/sec.

(a) First, rewrite the equation as:

$$V = \pi R h^2 - \frac{\pi}{3}h^3$$

Now take the derivative of the equation with respect to t:

$$\frac{dV}{dt} = 2\pi R h \frac{dh}{dt} - \pi h^2 \frac{dh}{dt}$$

If we plug in $\frac{dV}{dt} = 4$, $R = 6$, and $h = 2$, we get:

$$4 = 20\pi \frac{dh}{dt} \quad \text{or} \quad \frac{dh}{dt} = \frac{4}{20\pi} = \frac{1}{5\pi}$$

(b) Notice that we can construct a right triangle using the radius of the sphere and the radius of the surface of the water.

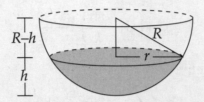

Notice that the distance from the center of the sphere to the surface of the water is $R - h$. Now, we can use the Pythagorean Theorem to find r:

$$R^2 = (R - h)^2 + r^2$$

We can rearrange this to get:

$$r = \sqrt{R^2 - (R - h)^2} = \sqrt{2Rh - h^2}$$

Because $R = 6$, we get:

$$r = \sqrt{12h - h^2}$$

(c) The area of the surface of the water is $A = \pi r^2$, where $r = \sqrt{12h - h^2}$. Thus, $A = \pi(12h - h^2)$.

Taking the derivative of the equation with respect to t, we get:

$$\frac{dA}{dt} = \pi\left(12\frac{dh}{dt} - 2h\frac{dh}{dt}\right)$$

We found in part (a) above that:

$$\frac{dh}{dt} = \frac{1}{5\pi}, \text{ so } \frac{dA}{dt} = \pi\left(\frac{12}{5\pi} - \frac{4}{5\pi}\right) = \frac{8}{5} \text{ in}^2/\text{sec}$$

PROBLEM 5. Let R be the region in the first quadrant bounded by $y^2 = x$ and $x^2 = y$.

(a) Find the area of region R.

First, let's sketch the region:

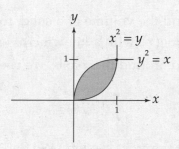

In order to find the area, we "slice" the region vertically and add up all of the slices. Now, we use the formula for the area of the region between $y = f(x)$ and $y = g(x)$, from $x = a$ to $x = b$:

$$\int_a^b [f(x) - g(x)]\, dx$$

We need to rewrite the equation $y^2 = x$ as $y = \sqrt{x}$ so that we can integrate with respect to x. Our integral for the area is:

$$\int_0^1 \left(\sqrt{x} - x^2\right) dx$$

Evaluating the integral, we get:

$$\left(\frac{2x^{\frac{3}{2}}}{3} - \frac{x^3}{3}\right)\Bigg|_0^1 = \frac{2}{3} - \frac{1}{3} = \frac{1}{3}$$

(b) In order to find the volume of a region between $y = f(x)$ and $y = g(x)$, from $x = a$ to $x = b$, when it is revolved around the x-axis, we use the formula:

$$\pi \int_a^b \left[f(x)^2 - g(x)^2\right] dx$$

Here, our integral for the area is:

$$\pi \int_0^1 \left(x - x^4\right) dx$$

Evaluating the integral, we get:

$$\pi\left(\frac{x^2}{2}-\frac{x^5}{5}\right)\bigg|_0^1 = \pi\left(\frac{1}{2}-\frac{1}{5}\right)=\frac{3\pi}{10}$$

(c) Whenever we want to find the volume of a solid, formed by the region between $y = f(x)$ and $y = g(x)$, with a known cross-section, from $x = a$ to $x = b$, when it is revolved around the x-axis, we use the formula:

$$\int_a^b A(x)\,dx$$

(Note: $A(x)$ is the area of the cross section.) We find the area of the cross-section by using the vertical slice formed by $f(x) - g(x)$, and then plugging it into the appropriate area formula. In the case of a circle, $f(x) - g(x)$ gives us the length of the diameter and we use the formula:

$$A(x) = \frac{\pi(diameter)^2}{4}$$

This gives us the integral:

$$\int_0^1 \frac{\pi}{4}\left(\sqrt{x}-x^2\right)^2 dx$$

Expand the integrand:

$$\int_0^1 \frac{\pi}{4}\left(\sqrt{x}-x^2\right)^2 dx = \frac{\pi}{4}\int_0^1\left(x-2x^{\frac{5}{2}}+x^4\right)dx$$

Evaluate the integral:

$$\frac{\pi}{4}\int_0^1\left(x-2x^{\frac{5}{2}}+x^4\right)dx = \frac{\pi}{4}\left(\frac{x^2}{2}-\frac{4x^{\frac{7}{2}}}{7}+\frac{x^5}{5}\right)\bigg|_0^1 = \frac{\pi}{4}\left(\frac{1}{2}-\frac{4}{7}+\frac{1}{5}\right)=\frac{9\pi}{280}$$

PROBLEM 6. An object moves with velocity $v(t) = t^2 - 8t + 7$.

(a) The velocity of an object is the derivative of its position with respect to time. Thus, if we want to find the position, we take the integral of velocity with respect to time:

$$s(t) = \int \left(t^2 - 8t + 7 \right) dt = \frac{t^3}{3} - \frac{8t^2}{2} + 7t + C = \frac{t^3}{3} - 4t^2 + 7t + C$$

(b) If we want to find when the particle is changing direction, we need to find where the velocity of the particle is zero:

$$v(t) = t^2 - 8t + 7 = (t - 1)(t - 7) = 0$$

Thus, at $t = 1$ or $t = 7$, the particle could be changing direction. To make sure, we need to check that the acceleration of the particle is <u>not</u> zero at those times. The acceleration of a particle is the derivative of the velocity with respect to time:

$$a(t) = 2t - 8$$

At $t = 1$:

$$a(1) = 2 - 8 = -6$$

It does not equal zero, so the particle is changing direction at $t = 1$.

At $t = 7$:

$$a(7) = 14 - 8 = 6$$

It does not equal zero, so the particle is changing direction at $t = 7$.

(c) If we want to find the total distance that a particle travels from time a to time b, we need to evaluate:

$$\int_a^b \left| v(t) \right| dt$$

This means that, over an interval where the particle's velocity is negative, we multiply the integral by -1. So, we need to find where the velocity is negative and where it is positive.

We know that the velocity is zero at $t = 1$ and at $t = 7$.

We can find that the velocity is positive when $t < 1$ and when $t > 7$, and that the velocity is negative when $1 < t < 7$.

Thus, the distance that the particle travels from $t = 0$ to $t = 4$ is:

$$\int_0^1 \left(t^2 - 8t + 7\right) dt - \int_1^4 \left(t^2 - 8t + 7\right) dt$$

Evaluating the integrals, we get:

$$\left(\frac{t^3}{3} - 4t^2 + 7t\right)\Bigg|_0^1 - \left(\frac{t^3}{3} - 4t^2 + 7t\right)\Bigg|_1^4 = \left(\frac{10}{3} - 0\right) - \left(-\frac{44}{3} - \frac{10}{3}\right) = \frac{64}{3}$$

26

The Princeton Review
AP Calculus AB
Practice Test 3

CALCULUS AB

SECTION I, Part A

Time—55 Minutes

Number of questions—28

A CALCULATOR MAY NOT BE USED ON THIS PART OF THE EXAMINATION

Directions: Solve each of the following problems, using the available space for scratchwork. After examining the form of the choices, decide which is the best of the choices given and fill in the corresponding oval on the answer sheet. No credit will be given for anything written in the test book. Do not spend too much time on any one problem.

In this test: Unless otherwise specified, the domain of a function f is assumed to be the set of all real numbers x for which $f(x)$ is a real number.

1. $\displaystyle\int_{\frac{\pi}{4}}^{x} \cos(2t)\, dt =$

   (A) $\cos(2x)$　　(B) $\dfrac{\sin(2x)-1}{2}$　　(C) $\cos(2x)-1$　　(D) $\sin(2x)$　　(E) $\dfrac{\sin(2x)}{2}$

2. What are the coordinates of the point of inflection on the graph of $y = x^3 - 15x^2 + 33x + 100$?

   (A) $(9, 0)$　　(B) $(5, -48)$　　(C) $(1, 119)$　　(D) $(9, -89)$　　(E) $(5, 15)$

GO ON TO THE NEXT PAGE

3. If $3x^2 - 2xy + 3y = 1$, then when $x = 2$, $\dfrac{dy}{dx} =$

(A) -12 (B) -10 (C) $-\dfrac{10}{7}$ (D) 12 (E) 32

---

4. $\displaystyle\int_{1}^{3} \frac{8}{x^3}\, dx =$

(A) $\dfrac{32}{9}$ (B) $\dfrac{40}{9}$ (C) 0 (D) $-\dfrac{40}{9}$ (E) $-\dfrac{32}{9}$

5.

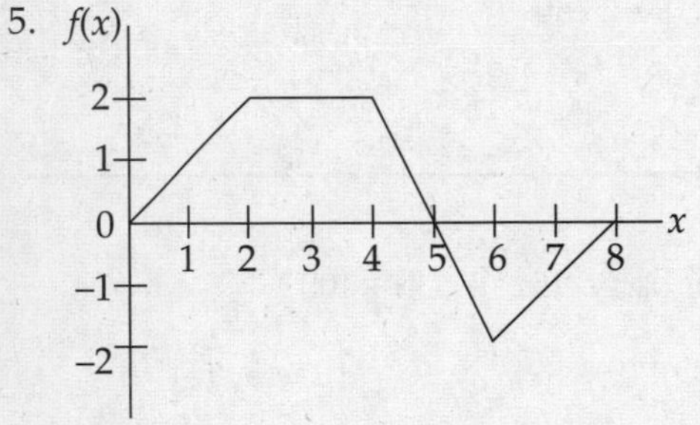

The graph of a piecewise linear function f, for $0 \le x \le 8$, is shown above. What is the value of $\displaystyle\int_{0}^{8} f(x)\, dx$?

(A) 1 (B) 4 (C) 8 (D) 10 (E) 13

GO ON TO THE NEXT PAGE

6. If f is continuous for $a \le x \le b$, then at any point $x = c$, where $a < c < b$, which of the following must be true?

(A) $f(c) = \dfrac{f(b) - f(a)}{b - a}$

(B) $f(a) = f(b)$

(C) $f(c) = 0$

(D) $\displaystyle\int_a^b f(x)\, dx = f(c)$.

(E) $\displaystyle\lim_{x \to c} f(x) = f(c)$

7. If $f(x) = x^2\sqrt{3x + 1}$, then $f'(x) =$

(A) $\dfrac{-3x^2 - 2x}{\sqrt{3x + 1}}$

(B) $\dfrac{9x^2 + 2x}{\sqrt{3x + 1}}$

(C) $\dfrac{-9x^2 + 4x}{2\sqrt{3x + 1}}$

(D) $\dfrac{15x^2 + 4x}{2\sqrt{3x + 1}}$

(E) $\dfrac{-9x^2 - 4x}{2\sqrt{3x + 1}}$

GO ON TO THE NEXT PAGE

8. What is the instantaneous rate of change at $t = -1$ of the function f, if $f(t) = \dfrac{t^3 + t}{4t + 1}$?

(A) $\dfrac{12}{9}$ (B) $\dfrac{4}{9}$ (C) $-\dfrac{20}{9}$ (D) $-\dfrac{4}{9}$ (E) $-\dfrac{12}{9}$

9. $\displaystyle\int_{2}^{e+1}\left(\dfrac{4}{x-1}\right)dx =$

(A) 4   (B) $4e$ (C) 0   (D) $-4e$ (E) -4

GO ON TO THE NEXT PAGE

10.

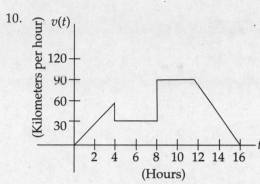

A car's velocity is shown on the graph above. Which of the following gives the total distance traveled from $t = 0$ to $t = 16$ (in kilometers)?

(A) 360 (B) 390 (C) 780 (D) 1000 (E) 1360

11. $\dfrac{d}{dx}\tan^2(4x) =$

(A) $8\tan(4x)$

(B) $4\sec^4(4x)$

(C) $8\tan(4x)\sec^2(4x)$

(D) $4\tan(4x)\sec^2(4x)$

(E) $8\sec^4(4x)$

GO ON TO THE NEXT PAGE

12. What is the equation of the line tangent to the graph of $y = \sin^2 x$ at $x = \dfrac{\pi}{4}$?

(A) $y - \dfrac{1}{2} = -\left(x - \dfrac{\pi}{4} \right)$

(B) $y - \dfrac{1}{2} = \left(x - \dfrac{\pi}{4} \right)$

(C) $y - \dfrac{1}{\sqrt{2}} = \left(x - \dfrac{\pi}{4} \right)$

(D) $y - \dfrac{1}{\sqrt{2}} = \dfrac{1}{2}\left(x - \dfrac{\pi}{4} \right)$

(E) $y - \dfrac{1}{2} = \dfrac{1}{2}\left(x - \dfrac{\pi}{4} \right)$

---

13. If the function $f(x) = \begin{cases} 3ax^2 + 2bx + 1; & x \le 1 \\ ax^4 - 4bx^2 - 3x; & x > 1 \end{cases}$ is differentiable for all real values of x, then $b =$

(A) $-\dfrac{11}{4}$ (B) $\dfrac{1}{4}$ (C) $-\dfrac{7}{16}$ (D) 0   (E) $-\dfrac{1}{4}$

GO ON TO THE NEXT PAGE

14. The graph of $y = x^4 + 8x^3 - 72x^2 + 4$ is concave down for

(A) $-6 < x < 2$

(B) $x > 2$

(C) $x < -6$

(D) $x < -3 - 3\sqrt{5}$ or $x > -3 + 3\sqrt{5}$

(E) $-3 - 3\sqrt{5} < x < -3 + 3\sqrt{5}$

---

15. If $f(x) = \dfrac{x^2 + 5x - 24}{x^2 + 10x + 16}$, then $\lim\limits_{x \to -8} f(x)$ is

(A) 0   (B) 1   (C) $-\dfrac{3}{2}$ (D) $\dfrac{11}{6}$ (E) Nonexistent

---

GO ON TO THE NEXT PAGE

16.

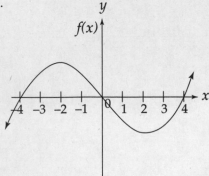

The graph of $f(x)$ is shown in the figure above. Which of the following could be the graph of $f'(x)$?

(A)

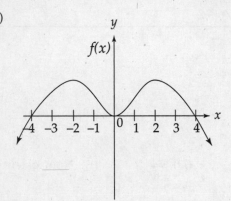

(D)

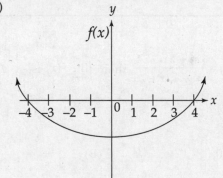

(B)

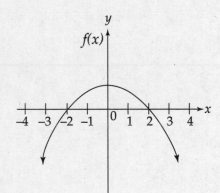

(E)

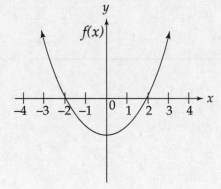

(C)

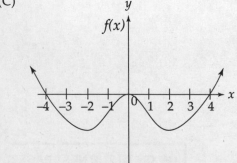

GO ON TO THE NEXT PAGE

17. If $f(x) = \ln(\cos(3x))$, then $f'(x) =$

(A) $-3\csc(3x)$

(B) $3\sec(3x)$

(C) $3\tan(3x)$

(D) $-3\tan(3x)$

(E) $-3\cot(3x)$

---

18. If $f(x) = \int\limits_{0}^{x+1} \sqrt[3]{t^2 - 1}\, dt$, then $f'(-4) =$

(A) $\sqrt[3]{-9}$　　　(B) -2　　　(C) 2　　　(D) $\sqrt[3]{15}$　　　(E) 0

---

19. A particle moves along the x-axis so that its position at time t, in seconds, is given by $x(t) = t^2 - 7t + 6$. For what value(s) of t is the velocity of the particle zero?

(A) 1　　　(B) 6　　　(C) 1 or 6　　　(D) 3.5　　　(E) 1 or 3.5 or 6

GO ON TO THE NEXT PAGE

20. $\int\limits_{0}^{\frac{\pi}{2}} \sin(2x)e^{\sin^2 x}\,dx =$

(A) e (B) $e - 1$ (C) $1 - e$ (D) $e + 1$ (E) 1

---

21. The average value of $\sec^2 x$ on the interval $\left[\dfrac{\pi}{6}, \dfrac{\pi}{4}\right]$ is

(A) $\dfrac{8}{\pi}$

(B) $\dfrac{12\sqrt{3} - 12}{\pi}$

(C) $\dfrac{12 - 4\sqrt{3}}{\pi}$

(D) $\dfrac{6\sqrt{2} - 6}{\pi}$

(E) $\dfrac{6 - 6\sqrt{2}}{\pi}$

GO ON TO THE NEXT PAGE

22. Find the area of the region bounded by the parabolas $y = x^2$ and $y = 6x - x^2$.

(A) 9   (B) 27   (C) 6   (D) –9   (E) –18

---

23. The function f is given by $f(x) = x^4 + 4x^3$. On which of the following intervals is f decreasing?

(A) $(-3, 0)$ (B) $(0, \infty)$ (C) $(-3, \infty)$ (D) $(-\infty, -3)$ (E) $(-\infty, 0)$

---

24. $\lim\limits_{x \to 0} \dfrac{\tan(3x) + 3x}{\sin(5x)} =$

(A) 0   (B) $\dfrac{3}{5}$ (C) 1   (D) $\dfrac{6}{5}$ (E) Nonexistent

GO ON TO THE NEXT PAGE

25. If the region enclosed by the y-axis, the curve $y = 4\sqrt{x}$, and the line $y = 8$ is revolved about the x-axis, the volume of the solid generated is

(A) $\dfrac{32\pi}{3}$

(B) 128π

(C) $\dfrac{128}{3}$

(D) 128

(E) $\dfrac{128\pi}{3}$

---

26. The maximum velocity attained on the interval $0 \le t \le 5$ by the particle whose displacement is given by $s(t) = 2t^3 - 12t^2 + 16t + 2$ is

(A) 286

(B) 46

(C) 16

(D) 0

(E) -8

---

27. The value of c that satisfies the Mean Value Theorem for derivatives on the interval $[0,5]$ for the function $f(x) = x^3 - 6x$ is

(A) $-\dfrac{5}{\sqrt{3}}$

(B) 0

(C) 1

(D) $\dfrac{5}{3}$

(E) $\dfrac{5}{\sqrt{3}}$

GO ON TO THE NEXT PAGE

28. If $f(x) = \sec(4x)$, then $f'\left(\dfrac{\pi}{16}\right)$ is

(A) $4\sqrt{2}$ (B) $\sqrt{2}$ (C) 0 (D) $\dfrac{1}{\sqrt{2}}$ (E) $\dfrac{4}{\sqrt{2}}$

STOP

END OF PART A SECTION I

IF YOU FINISH BEFORE TIME IS CALLED, YOU MAY CHECK YOUR WORK ON PART A ONLY.

DO NOT GO ON TO PART B UNTIL YOU ARE TOLD TO DO SO.

CALCULUS AB

SECTION I, Part B

Time—50 Minutes

Number of questions—17

A GRAPHING CALCULATOR IS REQUIRED FOR SOME QUESTIONS ON THIS PART OF THE EXAMINATION

Directions: Solve each of the following problems, using the available space for scratchwork. After examining the form of the choices, decide which is the best of the choices given and fill in the corresponding oval on the answer sheet. No credit will be given for anything written in the test book. Do not spend too much time on any one problem.

In this test:

1. The **exact** numerical value of the correct answer does not always appear among the choices given. When this happens, select from among the choices the number that best approximates the exact numerical value.

2. Unless otherwise specified, the domain of a function f is assumed to be the set of all real numbers x for which $f(x)$ is a real number.

29. If $f(x)$ is the function given by $f(x) = e^{3x} + 1$, at what value of x is the slope of the tangent line to $f(x)$ equal to 2?

(A) −.135   (B) 0   (C) .231   (D) −.366   (E) .693

30. The graph of the function $y = x^3 + 12x^2 + 15x + 3$ has a relative maximum at $x =$

(A) −10.613   (B) −.248   (C) −7.317   (D) −1.138   (E) −.683

GO ON TO THE NEXT PAGE

31. The side of a square is increasing at a constant rate of 0.4 cm/sec. In terms of the perimeter, P, what is the rate of change of the area of the square, in cm² / sec?

   (A) 0.05P (B) 0.2P (C) 0.4P (D) 6.4P (E) 51.2P

---

32. Let f be the function given by $f(x) = 3^x$. For what value of x is the slope of the line tangent to the curve at $(x, f(x))$ equal to 1?

   (A) 1.099   (B) .086   (C) 0   (D) –.086   (E) –1.099

---

33. Given f and g are differentiable functions and

$$f(a) = -4, \ g(a) = c, \ g(c) = 10, \ f(c) = 15$$

$$f'(a) = 8, \ g'(a) = b, \ g'(c) = 5, \ f'(c) = 6$$

If $h(x) = f(g(x))$, find $h'(a)$

   (A) 6b (B) 8b (C) –4b (D) 80   (E) 15b

GO ON TO THE NEXT PAGE

34. What is the area of the region in the first quadrant enclosed by the graph of $y = e^{\frac{-x^2}{4}}$ and the line $y = 0.5$?

   (A) 0.240   (B) 0.516   (C) 0.480   (D) 1.032   (E) 1.349

---

35. What is the trapezoidal approximation of $\int_0^3 e^x\, dx$ using $n = 4$ subintervals?

   (A) 6.407   (B) 13.565   (C) 19.972   (D) 27.879   (E) 34.944

---

36. The second derivative of a function f is given by $f''(x) = x\sin x - 2$. How many points of inflection does f have on the interval $(-10, 10)$?

   (A) Zero   (B) Two   (C) Four   (D) Six   (E) Eight

GO ON TO THE NEXT PAGE

37. $\lim\limits_{h \to 0} \dfrac{\sin\left(\dfrac{5\pi}{6} + h\right) - \dfrac{1}{2}}{h}$

(A) $\dfrac{\sqrt{3}}{2}$ (B) $\dfrac{1}{2}$ (C) 0 (D) $-\dfrac{1}{2}$ (E) $-\dfrac{\sqrt{3}}{2}$

38. $\dfrac{d}{dx} \displaystyle\int_{2x}^{5x} \cos t \, dt =$

(A) $5\cos 5x - 2\cos 2x$

(B) $5\sin 5x - 2\sin 2x$

(C) $\cos 5x - \cos 2x$

(D) $\sin 5x - \sin 2x$

(E) $\dfrac{1}{5}\cos 5x - \dfrac{1}{2}\sin 2x$

39. The base of a solid S is the region enclosed by the graph of $4x + 5y = 20$, the x-axis, and the y-axis. If the cross-sections of S perpendicular to the x-axis are semicircles, then the volume of S is

(A) $\dfrac{5\pi}{3}$ (B) $\dfrac{10\pi}{3}$ (C) $\dfrac{50\pi}{3}$ (D) $\dfrac{225\pi}{3}$ (E) $\dfrac{425\pi}{3}$

GO ON TO THE NEXT PAGE

40. Which of the following is an equation of the line tangent to the graph of $y = x^3 + x^2$ at $y = 3$?

(A) $y = 33x - 63$

(B) $y = 33x - 135$

(C) $y = 6.488x - 1.175$

(D) $y = 6.488x - 4.620$

(E) $y = 6.488x - 10.620$

41. If $f'(x) = \ln x - x + 2$, at which of the following values of x does f have a relative minimum value?

(A) 5.146   (B) 3.146   (C) 1.000   (D) 0.159   (E) 0

42. Find the total area of the region between the curve $y = \cos x$ and the x-axis from $x = 1$ to $x = 2$ radians.

(A) 0   (B) 0.068   (C) 0.249   (D) 1.751   (E) 2.592

GO ON TO THE NEXT PAGE

43. Let $f(x) = \int \cot x \, dx$; $0 < x < \pi$. If $f\left(\dfrac{\pi}{6}\right) = 1$, then $f(1) =$

(A) −1.861   (B) −0.480   (C) 0.134   (D) 0.524   (E) 1.521

---

44. A radioactive isotope, y, decays according to the equation $\dfrac{dy}{dt} = ky$, where k is a constant and t is measured in seconds. If the half-life of y is 1 minute, then the value of k is

(A) −41.589   (B) −0.012   (C) 0.027   (D) 0.693   (E) 98.923

GO ON TO THE NEXT PAGE

45.

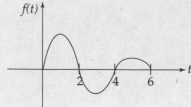

Let $g(x) = \int_0^x f(t)\,dt$, where $f(t)$ has the graph shown above. Which of the following could be the graph of g?

(A)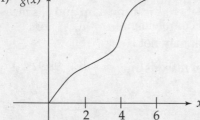

(B)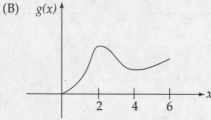

(C)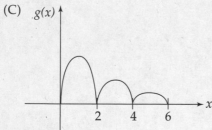

(D)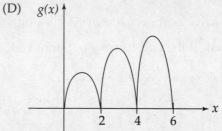

(E)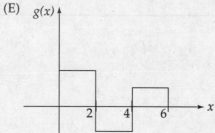

STOP

END OF SECTION I

IF YOU FINISH BEFORE TIME IS CALLED, YOU MAY CHECK YOUR WORK ON PART B ONLY.

DO NOT GO ON TO SECTION II UNTIL YOU ARE TOLD TO DO SO.

You may wish to look over the problems before starting to work on them, since it is not expected that everyone will be able to complete all parts of all problems. All problems are given equal weight, but the parts of a particular problem are not necessarily given equal weight.

A GRAPHING CALCULATOR IS REQUIRED FOR SOME PROBLEMS OR PARTS OF PROBLEMS ON THIS SECTION OF THE EXAMINATION.

- You should write all work for each part of each problem in the space provided for that part in the booklet. Be sure to write clearly and legibly. If you make an error, you may save time by crossing it out rather than trying to erase it. Erased or crossed-out work will not be graded.

- Show all your work. You will be graded on the correctness and completeness of your methods as well as your answers. Correct answers without supporting work may not receive credit.

- Justifications require that you give mathematical (noncalculator) reasons and that you clearly identify functions, graphs, tables, or other objects you use.

- You are permitted to use your calculator to solve an equation, find the derivative of a function at a point, or calculate the value of a definite integral. However, you must clearly indicate the setup of your problem, namely the equation, function, or integral you are using. If you use other built-in features or programs, you must show the mathematical steps necessary to produce your results.

- Your work must be expressed in standard mathematical notation rather than calculator syntax.

  For example, $\int_1^5 x^2 dx$ may not be written as fnInt (X², X, 1, 5).

- Unless otherwise specified, answers (numeric or algebraic) need not be simplified. If your answer is given as a decimal approximation, it should be correct to three places after the decimal point.

- Unless otherwise specified, the domain of a function f is assumed to be the set of all real numbers x for which $f(x)$ is a real number.

SECTION II, PART A
Time—45 minutes
Number of problems—3

A graphing calculator is required for some problems or parts of problems.

During the timed portion for Part A, you may work only on the problems in Part A.

On Part A, you are permitted to use your calculator to solve an equation, find the derivative of a function at a point, or calculate the value of a definite integral. However, you must clearly indicate the setup of your problem, namely the equation, function, or integral you are using. If you use other built-in features or programs, you must show the mathematical steps necessary to produce your results.

GO ON TO THE NEXT PAGE

1.

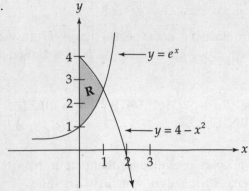

Let R be the region in the first quadrant shown in the figure above.

(a) Find the area of R.

(b) Find the volume of the solid generated when R is revolved about the x-axis.

(c) Find the volume of the solid generated when R is revolved about the line $x = -1$.

GO ON TO THE NEXT PAGE

2.

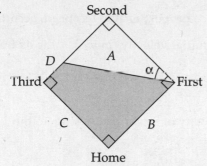

A baseball diamond is a square with each side 90 feet in length. A player runs from second base to third base at a rate of 18 ft/sec.

(a) At what rate is the player's distance from first base, A, changing when his distance from third base, D, is 22.5 feet?

(b) At what rate is angle α increasing when D is 22.5 feet?

(c) At what rate is the area of the trapezoidal region, formed by line segments A, B, C, and D, changing when D is 22.5 feet?

GO ON TO THE NEXT PAGE

3. A body is coasting to a stop and the only force acting on it is a resistance proportional to its speed, according to the equation $\frac{ds}{dt} = v_f = v_0 \, e^{-\left(\frac{k}{m}\right)t}$; $s(0) = 0$, where v_0 is the body's initial velocity (in m/s), v_f is its final velocity, m is its mass, k is a constant, and t is time.

(a) If a body with mass $m = 50$ kg and $k = 1.5$ kg/sec initially has a velocity of 30 m/s, how long, to the nearest second, will it take to slow to 1 m/s?

(b) How far, to the 10 nearest meters, will the body coast during the time it takes to slow from 30 m/s to 1 m/s?

(c) If the body coasts from 30 m/s to a stop, how far will it coast?

No calculator is allowed for these problems.

During the timed portion for Part B, you may continue to work on the problems in Part A without the use of any calculator.

4.

Three trains, A, B, and C each travel on a straight track for $0 \le t \le 16$ hours. The graphs above, which consist of line segments, show the velocities, in kilometers per hour, of trains A and B. The velocity of C is given by

$$v(t) = 8t - 0.25t^2$$

(Indicate units of measure for all answers.)

(a) Find the velocities of A and C at time $t = 6$ hours.

(b) Find the accelerations of B and C at time $t = 6$ hours.

(c) Find the positive difference between the total distance that A traveled and the total distance that B traveled in 16 hours.

(d) Find the total distance that C traveled in 16 hours.

GO ON TO THE NEXT PAGE

5.

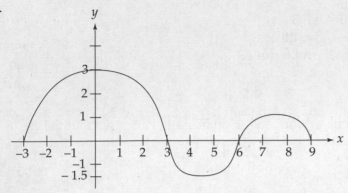

The figure above shows the graph of $g(x)$, where g is the derivative of the function f, for $-3 \le x \le 9$. The graph consists of three semicircular regions and has horizontal tangent lines at $x = 0$, $x = 4.5$, and $x = 7.5$.

(a) Find all values of x, for $-3 < x \le 9$, at which f attains a relative minimum. Justify your answer.

(b) Find all values of x, for $-3 < x \le 9$, at which f attains a relative maximum. Justify your answer.

(c) If $f(x) = \int_{-3}^{x} g(t)dt$, find $f(6)$.

(d) Find all points where $f''(x) = 0$.

GO ON TO THE NEXT PAGE

6. Consider the curve given by $x^2y - 4x + y^2 = 2$.

    (a) Find $\dfrac{dy}{dx}$.

    (b) Find $\dfrac{d^2y}{dx^2}$.

    (c) Find the equation of the tangent lines at each of the two points on the curve whose x-coordinate is 1.

END OF EXAMINATION

ANSWER KEY TO SECTION 1

1.	B	11.	C	21.	C	31.	B	41.	D
2.	E	12.	B	22.	A	32.	D	42.	C
3.	B	13.	B	23.	D	33.	A	43.	E
4.	A	14.	A	24.	D	34.	B	44.	B
5.	B	15.	D	25.	B	35.	C	45.	B
6.	E	16.	E	26.	B	36.	C		
7.	D	17.	D	27.	E	37.	E		
8.	D	18.	C	28.	A	38.	A		
9.	A	19.	D	29.	A	39.	B		
10.	C	20.	B	30.	C	40.	D		

27

Answers and Explanations to AB Practice Test 3

ANSWERS AND EXPLANATIONS TO SECTION 1

PROBLEM 1. $\displaystyle\int_{\frac{\pi}{4}}^{x} \cos(2t)\, dt =$

First, take the antiderivative: $\displaystyle\int \cos(2t)\, dt = \frac{1}{2}\sin(2t)$

Next, plug in x and $\dfrac{\pi}{4}$ for t and take the difference: $\dfrac{1}{2}\sin(2x) - \dfrac{1}{2}\sin\left(2\left(\dfrac{\pi}{4}\right)\right)$

This can be simplified to $\dfrac{\sin(2x)-1}{2}$.

The answer is (B).

PROBLEM 2. What are the coordinates of the point of inflection on the graph of $y = x^3 - 15x^2 + 33x + 100$?

In order to find the inflection point(s) of a polynomial, we need to find the values of x where its second derivative is zero.

First, we find the first and second derivative:

$$\frac{dy}{dx} = 3x^2 - 30x + 33$$

$$\frac{d^2y}{dx^2} = 6x - 30$$

Now, let's set the second derivative equal to zero and solve for x:

$$6x - 30 = 0; x = 5$$

In order to find the y-coordinate, we plug in 5 for x in the original equation:

$$y = 5^3 - 15\left(5^2\right) + 33(5) + 100 = 15$$

Therefore, the coordinates of the point of inflection are (5, 15).

The answer is (E).

PROBLEM 3. If $3x^2 - 2xy + 3y = 1$, then when $x = 2$, $\dfrac{dy}{dx} =$

We need to use implicit differentiation to find $\dfrac{dy}{dx}$:

$$6x - 2\left(x\frac{dy}{dx} + y\right) + 3\frac{dy}{dx} = 0$$

$$6x - 2x\frac{dy}{dx} - 2y + 3\frac{dy}{dx} = 0$$

Now, if we wanted to solve for $\dfrac{dy}{dx}$ in terms of x and y, we would have to do some algebra to isolate $\dfrac{dy}{dx}$. But, because we are asked to solve for $\dfrac{dy}{dx}$ at a specific value of x, we don't need to simplify.

We need to find the y-coordinate that corresponds to the x-coordinate $x = 2$. We plug $x = 2$ into the original equation and solve for y:

$$3(2)^2 - 2(2)y + 3y = 12 - y = 1$$
$$y = 11$$

Finally, we plug $x = 2$ and $y = 11$ into the derivative and we get:

$$6(2) - 2(2)\frac{dy}{dx} - 2(11) + 3\frac{dy}{dx} = 0$$

$$12 - 4\frac{dy}{dx} - 22 + 3\frac{dy}{dx} = 0$$

$$\frac{dy}{dx} = -10$$

The answer is (B).

PROBLEM 4. $\displaystyle\int_{1}^{3} \frac{8}{x^3}\, dx =$

First, rewrite the integral as: $\displaystyle\int_{1}^{3} 8x^{-3}dx =$

Using the power rule for integrals, which is $\displaystyle\int x^n\, dx = \frac{x^{n+1}}{n+1} + C$, we get:

$$\int 8x^{-3}\, dx = \frac{8}{-2}x^{-2} = -\frac{4}{x^2}$$

Next, plug in 3 and 1 for x and take the difference: $-\dfrac{4}{3^2}+\dfrac{4}{1^2}=-\dfrac{4}{9}+4=\dfrac{32}{9}$

The answer is (A).

PROBLEM 5.

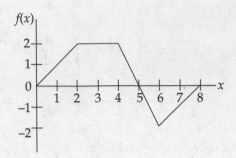

The graph of a piecewise linear function f, for $0 \le x \le 8$, is shown above. What is the

value of $\displaystyle\int_{0}^{8} f(x)\,dx$?

Here, we need to add the areas of the regions between the graph and the x-axis.
Note that the area of the region between 0 and 5 has a positive value and the area of
the region between 5 and 8 has a negative value. The area of the former region can
be found by calculating the area of a trapezoid with bases of 2 and 5, and a height
of 2. The area is $\dfrac{1}{2}(2+5)(2)=7$. The area of the latter region can be found by
calculating the area of a triangle with a base of 3 and a height of 2. The area is
$\dfrac{1}{2}(3)(2)=3$. Thus the value of the integral is $7-3=4$.

The answer is (B).

PROBLEM 6. If f is continuous for $a \le x \le b$, then at any point $x = c$, where $a < b < c$, which of
the following must be true?

In order for $f(x)$ to be continuous at a point c, there are three conditions that need
to be fulfilled:

(1) $f(c)$ exists

(2) $\displaystyle\lim_{x \to c} f(x)$ exists

(3) $\displaystyle\lim_{x \to c} f(x)= f(c)$

Answer choices (A), (B), (C), and (D) are not necessarily true.

The answer is (E).

PROBLEM 7. If $f(x) = x^2\sqrt{3x+1}$, then $f'(x) =$

Here we need to use the Product Rule, which is: If $f(x) = uv$, where u and v are both functions of x, then $f'(x) = u\dfrac{dv}{dx} + v\dfrac{du}{dx}$.

Here, we get: $f'(x) = x^2\left[\dfrac{1}{2}(3x+1)^{-\frac{1}{2}}(3)\right] + 2x\sqrt{3x+1}$

This can be simplified to: $\dfrac{3x^2}{2\sqrt{3x+1}} + 2x\sqrt{3x+1}$

Multiply the numerator and denominator of the second expression by $2\sqrt{3x+1}$ to get a common denominator : $\dfrac{3x^2}{2\sqrt{3x+1}} + 2x\sqrt{3x+1}\left(\dfrac{2\sqrt{3x+1}}{2\sqrt{3x+1}}\right)$

This simplifies to: $\dfrac{3x^2}{2\sqrt{3x+1}} + 4x\left(\dfrac{3x+1}{2\sqrt{3x+1}}\right) = \dfrac{3x^2}{2\sqrt{3x+1}} + \dfrac{12x^2+4x}{2\sqrt{3x+1}} = \dfrac{15x^2+4x}{2\sqrt{3x+1}}$

The answer is (D).

PROBLEM 8. What is the instantaneous rate of change at $t = -1$ of the function f, if $f(t) = \dfrac{t^3+t}{4t+1}$?

We find the instantaneous rate of change of the function by taking the derivative and plugging in $t = -1$.

We need to use the Quotient Rule, which is:

Given $f(x) = \dfrac{g(x)}{h(x)}$, then $f'(x) = \dfrac{h(x)g'(x) - g(x)h'(x)}{\left[h(x)\right]^2}$

Here, we have: $f'(t) = \dfrac{(4t+1)(3t^2+1) - (t^3+t)(4)}{(4t+1)^2}$

Next, plug in $t = -1$ and solve:

$$f'(-1) = \frac{\left(4(-1)+1\right)\left(3(-1)^2+1\right) - \left((-1)^3+(-1)\right)(4)}{\left(4(-1)+1\right)^2} = \frac{(-3)(4) - (-2)(4)}{(-3)^2} = -\frac{4}{9}$$

The answer is (D).

PROBLEM 9. $\displaystyle\int_{2}^{e+1}\left(\frac{4}{x-1}\right)dx =$

You should know that $\displaystyle\int\frac{dx}{x} = \ln|x| + C$.

We take the antiderivative and we get: $\displaystyle\int\left(\frac{4}{x-1}\right)dx = 4\ln|x-1| + C$

Next, Plug In $e + 1$ and 2 for x and take the difference: $4\ln(e) - 4\ln(1)$

You should know that $\ln e = 1$ and $\ln 1 = 0$. Thus we get: $4\ln(e) - 4\ln(1) = 4$

The answer is (A).

PROBLEM 10.

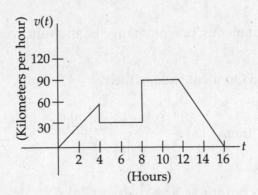

A car's velocity is shown on the graph above. Which of the following gives the total distance traveled from $t = 0$ to $t = 16$ (in kilometers)?

We find the total distance traveled by finding the area of the region between the curve and the x-axis. Normally, we would have to integrate but here we can find the area of the region easily because it consists of geometric objects whose areas are simple to calculate.

The area of the region between $t = 0$ and $t = 4$ can be found by calculating the area of a triangle with a base of 4 and a height of 60. The area is $\frac{1}{2}(4)(60) = 120$.

The area of the region between $t = 4$ and $t = 8$ can be found by calculating the area of a rectangle with a base of 4 and a height of 30.

The area is $(4)(30) = 120$.

The area of the region between $t = 8$ and $t = 16$ can be found by calculating the area of a trapezoid with bases of 4 and 8, and a height of 90 (or you could break it up into a rectangle and a triangle). The area is $\frac{1}{2}(4+8)(90) = 540$.

Thus the total distance traveled is $120 + 120 + 540 = 780$ kilometers.

The answer is (C).

PROBLEM 11. $\dfrac{d}{dx}\tan^2(4x) =$

The derivative of $\tan(u) = \sec^2 u \dfrac{du}{dx}$. Here, we need to use the Chain Rule:

$$\frac{d}{dx}\tan^2(4x) = 2\left[\tan(4x)\right]\left[\sec^2(4x)\right](4) = 8\left[\tan(4x)\right]\left[\sec^2(4x)\right]$$

The answer is (C).

PROBLEM 12. What is the equation of the line tangent to the graph of $y = \sin^2 x$ at $x = \dfrac{\pi}{4}$?

If we want to find the equation of the tangent line, first we need to find the y-coordinate that corresponds to $x = \dfrac{\pi}{4}$. It is: $y = \sin^2\left(\dfrac{\pi}{4}\right) = \left(\dfrac{1}{\sqrt{2}}\right)^2 = \dfrac{1}{2}$.

Next, we need to find the derivative of the curve at $x = \dfrac{\pi}{4}$, using the Chain Rule.

We get: $\dfrac{dy}{dx} = 2\sin x \cos x$. At $x = \dfrac{\pi}{4}$, $\dfrac{dy}{dx}\bigg|_{x=\frac{\pi}{4}} = 2\sin\left(\dfrac{\pi}{4}\right)\cos\left(\dfrac{\pi}{4}\right) = 2\left(\dfrac{1}{\sqrt{2}}\right)\left(\dfrac{1}{\sqrt{2}}\right) = 1$.

Now we have the slope of the tangent line and a point that it goes through. We can use the point-slope formula for the equation of a line, $(y - y_1) = m(x - x_1)$, and plug in what we have just found. We get: $\left(y - \dfrac{1}{2}\right) = (1)\left(x - \dfrac{\pi}{4}\right)$.

The answer is (B).

PROBLEM 13. If the function $f(x) = \begin{cases} 3ax^2 + 2bx + 1; \; x \le 1 \\ ax^4 - 4bx^2 - 3x; \; x > 1 \end{cases}$ is differentiable for all real values of x, then $b =$

In order to solve this for b, we need $f(x)$ to be differentiable at $x = 1$, which means that it must be continuous at $x = 1$. If we plug $x = 1$ into both pieces of this piecewise

function, we get: $f(x) = \begin{cases} 3a + 2b + 1; \; x \le 1 \\ a - 4b - 3; \; x > 1 \end{cases}$, so we need $3a + 2b + 1 = a - 4b - 3$, which

can be simplified to $2a + 6b = -4$.

Now, we take the derivative of both pieces of this function:

$$f'(x) = \begin{cases} 6ax + 2b; \; x < 1 \\ 4ax^3 - 8bx - 3; \; x > 1 \end{cases}$$

Then we plug in $x = 1$ and we get: $f'(x) = \begin{cases} 6a + 2b; \; x < 1 \\ 4a - 8b - 3; \; x > 1 \end{cases}$, so we

need $6a + 2b = 4a - 8b - 3$, which can be simplified to $2a + 10b = -3$

Solving the simultaneous equations, we get $a = -\dfrac{11}{4}$ and $b = \dfrac{1}{4}$.

The answer is (B).

PROBLEM 14. The graph of $y = x^4 + 8x^3 - 72x^2 + 4$ is concave down for

A graph is concave down where the second derivative is negative.

First, we find the first and second derivative:

$$\frac{dy}{dx} = 4x^3 + 24x^2 - 144x$$

$$\frac{d^2y}{dx^2} = 12x^2 + 48x - 144$$

Next, we want to determine on which intervals the second derivative of the function is positive and on which it is negative. We do this by finding where the second derivative is zero:

$$12x^2 + 48x - 144 = 0$$

$$x^2 + 4x - 12 = 0$$

$$(x+6)(x-2) = 0$$

$$x = -6 \text{ or } x = 2$$

We can test where the second derivative is positive and negative by picking a point in each of the three regions $-\infty < x < -6$, $-6 < x < 2$, and $2 < x < \infty$, plugging the point into the second derivative, and seeing what the sign of the answer is. You should find that the second derivative is negative on the interval $-6 < x < 2$.

The answer is (A).

PROBLEM 15. If $f(x) = \dfrac{x^2 + 5x - 24}{x^2 + 10x + 16}$, then $\displaystyle\lim_{x \to -8} f(x)$ is

First, try plugging $x = -8$ into $f(x) = \dfrac{x^2 + 5x - 24}{x^2 + 10x + 16}$

We get: $f(x) = \dfrac{(-8)^2 + 5(-8) - 24}{(-8)^2 + 10(-8) + 16} = \dfrac{0}{0}$. This does NOT necessarily mean that the limit does not exist. When we get a limit of the form $\dfrac{0}{0}$, we first try to simplify the function by factoring and canceling like terms. Here we get:

$$f(x) = \frac{x^2 + 5x - 24}{x^2 + 10x + 16} = \frac{(x+8)(x-3)}{(x+8)(x+2)} = \frac{(x-3)}{(x+2)}$$

Now, if we plug in $x = -8$, we get: $f(x) = \dfrac{(-8-3)}{(-8+2)} = \dfrac{-11}{-6} = \dfrac{11}{6}$

The answer is (D).

PROBLEM 16.

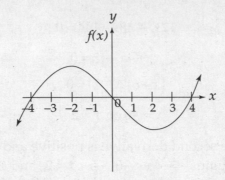

The graph of $f(x)$ is shown in the figure above. Which of the following could be the graph of $f'(x)$?

Here we want to examine the slopes of various pieces of the graph of $f(x)$. Notice that the graph has a positive slope from $x = -\infty$ to $x = -2$, where the slope is zero. Thus we are looking for a graph of $f'(x)$ that is positive from $x = -\infty$ to $x = -2$ and zero at $x = -2$. Next, notice that the graph of $f(x)$ has a negative slope from $x = -2$ to $x = 2$, where the slope is zero. Thus we are looking for a graph of $f'(x)$ that is negative from $x = -2$ to $x = 2$ and zero at $x = 2$. Finally, notice that the graph of $f(x)$ has a positive slope from $x = 2$ to $x = \infty$. Thus we are looking for a graph of $f'(x)$ that is positive from $x = 2$ to $x = \infty$. Graph (E) satisfies all of these requirements.

The answer is (E).

PROBLEM 17. If $f(x) = \ln(\cos(3x))$, then $f'(x) =$

Remember that $\dfrac{d}{dx}\ln(u(x)) = \dfrac{u'(x)}{u(x)}$.

We will need to use the Chain Rule to find the derivative:

$$f'(x) = \left(\frac{-\sin(3x)}{\cos(3x)}\right)(3) = -3\tan(3x)$$

The answer is (D).

PROBLEM 18. If $f(x) = \int_0^{x+1} \sqrt[3]{t^2 - 1}\, dt$, then $f'(-4)$

The Second Fundamental Theorem of calculus tells us how to find the derivative of an integral. It says that $\dfrac{d}{dx}\int_c^u f(t)\, dt = f(u)\dfrac{du}{dx}$, where c is a constant and u is a function of x.

Here we can use the theorem to get: $\dfrac{d}{dx}\int_0^{x+1} \sqrt[3]{t^2 - 1}\, dt = \sqrt[3]{(x+1)^2 - 1}$

Now we evaluate the expression at $x = -4$. We get: $\sqrt[3]{(-4+1)^2 - 1} = 2$

The answer is (C).

PROBLEM 19. A particle moves along the x-axis so that its position at time t, in seconds, is given by $x(t) = t^2 - 7t + 6$. For what value(s) of t is the velocity of the particle zero?

Velocity is the first derivative of position with respect to time.

The first derivative is: $v(t) = 2t - 7$.

Thus the velocity of the particle is zero at time $t = 3.5$ seconds.

The answer is (D).

PROBLEM 20. $\int_0^{\frac{\pi}{2}} \sin(2x)e^{\sin^2 x}\, dx =$

We can use u-substitution to evaluate the integral.

Let $u = \sin^2 x$ and $du = 2\sin x \cos x\, dx$. Next, recall from trigonometry that $2\sin x \cos x = \sin(2x)$. Now we can substitute into the integral $\int e^u\, du$, leaving out the limits of integration for the moment.

Evaluate the integral to get: $\int e^u\, du = e^u$

Now we substitute back to get: $e^{\sin^2 x}$

Finally, we evaluate at the limits of integration and we get:

$$e^{\sin^2 x}\Big|_0^{\frac{\pi}{2}} = e^{\sin^2\frac{\pi}{2}} - e^{\sin^2 0} = e - 1$$

The answer is (B).

PROBLEM 21. The average value of $\sec^2 x$ on the interval $\left[\dfrac{\pi}{6}, \dfrac{\pi}{4}\right]$ is

In order to find the average value, we use the Mean Value Theorem for integrals, which says that the average value of $f(x)$ on the interval $[a, b]$ is $\dfrac{1}{b-a}\displaystyle\int_a^b f(x)\,dx$.

Here, we have $\dfrac{1}{\dfrac{\pi}{4} - \dfrac{\pi}{6}}\displaystyle\int_{\frac{\pi}{6}}^{\frac{\pi}{4}} \sec^2 x\,dx$.

Next, recall that $\dfrac{d}{dx}\tan x = \sec^2 x$.

We evaluate the integral: $\dfrac{1}{\dfrac{\pi}{4} - \dfrac{\pi}{6}}\left(\tan x\right)_{\frac{\pi}{6}}^{\frac{\pi}{4}} = \dfrac{1}{\dfrac{\pi}{4} - \dfrac{\pi}{6}}\left[\tan\dfrac{\pi}{4} - \tan\dfrac{\pi}{6}\right] = \dfrac{1}{\dfrac{\pi}{4} - \dfrac{\pi}{6}}\left(1 - \dfrac{\sqrt{3}}{3}\right)$

Get a common denominator for each of the two expressions:

$$\dfrac{1}{\dfrac{\pi}{4} - \dfrac{\pi}{6}}\left(1 - \dfrac{\sqrt{3}}{3}\right) = \dfrac{1}{\dfrac{6\pi}{24} - \dfrac{4\pi}{24}}\left(\dfrac{3}{3} - \dfrac{\sqrt{3}}{3}\right)$$

We can simplify this to: $\dfrac{1}{\dfrac{2\pi}{24}}\left(\dfrac{3 - \sqrt{3}}{3}\right) = \dfrac{12}{\pi}\left(\dfrac{3 - \sqrt{3}}{3}\right) = \dfrac{12 - 4\sqrt{3}}{\pi}$

The answer is (C).

PROBLEM 22. Find the area of the region bounded by the parabolas $y = x^2$ and $y = 6x - x^2$.

First, we should graph the two curves:

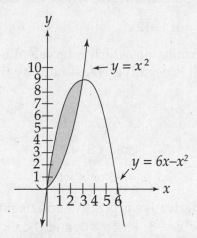

Next, we need to find the points of intersection of the two curves, which we do by setting them equal to each other and solving for x:

$$x^2 = 6x - x^2$$

$$2x^2 = 6x$$

$$2x^2 - 6x = 0$$

$$2x(x - 3) = 0$$

$$x = 0 \text{ or } x = 3$$

We can find the area between the two curves by integrating the top curve minus the bottom curve, using the points of intersection as the limits of integration. We get:

$$\int_0^3 \left[\left(6x - x^2 \right) - \left(x^2 \right) \right] dx$$

We evaluate the integral and we get: $\displaystyle \int_0^3 \left(6x - 2x^2 \right) dx = \left(3x^2 - \frac{2}{3}x^3 \right) \Big|_0^3 = 9$

The answer is (A).

PROBLEM 23. The function f is given by $f(x) = x^4 + 4x^3$. On which of the following intervals is f decreasing?

A function is decreasing on an interval where the derivative is negative.

The derivative is $f'(x) = 4x^3 + 12x^2$

Next, we want to determine on which intervals the derivative of the function is positive and on which it is negative. We do this by finding where the derivative is zero:

$$4x^3 + 12x^2 = 0$$

$$4x^2(x+3) = 0$$

$$x = -3 \text{ or } x = 0$$

We can test where the derivative is positive and negative by picking a point in each of the three regions $-\infty < x < -3$, $-3 < x < 0$, and $0 < x < \infty$, plugging the point into the derivative, and seeing what the sign of the answer is. Because x^2 is never negative, you should find that the derivative is negative on the interval $-\infty < x < -3$.

The answer is (D).

PROBLEM 24. $\displaystyle \lim_{x \to 0} \frac{\tan(3x) + 3x}{\sin(5x)} =$

We will need to use the fact that $\displaystyle \lim_{x \to 0} \frac{\sin x}{x} = 1$ to find the limit.

First, rewrite the limit as $\displaystyle \lim_{x \to 0} \frac{\dfrac{\sin(3x)}{\cos(3x)} + 3x}{\sin(5x)} =$

Next, break the expression into two rational expressions:

$$\lim_{x \to 0} \frac{\sin(3x)}{\sin(5x)\cos(3x)} + \frac{3x}{\sin(5x)} =$$

Which can be broken up further into:

$$\lim_{x \to 0} \frac{\sin(3x)}{\sin(5x)} \frac{1}{\cos(3x)} + \frac{3x}{\sin(5x)} =$$

We will evaluate the limit of each separately.

First expression:

Divide the top and bottom by x: $\displaystyle\lim_{x\to 0}\frac{\dfrac{\sin(3x)}{x}}{\dfrac{\sin(5x)}{x}}$.

Then multiply the top and bottom of the upper expression by 3, and the top and

bottom of the lower expression by 5: $\displaystyle\lim_{x\to 0}\frac{\dfrac{3\sin(3x)}{3x}}{\dfrac{5\sin(5x)}{5x}}$.

Now, if we take the limit, we get: $\displaystyle\lim_{x\to 0}\frac{\dfrac{3\sin(3x)}{3x}}{\dfrac{5\sin(5x)}{5x}}=\frac{3(1)}{5(1)}=\frac{3}{5}$.

Second expression:

This limit is straightforward: $\displaystyle\lim_{x\to 0}\frac{1}{\cos(3x)}=\frac{1}{\cos(0)}=1$

Third expression:

First, pull the constant, 3, out of the limit: $\displaystyle\lim_{x\to 0}\frac{3x}{\sin(5x)}=3\lim_{x\to 0}\frac{x}{\sin(5x)}$.

Now, if we multiply the top and bottom of the expression by 5, we get:

$\displaystyle 3\lim_{x\to 0}\frac{5x}{5\sin(5x)}$.

Now, if we take the limit, we get: $\displaystyle 3\lim_{x\to 0}\frac{5x}{5\sin(5x)}=3\left(\frac{1}{5}\right)=\frac{3}{5}$.

Combine the three numbers and we get: $\dfrac{3}{5}(1)+\dfrac{3}{5}=\dfrac{6}{5}$.

The answer is (D).

PROBLEM 25. If the region enclosed by the y-axis, the curve $y = 4\sqrt{x}$, and the line $y = 8$ is revolved about the x-axis, the volume of the solid generated is

First, we graph the curves:

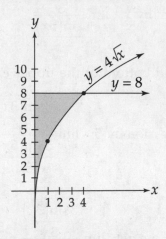

We can find the volume by taking a vertical slice of the region. The formula for the volume of a solid of revolution around the x-axis, using a vertical slice bounded from above by the curve $f(x)$ and from below by $g(x)$, on the interval $[a,b]$, is:

$$\pi \int_a^b \left[f(x)^2 - g(x)^2 \right] dx$$

The upper curve is $y = 8$ and the lower curve is $y = 4\sqrt{x}$.

Next, we need to find the point(s) of intersection of the two curves, which we do by setting them equal to each other and solving for x:

$$8 = 4\sqrt{x}$$

$$2 = \sqrt{x}$$

$$x = 4$$

Thus, the limits of integration are $x = 0$ and $x = 4$.

Now, we evaluate the integral:

$$\pi \int_0^4 \left[(8)^2 - \left[4\sqrt{x} \right]^2 \right] dx = \pi \int_0^4 (64 - 16x)\, dx = \pi \left(64x - 8x^2 \right) \Big|_0^4 = 128\pi$$

The answer is (B).

PROBLEM 26. The maximum velocity attained on the interval $0 \le t \le 5$ by the particle whose displacement is given by $s(t) = 2t^3 - 12t^2 + 16t + 2$ is

Velocity is the first derivative of position with respect to time.

The first derivative is:

$$v(t) = 6t^2 - 24t + 16$$

If we want to find the maximum velocity, we take the derivative of velocity (which is acceleration) and find where the derivative is zero:

$$v'(t) = 12t - 24$$

Next, we set the derivative equal to zero and solve for t, in order to find the critical value:

$$12t - 24 = 0$$

$$t = 2$$

Note that the second derivative of velocity is 12, which is positive. Remember the second derivative test: **If the sign of the second derivative at a critical value is positive, then the curve has a local minimum there. If the sign of the second derivative is negative, then the curve has a local maximum there.**

Thus, the velocity is a *minimum* at $t = 2$. In order to find where it has an absolute *maximum*, we plug the endpoints of the interval into the original equation for velocity, and the larger value will be the answer.

At $t = 0$ the velocity is 16. At $t = 5$, the velocity is 46.

The answer is (B).

PROBLEM 27. The value of c that satisfies the Mean Value Theorem for derivatives on the interval $[0,5]$ for the function $f(x) = x^3 - 6x$ is

The Mean Value Theorem for derivatives says that, given a function $f(x)$ which is continuous and differentiable on $[a,b]$, then there exists some value c on (a,b) where $\dfrac{f(b) - f(a)}{b - a} = f'(c)$.

Here, we have $\dfrac{f(b) - f(a)}{b - a} = \dfrac{f(5) - f(0)}{5 - 0} = \dfrac{95 - 0}{5} = 19$.

Plus, $f'(c) = 3c^2 - 6$, so we simply set $3c^2 - 6 = 19$. If we solve for c, we get: $c = \pm \dfrac{5}{\sqrt{3}}$.

Both of these values satisfy the Mean Value Theorem for derivatives, but only the positive value, $c = \dfrac{5}{\sqrt{3}}$, is in the interval.

The answer is (E).

PROBLEM 28. If $f(x) = \sec(4x)$, then $f'\left(\dfrac{\pi}{16}\right)$ is

Recall that $\dfrac{d}{dx} \sec x = \sec x \tan x$.

Therefore, using the Chain Rule, we get: $f'(x) = 4\sec(4x)\tan(4x)$

If we plug in $x = \dfrac{\pi}{16}$, we get: $f'(x) = 4\sec\left(\dfrac{\pi}{4}\right)\tan\left(\dfrac{\pi}{4}\right) = 4\sqrt{2}$

The answer is (A).

PROBLEM 29. If $f(x)$ is the function given by $f(x) = e^{3x} + 1$, at what value of x is the slope of the tangent line to $f(x)$ equal to 2?

The slope of the tangent line is the derivative of the function. We get: $f'(x) = 3e^{3x}$. Now we set the derivative equal to 2 and solve for x.

$$3e^{3x} = 2$$

$$e^{3x} = \frac{2}{3}$$

$$3x = \ln\frac{2}{3}$$

$$x = \frac{1}{3}\ln\frac{2}{3} \approx -.135$$

(Remember to round all answers to three decimal places on the AP exam.)

The answer is (A).

PROBLEM 30. The graph of the function $y = x^3 + 12x^2 + 15x + 3$ has a relative maximum at $x =$

First, let's find the derivative: $\dfrac{dy}{dx} = 3x^2 + 24x + 15$

Next, set the derivative equal to zero and solve for x.

$$3x^2 + 24x + 15 = 0$$
$$x^2 + 8x + 5 = 0$$

Using the quadratic formula (or your calculator), we get:

$$x = \frac{-8 \pm \sqrt{64 - 20}}{2} \approx -.683, -7.317$$

Let's use the second derivative test to determine which is the maximum. We take the second derivative and then plug in the critical values that we found when we set the first derivative equal to zero. **If the sign of the second derivative at a critical value is positive, then the curve has a local minimum there. If the sign of the second derivative is negative, then the curve has a local maximum there.**

The second derivative is: $\dfrac{d^2y}{dx^2} = 6x + 24$. The second derivative is negative at $x = -7.317$, so the curve has a local maximum there.

The answer is (C).

PROBLEM 31. The side of a square is increasing at a constant rate of 0.4 cm/sec. In terms of the perimeter, P, what is the rate of change of the area of the square, in cm²/sec?

The formula for the perimeter of a square is $P = 4s$, where s is the length of a side of the square.

If we differentiate this with respect to t, we get $\dfrac{dP}{dt} = 4\dfrac{ds}{dt}$. We plug in $\dfrac{ds}{dt} = 0.4$ and

we get $\dfrac{dP}{dt} = 4(0.4) = 1.6$

The formula for the area of a square is $A = s^2$. If we solve the perimeter equation for s in terms of P and substitute it into the area equation we get:

$$s = \frac{P}{4}, \text{ so } A = \left(\frac{P}{4}\right)^2 = \frac{P^2}{16}$$

If we differentiate this with respect to t, we get: $\dfrac{dA}{dt} = \dfrac{P}{8}\dfrac{dP}{dt}$

Now we plug in $\dfrac{dP}{dt} = 1.6$ and we get: $\dfrac{dA}{dt} = \dfrac{P}{8}(1.6) = 0.2P$

The answer is (B).

PROBLEM 32. Let f be the function given by $f(x) = 3^x$. For what value of x is the slope of the line tangent to the curve at $\big(x, f(x)\big)$ equal to 1?

The slope of the tangent line is the derivative of the function.

Recall that $\dfrac{d}{dx} a^x = a^x \ln a$. Here we get: $f'(x) = 3^x \ln 3$

Now we set the derivative equal to 1 and solve for x.

Using the calculator, we get: $3^x \ln 3 = 1$

$x \approx -.086$

The answer is (D).

PROBLEM 33. Given f and g are differentiable functions and

$$f(a) = -4, \quad g(a) = c, \quad g(c) = 10, \quad f(c) = 15$$

$$f'(a) = 8, \quad g'(a) = b, \quad g'(c) = 5, \quad f'(c) = 6$$

If $h(x) = f\big(g(x)\big)$, find $h'(a)$.

Use the Chain Rule to find $h'(a)$: $h'(x) = f'\big(g(x)\big)\big(g'(x)\big)$

We substitute a for x, and because $g(a) = c$, we get: $h'(a) = f'(c)\big(g'(a)\big) = 6b$

The answer is (A).

PROBLEM 34. What is the area of the region in the first quadrant enclosed by the graph of $y = e^{-\frac{x^2}{4}}$ and the line $y = 0.5$?

First, we should graph the two curves:

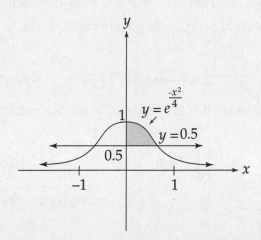

Next, we need to find the points of intersection of the two curves, which we do by setting them equal to each other and solving for x.

$$e^{-\frac{x^2}{4}} = 0.5$$

You will need to use a calculator to solve for x. The answers are (to three decimal places): $x = -1.665$ and $x = +1.665$.

We can find the area between the two curves by integrating the top curve minus the bottom curve, using the points of intersection as the limits of integration. Because we want to find the area in the first quadrant, we use 0 as the lower limit of integration. We get:

$$\int_0^{1.665} \left(e^{-\frac{x^2}{4}} - .5 \right) dx$$

We will need a calculator to evaluate this integral: $\int_0^{1.665} \left(e^{-\frac{x^2}{4}} - .5 \right) dx \approx 0.516$

The answer is (B).

PROBLEM 35. What is the trapezoidal approximation of $\int_{0}^{3} e^x \, dx$ using $n = 4$ subintervals?

The Trapezoid Rule enables us to approximate the area under a curve with a fair degree of accuracy. The rule says that the area between the x-axis and the curve $y = f(x)$, on the interval $[a,b]$, with n trapezoids, is:

$$\frac{1}{2}\frac{b-a}{n}\left[y_0 + 2y_1 + 2y_2 + 2y_3 + \ldots + 2y_{n-1} + y_n\right]$$

Using the rule here, with $n = 4$, $a = 0$, and $b = 3$, we get:

$$\frac{1}{2}\left(\frac{3}{4}\right)\left[e^0 + 2e^{\frac{3}{4}} + 2e^{\frac{6}{4}} + 2e^{\frac{9}{4}} + e^3\right] \approx 19.972$$

The answer is (C).

PROBLEM 36. The second derivative of a function f is given by $f''(x) = x\sin x - 2$. How many points of inflection does f have on the interval $(-10,10)$?

Use your calculator to graph the second derivative and count the number of times that it crosses the x-axis on the interval $(-10,10)$:

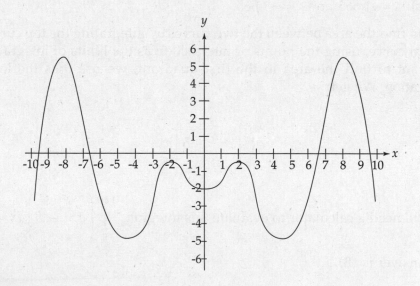

It crosses four times, so there are four points of inflection.

The answer is (C).

PROBLEM 37. $\lim\limits_{h \to 0} \dfrac{\sin\left(\dfrac{5\pi}{6}+h\right)-\dfrac{1}{2}}{h}$

Notice how this limit takes the form of the definition of the derivative, which is:

$$f'(x)=\lim_{h \to 0} \frac{f(x+h)-f(x)}{h}$$

Here, if we think of $f(x)$ as $\sin x$, then this expression gives the derivative of $\sin x$

at the point $x=\dfrac{5\pi}{6}$.

The derivative of $\sin x$ is $f'(x)=\cos x$. At $x=\dfrac{5\pi}{6}$, we get $f'\left(\dfrac{5\pi}{6}\right)=\cos\left(\dfrac{5\pi}{6}\right)=-\dfrac{\sqrt{3}}{2}$.

The answer is (E).

PROBLEM 38. $\dfrac{d}{dx}\displaystyle\int_{2x}^{5x} \cos t \; dt =$

The Second Fundamental Theorem of calculus tells us how to find the derivative of

an integral: $\dfrac{d}{dx}\displaystyle\int_{2x}^{5x} \cos t \; dt = 5\cos 5x - 2\cos 2x$, where u and v are functions of x.

Here we can use the theorem to get: $\dfrac{d}{dx}\displaystyle\int_{2x}^{5x} \cos t \; dt = 5\cos 5x - 2\cos 2x$

The answer is (A).

PROBLEM 39. The base of a solid S is the region enclosed by the graph of $4x + 5y = 20$, the x-axis, and the y-axis. If the cross-sections of S perpendicular to the x-axis are semicircles, then the volume of S is

First, sketch the region:

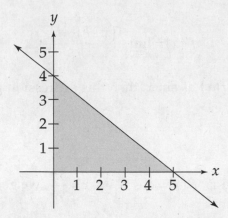

The rule for finding the volume of a solid with known cross-sections is $V = \int_a^b A(x)\,dx$, where A is the formula for the area of the cross-section. Here, x represents the diameter of a semi-circular cross-section.

The area of a semi-circle in terms of its diameter is $A = \pi \dfrac{d^2}{8}$. We find the length of the diameter by solving the equation $4x + 5y = 20$ for y: $y = \dfrac{20 - 4x}{5}$. Next, we need to find where the graph intersects the x-axis. You should get $x = 5$. Thus, we find the volume by evaluating the integral:

$$\int_0^5 \pi \frac{\left(\dfrac{20 - 4x}{5}\right)^2}{8}\, dx$$

This integral can be simplified to: $\dfrac{\pi}{200}\displaystyle\int_0^5 (20 - 4x)^2\, dx = \dfrac{\pi}{200}\displaystyle\int_0^5 \left(400 - 160x + 16x^2\right) dx$

You can evaluate the integral by hand or with a calculator. You should get:

$$\frac{\pi}{200}\int_0^5 \left(400 - 160x + 16x^2\right) dx = \frac{10\pi}{3}$$

The answer is (B).

PROBLEM 40. Which of the following is an equation of the line tangent to the graph of $y = x^3 + x^2$ at $y = 3$?

If we want to find the equation of the tangent line, first we need to find the x-coordinate that corresponds to $y = 3$. If you use your calculator to solve $x^3 + x^2 = 3$, you should get $x = 1.1746$.

Next, we need to find the derivative of the curve at $x = 1.1746$.

We get:

$$\frac{dy}{dx} = 3x^2 + 2x. \text{ At } x = 1.1746, \ \left.\frac{dy}{dx}\right|_{x=1.1746} = 3(1.1746)^2 + 2(1.1746) = 6.488$$

(Rounded to three decimal places).

Now we have the slope of the tangent line and a point that it goes through. We can use the point-slope formula for the equation of a line, $(y - y_1) = m(x - x_1)$, and plug in what we have just found. We get: $(y - 3) = (6.488)(x - 1.1746)$. This simplifies to $y = 6.488x - 4.620$

The answer is (D).

PROBLEM 41. If $f'(x) = \ln x - x + 2$, at which of the following values of x does f have a relative minimum value?

Set the derivative equal to zero and solve for x. Using your calculator, you should get $\ln x - x + 2 = 0$.

$x = 3.146$ or $x = 0.159$ (Rounded to three decimal places)

Let's use the second derivative test to determine which is the minimum. We take the second derivative and then plug in the critical values that we found when we set the first derivative equal to zero. **If the sign of the second derivative at a critical value is positive, then the curve has a local minimum there. If the sign of the second derivative is negative, then the curve has a local maximum there.**

The second derivative is: $f''(x) = \frac{1}{x} - 1$. The second derivative is positive at $x = 0.159$, so the curve has a local minimum there.

The answer is (D).

PROBLEM 42. Find the area of the region between the curve $y = \cos x$ and the x-axis from $x = 1$ to $x = 2$ radians.

First, we should graph the curve:

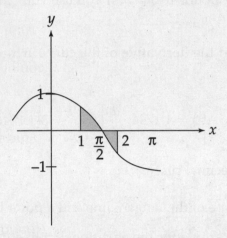

Note that the curve is above the x-axis from $x = 1$ to $x = \dfrac{\pi}{2}$ and below the x-axis from

$x = \dfrac{\pi}{2}$ to $x = 2$. Thus, we need to evaluate two integrals to find the area:

$$\int\limits_{1}^{\frac{\pi}{2}} \cos x\, dx + \int\limits_{\frac{\pi}{2}}^{2} \left(-\cos x\right) dx$$

We will need a calculator to evaluate these integrals:

$$\int\limits_{1}^{\frac{\pi}{2}} \cos x\, dx + \int\limits_{\frac{\pi}{2}}^{2} \left(-\cos x\right) dx \approx 0.249$$

The answer is (C).

PROBLEM 43. Let $f(x) = \int \cot x \, dx$; $0 < x < \pi$. If $f\left(\dfrac{\pi}{6}\right) = 1$, then $f(1) =$

We find $\int \cot x \, dx$ by rewriting the integral as $\int \dfrac{\cos x}{\sin x} \, dx$.

Then we use u-substitution. Let $u = \sin x$ and $du = \cos x$.

Substituting, we can get: $\int \dfrac{\cos x}{\sin x} \, dx = \int \dfrac{du}{u} = \ln|u| + C$. Then substituting back, we get: $\ln(\sin x) + C$ (we can get rid of the absolute value bars because sine is always positive on the interval).

Next, we use $f\left(\dfrac{\pi}{6}\right) = 1$ to solve for C. We get: $1 = \ln\left(\sin\dfrac{\pi}{6}\right) + C$

$$1 = \ln\left(\dfrac{1}{2}\right) + C$$

$$1 - \ln\left(\dfrac{1}{2}\right) = C = 1.693147$$

Thus, $f(x) = \ln(\sin x) + 1.693147$

At $x = 1$, we get $f(1) = \ln(\sin 1) + 1.693147 = 1.521$ (rounded to three decimal places).
The answer is (E).

PROBLEM 44. A radioactive isotope, y, decays according to the equation $\dfrac{dy}{dt} = ky$, where k is a constant and t is measured in seconds. If the half-life of y is 1 minute, then the value of k is

We solve this differential equation using separation of variables.

First, move the y to the left side and the dt to the right side, to get: $\dfrac{dy}{y} = k\,dt$.

Now, integrate both sides:

$$\int \dfrac{dy}{y} = k \int dt$$

$\ln y = kt + C$

Next, it's traditional to put the equation in terms of y. We do this by exponentiating both sides to the base e. We get: $y = e^{kt + c}$

Using the rules of exponents, we can rewrite this as: $y = e^{kt}e^{C}$. Finally, because e^{c} is a constant, we can rewrite the equation as: $y = Ce^{kt}$.

Now, we use the initial condition to solve for k. At time $t = 60$ (seconds), $y = \dfrac{1}{2}$.

We are assuming a starting amount of $y = 1$, which will make $C = 1$. Actually, we could assume any starting amount. The half-life tells us that there will be half that amount after 1 minute. Therefore:

$$\frac{1}{2} = e^{60k}$$

Solve for k: $k = \dfrac{1}{60}\ln\left(\dfrac{1}{2}\right)$

This gives us: $k = -0.012$ (rounded to three decimal places)

The answer is (B).

PROBLEM 45.

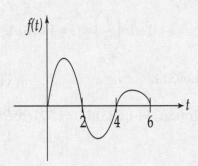

Let $g(x) = \int_{0}^{x} f(t)\, dt$, where $f(t)$ has the graph shown above. Which of the following could be the graph of g ?

The function $g(x) = \int_{0}^{x} f(t)\, dt$ is called an *accumulation function* and stands for the area between the curve and the x-axis to the point x. At $x = 0$, the area is 0, so $g(0) = 0$. From $x = 0$ to $x = 2$ the area grows, so $g(x)$ has a positive slope. Then from $x = 2$ to $x = 4$ the area shrinks (because we subtract the area of the region under the x-axis from the area of the region above it), so $g(x)$ has a negative slope. Finally, from $x = 4$ to $x = 6$ the area again grows, so $g(x)$ has a positive slope. The curve that best represents this is (B).

The answer is (B).

ANSWERS AND EXPLANATIONS TO SECTION II

PROBLEM 1.

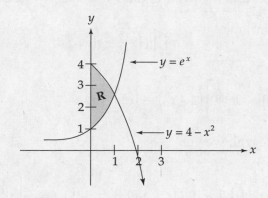

Let R be the region in the first quadrant shown in the figure above.

(a) Find the area of R.

(b) Find the volume of the solid generated when R is revolved about the x-axis.

(c) Find the volume of the solid generated when R is revolved about the line $x = 1$.

(a) In order to find the area, we "slice" the region vertically and add up all of the

slices. We use the formula for the area of the region between $y = f(x)$ and $y = g(x)$, from $x = a$ to $x = b$:

$$\int_a^b \left[f(x) - g(x) \right] dx.$$

Here, we have:

$$f(x) = 4 - x^2 \text{ and } g(x) = e^x$$

Next, we need to find the point of intersection in the first quadrant. Use your calculator to find that the point of intersection is $x = 1.058$ (rounded to three decimal places). Plugging into the formula, we get:

$$\int_0^{1.058} \left[(4 - x^2) - e^x \right] dx.$$

Evaluating the integral, we get: $\displaystyle \int_0^{1.058} \left[(4 - x^2) - e^x \right] dx = \left(4x - \frac{x^3}{3} - e^x \right)_0^{1.058} = 1.957$

(b) In order to find the volume of a region between $y = f(x)$ and $y = g(x)$, from $x = a$ to $x = b$, when it is revolved about the x-axis, we use the formula:

$$\pi \int_a^b \left[f(x)^2 - g(x)^2 \right] dx$$

Here our integral is: $\pi \displaystyle\int_0^{1.058} \left[\left(4 - x^2\right)^2 - \left(e^x\right)^2 \right] dx$

Evaluating the integral, we get:

$$\pi \int_0^{1.058} \left[\left(4 - x^2\right)\right]^2 - \left[e^x\right]^2 \, dx = \pi \int_0^{1.058} \left(16 - 8x^2 + x^4 - e^{2x}\right) dx = \pi \left[16x - \frac{8x^3}{3} + \frac{x^5}{5} - \frac{e^{2x}}{2} \right]_0^{1.058} = 32.629$$

(c) In order to find the volume of this region, if we want to use vertical slices, we will use the method of cylindrical shells. Also, because we are revolving about the line $x = -1$, we will need to add 1 to the radius of the cylindrical shell. We will use the formula:

$$2\pi \int_a^b (x+1)\left[f(x) - g(x) \right] dx.$$

Here, we get:

$$2\pi \int_0^{1.058} (x+1)\left[\left(4 - x^2\right) - e^x \right] dx$$

We suggest that you use your calculator to evaluate the integral:

$$2\pi \int_0^{1.058} (x+1)\left[\left(4 - x^2\right) - e^x \right] dx = 2\pi \int_0^{1.058} \left[4x - x^3 - xe^x + 4 - x^2 - e^x \right] dx = 17.059$$

PROBLEM 2.

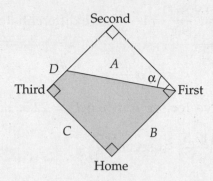

A baseball diamond is a square with each side 90 feet in length. A player runs from second base to third base at a rate of 18 ft/sec.

(a) At what rate is the player's distance from first base, A, changing when his distance from third base, D, is 22.5 feet?

(b) At what rate is angle α increasing when D is 22.5 feet?

(c) At what rate is the area of the trapezoidal region, formed by line segments A, B, C, and D, changing when D is 22.5 feet?

(a) A is related to D by the Pythagorean Theorem: $90^2 + (90 - D)^2 = A^2$. This can be simplified to: $16200 - 180D + D^2 = A^2$

Take the derivative of both sides with respect to t: $-180\dfrac{dD}{dt} + 2D\dfrac{dD}{dt} = 2A\dfrac{dA}{dt}$

Now, we are given that $\dfrac{dD}{dt} = -18$ (it's negative because D is shrinking) and $D = 22.5$. Next, we need to solve for A: $90^2 + (90 - 22.5)^2 = A^2$. You should get $A = 112.5$.

Now we can plug in and solve for $\dfrac{dA}{dt}$:

$$-180(-18) + 2(22.5)(-18) = 2(112.5)\dfrac{dA}{dt}$$

$$3240 - 810 = 225\dfrac{dA}{dt}$$

$$\dfrac{dA}{dt} = 10.8 \text{ ft/sec}$$

(b) Notice that $\tan\alpha = \dfrac{90-D}{90} = 1 - \dfrac{D}{90}$. We differentiate both sides with respect to t:

$$\sec^2\alpha\,\frac{d\alpha}{dt} = -\frac{1}{90}\frac{dD}{dt}$$

Next, we need to solve for $\sec^2\alpha$ when $D = 22.5$. From part (a), we know that

$A = 112.5$, so $\sec\alpha = \dfrac{112.5}{90}$, so $\sec^2\alpha = \dfrac{25}{16}$.

Now we plug in to solve for $\dfrac{d\alpha}{dt}$: $\left(\dfrac{25}{16}\right)\dfrac{d\alpha}{dt} = -\dfrac{1}{90}(-18)$

$$\frac{d\alpha}{dt} = \frac{16}{125} = 0.128 \text{ radians/sec}$$

(c) The area of the trapezoid is $a = \dfrac{1}{2}C(B+D)$. Notice that B and C are constants. We

differentiate both sides with respect to t: $\dfrac{da}{dt} = \dfrac{1}{2}C\dfrac{dD}{dt}$

Now, we plug in and solve for $\dfrac{da}{dt}$: $\dfrac{da}{dt} = \dfrac{1}{2}(90)(-18) = -810 \text{ ft}^2/\text{sec}$

PROBLEM 3. A body is coasting to a stop and the only force acting on it is a resistance proportional to its speed, according to the equation $\dfrac{ds}{dt} = v_f = v_0\, e^{-\left(\frac{k}{m}\right)t}$; $s(0) = 0$, where v_0 is the body's initial velocity (in m/s), v_f is its final velocity, m is its mass, k is a constant, and t is time.

(a) If a body, with mass $m = 50$ kg and $k = 1.5$ kg/sec, initially has a velocity of 30 m/s, how long, to the nearest second, will it take to slow to 1 m/s?

(b) How far, to the nearest 10 meters, will the body coast during the time it takes to slow from 30 m/s to 1 m/s?

(c) If the body coasts from 30 m/s to a stop, how far will it coast?

(a) We simply plug into the formula and solve for t.

We get:

$$v_f = v_0\, e^{-\left(\frac{k}{m}\right)t}$$

$$1 = 30\, e^{-\left(\frac{1.5}{50}\right)t}$$

Divide both sides by 30: $\dfrac{1}{30} = e^{-\left(\frac{1.5}{50}\right)t}$

Take the log of both sides: $\ln\dfrac{1}{30} = -\left(\dfrac{1.5}{50}\right)t$

Multiply both sides by $-\dfrac{50}{1.5}$: $-\dfrac{50}{1.5}\ln\dfrac{1}{30} = t \approx 113$ seconds

(b) Now we need to solve the differential equation $\dfrac{ds}{dt} = v_0\, e^{-\left(\frac{k}{m}\right)t}$, which we can do with separation of variables.

First, multiply both sides by dt: $ds = v_0\, e^{-\left(\frac{k}{m}\right)t}\, dt$

Integrate both sides: $\displaystyle\int ds = \int v_0\, e^{-\left(\frac{k}{m}\right)t}\, dt$

Evaluate the integrals: $s = -\dfrac{mv_0}{k}\, e^{-\left(\frac{k}{m}\right)t} + C$.

Now plug in the initial conditions to solve for C: $0 = -\dfrac{(50)(30)}{1.5}\, e^{-\left(\frac{1.5}{50}\right)(0)} + C$

$$C = \dfrac{(30)(50)}{1.5} = 1000$$

Therefore, $s = -\dfrac{mv_0}{k}\, e^{-\left(\frac{k}{m}\right)t} + 1000$. Now we plug in the time $t = 113$ that we found in part (a) as well as the initial conditions to solve for is:

$$s = -\dfrac{(50)30}{1.5}\, e^{-\left(\frac{1.5}{50}\right)113} + 1000 \approx 970 \text{ meters}$$

(c) Here, because the braking force is an exponential function, the object will coast to a stop after an infinite amount of time. In other words, we need to find:

$$\lim_{t \to \infty} s(t) = \lim_{t \to \infty} \left[1000 - 1000e^{-\left(\frac{k}{m}\right)t} \right] = 1000 \text{ meters}$$

PROBLEM 4.

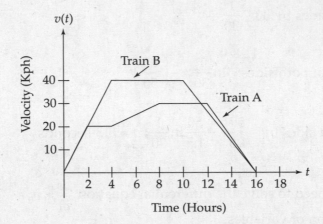

Three trains, A, B, and C, each travel on a straight track for $0 \le t \le 16$ hours. The graphs above, which consist of line segments, show the velocities, in kilometers per hour, of trains A and B. The velocity of C is given by $v(t) = 8t - 0.25t^2$.

(Indicate units of measure for all answers.)

(a) Find the velocities of A and C at time $t = 6$ hours.

(b) Find the accelerations of B and C at time $t = 6$ hours.

(c) Find the positive difference between the total distance that A traveled and the total distance that B traveled in 16 hours.

(d) Find the total distance that C traveled in 16 hours.

(a) We can find the velocity of train A at time $t = 6$ simply by reading the graph. We get $v_A(6) = 25$ kph. We find the velocity of train C at time $t = 6$ by plugging $t = 6$ into the formula. We get $v_C(6) = 8(6) - .25(6^2) = 39$ kilometers per hour.

(b) Acceleration is the derivative of velocity with respect to time. For train B, we look at the *slope* of the graph at time $t = 6$. We get: $a_B(6) = 0$ km/hr². For train C, we take the derivative of v. We get: $a(t) = 8 - .5t$. At time $t = 6$, we get $a_C(6) = 5$ km/hr².

(c) In order to find the total distance that train A traveled in 16 hours, we need to find the area under the graph. We can find this area by adding up the areas of the different geometric objects that are under the graph. From time $t = 0$ to $t = 2$, we need to find the area of a triangle with a base of 2 and a height of 20. The area is 20. Next, from time $t = 2$ to $t = 4$, we need to find the area of a rectangle with a base of 2 and a height of 20. The area is 40. Next, from time $t = 4$ to $t = 8$, we need to find the area of a trapezoid with bases of 20 and 30 and a height of 4. The area is 100. Next, from time $t = 8$ to $t = 12$, we need to find the area of a rectangle with a base of 4 and a height of 30. The area is 120. Finally, from time $t = 12$ to $t = 16$, we need to find the area of a triangle with a base of 4 and a height of 30. The area is 60. Thus the total distance that train A traveled is 340 km.

Let's repeat the process for train B. From time $t = 0$ to $t = 4$, we need to find the area of a triangle with a base of 4 and a height of 40. The area is 80. Next, from time $t = 4$ to $t = 10$, we need to find the area of a rectangle with a base of 6 and a height of 40. The area is 240. Finally, from time $t = 10$ to $t = 16$, we need to find the area of a triangle with a base of 6 and a height of 40. The area is 120. Thus the total distance that train B traveled is 440 km.

Therefore, the positive difference between their distances is 100 km.

(d) First, note that the graph of train C's velocity, $v(t) = 8t - 0.25t^2$, is above the x-axis on the entire interval. Therefore, in order to find the total distance traveled, we integrate $v(t)$ over the interval.

We get:

$$\int_0^{16} \left(8t - .25t^2\right) dt$$

Evaluate the integral: $\int_0^{16} \left(8t - .25t^2\right) dt = \left(4t^2 - \frac{t^3}{12}\right)_0^{16} = \frac{2048}{3}$ km

PROBLEM 5.

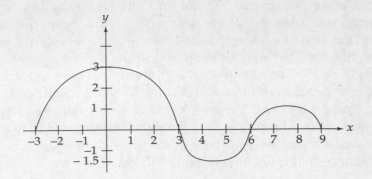

The figure above shows the graph of $g(x)$, where g is the derivative of the function f, for $-3 \le x \le 9$. The graph consists of three semicircular regions and has horizontal tangent lines at $x = 0$, $x = 4.5$, and $x = 7.5$.

(a) Find all values of x, for $-3 < x \le 9$, at which f attains a relative minimum. Justify your answer.

(b) Find all values of x, for $-3 < x \le 9$, at which f attains a relative maximum. Justify your answer.

(c) If $f(x) = \int_{-3}^{x} g(t)dt$, find $f(6)$.

(d) Find all points where $f''(x) = 0$.

(a) Because g is the derivative of the function f, f will attain a relative minimum at a point where $g = 0$ and where g is negative to the left of that point and positive to the right of it. This occurs at $x = 6$.

(b) Because g is the derivative of the function f, f will attain a relative maximum at a point where $g = 0$ and where g is positive to the left of that point and negative to the right of it. This occurs at $x = 3$.

(c) We are trying to find the area between the graph and the x-axis from $x = -3$ to $x = 6$. From $x = -3$ to $x = 3$, the region is a semicircle of radius 3, so the area is $\dfrac{9\pi}{2}$.

From $x = 3$ to $x = 6$, the region is a semicircle of radius $\dfrac{3}{2}$, so the area is $\dfrac{9\pi}{8}$. We subtract the latter region from the former to obtain: $\dfrac{9\pi}{2} - \dfrac{9\pi}{8} = \dfrac{27\pi}{8}$.

(d) Because $f''(x) = g'(x)$, we are looking for points were the derivative of g is zero. This occurs at the horizontal tangent lines at $x = 0$, $x = 4.5$, and $x = 7.5$.

PROBLEM 6. Consider the curve given by $x^2 y - 4x + y^2 = 2$.

(a) Find $\dfrac{dy}{dx}$.

(b) Find $\dfrac{d^2 y}{dx^2}$.

(c) Find the equation of the tangent lines at each of the two points on the curve whose x-coordinate is 1.

(a) We can find $\dfrac{dy}{dx}$ by implicit differentiation: $x^2 \dfrac{dy}{dx} + 2xy - 4 + 2y \dfrac{dy}{dx} = 0$.

Now we need to do some algebra to isolate $\dfrac{dy}{dx}$. First, we move all of the terms that do not contain $\dfrac{dy}{dx}$ to the right side of the equals sign:

$$x^2 \frac{dy}{dx} + 2y \frac{dy}{dx} = 4 - 2xy$$

Next, we factor out $\dfrac{dy}{dx}$: $\dfrac{dy}{dx}\left(x^2 + 2y\right) = 4 - 2xy$

Finally, we divide through by $\left(x^2 + 2y\right)$ to isolate $\dfrac{dy}{dx}$:

$$\frac{dy}{dx} = \frac{4 - 2xy}{x^2 + 2y}$$

(b) We need to use the Quotient Rule and implicit differentiation:

$$\frac{d^2 y}{dx^2} = \frac{\left(x^2 + 2y\right)\left(-2x \dfrac{dy}{dx} - 2y\right) - \left(4 - 2xy\right)\left(2x + 2 \dfrac{dy}{dx}\right)}{\left(x^2 + 2y\right)^2}$$

Next, substitute $\dfrac{dy}{dx} = \dfrac{4-2xy}{x^2+2y}$ into the derivative:

$$\frac{d^2y}{dx^2} = \frac{\left(x^2+2y\right)\left(-2x\left(\dfrac{4-2xy}{x^2+2y}\right)-2y\right)-\left(4-2xy\right)\left(2x+2\left(\dfrac{4-2xy}{x^2+2y}\right)\right)}{\left(x^2+2y\right)^2}$$

There is no need to simplify this.

(c) First, we need to find the y-coordinates that correspond to $x = 1$. We plug $x = 1$ into $x^2y-4x+y^2=2$, and rearrange a little, and we get: $y^2+y-6=0$.

Next, we factor the quadratic to get: $\left(y+3\right)\left(y-2\right)=0$, so we will be finding tangent lines at the coordinates $\left(1,-3\right)$ and $\left(1,2\right)$.

At $\left(1,-3\right)$, we get: $\dfrac{dy}{dx} = \dfrac{4-2(1)(-3)}{(1)^2+2(-3)} = \dfrac{10}{-5} = -2$

Therefore, the equation of the tangent line is: $y+3=-2\left(x-1\right)$

At $\left(1,2\right)$, we get: $\dfrac{dy}{dx} = \dfrac{4-2(1)(2)}{(1)^2+2(2)} = \dfrac{0}{5} = 0$

Therefore, the equation of the tangent line is: $y=2$

28

The Princeton Review AP Calculus BC Practice Test 1

<u>Directions</u>: Solve each of the following problems, using the available space for scratchwork. After examining the form of the choices, decide which is the best of the choices given and fill in the corresponding oval on the answer sheet. No credit will be given for anything written in the test book. Do not spend too much time on any one problem.

<u>In this test</u>: Unless otherwise specified, the domain of a function f is assumed to be the set of all real numbers x for which $f(x)$ is a real number.

1. If $7 = xy - e^{xy}$, then $\dfrac{dy}{dx} =$

   (A) $x - e^y$ (B) $y - e^x$ (C) $\dfrac{ye^{xy} + y}{x - xe^{xy}}$ (D) $\dfrac{-y}{x}$ (E) $\dfrac{ye^{xy} + y}{x + xe^{xy}}$

2. The volume of the solid that results when the area between the curve $y = e^x$ and the line $y = 0$, from $x = 1$ to $x = 2$, is revolved around the x-axis is

   (A) $2\pi(e^4 - e^2)$ (B) $\dfrac{\pi}{2}(e^4 - e^2)$ (C) $\dfrac{\pi}{2}(e^2 - e)$ (D) $2\pi(e^2 - e)$ (E) $2\pi e^2$

GO ON TO THE NEXT PAGE

3. $\displaystyle\int \frac{x-18}{(x+3)\,(x-4)}\,dx =$

(A) $\displaystyle\int \frac{5dx}{(x+3)\,(x-4)}$

(B) $\displaystyle\int \frac{dx}{(x+3)\,(x-4)}$

(C) $\displaystyle\int \frac{3dx}{x+3} + \int \frac{2dx}{x-4}$

(D) $\displaystyle\int \frac{15dx}{x+3} - \int \frac{14dx}{x-4}$

(E) $\displaystyle\int \frac{3dx}{x+3} - \int \frac{2dx}{x-4}$

---

4. If $y = 5x^2 + 4x$ and $x = \ln t$ then $\dfrac{dy}{dt} =$

(A) $\dfrac{10}{t} + 4$
(B) $10t\ln t + 4t$
(C) $\dfrac{10\ln t + 4}{t}$
(D) $\dfrac{5}{t^2} + \dfrac{4}{t}$
(E) $10\ln t + \dfrac{4}{t}$

GO ON TO THE NEXT PAGE

5. $\displaystyle\int_0^{\frac{\pi}{2}} \sin^5 x \cos x\, dx =$

(A) $\dfrac{1}{6}$ (B) $-\dfrac{1}{6}$ (C) 0   (D) –6   (E) 6

---

6. The tangent line to the curve $y = x^3 - 4x + 8$ at the point (2, 8) has an x-intercept at

(A) (–1, 0)   (B) (1, 0)   (C) (0, –8)   (D) (0, 8)   (E) (8, 0)

---

7. The graph in the xy–plane represented by $x = 3\sin(t)$ and $y = 2\cos(t)$ is

(A) a circle   (B) an ellipse   (C) a hyperbola   (D) a parabola   (E) a line

GO ON TO THE NEXT PAGE

8. $\int \dfrac{dx}{\sqrt{4-9x^2}} =$

(A) $\dfrac{1}{6}\sin^{-1}\left(\dfrac{3x}{2}\right)+C$

(B) $\dfrac{1}{2}\sin^{-1}\left(\dfrac{3x}{2}\right)+C$

(C) $6\sin^{-1}\left(\dfrac{3x}{2}\right)+C$

(D) $3\sin^{-1}\left(\dfrac{3x}{2}\right)+C$

(E) $\dfrac{1}{3}\sin^{-1}\left(\dfrac{3x}{2}\right)+C$

---

9. $\displaystyle\lim_{x\to\infty} 4x\sin\left(\dfrac{1}{x}\right)$ is

(A) 0   (B) 2   (C) 4   (D) 4π (E) nonexistent

GO ON TO THE NEXT PAGE

10. The position of a particle moving along the x-axis at time t is given by $x(t) = e^{\cos(2t)}, 0 \le t \le \pi$. For which of the following values of t will $x'(t) = 0$?

I. $t = 0$

II. $t = \dfrac{\pi}{2}$

III. $t = \pi$

(A) I only   (B) II only   (C) I and III only   (D) I and II only   (E) I, II, and III

---

11. $\displaystyle\lim_{h \to 0} \frac{\sec(\pi + h) - \sec(\pi)}{h} =$

(A) -1 (B) 0 (C) $\dfrac{1}{\sqrt{2}}$ (D) 1 (E) $\sqrt{2}$

---

12. Use differentials to approximate the change in the volume of a cube when the side is decreased from 8 to 7.99 cm. (in cm^3)

(A) -19.2

(B) -15.36

(C) -1.92

(D) -0.01

(E) -0.0001

GO ON TO THE NEXT PAGE

13. The radius of convergence of $\sum_{n=1}^{\infty} \frac{a^n}{(x+2)^n}$; $a > 0$ is

   (A) $(a-2) \leq x \leq (a+2)$
   (B) $(a-2) < x < (a+2)$
   (C) $(-a-2) > x > (a-2)$
   (D) $(a-2) > x > (-a-2)$
   (E) $(a-2) \leq x \leq (-a-2)$

14. $\int_0^1 \sin^{-1}(x)\,dx =$

   (A) 0
   (B) $\frac{\pi+2}{2}$
   (C) $\frac{\pi-2}{2}$
   (D) $\frac{\pi}{2}$
   (E) $\frac{-\pi}{2}$

15. The equation of the line *normal* to $y = \sqrt{\dfrac{5-x^2}{5+x^2}}$ at $x = 2$ is

   (A) $81x - 60y = 142$
   (B) $81x + 60y = 182$
   (C) $20x + 27y = 49$
   (D) $20x + 27y = 31$
   (E) $81x - 60y = 182$

GO ON TO THE NEXT PAGE

16. If c satisfies the conclusion of the Mean Value Theorem for derivatives for $f(x) = 2 \sin x$ on the interval $[0, \pi]$, then c could be

(A) 0

(B) $\dfrac{\pi}{4}$

(C) $\dfrac{\pi}{2}$

(D) π

(E) There is no value of c on $\left[0, \pi \right]$

17. The average value of $f(x) = x \ln x$ on the interval $[1, e]$ is

(A) $\dfrac{e^2 + 1}{4}$

(B) $\dfrac{e^2 + 1}{4(e+1)}$

(C) $\dfrac{e + 1}{4}$

(D) $\dfrac{e^2 + 1}{4(e-1)}$

(E) $\dfrac{3e^2 + 1}{4(e-1)}$

18. A 17-foot ladder is sliding down a wall at a rate of –5 feet/sec. When the top of the ladder is 8 feet from the ground, how fast is the foot of the ladder sliding away from the wall (in feet/sec)?

(A) $\dfrac{75}{8}$

(B) $\dfrac{8}{3}$

(C) $\dfrac{3}{8}$

(D) –16

(E) $\dfrac{-75}{3}$

GO ON TO THE NEXT PAGE

19. If $\dfrac{dy}{dx} = 3y\cos x$, and $y = 8$ when $x = 0$, then $y =$

(A) $8e^{3\sin x}$ (B) $8e^{3\cos x}$ (C) $8e^{3\sin x} + 3$ (D) $3\dfrac{y^2}{2}\cos x + 8$ (E) $3\dfrac{y^2}{2}\sin x + 8$

---

20. The length of the curve determined by $x = 3t$ and $y = 2t^2$ from $t = 0$ to $t = 9$ is

(A) $\displaystyle\int_0^9 \sqrt{9t^2 + 4t^4}\,dt$

(B) $\displaystyle\int_0^{162} \sqrt{9 - 16t^2}\,dt$

(C) $\displaystyle\int_0^{162} \sqrt{9 + 16t^2}\,dt$

(D) $\displaystyle\int_0^3 \sqrt{9 - 16t^2}\,dt$

(E) $\displaystyle\int_0^9 \sqrt{9 + 16t^2}\,dt$

GO ON TO THE NEXT PAGE

21. If a particle moves in the xy-plane so that at time $t > 0$ its position vector is $\left(e^{t^2}, e^{-t^3}\right)$, then its velocity vector at time $t = 3$ is

(A) $\left(\ln 6, \ln(-27)\right)$

(B) $\left(\ln 9, \ln(-27)\right)$

(C) (e^9, e^{-27})

(D) $(6e^9, -27e^{-27})$

(E) $(9e^9, -27e^{-27})$

---

22. The graph of $f(x) = \sqrt{11 + x^2}$ has a point of inflection at

(A) $\left(0, \sqrt{11}\right)$

(B) $\left(-\sqrt{11}, 0\right)$

(C) $\left(0, -\sqrt{11}\right)$

(D) $\left(\sqrt{\dfrac{11}{2}}, \sqrt{\dfrac{33}{2}}\right)$

(E) There is no point of inflection.

GO ON TO THE NEXT PAGE

23. What is the volume of the solid generated by rotating about the y-axis the region enclosed by $y = \sin x$ and the x-axis, from $x = 0$ to $x = \pi$?

(A) π^2 (B) $2\pi^2$ (C) $4\pi^2$ (D) 2   (E) 4

24. $\displaystyle\int_{\frac{2}{\pi}}^{\infty} \frac{\sin\left(\frac{1}{t}\right)}{t^2}\,dt =$

(A) 1   (B) 0   (C) –1   (D) 2   (E) Undefined

25. A rectangle is to be inscribed between the parabola $y = 4 - x^2$ and the x-axis, with its base on the x-axis. A value of x that maximizes the area of the rectangle is

(A) 0   (B) $\dfrac{2}{\sqrt{3}}$ (C) $\dfrac{2}{3}$ (D) $\dfrac{4}{3}$ (E) $\dfrac{\sqrt{3}}{2}$

GO ON TO THE NEXT PAGE

26. $\displaystyle\int \frac{dx}{\sqrt{9-x^2}} =$

(A) $\sin^{-1} 3x + C$

(B) $\ln\left|x + \sqrt{9-x^2}\right| + C$

(C) $\dfrac{1}{3}\sin^{-1}x + C$

(D) $\sin^{-1}\dfrac{x}{3} + C$

(E) $\dfrac{1}{3}\ln\left|x + \sqrt{9-x^2}\right| + C$

27. Find $\displaystyle\lim_{x\to\infty} x^{\frac{1}{x}}$

(A) 0   (B) 1   (C) ∞ (D) -1 (E) $-\infty$

GO ON TO THE NEXT PAGE

28. What is the sum of the Maclaurin series $\pi - \dfrac{\pi^3}{3!} + \dfrac{\pi^5}{5!} - \dfrac{\pi^7}{7!} + \ldots + (-1)^n \dfrac{\pi^{2n+1}}{(2n+1)!} + \ldots$?

(A) 1 (B) 0 (C) –1 (D) e (E) There is no sum.

STOP

END OF PART A SECTION I

IF YOU FINISH BEFORE TIME IS CALLED, YOU MAY CHECK YOUR WORK ON PART A ONLY.

DO NOT GO ON TO PART B UNTIL YOU ARE TOLD TO DO SO.

CALCULUS BC

SECTION I, Part B

Time—50 Minutes

Number of questions—17

A GRAPHING CALCULATOR IS REQUIRED FOR SOME QUESTIONS ON THIS PART OF THE EXAMINATION

Directions: Solve each of the following problems, using the available space for scratchwork. After examining the form of the choices, decide which is the best of the choices given and fill in the corresponding oval on the answer sheet. No credit will be given for anything written in the test book. Do not spend too much time on any one problem.

In this test:

1. The **exact** numerical value of the correct answer does not always appear among the choices given. When this happens, select from among the choices the number that best approximates the exact numerical value.

2. Unless otherwise specified, the domain of a function f is assumed to be the set of all real numbers x for which $f(x)$ is a real number.

29. The first three non-zero terms in the Taylor series about $x = 0$ for $f(x) = \cos x$

(A) $x + \dfrac{x^3}{3!} + \dfrac{x^5}{5!}$

(B) $x - \dfrac{x^3}{3!} + \dfrac{x^5}{5!}$

(C) $1 - \dfrac{x^2}{2!} + \dfrac{x^4}{4!}$

(D) $1 - \dfrac{x^2}{2!} - \dfrac{x^4}{4!}$

(E) $1 + \dfrac{x^2}{2!} + \dfrac{x^4}{4!}$

GO ON TO THE NEXT PAGE

30. $\displaystyle\int \cos^3 x \, dx =$

(A) $\dfrac{\cos^4 x}{4} + C$

(B) $\dfrac{\sin^4 x}{4} + C$

(C) $\sin x - \dfrac{\sin^3 x}{3} + C$

(D) $\sin x + \dfrac{\sin^3 x}{3} + C$

(E) $\sin^3 x + C$

---

31. If $f(x) = (3x)^{(3x)}$ then $f'(x) =$

(A) $(3x)^{(3x)}(3\ln(3x) + 3)$

(B) $(3x)^{(3x)}(3\ln(3x) + 3x)$

(C) $(9x)^{(3x)}(\ln(3x) + 1)$

(D) $(3x)^{(3x-1)}(3x)$

(E) $(3x)^{(3x-1)}(9x)$

GO ON TO THE NEXT PAGE

32. To what limit does the sequence $S_n = \dfrac{3+n}{3^n}$ converge as n approaches infinity?

   (A) 1   (B) $\dfrac{1}{3}$ (C) 0   (D) ∞ (E) 3

---

33. $\displaystyle\int \dfrac{18x - 17}{(2x - 3)\,(x + 1)}\,dx =$

   (A) $8\ln|2x - 3| + 7\ln|x + 1| + C$

   (B) $2\ln|2x - 3| + 7\ln|x + 1| + C$

   (C) $4\ln|2x - 3| + 7\ln|x + 1| + C$

   (D) $7\ln|2x - 3| + 2\ln|x + 1| + C$

   (E) $\dfrac{7}{2}\ln|2x - 3| + 4\ln|x + 1| + C$

---

34. A particle moves along a path described by $x = \cos^3 t$ and $y = \sin^3 t$. The distance that the particle travels along the path from $t = 0$ to $t = \dfrac{\pi}{2}$ is

   (A) 0.75   (B) 1.50   (C) 0   (D) –3.50   (E) –0.75

GO ON TO THE NEXT PAGE

35. The sale price of an item is $800 - 35x$ dollars and the total manufacturing cost is $2x^3 - 140x^2 + 2,600x + 10,000$ dollars, where x is the number of items. What number of items should be manufactured in order to optimize the manufacturer's total profit?

(A) 35   (B) 25   (C) 10   (D) 15   (E) 20

36. The area enclosed by the polar equation $r = 4 + \cos\theta$, for $0 \le \theta \le 2\pi$, is

(A) 0   (B) $\dfrac{9\pi}{2}$ (C) 18π (D) $\dfrac{33\pi}{2}$ (E) $\dfrac{33\pi}{4}$

37. Use the trapezoid rule with $n = 4$ to approximate the area between the curve $y = x^3 - x^2$ and the x-axis from $x = 3$ to $x = 4$.

(A) 35.266   (B) 27.766   (C) 63.031   (D) 31.516   (E) 25.125

GO ON TO THE NEXT PAGE

38. If $f(x) = \sum_{k=0}^{\infty} (\cos^2 x)^k$, then $f\left(\dfrac{\pi}{4}\right)$ is

(A) −2   (B) −1   (C) 0   (D) 1   (E) 2

---

39. The volume of the solid that results when the area between the graph of $y = x^2 + 2$ and the graph of $y = 10 - x^2$ from $x = 0$ to $x = 2$ is rotated around the x-axis is

(A) $2\pi \displaystyle\int_0^2 y\left(\sqrt{y-2}\right)dy + 2\pi \int_0^2 y\left(\sqrt{10-y}\right)dy$

(B) $2\pi \displaystyle\int_2^6 y\left(\sqrt{y-2}\right)dy + 2\pi \int_6^{10} y\left(\sqrt{10-y}\right)dy$

(C) $2\pi \displaystyle\int_2^6 y\left(\sqrt{y-2}\right)dy - 2\pi \int_6^{10} y\left(\sqrt{10-y}\right)dy$

(D) $2\pi \displaystyle\int_0^2 y\left(\sqrt{y-2}\right)dy - 2\pi \int_0^2 y\left(\sqrt{10-y}\right)dy$

(E) $2\pi \displaystyle\int_0^2 y\left(\sqrt{10-y}\right)dy - 2\pi \int_0^2 y\left(\sqrt{y-2}\right)dy$

---

40. $\displaystyle\int_0^4 \dfrac{dx}{\sqrt{9+x^2}} =$

(A) ln3   (B) ln4   (C) −ln2   (D) −ln4   (E) Undefined

41. The rate that an object cools is directly proportional to the difference between its temperature (in Kelvins) at that time and the surrounding temperature (in Kelvins). If an object is initially at $35K$, and the surrounding temperature remains constant at $10K$, it takes 5 minutes for the object to cool to $25K$. How long will it take for the object to cool to $20K$?

(A) 6.66 min.   (B) 7.50 min.   (C) 7.52 min.   (D) 8.97 min.   (E) 10.00 min.

42. $\int e^x \cos x \, dx =$

(A) $\dfrac{e^x}{2}(\sin x + \cos x) + C$

(B) $\dfrac{e^x}{2}(\sin x - \cos x) + C$

(C) $\dfrac{e^x}{2}(\cos x - \sin x) + C$

(D) $2e^x(\sin x + \cos x) + C$

(E) $e^x(\sin x + \cos x) + C$

43. Two particles leave the origin at the same time and move along the y-axis with their respective positions determined by the functions $y_1 = \cos 2t$ and $y_2 = 4 \sin t$ for $0 < t < 6$. For how many values of t do the particles have the same acceleration?

(A) 0   (B) 1   (C) 2   (D) 3   (E) 4

GO ON TO THE NEXT PAGE

44. The minimum value of the function $y = x^3 - 7x + 11$, $x \geq 0$, is approximately

   (A) 18.128   (B) 9.283   (C) 6.698   (D) 5.513   (E) 3.872

---

45. Use Euler's Method with $h = 0.2$ to estimate $y(1)$, if $y' = y$ and $y(0) = 1$.

   (A) 1.200   (B) 2.075   (C) 2.488   (D) 4.838   (E) 9.677

STOP

END OF SECTION I

IF YOU FINISH BEFORE TIME IS CALLED, YOU MAY CHECK YOUR WORK ON THIS SECTION.

DO NOT GO ON TO SECTION II UNTIL YOU ARE TOLD TO DO SO.

SECTION II
GENERAL INSTRUCTIONS

You may wish to look over the problems before starting to work on them, since it is not expected that everyone will be able to complete all parts of all problems. All problems are given equal weight, but the parts of a particular problem are not necessarily given equal weight.

A GRAPHING CALCULATOR IS REQUIRED FOR SOME PROBLEMS OR PARTS OF PROBLEMS ON THIS SECTION OF THE EXAMINATION.

- You should write all work for each part of each problem in the space provided for that part in the booklet. Be sure to write clearly and legibly. If you make an error, you may save time by crossing it out rather than trying to erase it. Erased or crossed-out work will not be graded.

- Show all your work. You will be graded on the correctness and completeness of your methods as well as your answers. Correct answers without supporting work may not receive credit.

- Justifications require that you give mathematical (noncalculator) reasons and that you clearly identify functions, graphs, tables, or other objects you use.

- You are permitted to use your calculator to solve an equation, find the derivative of a function at a point, or calculate the value of a definite integral. However, you must clearly indicate the setup of your problem, namely the equation, function, or integral you are using. If you use other built-in features or programs, you must show the mathematical steps necessary to produce your results.

- Your work must be expressed in standard mathematical notation rather than calculator syntax.

  For example, $\int_{1}^{5} x^2 dx$ may not be written as fnInt (X², X, 1, 5).

- Unless otherwise specified, answers (numeric or algebraic) need not be simplified. If your answer is given as a decimal approximation, it should be correct to three places after the decimal point.

- Unless otherwise specified, the domain of a function f is assumed to be the set of all real numbers x for which $f(x)$ is a real number.

SECTION II, PART A
Time—45 minutes
Number of problems—3

A graphing calculator is required for some problems or parts of problems.

During the timed portion for Part A, you may work only on the problems in Part A.

On Part A, you are permitted to use your calculator to solve an equation, find the derivative of a function at a point, or calculate the value of a definite integral. However, you must clearly indicate the setup of your problem, namely the equation, function, or integral you are using. If you use other built-in features or programs, you must show the mathematical steps necessary to produce your results.

GO ON TO THE NEXT PAGE

1. Two particles travel in the xy-plane. For time $t \geq 0$, the position of particle A is given by $x = t + 1$ and $y = (t + 1)^2 - 2t - 2$, and the position of particle B is given by $x = 4t - 2$ and $y = -2t + 2$.

   (a) Find the velocity vector for each particle at time $t = 2$.

   (b) Set up an integral expression for the distance traveled by particle A from time $t = 1$ to $t = 3$. <u>Do not evaluate the integral</u>.

   (c) At what time do the two particles collide? Justify your answer.

   (d) Sketch the path of both particles from time $t = 0$ to $t = 4$. Indicate the direction of each particle along its path.

---

2. Let f be the function given by $f(x) = 2x^4 - 4x^2 + 1$.

   (a) Find an equation of the line tangent to the graph at $(-2, 17)$. Verify your answer.

   (b) Find the x and y-coordinates of the relative maxima and relative minima.

   (c) Find the x-coordinates of the points of inflection. Verify your answer.

---

3. Water is draining at the rate of 48πft³/sec from the vertex at the bottom of a conical tank whose diameter at its base is 40 feet and whose height is 60 feet.

   (a) Find an expression for the volume of water (in ft³) in the tank in terms of its radius at the surface of the water.

   (b) At what rate (in ft/sec) is the radius of the water in the tank shrinking when the radius is 16 feet?

   (c) How fast (in ft/sec) is the height of the water in the tank dropping at the instant that the radius is 16 feet?

PART B
Time—45 minutes
Number of problems—3

No calculator is allowed for these problems.

During the timed portion for Part B, you may continue to work on the problems in Part A without the use of any calculator.

---

4. Let f be the function given by $f(x) = e^{-4x^2}$

   (a) Find the first four non-zero terms and the general term of the power series for $f(x)$ about $x = 0$.

   (b) Find the interval of convergence of the power series for $f(x)$ about $x = 0$. Show the analysis that leads to your conclusion.

   (c) Use term-by-term differentiation to show that $f'(x) = -8xe^{-4x^2}$

---

5. Let R be the region enclosed by the graphs of $y = 2\ln x$ and $y = \frac{x}{2}$, and the lines $x = 2$ and $x = 8$.

   (a) Find the area of R.

   (b) Set up, but do not integrate, an integral expression, in terms of a single variable, for the volume of the solid generated when R is revolved about the x-axis.

   (c) Set up, but do not integrate, an integral expression, in terms of a single variable, for the volume of the solid generated when R is revolved about the line $x = -1$.

GO ON TO THE NEXT PAGE

6. Let f and g be functions that are differentiable throughout their domains and that have the following properties:

   (i) $f(x + y) = f(x)g(y) + g(x)f(y)$

   (ii) $\lim_{a \to 0} f(a) = 0$

   (iii) $\lim_{h \to 0} \dfrac{g(h) - 1}{h} = 0$

   (iv) $f'(0) = 1$

   (a) Use L'Hôpital's Rule to show that $\lim_{a \to 0} \dfrac{f(a)}{a} = 1$.

   (b) Use the definition of the derivative to show that $f'(x) = g(x)$.

   (c) Find $\displaystyle\int \dfrac{g(x)}{f(x)}\,dx$

END OF EXAMINATION

ANSWER KEY TO SECTION I

1.	D	11.	B	21.	D	31.	A	41.	D
2.	B	12.	C	22.	E	32.	C	42.	A
3.	E	13.	C	23.	B	33.	B	43.	D
4.	C	14.	C	24.	A	34.	B	44.	E
5.	A	15.	A	25.	B	35.	E	45.	C
6.	B	16.	C	26.	D	36.	D		
7.	B	17.	D	27.	B	37.	D		
8.	E	18.	B	28.	B	38.	E		
9.	C	19.	A	29.	C	39.	B		
10.	E	20.	E	30.	C	40.	A		

29

Answers and Explanations to BC Practice Test 1

ANSWERS AND EXPLANATIONS TO SECTION I

PROBLEM 1. If $7 = xy - e^{xy}$, then $\dfrac{dy}{dx} =$

We need to use implicit differentiation to solve this problem.

Step 1: $0 = \left(x\dfrac{dy}{dx} + y\dfrac{dx}{dx} \right) - \left[\left(x\dfrac{dy}{dx} + y\dfrac{dx}{dx} \right)e^{xy} \right]$ *Remember:* $\dfrac{dx}{dx} = 1$

Step 2: $0 = \left(x\dfrac{dy}{dx} + y \right) - \left[\left(x\dfrac{dy}{dx} + y \right)e^{xy} \right]$

Step 3: $0 = \left(x\dfrac{dy}{dx} + y \right) - xe^{xy}\dfrac{dy}{dx} - ye^{xy}$

Step 4: $ye^{xy} - y = x\dfrac{dy}{dx} - xe^{xy}\dfrac{dy}{dx}$

Step 5: $ye^{xy} - y = \dfrac{dy}{dx}\left(x - xe^{xy} \right)$

Step 6: $\dfrac{\left(ye^{xy} - y \right)}{\left(x - xe^{xy} \right)} = \dfrac{dy}{dx}$

Step 7: $\dfrac{\left(ye^{xy} - y \right)}{\left(x - xe^{xy} \right)} = \dfrac{y\left(e^{xy} - 1 \right)}{x\left(1 - e^{xy} \right)} = \dfrac{-y}{x}$

The answer is (D).

PROBLEM 2. The volume of the solid that results when the area between the curve $y = e^x$ and the line $y = 0$, from $x = 1$ to $x = 2$, is revolved around the *x-axis* is

Step 1: We need to use the formula for finding the volume of a solid of revolution. The equations in the problems are given to us in terms of x, and we are rotating around the *x-axis*, so we can use the method of washers. The curve $y = e^x$ is always above the curve $y = 0$ (which is the *x-axis*), so we don't have to break this up into two integrals.

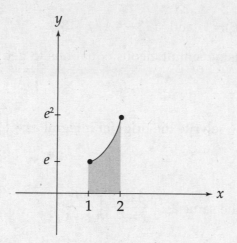

Therefore, the integral will be: $\pi\displaystyle\int_1^2\left(\left(e^x\right)^2-0^2\right)dx$

Step 2: $\pi\displaystyle\int_1^2\left(\left(e^x\right)^2-0^2\right)dx=\pi\int_1^2 e^{2x}dx$

Step 3: $\pi\displaystyle\int_1^2 e^{2x}dx=\pi\left(\dfrac{1}{2}e^{2x}\right)\Big|_1^2$

Step 4: $\pi\left(\dfrac{1}{2}e^{2x}\right)\Big|_1^2=\pi\left(\dfrac{1}{2}e^4-\dfrac{1}{2}e^2\right)$

Step 5: $\pi\left(\dfrac{1}{2}e^4-\dfrac{1}{2}e^2\right)=\dfrac{\pi}{2}\left(e^4-e^2\right)$

The answer is (B).

PROBLEM 3. $\displaystyle\int\dfrac{x-18}{(x+3)(x-4)}\,dx=$

Step 1: We need to use partial fractions to evaluate this integral.

First, we write the integrand as: $\dfrac{x-18}{(x+3)(x-4)}=\dfrac{A}{(x+3)}+\dfrac{B}{(x-4)}$

Step 2: Multiply both sides by: $(x+3)\,(x-4)$

Step 3: Now we have: $x-18=A(x-4)+B(x+3)$

Step 4: $x-18=Ax-4A+Bx+3B$

Step 5: $x-18=(Ax+Bx)+(3B-4A)$

Step 6: $x-18=x(A+B)+(3B-4A)$

Step 7: Thus: $(A+B)=1$ and $(3B-4A)=-18$

Step 8: Solve this using simultaneous equations to get: $A = 3$ and $B = -2$

Step 9: We can now rewrite the original integral as: $\displaystyle\int\left(\frac{3}{x+3}+\frac{-2}{x-4}\right)dx$

Step 10: Which is the same as: $\displaystyle\int\frac{3dx}{x+3}-\int\frac{2dx}{x-4}$

The answer is (E).

PROBLEM 4. If $y = 5x^2 + 4x$ and $x = \ln t$ then $\dfrac{dy}{dt} =$

We can solve this problem with the Chain Rule.

Step 1: $\dfrac{dy}{dx} = 10x + 4$

Step 2: $\dfrac{dx}{dt} = \dfrac{1}{t}$

Step 3: $\dfrac{dy}{dt} = \dfrac{dy}{dx}\dfrac{dx}{dt}$ so $\dfrac{dy}{dt} = (10x+4)\left(\dfrac{1}{t}\right)$

Step 4: Substitute for x so that $\dfrac{dy}{dt} = (10\ln t + 4)\left(\dfrac{1}{t}\right) = \dfrac{10\ln t + 4}{t}$

The answer is (C).

You could also have solved this by first substituting for x in the original equation and getting y in terms of t, and then differentiating with the Chain Rule.

PROBLEM 5. $\displaystyle\int_0^{\frac{\pi}{2}}\sin^5 x\cos x\,dx =$

This trigonometric integral is solved by using u-substitution.

Step 1: Let $\begin{aligned}u &= \sin x\\ du &= \cos x\,dx\end{aligned}$

Step 2: The integral is now written as: $\int_0^1 u^5 \, du =$

Note: The limits of integration change because:

$$u = \sin\frac{\pi}{2} = 1 \text{ and } u = \sin 0 = 0$$

Step 3: $\int_0^1 u^5 \, du = \left. \frac{u^6}{6} \right|_0^1$

Step 4: $\left. \frac{u^6}{6} \right|_0^1 = \frac{1}{6} - 0 = \frac{1}{6}$

The answer is (A).

PROBLEM 6. The tangent line to the curve $y = x^3 - 4x + 8$ at the point (2,8) has an x-intercept at

Step 1: First find the slope of the tangent line: $\frac{dy}{dx} = 3x^2 - 4$

Step 2: Plug 2 into $\frac{dy}{dx} = 3(2)^2 - 4 = 12 - 4 = 8$.

This means that the slope of the tangent line at $x = 2$ is 8.

Step 3: Then the equation of the tangent line is $(y - 8) = 8(x - 2)$.

Step 4: The x-intercept is found by plugging in $y = 0$ and solving for x:

$$0 - 8 = 8(x - 2)$$

Therefore, $x = 1$.

The answer is (B).

PROBLEM 7. The graph in the xy-plane represented by $x = 3\sin(t)$ and $y = 2\cos(t)$ is

This is a parametric equation and is solved by eliminating t from the equations and finding a direct relationship between y and x. These problems can often be quite difficult, but, fortunately, on the AP exam, they only give very easy versions of parametric equations.

Step 1: $\frac{x}{3} = \sin(t)$ and $\frac{y}{2} = \cos(t)$

Step 2: Because $\sin^2(t) + \cos^2(t) = 1$, we can substitute and we get $\left(\dfrac{x}{3}\right)^2 + \left(\dfrac{y}{2}\right)^2 = 1$. This is an ellipse.

The answer is (B).

PROBLEM 8. $\displaystyle\int \dfrac{dx}{\sqrt{4-9x^2}} =$

You should recognize this as an inverse trigonometric integral of the form $\dfrac{du}{\sqrt{1-u^2}}$, which is $\sin^{-1}(u)$. You also should know this by looking at the answer choices. One of the difficulties of the AP exam is that you are required to recognize many different types of integrals by sight, and to know which techniques to use to solve them.

Step 1: First, we need to use a little algebra to convert the integrand to the form:

$$\dfrac{du}{\sqrt{1-u^2}}$$

Rewrite: $\sqrt{\left(4-9x^2\right)} = \sqrt{4\left(1-\dfrac{9x^2}{4}\right)} = 2\sqrt{\left(1-\dfrac{9x^2}{4}\right)} = 2\sqrt{1-\left(\dfrac{3x}{2}\right)^2}$

The integral then becomes: $\displaystyle\int \dfrac{dx}{\sqrt{4-9x^2}} = \int \dfrac{dx}{\left(2\sqrt{1-\left(\dfrac{3x}{2}\right)^2}\right)} = \dfrac{1}{2}\int \dfrac{dx}{\sqrt{1-\left(\dfrac{3x}{2}\right)^2}}$

Step 2: Now we can use *u*-substitution. Let $u = \dfrac{3x}{2}$ and $du = \dfrac{3}{2}dx$ and $\dfrac{2}{3}du = dx$.

We can now rewrite the integral as: $\displaystyle\int \dfrac{dx}{\sqrt{4-9x^2}} = \left(\dfrac{1}{2}\right)\left(\dfrac{2}{3}\right)\int \dfrac{du}{\sqrt{1-u^2}} = \dfrac{1}{3}\int \dfrac{du}{\sqrt{1-u^2}}$

Step 3: You should have memorized this last integral. It is: $\left(\dfrac{1}{3}\right)\sin^{-1}(u) + C$

Step 4: Now reverse the *u*-substitution and we have:

$$\left(\dfrac{1}{3}\right)\sin^{-1}(u) + C = \left(\dfrac{1}{3}\right)\sin^{-1}\left(\dfrac{3x}{2}\right) + C$$

The answer is (E).

PROBLEM 9. $\lim\limits_{x\to\infty} 4x\sin\left(\dfrac{1}{x}\right) =$

To solve this problem, you need to remember how to evaluate limits, particularly of trigonometric functions.

Step 1: As you should recall, the $\lim\limits_{x\to0}\dfrac{\sin x}{x} = 1$. (This can be shown with L'Hôpital's Rule. Differentiate the top and bottom of the limit to obtain $\lim\limits_{x\to0}\dfrac{\cos x}{1}$, which just equals 1.) Thus, we need to find a way to convert this integral into one that looks like $\dfrac{\sin x}{x}$.

We can do this with a simple substitution. Let $y = \dfrac{1}{x}$. Now we can change this limit from $\lim\limits_{x\to\infty} 4x\sin\left(\dfrac{1}{x}\right)$ to $\lim\limits_{y\to0} 4\left(\dfrac{\sin y}{y}\right)$.

Step 2: $\lim\limits_{y\to0} 4\left(\dfrac{\sin y}{y}\right) = 4(1) = 4$

The answer is (C).

PROBLEM 10. The position of a particle moving along the x-axis at time t is given by $x(t) = e^{\cos(2t)}$, $0 \le t \le \pi$. For which of the following values of t will $x'(t) = 0$?

This problem requires you to know derivatives of exponential functions and derivatives of trigonometric functions. Also, whenever you are given restrictions on the domain of a function, pay careful attention to the restrictions.

Step 1: $x'(t) = e^{\cos(2t)}\left(-2\sin(2t)\right)$

Step 2: Now that we have the derivative, set it equal to zero:

$$e^{\cos(2t)}\left(-2\sin(2t)\right) = 0$$

Step 3: Because $e^{\cos(2t)}$ can never equal zero (Did you know this? Make sure that you do!), we only have to set $-2\sin(2t)$ equal to zero. This will be true wherever $\sin(2t) = 0$. This will occur whenever $2t = 0$, π, 2π,... or when $t = 0$, $\dfrac{\pi}{2}$, π,... Thus all three roman numeral answer choices work.

The answer is (E).

PROBLEM 11. $\lim\limits_{h \to 0} \dfrac{\sec(\pi + h) - \sec(\pi)}{h} =$

This may *appear* to be a limit problem, but it is *actually* testing to see whether you know the definition of the derivative.

Step 1: You should recall that $\lim\limits_{h \to 0} \dfrac{f(x+h) - f(x)}{h} = f'(x)$. Thus, if we replace $f(x)$ with $\sec(x)$, we can rewrite the problem as:

$$\lim\limits_{h \to 0} \frac{\sec(x+h) - \sec(x)}{h} = \big[\sec(x)\big]'$$

Step 2: The derivative of $\sec(x)$ is $\sec(x)\tan(x)$. Thus,

$$\lim\limits_{h \to 0} \frac{\sec(\pi + h) - \sec(\pi)}{h} = \sec(\pi)\tan(\pi)$$

Step 3: Because $\sec(\pi) = -1$ and $\tan(\pi) = 0$, this is equal to 0.

The answer is (B).

PROBLEM 12. Use differentials to approximate the change in the volume of a cube when the side is decreased from 8 to 7.99 cm (in cm^3).

The volume of a cube is $V = x^3$. Using differentials, the change will be: $dV = 3x^2\, dx$

Substitute in $x = 8$ and $dx = -.01$, and we get:

$$dV = 3(8^2)(-.01)$$

$$dV = -1.92$$

The answer is (C).

PROBLEM 13. The radius of convergence of $\displaystyle\sum_{n=1}^{\infty} \frac{a^n}{(x+2)^n}$; $a > 0$ is

Step 1: An infinite series of the form $\displaystyle\sum_{n=0}^{\infty} r^n$ will converge if $|r| < 1$. So all we have to do is to set $\left|\dfrac{a}{x+2}\right| < 1$.

Step 2: $\left|\dfrac{a}{x+2}\right| < 1$ means that $-1 < \dfrac{a}{x+2} < 1$. We can rewrite this as $-1 > \dfrac{x+2}{a} > 1$.

Step 3: Now we have $-a > x + 2 > a$ or $-a - 2 > x > a - 2$.

The answer is (C).

PROBLEM 14. $\int_0^1 \sin^{-1}(x)dx =$

Step 1: Your first reaction to this integral may very well be "I don't know how to find the integral of an inverse trigonometric function. I only know how to find the derivative of an inverse trigonometric function!" That's okay. This is actually an integration by parts problem. First of all, we are going to ignore the limits of integration until the end of this problem, and just focus on finding the integral itself. As you should recall, the formula for integration by parts is:

$$\int u\,dv = uv - \int v\,du$$

Step 2: Let: $u = \sin^{-1} x$ and $dv = dx$.

Then: $du = \dfrac{dx}{\sqrt{1-x^2}}$ and $v = x$

Now, using integration by parts, we have: $\int \sin^{-1}(x)dx = x\sin^{-1}(x) - \int \dfrac{xdx}{\sqrt{1-x^2}}$

Step 3: We can now solve this latter integral with u-substitution.

Let $u = 1 - x^2$ and $du = -2xdx$:

$$\frac{-1}{2}du = xdx$$

Then we have: $\int \dfrac{dx}{\sqrt{1-x^2}} = \dfrac{-1}{2}\int u^{\frac{-1}{2}}\,du = -u^{\frac{1}{2}}$

Step 4: Substituting back for u gives us: $\int \sin^{-1}(x)dx = x\sin^{-1}(x) + \sqrt{(1-x^2)}$

Step 5: Now we evaluate at the limits of integration:

$$\left(x\sin^{-1}x + \sqrt{1-x^2}\right)\Big|_0^1 = \left((1)\sin^{-1}(1) + \sqrt{0}\right) - \left(0\sin^{-1}0 + \sqrt{1}\right) = \left(\frac{\pi}{2}\right) - (1) = \frac{\pi-2}{2}$$

The answer is (C).

PROBLEM 15. The equation of the line *normal* to $y = \sqrt{\dfrac{5-x^2}{5+x^2}}$ at $x = 2$ is

Step 1: This problem requires you to know how to find equations of tangent lines. We will use the slope-intercept formula of a line: $(y - y_1) = m(x - x_1)$.

Step 2: When $x = 2$, $y = \sqrt{\dfrac{5-(2^2)}{5+(2^2)}} = \sqrt{\dfrac{5-4}{5+4}} = \sqrt{\dfrac{1}{9}} = \dfrac{1}{3}$, so

$$x_1 = 2 \quad \text{and} \quad y_1 = \frac{1}{3}$$

Step 3: $\dfrac{dy}{dx} = \dfrac{1}{2}\left(\dfrac{5-x^2}{5+x^2}\right)^{\frac{-1}{2}}\left(\dfrac{(5+x^2)(-2x)-(5-x^2)(2x)}{(5+x^2)^2}\right)$ This would now require some

messy algebra to simplify, but fortunately we don't have to. We can plug in 2 for x

right now and solve for $\dfrac{dy}{dx} = \dfrac{1}{2}\left(\dfrac{5-2^2}{5+2^2}\right)^{\frac{-1}{2}}\left(\dfrac{(5+2^2)(-4)-(5-2^2)(4)}{(5+2^2)^2}\right)$,

which simplifies to $\dfrac{1}{2}\left(\dfrac{1}{9}\right)^{\frac{-1}{2}}\left(\dfrac{(9)(-4)-(1)(4)}{(9)^2}\right) = \dfrac{3}{2}\left(\dfrac{-36-4}{81}\right) = \dfrac{-20}{27}$.

Step 4: If we were finding the equation of a *tangent line*, we would use $\dfrac{-20}{27}$ for m in the equation, but, as you should recall, because we are finding the equation of the *normal line*, we use the *negative reciprocal* of $\dfrac{-20}{27}$ for m, which is $\dfrac{27}{20}$ and plug it into the equation of the line.

Step 5: Now we have $(y - y_1) = m(x - x_1)$ which becomes $y - \dfrac{1}{3} = \dfrac{27}{20}(x - 2)$.

Multiply through by 60 to get: $60y - 20 = 81x - 162$ or $81x - 60y = 142$.

The answer is (A).

PROBLEM 16. If c satisfies the conclusion of the Mean Value Theorem for derivatives for $f(x) = 2\sin x$ on the interval $[0, \pi]$, then c is

Step 1: The Mean Value Theorem for derivatives states that if a function is differentiable on an interval $[a, b]$, then there exists some value c in that interval where
$$\frac{f(b)-f(a)}{b-a} = f'(c)$$

Step 2: $\dfrac{f(b)-f(a)}{b-a}=\dfrac{2\sin\pi-2\sin 0}{\pi-0}=\dfrac{0}{\pi}=0$

Step 3: Thus $f'(c)=0$. Because $f'(c)=2\cos(c)$, we need to know what value of c makes $2\cos(c)=0$. The value is $\dfrac{\pi}{2}$.

The answer is (C).

PROBLEM 17. The average value of $f(x)=x\ln x$ on the interval $[1, e]$ is

This problem requires you to be familiar with the Mean Value Theorem for integrals, which we use to find the average value of a function.

Step 1: If you want to find the average value of $f(x)$ on an interval $[a, b]$, you need to evaluate the integral $\dfrac{1}{b-a}\displaystyle\int_a^b f(x)dx$. So here we would evaluate the integral $\dfrac{1}{e-1}\displaystyle\int_1^e x\ln x\,dx$.

Step 2: We are going to need to do integration by parts to evaluate this integral. Let's ignore the limits of integration for now and just do the integration:

Let $u=\ln x$ and $dv=xdx$.

Then: $du=\dfrac{1}{x}dx$ and $v=\dfrac{x^2}{2}$

Now the integral becomes: $\displaystyle\int x\ln x\,dx=\dfrac{x^2}{2}\ln x-\int\left(\dfrac{x^2}{2}\right)\left(\dfrac{1}{x}\right)dx=\dfrac{x^2}{2}\ln x-\dfrac{1}{2}\int x\,dx$

Thus we have: $\displaystyle\int_1^e x\ln x\,dx=\left(\dfrac{x^2}{2}\ln x-\dfrac{x^2}{4}\right)\Big|_1^e$

Step 3: $\left(\dfrac{x^2}{2}\ln x-\dfrac{x^2}{4}\right)\Big|_1^e=\left(\dfrac{e^2}{2}\ln e-\dfrac{e^2}{4}\right)-\left(\dfrac{1}{2}\ln 1-\dfrac{1}{4}\right)=\left(\dfrac{e^2}{2}-\dfrac{e^2}{4}+\dfrac{1}{4}\right)$

This can be simplified to: $\dfrac{e^2+1}{4}$

Step 4: Don't forget to multiply by $\dfrac{1}{e-1}$. This gives the final result of: $\dfrac{e^2+1}{4(e-1)}$.

The answer is (D).

PROBLEM 18. A 17 foot ladder is sliding down a wall at a rate of –5 feet/sec. When the top of the ladder is 8 feet from the ground, how fast is the foot of the ladder sliding away from the wall (in feet/sec)?

Step 1: The ladder forms a right triangle with the wall, with the ladder itself as the hypotenuse. Whenever we see right triangles in related rates problems, we look to use the Pythagorean Theorem.

Call the distance from the top of the ladder to the ground y, and the distance from the foot of the ladder to the wall x. Then the rate at which the top of the ladder is sliding down the wall is $\dfrac{dy}{dt}$, and the rate at which the foot of the ladder is sliding away from the wall is $\dfrac{dx}{dt}$, which is what we need to find. Now we use the Pythagorean Theorem to set up the relationships: $x^2 + y^2 = 17^2$

Step 2: Differentiating both sides we obtain: $2x\dfrac{dx}{dt} + 2y\dfrac{dy}{dt} = 0$

Step 3: Because of the Pythagorean Theorem, we also know that, when $y = 8$, $x = 15$.

Step 4: Now we plug everything into the equation from Step 2 and solve for $\dfrac{dx}{dt}$:

$$2(15)\dfrac{dx}{dt} + 2(8)(-5) = 0 \quad \text{and} \quad \dfrac{dx}{dt} = \dfrac{8}{3}$$

The answer is (B).

PROBLEM 19. If $\dfrac{dy}{dx} = 3y\cos x$, and $y = 8$ when $x = 0$, then $y =$

Step 1: Separate the variables, by putting all of the terms containing y on the left hand side of the equals sign, and all of the terms containing x on the right hand side:

$$\dfrac{dy}{y} = 3\cos x \, dx$$

Step 2: Integrate both sides:

$$\int \dfrac{dy}{y} = 3\int \cos x \, dx$$

$$\ln y = 3\sin x + C$$

Whenever we have a differential equation where the solution is in terms of $\ln y$, we always solve the equation for y. This involves raising e to the power of each side. This gives us: $e^{\ln y} = e^{3\sin x + C}$; $y = e^{3\sin x} e^C$; $y = Ce^{3\sin x}$. Now you should notice that e^C is just a constant, so we call that C, and write the equation as:

$$y = Ce^{3\sin x}$$

Step 3: Now plug in $y = 8$ and $x = 0$ in order to solve for C:

$$8 = Ce^{3\sin 0} = Ce^0 = C$$
$$8 = C$$

Step 4: This gives the final equation of $y = 8e^{3\sin x}$.

The answer is (A).

PROBLEM 20. The length of the curve determined by $x = 3t$ and $y = 2t^2$ from $t = 0$ to $t = 9$ is

This problem requires you to find an Arc Length. This is a simple integral formula.

Step 1: The formula for the arc length of a curve given in parametric form on the interval $[a, b]$ is:

$$\int_a^b \sqrt{\left(\frac{dx}{dt}\right)^2 + \left(\frac{dy}{dt}\right)^2}\, dt$$

Step 2: $\dfrac{dx}{dt} = 3$ and $\dfrac{dy}{dt} = 4t$, so $\int_a^b \sqrt{\left(\dfrac{dx}{dt}\right)^2 + \left(\dfrac{dy}{dt}\right)^2}\, dt = \int_0^9 \sqrt{3^2 + (4t)^2}\, dt$

Step 3: $\int_0^9 \sqrt{3^2 + (4t)^2}\, dt = \int_0^9 \sqrt{9 + 16t^2}\, dt$

The answer is (E).

PROBLEM 21. If a particle moves in the xy-plane so that at time $t > 0$ its position vector is $\left(e^{t^2}, e^{-t^3}\right)$ then its velocity vector at time $t = 3$ is

This problem requires you to know how to find the velocity of a moving object.

Step 1: All you need to do to find the velocity of a moving object at a particular instant in time is to take the derivative of its position function at that time; the derivative of $e^{t^2} = 2te^{t^2}$ and the derivative of $e^{-t^3} = -3t^2e^{-t^3}$.

Step 2: Now we plug in 3 for t and we get: $2te^{t^2} = 6e^9$ and $-3t^2e^{-t^3} = -27e^{-27}$

The answer is (D).

PROBLEM 22. The graph of $f(x) = \sqrt{11 + x^2}$ has a point of inflection at

This problem requires you to know how to find the critical points on a graph, which is a crucial part of graphing functions.

Step 1: The points of inflection on a graph are generally at points where the second derivative is zero, but not necessarily at *all* points where the second derivative is zero. The good thing about the AP exam is that, in the multiple choice part of the test, you do not have to worry about exceptions to the second derivative rule. Thus, all we have to do here is to take the second derivative of the function and set it equal to zero:

$$f'(x) = \frac{1}{2}\left(11 + x^2\right)^{\frac{-1}{2}}(2x) = \frac{x}{\left(11 + x^2\right)^{\frac{1}{2}}}$$

and

$$f''(x) = \frac{\left(11 + x^2\right)^{\frac{1}{2}}(1) - (x)\frac{1}{2}\left(11 + x^2\right)^{\frac{-1}{2}}(2x)}{\left(11 + x^2\right)}$$

$$= \frac{\left(11 + x^2\right)^{\frac{1}{2}} - \dfrac{x^2}{\left(11 + x^2\right)^{\frac{1}{2}}}}{\left(11 + x^2\right)^{\frac{1}{2}}}$$

$$= \frac{\left(11 + x^2\right) - x^2}{\left(11 + x^2\right)^{\frac{3}{2}}}$$

$$= \frac{11}{\left(11 + x^2\right)^{\frac{3}{2}}}$$

Step 2: When we are setting a rational function equal to zero, all we have to do is set the numerator equal to zero, and that value will be our point of inflection. Always double check that the value that makes the numerator equal to zero does not also make the DENOMINATOR equal to zero. If it does, this is NOT necessarily a point of inflection. Here, there is no point where 11 equals zero, so there is no point of inflection.

The answer is (E).

PROBLEM 23. What is the volume of the solid generated by rotating about the y-axis the region enclosed by $y = \sin x$ and the x-axis, from $x = 0$ to $x = \pi$?

This problem requires us to find the volume of a solid of revolution.

Step 1: Whenever you find the volume of a solid of revolution, you should first draw the graph of the equation so that you are sure of exactly what the curve looks like. You can graph this easily on your calculator, and should get something that looks like this:

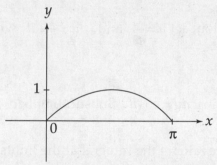

Step 2: Because we are revolving this curve around the y-axis, it will be easier to use the "shells" formula than the "washers" formula.

Using this formula, we get: $2\pi \int_0^\pi x \sin x\, dx$. This is one of our basic integration by parts integrals.

Let $u = x$ and $dv = \sin x\, dx$.

Then: $du = dx$ and $v = -\cos x$

then,

$$\int x \sin x\, dx = -x \cos x + \int \cos x\, dx = -x \cos x + \sin x$$

Step 3: Now we evaluate at the limits of integration and we get:

$$2\pi(-x \cos x + \sin x)\big|_0^\pi = 2\pi\big[(-\pi \cos \pi + \sin \pi) - (0 + \sin 0)\big] = 2\pi^2$$

The answer is (B).

PROBLEM 24. $\displaystyle\int_{\frac{2}{\pi}}^{\infty} \frac{\sin\left(\frac{1}{t}\right)}{t^2} dt =$

This is an improper integral. As with many of the more difficult topics in calculus, the AP examination only tends to ask us to solve very straightforward improper Integrals. The trick is to change the improper integral into a proper one.

Step 1: First, we need to rewrite the integral as a limit. Let $a = \infty$, and evaluate:

$\displaystyle\lim_{a\to\infty}\int_{\frac{2}{\pi}}^{a} \frac{\sin\left(\frac{1}{t}\right)}{t^2} dt$. This gets rid of the "infinity problem."

At this point, we ignore the limits of integration while we figure out how to do the integral.

Using u-substitution, let $u = \dfrac{1}{t}$ and $du = \dfrac{-1}{t^2} dt$, which gives us:

$\displaystyle\int \frac{\sin\left(\frac{1}{t}\right)}{t^2} dt = -\int \sin u\, du = \cos u$. Substituting back, we get $\cos\dfrac{1}{t}\bigg|_{\frac{2}{\pi}}^{a}$

Step 2: Now we evaluate the integral at the limits of integration and get:

$$\cos\frac{1}{t}\bigg|_{\frac{2}{\pi}}^{a} = \cos\frac{1}{a} - \cos\frac{\pi}{2} = \cos\frac{1}{a}$$

Step 3: Finally, we take the limit and we get: $\displaystyle\lim_{a\to\infty}\cos\frac{1}{a} = \cos 0 = 1$

The answer is (A).

PROBLEM 25. A rectangle is to be inscribed between the parabola $y = 4 - x^2$ and the x-axis, with its base on the x-axis. The value of x that maximizes the area of the rectangle is

This is a maximum/minimum problem. It is usually helpful to draw a picture first, so we know what we are looking for.

Step 1: If we graph $y = 4 - x^2$ and sketch in a rectangle, we get something like this:

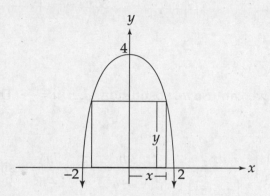

Step 2: Notice that the length of the base of the rectangle is $2x$ and the height of the rectangle is y. This means that the area of the rectangle is: $A = 2xy$. If we substitute $4 - x^2$ for y, we get: $A = 2x\left(4 - x^2\right) = 8x - 2x^3$.

Step 3: If we want to find the maximum area, all we have to do is take the derivative of A and set it equal to zero:

$$\frac{dA}{dx} = 8 - 6x^2 = 0$$

$$8 = 6x^2$$

$$x = \pm\sqrt{\frac{4}{3}} = \pm\frac{2}{\sqrt{3}}$$

Because the answer is looking for a length, we are satisfied with the positive answer. Besides, $-\frac{2}{\sqrt{3}}$ isn't an answer choice.

The answer is (B).

PROBLEM 26. $\displaystyle\int \frac{dx}{\sqrt{9 - x^2}} =$

If you look at this integral, you should notice that it is similar to the integral:

$$\int \frac{dx}{\sqrt{1 - x^2}} = \sin^{-1} x + C$$

Step 1: If we factor 9 out of the radicand, we can convert our integral into the one above:

$$\int \frac{dx}{\sqrt{9-x^2}} = \int \frac{dx}{\sqrt{9\left(1-\frac{x^2}{9}\right)}} = \int \frac{dx}{3\sqrt{\left(1-\frac{x^2}{9}\right)}} = \frac{1}{3}\int \frac{dx}{\sqrt{\left(1-\frac{x^2}{9}\right)}}$$

Step 2: Now we can use u-substitution. Let $u = \frac{x}{3}$. Then $du = \frac{1}{3}dx$ and $3du = dx$. We get:

$$\frac{1}{3}\int \frac{dx}{\sqrt{\left(1-\frac{x^2}{9}\right)}} = \frac{1}{3}\int \frac{3du}{\sqrt{1-u^2}} = \int \frac{du}{\sqrt{1-u^2}} = \sin^{-1}u + C$$

Step 3: Substituting back, we get:

$$\sin^{-1}\frac{x}{3} + C$$

The answer is (D).

PROBLEM 27. Find $\lim\limits_{x\to\infty} x^{\frac{1}{x}}$

This is a limit of an *indeterminate form*. We use L'Hôpital's Rule to evaluate these limits, but we need to get this into the form $\frac{f(x)}{g(x)}$ so that we can take the derivative of the top and bottom. We do this using logarithms.

Step 1: First, let $y = x^{\frac{1}{x}}$

Step 2: Now, take the log of both sides (remember, when we say log, we mean *natural log*, not *common log*).

We get $\ln y = \ln x^{\frac{1}{x}}$, which we can rewrite, using log rules, as $\frac{1}{x}\ln x$ or $\frac{\ln x}{x}$

Step 3: Now we can use L'Hôpital's Rule. Take the derivative of the top and bottom.

$$\lim_{x\to\infty} \frac{\ln x}{x} = \lim_{x\to\infty} \frac{\frac{1}{x}}{1} = 0$$

Be careful! This is NOT the answer! We just found that the limit of $\ln y \to 0$, therefore, $y \to e^0 = 1$. Whenever you use this technique, remember to reverse the logarithm at the end.

The answer is (B).

PROBLEM 28. What is the sum of the Maclaurin series $\pi - \dfrac{\pi^3}{3!} + \dfrac{\pi^5}{5!} - \dfrac{\pi^7}{7!} + \ldots$ $+ (-1)^n \dfrac{\pi^{2n+1}}{(2n+1)!} + \ldots$?

This series is of the form $x - \dfrac{x^3}{3!} + \dfrac{x^5}{5!} - \dfrac{x^7}{7!} + \ldots + (-1)^n \dfrac{x^{2n+1}}{(2n+1)!} + \ldots$. This, as we know,

is the Maclaurin series expansion of $\sin x$. In the problem, we simply have π instead of x. Therefore, this is equal to $\sin \pi = 0$.

The answer is (B).

PROBLEM 29. The first three non-zero terms in the Taylor series about $x = 0$ of $\cos x$ are

This is a Taylor series problem. There are four Taylor series that you should memorize. *This is one of them.* But just in case you didn't memorize it ...

Step 1: The formula for a Taylor series about the point $x = a$ is:

$$f(a) + f'(a)(x-a) + f''(a)\frac{(x-a)^2}{2!} + f'''(a)\frac{(x-a)^3}{3!} + \ldots + f^{(n)}(a)\frac{(x-a)^n}{n!} + \ldots$$

Step 2: First, let's take the first few derivatives of $\cos x$:

$$f(x) = \cos x$$
$$f'(x) = -\sin x$$
$$f''(x) = -\cos x$$
$$f'''(x) = \sin x$$
$$f^{(4)}(x) = \cos x$$

Step 3: Next, we evaluate each of these at $a = 0$:

$$f(0) = \cos 0 = 1$$
$$f'(0) = -\sin 0 = 0$$
$$f''(0) = -\cos 0 = -1$$
$$f'''(0) = \sin 0 = 0$$
$$f^{(4)}(0) = \cos 0 = 1$$

Step 4: Now if we plug in 0 for a throughout the formula we get:

$$f(0)+f'(0)(x)+f''(0)\frac{(x)^2}{2!}+f'''(0)\frac{(x)^3}{3!}+f^{(4)}(0)\frac{(x)^4}{4!}+...$$

$$=1+(0)(x)+(-1)\left(\frac{x^2}{2!}\right)+(0)\left(\frac{x^3}{3!}\right)+(1)\left(\frac{x^4}{4!}\right)+...$$

$$=1+0-\frac{x^2}{2!}+0+\frac{x^4}{4!}=1-\frac{x^2}{2!}+\frac{x^4}{4!}$$

The answer is (C).

You should make sure to memorize the four Taylor series in the unit. One of them almost always shows up on the AP examination!

PROBLEM 30. $\int \cos^3 x \, dx =$

This is a trigonometric integral. Generally, these are solved by using the trigonometric substitutions that you learned in precalculus. If you are unfamiliar with these, you should go back and review them.

Step 1: First, rewrite $\cos^3 x$ as $\cos x(\cos^2 x)$. Then, because $\cos^2 x = (1-\sin^2 x)$, we can rewrite the integral as:

$$\int \cos^3 x \, dx = \int \cos x(1-\sin^2 x)dx = \int \cos x \, dx - \int \cos x \sin^2 x \, dx$$

Step 2: The first integral is easy: $\int \cos x \, dx = \sin x$. We do the second integral with u-substitution.

Let $u = \sin x$ and $du = \cos x dx$. Then $\int \cos x \sin^2 x \, dx = \int u^2 du = \frac{u^3}{3}+C$

Substituting back for u and combining, gives us:

$$\int \cos x \, dx - \int \cos x \sin^2 x \, dx = \sin x - \frac{\sin^3 x}{3}+C$$

The answer is (C).

PROBLEM 31. If $f(x) = (3x)^{(3x)}$ then $f'(x) =$

This problem requires us to find the derivative of an exponential function. Any power of x can be written as a power of e, which is what we will use to do this derivative.

Step 1: Rewrite $(3x)^{(3x)}$ as $e^{(3x)\ln(3x)}$. Now, we can take the derivative of this using the Chain Rule and the Product Rule.

Step 2: $f'(x) = \left[(3x)\left(\dfrac{3}{3x}\right) + 3\ln(3x) \right] e^{(3x)\ln(3x)} = (3 + 3\ln(3x)) e^{(3x)\ln(3x)}$

Step 3: Now, replacing $e^{(3x)\ln(3x)}$ with $(3x)^{(3x)}$, gives us $(3x)^{(3x)}(3 + 3\ln(3x))$.

The answer is (A).

PROBLEM 32. To what limit does the sequence $s_n = \dfrac{3+n}{3^n}$ converge as n approaches infinity?

This will require us to use one of the convergence tests for Infinite series. If we use the ratio test, we will be able to tell if the sequence converges, and, if so, to what value.

Step 1: $s_n = \dfrac{3+n}{3^n}$ and $s_{n+1} = \dfrac{4+n}{3^{n+1}}$. So the ratio test says that, if $\lim\limits_{n \to \infty} \left| \dfrac{s_{n+1}}{s_n} \right| < 1$, then the sequence will converge to zero, and if $\lim\limits_{n \to \infty} \left| \dfrac{s_{n+1}}{s_n} \right| > 1$, then the series diverges–in other words, it has no limit.

Step 2: $\dfrac{s_{n+1}}{s_n} = \dfrac{\dfrac{4+n}{3^{n+1}}}{\dfrac{3+n}{3^n}} = \dfrac{4+n}{3+n}\left(\dfrac{3^n}{3^{n+1}}\right) = \dfrac{1}{3}\left(\dfrac{4+n}{3+n}\right)$

If we take the limit, $\lim\limits_{n \to \infty} \dfrac{1}{3}\left(\dfrac{4+n}{3+n}\right) = \dfrac{1}{3}$.

Because this is less than one, the sequence converges to zero.

The answer is (C).

PROBLEM 33. $\displaystyle\int \dfrac{18x - 17}{(2x-3)(x+1)}\, dx =$

This is another partial fractions integral.

Step 1: Write the integrand as: $\dfrac{18x-17}{(2x-3)(x+1)} = \dfrac{A}{(2x-3)} + \dfrac{B}{(x+1)}$

Step 2: Multiply both sides by: $(2x - 3)(x + 1)$

Step 3: Now we have: $18x - 17 = A(x + 1) + B(2x - 3)$

Step 4: $18x - 17 = Ax + A + 2Bx - 3B$

Step 5: $18x - 17 = (Ax + 2Bx) + (A - 3B)$

Step 6: $18x - 17 = x(A + 2B) + (A - 3B)$

Step 7: Thus: $(A + 2B) = 18$ and $(A - 3B) = -17$

Step 8: Solve this using simultaneous equations to get: $A = 4$ and $B = 7$

Step 9: We can now rewrite the original integral as:

$$\int \left(\frac{4}{2x-3} + \frac{7}{x+1} \right) dx = 4\int \frac{dx}{2x-3} + 7\int \frac{dx}{x+1}$$

Step 10: These are both basic *ln* integrals, and we get:

$$4\int \frac{dx}{2x-3} + 7\int \frac{dx}{x+1} = 2\ln|2x-3| + 7\ln|x+1| + C$$

The answer is (B).

PROBLEM 34. A particle moves along a path described by $x = \cos^3 t$ and $y = \sin^3 t$. Find the distance that the particle travels along the path from $t = 0$ to $t = \dfrac{\pi}{2}$.

This is another arc length problem.

Step 1: The formula for the arc length of a curve given in parametric form on the interval $[a,b]$ is: $\displaystyle\int_a^b \sqrt{\left(\frac{dx}{dt}\right)^2 + \left(\frac{dy}{dt}\right)^2}\, dt$

Step 2: $\dfrac{dx}{dt} = -3\cos^2 t \sin t$ and $\dfrac{dy}{dt} = 3\sin^2 t \cos t$, so:

$$\int_a^b \sqrt{\left(\frac{dx}{dt}\right)^2 + \left(\frac{dy}{dt}\right)^2}\, dt = \int_0^{\frac{\pi}{2}} \sqrt{\left(-3\cos^2 t \sin t\right)^2 + \left(3\sin^2 t \cos t\right)^2}\, dt$$

$$= \int_0^{\frac{\pi}{2}} \sqrt{\left(9\cos^4 t \sin^2 t\right) + \left(9\sin^4 t \cos^2 t\right)}\, dt$$

Step 3: Now you have a choice. Integrate this using your calculator. You should get 1.5.

If you are not comfortable with this on the calculator, or if you prefer to do the integration, you need to do the following. Reduce the integrand by factoring out $\sin^2 t \cos^2 t$ and we get:

$$\int_0^{\frac{\pi}{2}} \sqrt{9\left(\sin^2 t \cos^2 t\right)\left(\sin^2 t + \cos^2 t\right)}\,dt = \int_0^{\frac{\pi}{2}} \sqrt{9\left(\sin^2 t \cos^2 t\right)(1)}\,dt$$

$$\int_0^{\frac{\pi}{2}} \sqrt{9\sin^2 t \cos^2 t}\,dt = \int_0^{\frac{\pi}{2}} 3\sin t \cos t\,dt$$

Step 4: Using u-substitution, let $u = \sin t$ and $du = \cos t$. Then we get:

$$\int_0^{\frac{\pi}{2}} 3\sin t \cos t\,dt = 3\int_0^1 u\,du = 3\left(\frac{u^2}{2}\right)\Bigg|_0^1 = \frac{3}{2}$$

The answer is (B).

Problem 35. The sales price of an item is $800 - 35x$ dollars and the total manufacturing cost is $2x^3 - 140x^2 + 2,600x + 10,000$ dollars, where x is the number of items. What number of items should be manufactured in order to optimize the manufacturer's total profit?

Anytime that you see the word "optimize," you will be doing a maximum/minimum problem. The profit is the number of items sold times the difference between the sales price of each object and its cost. The number of items is x, so the total sales price is $800x - 35x^2$.

Step 1: Let P equal profit:

$P = 800x - 35x^2 - (2x^3 - 140x^2 + 2600x + 10000) = -2x^3 + 105x^2 - 1800x - 10000$

Step 2: $\dfrac{dP}{dx} = -6x^2 + 210x - 1800$. Setting it equal to 0 we get:

$$-6x^2 + 210x - 1800 = 0$$

$$x^2 - 35x + 300 = 0$$

$$(x - 20)(x - 15) = 0$$

$$x = 15, 20$$

Step 3: In order to determine which of these is the maximum and which is the minimum, use the second derivative test. The second derivative of profit is $\dfrac{d^2 P}{dx^2} = -12x + 210$. At $x = 15$, we get $\dfrac{d^2 P}{dx^2} = 30$, so this is a minimum. At $x = 20$, we get $\dfrac{d^2 P}{dx^2} = -30$, so this is a maximum. Therefore, the optimum number of units is 20.

The answer is (E).

PROBLEM 36. Find the area enclosed by the polar equation $r = 4 + \cos\theta$ for $0 \le \theta \le 2\pi$.

Step 1: This problem requires you to know the polar formula for finding the area of a region. The formula is $Area = \dfrac{1}{2}\displaystyle\int_{\theta=a}^{\theta=b} r^2 \, d\theta$.

$\dfrac{1}{2}\displaystyle\int_{\theta=a}^{\theta=b} r^2 \, d\theta = \dfrac{1}{2}\displaystyle\int_{0}^{2\pi} (4 + \cos\theta)^2 \, d\theta$. Use your calculator to get 51.8363.

The answer is (D).

If you don't want to do this integral with the calculator, do the following:

If we expand the integrand, we will get three integrals:

$$\frac{1}{2}\int_{0}^{2\pi}(4+\cos\theta)^2 \, d\theta = \frac{1}{2}\int_{0}^{2\pi}16 \, d\theta + \frac{1}{2}\int_{0}^{2\pi}8\cos\theta \, d\theta + \frac{1}{2}\int_{0}^{2\pi}\cos^2\theta \, d\theta$$

The first two integrals are easy and give us:

$$\frac{1}{2}(16\theta)\Big|_{0}^{2\pi} + \frac{1}{2}(8\sin\theta)\Big|_{0}^{2\pi} + \frac{1}{2}\int_{0}^{2\pi}\cos^2\theta \, d\theta$$

Evaluating the first two integrals, we get $(8\theta)\Big|_{0}^{2\pi} + (4\sin\theta)\Big|_{0}^{2\pi} = 16\pi$.

Step 2: We do the third integral using a trigonometric substitution:

$$\frac{1}{2}\int_{0}^{2\pi}\cos^2\theta \, d\theta = \frac{1}{2}\int_{0}^{2\pi}\frac{1+\cos 2\theta}{2} \, d\theta$$

If we simplify this integral, we get:

$$\frac{1}{2}\int_{0}^{2\pi}\frac{1}{2} \, d\theta + \frac{1}{2}\int_{0}^{2\pi}\frac{\cos 2\theta}{2} = \frac{1}{4}\theta\Big|_{0}^{2\pi} + \frac{1}{8}\sin 2\theta\Big|_{0}^{2\pi} = \frac{\pi}{2}$$

If we add $16\pi + \dfrac{\pi}{2}$, we get $\dfrac{33\pi}{2}$.

The answer is (D).

PROBLEM 37. Use the Trapezoid Rule with $n = 4$ to approximate the area between the curve $f(x) = x^3 - x^2$ and the x-axis from $x = 3$ to $x = 4$.

This problem will require you to be familiar with the Trapezoid Rule. This is very easy to do on the calculator, and some of you may even have written programs to evaluate this. Even if you haven't, the formula is easy. The area under a curve from $x = a$ to $x = b$, divided into n intervals is approximated by the Trapezoid Rule and is:

$$\left(\frac{1}{2}\right)\left(\frac{b-a}{n}\right)\left[y_0 + 2y_1 + 2y_2 + 2y_3 \ldots + 2y_{n-2} + 2y_{n-1} + y_n\right]$$

This formula may look scary, but it actually is quite simple, and the AP examination never uses a very large value for n anyway.

Step 1: $\dfrac{b-a}{n} = \dfrac{4-3}{4} = \dfrac{1}{4}$

Plugging into the formula, we get:

$$\frac{1}{8}\left[\left(3^3 - 3^2\right) + 2\left(3.25^3 - 3.25^2\right) + 2\left(3.5^3 - 3.5^2\right) + 2\left(3.75^3 - 3.75^2\right) + \left(4^3 - 4^2\right)\right]$$

This is easy to plug into your calculator and you will get 31.516.

The answer is (D).

PROBLEM 38. If $f(x) = \displaystyle\sum_{k=0}^{\infty} \left(\cos^2 x\right)^k$, then $f\left(\dfrac{\pi}{4}\right)$ is

Step 1: If a series is of the form $\displaystyle\sum_{n=0}^{\infty} ar^n$, and $|r| < 1$ then the sum of the series is

$(a)\left(\dfrac{1}{1-r}\right)$, where a is the first term. (Notice that if the series went from one to

infinity, instead of zero to infinity, then the formula would be $(a)\left(\dfrac{r}{1-r}\right)$. Be careful

that you memorize the correct formula. You could avoid this confusion by deriving

the formula as you do the problem. To learn how to do that, refer to the unit on

Infinite Series.) Here r is $\cos^2 x$ and a is 1, and $\left|\cos^2 x\right| < 1$. This is very important.

If $|r| \geq 1$ the formula doesn't work. So the sum is $(1)\left(\dfrac{1}{1 - \cos^2 x}\right)$.

Using trigonometric substitution, this sum can be simplified to: $(1) - \dfrac{1}{\sin^2 x}$.

Now if we plug in $\dfrac{\pi}{4}$ for x, we get: $(1)\left(\dfrac{1}{\sin^2\left(\dfrac{\pi}{4}\right)}\right) = 2$.

The answer is (E).

PROBLEM 39. The volume of the solid that results when the area between the graph of $y = x^2 + 2$ and the graph of $y = 10 - x^2$ from $x = 0$ to $x = 2$ is rotated around the x-axis is:

This is another volume of a solid of revolution problem. As you should have noticed by now, these are very popular on the AP Examination and show up in both the multiple choice section and in the Free-Response section. If you are not good at these, go back and review the unit carefully. You cannot afford to get these wrong on the AP exam! The good thing about this volume problem is that it is in the calculator part of the Multiple-Choice section, so you can use a program and your graphing calculator to assist you with this problem.

Step 1: First, graph the two curves on the same set of axes. The graph should look like this:

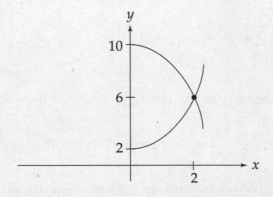

Step 2: Now look at the answer choices. Notice that each answer choice is the sum of two integrals, and all of the functions are in terms of y. This means that you are going to have to use the method of shells, and that you will have to convert the functions from being in terms of x to being in terms of y. Also, when you make a horizontal slice in this region, you are using different curves above and below the intersection point, so you will have to do two integrals. Okay. One thing at a time.

Step 3: First let's find where the two curves intersect. We can do this either with the calculator or algebraically.

Algebraically, we set the two equations equal to each other:

$$x^2 + 2 = 10 - x^2$$
$$2x^2 = 8$$
$$x^2 = 4$$
$$x = \pm 2$$

We will use $x = 2$, and plugging in 2 for x, we get $y = 6$.

Now we have to find what y is when $x = 0$. On the lower curve, $y = 2$. On the higher curve, $y = 10$. These then are our limits of integration. We will have two integrals, one from 2 to 6, the other from 6 to 10. By process of elimination, this means that the answer can only be (B) or (C).

Step 4: Now we have to convert each of the equations to being in terms of y:

$$y = x^2 + 2 \qquad y = 10 - x^2$$
$$x^2 = y - 2 \qquad x^2 = 10 - y$$
$$x = \pm\sqrt{y - 2} \qquad x = \pm\sqrt{10 - y}$$

Step 5: We are only concerned with the positive roots for this region, so using the Shells formula, we get that the volume is $2\pi\int_2^6 y\left(\sqrt{y-2}\right)dy + 2\pi\int_6^{10} y\left(\sqrt{10-y}\right)dy$.

The answer is (B).

PROBLEM 40. $\displaystyle\int_0^4 \frac{dx}{\sqrt{9+x^2}} =$

Remember, this is the calculator part of the test. You can simply evaluate this on your calculator using **fnint**. If you are not comfortable with this, we will show you how to do this algebraically. This integral requires a trigonometric substitution. These types of integrals require a lot of algebra, so you should leave them for the second pass.

Step 1: Using your calculator, enter **fnint** $((1/(\sqrt{(9+x^2)})), x, 0, 4)$. You should get 1.0986. Evaluate each of the answer choices to see which has the same value, or which is closest.

The answer is (A).

Step 2: If you are not using your calculator, you first have to do a substitution. Let's ignore the limits of integration for now, and just evaluate the integral. Whenever we have an integral of the form $\sqrt{(a^2 + x^2)}$, we do the substitution $x = a\tan\theta$. So here we let $x = 3\tan\theta$ and $dx = 3\sec^2\theta\,d\theta$.

Substituting into the integrand, we get: $\displaystyle\int\frac{dx}{\sqrt{9+x^2}} = \int\frac{3\sec^2\theta}{\sqrt{9+9\tan^2\theta}}\,d\theta$

If we factor 9 out of the radical in the denominator, we get :

$$\int \frac{3\sec^2\theta}{\sqrt{9+9\tan^2\theta}}\,d\theta = \int \frac{3\sec^2\theta}{3\sqrt{1+\tan^2\theta}}\,d\theta = \int \frac{\sec^2\theta}{\sec\theta}\,d\theta = \int \sec\theta\,d\theta$$

You should have memorized this integral. It is $\ln|\sec\theta + \tan\theta|$.

Step 3: Now we want to evaluate the limits of integration, but in order to do that, we should substitute back for x. If $x = 3\tan\theta$ then $\frac{x}{3} = \tan\theta$. Using the

Pythagorean Theorem, $\frac{\sqrt{9+x^2}}{3} = \sec\theta$.

So now we have $\ln|\sec\theta + \tan\theta| = \ln\left|\frac{\sqrt{9+x^2}}{3} + \frac{x}{3}\right|$. If we evaluate the limits of integra-

tion, we get:

$$\ln\left|\frac{\sqrt{9+x^2}}{3} + \frac{x}{3}\right|_0^4 = \ln\left|\frac{5}{3} + \frac{4}{3}\right| - \ln|1| = \ln 3$$

The answer is (A).

PROBLEM 41. The rate that an object cools is directly proportional to the difference between its temperature (in Kelvin) at that time and the surrounding temperature (in Kelvin). If an object is initially at $35K$, and the surrounding temperature remains constant at $10K$, it takes 5 minutes for the object to cool to $25K$. How long will it take for the object to cool to $20K$?

This is a differential equation. Each AP examination tends to contain one differential equation word problem. They usually give you the same type of equation and are actually not terribly difficult, once you understand the question.

Step 1: The first sentence tells us what the equation is going to be. Let T stand for temperature at a particular time, and S stand for the surrounding temperature. Then our equation is: $\frac{dT}{dt} = k(T - S)$. Time is always represented by t, and k is a constant.

This equation is solvable using separation of variables. Put everything that contains a T on the left side, and everything that contains a t on the right side:

$$\frac{dT}{(T-S)} = kdt$$

If we integrate both sides we get: $\int \frac{dT}{(T-S)} = k \int dt$

And performing the integration gives us: $\ln|T-S| = kt + C$.

Step 2: Whenever we have an equation of this form, we then exponentiate both sides, giving us:

$$|T-S| = e^{kt+C} \text{ or } |T-S| = Ce^{kt}$$

If we plug in the rest of the information from the problem, we can solve for the constants k and C.

The initial temperature tells us that at time $t = 0$, $T = 35$, and $S = 10$.

So $|35-10| = Ce^{k(0)}$ and $25 = C$

Then at time $t = 5$, $T = 25$. So:

$$|25-10| = 25e^{k(5)}$$

$$15 = 25e^{k(5)}$$

$$\frac{3}{5} = e^{5k}$$

$$\frac{1}{5}\ln\left(\frac{3}{5}\right) = k$$

This gives us the final equation $|T-10| = 25e^{\left(\frac{1}{5}\ln\left(\frac{3}{5}\right)\right)(t)}$.

Step 3: Finally, we plug in the last bit of information, that $T = 20$ to solve for t.

$$|20-10| = 25e^{\left(\frac{1}{5}\ln\left(\frac{3}{5}\right)\right)(t)}$$

$$\frac{2}{5} = e^{\left(\frac{1}{5}\ln\left(\frac{3}{5}\right)\right)(t)}$$

$$\ln\frac{2}{5} = \frac{1}{5}\ln\left(\frac{3}{5}\right)(t)$$

$$5\frac{\ln\dfrac{2}{5}}{\ln\dfrac{3}{5}} = t$$

$$t = 8.97$$

The answer is (D).

PROBLEM 42. $\displaystyle\int e^x \cos x\, dx =$

You should recognize this integral as an elementary integration by parts integral. If so, this won't be very hard to do.

Step 1: Let $u = e^x$ and $dv = \cos x\, dx$.

$du = e^x dx \qquad v = \sin x$

Then we have: $\displaystyle\int e^x \cos x\, dx = e^x \sin x - \int e^x \sin x\, dx$

Step 2: We need to do integration by parts *a second time* to evaluate the second integral:

Let $u = e^x$ and $dv = \sin x\, dx$.

$du = e^x dx \qquad v = -\cos x$

Now we have: $\displaystyle\int e^x \cos x\, dx = e^x \sin x + e^x \cos x - \int e^x \cos x\, dx$

Step 3: Although this looks as if we are back where we started, and will have to do a *third* integration, if we add $\displaystyle\int e^x \cos x\, dx$ to both sides we get:

$$2\int e^x \cos x\, dx = e^x \sin x + e^x \cos x$$

Now if we divide both sides by 2 we get:

$$\int e^x \cos x \, dx = \frac{e^x \sin x + e^x \cos x}{2}$$

The answer is (A).

PROBLEM 43. Two particles leave the origin at the same time and move along the y-axis with their respective positions determined by the functions $y_1 = \cos 2t$ and $y_2 = 4 \sin t$ for $0 < t < 6$. For how many values of t do the particles have the same acceleration?

If you want to find acceleration, all you have to do is take the second derivative of the position functions.

Step 1:

$$\frac{dy_1}{dx} = -2\sin 2t \text{ and } \frac{dy_2}{dx} = 4\cos t$$

$$\frac{d^2 y_1}{dx^2} = -4\cos 2t \text{ and } \frac{d^2 y_2}{dx^2} = -4\sin t$$

Step 2: Now all we have to do is to graph both of these equations on the same set of axes on a calculator. You should make the window from $x = 0$ to $x = 7$ (leave yourself a little room so that you can see the whole range that you need). You should get a picture that looks like this:

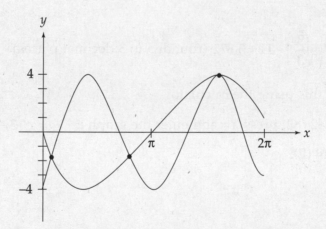

Where the graphs intersect, the acceleration is the same. There are three points of intersection.

The answer is (D).

PROBLEM 44: The minimum value of the function $y = x^3 - 7x + 11$, $x \geq 0$, is approximately

You have two options. First, let's do the problem without using the calculator.

If we want to find the minimum, we take the derivative and set it equal to zero. We

get: $\dfrac{dy}{dx} = 3x^2 - 7 = 0$. Now we solve for x:

$$3x^2 = 7$$

$$x^2 = \frac{7}{3}$$

$$x = \pm\sqrt{\frac{7}{3}}$$

We are only concerned with positive values of x (note the restriction in the problem),

so let's look at $x = \sqrt{\dfrac{7}{3}}$. First, we have to determine whether this is a minimum or

a maximum. The simplest way to do this is with the second derivative test. Take the

second derivative and we get: $\dfrac{d^2y}{dx^2} = 6x$. Now, plug in $x = \sqrt{\dfrac{7}{3}}$. The second deriva-

tive is positive there, so the point is a minimum.

Now, we plug $x = \sqrt{\dfrac{7}{3}}$ back into the original equation to find the y value.

$$y = \left(\sqrt{\frac{7}{3}}\right)^3 - 7\left(\sqrt{\frac{7}{3}}\right) + 11 \approx 3.872 \text{ (rounded to 3 decimal places)}.$$

Now let's do this using the calculator.

Using the TI 82/83, press **Y=** and enter the graph as $Y_1 = x^\wedge 3 - 7x + 11$.

The answer is (E).

PROBLEM 45: Use Euler's Method with $h = 0.2$ to estimate $y(1)$, if $y' = y$ and $y(0) = 1$.

We are given that the curve goes through the point $(0,1)$. We will call the coordinates of this point $x_0 = 0$ and $y_0 = 1$. The slope is found by plugging $y_0 = 1$ into $y' = y$, so we have an initial slope of $y_0' = 1$.

Now we need to find the next set of points.

Step 1: Increase x_0 by h to get x_1:

$$x_1 = 0.2$$

Step 2: Multiply h by y_0' and add to y_0 to get y_1:

$$y_1 = 1 + 0.2(1) = 1.2$$

Step 3: Find y_1' by plugging y_1 into the equation for y':

$$y_1' = 1.2$$

Repeat until you get to $x = 1$.

Step 1: Increase x_1 by h to get x_2:

$$x_2 = 0.4$$

Step 2: Multiply h by y_1' and add to y_1 to get y_2:

$$y_2 = 1.2 + 0.2(1.2) = 1.44$$

Step 3: Find y_2' by plugging y_2 into the equation for y':

$$y_2' = 1.44$$

Step 1: $x_3 = x_2 + h$:

$$x_3 = 0.6$$

Step 2: $y_3 = y_2 + h(y_2')$:

$$y_3 = 1.44 + 0.2(1.44) = 1.728$$

Step 3: $y_3' = y_3$:

$$y_3' = 1.728$$

Step 1: $x_4 = x_3 + h$:

$$x_4 = 0.8$$

Step 2: $y_4 = y_3 + h(y_3')$:

$$y_4 = 1.728 + 0.2(1.728) = 2.0736$$

Step 3: $y_4' = y_4$:

$$y_4' = 2.0736$$

Step 1: $x_5 = x_4 + h$:

$$x_5 = 1.0$$

Step 2: $y_5 = y_4 + h(y_4')$:

$$y_5 = 2.0736 + 0.2(2.0736) = 2.48832$$

We don't need to go any farther because we are asked for the value of y when $x = 1$.

The answer is $y = 2.48832$.

The answer is (C).

ANSWERS AND EXPLANATIONS TO SECTION II

Problem 1. Two particles travel in the xy-plane. For time $t \geq 0$, the position of particle A is given by $x = t + 1$ and $y = (t + 1)^2 - 2t - 2$, and the position of particle B is given by $x = 4t - 2$ and $y = -2t + 2$.

(a) Find the velocity vector for each particle at time $t = 2$.

Step 1: Because velocity is the derivative of position with respect to time, all we have to do is take the derivative of each of the position functions.

Particle A: The position of the x-coordinate is $t + 1$, the x-component of the velocity is 1.
The position of the y-coordinate is $(t + 1)^2 - 2t - 1$, the y-component of the velocity is $2(t + 1)(1) - 2 = 2t$

Particle B: The position of the x-coordinate is $4t - 2$, the x-component of the velocity is 4.
The position of the y-coordinate is $-2t + 2$, the y-component of the velocity is -2.

Step 2: Now all we have to do is plug in.

At $t = 2$, particle A's velocity vector is (1, 4).

At $t = 2$, particle B's velocity vector is (4, −2).

(b) Set up an integral expression for the distance traveled by particle A from time $t = 1$ to $t = 3$. Do not evaluate the integral.

Step 1: We are being asked to find the arc length of a curve in parametric form. The

formula is: $\int_a^b \sqrt{\left(\dfrac{dx}{dt}\right)^2 + \left(\dfrac{dy}{dt}\right)^2}\, dt$, where the starting time is a, and the ending time is b.

Plugging into the formula, we get: $\int_1^3 \sqrt{(1)^2 + (2t)^2}\, dt = \int_1^3 \sqrt{1 + 4t^2}\, dt$

(c) At what time do the two particles collide? Justify your answer.

Step 1: The particles collide when they have the same x and y-coordinates. If we set the equations for the x-coordinates of the two particles equal we get:

$$t + 1 = 4t - 2 \text{ so } t = 1$$

At this time, the y-coordinate for particle A is: $(1+1)^2 - 2(1) - 2 = 0$

The y-coordinate for particle B is: $-2(1) + 2 = 0$. These are the same, so at time $t = 1$, the two particles collide.

(d) Sketch the path of both particles from time $t = 0$ to $t = 4$. Indicate the direction of each particle along its path.

By shifting the calculator into parametric mode, setting the window to match the one below, and inserting the equations for particles A and B into $x_1, y_1, x_2,$ and y_2 respectively, we get:

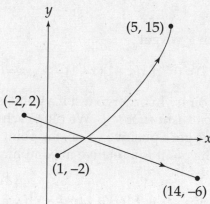

PROBLEM 2. Let f be the function given by $y = f(x) = 2x^4 - 4x^2 + 1$.

(a) Find an equation of the line tangent to the graph at $(-2, 17)$.

In order to find the equation of a tangent line at a particular point we need to take the derivative of the function and plug in the x and y values at that point to give us the slope of the line.

Step 1: The derivative is: $f'(x) = 8x^3 - 8x$. If we plug in $x = -2$, we get:

$$f'(-2) = 8\,(-2)^3 - 8\,(-2) = -48.$$

This is the slope m.

Step 2: Now we use the slope-intercept form of the equation of a line, $y - y_1 = m\,(x - x_1)$, and plug in the appropriate values of x, y, and m.

$$y - 17 = -48\,(x + 2)$$

If we simplify this we get $y = -48x - 79$.

(b) Find the x and y-coordinates of the relative maxima and relative minima.

If we want to find the maxima/minima, we need to take the derivative and set it equal to zero. The values that we get are called critical points. We will then test each point to see if it is a maximum or a minimum.

Step 1: We already have the first derivative from part (a), so we can just set it equal to zero: $8x^3 - 8x = 0$.

If we now solve this for x we get:

$$8x(x^2 - 1) = 0 \quad 8x(x+1)(x-1) = 0 \quad x = 0, 1, -1$$

These are our critical points. In order to test if a point is a maximum or a minimum, we usually use the *second derivative test*. We plug each of the critical points into the second derivative. If we get a positive value, the point is a relative minimum. If we get a negative value, the point is a relative maximum. If we get zero, the point is a point of inflection.

Step 2: The second derivative is $f''(x) = 24x^2 - 8$. If we plug in the critical points we get:

$$f''(0) = 24(0)^2 - 8 = -8$$
$$f''(1) = 24(1)^2 - 8 = 16$$
$$f''(-1) = 24(-1)^2 - 8 = 16$$

So $x = 0$ is a relative maximum, and $x = 1, -1$ are relative minima.

Step 3: In order to find the y-coordinates, we plug the x values back into the original equation, and solve:

$$f(0) = 1$$
$$f(1) = -1$$
$$f(-1) = -1$$

and our points are

(0, 1) is a relative maximum

(1, –1) is a relative minimum

(–1, –1) is a relative minimum

(c) Find the x-coordinates of the points of inflection. Verify your answer.

If we want to find the points of inflection, we set the second derivative equal to zero. The values that we get are the x-coordinates of the points of inflection.

Step 1: We already have the second derivative from part (b), so all we have to do is set it equal to zero and solve for x:

$$24x^2 - 8 = 0 \quad x^2 = \frac{1}{3} \quad x = \pm\sqrt{\frac{1}{3}}$$

PROBLEM 3: Water is draining at the rate of $48\,\pi\,\text{ft}^3$ from a conical tank whose diameter at its base is 40 feet and whose height is 60 feet.

(a) Find an expression for the volume of water (in ft^3) in the tank in terms of its radius.

The formula for the volume of a cone is: $V = \frac{1}{3}\pi R^2 H$, where R is the radius of the cone, and H is the height. The ratio of the height of a cone to its radius is constant at any point on the edge of the cone, so we also know that $\frac{H}{R} = \frac{60}{20} = 3$ (remember that the radius is half the diameter). If we solve this for H and substitute, we get:

$$H = 3R$$
$$V = \frac{1}{3}\pi R^2(3R) = \pi R^3$$

(b) At what rate (in ft/sec) is the radius of the water in the tank shrinking when the radius is 16 feet?

Step 1: This is a related rates question. We now have a formula for the volume of the cone in terms of its radius, so if we differentiate it in terms of t we should be able to solve for the rate of change of the radius $\dfrac{dR}{dt}$.

We are given that the rate of change of the volume and the radius are, respectively:

$$\frac{dV}{dt} = 48\pi \text{ and } R = 16$$

Differentiating the formula for the volume, we get: $\dfrac{dV}{dt} = 3\pi R^2 \dfrac{dR}{dt}$

Now we plug in and get: $48\pi = 3\pi 16^2 \dfrac{dR}{dt}$. Finally, if we solve for $\dfrac{dR}{dt}$, we get:

$$\frac{dR}{dt} = \frac{1}{16} \text{ ft/sec.}$$

(c) How fast (in ft/sec) is the height of the water in the tank dropping at the instant that the radius is 16 feet?

Step 1: This is the same idea as the previous problem, except that we want to solve for $\dfrac{dH}{dt}$. In order to do this, we need to go back to our ratio of height to radius and solve it for the radius:

$$\frac{H}{R} = 3 \quad \text{or} \quad \frac{H}{3} = R$$

Substituting for R in the original equation, we get: $V = \dfrac{1}{3}\pi \left(\dfrac{H}{3}\right)^2 H = \dfrac{\pi H^3}{27}$

Step 2: Now we need to know what H is when R is 16. Using our ratio:

$$H = 3(16) = 48$$

Step 3: Now if we differentiate we get: $\dfrac{dV}{dt} = \dfrac{\pi H^2}{9}\dfrac{dH}{dt}$

Now we plug in and solve:

$$48\pi = \frac{\pi(48)^2}{9}\frac{dH}{dt}$$

$$\frac{dH}{dt} = \frac{3}{16}$$

One should also note that, because $H = 3R$, $\frac{dH}{dt} = 3\frac{dR}{dt}$ in part (b), we merely had to multiply it by 3 to find the answer for part (c).

PROBLEM 4. Let f be the function given by $f(x) = e^{-4x^2}$

(a) Find the first four non-zero terms and the general term of the power series for $f(x)$ about $x = 0$.

Step 1: If we want to find the power series we need to do the Taylor series expansion for $f(x)$. The formula for a Taylor series about the point $x = a$ is:

$$f(a) + f'(a)(x-a) + f''(a)\frac{(x-a)^2}{2!} + f'''(a)\frac{(x-a)^3}{3!} + \ldots + f^{(n)}(a)\frac{(x-a)^n}{n!} + \ldots$$

Here, $a = 0$ and $f(x) = e^{-4x^2}$. You should have memorized the Taylor series expansion $e^u = 1 + u + \frac{u^2}{2} + \frac{u^3}{3!} + \ldots + \frac{u^n}{n!} + \ldots$, so you don't have to do all of the work here. You can just substitute

$-4x^2$ for u:

$$e^{-4x^2} = 1 + \left(-4x^2\right) + \frac{\left(-4x^2\right)^2}{2} + \frac{\left(-4x^2\right)^3}{3!} = 1 - 4x^2 + 8x^4 - \frac{32x^6}{3}$$

Step 2: The general term is: $\dfrac{(-1)^n 2^{2n} x^{2n}}{n!}$

(b) Find the interval of convergence of the power series for $f(x)$ about $x = 0$. Show the analysis that leads to your conclusion.

Step 1: The series for e^{-u^2} converges for $-\infty < u < \infty$. So the series for $f(x) = e^{-4x^2}$ converges if $-\infty < 2x < \infty$. Thus, it converges if $-\infty < x < \infty$.

(c) Use term-by-term differentiation to show that: $f'(x) = -8xe^{-4x^2}$

Step 1: First we differentiate the individual terms of the power series:

$$f(x) = 1 - 4x^2 + 8x^4 - \frac{32x^6}{3} + \ldots + \frac{(-1)^n 2^{2n} x^{2n}}{n!}$$

$$f'(x) = 0 - 8x + 32x^3 - 64x^5 + \ldots + \frac{(-1)^n 2^{2n}(2n)x^{2n-1}}{n!}$$

$$= -8x + 32x^3 - 64x^5 + \ldots + \frac{(-1)^n 2^{2n+1} x^{2n-1}}{(n-1)!}$$

Step 2: Next, we multiply $-8x$ by the individual terms of the power series and compare to the result of step 1:

$$-8xf(x) = 1(-8x) - 4x^2(-8x) + 8x^4(-8x) - \frac{32x^6}{3}(-8x) + ... + \frac{(-1)^n 2^{2n} x^{2n}}{n!}(-8x)$$

$$= -8x + 32x^3 - 64x^5 + ... + \frac{(-1)^{n+1} 2^{2n+3} x^{2n+1}}{n!}$$

Step 3: If we substitute $n - 1$ for n, we can make the general terms match exactly.

$$\frac{(-1)^{(n-1)+1} 2^{2(n-1)+3} x^{2(n-1)+1}}{(n-1)!} = \frac{(-1)^n 2^{2n+1} x^{2n-1}}{(n-1)!}$$

PROBLEM 5. Let R be the region enclosed by the graphs of $y = 2\ln x$ and $y = \dfrac{x}{2}$, and the lines $x = 2$ and $x = 8$.

(a) Find the area of R.

Step 1: If there are two curves, $f(x)$ and $g(x)$, where $f(x)$ is always above $g(x)$, on the interval $[a, b]$, then the area of the region between the two curves is found by:

$$\int_a^b (f(x) - g(x)) dx$$

In order to determine whether one of the curves is above the other, we can graph them on the calculator.

The graph looks like this:

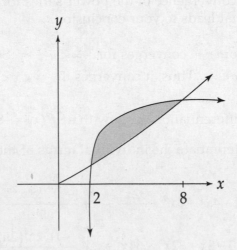

As we can see, the graph of $y = 2\ln x$ is above $y = \dfrac{x}{2}$ on the entire interval, so all we

have to do is evaluate the integral $\displaystyle\int_2^8 \left(2\ln x - \dfrac{x}{2}\right) dx =$.

Step 2: We can do the integration one of two ways—on the calculator or analytically.

Calculator: You should get 3.498

Analytically: $\displaystyle\int_2^8 \left(2\ln x - \dfrac{x}{2}\right) dx = 2\int_2^8 \ln x\, dx - \dfrac{1}{2}\int_2^8 x\, dx =$

$$2(x\ln x - x)\Big|_2^8 - \dfrac{1}{2}\left(\dfrac{x^2}{2}\right)\Big|_2^8 = 18.498 - 15 = 3.498$$

By the way, you should have memorized $\displaystyle\int \ln x\, dx = x\ln x - x$, or you can do it as one of the basic integration by parts integrals.

(b) Set up, <u>but do not integrate</u>, an integral expression, in terms of a single variable, for the volume of the solid generated when R is revolved about the x-axis.

Step 1: If there are two curves, $f(x)$ and $g(x)$, where $f(x)$ is always above $g(x)$, on the interval $[a,b]$, then the volume of the solid generated when the region is revolved about the x-axis is found by using the method of washers:

$$\pi\int_a^b \left[f(x)\right]^2 - \left[g(x)\right]^2 dx$$

Here, we already know that $f(x)$ is above $g(x)$ on the interval, so the integral we need

to evaluate is: $\pi\displaystyle\int_2^8 [2\ln x]^2 - \left[\dfrac{x}{2}\right]^2 dx$.

(c) Set up, <u>but do not integrate</u>, an integral expression, in terms of a single variable, for the volume of the solid generated when R is revolved about the line $x = -1$.

Step 1: Now we have to revolve the area around a <u>vertical</u> axis. If there are two curves, $f(x)$ and $g(x)$, where $f(x)$ is always above $g(x)$, on the interval $[a,b]$, then the volume of the solid generated when the region is revolved about the y-axis is found by using the method of shells:

$$2\pi\int_a^b x\left[f(x) - g(x)\right] dx$$

When we are rotating around a vertical axis, we use the same formula as when we rotate around the y-axis, but we have to account for the shift away from $x = 0$. Here we have a curve that is 1 unit farther away from the line $x = -1$ than it is from the y-axis, so we add 1 to the radius of the shell (for a more detailed explanation of shifting axes, see the unit on finding the volume of a solid of revolution). This gives us the equation:

$$2\pi \int_2^8 (x+1)\left[2\ln x - \frac{x}{2}\right] dx$$

PROBLEM 6. Let f and g be functions that are differentiable throughout their domains and that have the following properties:

(i) $f(x+y) = f(x)g(y) + g(x)f(y)$

(ii) $\lim_{a \to 0} f(a) = 0$

(iii) $\lim_{h \to 0} \dfrac{g(h)-1}{h} = 0$

(iv) $f'(0) = 1$

(a) Use L'Hôpital's Rule to show that $\lim_{a \to 0} \dfrac{f(a)}{a} = 1$.

Step 1: L'Hôpital's Rule states that if a function is of the indeterminate form $\dfrac{0}{0}$, then the limit of the derivatives of the numerator is the same as the limit of the original quotient. In other words, if we differentiate the top and bottom of the quotient, we will get the limit. First, we have to show that the quotient gives us an indeterminate form:

$$\lim_{a \to 0} \frac{f(a)}{a} = \frac{0}{0} \text{ (using property (ii))}$$

Next, we differentiate the top and bottom and take the limit:

$$\lim_{a \to 0} \frac{f(a)}{a} = \lim_{a \to 0} \frac{f'(a)}{1} = f'(0) = 1 \text{ (using property (iv))}$$

(b) Use the definition of the derivative to show that $f'(x) = g(x)$.

Step 1: The definition of the derivative states: $f'(x) = \lim_{h \to 0} \dfrac{f(x+h)-f(x)}{h}$

If we substitute into the formula, we get:

$$f'(x) = \lim_{h \to 0} \frac{f(x+h) - f(x)}{h} = \lim_{h \to 0} \frac{f(x)g(h) + g(x)f(h) - f(x)}{h} \text{ (using property (i))}$$

$$= \lim_{h \to 0} \frac{[g(h) - 1]f(x) + g(x)f(h)}{h} = \lim_{h \to 0} \frac{[g(h) - 1]f(x)}{h} + \frac{g(x)f(h)}{h}$$

$$\lim_{h \to 0} f(x) \frac{[g(h) - 1]}{h} + g(x)\frac{f(h)}{h} = [f(x)](0) + g(x)(1) = g(x) \text{ (using property (iii))}$$

(c) Find $\int \dfrac{g(x)}{f(x)} dx$.

Step 1: Using u-substitution, let $u = f(x)$ and $du = f'(x) = g(x)$. Then we have:

$$\int \frac{g(x)}{f(x)} dx = \int \frac{du}{u} = \ln|u| + C = \ln|f(x)| + C$$

30

The Princeton Review
AP Calculus BC
Practice Test 2

CALCULUS BC

SECTION I, Part A

Time—55 Minutes

Number of questions—28

A CALCULATOR MAY NOT BE USED ON THIS PART OF THE EXAMINATION

<u>Directions</u>: Solve each of the following problems, using the available space for scratchwork. After examining the form of the choices, decide which is the best of the choices given and fill in the corresponding oval on the answer sheet. No credit will be given for anything written in the test book. Do not spend too much time on any one problem.

<u>In this test</u>: Unless other wise specified, the domain of a function f is assumed to be the set of all real numbers x for which $f(x)$ is a real number.

1. What is the slope of the line tangent to the curve $x^2 + 2xy + 3y^2 = 2$ when $y = 1$?

(A) $-\dfrac{1}{2}$ (B) $-\dfrac{1}{8}$ (C) -1 (D) 0 (E) $\dfrac{1}{8}$

2. $\displaystyle\int_{-1}^{1} x e^{x^2}\,dx =$

(A) $-e$ (B) $-\dfrac{e}{2}$ (C) 0 (D) $\dfrac{e}{2}$ (E) e

GO ON TO THE NEXT PAGE

3. If, for $t > 0$, $x = t^2$ and $y = \cos\left(t^2\right)$, then $\dfrac{dy}{dx} =$

(A) $\cos\left(t^2\right)$ (B) $-\sin\left(t^2\right)$ (C) $-\sin(2t)$ (D) $\sin\left(t^2\right)$ (E) $\cos(2t)$

---

4. The function $f(x) = 4x^3 - 8x^2 + 1$ on the interval $[-1, 1]$ has an absolute minimum at $x =$

(A) -11 (B) -1 (C) 0 (D) 1 (E) $\dfrac{4}{3}$

---

5. $\displaystyle\int \dfrac{x\,dx}{x^2 + 5x + 6} =$

(A) $\ln\left|\dfrac{(x+3)^3}{(x+2)^2}\right| + C$

(B) $\ln\left|(x+3)^3(x+2)^2\right| + C$

(C) $\ln\left|\dfrac{(x+2)^2}{(x+3)^3}\right| + C$

(D) $\ln\left|(x+3)^2(x+2)^3\right| + C$

(E) $\ln\left|(x+3)(x+2)\right| + C$

GO ON TO THE NEXT PAGE

6. $\dfrac{d}{dx}\left(x^2 \sin^2 x\right) =$

(A) $2x \sin 2x$

(B) $2x \cos^2 x$

(C) $x \sin 2x$

(D) $2x \sin^2 x + x^2 \cos^2 x$

(E) $2x \sin^2 x + x^2 \sin 2x$

---

7. The line normal to the curve $y = \dfrac{x^2 - 1}{x^2 + 1}$ at $x = 2$ has slope

(A) $-\dfrac{8}{25}$ (B) $-\dfrac{25}{8}$ (C) 1 (D) $\dfrac{8}{25}$ (E) -1

GO ON TO THE NEXT PAGE

8. If f and g are differentiable functions and $h(x) = f(x)e^{g(x)}$, then $h'(x) =$

(A) $f'(x)e^{g'(x)}$

(B) $f'(x)e^{g(x)} + f(x)e^{g'(x)}$

(C) $e^{g(x)}[f'(x) + f(x)g'(x)]$

(D) $e^{g(x)}[f'(x) + 1]$

(E) $e^{g'(x)}[f'(x) + g'(x)]$

GO ON TO THE NEXT PAGE

9.

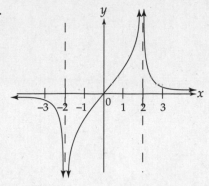

The graph of $y = f(x)$ is shown above. Which of the following could be the graph of $y = f'(x)$?

(A)

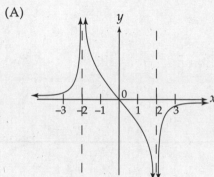

(D)

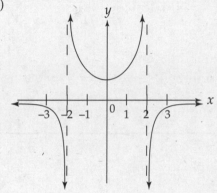

(B)

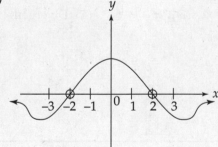

(E)

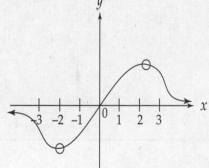

(C)

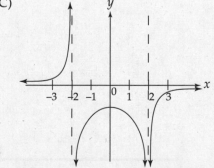

GO ON TO THE NEXT PAGE

10. $\displaystyle\int_{e}^{e^2}\left(\sqrt{x}+\frac{1}{\sqrt{x}}\right)^2 dx =$

(A) $\dfrac{e^4}{2}+2e^2+2$

(B) $\dfrac{e^2}{2}+2e+1$

(C) e^4+2e^2+e

(D) $\dfrac{e^4}{2}+\dfrac{3e^2}{2}-2e+1$

(E) $\dfrac{e^4}{2}+e^2+e$

11. $\displaystyle\int_{4}^{\infty}\frac{dx}{x^2+16}$

(A) $\dfrac{\pi}{16}$ (B) $\dfrac{\pi}{4}$ (C) $\dfrac{\pi}{2}$ (D) π (E) Divergent

GO ON TO THE NEXT PAGE

12. What is the equation of the line tangent to the graph of $y = \sin^2 x$ at $x = \dfrac{\pi}{4}$?

(A) $y - \dfrac{1}{2} = -\left(x - \dfrac{\pi}{4} \right)$

(B) $y - \dfrac{1}{2} = \left(x - \dfrac{\pi}{4} \right)$

(C) $y - \dfrac{1}{\sqrt{2}} = \left(x - \dfrac{\pi}{4} \right)$

(D) $y - \dfrac{1}{\sqrt{2}} = \dfrac{1}{2}\left(x - \dfrac{\pi}{4} \right)$

(E) $y - \dfrac{1}{2} = \dfrac{1}{2}\left(x - \dfrac{\pi}{4} \right)$

---

13. If $f(x) = \begin{cases} ax^2 + 3ax + 5 ; & x \geq 2 \\ 4ax^3 - 6ax^2 + 9 ; & x < 2 \end{cases}$, find the value of a that makes $f(x)$ continuous for all real values of x.

(A) –1   (B) 0   (C) 1   (D) 2   (E) 4

GO ON TO THE NEXT PAGE

14. $\int x\sin(2x)\,dx =$

(A) $-\dfrac{x^2}{2}\cos(2x)+C$

(B) $-\dfrac{x^2}{4}\cos(2x)+C$

(C) $-\dfrac{x}{2}\cos(2x)+\dfrac{1}{4}\sin(2x)+C$

(D) $-\dfrac{x}{2}\cos(2x)+\dfrac{1}{2}\cos(2x)+C$

(E) $-\dfrac{1}{2}\cos(2x)+\dfrac{1}{4}\sin(2x)+C$

15. If $f(x)=\dfrac{x^2+5x-24}{x^2+10x+16}$, then $\lim\limits_{x\to-8}f(x)$ is

(A) 0   (B) 1   (C) $-\dfrac{3}{2}$ (D) $\dfrac{11}{6}$ (E) Nonexistent

GO ON TO THE NEXT PAGE

16. What is the approximation of the value of e^3 obtained by using the fourth-degree Taylor polynomial about $x = 0$ for e^x?

(A) $1 + 3 + \dfrac{3^2}{2} + 3^2 + \dfrac{3^4}{4}$

(B) $1 + 3 + \dfrac{3^2}{2!} + \dfrac{3^3}{3!} + \dfrac{3^4}{4!}$

(C) $1 - 3 + \dfrac{3^2}{2!} - \dfrac{3^3}{3!} + \dfrac{3^4}{4!}$

(D) $1 - 3 + \dfrac{3^2}{2} - 3^2 + \dfrac{3^4}{4}$

(E) $1 - \dfrac{3^2}{2!} + \dfrac{3^4}{4!}$

_____

17. A rock is thrown straight upward with an initial velocity of 50 m/s from a point 100 m above the ground. If the acceleration of the rock at any time t is $a = -10$ m/s^2, what is the maximum height of the rock (in meters)?

(A) 125   (B) 150   (C) 175   (D) 200   (E) 225

GO ON TO THE NEXT PAGE

18. The sum of the infinite geometric series $2 - \dfrac{2}{3} + \dfrac{2}{9} - \dfrac{2}{27} + \ldots$ is

(A) −6   (B) −3   (C) 0   (D) $\dfrac{3}{7}$ (E) $\dfrac{3}{2}$

---

19. What are all values of x for which the series $\displaystyle\sum_{n=1}^{\infty} \dfrac{(x-3)^n}{n^2(5^n)}$ converges?

(A) $-2 \le x \le 8$

(B) $-2 < x \le 8$

(C) $-2 \le x < 8$

(D) $-5 \le x \le 5$

(E) $-5 \le x < 5$

---

20. Find the area inside one loop of the curve $r = \sin 2\theta$.

(A) $\dfrac{\pi}{16}$ (B) $\dfrac{\pi}{8}$ (C) $\dfrac{\pi}{4}$ (D) $\dfrac{\pi}{2}$ (E) π

GO ON TO THE NEXT PAGE

21. The average value of $\sec^2 x$ on the interval $\left[\dfrac{\pi}{6}, \dfrac{\pi}{4}\right]$ is

(A) $\dfrac{8}{\pi}$

(B) $\dfrac{12\sqrt{3} - 12}{\pi}$

(C) $\dfrac{12 - 4\sqrt{3}}{\pi}$

(D) $\dfrac{6\sqrt{2} - 6}{\pi}$

(E) $\dfrac{6 - 6\sqrt{2}}{\pi}$

---

22. Find the length of the arc of the curve defined by $x = \dfrac{1}{2}t^2$ and $y = \dfrac{1}{9}(6t + 9)^{\frac{3}{2}}$, from $t = 0$ to $t = 2$.

(A) 8   (B) 10   (C) 12   (D) 14   (E) 16

GO ON TO THE NEXT PAGE

23. The function f is given by $f(x) = x^4 + 4x^3$. On which of the following intervals is f decreasing?

(A) $(-3, 0)$ (B) $(0, \infty)$ (C) $(-3, \infty)$ (D) $(-\infty, -3)$ (E) $(-\infty, 0)$

24. Which of the following series converge(s)?

I. $\displaystyle\sum_{n=1}^{\infty} \frac{(-1)^n}{n}$

II. $\displaystyle\sum_{n=1}^{\infty} \frac{1}{\sqrt{n^3}}$

III. $\displaystyle\sum_{n=1}^{\infty} \frac{1}{\sqrt[3]{n^2}}$

(A) I only   (B) II only   (C) I and II   (D) I and III   (E) I, II, and III

25. Given the differential equation $\dfrac{dz}{dt} = z\left(4 - \dfrac{z}{100}\right)$, where $z(0) = 50$, what is $\lim\limits_{t \to \infty} z(t)$?

(A) 400   (B) 200   (C) 100   (D) 50   (E) 4

GO ON TO THE NEXT PAGE

26.

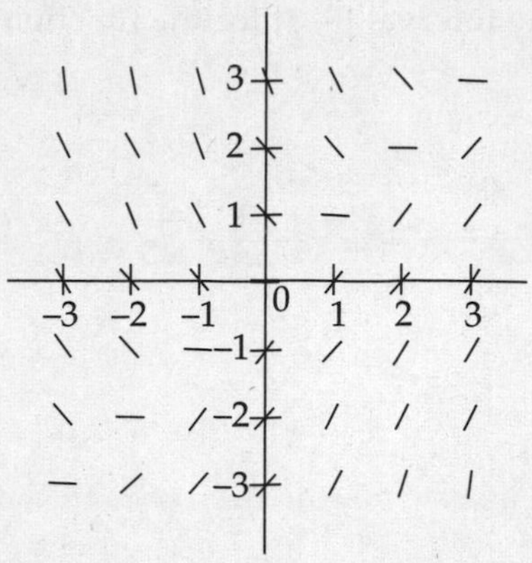

The slope field shown above corresponds to which of the following differential equations?

(A) $\dfrac{dy}{dx} = \dfrac{x}{y}$

(B) $\dfrac{dy}{dx} = \dfrac{y}{x}$

(C) $\dfrac{dy}{dx} = xy$

(D) $\dfrac{dy}{dx} = x - y$

(E) $\dfrac{dy}{dx} = x + y$

GO ON TO THE NEXT PAGE

27. The value of c that satisfies the mean value theorem for derivatives on the interval $[0, 5]$ for the function $f(x) = x^3 - 6x$ is

(A) $-\dfrac{5}{\sqrt{3}}$ (B) 0   (C) 1   (D) $\dfrac{5}{3}$ (E) $\dfrac{5}{\sqrt{3}}$

28.

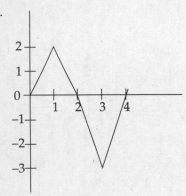

The graph of f is shown in the figure above. If $g(x) = \int\limits_{0}^{x} f(t)\,dt$, for what positive value of x does $g(x)$ have a minimum?

(A) 0   (B) 1   (C) 2   (D) 3   (E) 4

STOP

END OF PART A SECTION I

IF YOU FINISH BEFORE TIME IS CALLED, YOU MAY CHECK YOUR WORK ON PART A ONLY.

DO NOT GO ON TO PART B UNTIL YOU ARE TOLD TO DO SO.

CALCULUS BC

SECTION I, Part B

Time—50 Minutes

Number of questions—17

A GRAPHING CALCULATOR IS REQUIRED FOR SOME QUESTIONS ON THIS PART OF THE EXAMINATION

<u>Directions</u>: Solve each of the following problems, using the available space for scratchwork. After examining the form of the choices, decide which is the best of the choices given and fill in the corresponding oval on the answer sheet. No credit will be given for anything written in the test book. Do not spend too much time on any one problem.

<u>In this test</u>:

(1) The exact numerical value of the correct answer does not always appear among the choices given. When this happens, select from among the choices the number that best approximates the exact numerical value.

(2) Unless otherwise specified, the domain of a function f is assumed to be the set of all real numbers x for which $f(x)$ is a real number.

29. If $f(x)$ is the function given by $f(x) = e^{3x} + 1$, at what value of x is the slope of the tangent line to $f(x)$ equal to 2?

(A) −.135   (B) 0   (C) .231   (D) −.366   (E) .693

GO ON TO THE NEXT PAGE

30. If $y = (\sin x)^{e^x}$, then, when defined, $y' =$

(A) $(\sin x)^{e^x}(\cos x)$

(B) $(\cos x)^{e^x}$

(C) $e^x(\cot x + \ln(\sin x))$

(D) $e^x(\sin x)^{e^x}(\cot x + \ln(\sin x))$

(E) $e^x(\sin x)^{e^x}(\cot x)$

31. The side of a square is increasing at a constant rate of 0.4 cm/sec. In terms of the perimeter, P, what is the rate of change of the area of the square, in cm²/sec?

(A) $0.05P$ (B) $0.2P$ (C) $0.4P$ (D) $6.4P$ (E) $51.2P$

GO ON TO THE NEXT PAGE

32. If f is a vector-valued function defined by $f(t) = \left(\sin 2t, \sin^2 t\right)$, then $f''(t) =$

   (A) $\left(-4\sin 2t, 2\cos 2t\right)$

   (B) $\left(-\sin 2t, -\cos^2 t\right)$

   (C) $\left(4\sin 2t, \cos^2 t\right)$

   (D) $\left(4\sin 2t, -2\cos 2t\right)$

   (E) $\left(2\cos 2t, -4\sin 2t\right)$

---

33. The height of a mass hanging from a spring at time t seconds, where $t > 0$, is given by $h(t) = 12 - 4\cos(2t)$. In the first two seconds, how many times is the velocity of the mass equal to 0?

   (A) 0 (B) 1 (C) 2 (D) 3 (E) 4

GO ON TO THE NEXT PAGE

34. $\lim\limits_{h \to 0} \dfrac{\tan^{-1}(1+h) - \dfrac{\pi}{4}}{h} =$

(A) 2   (B) $\dfrac{4}{4 + \pi^2}$ (C) $\dfrac{16}{16 + \pi^2}$ (D) $\dfrac{1}{2}$ (E) Nonexistent

---

35. What is the trapezoidal approximation of $\int\limits_{0}^{3} e^x dx$ using $n = 4$ subintervals?

(A) 6.407   (B) 13.565   (C) 19.972   (D) 27.879   (E) 34.944

---

36. Given $x^2 y + x^2 = y^2 + 1$, find $\dfrac{d^2 y}{dx^2}$ at $(1,1)$.

(A) 36   (B) 12   (C) −4   (D) −12   (E) −36

GO ON TO THE NEXT PAGE

37. If $\int\limits_{-2}^{4} f(x)dx = a$ and $\int\limits_{3}^{4} f(x)dx = b$, then $\int\limits_{3}^{-2} f(x)\,dx =$

   (A) $a+b$ (B) $a-2b$ (C) $a-b$ (D) $b-a$ (E) $2b-a$

38. $\dfrac{d}{dx}\int\limits_{2x}^{5x} \cos t\; dt =$

   (A) $5\cos 5x - 2\cos 2x$

   (B) $5\sin 5x - 2\sin 2x$

   (C) $\cos 5x - \cos 2x$

   (D) $\sin 5x - \sin 2x$

   (E) $\dfrac{1}{5}\cos 5x - \dfrac{1}{2}\sin 2x$

GO ON TO THE NEXT PAGE

39. Using the Taylor series about $x = 0$ for $\sin x$, approximate $\sin(0.4)$ to four decimal places.

(A) $0.4 + \dfrac{(0.4)^3}{3!} + \dfrac{(0.4)^5}{5!}$

(B) $0.4 - \dfrac{(0.4)^3}{3!} + \dfrac{(0.4)^5}{5!}$

(C) $0.4 - \dfrac{(0.4)^3}{3} + \dfrac{(0.4)^5}{5}$

(D) $0.4 + \dfrac{(0.4)^2}{2!} + \dfrac{(0.4)^3}{3!} + \dfrac{(0.4)^4}{4!} + \dfrac{(0.4)^5}{5!}$

(E) $0.4 - \dfrac{(0.4)^2}{2!} + \dfrac{(0.4)^3}{3!} - \dfrac{(0.4)^4}{4!} + \dfrac{(0.4)^5}{5!}$

40. Let R be the region in the first quadrant between the graphs of $y = e^{-x}$, $y = \sin x$, and the y-axis. The volume of the solid that results when R is revolved about the x-axis is

(A) –0.888   (B) –0.869   (C) 0.277   (D) 0.869   (E) 0.888

41. Use Euler's Method, with $h = 0.2$ to estimate $y(3)$, if $\dfrac{dy}{dx} = 2y - 4x$ and $y(2) = 6$.

(A) 9.684   (B) 10.442   (C) 12.378   (D) 12.756   (E) 18.426

---

42. $\displaystyle\int \sec^4 x \, dx =$

(A) $\tan^4 x + C$

(B) $\tan x + \dfrac{1}{3}\tan^3 x + C$

(C) $\tan^2 x + C$

(D) $\dfrac{\sec^5 x}{5} + C$

(E) $\sec^2 x \tan^2 x + C$

---

43. Let $f(x) = \displaystyle\int \cot x \, dx$; $0 < x < \pi$. If $f\left(\dfrac{\pi}{6}\right) = 1$, then $f(1) =$

(A) −1.861   (B) −0.480   (C) 0.134   (D) 0.524   (E) 1.521

GO ON TO THE NEXT PAGE

44. $\int \sqrt{4-x^2}\,dx =$

(A) $\frac{2}{3}\left(4-x^2\right)^{\frac{3}{2}}+C$

(B) $2\sin^{-1}\left(\frac{x}{2}\right)+x\sqrt{4-x^2}+C$

(C) $2\sin^{-1}\left(\frac{x}{2}\right)+\frac{x}{2}\sqrt{4-x^2}+C$

(D) $\frac{2}{3}\left(4-x^2\right)^{\frac{3}{2}}+C$

(E) $2\sin^{-1}\left(\frac{x}{2}\right)+4x\sqrt{4-x^2}+C$

---

45. A force of 250 N is required to stretch a spring 5 m from rest. Using Hooke's law, $F = kx$, how much work, in Joules, is required to stretch the spring 7 m from rest?

(A) 14.286   (B) 71.429   (C) 245   (D) 490   (E) 1225

STOP

END OF SECTION I

IF YOU FINISH BEFORE TIME IS CALLED, YOU MAY CHECK YOUR WORK ON PART B ONLY.

DO NOT GO ON TO SECTION II UNTIL YOU ARE TOLD TO DO SO.

SECTION II
GENERAL INSTRUCTIONS

You may wish to look over the problems before starting to work on them, since it is not expected that everyone will be able to complete all parts of all problems. All problems are given equal weight, but the parts of a particular problem are not necessarily given equal weight.

A GRAPHING CALCULATOR IS REQUIRED FOR SOME PROBLEMS OR PARTS OF PROBLEMS ON THIS SECTION OF THE EXAMINATION.

- You should write all work for each part of each problem in the space provided for that part in the booklet. Be sure to write clearly and legibly. If you make an error, you may save time by crossing it out rather than trying to erase it. Erased or crossed-out work will not be graded.

- Show all your work. You will be graded on the correctness and completeness of your methods as well as your answers. Correct answers without supporting work may not receive credit.

- Justifications require that you give mathematical (noncalculator) reasons and that you clearly identify functions, graphs, tables, or other objects you use.

- You are permitted to use your calculator to solve an equation, find the derivative of a function at a point, or calculate the value of a definite integral. However, you must clearly indicate the setup of your problem, namely the equation, function, or integral you are using. If you use other built-in features or programs, you must show the mathematical steps necessary to produce your results.

- Your work must be expressed in standard mathematical notation rather than calculator syntax.

  For example, $\int_1^5 x^2 dx$ may not be written as fnInt $(X^2, X, 1, 5)$.

- Unless otherwise specified, answers (numeric or algebraic) need not be simplified. If your answer is given as a decimal approximation, it should be correct to three places after the decimal point.

- Unless otherwise specified, the domain of a function f is assumed to be the set of all real numbers x for which $f(x)$ is a real number.

SECTION II, PART A
Time—45 minutes
Number of problems—3

A graphing calculator is required for some problems or parts of problems.

During the timed portion for Part A, you may work only on the problems in Part A.

On Part A, you are permitted to use your calculator to solve an equation, find the derivative of a function at a point, or calculate the value of a definite integral. However, you must clearly indicate the setup of your problem, namely the equation, function, or integral you are using. If you use other built-in features or programs, you must show the mathematical steps necessary to produce your results.

GO ON TO THE NEXT PAGE

1. An object moving along a curve in the xy-plane has its position given by $\left(x(t), y(t)\right)$ at time t seconds, $0 \le t \le 1$, with $\dfrac{dx}{dt} = 8t\cos t$ units/sec and $\dfrac{dy}{dt} = 8t\sin t$ units/sec.

At time $t = 0$, the object is located at (5, 11).

(a) Find the speed of the object at time $t = 1$.

(b) Find the length of the arc described by the curve's position from time $t = 0$ to time $t = 1$.

(c) Find the location of the object at time $t = \dfrac{\pi}{2}$.

2.

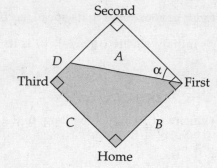

A baseball diamond is a square with each side 90 feet in length. A player runs from second base to third base at a rate of 18 ft/sec.

(a) At what rate is the player's distance from first base, A, changing when his distance from third base, D, is 22.5 feet?

(b) At what rate is angle α increasing when D is 22.5 feet?

(c) At what rate is the area of the trapezoidal region, formed by line segments A, B, C, and D, changing when D is 22.5 feet?

GO ON TO THE NEXT PAGE

3. A body is coasting to a stop and the only force acting on it is a resistance proportional to its speed, according to the equation $\frac{ds}{dt} = v_f = v_0\, e^{-\left(\frac{k}{m}\right)t}$; $s(0) = 0$, where v_0 is the body's initial velocity (in m/s), v_f is its final velocity, m is its mass, k is a constant, and t is time.

(a) If a body with mass $m = 50$ kg and $k = 1.5$ kg/sec initially has a velocity of 30 m/s, how long, to the nearest second, will it take to slow to 1 m/s?

(b) How far, to the nearest 10 meters, will the body coast during the time it takes to slow from 30 m/s to 1 m/s?

(c) If the body coasts from 30 m/s to a stop, how far will it coast?

No calculator is allowed for these problems.

During the timed portion for Part B, you may continue to work on the problems in Part A without the use of any calculator.

4.

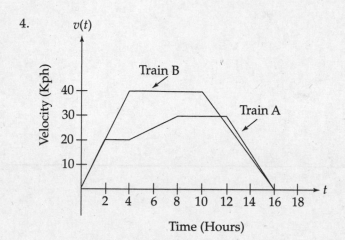

Three trains, A, B, and C each travel on a straight track for $0 \le t \le 16$ hours. The graphs above, which consist of line segments, show the velocities, in kilometers per hour, of trains A and B. The velocity of C is given by $v(t) = 8t - 0.25t^2$.

(Indicate units of measure for all answers.)

(a) Find the velocities of A and C at time $t = 6$ hours.

(b) Find the accelerations of B and C at time $t = 6$ hours.

(c) Find the positive difference between the total distance that A traveled and the total distance that B traveled in 16 hours.

(d) Find the total distance that C traveled in 16 hours.

GO ON TO THE NEXT PAGE

5. Let y be the function satisfying $f'(x) = x(1 - f(x))$; $f(0) = 10$.

(a) Use Euler's Method, starting at $x = 0$, with step size of 0.5 to approximate $f(x)$ at $x = 1$.

(b) Find an exact solution for $f(x)$ when $x = 1$.

(c) Evaluate $\int_0^\infty x(1 - f(x))dx$.

---

6. Given $f(x) = \tan^{-1}(x)$ and $g(x) = \dfrac{1}{1 + x}$, for $|x| \le 1$.

(a) Find the fifth-degree Taylor polynomial and general expression for $g(x)$ about $x = 0$.

(b) Given that $\dfrac{d}{dx}\tan^{-1}x = \dfrac{1}{1 + x^2}$, for $|x| \le 1$, use the result of part (a) to find the fifth-degree Taylor polynomial and general expression for $f(x)$ about $x = 0$.

(c) Use the fifth-degree Taylor polynomial to estimate $f\left(\dfrac{1}{10}\right)$.

END OF EXAMINATION

ANSWER KEY TO SECTION I

1. D	11. A	21. C	31. B	41. C
2. C	12. B	22. A	32. A	42. B
3. B	13. D	23. D	33. B	43. E
4. B	14. C	24. C	34. D	44. C
5. A	15. D	25. A	35. C	45. E
6. E	16. B	26. D	36. D	
7. B	17. E	27. E	37. D	
8. C	18. E	28. E	38. A	
9. D	19. A	29. A	39. B	
10. D	20. B	30. D	40. E	

31

Answers and Explanations to BC Practice Test 2

ANSWERS AND EXPLANATIONS TO SECTION 1

PROBLEM 1. What is the slope of the line tangent to the curve $x^2 + 2xy + 3y^2 = 2$ when $y = 1$?

We need to use implicit differentiation to find $\dfrac{dy}{dx}$.

$$2x + 2\left(x\frac{dy}{dx} + y\right) + 6y\frac{dy}{dx} = 0$$

$$2x + 2x\frac{dy}{dx} + 2y + 6y\frac{dy}{dx} = 0$$

Now, if we wanted to solve for $\dfrac{dy}{dx}$ in terms of x and y, we would have to do some algebra to isolate $\dfrac{dy}{dx}$. But, because we are asked to solve for $\dfrac{dy}{dx}$ at a specific value of x, we don't need to simplify.

We need to find the x-coordinate that corresponds to the y-coordinate $y = 1$. We plug $y = 1$ into the equation and solve for x:

$$x^2 + 2x(1) + 3(1)^2 = 2$$

$$x^2 + 2x + 3 = 2$$

$$x^2 + 2x + 1 = 0$$

$$(x+1)^2 = 0$$

$$x = -1$$

Finally, we plug $x = -1$ and $y = 1$ into the derivative and we get:

$$2(-1) + 2(-1)\frac{dy}{dx} + 2(1) + 6(1)\frac{dy}{dx} = 0$$

$$-2 - 2\frac{dy}{dx} + 2 + 6\frac{dy}{dx} = 0$$

$$\frac{dy}{dx} = 0$$

The answer is (D).

PROBLEM 2. $\displaystyle\int_{-1}^{1} xe^{x^2}\,dx =$

We can use u-substitution to evaluate the integral.

Let $u = x^2$ and $du = 2xdx$. Then $\dfrac{1}{2}du = x\,dx$.

Now we substitute into the integral $\dfrac{1}{2}\displaystyle\int e^u\,du$, leaving out the limits of integration for the moment.

Evaluate the integral to get: $\dfrac{1}{2}\displaystyle\int e^u\,du = \dfrac{1}{2}e^u$

Now we substitute back to get: $\dfrac{1}{2}e^{x^2}$

Finally, we evaluate at the limits of integration and we get: $\dfrac{1}{2}e^{x^2}\Big|_{-1}^{1} = \dfrac{1}{2}e - \dfrac{1}{2}e = 0$

The answer is (C).

PROBLEM 3. If, for $t > 0$, $x = t^2$ and $y = \cos\!\left(t^2\right)$, then $\dfrac{dy}{dx} =$

If we have a pair of parametric equations, $x(t)$ and $y(t)$, then: $\dfrac{dy}{dx} = \dfrac{\dfrac{dy}{dt}}{\dfrac{dx}{dt}}$

Here we get: $\dfrac{dy}{dt} = -2t\sin\!\left(t^2\right)$ and $\dfrac{dx}{dt} = 2t$

Then: $\dfrac{dy}{dx} = \dfrac{-2t\sin\!\left(t^2\right)}{2t} = -\sin\!\left(t^2\right)$

The answer is (B).

PROBLEM 4. The function $f(x) = 4x^3 - 8x^2 + 1$ on the interval $[-1, 1]$ has an absolute minimum at $x =$

If we want to find the minimum, we take the derivative and find where the derivative is zero:

$$f'(x) = 12x^2 - 16x$$

Next, we set the derivative equal to zero and solve for x, in order to find the critical values:

$$12x^2 - 16x = 0$$

$$4x(3x - 4) = 0$$

$$x = 0 \text{ or } x = \frac{4}{3}$$

Next, we can use the second derivative test to determine which critical value is a minimum and which is a maximum.

Remember the second derivative test: **If the sign of the second derivative at a critical value is positive, then the curve has a local minimum there. If the sign of the second derivative is negative, then the curve has a local maximum there.**

We take the second derivative: $f'(x) = 24x - 16$

This is negative at $x = 0$ and positive at $x = \frac{4}{3}$. This means that the curve has a *relative* minimum at $x = \frac{4}{3}$, but, this value is outside of the interval $[-1, 1]$. So, in order to find where it has an absolute *minimum*, we plug the endpoints of the interval into the original equation, and the smaller value will be the answer.

At $x = -1$, the value is $f(-1) = -11$. At $x = 1$, the value is $f(1) = -3$.

The answer is (B).

PROBLEM 5. $\displaystyle\int \frac{x\,dx}{x^2 + 5x + 6} =$

Whenever we have an integrand that is a rational expression, we can often use the method of partial fractions to rewrite the integral in a form in which it's easy to evaluate.

First, separate the denominator into its two components and place the constants A and B in the numerators of the fractions and the components into the denominators. Set their sum equal to the original rational expression.

$$\frac{A}{x+3} + \frac{B}{x+2} = \frac{x}{(x+3)(x+2)}$$

Now we want to solve for the constants A and B. First, multiply through by $(x+3)(x+2)$ to clear the denominators:

$$(x+3)(x+2)\left[\frac{A}{x+3} + \frac{B}{x+2}\right] = x$$

$$A(x+2) + B(x+3) = x$$

Now distribute, then group, the terms on the left side:

$$Ax + 2A + Bx + 3B = x$$

$$Ax + Bx + 2A + 3B = x$$

$$(A+B)x + (2A+3B) = x$$

In order for this last equation to be true, we need $A + B = 1$ and $2A + 3B = 0$.

If we solve these simultaneous equations, we get: $A = 3$ and $B = -2$.

Now that we have done the partial fraction decomposition, we can rewrite the

original integral as: $\int\left[\dfrac{3}{x+3} - \dfrac{2}{x+2}\right]dx$. This is now simple to evaluate:

$$\int\left[\frac{3}{x+3} - \frac{2}{x+2}\right]dx = 3\int\frac{dx}{x+3} - 2\int\frac{dx}{x+2} = 3\ln|x+3| - 2\ln|x+2| + C$$

Using the rules of logarithms, the answer can be rewritten as: $\ln\left|\dfrac{(x+3)^3}{(x+2)^2}\right| + C$

The answer is (A).

PROBLEM 6. $\dfrac{d}{dx}\left(x^2 \sin^2 x\right) =$

Here we need to use the Product Rule, which is: If $f(x) = uv$, where u and v are both

functions of x, then $f'(x) = u\dfrac{dv}{dx} + v\dfrac{du}{dx}$.

We get: $\dfrac{d}{dx}\left(x^2 \sin^2 x\right) = 2x\sin^2 x + x^2\left(2\sin x\cos x\right)$

This can be simplified to: $2x\sin^2 x + x^2\sin 2x$

The answer is (E).

PROBLEM 7. The line normal to the curve $y = \dfrac{x^2-1}{x^2+1}$ at $x = 2$ has slope

The normal line to a curve at a point is perpendicular to the tangent line at the same point. Thus, the slope of the normal line is the negative reciprocal of the slope of the tangent line. We find the slope of the tangent line by finding the derivative and evaluating it at the point.

We need to use the Quotient Rule, which is:

Given $y = \dfrac{g(x)}{h(x)}$, then: $\dfrac{dy}{dx} = \dfrac{h(x)g'(x) - g(x)h'(x)}{[h(x)]^2}$

Here, we have: $\dfrac{dy}{dx} = \dfrac{(x^2+1)(2x) - (x^2-1)(2x)}{(x^2+1)^2}$

Next, plug in $x = 2$ and solve: $\dfrac{dy}{dx}\bigg|_{x=2} = \dfrac{(4+1)(4) - (4-1)(4)}{(4+1)^2} = \dfrac{8}{25}$

Therefore, the slope of the normal line is: $-\dfrac{25}{8}$

The answer is (B).

PROBLEM 8. If f and g are differentiable functions and $h(x) = f(x)e^{g(x)}$, then $h'(x) =$

Here we need to use the Product Rule, which is: If $f(x) = uv$, where u and v are both

functions of x, then $f'(x) = u\dfrac{dv}{dx} + v\dfrac{du}{dx}$.

We get: $h'(x) = f'(x)e^{g(x)} + f(x)\left[e^{g(x)}g'(x)\right]$

This can be simplified to: $h'(x) = e^{g(x)}\left[f'(x) + f(x)g'(x)\right]$

The answer is (C).

PROBLEM 9.

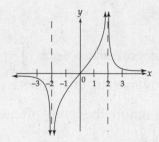

The graph of $y = f(x)$ is shown above. Which of the following could be the graph of $y = f'(x)$?

Here we want to examine the slopes of various pieces of the graph of $f(x)$. Notice that the graph starts with a slope of approximately zero and has a negative slope from $x = -\infty$ to $x = -2$, where the slope is $-\infty$. Thus we are looking for a graph of $f'(x)$ that is negative from $x = -\infty$ to $x = -2$ and undefined at $x = -2$. Next, notice that the graph of $f(x)$ has a positive slope from $x = -2$ to $x = 2$ and that the slope shrinks from ∞ to approximately one and then grows to ∞. Thus we are looking for a graph of $f'(x)$ that is positive from $x = -2$ to $x = 2$ and approximately equal to one at $x = 0$. Finally, notice that the graph of $f(x)$ has a negative slope from $x = 2$ to $x = \infty$, where the slope starts at $-\infty$ and grows to approximately zero. Thus we are looking for a graph of $f'(x)$ that is negative from $x = 2$ to $x = \infty$, where it is approximately zero. Graph (D) satisfies all of these requirements.

The answer is (D).

PROBLEM 10. $\displaystyle\int_{e}^{e^2}\left(\sqrt{x} + \frac{1}{\sqrt{x}}\right)^2 dx =$

First, expand the integrand: $\displaystyle\int_{e}^{e^2}\left(\sqrt{x} + \frac{1}{\sqrt{x}}\right)^2 dx = \int_{e}^{e^2}\left(x + 2 + \frac{1}{x}\right) dx$

Next, evaluate the integral:

$$\int_{e}^{e^2}\left(x + 2 + \frac{1}{x}\right) dx = \left(\frac{x^2}{2} + 2x + \ln|x|\right)\Bigg|_{e}^{e^2} = \left(\frac{e^4}{2} + 2e^2 + \ln e^2\right) - \left(\frac{e^2}{2} + 2e + \ln e\right) = \frac{e^4}{2} + \frac{3e^2}{2} - 2e + 1$$

The answer is (D).

PROBLEM 11. $\displaystyle\int_{4}^{\infty}\frac{dx}{x^2+16}$

Whenever we have an integral of the form $\displaystyle\int\frac{dx}{a^2+x^2}$, where a is a constant, the integral is going to be an inverse tangent. So let's put the integrand into the desired form. Also, we're going to ignore the limits of integration until after we have done the antidifferentiation.

First divide the numerator and the denominator by 16: $\displaystyle\int\frac{dx}{x^2+16}=\frac{1}{16}\int\frac{dx}{\left(1+\dfrac{x^2}{16}\right)}$

Next, we do u-substitution. Let $u=\dfrac{x}{4}$ and $du=\dfrac{dx}{4}$ or $4du=dx$.

Substitute into the integrand: $\displaystyle\frac{1}{16}\int\frac{dx}{\left(1+\dfrac{x^2}{16}\right)}=\frac{1}{16}\int\frac{4du}{\left(1+u^2\right)}=\frac{1}{4}\int\frac{du}{\left(1+u^2\right)}$

Evaluate the integral: $\displaystyle\frac{1}{4}\int\frac{du}{\left(1+u^2\right)}=\frac{1}{4}\tan^{-1}u$

Substitute back to get: $\displaystyle\frac{1}{4}\tan^{-1}\left(\frac{x}{4}\right)$

Now we can evaluate the function at the limits of integration:

$$\left[\frac{1}{4}\tan^{-1}\left(\frac{x}{4}\right)\right]_{4}^{\infty}=\frac{1}{4}\left[\tan^{-1}\infty-\tan^{-1}1\right]=\frac{1}{4}\left[\frac{\pi}{2}-\frac{\pi}{4}\right]=\frac{\pi}{16}$$

The answer is (A).

PROBLEM 12. What is the equation of the line tangent to the graph of $y=\sin^2 x$ at $x=\dfrac{\pi}{4}$?

If we want to find the equation of the tangent line, first we need to find the y-coordinate that corresponds to $x=\dfrac{\pi}{4}$. It is: $y=\sin^2\left(\dfrac{\pi}{4}\right)=\left(\dfrac{1}{\sqrt{2}}\right)^2=\dfrac{1}{2}$

Next, we need to find the derivative of the curve at $x = \frac{\pi}{4}$, using the Chain Rule.

We get: $\frac{dy}{dx} = 2\sin x \cos x$. At $x = \frac{\pi}{4}$, $\frac{dy}{dx}\Big|_{x=\frac{\pi}{4}} = 2\sin\left(\frac{\pi}{4}\right)\cos\left(\frac{\pi}{4}\right) = 2\left(\frac{1}{\sqrt{2}}\right)\left(\frac{1}{\sqrt{2}}\right) = 1$

Now we have the slope of the tangent line and a point that it goes through. We can use the point-slope formula for the equation of a line, $(y - y_1) = m(x - x_1)$, and plug in what we have just found. We get: $\left(y - \frac{1}{2}\right) = (1)\left(x - \frac{\pi}{4}\right)$

The answer is (B).

PROBLEM 13. If $f(x) = \begin{cases} ax^2 + 3ax + 5 \, ; \ x \geq 2 \\ 4ax^3 - 6ax^2 + 9 \, ; \ x < 2 \end{cases}$, find the value of a that makes $f(x)$ continuous for all real values of x.

A polynomial is continuous everywhere on its domain, so we need to find a value of a such that $f(x)$ is continuous at $x = 2$. This means that $\lim\limits_{x \to 2^-} f(x)$ must equal $\lim\limits_{x \to 2^+} f(x)$. In other words, if we plug $x = 2$ into both pieces of this piecewise function, we need to get the same value:

$f(x) = \begin{cases} a(2)^2 + 3a(2) + 5 \, ; \ x \geq 2 \\ 4a(2)^3 - 6a(2)^2 + 9 \, ; \ x < 2 \end{cases}$, so we need $10a + 5 = 8a + 9$ and, therefore, $a = 2$.

The answer is (D).

PROBLEM 14. $\int x\sin(2x)dx =$

We can evaluate this integral using integration by parts. Here, we let $u = x$ and $dv = \sin(2x)^{dx}$. Then $du = dx$ and $v = -\frac{1}{2}\cos(2x)$.

The rule for integration by parts says that $\int u \, dv = uv - \int v \, du$.

Substituting the terms, we get: $\int x\sin(2x)dx = -\frac{x}{2}\cos(2x) + \frac{1}{2}\int \cos(2x) \, dx$

Now, we integrate the second term, which gives us:

$$\int x\sin(2x)dx = -\frac{x}{2}\cos(2x) + \frac{1}{4}\sin(2x) + C$$

The answer is (C).

PROBLEM 15. If $f(x) = \dfrac{x^2 + 5x - 24}{x^2 + 10x + 16}$, then $\lim\limits_{x \to -8} f(x)$ is

First, try plugging $x = -8$ into $f(x) = \dfrac{x^2 + 5x - 24}{x^2 + 10x + 16}$.

We get: $f(x) = \dfrac{(-8)^2 + 5(-8) - 24}{(-8)^2 + 10(-8) + 16} = \dfrac{0}{0}$. This does NOT necessarily mean that the limit

does not exist. When we get a limit of the form $\dfrac{0}{0}$, we first try to simplify the function

by factoring and canceling like terms. Here we get:

$$f(x) = \frac{x^2 + 5x - 24}{x^2 + 10x + 16} = \frac{(x+8)(x-3)}{(x+8)(x+2)} = \frac{(x-3)}{(x+2)}$$

Now, if we plug in $x = -8$, we get: $f(x) = \dfrac{(-8-3)}{(-8+2)} = \dfrac{-11}{-6} = \dfrac{11}{6}$

The answer is (D).

PROBLEM 16. What is the approximation of the value of e^3 obtained by using the fourth-degree Taylor polynomial about $x = 0$ for e^x?

The Taylor series for e^x about $x = 0$ is $e^x = 1 + x + \dfrac{x^2}{2!} + \dfrac{x^3}{3!} + \dfrac{x^4}{4!} + \ldots$

Here, we simply substitute 3 for x in the series and we get:

$$e^3 = 1 + 3 + \frac{3^2}{2!} + \frac{3^3}{3!} + \frac{3^4}{4!} + \ldots$$

The answer is (B).

PROBLEM 17. A rock is thrown straight upward with an initial velocity of 50 m/s from a point 100 m above the ground. If the acceleration of the rock at any time t is $a = -10$ m/s^2, what is the maximum height of the rock (in meters)?

Because the derivative of velocity with respect to time is acceleration, we have:

$$v(t) = \int -10 \, dt = -10t + C$$

Now we can plug in the initial condition to solve for the constant:

$$50 = -10(0) + C$$

$$C = 50$$

Therefore, the velocity function is: $v(t) = -10t + 50$

Note that the velocity is zero at $t = 5$

Next, because the derivative of position with respect to time is velocity, we have:

$$s(t) = \int (-10t + 50) \, dt = -5t^2 + 50t + C$$

Now we can plug in the initial condition to solve for the constant:

$$100 = -5(0)^2 + 50(0) + C$$
$$C = 100$$

Therefore, the position function is: $s(t) = -5t^2 + 50t + 100$

The maximum height occurs when the velocity is zero, so we plug $t = 5$ into the position function to get: $s(5) = -5(5)^2 + 50(5) + 100 = 225$

The answer is (E).

PROBLEM 18. The sum of the infinite geometric series $2 - \dfrac{2}{3} + \dfrac{2}{9} - \dfrac{2}{27} + \dots$ is

This is the geometric series $\displaystyle\sum_{n=0}^{\infty} 2\left(-\dfrac{1}{3}\right)^n$. The sum of an infinite series of the form

$\displaystyle\sum_{n=0}^{\infty} ar^n$ is: $S = \dfrac{a}{1-r}$. Here, the sum is: $S = \dfrac{2}{1 - \left(-\dfrac{1}{3}\right)} = \dfrac{2}{\dfrac{4}{3}} = \dfrac{3}{2}$

The answer is (E).

PROBLEM 19. What are all values of x for which the series $\sum_{n=1}^{\infty} \dfrac{(x-3)^n}{n^2(5^n)}$ converges?

Use the Ratio Test to determine the interval of convergence.

We get: $\lim\limits_{n\to\infty} \dfrac{\dfrac{(x-3)^{n+1}}{(n+1)^2(5^{n+1})}}{\dfrac{(x-3)^n}{(n)^2(5^n)}} = \lim\limits_{n\to\infty} \dfrac{(x-3)^{n+1}}{(n+1)^2(5^{n+1})} \dfrac{(n)^2(5^n)}{(x-3)^n} = \lim\limits_{n\to\infty} \dfrac{x-3}{5} \dfrac{(n)^2}{(n+1)^2} = \dfrac{x-3}{5}$

This converges if $\left|\dfrac{x-3}{5}\right| < 1$ or $-1 < \dfrac{x-3}{5} < 1$ and diverges if $\left|\dfrac{x-3}{5}\right| > 1$.

Thus the series converges when $-2 < x < 8$.

Now, we need to test whether the series converges at the endpoints of this interval.

When $x = 8$, we get the series $\sum_{n=1}^{\infty} \dfrac{1}{n^2}$, which converges, and when $x = -2$, we get the

alternating series $\sum_{n=1}^{\infty} \dfrac{(-1)^n}{n^2}$, which also converges. Thus, the series converges when

$-2 \leq x \leq 8$.

The answer is (A).

PROBLEM 20. Find the area inside one loop of the curve $r = \sin 2\theta$.

First, let's graph the curve:

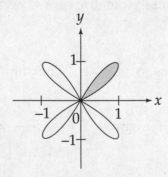

Let's find the area of the loop in the first quadrant, which is the interval from $\theta = 0$

to $\theta = \dfrac{\pi}{2}$. We find the area of a polar graph by evaluating $A = \dfrac{1}{2} \displaystyle\int_{0}^{\frac{\pi}{2}} r^2 d\theta$.

Thus, we need to evaluate: $A = \dfrac{1}{2}\displaystyle\int_0^{\frac{\pi}{2}} \sin^2(2\theta)\,d\theta$

Next, we need to do a trigonometric substitution to evaluate this integral. Recall that $\cos 2\theta = 1 - 2\sin^2\theta$. We can rearrange this to obtain $\sin^2\theta = \dfrac{1 - \cos 2\theta}{2}$, or in this case,

$\sin^2 2\theta = \dfrac{1 - \cos 4\theta}{2}$.

Thus, we can rewrite the integral: $A = \dfrac{1}{2}\displaystyle\int_0^{\frac{\pi}{2}} \dfrac{1 - \cos(4\theta)}{2}\,d\theta$

Now we can evaluate this integral:

$$\int \frac{1 - \cos(4\theta)}{2}\,d\theta = \int \frac{d\theta}{2} - \int \frac{\cos(4\theta)}{2}\,d\theta = \frac{\theta}{2} - \frac{\sin(4\theta)}{8}$$

Now we evaluate the integral at the limits of integration:

$$\frac{1}{2}\left(\frac{\theta}{2} - \frac{\sin(4\theta)}{8}\right)\Bigg|_0^{\frac{\pi}{2}} = \frac{1}{2}\left(\frac{\pi}{4} - \frac{\sin(2\pi)}{8}\right) - \frac{1}{2}\left(0 - \frac{\sin(0)}{8}\right) = \frac{\pi}{8}$$

The answer is (B).

PROBLEM 21. The average value of $\sec^2 x$ on the interval $\left[\dfrac{\pi}{6}, \dfrac{\pi}{4}\right]$ is

In order to find the average value, we use the Mean Value Theorem for integrals, which says that the average value of $f(x)$ on the interval $[a, b]$ is $\dfrac{1}{b-a}\displaystyle\int_a^b f(x)\,dx$.

Here, we have: $\dfrac{1}{\dfrac{\pi}{4} - \dfrac{\pi}{6}} \displaystyle\int_{\frac{\pi}{6}}^{\frac{\pi}{4}} \sec^2 x\,dx$

Next, recall that: $\dfrac{d}{dx}\tan x = \sec^2 x$

We evaluate the integral: $\dfrac{1}{\dfrac{\pi}{4} - \dfrac{\pi}{6}}(\tan x)\Big|_{\frac{\pi}{6}}^{\frac{\pi}{4}} = \dfrac{1}{\dfrac{\pi}{4} - \dfrac{\pi}{6}}\left[\tan\dfrac{\pi}{4} - \tan\dfrac{\pi}{6}\right] = \dfrac{1}{\dfrac{\pi}{4} - \dfrac{\pi}{6}}\left(1 - \dfrac{\sqrt{3}}{3}\right)$

Next, we need to do a little algebra. Get a common denominator for each of the two expressions: $\dfrac{1}{\dfrac{\pi}{4} - \dfrac{\pi}{6}}\left(1 - \dfrac{\sqrt{3}}{3}\right) = \dfrac{1}{\dfrac{6\pi}{24} - \dfrac{4\pi}{24}}\left(\dfrac{3}{3} - \dfrac{\sqrt{3}}{3}\right)$

We can simplify this to: $\dfrac{1}{\dfrac{2\pi}{24}}\left(\dfrac{3 - \sqrt{3}}{3}\right) = \dfrac{12}{\pi}\left(\dfrac{3 - \sqrt{3}}{3}\right) = \dfrac{12 - 4\sqrt{3}}{\pi}$

The answer is (C).

PROBLEM 22. Find the length of the arc of the curve defined by $x = \dfrac{1}{2}t^2$ and $y = \dfrac{1}{9}(6t + 9)^{\frac{3}{2}}$, from $t = 0$ to $t = 2$.

We can find the length of a parametric curve on the interval $[a, b]$ by evaluating the integral: $\displaystyle\int_a^b \sqrt{\left(\dfrac{dx}{dt}\right)^2 + \left(\dfrac{dy}{dt}\right)^2}\, dt$

First, we take the derivatives: $\dfrac{dx}{dt} = t$ and $\dfrac{dy}{dt} = \sqrt{6t + 9}$

Now, square the derivatives: $\left(\dfrac{dx}{dt}\right)^2 = t^2$ and $\left(\dfrac{dy}{dt}\right)^2 = 6t + 9$

Now, we plug this into the formula and we get:

$$\int_0^2 \sqrt{t^2 + 6t + 9}\, dt = \int_0^2 \sqrt{(t+3)^2}\, dt = \int_0^2 (t+3)\, dt = \left(\dfrac{t^2}{2} + 3t\right)_0^2 = 8$$

The answer is (A).

PROBLEM 23. The function f is given by $f(x) = x^4 + 4x^3$. On which of the following intervals is f decreasing?

A function is decreasing on an interval where the derivative is negative.

The derivative is: $f'(x) = 4x^3 + 12x^2$

Next, we want to determine on which intervals the derivative of the function is positive and on which it is negative. We do this by finding where the derivative is zero:

$$4x^3 + 12x^2 = 0$$

$$4x^2(x+3) = 0$$

$$x = -3 \text{ or } x = 0$$

We can test where the derivative is positive and negative by picking a point in each of the three regions $-\infty < x < -3$, $-3 < x < 0$, and $0 < x < \infty$, plugging the point into the derivative, and seeing what the sign of the answer is. You should find that the derivative is negative on the interval $-\infty < x < -3$.

The answer is (D).

PROBLEM 24. Which of the following series converge(s)?

I. $\displaystyle\sum_{n=1}^{\infty} \frac{(-1)^n}{n}$ II. $\displaystyle\sum_{n=1}^{\infty} \frac{1}{\sqrt{n^3}}$ III. $\displaystyle\sum_{n=1}^{\infty} \frac{1}{\sqrt[3]{n^2}}$

Series I: You might recognize this as the Alternating Harmonic series, which converges. If you don't, use the alternating series test, which says that, in order for an alternating series $\displaystyle\sum_{n=1}^{\infty} (-1)^n a_n$ to converge: (1) $a_{n+1} < a_n$; (2) $\displaystyle\lim_{n \to \infty} a_n = 0$; and (3) $a_n > 0$. This series satisfies these conditions, so it converges.

Series II: We can rewrite this series as $\displaystyle\sum_{n=1}^{\infty} \frac{1}{n^{\frac{3}{2}}}$, which is a p-series. A p-series is a series of the form $\displaystyle\sum_{n=1}^{\infty} \frac{1}{n^p}$, which converges if $p > 1$ and diverges if $p < 1$. Thus, this series converges.

Series III: We can rewrite this series as $\displaystyle\sum_{n=1}^{\infty} \frac{1}{n^{\frac{2}{3}}}$, which is also a p-series. Because $p < 1$, this series diverges.

The answer is (C).

PROBLEM 25. Given the differential equation $\dfrac{dz}{dt} = z\left(4 - \dfrac{z}{100}\right)$, where $z(0) = 50$, what is $\lim\limits_{t\to\infty} z(t)$?

We can solve this differential equation by separation of variables:

$$\int \frac{dz}{z\left(4 - \dfrac{z}{100}\right)} = \int dt$$

The integral on the right is trivial. We get $t + C$.

The one on the left will require the Method of Partial Fractions. First, separate the denominator into its two components and place the constants A and B in the numerators of the fractions and the components into the denominators. Set their sum equal to the original rational expression: $\quad \dfrac{A}{z} + \dfrac{B}{4 - \dfrac{z}{100}} = \dfrac{1}{z\left(4 - \dfrac{z}{100}\right)}$.

Now we want to solve for the constants A and B. First, multiply through by $z\left(4 - \dfrac{z}{100}\right)$ to clear the denominators:

$$z\left(4 - \frac{z}{100}\right)\left[\frac{A}{z} + \frac{B}{\left(4 - \dfrac{z}{100}\right)}\right] = 1$$

$$A\left(4 - \frac{z}{100}\right) + Bz = 1$$

Now distribute, then group, the terms on the left side:

$$4A - A\frac{z}{100} + Bz = 1$$

$$z\left(B - \frac{A}{100}\right) + 4A = 1$$

In order for this last equation to be true, we need: $4A = 1$ and $B - \dfrac{A}{100} = 0$

If we solve these simultaneous equations, we get: $A = \dfrac{1}{4}$ and $B = \dfrac{1}{400}$.

Now that we have done the partial fraction decomposition, we can rewrite the

original integral as: $\displaystyle\int \dfrac{\frac{1}{4}}{z} + \dfrac{\frac{1}{400}}{\left(4 - \frac{z}{100}\right)} \, dz$. This is now simple to evaluate:

$$\int \dfrac{\frac{1}{4}}{z} + \dfrac{\frac{1}{400}}{\left(4 - \frac{z}{100}\right)} \, dz = \dfrac{1}{4}\int \dfrac{dz}{z} + \dfrac{1}{400}\int \dfrac{dz}{\left(4 - \frac{z}{100}\right)} = \dfrac{1}{4}\ln|z| - \dfrac{1}{4}\ln\left|4 - \dfrac{z}{100}\right| + C$$

We can rewrite this with the laws of logarithms to get:

$$\dfrac{1}{4}\ln|z| - \dfrac{1}{4}\ln\left|4 - \dfrac{z}{100}\right| = \ln\left(\dfrac{100z}{400 - z}\right)^{\frac{1}{4}}$$

Thus, the solution to the differential equation is $\ln\left(\dfrac{100z}{400 - z}\right)^{\frac{1}{4}} = t + C$. We will need to do some algebra to rearrange the equation. First, exponentiate both sides to base e:

$$\left(\dfrac{100z}{400 - z}\right)^{\frac{1}{4}} = e^{t+C}$$

Then, because $e^{t+C} = e^t e^C$, and because e^C is a constant, we get: $\left(\dfrac{100z}{400 - z}\right)^{\frac{1}{4}} = Ce^t$

Next, raise both sides to the fourth power: $\left(\dfrac{100z}{400 - z}\right) = Ce^{4t}$

Invert both sides: $\left(\dfrac{400 - z}{100z}\right) = Ce^{-4t}$

Break the left side into two fractions: $\dfrac{4}{z} - \dfrac{1}{100} = Ce^{-4t}$

Add $\dfrac{1}{100}$ to both sides: $\dfrac{4}{z} = \dfrac{1}{100} + Ce^{-4t} = \dfrac{Ce^{-4t} + 1}{100}$

Invert both sides (again): $\dfrac{z}{4} = \dfrac{100}{Ce^{-4t}+1}$

Finally: $z(t) = \dfrac{400}{Ce^{-4t}+1}$ (Whew!)

Now, we can take the limit: $\displaystyle\lim_{t\to\infty}\dfrac{400}{Ce^{-4t}+1} = 400$

The answer is (A).

PROBLEM 26.

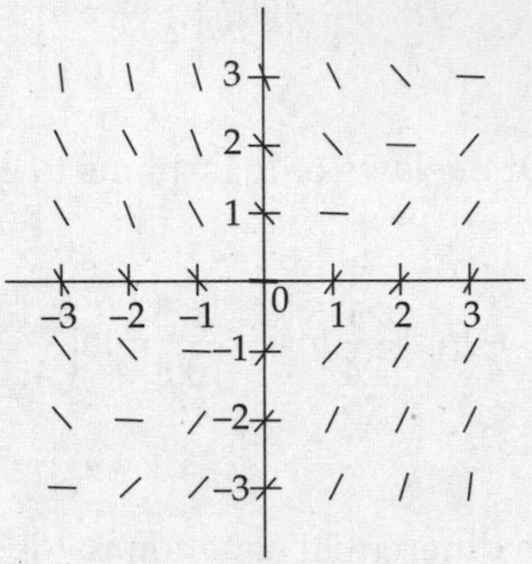

The slope field shown above corresponds to which of the following differential equations?

Notice that the slope of the differential equation is zero (horizontal tangent) at the origin. This eliminates answer choices (A) and (B) because they are undefined at the origin (so they would show a vertical tangent there). Next, notice that the slope is positive at (1, 0). This eliminates answer choice (C), which is zero on both axes. Finally, notice that the slope is negative at (0, 1), which eliminates answer choice (E), which is positive there.

The answer is (D).

PROBLEM 27. The value of c that satisfies the Mean Value Theorem for derivatives on the interval [0, 5] for the function $f(x) = x^3 - 6x$ is

The Mean Value Theorem for derivatives says that, given a function $f(x)$ which is continuous and differentiable on $[a, b]$, then there exists some value c on (a, b) where:

$$\dfrac{f(b)-f(a)}{b-a} = f'(c)$$

Here, we have: $\dfrac{f(b)-f(a)}{b-a} = \dfrac{f(5)-f(0)}{5-0} = \dfrac{95-0}{5} = 19$

Plus, $f'(c) = 3c^2 - 6$, so we simply set $3c^2 - 6 = 19$. If we solve for c, we get: $c = \pm\dfrac{5}{\sqrt{3}}$. Both of these values satisfy the Mean Value Theorem for derivatives, but only the positive value, $c = \dfrac{5}{\sqrt{3}}$, is in the interval.

The answer is (E).

PROBLEM 28.

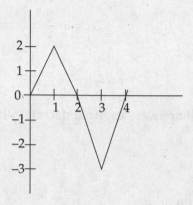

The graph of f is shown in the figure above. If $g(x) = \displaystyle\int_0^x f(t)\,dt$, for what positive value of x does $g(x)$ have a minimum?

If we want to find where $g(x)$ is a minimum, we can look at $g'(x)$. The Second Fundamental Theorem of Calculus tells us how to find the derivative of an integral: $\dfrac{d}{dx}\displaystyle\int_c^x f(t)\,dt = f(x)$, where c is a constant. Thus, $g'(x) = f(x)$. The graph of f is zero at $x = 0$, $x = 2$, and $x = 4$. We can eliminate $x = 0$ because we are looking for a *positive* value of x. Next, notice that f is negative to the left of $x = 4$ and positive to the right of $x = 4$. Thus, $g(x)$ has a minimum at $x = 4$.

We also could have found the answer geometrically. The function $g(x) = \displaystyle\int_0^x f(t)\,dt$ is called an *accumulation function* and stands for the area between the curve and the x-axis to the point x. Thus, the value of g grows from $x = 0$ to $x = 2$. Then, because we subtract the area under the x-axis from the area above it, the value of g shrinks from $x = 2$ to $x = 4$. The value begins to grow again after $x = 4$.

The answer is (E).

PROBLEM 29. If $f(x)$ is the function given by $f(x) = e^{3x} + 1$, at what value of x is the slope of the tangent line to $f(x)$ equal to 2?

The slope of the tangent line is the derivative of the function. We get: $f'(x) = 3e^{3x}$
Now we set the derivative equal to 2 and solve for x:

$$3e^{3x} = 2$$

$$e^{3x} = \frac{2}{3}$$

$$3x = \ln\frac{2}{3}$$

$$x = \frac{1}{3}\ln\frac{2}{3} \approx -.135$$

(Remember to round all answers to three decimal places on the AP exam.)

The answer is (A).

PROBLEM 30. If $y = (\sin x)^{e^x}$, then $y' =$

We need to use logarithmic differentiation to find the derivative. First, take the log

of both sides: $\ln y = \ln\left[(\sin x)^{e^x}\right]$

Next, on the right side, put the power in front of the log: $\ln y = e^x \ln(\sin x)$

Next, take the derivative of both sides: $\dfrac{1}{y}\dfrac{dy}{dx} = e^x \ln(\sin x) + e^x \dfrac{\cos x}{\sin x}$

This can be simplified to: $\dfrac{1}{y}\dfrac{dy}{dx} = e^x \ln(\sin x) + e^x \cot x$

Multiply both sides by y: $\dfrac{dy}{dx} = y\left[e^x \ln(\sin x) + e^x \cot x\right]$

Substitute $y = (\sin x)^{e^x}$ for y on the right side: $\dfrac{dy}{dx} = (\sin x)^{e^x}\left[e^x \ln(\sin x) + e^x \cot x\right]$

Finally, factor out e^x to obtain: $\dfrac{dy}{dx} = e^x(\sin x)^{e^x}\left[\ln(\sin x) + \cot x\right]$

The answer is (D).

Problem 31. The side of a square is increasing at a constant rate of 0.4 cm/sec. In terms of the perimeter, P, what is the rate of change of the area of the square, in cm²/sec?

The formula for the perimeter of a square is $P = 4s$, where s is the length of a side of the square.

If we differentiate this with respect to t, we get $\dfrac{dP}{dt} = 4\dfrac{ds}{dt}$. We plug in $\dfrac{ds}{dt} = 0.4$ and we get: $\dfrac{dP}{dt} = 4(0.4) = 1.6$

The formula for the area of a square is $A = s^2$. If we solve the perimeter equation for s in terms of P and substitute it into the area equation we get:

$$s = \frac{P}{4}, \text{ so } A = \left(\frac{P}{4}\right)^2 = \frac{P^2}{16}$$

If we differentiate this with respect to t, we get: $\dfrac{dA}{dt} = \dfrac{P}{8}\dfrac{dP}{dt}$

Now we plug in $\dfrac{dP}{dt} = 1.6$ and we get: $\dfrac{dA}{dt} = \dfrac{P}{8}(1.6) = 0.2P$

The answer is (B).

Problem 32. If f is a vector-valued function defined by $f(t) = \left(\sin 2t, \sin^2 t\right)$, then $f''(t) =$

The acceleration vector is the second derivative of the position vector (the velocity vector is the first derivative).

The velocity vector of this particle is: $\left(2\cos 2t, 2\sin t \cos t\right)$

This can be simplified to: $\left(2\cos 2t, \sin 2t\right)$

The acceleration vector is: $\left(-4\sin 2t, 2\cos 2t\right)$

The answer is (A).

Problem 33. The height of a mass hanging from a spring at time t seconds, where $t > 0$, is given by $h(t) = 12 - 4\cos(2t)$. In the first two seconds, how many times is the velocity of the mass equal to 0?

The velocity of the mass is the first derivative of the height: $v(t) = 8\sin(2t)$

Now, graph the equation to find how many times the graph of $v(t)$ crosses the t-axis between $t = 0$ and $t = 2$. Or you should know that this is a sine graph with an amplitude of 8 and a period of π, which will cross the t-axis once on the interval at $t = \dfrac{\pi}{2}$.

The answer is (B).

PROBLEM 34. $\displaystyle\lim_{h\to 0} \frac{\tan^{-1}(1+h) - \dfrac{\pi}{4}}{h} =$

Notice how this limit takes the form of the definition of the derivative, which is:

$$f'(x) = \lim_{h\to 0} \frac{f(x+h) - f(x)}{h}$$

Here, if we think of $f(x)$ as $\tan^{-1} x$, then this expression gives the derivative of $\tan^{-1} x$ at the point $x = 1$.

The derivative of $\tan^{-1} x$ is $f'(x) = \dfrac{1}{1+x^2}$. At $x = 1$, we get:

$$f'(1) = \frac{1}{2}$$

The answer is (D).

PROBLEM 35. What is the trapezoidal approximation of $\displaystyle\int_0^3 e^x dx$ using $n = 4$ subintervals?

The Trapezoid Rule enables us to approximate the area under a curve with a fair degree of accuracy. The rule says that the area between the x-axis and the curve $y = f(x)$, on the interval $[a,b]$, with n trapezoids, is:

$$\frac{1}{2}\frac{b-a}{n}\left[y_0 + 2y_1 + 2y_2 + 2y_3 + \ldots + 2y_{n-1} + y_n\right]$$

Using the rule here, with $n = 4$, $a = 0$, and $b = 3$, we get:

$$\frac{1}{2} \cdot \frac{3}{4}\left[e^0 + 2e^{\frac{3}{4}} + 2e^{\frac{6}{4}} + 2e^{\frac{9}{4}} + e^3\right] \approx 19.972$$

The answer is (C).

PROBLEM 36. Given $x^2 y + x^2 = y^2 + 1$, find $\dfrac{d^2 y}{dx^2}$ at $(1,1)$.

Use implicit differentiation to find $\dfrac{dy}{dx}$: $\quad x^2 \dfrac{dy}{dx} + 2xy + 2x = 2y \dfrac{dy}{dx}$

Now we want to isolate $\dfrac{dy}{dx}$, which will take some algebra.

First, put all of the terms containing $\dfrac{dy}{dx}$ on one side of the equals sign and all of the other terms on the other side: $\quad 2xy + 2x = 2y \dfrac{dy}{dx} - x^2 \dfrac{dy}{dx}$

Next, factor $\dfrac{dy}{dx}$ out of the right hand side: $\quad 2xy + 2x = \dfrac{dy}{dx}\left(2y - x^2\right)$

Finally, divide both sides by $\left(2y - x^2\right)$ to isolate $\dfrac{dy}{dx}$: $\quad \dfrac{dy}{dx} = \dfrac{2xy + 2x}{2y - x^2}$

At $(1,1)$, we get: $\quad \dfrac{dy}{dx} = \dfrac{2+2}{2-1} = 4$

Now, we can find the second derivative by again performing implicit differentiation:

$$\frac{d^2 y}{dx^2} = \frac{\left(2y - x^2\right)\left(2x\dfrac{dy}{dx} + 2y + 2\right) - \left(2xy + 2x\right)\left(2\dfrac{dy}{dx} - 2x\right)}{\left(2y - x^2\right)^2}$$

At $(1,1)$, we get: $\quad \dfrac{d^2 y}{dx^2} = \dfrac{(2-1)(8+2+2) - (2+2)(8-2)}{(2-1)^2} = \dfrac{12 - 24}{1} = -12$

The answer is (D).

PROBLEM 37. If $\int_{-2}^{4} f(x)dx = a$ and $\int_{3}^{4} f(x)dx = b$, then $\int_{3}^{-2} f(x)\,dx =$

Because the integral of a function can be interpreted as the area between the function and the curve, we can say that $\int_{a}^{b} f(x)\,dx = \int_{a}^{c} f(x)\,dx + \int_{c}^{b} f(x)\,dx$, where c is a point in the interval (a,b). Here we have: $\int_{-2}^{4} f(x)dx = \int_{-2}^{3} f(x)dx + \int_{3}^{4} f(x)dx$. We can rearrange this to: $\int_{-2}^{4} f(x)dx - \int_{3}^{4} f(x)dx = \int_{-2}^{3} f(x)dx$. This means that $a - b = \int_{-2}^{3} f(x)dx$. Finally, we know that $\int_{a}^{b} f(x)dx = -\int_{b}^{a} f(x)dx$, so $b - a = \int_{3}^{-2} f(x)dx$.

The answer is (D).

PROBLEM 38. $\dfrac{d}{dx} \displaystyle\int_{2x}^{5x} \cos t\, dt =$

The Second Fundamental Theorem of Calculus tells us how to find the derivative of an integral: $\dfrac{d}{dx} \displaystyle\int_{v}^{u} f(t)\, dt = f(u)\dfrac{du}{dx} - f(v)\dfrac{dv}{dx}$, where u and v are functions of x.

Here we can use the theorem to get: $\dfrac{d}{dx} \displaystyle\int_{2x}^{5x} \cos t\, dt = 5\cos 5x - 2\cos 2x$.

The answer is (A).

PROBLEM 39. Using the Taylor series about $x = 0$ for $\sin x$, approximate $\sin(0.4)$ to four decimal places.

We are given that $\sin x = x - \dfrac{x^3}{3!} + \dfrac{x^5}{5!} + \ldots$

Here, we simply substitute 0.4 for x in the series and we get:

$$\sin 0.4 = 0.4 - \frac{(0.4)^3}{3!} + \frac{(0.4)^5}{5!} + \ldots$$

Find the value on your calculator. Keep adding terms until you get four decimal places of accuracy. You should get: $\sin(0.4) = 0.3894$. If you only got 0.3893, you didn't use enough terms (you need to use the fifth power term).

The answer is (B).

PROBLEM 40. Let R be the region in the first quadrant between the graphs of $y = e^{-x}$, $y = \sin x$, and the y-axis. The volume of the solid that results when R is revolved about the x-axis is

First, we graph the curves:

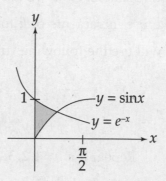

We can find the volume by taking a vertical slice of the region. The formula for the volume of a solid of revolution around the y-axis, using a vertical slice bounded from above by the curve $f(x)$ and from below by $g(x)$, on the interval $[a, b]$, is:

$$\pi \int_a^b \left[f(x)^2 - g(x)^2 \right] dx$$

The upper curve is $y = e^{-x}$ and the lower curve is $y = \sin x$.

Next, we need to find the point(s) of intersection of the two curves with a calculator (Good luck doing it by hand!), which we do by setting them equal to each other and solving for x. You should get approximately: $x = 0.589$ (remember to round to three decimal places on the AP).

Thus, the limits of integration are $x = 0$ and $x = 0.589$.

Now, we evaluate the integral:

$$\pi \int_0^{0.589} \left[\left(e^{-x}\right)^2 - \left(\sin^2 x\right) \right] dx = \pi \int_0^{0.589} \left(e^{-2x} - \sin^2 x\right) dx$$

We can evaluate this integral by hand but, because we will need a calculator to find the answer, we might as well use it to evaluate the integral.

We get: $\pi\int_{0}^{0.589}\left(e^{-2x}-\sin^2 x\right)dx=0.888$ (rounded to three decimal places).

The answer is (E).

PROBLEM 41. Use Euler's Method, with $h=0.2$ to estimate $y(3)$, if $\dfrac{dy}{dx}=2y-4x$ and $y(2)=6$.

We can use Euler's Method to find an approximate answer to the differential equation. The method is quite simple. First, we need a starting point, (x_0, y_0) and an initial slope, y_0'. Next, we use increments of h to come up with approximations. Each new approximation will use the following rules:

$$x_n = x_{n-1} + h$$

$$y_n = y_{n-1} + h \cdot y_{n-1}'$$

Repeat for $n = 1, 2, 3, \ldots$

We are given that the curve goes through the point $(2, 6)$. We will call the coordinates of this point $x_0 = 2$ and $y_0 = 6$. The slope is found by plugging these coordinates into $y' = 2y - 4x$, so we have an initial slope of $y_0' = 4$.
Now we need to find the next set of points.

Step 1: Increase x_0 by h to get x_1: $x_1 = 2.2$

Step 2: Multiply h by y_0' and add to y_0 to get y_1: $y_1 = 6 + 0.2(4) = 6.8$

Step 3: Find y_1' by plugging x_1 and y_1 into the equation for y':

$$y_1' = 2(6.8) - 4(2.2) = 4.8$$

Repeat until we get to the desired point (in this case $x = 3$).

Step 1: Increase x_1 by h to get x_2: $x_2 = 2.4$

Step 2: Multiply h by y_1' and add to y_1 to get y_2: $y_2 = 6.8 + 0.2(4.8) = 7.76$

Step 3: Find y_2' by plugging x_2 and y_2 into the equation for y':

$$y_2' = 2(7.76) - 4(2.4) = 5.92$$

Step 1: $x_3 = x_2 + h$: $x_3 = 2.6$

Step 2: $y_3 = y_2 + h(y_2')$: $y_3 = 7.76 + 0.2(5.92) = 8.944$

Step 3: $y_3' = 2(y_3) - 4(x_3)$: $y_3' = 2(8.944) - 4(2.6) = 7.488$

Step 1: $x_4 = x_3 + h$: $x_4 = 2.8$

Step 2: $y_4 = y_3 + h(y_3')$: $y_4 = 8.944 + 0.2(7.488) = 10.4416$

Step 3: $y_4' = 2(y_4) - 4(x_4)$: $y_4' = 2(10.4416) - 4(2.8) = 9.6832$

Step 1: $x_5 = x_4 + h$: $x_5 = 3$

Step 2: $y_5 = y_4 + h(y_4')$: $y_5 = 10.4416 + 0.2(9.6832) = 12.378$

The answer is (C).

PROBLEM 42. $\int \sec^4 x \, dx =$

First, break up the integrand: $\int \sec^4 x \, dx = \int (\sec^2 x)(\sec^2 x) dx$

Next, use the trig identity $1 + \tan^2 x = \sec^2 x$ to rewrite the integral:

$$\int (\sec^2 x)(\sec^2 x) dx = \int (1 + \tan^2 x)(\sec^2 x) dx = \int (\sec^2 x + \sec^2 x \tan^2 x) dx$$

We can evaluate these integrals separately.

The left one is easy: $\int \sec^2 x \, dx = \tan x + C$

We will use u-substitution for the right one. Let $u = \tan x$ and $du = \sec^2 x \, dx$. Then

substitute into the integral and integrate: $\int \sec^2 x \tan^2 x \, dx = \int u^2 du = \frac{1}{3} u^3 + C$

Now substitute back: $\frac{1}{3} \tan^3 x + C$

Combine the two integrals to get: $\tan x + \frac{1}{3} \tan^3 x + C$

The answer is (B).

PROBLEM 43. Let $f(x) = \int \cot x \, dx$; $0 < x < \pi$. If $f\left(\dfrac{\pi}{6}\right) = 1$, then $f(1) =$

We find $\int \cot x \, dx$ by rewriting the integral as $\int \dfrac{\cos x}{\sin x} \, dx$. Then we use u-substitution. Let $u = \sin x$ and $du = \cos x$. Substituting, we can get:

$$\int \frac{\cos x}{\sin x} \, dx = \int \frac{du}{u} = \ln|u| + C$$

Then substituting back, we get: $\ln(\sin x) + C$ (We can get rid of the absolute value bars because sine is always positive on the interval.). Next, we use $f\left(\dfrac{\pi}{6}\right) = 1$ to solve for C.

We get:

$$1 = \ln\left(\sin\frac{\pi}{6}\right) + C$$

$$1 = \ln\left(\frac{1}{2}\right) + C$$

$$1 - \ln\left(\frac{1}{2}\right) = C = 1.693147$$

Thus: $f(x) = \ln(\sin x) + 1.693147$

At $x = 1$, we get $f(1) = \ln(\sin 1) + 1.693147 = 1.521$ (rounded to three decimal places).

The answer is (E).

PROBLEM 44. $\int \sqrt{4 - x^2} \, dx =$

We solve an integral of the form $\sqrt{a^2 - x^2}$ by performing the trig substitution $x = a \sin \theta$. Here we will use $x = 2\sin\theta$, which means that $dx = 2\cos\theta \, d\theta$. We get: $\int \left[\sqrt{4 - 4\sin^2\theta} (2\cos\theta) \right] d\theta$. Next, factor out the 4: $\int 4\sqrt{1 - \sin^2\theta} \cos\theta \, d\theta$.

Next, simplify the radicand: $\int 4\sqrt{\cos^2\theta} \cos\theta \, d\theta$, which gives us: $4\int \cos^2\theta \, d\theta$. Now we need to use another trig identity. Recall that $\cos 2\theta = 2\cos^2\theta - 1$, which can be rewritten as $\cos^2\theta = \dfrac{1 + \cos 2\theta}{2}$.

Now we can rewrite the integral: $4\int \cos^2\theta\, d\theta = 4\int \dfrac{1+\cos 2\theta}{2}\, d\theta = 2\int (1+\cos 2\theta)\, d\theta$

Integrate: $2\int (1+\cos 2\theta)\, d\theta = 2\theta + \sin 2\theta + C$

Now we have to substitute back.

Because $x = 2\sin\theta$, we know that $\theta = \sin^{-1}\left(\dfrac{x}{2}\right)$ and that $\cos\theta = \dfrac{\sqrt{4-x^2}}{2}$.

This gives us: $2\theta + \sin 2\theta + C = 2\sin^{-1}\left(\dfrac{x}{2}\right) + \dfrac{x}{2}\sqrt{4-x^2} + C$

The answer is (C).

PROBLEM 45. A force of 250 N is required to stretch a spring 5 m from rest. Using Hooke's law, $F = kx$, how much work, in Joules, is required to stretch the spring 7 m from rest?

Hooke's law says that the force needed to compress or stretch a spring from its natural state is $F = kx$, where k is the spring constant. We can find the value of k from the initial information, namely $F = 250$ N for a stretch of 5 m. Thus, we can solve to find the value of k : $k = 250/5 = 50$ N/m.

We find the work done by a variable force along the x-axis from $x = a$ to $x = b$ by evaluating the integral for the Work, $W = \int_a^b F(x)dx.$

Using the information we have: $W = \int_a^b F(x)dx = \dfrac{1}{2}kx^2 \,\big|_0^7 = \dfrac{1}{2}50(7)^2 = 1225\,\text{N}$

The correct answer is (E).

ANSWERS AND EXPLANATIONS TO SECTION II

PROBLEM 1. An object moving along a curve in the xy-plane has its position given by $(x(t), y(t))$ at time t seconds, $0 \le t \le 1$, with $\dfrac{dx}{dt} = 8t\cos t$ units/sec and $\dfrac{dy}{dt} = 8t\sin t$ units/sec.

At time $t = 0$, the object is located at $(5, 11)$.

(a) Find the speed of the object at time $t = 1$.

(b) Find the length of the arc described by the curve's position from time $t = 0$ to time $t = 1$.

(c) Find the location of the object at time $t = \dfrac{\pi}{2}$.

(a) The equation for the speed of an object is $speed = \sqrt{\left(\dfrac{dx}{dt}\right)^2 + \left(\dfrac{dy}{dt}\right)^2}$

Here, we get: $speed = \sqrt{\left(8t\cos t\right)^2 + \left(8t\sin t\right)^2}$

This can be simplified to: $speed = \sqrt{64t^2\cos^2 t + 64t^2\sin^2 t} = 8t\sqrt{\cos^2 t + \sin^2 t} = 8t$

Thus, the speed of the object at time $t = 1$ is 8.

(b) We can find the length of a parametric curve $(x(t), y(t))$, on the interval $[a, b]$, by

evaluating the integral: $\displaystyle\int_a^b \sqrt{\left(\dfrac{dx}{dt}\right)^2 + \left(\dfrac{dy}{dt}\right)^2}\, dt$

We found the integrand in part (a): $\sqrt{\left(\dfrac{dx}{dt}\right)^2 + \left(\dfrac{dy}{dt}\right)^2} = 8t$. Thus, all we have to do is integrate this with respect to t from $t = 0$ to $t = 1$.

We get: $\displaystyle\int_0^1 8t\, dt = \left(4t^2\right)\Big|_0^1 = 4$

(c) First, we will need to find the equations for the coordinates, which we can do by

solving the differential equations. Let's find x: $\dfrac{dx}{dt} = 8t\cos t$.

We can solve this by separation of variables: First, we move dt to the right side of the equals sign: $dx = 8t\cos t\, dt$

Integrate both sides (pulling the constant out of the integrand): $\displaystyle\int dx = 8\int t\cos t\, dt$

The integral on the left is trivial: $\displaystyle\int dx = x$

We will need to use integration by parts to solve the integral on the right.

The rule for integration by parts says that: $\displaystyle\int u\, dv = uv - \int v\, du$

Here, we let: $u = t$ and $dv = \cos t\, dt$. Then: $du = dt$ and $v = \sin t$

Substituting the terms we get: $8\int t\cos t\, dt = 8t\sin t - 8\int \sin t\, dt$

Now, we integrate the second term, which gives us: $8\int t\cos t\, dt = 8t\sin t + 8\cos t + C$

Thus, the x-coordinate is: $x(t) = 8t\sin t + 8\cos t + C$

Now, we plug in the initial condition: $5 = (8)(0)\sin(0) + (8)\cos(0) + C$

This means that $C = -3$, so the equation for the x-coordinate is:

$$x(t) = 8t\sin t + 8\cos t - 3$$

Now let's find y: $\dfrac{dy}{dt} = 8t\sin t$

First, move dt to the right side of the equals sign: $dy = 8t\sin t\, dt$

Integrate both sides (pulling the constant out of the integrand): $\displaystyle\int dy = 8\int t\sin t\, dt$

The integral on the left is trivial: $\displaystyle\int dy = y$

Again, we will need to use integration by parts to solve the integral on the right.

Here, we let: $u = t$ and $dv = \sin t\, dt$. Then: $du = dt$ and $v = -\cos t$.

Substituting the terms we get: $8\int t\sin t\, dt = -8t\cos t + 8\int\cos t\, dt$

Now, we integrate the second term, which gives us: $8\int t\sin t\, dt = -8t\cos t + 8\sin t + C$

Thus, the y-coordinate is: $y(t) = -8t\cos t + 8\sin t + C$

Now, we plug in the initial condition: $11 = -(8)(0)\cos(0) + (8)\sin(0) + C$

This means that $C = 11$, so the equation for the y-coordinate is:

$$y(t) = -8t\cos t + 8\sin t + 11$$

Finally, we plug $t = \dfrac{\pi}{2}$ into the equations for the coordinates:

$$x\left(\frac{\pi}{2}\right) = (8)\left(\frac{\pi}{2}\right)\sin\left(\frac{\pi}{2}\right) + (8)\cos\left(\frac{\pi}{2}\right) - 3 = 4\pi - 3$$

$$y\left(\frac{\pi}{2}\right) = -(8)\left(\frac{\pi}{2}\right)\cos\left(\frac{\pi}{2}\right) + (8)\sin\left(\frac{\pi}{2}\right) + 11 = 19$$

Therefore, the object's location at time $t = \dfrac{\pi}{2}$ is $(4\pi - 3, 19)$.

PROBLEM 2.

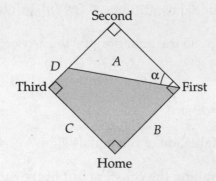

Second

Third

First

Home

A baseball diamond is a square with each side 90 feet in length. A player runs from second base to third base at a rate of 18 ft/sec.

(a) At what rate is the player's distance from first base, A, changing when his distance from third base, D, is 22.5 feet?

(b) At what rate is angle α increasing when D is 22.5 feet?

(c) At what rate is the area of the trapezoidal region, formed by line segments A, B, C, and D, changing when D is 22.5 feet?

(a) A is related to D by the Pythagorean theorem: $90^2 + (90 - D)^2 = A^2$. This can be simplified to: $16200 - 180D + D^2 = A^2$

Take the derivative of both sides with respect to t: $-180\dfrac{dD}{dt} + 2D\dfrac{dD}{dt} = 2A\dfrac{dA}{dt}$

Now, we are given that $\dfrac{dD}{dt} = -18$ (it's negative because D is shrinking) and $D = 22.5$.

Next, we need to solve for A: $90^2 + (90 - 22.5)^2 = A^2$. You should get $A = 112.5$.

Now we can plug in and solve for $\dfrac{dA}{dt}$:

$$-180(-18) + 2(22.5)(-18) = 2(112.5)\dfrac{dA}{dt}$$

$$3240 - 810 = 225\dfrac{dA}{dt}$$

$$\dfrac{dA}{dt} = 10.8 \text{ ft/sec}$$

(b) Notice that $\tan\alpha = \dfrac{90-D}{90} = 1 - \dfrac{D}{90}$. We differentiate both sides with respect to t:

$$\sec^2\alpha\,\frac{d\alpha}{dt} = -\frac{1}{90}\frac{dD}{dt}$$

Next, we need to solve for $\sec^2\alpha$ when $D = 22.5$. From part (a), we know that

$A = 112.5$, so $\sec\alpha = \dfrac{112.5}{90}$, so $\sec^2\alpha = \dfrac{25}{16}$.

Now we plug in to solve for $\dfrac{d\alpha}{dt}$: $\quad \left(\dfrac{25}{16}\right)\dfrac{d\alpha}{dt} = -\dfrac{1}{90}(-18)$

$$\frac{d\alpha}{dt} = \frac{16}{125} = 0.128 \text{ radians/sec}$$

(c) The area of the trapezoid is $a = \dfrac{1}{2}C(B+D)$. Notice that B and C are constants. We

differentiate both sides with respect to t: $\quad \dfrac{da}{dt} = \dfrac{1}{2}C\dfrac{dD}{dt}$

Now we plug in and solve for $\dfrac{da}{dt}$: $\quad \dfrac{da}{dt} = \dfrac{1}{2}(90)(-18) = -810 \text{ ft}^2/\text{sec}$

PROBLEM 3. A body is coasting to a stop and the only force acting on it is a resistance proportional to its speed, according to the equation $\dfrac{ds}{dt} = v_f = v_0\, e^{-\left(\frac{k}{m}\right)t}$; $s(0) = 0$, where v_0 is the body's initial velocity (in m/s), v_f is the its final velocity, m is its mass, k is a constant, and t is time.

(a) If a body with mass $m = 50$ kg and $k = 1.5$ kg/sec, initially has a velocity of 30 m/s, how long, to the nearest second, will it take to slow to 1 m/s?

(b) How far, to the 10 nearest meters, will the body coast during the time it takes to slow from 30 m/s to 1 m/s?

(c) If the body coasts from 30 m/s to a stop, how far will it coast?

(a) We simply plug into the formula and solve for t.

We get: $\quad v_f = v_0\, e^{-\left(\frac{k}{m}\right)t} \quad 1 = 30\, e^{-\left(\frac{1.5}{50}\right)t}$

Divide both sides by 30: $\dfrac{1}{30} = e^{-\left(\frac{1.5}{50}\right)t}$

Take the log of both sides: $\ln\dfrac{1}{30} = --\left(\dfrac{1.5}{50}\right)t$

Multiply both sides by $\dfrac{50}{1.5}$: $-\dfrac{50}{1.5}\ln\dfrac{1}{30} = t \approx 113$ seconds

(b) Now we need to solve the differential equation $\dfrac{ds}{dt} = v_0\, e^{-\left(\frac{k}{m}\right)t}$, which we can do

with separation of variables. First, multiply both sides by dt: $ds = v_0\, e^{-\left(\frac{k}{m}\right)t}\, dt$

Integrate both sides: $\displaystyle\int ds = \int v_0\, e^{-\left(\frac{k}{m}\right)t}\, dt$

Evaluate the integrals: $s = -\dfrac{mv_0}{k}\, e^{-\left(\frac{k}{m}\right)t} + C$

Now plug in the initial conditions to solve for C:

$$0 = -\dfrac{(50)(30)}{1.5}\, e^{-\left(\frac{1.5}{50}\right)(0)} + C$$

$$C = \dfrac{(30)(50)}{1.5} = 1000$$

Therefore, $s = -\dfrac{mv_0}{k}\, e^{-\left(\frac{k}{m}\right)t} + 1000$. Now we plug in the time $t = 113$ that we found in part (a) as well as the initial conditions to solve for s:

$$s = -\dfrac{(50)30}{1.5}\, e^{-\left(\frac{1.5}{50}\right)113} + 1000 \approx 970 \text{ meters}$$

(c) Here, because the braking force is an exponential function, the object will coast to a stop after an infinite amount of time. In other words, we need to find

$$\lim_{t\to\infty} s(t) = \lim_{t\to\infty}\left[1000 - 1000e^{-\left(\frac{k}{m}\right)t}\right] = 1000 \text{ meters}$$

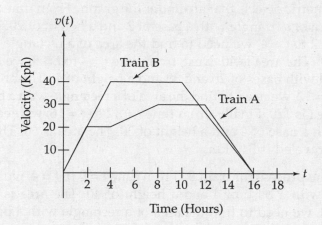

Three trains, A, B, and C, each travel on a straight track for $0 \le t \le 16$ hours. The graphs above, which consist of line segments, show the velocities, in kilometers per hour, of trains A and B. The velocity of C is given by $v(t) = 8t - 0.25t^2$.

(Indicate units of measure for all answers.)

(a) Find the velocities of A and C at time $t = 6$ hours.

(b) Find the accelerations of B and C at time $t = 6$ hours.

(c) Find the positive difference between the total distance that A traveled and the total distance that B traveled in 16 hours.

(d) Find the total distance that C traveled in 16 hours.

(a) We can find the velocity of train A at time $t = 6$ simply by reading the graph. We get $v_A(6) = 25$ km/hr. We find the velocity of train C at time $t = 6$ by plugging $t = 6$ into the formula. We get $v_C(6) = 8(6) - .25(6^2) = 39$ kilometers per hour.

(b) Acceleration is the derivative of velocity with respect to time. For train B, we look at the *slope* of the graph at time $t = 6$. We get: $a_B(6) = 0$ km/hr². For train C, we take the derivative of v. We get: $a(t) = 8 - .5t$. At time $t = 6$, we get $a_C(6) = 5$ km/hr².

(c) In order to find the total distance that train A traveled in 16 hours, we need to find the area under the graph. We can find this area by adding up the areas of the different geometric objects that are under the graph. From time $t = 0$ to $t = 2$, we need to find the area of a triangle with a base of 2 and a height of 20. The area is 20. Next, from time $t = 2$ to $t = 4$, we need to find the area of a rectangle with a base of 2 and a height of 20. The area is 40. Next, from time $t = 4$ to $t = 8$, we need to find the area of a trapezoid with bases of 20 and 30 and a height of 4. The area is 100. Next, from time $t = 8$ to $t = 12$, we need to find the area of a rectangle with a base of 4 and a height of 30. The area is 120. Finally, from time $t = 12$ to $t = 16$, we need to find the area of a triangle with a base of 4 and a height of 30. The area is 60. Thus the total distance that train A traveled is 340 km.

Let's repeat the process for train B. From time $t = 0$ to $t = 4$, we need to find the area of a triangle with a base of 4 and a height of 40. The area is 80. Next, from time $t = 4$ to $t = 10$, we need to find the area of a rectangle with a base of 6 and a height of 40. The area is 240. Finally, from time $t = 10$ to $t = 16$, we need to find the area of a triangle with a base of 6 and a height of 40. The area is 120. Thus the total distance that train B traveled is 440 km.

Therefore, the positive difference between their distances is 100 km.

(d) First, note that the graph of train C's velocity, $v(t) = 8t - 0.25t^2$, is above the x-axis on the entire interval. Therefore, in order to find the total distance traveled, we integrate $v(t)$ over the interval.

We get: $\displaystyle\int_0^{16} \left(8t - .25t^2\right) dt$

Evaluate the integral: $\displaystyle\int_0^{16} \left(8t - .25t^2\right) dt = \left(4t^2 - \frac{t^3}{12}\right)\Bigg|_0^{16} = \frac{2048}{3}$ km

PROBLEM 5. Let y be the function satisfying $f'(x) = x\left(1 - f(x)\right)$; $f(0) = 10$.

(a) Use Euler's Method, starting at $x = 0$, with step size of 0.5 to approximate $f(x)$ at $x = 1$.

(b) Find an exact solution for $f(x)$ when $x = 1$.

(c) Evaluate $\displaystyle\int_0^{\infty} x\left(1 - f(x)\right) dx$.

(a) We use Euler's Method to find an approximate answer to the differential equation. First, we need a starting point (x_0, y_0), and an initial slope, y_0'. (Note that here $f(x) = y$.) Next, we use increments of h to come up with approximations. Each new approximation will use the following rules:

$$x_n = x_{n-1} + h$$

$$y_n = y_{n-1} + h \cdot y_{n-1}'$$

Repeat for $n = 1, 2, 3, \ldots$

We are given that the curve goes through the point (0, 10). We will call the coordinates of this point $x_0 = 0$ and $y_0 = 10$. The slope is found by plugging these coordinates into $y' = x(1-y)$, so we have an initial slope of $y_0' = 0$.

Now we need to find the next set of points.

Step 1: Increase x_0 by h to get x_1: $x_1 = 0.5$

Step 2: Multiply h by y_0' and add to y_0 to get y_1: $y_1 = 10 + 0.5(0) = 10$

Step 3: Find y_1' by plugging x_1 and y_1 into the equation for y':

$$y_1' = (0.5)(1 - 10) = -4.5$$

Repeat until we get to the desired point (in this case $x = 1$).

Step 1: Increase x_1 by h to get x_2: $x_2 = 1$

Step 2: Multiply h by y_1' and add to y_1 to get y_2:

$$y_2 = 10 + 0.5(-4.5) = 7.75$$

(b) Here, we need to solve the differential equation $\frac{dy}{dx} = x(1-y)$. We can use separation of variables. Move the term containing y to the left side and the dx to the right side.

We get: $\dfrac{dy}{(1-y)} = x \, dx$

Integrate both sides:

$$\int \frac{dy}{(1-y)} = \int x \, dx$$

$$-\ln|1-y| = \frac{x^2}{2} + C$$

It's traditional to isolate y. First, exponentiate both sides to base e: $|1-y| = e^{-\frac{x^2}{2}+C}$

Next, use the rules of exponents to rewrite this: $|1-y| = e^C e^{-\frac{x^2}{2}}$.

Because e^C is a constant, we can rewrite this as: $|1-y| = Ce^{-\frac{x^2}{2}}$

Finally, we isolate y: $y = 1 - Ce^{-\frac{x^2}{2}}$

Now, we use the initial condition to solve for C: $10 = 1 - Ce^0$.

Therefore: $C = -9$

Thus, because $f(x) = y$, the exact solution is: $f(x) = 1 + 9e^{-\frac{x^2}{2}}$

Therefore: $f(1) = 1 + 9e^{-\frac{1}{2}}$

(c) Using the Fundamental Theorem of calculus, we know that:

$$\int_a^b f'(x)dx = f(b) - f(a).$$

In part (b), we found that $f(x) = 1 + 9e^{-\frac{x^2}{2}}$, so here we need to evaluate f at infinity and at zero.

We can find f at infinity using limits: $\lim_{x \to \infty} f(x) = \lim_{x \to \infty} 1 + 9e^{-\frac{x^2}{2}} = 1$

We can find f at zero by plugging in: $f(0) = 1 + 9e^0 = 10$

Therefore: $\int_0^\infty x(1 - f(x))dx = 1 - 10 = -9$

PROBLEM 6. Given $f(x) = \tan^{-1}(x)$ and $g(x) = \dfrac{1}{1+x}$, for $|x| \leq 1$

(a) Find the fifth-degree Taylor polynomial and general expression for $g(x)$ about $x = 0$.

(b) Given that $\dfrac{d}{dx} \tan^{-1} x = \dfrac{1}{1+x^2}$, for $|x| \leq 1$, use the result of part (a) to find the fifth-degree Taylor polynomial and general expression for $f(x)$ about $x = 0$.

(c) Use the fifth-degree Taylor polynomial to estimate $f\left(\dfrac{1}{10}\right)$.

(a) The formula for a Taylor polynomial of order n about $x = a$ is:

$$P_n(x) = f(a) + f'(a)(x-a) + \frac{f''(a)}{2!}(x-a)^2 + \ldots + \frac{f^{(k)}(a)}{k!}(x-a)^k + \ldots + \frac{f^{(n)}(a)}{n!}(x-a)^n$$

First, we need to find the derivatives of $g(x) = \dfrac{1}{1+x}$:

$$g'(x) = -(1+x)^{-2}$$

$$g''(x) = 2(1+x)^{-3}$$

$$g^{(3)}(x) = -6(1+x)^{-4}$$

$$g^{(4)}(x) = 24(1+x)^{-5}$$

$$g^{(5)}(x) = -120(1+x)^{-6}$$

Next, evaluate the derivatives about $x = 0$:

$$g(0) = 1; \quad g'(0) = -1; \quad g''(0) = 2; \quad g^{(3)}(0) = -6; \quad g^{(4)}(0) = 24; \quad g^{(5)}(0) = -120$$

Now, if we plug in the formula for the Taylor polynomial, we get:

$$g(x) = \frac{1}{1+x} = 1 - x + x^2 - x^3 + x^4 - x^5$$

The general expression is: $g(x) = \displaystyle\sum_{n=0}^{\infty} (-1)^n x^n$

(b) We can find the Taylor polynomial for $\dfrac{1}{1+x^2}$ by substituting x^2 for x in the

formula above. We get: $\dfrac{1}{1+x^2} = 1 - x^2 + x^4 - x^6 + \ldots$ (actually, we don't need the last

term). Then, because $\dfrac{d}{dx}\tan^{-1}x = \dfrac{1}{1+x^2}$, if we perform term-by-term integration on

the series for $\dfrac{1}{1+x^2}$ we will get the Taylor polynomial for $\tan^{-1}x$.

We get: $\tan^{-1}x = \displaystyle\int\left(1 - x^2 + x^4\right)dx = x - \dfrac{x^3}{3} + \dfrac{x^5}{5} + C$. Because $\tan^{-1}(0) = 0$, $C = 0$, and

thus the general expression for $f(x)$ is: $\tan^{-1}x = \displaystyle\sum_{n=0}^{\infty}(-1)^n\,\dfrac{x^{2n+1}}{2n+1}$.

(c) We can estimate $f\left(\dfrac{1}{10}\right)$ simply by plugging into the expression that we found in

part (b). We get: $f\left(\dfrac{1}{10}\right) = \left(\dfrac{1}{10}\right) - \dfrac{\left(\dfrac{1}{10}\right)^3}{3} + \dfrac{\left(\dfrac{1}{10}\right)^5}{5} = \dfrac{1}{10} - \dfrac{1}{3000} + \dfrac{1}{500000}$, which you

don't need to simplify.

Appendix

DERIVATIVES AND INTEGRALS THAT YOU SHOULD KNOW

1. $\dfrac{d}{dx}[ku] = k\dfrac{du}{dx}$

2. $\dfrac{d}{dx}[k] = 0$

3. $\dfrac{d}{dx}[uv] = u\dfrac{dv}{dx} + v\dfrac{du}{dx}$

4. $\dfrac{d}{dx}\left[\dfrac{u}{v}\right] = \dfrac{v\dfrac{du}{dx} - u\dfrac{dv}{dx}}{v^2}$

5. $\dfrac{d}{dx}[e^u] = e^u\dfrac{du}{dx}$

6. $\dfrac{d}{dx}[\ln u] = \dfrac{1}{u}\dfrac{du}{dx}$

7. $\dfrac{d}{dx}[\sin u] = \cos u\dfrac{du}{dx}$

8. $\dfrac{d}{dx}[\cos u] = -\sin u\dfrac{du}{dx}$

9. $\dfrac{d}{dx}[\tan u] = \sec^2 u\dfrac{du}{dx}$

10. $\dfrac{d}{dx}[\cot u] = -\csc^2 u\dfrac{du}{dx}$

11. $\dfrac{d}{dx}[\sec u] = \sec u\tan u\dfrac{du}{dx}$

12. $\dfrac{d}{dx}[\csc u] = -\csc u\cot u\dfrac{du}{dx}$

13. $\dfrac{d}{dx}[\sin^{-1} u] = \dfrac{1}{\sqrt{1-u^2}}\dfrac{du}{dx}$

14. $\dfrac{d}{dx}[\tan^{-1} u] = \dfrac{1}{1+u^2}\dfrac{du}{dx}$

15. $\dfrac{d}{dx}[\sec^{-1} u] = \dfrac{1}{|u|\sqrt{u^2-1}}\dfrac{du}{dx}$

---

1. $\displaystyle\int k\,du = ku + C$

2. $\displaystyle\int u^n\,du = \dfrac{u^{n+1}}{n+1} + C;\ n \neq -1$

3. $\displaystyle\int \dfrac{du}{u} = \ln|u| + C$

4. $\displaystyle\int e^u\,du = e^u + C$

5. $\displaystyle\int \sin u\,du = -\cos u + C$

6. $\displaystyle\int \cos u\,du = \sin u + C$

7. $\displaystyle\int \tan u\,du = -\ln|\cos u| + C$

8. $\displaystyle\int \cot u\,du = \ln|\sin u| + C$

9. $\displaystyle\int \sec u\,du = \ln|\sec u + \tan u| + C$

10. $\displaystyle\int \csc u\,du = -\ln|\csc u + \cot u| + C$

11. $\displaystyle\int \sec^2 u\,du = \tan u + C$

12. $\displaystyle\int \csc^2 u\,du = -\cot u + C$

13. $\displaystyle\int \sec u\tan u\,du = \sec u + C$

14. $\displaystyle\int \csc u\cot u\,du = -\csc u + C$

15. $\displaystyle\int \dfrac{du}{\sqrt{a^2-u^2}} = \sin^{-1}\dfrac{|u|}{a} + C;\ |u| < a$

16. $\displaystyle\int \dfrac{du}{a^2+u^2}du = \dfrac{1}{a}\tan^{-1}\dfrac{u}{a} + C$

17. $\displaystyle\int \dfrac{du}{u\sqrt{u^2-a^2}} = \dfrac{1}{a}\sec^{-1}\dfrac{u}{a} + C;\ |u| > a$

PREREQUISITE MATHEMATICS

One of the biggest problems that students have with calculus is that their algebra, geometry, and trigonometry are not solid enough. In calculus, you'll be expected to do a lot of graphing. This requires more than just graphing equations with your calculator. You'll be expected to look at an equation and have a "feel" for what the graph looks like. You'll be expected to factor, combine, simplify, and otherwise rearrange algebraic expressions. You'll be expected to know your formulas for the volume and area of various shapes. You'll be expected to remember trigonometric ratios, their values at special angles, and various identities. You'll be expected to be comfortable with logarithms. And so on. Throughout this book, we spend a lot of time reminding you of these things as they come up, but we thought we should summarize them here at the end.

POWERS

When you multiply exponential expressions with like bases, you add the powers.

$$x^a \cdot x^b = x^{a+b}$$

When you divide exponentiated expressions with like bases, you subtract the powers.

$$\frac{x^a}{x^b} = x^{a-b}$$

When you raise an exponentiated expression to a power, you multiply the powers.

$$\left(x^a\right)^b = x^{ab}$$

When you raise an expression to a fractional power, the denominator of the fraction is the root of the expression, and the numerator is the power.

$$x^{\frac{a}{b}} = \sqrt[b]{x^a}$$

When you raise an expression to the power of zero, you get one.

$$x^0 = 1$$

When you raise an expression to the power of one, you get the expression.

$$x^1 = x$$

When you raise an expression to a negative power, you get the reciprocal of the expression to the absolute value of the power.

$$x^{-a} = \frac{1}{x^a}$$

LOGARITHMS

A logarithm is the power to which you raise a base, in order to get a value. In other words, $\log_b x = a$ means that $b^a = x$. There are several rules of logarithms that you should be familiar with.

When you take the logarithm of the product of two expressions, you add the logarithms.

$$\log(ab) = \log a + \log b$$

When you take the logarithm of the quotient of two expressions, you subtract the logarithms.

$$\log\left(\frac{a}{b}\right) = \log a - \log b$$

When you take the logarithm of an expression to a power, you multiply the logarithm by the power.

$$\log\left(a^b\right) = b \log a$$

The logarithm of 1 is zero.

$$\log 1 = 0$$

The logarithm of its base is 1.

$$\log_b b = 1$$

You cannot take the logarithm of zero or of a negative number.

In calculus, and virtually all mathematics beyond calculus, you will work with natural logarithms. These are logs with base e and are denoted by ln. Thus, you should know the following:

$$\ln 1 = 0$$
$$\ln e = 1$$
$$\ln e^x = x$$
$$e^{\ln x} = x$$

The change of base rule is: $\log_b x = \dfrac{\ln x}{\ln b}$

GEOMETRY

The area of a triangle is $\frac{1}{2}(base)(height)$.

The area of a rectangle is $(base)(height)$.

The area of a trapezoid is $\frac{1}{2}(base_1 + base_2)(height)$.

The area of a circle is πr^2.

The circumference of a circle is $2\pi r$.

The Pythagorean Theorem states that the sum of the squares of the legs of a right triangle equals the square of the hypotenuse. This is more commonly stated as $a^2 + b^2 = c^2$ where c equals the length of the hypotenuse.

The volume of a right circular cylinder is $\pi r^2 h$.

The surface area of a right circular cylinder is $2\pi rh$.

The volume of a right circular cone is $\frac{1}{3}\pi r^2 h$.

The volume of a sphere is $\frac{4}{3}\pi r^3$.

The surface area of a sphere is $4\pi r^2$.

TRIGONOMETRY

Given a right triangle with sides x, y, and r and angle θ below:

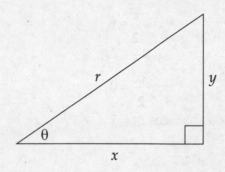

$$\sin\theta = \frac{y}{r} \qquad \csc\theta = \frac{r}{y} \qquad \text{Thus, } \sin\theta = \frac{1}{\csc\theta}$$

$$\cos\theta = \frac{x}{r} \qquad \sec\theta = \frac{r}{x} \qquad \text{Thus, } \cos\theta = \frac{1}{\sec\theta}$$

$$\tan\theta = \frac{y}{x} \qquad \cot\theta = \frac{x}{y} \qquad \text{Thus, } \tan\theta = \frac{1}{\cot\theta}$$

$$\sin 2\theta = 2\sin\theta\,\cos\theta \qquad \cos 2\theta = 1 - 2\sin^2\theta \qquad \sin^2\theta + \cos^2\theta = 1$$

$$\cos 2\theta = \cos^2\theta - \sin^2\theta \qquad \cos 2\theta = 2\cos^2\theta - 1 \qquad 1 + \tan^2\theta = \sec^2\theta$$

$$\cos^2\theta = \frac{1+\cos 2\theta}{2} \qquad \sin^2\theta = \frac{1-\cos 2\theta}{2} \qquad 1 + \cot^2\theta = \csc^2\theta$$

$$\sin(A + B) = \sin A \cos B + \cos A \sin B$$
$$\sin(A - B) = \sin A \cos B - \cos A \sin B$$
$$\cos(A + B) = \cos A \cos B - \sin A \sin B$$
$$\cos(A - B) = \cos A \cos B + \sin A \sin B$$

You must be able to work in radians and know that $2\pi = 360°$.

You should know the following:

$$\sin 0 = 0 \qquad\qquad \cos 0 = 1 \qquad\qquad \tan 0 = 0$$

$$\sin\frac{\pi}{6} = \frac{1}{2} \qquad\qquad \cos\frac{\pi}{6} = \frac{\sqrt{3}}{2} \qquad\qquad \tan\frac{\pi}{6} = \frac{1}{\sqrt{3}}$$

$$\sin\frac{\pi}{4} = \frac{1}{\sqrt{2}} \qquad\qquad \cos\frac{\pi}{4} = \frac{1}{\sqrt{2}} \qquad\qquad \tan\frac{\pi}{4} = 1$$

$$\sin\frac{\pi}{3} = \frac{\sqrt{3}}{2} \qquad\qquad \cos\frac{\pi}{3} = \frac{1}{2} \qquad\qquad \tan\frac{\pi}{3} = \sqrt{3}$$

$$\sin\frac{\pi}{2} = 1 \qquad\qquad \cos\frac{\pi}{2} = 0 \qquad\qquad \tan\frac{\pi}{2} = \infty$$

$$\sin\pi = 0 \qquad\qquad \cos\pi = -1 \qquad\qquad \tan\pi = 0$$

$$\sin\frac{3\pi}{2} = -1 \qquad\qquad \cos\frac{3\pi}{2} = 0 \qquad\qquad \tan\frac{3\pi}{2} = \infty$$

$$\sin 2\pi = 0 \qquad\qquad \cos 2\pi = 1 \qquad\qquad \tan 2\pi = 0$$

Completely darken bubbles with a No. 2 pencil. If you make a mistake, be sure to erase mark completely. Erase all stray marks.

1.

YOUR NAME: _____
(Print)

                Last   First   M.I.

SIGNATURE: _____   DATE: __/__/__

HOME ADDRESS: _____
(Print)
                Number and Street

_____
     City   State   Zip Code

PHONE NO.: _____
(Print)

IMPORTANT: Please fill in these boxes exactly as shown on the back cover of your test book.

2. TEST FORM

3. TEST CODE

4. REGISTRATION NUMBER

0	A	0	0	0	0	0	0	0	0	0	0
1	B	1	1	1	1	1	1	1	1	1	1
2	C	2	2	2	2	2	2	2	2	2	2
3	D	3	3	3	3	3	3	3	3	3	3
4	E	4	4	4	4	4	4	4	4	4	4
5	F	5	5	5	5	5	5	5	5	5	5
6	G	6	6	6	6	6	6	6	6	6	6
7		7	7	7	7	7	7	7	7	7	7
8		8	8	8	8	8	8	8	8	8	8
9		9	9	9	9	9	9	9	9	9	9

6. DATE OF BIRTH

Month		Day		Year	
⊂ ⊃ JAN					
⊂ ⊃ FEB					
⊂ ⊃ MAR	0	0	0	0	
⊂ ⊃ APR	1	1	1	1	
⊂ ⊃ MAY	2	2	2	2	
⊂ ⊃ JUN	3	3	3	3	
⊂ ⊃ JUL		4	4	4	
⊂ ⊃ AUG		5	5	5	
⊂ ⊃ SEP		6	6	6	
⊂ ⊃ OCT		7	7	7	
⊂ ⊃ NOV		8	8	8	
⊂ ⊃ DEC		9	9	9	

7. SEX
⊂ ⊃ MALE
⊂ ⊃ FEMALE

The Princeton Review

5. YOUR NAME

First 4 letters of last name				FIRST INIT	MID INIT
A	A	A	A	A	A
B	B	B	B	B	B
C	C	C	C	C	C
D	D	D	D	D	D
E	E	E	E	E	E
F	F	F	F	F	F
G	G	G	G	G	G
H	H	H	H	H	H
I	I	I	I	I	I
J	J	J	J	J	J
K	K	K	K	K	K
L	L	L	L	L	L
M	M	M	M	M	M
N	N	N	N	N	N
O	O	O	O	O	O
P	P	P	P	P	P
Q	Q	Q	Q	Q	Q
R	R	R	R	R	R
S	S	S	S	S	S
T	T	T	T	T	T
U	U	U	U	U	U
V	V	V	V	V	V
W	W	W	W	W	W
X	X	X	X	X	X
Y	Y	Y	Y	Y	Y
Z	Z	Z	Z	Z	Z

1 ⊂A⊃ ⊂B⊃ ⊂C⊃ ⊂D⊃ ⊂E⊃   24 ⊂A⊃ ⊂B⊃ ⊂C⊃ ⊂D⊃ ⊂E⊃
2 ⊂A⊃ ⊂B⊃ ⊂C⊃ ⊂D⊃ ⊂E⊃   25 ⊂A⊃ ⊂B⊃ ⊂C⊃ ⊂D⊃ ⊂E⊃
3 ⊂A⊃ ⊂B⊃ ⊂C⊃ ⊂D⊃ ⊂E⊃   26 ⊂A⊃ ⊂B⊃ ⊂C⊃ ⊂D⊃ ⊂E⊃
4 ⊂A⊃ ⊂B⊃ ⊂C⊃ ⊂D⊃ ⊂E⊃   27 ⊂A⊃ ⊂B⊃ ⊂C⊃ ⊂D⊃ ⊂E⊃
5 ⊂A⊃ ⊂B⊃ ⊂C⊃ ⊂D⊃ ⊂E⊃   28 ⊂A⊃ ⊂B⊃ ⊂C⊃ ⊂D⊃ ⊂E⊃
6 ⊂A⊃ ⊂B⊃ ⊂C⊃ ⊂D⊃ ⊂E⊃   29 ⊂A⊃ ⊂B⊃ ⊂C⊃ ⊂D⊃ ⊂E⊃
7 ⊂A⊃ ⊂B⊃ ⊂C⊃ ⊂D⊃ ⊂E⊃   30 ⊂A⊃ ⊂B⊃ ⊂C⊃ ⊂D⊃ ⊂E⊃
8 ⊂A⊃ ⊂B⊃ ⊂C⊃ ⊂D⊃ ⊂E⊃   31 ⊂A⊃ ⊂B⊃ ⊂C⊃ ⊂D⊃ ⊂E⊃
9 ⊂A⊃ ⊂B⊃ ⊂C⊃ ⊂D⊃ ⊂E⊃   32 ⊂A⊃ ⊂B⊃ ⊂C⊃ ⊂D⊃ ⊂E⊃
10 ⊂A⊃ ⊂B⊃ ⊂C⊃ ⊂D⊃ ⊂E⊃   33 ⊂A⊃ ⊂B⊃ ⊂C⊃ ⊂D⊃ ⊂E⊃
11 ⊂A⊃ ⊂B⊃ ⊂C⊃ ⊂D⊃ ⊂E⊃   34 ⊂A⊃ ⊂B⊃ ⊂C⊃ ⊂D⊃ ⊂E⊃
12 ⊂A⊃ ⊂B⊃ ⊂C⊃ ⊂D⊃ ⊂E⊃   35 ⊂A⊃ ⊂B⊃ ⊂C⊃ ⊂D⊃ ⊂E⊃
13 ⊂A⊃ ⊂B⊃ ⊂C⊃ ⊂D⊃ ⊂E⊃   36 ⊂A⊃ ⊂B⊃ ⊂C⊃ ⊂D⊃ ⊂E⊃
14 ⊂A⊃ ⊂B⊃ ⊂C⊃ ⊂D⊃ ⊂E⊃   37 ⊂A⊃ ⊂B⊃ ⊂C⊃ ⊂D⊃ ⊂E⊃
15 ⊂A⊃ ⊂B⊃ ⊂C⊃ ⊂D⊃ ⊂E⊃   38 ⊂A⊃ ⊂B⊃ ⊂C⊃ ⊂D⊃ ⊂E⊃
16 ⊂A⊃ ⊂B⊃ ⊂C⊃ ⊂D⊃ ⊂E⊃   39 ⊂A⊃ ⊂B⊃ ⊂C⊃ ⊂D⊃ ⊂E⊃
17 ⊂A⊃ ⊂B⊃ ⊂C⊃ ⊂D⊃ ⊂E⊃   40 ⊂A⊃ ⊂B⊃ ⊂C⊃ ⊂D⊃ ⊂E⊃
18 ⊂A⊃ ⊂B⊃ ⊂C⊃ ⊂D⊃ ⊂E⊃   41 ⊂A⊃ ⊂B⊃ ⊂C⊃ ⊂D⊃ ⊂E⊃
19 ⊂A⊃ ⊂B⊃ ⊂C⊃ ⊂D⊃ ⊂E⊃   42 ⊂A⊃ ⊂B⊃ ⊂C⊃ ⊂D⊃ ⊂E⊃
20 ⊂A⊃ ⊂B⊃ ⊂C⊃ ⊂D⊃ ⊂E⊃   43 ⊂A⊃ ⊂B⊃ ⊂C⊃ ⊂D⊃ ⊂E⊃
21 ⊂A⊃ ⊂B⊃ ⊂C⊃ ⊂D⊃ ⊂E⊃   44 ⊂A⊃ ⊂B⊃ ⊂C⊃ ⊂D⊃ ⊂E⊃
22 ⊂A⊃ ⊂B⊃ ⊂C⊃ ⊂D⊃ ⊂E⊃   45 ⊂A⊃ ⊂B⊃ ⊂C⊃ ⊂D⊃ ⊂E⊃
23 ⊂A⊃ ⊂B⊃ ⊂C⊃ ⊂D⊃ ⊂E⊃

The Princeton Review

1.

YOUR NAME: _____
(Print)   Last   First   M.I.

SIGNATURE: _____   DATE: ___ / ___ / ___

HOME ADDRESS: _____
(Print)   Number and Street

_____
City   State   Zip Code

PHONE NO.: _____
(Print)

IMPORTANT: Please fill in these boxes exactly as shown on the back cover of your test book.

2. TEST FORM

3. TEST CODE

c0⊃	cA⊃	c0⊃	c0⊃	c0⊃	c0⊃	c0⊃	c0⊃	c0⊃	c0⊃	c0⊃
c1⊃	cB⊃	c1⊃	c1⊃	c1⊃	c1⊃	c1⊃	c1⊃	c1⊃	c1⊃	c1⊃
c2⊃	cC⊃	c2⊃	c2⊃	c2⊃	c2⊃	c2⊃	c2⊃	c2⊃	c2⊃	c2⊃
c3⊃	cD⊃	c3⊃	c3⊃	c3⊃	c3⊃	c3⊃	c3⊃	c3⊃	c3⊃	c3⊃
c4⊃	cE⊃	c4⊃	c4⊃	c4⊃	c4⊃	c4⊃	c4⊃	c4⊃	c4⊃	c4⊃
c5⊃	cF⊃	c5⊃	c5⊃	c5⊃	c5⊃	c5⊃	c5⊃	c5⊃	c5⊃	c5⊃
c6⊃	cG⊃	c6⊃	c6⊃	c6⊃	c6⊃	c6⊃	c6⊃	c6⊃	c6⊃	c6⊃
c7⊃		c7⊃	c7⊃	c7⊃	c7⊃	c7⊃	c7⊃	c7⊃	c7⊃	c7⊃
c8⊃		c8⊃	c8⊃	c8⊃	c8⊃	c8⊃	c8⊃	c8⊃	c8⊃	c8⊃
c9⊃		c9⊃	c9⊃	c9⊃	c9⊃	c9⊃	c9⊃	c9⊃	c9⊃	c9⊃

4. REGISTRATION NUMBER

6. DATE OF BIRTH

Month		Day		Year	
c ⊃ JAN					
c ⊃ FEB					
c ⊃ MAR	c0⊃	c0⊃	c0⊃	c0⊃	
c ⊃ APR	c1⊃	c1⊃	c1⊃	c1⊃	
c ⊃ MAY	c2⊃	c2⊃	c2⊃	c2⊃	
c ⊃ JUN	c3⊃	c3⊃	c3⊃	c3⊃	
c ⊃ JUL		c4⊃	c4⊃	c4⊃	
c ⊃ AUG		c5⊃	c5⊃	c5⊃	
c ⊃ SEP		c6⊃	c6⊃	c6⊃	
c ⊃ OCT		c7⊃	c7⊃	c7⊃	
c ⊃ NOV		c8⊃	c8⊃	c8⊃	
c ⊃ DEC		c9⊃	c9⊃	c9⊃	

7. SEX

c ⊃ MALE
c ⊃ FEMALE

The Princeton Review

5. YOUR NAME

First 4 letters of last name				FIRST INIT	MID INIT
cA⊃	cA⊃	cA⊃	cA⊃	cA⊃	cA⊃
cB⊃	cB⊃	cB⊃	cB⊃	cB⊃	cB⊃
cC⊃	cC⊃	cC⊃	cC⊃	cC⊃	cC⊃
cD⊃	cD⊃	cD⊃	cD⊃	cD⊃	cD⊃
cE⊃	cE⊃	cE⊃	cE⊃	cE⊃	cE⊃
cF⊃	cF⊃	cF⊃	cF⊃	cF⊃	cF⊃
cG⊃	cG⊃	cG⊃	cG⊃	cG⊃	cG⊃
cH⊃	cH⊃	cH⊃	cH⊃	cH⊃	cH⊃
cI⊃	cI⊃	cI⊃	cI⊃	cI⊃	cI⊃
cJ⊃	cJ⊃	cJ⊃	cJ⊃	cJ⊃	cJ⊃
cK⊃	cK⊃	cK⊃	cK⊃	cK⊃	cK⊃
cL⊃	cL⊃	cL⊃	cL⊃	cL⊃	cL⊃
cM⊃	cM⊃	cM⊃	cM⊃	cM⊃	cM⊃
cN⊃	cN⊃	cN⊃	cN⊃	cN⊃	cN⊃
cO⊃	cO⊃	cO⊃	cO⊃	cO⊃	cO⊃
cP⊃	cP⊃	cP⊃	cP⊃	cP⊃	cP⊃
cQ⊃	cQ⊃	cQ⊃	cQ⊃	cQ⊃	cQ⊃
cR⊃	cR⊃	cR⊃	cR⊃	cR⊃	cR⊃
cS⊃	cS⊃	cS⊃	cS⊃	cS⊃	cS⊃
cT⊃	cT⊃	cT⊃	cT⊃	cT⊃	cT⊃
cU⊃	cU⊃	cU⊃	cU⊃	cU⊃	cU⊃
cV⊃	cV⊃	cV⊃	cV⊃	cV⊃	cV⊃
cW⊃	cW⊃	cW⊃	cW⊃	cW⊃	cW⊃
cX⊃	cX⊃	cX⊃	cX⊃	cX⊃	cX⊃
cY⊃	cY⊃	cY⊃	cY⊃	cY⊃	cY⊃
cZ⊃	cZ⊃	cZ⊃	cZ⊃	cZ⊃	cZ⊃

1 cA⊃ cB⊃ cC⊃ cD⊃ cE⊃
2 cA⊃ cB⊃ cC⊃ cD⊃ cE⊃
3 cA⊃ cB⊃ cC⊃ cD⊃ cE⊃
4 cA⊃ cB⊃ cC⊃ cD⊃ cE⊃
5 cA⊃ cB⊃ cC⊃ cD⊃ cE⊃
6 cA⊃ cB⊃ cC⊃ cD⊃ cE⊃
7 cA⊃ cB⊃ cC⊃ cD⊃ cE⊃
8 cA⊃ cB⊃ cC⊃ cD⊃ cE⊃
9 cA⊃ cB⊃ cC⊃ cD⊃ cE⊃
10 cA⊃ cB⊃ cC⊃ cD⊃ cE⊃
11 cA⊃ cB⊃ cC⊃ cD⊃ cE⊃
12 cA⊃ cB⊃ cC⊃ cD⊃ cE⊃
13 cA⊃ cB⊃ cC⊃ cD⊃ cE⊃
14 cA⊃ cB⊃ cC⊃ cD⊃ cE⊃
15 cA⊃ cB⊃ cC⊃ cD⊃ cE⊃
16 cA⊃ cB⊃ cC⊃ cD⊃ cE⊃
17 cA⊃ cB⊃ cC⊃ cD⊃ cE⊃
18 cA⊃ cB⊃ cC⊃ cD⊃ cE⊃
19 cA⊃ cB⊃ cC⊃ cD⊃ cE⊃
20 cA⊃ cB⊃ cC⊃ cD⊃ cE⊃
21 cA⊃ cB⊃ cC⊃ cD⊃ cE⊃
22 cA⊃ cB⊃ cC⊃ cD⊃ cE⊃
23 cA⊃ cB⊃ cC⊃ cD⊃ cE⊃

24 cA⊃ cB⊃ cC⊃ cD⊃ cE⊃
25 cA⊃ cB⊃ cC⊃ cD⊃ cE⊃
26 cA⊃ cB⊃ cC⊃ cD⊃ cE⊃
27 cA⊃ cB⊃ cC⊃ cD⊃ cE⊃
28 cA⊃ cB⊃ cC⊃ cD⊃ cE⊃
29 cA⊃ cB⊃ cC⊃ cD⊃ cE⊃
30 cA⊃ cB⊃ cC⊃ cD⊃ cE⊃
31 cA⊃ cB⊃ cC⊃ cD⊃ cE⊃
32 cA⊃ cB⊃ cC⊃ cD⊃ cE⊃
33 cA⊃ cB⊃ cC⊃ cD⊃ cE⊃
34 cA⊃ cB⊃ cC⊃ cD⊃ cE⊃
35 cA⊃ cB⊃ cC⊃ cD⊃ cE⊃
36 cA⊃ cB⊃ cC⊃ cD⊃ cE⊃
37 cA⊃ cB⊃ cC⊃ cD⊃ cE⊃
38 cA⊃ cB⊃ cC⊃ cD⊃ cE⊃
39 cA⊃ cB⊃ cC⊃ cD⊃ cE⊃
40 cA⊃ cB⊃ cC⊃ cD⊃ cE⊃
41 cA⊃ cB⊃ cC⊃ cD⊃ cE⊃
42 cA⊃ cB⊃ cC⊃ cD⊃ cE⊃
43 cA⊃ cB⊃ cC⊃ cD⊃ cE⊃
44 cA⊃ cB⊃ cC⊃ cD⊃ cE⊃
45 cA⊃ cB⊃ cC⊃ cD⊃ cE⊃

The Princeton Review

Completely darken bubbles with a No. 2 pencil. If you make a mistake, be sure to erase mark completely. Erase all stray marks.

1.

YOUR NAME: _____
(Print)　　　　　Last　　　　　　　First　　　　　　　M.I.

SIGNATURE: _____　DATE: ___/___/___

HOME ADDRESS: _____
(Print)　　　　　　　Number and Street

_____
City　　　　　　State　　　　　　Zip Code

PHONE NO.: _____
(Print)

IMPORTANT: Please fill in these boxes exactly as shown on the back cover of your test book.

2. TEST FORM

_____

6. DATE OF BIRTH

Month		Day	Year
⊂　⊃ JAN			
⊂　⊃ FEB			
⊂　⊃ MAR	⊂0⊃	⊂0⊃　⊂0⊃	⊂0⊃
⊂　⊃ APR	⊂1⊃	⊂1⊃　⊂1⊃	⊂1⊃
⊂　⊃ MAY	⊂2⊃	⊂2⊃　⊂2⊃	⊂2⊃
⊂　⊃ JUN	⊂3⊃	⊂3⊃　⊂3⊃	⊂3⊃
⊂　⊃ JUL		⊂4⊃　⊂4⊃	⊂4⊃
⊂　⊃ AUG		⊂5⊃　⊂5⊃	⊂5⊃
⊂　⊃ SEP		⊂6⊃　⊂6⊃	⊂6⊃
⊂　⊃ OCT		⊂7⊃　⊂7⊃	⊂7⊃
⊂　⊃ NOV		⊂8⊃　⊂8⊃	⊂8⊃
⊂　⊃ DEC		⊂9⊃　⊂9⊃	⊂9⊃

3. TEST CODE　　4. REGISTRATION NUMBER

⊂0⊃	⊂A⊃	⊂0⊃	⊂0⊃	⊂0⊃	⊂0⊃	⊂0⊃	⊂0⊃	⊂0⊃	⊂0⊃
⊂1⊃	⊂B⊃	⊂1⊃	⊂1⊃	⊂1⊃	⊂1⊃	⊂1⊃	⊂1⊃	⊂1⊃	⊂1⊃
⊂2⊃	⊂C⊃	⊂2⊃	⊂2⊃	⊂2⊃	⊂2⊃	⊂2⊃	⊂2⊃	⊂2⊃	⊂2⊃
⊂3⊃	⊂D⊃	⊂3⊃	⊂3⊃	⊂3⊃	⊂3⊃	⊂3⊃	⊂3⊃	⊂3⊃	⊂3⊃
⊂4⊃	⊂E⊃	⊂4⊃	⊂4⊃	⊂4⊃	⊂4⊃	⊂4⊃	⊂4⊃	⊂4⊃	⊂4⊃
⊂5⊃	⊂F⊃	⊂5⊃	⊂5⊃	⊂5⊃	⊂5⊃	⊂5⊃	⊂5⊃	⊂5⊃	⊂5⊃
⊂6⊃	⊂G⊃	⊂6⊃	⊂6⊃	⊂6⊃	⊂6⊃	⊂6⊃	⊂6⊃	⊂6⊃	⊂6⊃
⊂7⊃		⊂7⊃	⊂7⊃	⊂7⊃	⊂7⊃	⊂7⊃	⊂7⊃	⊂7⊃	⊂7⊃
⊂8⊃		⊂8⊃	⊂8⊃	⊂8⊃	⊂8⊃	⊂8⊃	⊂8⊃	⊂8⊃	⊂8⊃
⊂9⊃		⊂9⊃	⊂9⊃	⊂9⊃	⊂9⊃	⊂9⊃	⊂9⊃	⊂9⊃	⊂9⊃

7. SEX

⊂　⊃ MALE
⊂　⊃ FEMALE

The Princeton Review

5. YOUR NAME

First 4 letters of last name				FIRST INIT	MID INIT
⊂A⊃	⊂A⊃	⊂A⊃	⊂A⊃	⊂A⊃	⊂A⊃
⊂B⊃	⊂B⊃	⊂B⊃	⊂B⊃	⊂B⊃	⊂B⊃
⊂C⊃	⊂C⊃	⊂C⊃	⊂C⊃	⊂C⊃	⊂C⊃
⊂D⊃	⊂D⊃	⊂D⊃	⊂D⊃	⊂D⊃	⊂D⊃
⊂E⊃	⊂E⊃	⊂E⊃	⊂E⊃	⊂E⊃	⊂E⊃
⊂F⊃	⊂F⊃	⊂F⊃	⊂F⊃	⊂F⊃	⊂F⊃
⊂G⊃	⊂G⊃	⊂G⊃	⊂G⊃	⊂G⊃	⊂G⊃
⊂H⊃	⊂H⊃	⊂H⊃	⊂H⊃	⊂H⊃	⊂H⊃
⊂I⊃	⊂I⊃	⊂I⊃	⊂I⊃	⊂I⊃	⊂I⊃
⊂J⊃	⊂J⊃	⊂J⊃	⊂J⊃	⊂J⊃	⊂J⊃
⊂K⊃	⊂K⊃	⊂K⊃	⊂K⊃	⊂K⊃	⊂K⊃
⊂L⊃	⊂L⊃	⊂L⊃	⊂L⊃	⊂L⊃	⊂L⊃
⊂M⊃	⊂M⊃	⊂M⊃	⊂M⊃	⊂M⊃	⊂M⊃
⊂N⊃	⊂N⊃	⊂N⊃	⊂N⊃	⊂N⊃	⊂N⊃
⊂O⊃	⊂O⊃	⊂O⊃	⊂O⊃	⊂O⊃	⊂O⊃
⊂P⊃	⊂P⊃	⊂P⊃	⊂P⊃	⊂P⊃	⊂P⊃
⊂Q⊃	⊂Q⊃	⊂Q⊃	⊂Q⊃	⊂Q⊃	⊂Q⊃
⊂R⊃	⊂R⊃	⊂R⊃	⊂R⊃	⊂R⊃	⊂R⊃
⊂S⊃	⊂S⊃	⊂S⊃	⊂S⊃	⊂S⊃	⊂S⊃
⊂T⊃	⊂T⊃	⊂T⊃	⊂T⊃	⊂T⊃	⊂T⊃
⊂U⊃	⊂U⊃	⊂U⊃	⊂U⊃	⊂U⊃	⊂U⊃
⊂V⊃	⊂V⊃	⊂V⊃	⊂V⊃	⊂V⊃	⊂V⊃
⊂W⊃	⊂W⊃	⊂W⊃	⊂W⊃	⊂W⊃	⊂W⊃
⊂X⊃	⊂X⊃	⊂X⊃	⊂X⊃	⊂X⊃	⊂X⊃
⊂Y⊃	⊂Y⊃	⊂Y⊃	⊂Y⊃	⊂Y⊃	⊂Y⊃
⊂Z⊃	⊂Z⊃	⊂Z⊃	⊂Z⊃	⊂Z⊃	⊂Z⊃

1 ⊂A⊃ ⊂B⊃ ⊂C⊃ ⊂D⊃ ⊂E⊃
2 ⊂A⊃ ⊂B⊃ ⊂C⊃ ⊂D⊃ ⊂E⊃
3 ⊂A⊃ ⊂B⊃ ⊂C⊃ ⊂D⊃ ⊂E⊃
4 ⊂A⊃ ⊂B⊃ ⊂C⊃ ⊂D⊃ ⊂E⊃
5 ⊂A⊃ ⊂B⊃ ⊂C⊃ ⊂D⊃ ⊂E⊃
6 ⊂A⊃ ⊂B⊃ ⊂C⊃ ⊂D⊃ ⊂E⊃
7 ⊂A⊃ ⊂B⊃ ⊂C⊃ ⊂D⊃ ⊂E⊃
8 ⊂A⊃ ⊂B⊃ ⊂C⊃ ⊂D⊃ ⊂E⊃
9 ⊂A⊃ ⊂B⊃ ⊂C⊃ ⊂D⊃ ⊂E⊃
10 ⊂A⊃ ⊂B⊃ ⊂C⊃ ⊂D⊃ ⊂E⊃
11 ⊂A⊃ ⊂B⊃ ⊂C⊃ ⊂D⊃ ⊂E⊃
12 ⊂A⊃ ⊂B⊃ ⊂C⊃ ⊂D⊃ ⊂E⊃
13 ⊂A⊃ ⊂B⊃ ⊂C⊃ ⊂D⊃ ⊂E⊃
14 ⊂A⊃ ⊂B⊃ ⊂C⊃ ⊂D⊃ ⊂E⊃
15 ⊂A⊃ ⊂B⊃ ⊂C⊃ ⊂D⊃ ⊂E⊃
16 ⊂A⊃ ⊂B⊃ ⊂C⊃ ⊂D⊃ ⊂E⊃
17 ⊂A⊃ ⊂B⊃ ⊂C⊃ ⊂D⊃ ⊂E⊃
18 ⊂A⊃ ⊂B⊃ ⊂C⊃ ⊂D⊃ ⊂E⊃
19 ⊂A⊃ ⊂B⊃ ⊂C⊃ ⊂D⊃ ⊂E⊃
20 ⊂A⊃ ⊂B⊃ ⊂C⊃ ⊂D⊃ ⊂E⊃
21 ⊂A⊃ ⊂B⊃ ⊂C⊃ ⊂D⊃ ⊂E⊃
22 ⊂A⊃ ⊂B⊃ ⊂C⊃ ⊂D⊃ ⊂E⊃
23 ⊂A⊃ ⊂B⊃ ⊂C⊃ ⊂D⊃ ⊂E⊃

24 ⊂A⊃ ⊂B⊃ ⊂C⊃ ⊂D⊃ ⊂E⊃
25 ⊂A⊃ ⊂B⊃ ⊂C⊃ ⊂D⊃ ⊂E⊃
26 ⊂A⊃ ⊂B⊃ ⊂C⊃ ⊂D⊃ ⊂E⊃
27 ⊂A⊃ ⊂B⊃ ⊂C⊃ ⊂D⊃ ⊂E⊃
28 ⊂A⊃ ⊂B⊃ ⊂C⊃ ⊂D⊃ ⊂E⊃
29 ⊂A⊃ ⊂B⊃ ⊂C⊃ ⊂D⊃ ⊂E⊃
30 ⊂A⊃ ⊂B⊃ ⊂C⊃ ⊂D⊃ ⊂E⊃
31 ⊂A⊃ ⊂B⊃ ⊂C⊃ ⊂D⊃ ⊂E⊃
32 ⊂A⊃ ⊂B⊃ ⊂C⊃ ⊂D⊃ ⊂E⊃
33 ⊂A⊃ ⊂B⊃ ⊂C⊃ ⊂D⊃ ⊂E⊃
34 ⊂A⊃ ⊂B⊃ ⊂C⊃ ⊂D⊃ ⊂E⊃
35 ⊂A⊃ ⊂B⊃ ⊂C⊃ ⊂D⊃ ⊂E⊃
36 ⊂A⊃ ⊂B⊃ ⊂C⊃ ⊂D⊃ ⊂E⊃
37 ⊂A⊃ ⊂B⊃ ⊂C⊃ ⊂D⊃ ⊂E⊃
38 ⊂A⊃ ⊂B⊃ ⊂C⊃ ⊂D⊃ ⊂E⊃
39 ⊂A⊃ ⊂B⊃ ⊂C⊃ ⊂D⊃ ⊂E⊃
40 ⊂A⊃ ⊂B⊃ ⊂C⊃ ⊂D⊃ ⊂E⊃
41 ⊂A⊃ ⊂B⊃ ⊂C⊃ ⊂D⊃ ⊂E⊃
42 ⊂A⊃ ⊂B⊃ ⊂C⊃ ⊂D⊃ ⊂E⊃
43 ⊂A⊃ ⊂B⊃ ⊂C⊃ ⊂D⊃ ⊂E⊃
44 ⊂A⊃ ⊂B⊃ ⊂C⊃ ⊂D⊃ ⊂E⊃
45 ⊂A⊃ ⊂B⊃ ⊂C⊃ ⊂D⊃ ⊂E⊃

The Princeton Review

Completely darken bubbles with a No. 2 pencil. If you make a mistake, be sure to erase mark completely. Erase all stray marks.

1.

YOUR NAME: _____
(Print)   Last   First   M.I.

SIGNATURE: _____ DATE: __/__/__

HOME ADDRESS: _____
(Print)   Number and Street

_____
City   State   Zip Code

PHONE NO.: _____
(Print)

IMPORTANT: Please fill in these boxes exactly as shown on the back cover of your test book.

2. TEST FORM

_____

3. TEST CODE

⊂0⊃	⊂A⊃	⊂0⊃	⊂0⊃	⊂0⊃	⊂0⊃	⊂0⊃	⊂0⊃	⊂0⊃	⊂0⊃	⊂0⊃
⊂1⊃	⊂B⊃	⊂1⊃	⊂1⊃	⊂1⊃	⊂1⊃	⊂1⊃	⊂1⊃	⊂1⊃	⊂1⊃	⊂1⊃
⊂2⊃	⊂C⊃	⊂2⊃	⊂2⊃	⊂2⊃	⊂2⊃	⊂2⊃	⊂2⊃	⊂2⊃	⊂2⊃	⊂2⊃
⊂3⊃	⊂D⊃	⊂3⊃	⊂3⊃	⊂3⊃	⊂3⊃	⊂3⊃	⊂3⊃	⊂3⊃	⊂3⊃	⊂3⊃
⊂4⊃	⊂E⊃	⊂4⊃	⊂4⊃	⊂4⊃	⊂4⊃	⊂4⊃	⊂4⊃	⊂4⊃	⊂4⊃	⊂4⊃
⊂5⊃	⊂F⊃	⊂5⊃	⊂5⊃	⊂5⊃	⊂5⊃	⊂5⊃	⊂5⊃	⊂5⊃	⊂5⊃	⊂5⊃
⊂6⊃	⊂G⊃	⊂6⊃	⊂6⊃	⊂6⊃	⊂6⊃	⊂6⊃	⊂6⊃	⊂6⊃	⊂6⊃	⊂6⊃
⊂7⊃		⊂7⊃	⊂7⊃	⊂7⊃	⊂7⊃	⊂7⊃	⊂7⊃	⊂7⊃	⊂7⊃	⊂7⊃
⊂8⊃		⊂8⊃	⊂8⊃	⊂8⊃	⊂8⊃	⊂8⊃	⊂8⊃	⊂8⊃	⊂8⊃	⊂8⊃
⊂9⊃		⊂9⊃	⊂9⊃	⊂9⊃	⊂9⊃	⊂9⊃	⊂9⊃	⊂9⊃	⊂9⊃	⊂9⊃

4. REGISTRATION NUMBER

6. DATE OF BIRTH

Month		Day		Year	
⊂ ⊃ JAN					
⊂ ⊃ FEB					
⊂ ⊃ MAR	⊂0⊃	⊂0⊃	⊂0⊃	⊂0⊃
⊂ ⊃ APR	⊂1⊃	⊂1⊃	⊂1⊃	⊂1⊃
⊂ ⊃ MAY	⊂2⊃	⊂2⊃	⊂2⊃	⊂2⊃
⊂ ⊃ JUN	⊂3⊃	⊂3⊃	⊂3⊃	⊂3⊃
⊂ ⊃ JUL		⊂4⊃	⊂4⊃	⊂4⊃
⊂ ⊃ AUG		⊂5⊃	⊂5⊃	⊂5⊃
⊂ ⊃ SEP		⊂6⊃	⊂6⊃	⊂6⊃
⊂ ⊃ OCT		⊂7⊃	⊂7⊃	⊂7⊃
⊂ ⊃ NOV		⊂8⊃	⊂8⊃	⊂8⊃
⊂ ⊃ DEC		⊂9⊃	⊂9⊃	⊂9⊃

7. SEX

⊂ ⊃ MALE
⊂ ⊃ FEMALE

 The Princeton Review

5. YOUR NAME

First 4 letters of last name				FIRST INIT	MID INIT
⊂A⊃	⊂A⊃	⊂A⊃	⊂A⊃	⊂A⊃	⊂A⊃
⊂B⊃	⊂B⊃	⊂B⊃	⊂B⊃	⊂B⊃	⊂B⊃
⊂C⊃	⊂C⊃	⊂C⊃	⊂C⊃	⊂C⊃	⊂C⊃
⊂D⊃	⊂D⊃	⊂D⊃	⊂D⊃	⊂D⊃	⊂D⊃
⊂E⊃	⊂E⊃	⊂E⊃	⊂E⊃	⊂E⊃	⊂E⊃
⊂F⊃	⊂F⊃	⊂F⊃	⊂F⊃	⊂F⊃	⊂F⊃
⊂G⊃	⊂G⊃	⊂G⊃	⊂G⊃	⊂G⊃	⊂G⊃
⊂H⊃	⊂H⊃	⊂H⊃	⊂H⊃	⊂H⊃	⊂H⊃
⊂I⊃	⊂I⊃	⊂I⊃	⊂I⊃	⊂I⊃	⊂I⊃
⊂J⊃	⊂J⊃	⊂J⊃	⊂J⊃	⊂J⊃	⊂J⊃
⊂K⊃	⊂K⊃	⊂K⊃	⊂K⊃	⊂K⊃	⊂K⊃
⊂L⊃	⊂L⊃	⊂L⊃	⊂L⊃	⊂L⊃	⊂L⊃
⊂M⊃	⊂M⊃	⊂M⊃	⊂M⊃	⊂M⊃	⊂M⊃
⊂N⊃	⊂N⊃	⊂N⊃	⊂N⊃	⊂N⊃	⊂N⊃
⊂O⊃	⊂O⊃	⊂O⊃	⊂O⊃	⊂O⊃	⊂O⊃
⊂P⊃	⊂P⊃	⊂P⊃	⊂P⊃	⊂P⊃	⊂P⊃
⊂Q⊃	⊂Q⊃	⊂Q⊃	⊂Q⊃	⊂Q⊃	⊂Q⊃
⊂R⊃	⊂R⊃	⊂R⊃	⊂R⊃	⊂R⊃	⊂R⊃
⊂S⊃	⊂S⊃	⊂S⊃	⊂S⊃	⊂S⊃	⊂S⊃
⊂T⊃	⊂T⊃	⊂T⊃	⊂T⊃	⊂T⊃	⊂T⊃
⊂U⊃	⊂U⊃	⊂U⊃	⊂U⊃	⊂U⊃	⊂U⊃
⊂V⊃	⊂V⊃	⊂V⊃	⊂V⊃	⊂V⊃	⊂V⊃
⊂W⊃	⊂W⊃	⊂W⊃	⊂W⊃	⊂W⊃	⊂W⊃
⊂X⊃	⊂X⊃	⊂X⊃	⊂X⊃	⊂X⊃	⊂X⊃
⊂Y⊃	⊂Y⊃	⊂Y⊃	⊂Y⊃	⊂Y⊃	⊂Y⊃
⊂Z⊃	⊂Z⊃	⊂Z⊃	⊂Z⊃	⊂Z⊃	⊂Z⊃

1 ⊂A⊃ ⊂B⊃ ⊂C⊃ ⊂D⊃ ⊂E⊃
2 ⊂A⊃ ⊂B⊃ ⊂C⊃ ⊂D⊃ ⊂E⊃
3 ⊂A⊃ ⊂B⊃ ⊂C⊃ ⊂D⊃ ⊂E⊃
4 ⊂A⊃ ⊂B⊃ ⊂C⊃ ⊂D⊃ ⊂E⊃
5 ⊂A⊃ ⊂B⊃ ⊂C⊃ ⊂D⊃ ⊂E⊃
6 ⊂A⊃ ⊂B⊃ ⊂C⊃ ⊂D⊃ ⊂E⊃
7 ⊂A⊃ ⊂B⊃ ⊂C⊃ ⊂D⊃ ⊂E⊃
8 ⊂A⊃ ⊂B⊃ ⊂C⊃ ⊂D⊃ ⊂E⊃
9 ⊂A⊃ ⊂B⊃ ⊂C⊃ ⊂D⊃ ⊂E⊃
10 ⊂A⊃ ⊂B⊃ ⊂C⊃ ⊂D⊃ ⊂E⊃
11 ⊂A⊃ ⊂B⊃ ⊂C⊃ ⊂D⊃ ⊂E⊃
12 ⊂A⊃ ⊂B⊃ ⊂C⊃ ⊂D⊃ ⊂E⊃
13 ⊂A⊃ ⊂B⊃ ⊂C⊃ ⊂D⊃ ⊂E⊃
14 ⊂A⊃ ⊂B⊃ ⊂C⊃ ⊂D⊃ ⊂E⊃
15 ⊂A⊃ ⊂B⊃ ⊂C⊃ ⊂D⊃ ⊂E⊃
16 ⊂A⊃ ⊂B⊃ ⊂C⊃ ⊂D⊃ ⊂E⊃
17 ⊂A⊃ ⊂B⊃ ⊂C⊃ ⊂D⊃ ⊂E⊃
18 ⊂A⊃ ⊂B⊃ ⊂C⊃ ⊂D⊃ ⊂E⊃
19 ⊂A⊃ ⊂B⊃ ⊂C⊃ ⊂D⊃ ⊂E⊃
20 ⊂A⊃ ⊂B⊃ ⊂C⊃ ⊂D⊃ ⊂E⊃
21 ⊂A⊃ ⊂B⊃ ⊂C⊃ ⊂D⊃ ⊂E⊃
22 ⊂A⊃ ⊂B⊃ ⊂C⊃ ⊂D⊃ ⊂E⊃
23 ⊂A⊃ ⊂B⊃ ⊂C⊃ ⊂D⊃ ⊂E⊃

24 ⊂A⊃ ⊂B⊃ ⊂C⊃ ⊂D⊃ ⊂E⊃
25 ⊂A⊃ ⊂B⊃ ⊂C⊃ ⊂D⊃ ⊂E⊃
26 ⊂A⊃ ⊂B⊃ ⊂C⊃ ⊂D⊃ ⊂E⊃
27 ⊂A⊃ ⊂B⊃ ⊂C⊃ ⊂D⊃ ⊂E⊃
28 ⊂A⊃ ⊂B⊃ ⊂C⊃ ⊂D⊃ ⊂E⊃
29 ⊂A⊃ ⊂B⊃ ⊂C⊃ ⊂D⊃ ⊂E⊃
30 ⊂A⊃ ⊂B⊃ ⊂C⊃ ⊂D⊃ ⊂E⊃
31 ⊂A⊃ ⊂B⊃ ⊂C⊃ ⊂D⊃ ⊂E⊃
32 ⊂A⊃ ⊂B⊃ ⊂C⊃ ⊂D⊃ ⊂E⊃
33 ⊂A⊃ ⊂B⊃ ⊂C⊃ ⊂D⊃ ⊂E⊃
34 ⊂A⊃ ⊂B⊃ ⊂C⊃ ⊂D⊃ ⊂E⊃
35 ⊂A⊃ ⊂B⊃ ⊂C⊃ ⊂D⊃ ⊂E⊃
36 ⊂A⊃ ⊂B⊃ ⊂C⊃ ⊂D⊃ ⊂E⊃
37 ⊂A⊃ ⊂B⊃ ⊂C⊃ ⊂D⊃ ⊂E⊃
38 ⊂A⊃ ⊂B⊃ ⊂C⊃ ⊂D⊃ ⊂E⊃
39 ⊂A⊃ ⊂B⊃ ⊂C⊃ ⊂D⊃ ⊂E⊃
40 ⊂A⊃ ⊂B⊃ ⊂C⊃ ⊂D⊃ ⊂E⊃
41 ⊂A⊃ ⊂B⊃ ⊂C⊃ ⊂D⊃ ⊂E⊃
42 ⊂A⊃ ⊂B⊃ ⊂C⊃ ⊂D⊃ ⊂E⊃
43 ⊂A⊃ ⊂B⊃ ⊂C⊃ ⊂D⊃ ⊂E⊃
44 ⊂A⊃ ⊂B⊃ ⊂C⊃ ⊂D⊃ ⊂E⊃
45 ⊂A⊃ ⊂B⊃ ⊂C⊃ ⊂D⊃ ⊂E⊃

The Princeton Review

Completely darken bubbles with a No. 2 pencil. If you make a mistake, be sure to erase mark completely. Erase all stray marks.

1.

YOUR NAME: _____
(Print)   Last   First   M.I.

SIGNATURE: _____ DATE: __ / __ / __

HOME ADDRESS: _____
(Print)   Number and Street

_____
     City   State   Zip Code

PHONE NO.: _____
(Print)

IMPORTANT: Please fill in these boxes exactly as shown on the back cover of your test book.

2. TEST FORM

3. TEST CODE

4. REGISTRATION NUMBER

5. YOUR NAME

First 4 letters of last name				FIRST INIT	MID INIT

6. DATE OF BIRTH

Month	Day		Year	
JAN				
FEB				
MAR	0	0	0	0
APR	1	1	1	1
MAY	2	2	2	2
JUN	3	3	3	3
JUL		4	4	4
AUG		5	5	5
SEP		6	6	6
OCT		7	7	7
NOV		8	8	8
DEC		9	9	9

7. SEX

MALE
FEMALE

The Princeton Review

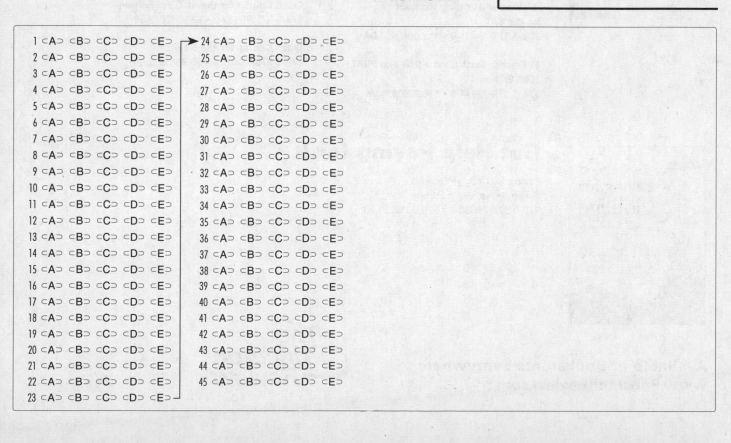

1 A B C D E
2 A B C D E
3 A B C D E
4 A B C D E
5 A B C D E
6 A B C D E
7 A B C D E
8 A B C D E
9 A B C D E
10 A B C D E
11 A B C D E
12 A B C D E
13 A B C D E
14 A B C D E
15 A B C D E
16 A B C D E
17 A B C D E
18 A B C D E
19 A B C D E
20 A B C D E
21 A B C D E
22 A B C D E
23 A B C D E

24 A B C D E
25 A B C D E
26 A B C D E
27 A B C D E
28 A B C D E
29 A B C D E
30 A B C D E
31 A B C D E
32 A B C D E
33 A B C D E
34 A B C D E
35 A B C D E
36 A B C D E
37 A B C D E
38 A B C D E
39 A B C D E
40 A B C D E
41 A B C D E
42 A B C D E
43 A B C D E
44 A B C D E
45 A B C D E

Our Books Help You Navigate the College Admissions Process

AP Exams

Cracking the AP Biology Exam,
2008 Edition
978-0-375-76640-4 • $18.00/C$22.00

Cracking the AP Calculus AB & BC Exams,
2008 Edition
978-0-375-76641-1 • $19.00/C$23.00

Cracking the AP Chemistry Exam,
2008 Edition
978-0-375-76642-8 • $18.00/C$22.00

**Cracking the AP Computer Science
A & AB Exams,** 2006–2007 Edition
978-0-375-76528-5 • $19.00/C$27.00

**Cracking the AP Economics (Macro &
Micro) Exams,** 2008 Edition
978-0-375-42841-8 • $18.00/C$22.00

**Cracking the AP English Language and
Composition Exam,** 2008 Edition
978-0-375-42842-5 • $18.00/C$22.00

Cracking the AP English Literature Exam,
2008 Edition
978-0-375-42843-2 • $18.00/C$22.00

**Cracking the AP Environmental
Science Exam,** 2008 Edition
978-0-375-42844-9 • $18.00/C$22.00

Cracking the AP European History Exam,
2008 Edition
978-0-375-42845-6 • $18.00/C$22.00

Cracking the AP Physics B Exam,
2008 Edition
978-0-375-42846-3 • $18.00/C$22.00

Cracking the AP Physics C Exam,
2008 Edition
978-0-375-42854-8 • $18.00/C$22.00

Cracking the AP Psychology Exam,
2008 Edition
978-0-375-42847-0 • $18.00/C$22.00

**Cracking the AP Spanish Exam,
with Audio CD,** 2008 Edition
978-0-375-42848-7 • $24.95/$29.95

Cracking the AP Statistics Exam,
2008 Edition
978-0-375-42849-4 • $19.00/C$23.00

**Cracking the AP U.S. Government
and Politics Exam,** 2008 Edition
978-0-375-42850-0 • $18.00/C$22.00

Cracking the AP U.S. History Exam,
2008 Edition
978-0-375-42851-7 • $18.00/C$22.00

Cracking the AP World History Exam,
2008 Edition
978-0-375-42852-4 • $18.00/C$22.00

SAT Subject Tests

**Cracking the SAT Biology E/M
Subject Test,** 2007–2008 Edition
978-0-375-76588-9 • $19.00/C$25.00

Cracking the SAT Chemistry Subject Test,
2007–2008 Edition
978-0-375-76589-6 • $18.00/C$22.00

Cracking the SAT French Subject Test,
2007–2008 Edition
978-0-375-76590-2 • $18.00/C$22.00

Cracking the SAT Literature Subject Test,
2007–2008 Edition
978-0-375-76592-6 • $18.00/C$22.00

**Cracking the SAT Math 1 and 2
Subject Tests,** 2007–2008 Edition
978-0-375-76593-3 • $19.00/C$25.00

Cracking the SAT Physics Subject Test,
2007–2008 Edition
978-0-375-76594-0 • $19.00/C$25.00

Cracking the SAT Spanish Subject Test,
2007–2008 Edition
978-0-375-76595-7 • $18.00/C$22.00

**Cracking the SAT U.S. & World History
Subject Tests,** 2007–2008 Edition
978-0-375-76591-9 • $19.00/C$25.00